United States Past and Future

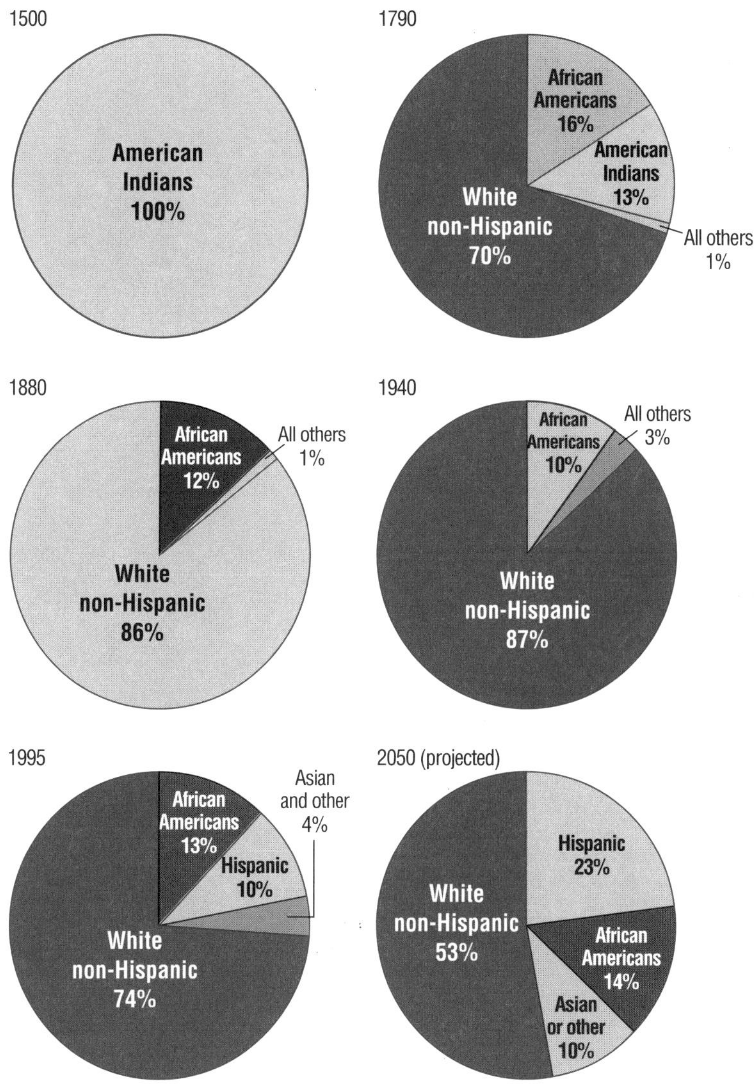

Sources: author's estimates, Bureau of the Census 1975, Day 1996, Thornton 1987

RACIAL AND ETHNIC GROUPS

Eighth Edition

Richard T. Schaefer
DePaul University

Prentice Hall
Upper Saddle River, New Jersey 07458

Library of Congress Cataloging-in-Publication Data

Schaefer, Richard T.
Racial and ethnic groups / Richard T. Schaefer.—8th ed.
p. cm.
Includes bibliographical references and index.
ISBN 0-321-04458-4 (hardcover)
1. Minorities—United States. 2. United States—Race relations.
3. United States—Ethnic relations. 4. Prejudices—United States.
I. Title
E184.A1S3 2000 97-22579
305.8' 00973—dc21 CIP

Editorial Director: Charlyce Jones Owen
Editor-in-Chief: Nancy Roberts
Managing Editor: Sharon Chambliss
Development Editor-in-Chief: Susanna Lesan
Director of Production and Manufacturing: Barbara Kittle
Manufacturing Manager: Nick Sklitsis
Prepress and Manufacturing Buyer: Mary Ann Gloriande
Director of Marketing: Gina Sluss
Marketing Manager: Christopher DeJohn
Creative Design Director: Leslie Osher
Interior Designer: Thomas Nery
Art Director: Nancy Wells
Cover Designer: Nancy Wells
Photo Research: Julie Tesser
Electronic Page Makeup: Electronic Publishing Services Inc., NYC

Photo Acknowledgments appear on p. 541, which constitute a continuation of the copyright page.

Printed in the United States of America
10 9 8 7 6 5 4 3 2 1

ISBN 0-321-04458-4

Prentice-Hall International (UK) *Limited, London*
Prentice-Hall of Australia Pty. Limited, *Sydney*
Prentice-Hall Canada Inc., *Toronto*
Prentice-Hall Hispanoamericana, S.A., *Mexico*
Prentice-Hall of India Private Limited, *New Delhi*
Prentice-Hall of Japan, Inc., *Tokyo*
Simon & Schuster Asia Pte. Ltd., *Singapore*
Editora Prentice-Hall do Brasil, Ltda., *Rio de Janeiro*

To the students in my classes who assist me
in understanding a multicultural society.

Brief Contents

CONTENTS

Part 2 Ethnic and Religious Sources of Conflict

Part 3 Major Racial and Ethnic Minority Groups in the United States

PREFACE

Race and ethnicity remain firmly a part of the national agenda. Twenty-three years ago, when the first edition of this book was being written, it was noted that race is not a static phenomenon and that while always a part of the social reality, specific aspects change. At that time the presence of a new immigrant group, the Vietnamese, was duly noted, and the efforts to define affirmative action were described. Today we seek to describe the growing presence of El Salvadorans and Haitians and the attempts to dismantle affirmative action.

Specific issues may change over time, but they continue to play out against a backdrop of discrimination that is rooted in the social structure and changing population composition as influenced by immigration patterns and reproduction patterns. One unanticipated change is that the breakup of the Soviet Union and further disinterest of the major industrial powers in the political and social events in Africa, Latin America, and much of Asia has made ethnic, language, and religious divisions even more the source of antagonism between and within nations. The old ideological debates about communism and capitalism have been replaced by emotional divisions over religious dogma and cultural traditions.

We continue to be reminded about the importance of the social construction of many aspects of racial and ethnic relations. What constitutes a race in terms of identity? What meaning does race and ethnicity have amidst the growing number of interracial marriages and marriages across cultural boundaries? Beyond the spectrum of race and ethnicity, we see the socially constructed meaning attached to all religions as members debate who is the "true" keeper of the faith. As we consider matters of gender, we see again that differences are largely the result of social constructions. And finally as we consider all groups that have been subjected to discrimination, such as the disabled, the elderly, and gays and lesbians, we see, in a similar manner, the power of labeling. The very issue of national identity is also a part of the agenda. The public and politicians alike question, "How many immigrants can we accept?" and "How much should be done to make up for past discrimination?" We are also witnessing the emergence of race, ethnicity, and national identity as global issues.

Changes in the Eighth Edition

As with all previous editions, every line, every source, and every number has been rechecked for its currency. We pride ourselves on providing the most current information possible to document the patterns in intergroup relations both in the United States and abroad.

Relevant scholarly findings in a variety of disciplines including economics, anthropology, and communication sciences have been incorporated. The feature

"Listen to Their Voices" appears in every chapter. These selections include excerpts from the writings or speeches of noted members of racial and ethnic groups such as Martin Luther King, Jr., Rosario Ferré, Elie Wiesel, Patricia J. Williams, and Nelson Mandela. Their writings will help students appreciate both the emotional and the intellectual energies felt by subordinate groups.

The eighth edition includes the following additions and changes:

An Internet Exercise is included at the end of every chapter to offer a way to continue learning via the WEB.

The Intergroup Relations Continuum presented in Chapter 1 has been reintroduced in later chapters to provide a connection between the coverage of specific groups and the introductory material (Chapters 1, 6, 8, 10, 12, 13, and 15).

An expansion of the discussion on racial identity to include biracial children and the debate over the "race question" to be included in Census 2000 (Chapter 1).

The world systems theory of Immanuel Wallerstein is outlined in Chapter 1 as it applies to race and ethnicity and later reintroduced in Chapters 10 and 15.

A look back after five years at the continuing legacy of *The Bell Curve* by Charles Murray and Richard Herrenstein (Chapter 1).

The definition of hate crimes and increasing efforts to tabulate their occurrence in the United States (Chapter 2).

The role of race in everyday behavior is considered in a new "Listen to Their Voices" entitled "Just Walk On By" by Staples (Chapter 3).

Sociologist William Julius Wilson offers his insight in a new "Listen to Their Voices" entitled "When Work Disappears" (Chapter 3).

Description of environmental justice as another, but often overlooked, form of discrimination (Chapter 3).

A new "Listen to Their Voices" entitled "Roots" by Raffi Ishkanian (Chapter 4).

A case study of the Amish is used to introduce the impact that laws and court decisions can have on a religious group (Chapter 5).

"Whiteness" as reflected in the growing consideration of white studies in academe is introduced to students in the context of ethnicity (Chapter 5).

A new "Listen to Their Voices" entitled "When the Boats Arrived" by Diane Glancy (Chapter 5).

Casino gambling receives special attention as a section within the consideration of economic development and tribal people in the United States (Chapter 6).

A controversy straight out of the sports pages is addressed by Tim Giago in a new "Listen to Their Voices" entitled "Honor Another Race of People as Mascots" (Chapter 6).

A new "Listen to Their Voices" entitled "Of Race and Risk" by Patricia J. Williams (Chapter 8).

A new "Listen to Their Voices" entitled "Language Is a Bridge to Culture" by Adela de la Torre (Chapter 9).

A new "Listen to Their Voices" entitled "Puerto Rico, U.S.A." by Rosario Ferré (Chapter 10).

Reorganization of chapters gives a clearer representation of the unique experiences of Mexican Americans and Puerto Ricans as well as Chinese Americans and Japanese Americans (Chapters 10 and 12).

A new "Listen to Their Voices" entitled "In Search of Bruce Lee's Grave" by Shanlon Wu (Chapter 11).

A new "Listen to Their Voices" entitled "I Was a Member of Kung Fu Crew" by Henry Han Xi Lau (Chapter 12).

The expansion of background information on the Holocaust by Pulitzer prize-winner Elie Wiesel (Chapter 13).

Arlie Russell Hochschild perceptively looks at work and the family in a new "Listen to Their Voices" entitled "Time for Change" (Chapter 14).

Inclusion of a comparison statistical table to assist in understanding the different nations under study in the cross-cultural comparison (Chapter 15).

The 1998 Northern Ireland Accord is considered in light of the history of the long-standing Protestant-Roman Catholic conflict (Chapter 15).

A new "Listen to Their Voices" entitled "Is the Disability Law Creating a Handicap?" by Kathi Wolfe (Chapter 16).

The inclusion at the end of chapters of both Review Questions and Critical Thinking Questions (all chapters).

Inclusion as an endpaper a figure dramatizing the changing racial and ethnic composition of the United States (inside front cover).

Expansion of Internet Resource Directory (preceding the Glossary).

There are a total of 17 new tables and 32 new figures, and nine glossary terms have been added. In addition, photographs, maps, and political cartoons have been updated.

Complete Coverage in Four Parts

Any constructive discussion of racial and ethnic minorities must do more than merely describe events. Part One, "Perspectives on Racial and Ethnic Groups," includes the relevant theories and operational definitions that ground the study of race and ethnic relations in the social sciences. We specifically present the functionalist, conflict, and labeling theories of sociology in their relation to the study of race and ethnicity. We show the relationship between subordinate groups and the study of stratification. They will also be introduced to the dual labor market theory and the irregular economy from economics and reference group theory from psychology. The extensive treatment of prejudice and discrimination covers anti-White prejudice as well as the more familiar topic of bigotry aimed at subordinate groups. Discrimination is analyzed from an economic perspective, including the latest efforts to document discrimination in environmental issues such as location of toxic waste facilities and the move to dismantle affirmative action.

In Part Two, "Ethnic and Religious Sources of Conflict," we examine some often-ignored sources of intergroup conflict in the United States: White ethnic groups and religious minorities. Diversity in the United States is readily apparent when we look at the ethnic and religious groups that have resulted from waves of immigration. Refugees, now primarily from Haiti and Central America, also continue to raise major issues.

Any student needs to be familiar with the past to understand present forms of discrimination and subordination. Part Three, "Major Racial and Ethnic Minority Groups in the United States," brings into sharper focus the history and contemporary status of Native Americans, African Americans, Hispanics, Asian Americans, and Jews in the United States. Social institutions such as family, education, politics, health care, religion, and the economy receive special attention for the subordinate groups. The author contends that institutional discrimination, rather than individual action, is the source of conflict between the subordinate and dominant elements in the United States.

Part Four, "Other Patterns of Dominance," includes topics related to American racial and ethnic relations. The author recognizes, as have Gunnar Myrdal and Helen Mayer Hacker before, that relations between women and men resemble those between Blacks and Whites. Therefore, in this book, we consider the position of women as a subordinate group. Since the first edition of *Racial and Ethnic Groups*, published over twenty years ago, debates over equal rights and abortion have shown no sign of resolution. For women of color, we document the double jeopardy suffered because of subordinate status twice over: race and gender.

Perhaps we can best comprehend intergroup conflict in the United States by comparing it to the ethnic hostilities in other nations. The similarities and differences between the United States and other societies treated in this book are striking. Again, as in the seventh edition, we examine the tensions in Canada, Israel, Mexico, Northern Ireland, and South Africa to document further the diversity of intergroup conflict.

The final chapter highlights other groups that have been the subject of exclusion—the aged, people with disabilities, and gay men and lesbians. This chapter also includes a concluding section that ties together thematically the forces of dominance-subordination that have been the subject of this book.

Features to Aid Students

Several features are included in the text to facilitate student learning. A "Chapter Outline" appears at the beginning of each chapter and is followed by "Highlights," a short section alerting students to important issues and topics to be addressed. To help students review, each chapter ends with a summary "Conclusion." A bibliography,

"For Further Information," provides references for additional research. The "Key Terms" are highlighted in bold when they are first introduced in the text and are listed with page numbers at the conclusion of each chapter. Periodically throughout the book the Intergroup Relations Continuum first presented in Chapter 1 is repeated to reinforce major concepts while addressing the unique social circumstances of individual racial and ethnic groups. In addition there is an end-of-book "Glossary" with full definitions referenced to chapter numbers. In this edition are both "Review Questions" and "Critical Thinking Questions." The "Review Questions" are intended to remind the reader of major points while the "Critical Thinking Questions" encourage students to think more deeply about some of the major issues raised in the chapter. A new section includes an Internet Exercise that allows students to do some critical thinking via the WEB. As a part of each chapter is a section "For Further Information" that highlights recent books and presents a list of relevant journals. An "Internet Resource Directory" has been expanded to allow access to the latest electronic sources. An extensive illustration program, which includes maps and political cartoons, expands the text discussion and provokes thought.

Ancillary Materials

The ancillary materials that accompany this textbook have been carefully created to enhance the topics being discussed. We again offer a Student Study Guide to accompany *Racial and Ethnic Groups*. Written by Noel Barker at DePaul University, it includes learning objectives, exercises keyed to the learning objectives, suggestions for additional research, and practice tests. For the instructor, an Instructor's Manual and Test Bank, written by Jody Anderson Wetzler at Minnesota State University, Mankato, includes chapter overviews, key term identification exercises, discussion questions, topics for class discussion, audiovisual resources, and test questions in both multiple-choice and essay format. The test bank portion of the manual is available in the computerized Prentice Hall Custom Test, which allows you to create your own personalized exams. It is available in both Windows and Macintosh formats.

In tandem with the text, students and professors can now take full advantage of the World Wide Web to enrich their study of racial and ethnic groups. The Schaefer *Companion Website* correlates the text with related material available on the Internet. Features of the Web site include chapter objectives and study questions, as well as links to interesting material and information from other sites on the Web that can reinforce and enhance the content of each chapter. You can reach the site at HYPERLINK http://www.prenhall.com/schaefer # http://www.prenhall.com/schaefer.

Sociology on the Internet: A Prentice Hall Guide, 1999–2000 introduces students to the origin and innovations behind the Internet and provides clear strategies for navigating the complexity of the Internet and World Wide Web. Exercises within and at the end of the chapters allow students to practice searching for the myriad resources available to the student of sociology. This 96-page supplementary book is free to students when shrinkwrapped as a package with *Racial and Ethnic Groups*.

Changes in race and ethnic relations will continue because these relations are a part of our constantly changing behavior. *Racial and Ethnic Groups* gives the reader a firm knowledge of the past and the present, as well as a sufficient conceptual understanding to prepare for the future.

Acknowledgments

This eighth edition benefited from the thoughtful reaction of my students in classes at DePaul University and, previously, Western Illinois University, where special programs enabled me to teach the race and ethnicity course to older students through independent home study; to inmates at a maximum-security prison; and to undergraduates. This edition also benefits from my past collaborative writing experiences on other projects with Jinny Joyner and Robert P. Lamm. John Tenuto of College of Lake County (Illinois) developed the Internet Exercises and assisted with the Internet Resource Directory.

The eighth edition was improved by the suggestions of Bonnijean Korn Ach, Chapman University; Terrance Brungardt, Saint Mary College; Michael Collins, University of Wisconsin-Fox Valley; William Egelman, Iona College; Whitney Garcia, Townson University; Roger Guy, Texas Lutheran University; Leilani Holmes, Grossmont College; Walter Konetschni, Shippensburg University; Sharon Linzey, George Fox University; Alvaro Nieves, Wheaton College; Yaw Oheneba Sakyi, SUNY-Potsdam; S. Daniel Schwartz, Pima Community College; Nancy Terjesen, Kent State University; and Richard Wedeking, Iowa Central Community College. I would also like to thank my editors Sharon Chambliss, Nancy Roberts, Lisa Ziccardi, Priscilla McGeehon, and Lisa Pinto for their patience in the development of this greatly revised edition. They make a great team in the production of academic books from which I have fortunately benefited. This edition also directly reflects the editorial skills of Alan McClare on three previous editions. Julie Tesser facilitated the development of the photograph program for this edition. Lake Lloyd guided me through the production process. In addition, I am appreciative of the assistance of Karen Nelson in assembling the reference list.

The task of writing and researching is often a lonely one. I have always found it an enriching experience, mostly because of the supportive home I share with my wife, Sandy. She knows so well my appreciation and gratitude now as in the past and in the future.

Richard T. Schaefer

1

Understanding Race and Ethnicity

CHAPTER OUTLINE

What Is a Subordinate Group?

Types of Subordinate Groups
- Racial Groups
- Ethnic Groups
- Religious Groups
- Gender Groups
- Other Subordinate Groups

Race
- Biological Meaning
- Social Construction of Race
- Census 2000

Sociology and the Study of Race and Ethnicity
- Stratification by Class and Gender
- Theoretical Perspectives

The Creation of Subordinate-Group Status
- Migration
- Annexation
- Colonialism

The Consequences of Subordinate-Group Status
- Extermination
- Expulsion
- Secession
- Segregation
- Fusion
- Assimilation
- The Pluralist Perspective

Who Am I?

Resistance and Change

Conclusion

Key Terms

Review Questions

Critical Thinking

Internet Exercise

For Further Information

HIGHLIGHTS

Minority groups are subordinated in terms of power and privilege to the majority, or dominant, group. A minority is defined not by being outnumbered, but by five characteristics: unequal treatment, distinguishing physical or cultural traits, involuntary membership, in-group marriage, and awareness of subordination. Subordinate groups are classified in terms of race, ethnicity, religion, and gender. The social importance of race is significant through a process of racial formation; its biological significance is uncertain. The theoretical perspectives of functionalism, conflict theory, and labeling offer insights into the sociology of intergroup relations.

Immigration, annexation, and colonialism are processes that may create subordinate groups. Other processes such as expulsion may remove the presence of a subordinate group. Significant for race and ethnic relations in the United States today is the distinction between assimilation and pluralism. The former demands subordinate-group conformity to the dominant group, and the latter implies mutual respect among diverse groups.

Schoolteacher Susan Litwinetz can say "How are you?" in seven languages, "Please be quiet" in four. Her students in Annandale, Virginia, who fled certain death in Iraq and civil war in the African country Sierra Leone, now face a new struggle with language in the United States. They learn English one picture at a time; occasionally, she speaks to them in their native languages and immediately they beam with recognition.

"When I say goodbye in Farsi, their eyes light up," says Litwinetz, who has taught English to immigrant students for seven years. "But one ***Tashakur*** is worth a million 'thank yous.'"(Jones 1997:1A).

The students in this Virginia suburb of Washington, D.C., are both typical and unique. They are typical because throughout the United States, students discover racial and ethnic diversity first-hand from their classmates. Religious holidays are not automatically shared. Favorite recreational activities may be different. But Annandale is different in its extreme diversity—there are students in this one school district from 182 countries, speaking more than 100 languages. Available information indicates that there at are least four other school districts in which more than 100 languages are spoken, so this degree of cultural diversity is unusual, but the issues it raises are not.

We also must consider these schools against the backdrop of race and ethnicity globally—currently 6,701 are languages spoken in the 228 countries of the world. Even on the level of everyday life, tensions over group differences emerge. People on two continents were stunned in 1998 when a Black American marine was beaten severely by a band of Russian skinheads. The attack was carried out in daylight in a Moscow city park. Foreign students from Asia and Africa said they were not surprised by the attack and that their complaints routinely go unnoticed by the local police. Further, it was noted critically by Human Rights Watch that during a recent celebration of the 850th anniversary of Moscow, the city cleared the streets of people from Third World countries hoping to minimize intergroup problems. Tensions defined by race and ethnicity know no boundaries (Gordon 1998; Mutiso 1998).

Is the diversity we find present in the United Sates in general and in most schools specifically a strength to build upon or a challenge to address? There is not a lack of views on this subject, which has been debated for the last 400 years in the area we now know as the United States.

We expect issues of race and ethnicity to emerge in certain aspects of our lives, such as education, the economy, and the courts, but it also emerges where it may not be expected. For example, baseball star Henry Aaron passed Babe Ruth's career record for home runs in 1969. Despite this achievement, which even today no player is likely to equal, Aaron received racially linked death threats and hate mail because he had usurped a White man's place in history. Moreover, Aaron received few invitations for commercial endorsements, which instead went to White players who had more modest careers. Racial issues also exist in the music industry. The lyrics of some rap and rock music have promoted racism by emphasizing violence against other groups. The college campus is also not exempt from issues of race, ethnicity, and gender. Many universities with diverse populations, such as Stanford University and the University of Wisconsin, have instituted codes prohibiting discrimination or victimization of students on the basis of race, ethnicity, gender, or sexual preference.

People in the United States and elsewhere are also, often reluctantly, beginning to consider that the same principles that guarantee equality based on race or gender can apply to other groups who are discriminated against. There have been growing efforts to ensure the same rights and privileges to all people regardless of age, disability, or sexual orientation. These concerns are emerging even as the old divisions

Lana Sofy, a Kurd from Iraq, shares a laugh with Leyla Dawoudi, an Iranian. They attend Annandale High School, where diversity is commonplace.

over race, ethnicity, and religion continue to fester and occasionally explode into violence that envelops entire nations.

In 1997, there was one major armed conflict between countries (India and Pakistan), but twenty-four major armed conflicts within countries. In the vast majority of these, issues of ethnicity, race, language, or religion were central to the conflict or served to inflame the emotions of the combatants. We will frequently make reference to how these social characteristics create boundaries that transcend any politically defined borders (Mutiso 1998).

Quick—imagine an American. Is your image of someone White? By the middle of the next century, according to best estimates, most people in the United States will not be (Tilove 1998).

Tensions in the United States arise in an extremely diverse nation, as shown in Table 1.1. At present, 15 percent of the population are members of racial minorities, and another 9 percent are Hispanic. These percentages represent one of four people in the United States, without counting White ethnic groups. African Americans, Hispanics, and Asian Americans already outnumber Whites in fifteen of the twenty-eight largest cities. The trend is toward even greater diversity between 1995 and 2050, as shown in Figure 1.1. The population in the United States is expected to rise from 24 percent Black-Hispanic-Asian-Native American to 47 percent. While the composition of the population is changing, the problems of prejudice, discrimination, and mistrust remain.

Table 1.1 Racial and Ethnic Groups in the United States, 1990

Classification	Number in Thousands	Percentage of Total Population
Racial groups		
Whites	199,686	80.3
Blacks/African Americans	29,986	12.1
Native Americans, Eskimos, Aleuts	1,959	0.8
Chinese	1,645	0.7
Filipinos	1,407	0.6
Japanese	848	0.3
Asian Indians	815	0.3
Koreans	799	0.3
Vietnamese	615	0.2
Laotians	149	0.1
Cambodians	147	0.1
Ethnic groups		
White ancestry (single or mixed)		
Germans	57,986	23.3
Irish	38,740	15.6
English	32,656	13.1
Italians	14,715	5.9
French	10,321	4.1
Poles	9,366	3.8
Jews	5,935	2.6
Hispanics (or Latinos)	22,354	9.0
Mexican Americans	13,496	5.4
Puerto Ricans	2,728	1.0
Cubans	1,044	0.4
Other	5,086	2.2
Total (all groups)	248,710	

Source: Bureau of the Census 1992:24–25; 1993a:18, 51.

Note: Percentages do not total 100 percent, and subheads do not add up to figures in major heads, because of overlap between groups (e.g., Polish-American Jews or people of mixed ancestry, such as Irish and Italian). Therefore, numbers and percentages should be considered approximations. Data on Jews are for 1989.

What Is a Subordinate Group?

Identifying a subordinate group or a minority in a society would seem to be a simple enough task: groups with fewer members. In the United States, those groups readily identified as minorities—Blacks and Native Americans, for example—are outnumbered by non-Blacks and non-Native Americans. However, minority status is not necessarily the result of being outnumbered. A social minority need not be a mathematical one. A **minority group** is a subordinate group whose members have significantly less control or power over their own lives than do the members of a dominant or majority group. However, minority means the same as subordinate, and dominant is used interchangeably with majority.

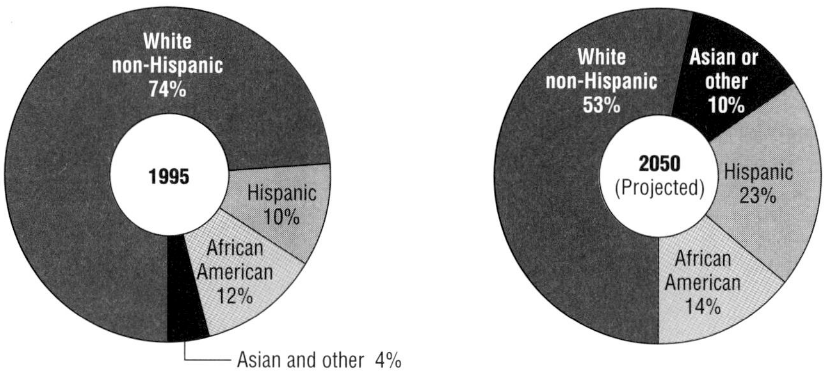

Figure 1.1 Population of the United States by Race and Ethnicity, 1995 and 2050 (Projected)

According to projections by the Bureau of the Census, the proportion of residents of the United States who are White and non-Hispanic will decrease significantly by the year 2050. By contrast, there will be a striking rise in the proportion of both Hispanic Americans and Asian Americans.

Source: Day 1996.

Confronted with evidence that a particular minority in the United States is subordinate to the majority, some individuals will respond, "Why not? After all, this is a democracy, and so the majority rules." The subordination of a minority, however, involves more than its inability to rule over society. A member of a subordinate or minority group experiences a narrowing of life's opportunities—for success, education, wealth, the pursuit of happiness—that goes beyond any personal shortcoming he or she may have. A minority group does not share in proportion to its numbers what a given society, such as the United States, defines as valuable.

Being superior in numbers does not guarantee a group control over its destiny and assure it of majority status. In 1920, the majority of people in Mississippi and South Carolina were African Americans. Yet African Americans did not have as much significant control over their lives as Whites, let alone control the states of Mississippi and South Carolina. Throughout the United States today are counties or neighborhoods in which the majority of people are African American, Native American, or Hispanic, but White Americans are the dominant force. Nationally, 51.2 percent of the population is female, but males still dominate positions of authority and wealth well in excess of their numbers.

A minority or subordinate group has five characteristics: unequal treatment, distinguishing physical or cultural traits, involuntary membership, awareness of subordination, and in-group marriage (Wagley and Harris 1958).

1. Members of a minority experience unequal treatment and have less power over their lives than members of a dominant group have over theirs. Prejudice, discrimination, segregation, and even extermination create this social inequality.

2. Members of a minority group share physical or cultural characteristics that distinguish them from the dominant group, such as skin color or language. Each society has its own arbitrary standard for determining which characteristics are most important in defining dominant and minority groups.
3. Membership in a dominant or minority group is not voluntary: People are born into the group. A person does not choose to be an African American or a White.
4. Minority-group members have a strong sense of group solidarity. William Graham Sumner, writing in 1906, noted that individuals make distinctions between members of their own group (the in-group) and everyone else (the out-group). When a group is the object of long-term prejudice and discrimination, the feeling of us versus them can and often does become extremely intense.
5. Members of a minority generally marry others from the same group. A member of a dominant group is often unwilling to join a supposedly inferior minority by marrying one of its members. In addition, the minority group's sense of solidarity encourages marriage within the group and discourages marriage to outsiders.

Types of Subordinate Groups

There are four types of minority or subordinate groups. All four, except where noted, have the five properties outlined. The four criteria for classifying minority groups are race, ethnicity, religion, and gender.

RACIAL GROUPS

The term **racial group** is reserved for those minorities and the corresponding majorities that are classified according to obvious physical differences. Notice the two crucial words in the definition: ***obvious*** and ***physical***. What is obvious? Hair color? Shape of an earlobe? Presence of body hair? To whom are these differences obvious, and why? Each society defines what it finds obvious.

In the United States, skin color is one obvious difference. On a cold winter day with clothing covering all but one's head, however, skin color may be less obvious than hair color. Yet people in the United States have learned informally that skin color is important, and hair color is unimportant. We need to say more than that. In the United States, people have traditionally classified and classify themselves as either Black or White. There is no in-between state except for people readily identified as Native Americans or Asian Americans. Later in this chapter we will explore this issue more deeply and see how such assumptions have very complex implications.

Other societies use skin color as a standard but may have a more elaborate system of classification. In Brazil, where hostility among races is less than in the United States, numerous categories identify people on the basis of skin color. In the United States, a person is Black or White. In Brazil, a variety of terms, such as ***cafuso***, ***mazombo***, ***preto***, and ***escuro***, are applied to describe various combinations of skin color, facial features, and hair texture. What makes differences obvious is subject to a society's definition.

The designation of a racial group emphasizes physical differences as opposed to cultural distinctions. In the United States, minority races include Blacks, Native Americans (or American Indians), Japanese Americans, Chinese Americans, Arab Americans, Filipinos, Hawaiians, and other Asian peoples. The issue of race and racial differences has been an important one, not only in the United States but throughout the entire sphere of European influence. Later in this chapter we will examine race and its significance more closely. We should not forget that Whites are a race too. As we will consider in Chapter 5, who is White has been subject to change over time as certain European groups were felt historically not to be deserving of being considered White, but over time, partly to compete against a growing Black population, the whiting of some Euro-Americans occurred.

ETHNIC GROUPS

Ethnic minority groups are differentiated from the dominant group on the basis of cultural differences, such as language, attitudes toward marriage and parenting, and food habits. **Ethnic groups** are groups set apart from others because of their national origin or distinctive cultural patterns.

Ethnic groups in the United States include a grouping that we refer to collectively as Hispanics or Latinos, including Mexican Americans (Chicanos), Puerto Ricans, Cubans, and other Latin Americans in the United States. Hispanics can be either Black or White as, for example, in the case of a dark-skinned Puerto Rican who may be taken as Black in central Texas but be viewed as a Puerto Rican in New York City. The ethnic-group category also includes White ethnics, such as Irish Americans, Polish Americans, and Norwegian Americans.

The cultural traits that make groups distinctive usually originate from their homeland or, for Jews, from a long history of being segregated and prohibited from becoming a part of the host society. An immigrant group, once in the United States, may maintain distinctive cultural practices through associations, clubs, and worship. Ethnic enclaves such as a Little Italy or a Greektown in urban areas also perpetuate cultural distinctiveness.

Some of the racial groups discussed in the preceding section may also have unique cultural traditions, as we can readily see in the many Chinatowns throughout the United States. For racial groups, however, the physical distinctiveness and not the cultural differences generally prove to be the barrier to acceptance by the host society. For example, Chinese Americans who are faithful Protestants and know the names of all the members of the Baseball Hall of Fame may be bearers of American culture. Yet these Chinese Americans are still part of a minority because they are seen as physically different.

Ethnicity continues to be important, as recent events in Bosnia and other parts of Eastern Europe have demonstrated. By comparison, however, race is even more significant worldwide. Almost a century ago, African American sociologist W. E. B. Du Bois, addressing an audience in London, called attention to the overwhelming importance of the color line throughout the world. In "Listen to Their Voices," we

LISTEN TO THEIR VOICES

Problem of the Color-Line

W. E. B. DuBois

In the metropolis of the modern world, in this the closing year of the nineteenth century, there has been assembled a congress of men and women of African blood, to deliberate solemnly upon the present situation and outlook of the darker races of mankind. The problem of the twentieth century is the problem of the color-line, the question as to how far differences of race—which show themselves chiefly in the color of the skin and the texture of the hair—will hereafter be made the basis of denying to over half the world the right of sharing to their utmost ability the opportunities and privileges of modern civilization....

Let the world take no backward step in that slow but sure progress which has successively refused to let the spirit of class, of caste, of privilege, or of birth, debar from life, liberty and the pursuit of happiness a striving human soul.

Let not color or race be a feature of distinction between white and black men, regardless of worth or ability....

Thus we appeal with boldness and confidence to the Great Powers of the civilized world, trusting in the wide spirit of humanity, and the deep sense of justice of our age, for a generous recognition of the righteousness of our cause.

From *An ABC of Color,* pp. 20–21, 23, by W.E.B. DuBois.

read the remarks of Du Bois, the first Black person to receive a doctorate from Harvard, who later helped to organize the National Association for the Advancement of Colored People (NAACP). Du Bois's observances give us a historic perspective on the struggle for equality. We can look ahead—knowing how far we have come and speculating on how much further we have to go.

RELIGIOUS GROUPS

Association with a religion other than the dominant faith is the third basis for minority-group status. In the United States, Protestants, as a group, outnumber members of all other religions. Roman Catholics form the largest minority religion. Chapter 5, focusing on Roman Catholics and other minority faiths, details how all five properties of a minority group apply to such faiths in the United States.

Religious minorities include such groups as the Church of Jesus Christ of Latter-Day Saints (the Mormons), the Hutterites, the Amish, the Muslims, and Buddhists. Cults or sects associated with such things as animal sacrifice, doomsday prophecy, demon worship, or the use of snakes in a ritualistic fashion would also constitute minorities. Jews are excluded from this category and placed among ethnic groups. Culture is a more important defining trait for Jewish people worldwide than is religious dogma. Jewish Americans share a cultural tradition that goes beyond theology. In this sense, it is appropriate to view them as an ethnic group rather than as members of a religious faith.

GENDER GROUPS

Gender is another attribute that creates dominant and subordinate groups. Males are the social majority; females, although more numerous, are relegated to the position of the social minority. Women are considered a minority even though they do not exhibit all the characteristics outlined earlier (there is, for example, little in-group marriage). Women encounter prejudice and discrimination and are physically distinguishable. Group membership is involuntary, and many women have developed a sense of sisterhood.

Women who are members of racial and ethnic minorities face a special challenge to achieving equality. They suffer from double jeopardy because they belong to two separate minority groups: a racial or ethnic group plus a subordinate gender group. The 1991 U.S. Senate confirmation hearing for Clarence Thomas as a justice of the U.S. Supreme Court provides a noteworthy example. When an African American, Anita Hill, charged Thomas (also an African American) with sexual harassment, she faced an all-White, all-male panel of U.S. senators. Critics of the hearings,

Given the diversity in the nation, the workplace is increasingly a place where intergroup tensions may develop.

in which Hill's testimony was essentially discounted and Thomas's appointment recommended, questioned whether Hill's gender, especially, made her less credible to the male panel than Thomas—reaffirming the interconnectedness of race and gender in contemporary society.

OTHER SUBORDINATE GROUPS

This book focuses on groups that meet a set of criteria for subordinate status. People encounter prejudice or are excluded from full participation in society for many reasons. Racial, ethnic, religious, and gender barriers are the main ones, but there are others. Age, disabilities, and sexual orientation are among the factors that are used to subordinate groups of people. As a result, in Chapter 16 we will go beyond the original scope and title of the book and consider other groups of people who have been excluded from all that society offers and witness their fight against prejudice and discrimination.

Race

Race has many meanings for many people. Often these meanings are inaccurate and based on theories discarded by scientists generations ago. As we will see, race is a socially constructed concept.

BIOLOGICAL MEANING

The way the term race has been used by some people to apply to human beings lacks any scientific meaning. We cannot identify today distinctive physical characteristics for groups of human beings the way scientists do to distinguish one species of animal from another. The idea of **biological race** is based on the mistaken notion of a genetically isolated group.

Even among past proponents that sharp, scientific divisions exist among humans, there were endless debates over what the races of the world were. Given people's frequent migration, exploration, and invasions, pure genetic types have not existed for some time, if they ever did. There are no mutually exclusive races. Skin color among African Americans varies tremendously, as it does among White Americans. There is even an overlapping of dark-skinned Whites and light-skinned African Americans. If we grouped people by genetic resistance to malaria and by fingerprint patterns, Norwegians and many African groups would be of the same race. If we grouped people by some digestive capacities, some Africans, Asians, and southern Europeans would be of one group and West Africans and northern Europeans of another (R. Leehotz 1995; E. Shanklin 1994).

Biologically there are no pure, distinct races. For example, blood type cannot determine racial groups with any accuracy. Furthermore, applying pure racial types to humans is problematic because of interbreeding. Despite continuing prejudice about Black–White marriages, a large number of Whites have African American ancestry. Scientists, using various techniques, maintain that the proportion of African Americans with White ancestry is between 20 and 75 percent. Despite the extremely wide range of these estimates, the mixed ancestry of today's Blacks and Whites is part of the biological reality of race (M. Herskovits 1930:15; D. Roberts 1955).

Research has been conducted to determine whether personality characteristics such as temperament and nervous habits are inherited among minority groups. Not surprisingly, the question of whether races have different innate levels of intelligence has led to the most explosive controversy.

Typically, intelligence is summarized in an **intelligence quotient**, or IQ, where 100 represents average intelligence and higher scores represent greater intelligence. It should be noted that there is little consensus over just what intelligence is, other than as defined by such IQ tests. Intelligence tests are adjusted for a person's age, so that ten-year-olds take a very different test from someone aged twenty. While research does show that certain learning strategies can improve a person's IQ, generally IQ remains stable as one ages.

A great deal of debate continues over the accuracy of these tests. Are they biased toward people who come to the tests with knowledge similar to that of the test writers? Consider the following two questions used on standard tests:

1. Runner: Marathon (A) envoy: embassy, (B) oarsman: regatta, (C) martyr: massacre, (D) referee: tournament.
2. Your mother sends you to a store to get a loaf of bread. The store is closed. What should you do? (A) return home, (B) go to the next store, (C) wait until it opens, (D) ask a stranger for advice.

Both correct answers are B. But is a lower-class youth likely to know, in the first question, what a regatta is? Skeptics argue that such test questions do not truly measure intellectual potential. Inner-city youths have been shown often to respond with A to the second question, as that may be the only store with which the family has credit. Youths in rural areas, where the next store may be miles away, are also unlikely to respond with the designated correct answer. The issue of culture bias in tests remains an unresolved concern. The most recent research shows that differences in intelligence scores between Blacks and Whites are virtually eliminated when adjustments are made for social and economic characteristics (Brooks-Gunn et al. 1996; J. Kagan 1971; Herrnstein and Murray 1994:30).

The second issue, trying to associate these results with certain subpopulations such as races, also has a long history. In the past, a few have contended that, as a group, Whites have more intelligence on average than Blacks. All researchers agree that within-group differences are greater than any speculated differences among groups. The range of intelligence among, for example, Korean Americans is much greater than any average difference between them as a group and Japanese Americans.

The third issue relates to the subpopulations themselves. If Blacks or Whites are not mutually exclusive biologically, how can there be measurable differences? Many Whites and most Blacks have mixed ancestry that complicates the inheritance issue. Both groups reflect a rich heritage of very dissimilar populations from Swedes to Slovaks and Zulus to Tutus.

In 1994, an 845-page book unleashed a new national debate on the issue of IQ. The latest research effort of psychologist Richard J. Herrnstein and social scientist

Charles Murray (1994), published in ***The Bell Curve***, concluded that 60 percent of IQ is inheritable, and that racial groups offer a convenient means to generalize about any differences in intelligence. Unlike most other proponents of the race–IQ link, the authors offer policy suggestions that include ending welfare to discourage births among low-IQ poor women, and changing immigration laws so that the IQ pool in the United States is not diminished. Herrenstein and Murray even made generalizations about IQ levels among Asians and Hispanics in the United States—groups subject to even more intermarriage. It is not possible to generalize about absolute differences between groups, such as Latinos versus Whites, when close to half of Latinos in the United States marry non-Hispanics.

Years later, the mere mention of "the bell curve" signals to many the belief in a racial hierarchy with Whites toward the top and Blacks near the bottom. The research present then and repeated today points to the difficulty in definitions: what is intelligence and what constitutes a racial group given generations, if not centuries, of intermarriage? How can we speak of definitive inherited racial differences if there has been intermarriage between people of every color? Furthermore, as people on both sides of the debate have noted, regardless of the findings we would still want to strive to maximize the talents of each individual. All research shows that the differences within a group are much greater than any alleged differences between group averages (Cullen et al. 1997; Jencks and Phillips 1998).

All these issues and controversial research have led to the basic question of what difference it would make even if there were significant differences. No researcher believes that race can be used to predict one's intelligence. Also, there is a general agreement that certain intervention strategies can improve scholastic achievement and even intelligence as defined by standard tests. Should we mount efforts to upgrade the abilities of those alleged to be below average? These debates tend to contribute to a sense of hopelessness among some policy makers who think that biology is destiny, rather than causing them to rethink the issue or expand positive intervention efforts (E. Dionne 1994).

Why does such IQ research reemerge if the data are subject to different interpretations? The argument that "we" are superior to "them" is very appealing to the dominant group. It justifies receiving opportunities that are denied to others. For example, the authors of ***The Bell Curve*** argue that intelligence significantly determines the poverty problem in the United States. We can anticipate that the debate over IQ and the allegations of significant group differences will continue. Policy makers need to acknowledge the difficulty in using race in any biologically significant manner.

SOCIAL CONSTRUCTION OF RACE

If race does not distinguish humans from one another biologically, why does it seem to be so important? It is important because of the social meaning that people have attached to it. The 1950 UNESCO Statement on Race maintains that "for all practical social purposes 'race' is not so much a biological phenomenon as a social myth" (A. Montagu 1972:118). Adolf Hitler expressed concern over the "Jewish race" and translated this concern into Nazi death camps. Winston Churchill spoke proudly of the "British race" and used that pride to spur a nation to fight. Evidently, race was a useful political tool for two rather different leaders in the 1930s and 1940s.

People could speculate that if human groups have obvious physical differences, then they could have corresponding mental or personality differences. No one disagrees that people differ in temperament, potential to learn, and sense of humor. In its social sense, race implies that groups that differ physically also bear distinctive emotional and mental abilities or disabilities. These beliefs are based on the notion that humankind can be divided into distinct groups. We have already seen the difficulties associated with pigeonholing people into racial categories. Despite these difficulties, belief in the inheritance of behavior patterns and in an association between physical and cultural traits is widespread. It is called **racism** when this belief is coupled with the feeling that certain groups or races are inherently superior to others. Racism is a doctrine of racial supremacy, stating that one race is superior to another (see also Bonilla-Silva 1996).

We questioned the biological significance of race in the previous section. In modern complex industrial societies, we find little adaptive utility in the presence or absence of prominent chins, epicanthic folds of the eyelids, or the comparative amount of melanin in the skin. What is important is not that people are genetically different but that they approach one another with dissimilar perspectives. It is in the social setting that race is decisive. Race is significant because people have given it significance.

Race definitions are crystallized through what Michael Omi and Howard Winant (1994) called **racial formation**. Racial formation is a sociohistorical process by which racial categories are created, inhibited, transformed, and destroyed. Those in power define groups of people in a certain way that depends on a racist social structure. The Native Americans and the creation of the reservation system in the latter 1800s would be an example of this racial formation. Previously distinctive tribes, the federal American Indian policy created a single group where one had not existed. No one—absolutely no one—escapes the extent and frequency to which we are subjected to racial formation.

In the South of the United States the social construction of race was known as the "one-drop rule." This tradition stipulated that if a person had even a single drop of "Black blood," that person was defined and viewed as Black. Today children of biracial or multiracial marriages try to build their own identity in a United States that seems intent on placing them in some single traditional category (S. Love 1996; R. Schaefer 1996).

A particularly sobering aspect of racial formation is that the United States is exporting this development. Just as this nation promotes tastes in music and television, the racial identities in the United States are being internationalized. While the United States is certainly not responsible for racial, ethnic, and religious tensions, we have been contributing to the defining of racial awareness (H. Winant 1994:20).

CENSUS 2000

Only six questions are asked of every person in the United States on Census Day, April 18, 2000—and two of them deal with ethnicity and race. As you can see in the reproduction from official Census materials in Figure 1.2, people are first asked to indicate whether they are Spanish/Hispanic/Latino, and if they are, what specific Hispanic group they are. Then, in the next question, people again are asked to check off ***one or more*** racial groups. In the longer questionnaire form given to a sample of about one-sixth of the entire population, a series of five questions asks people to indicate in what country they were born, their citizenship status, and to identify their ancestry or ethnic origin (for example, Italian, Jamaican, and so on).

Census 2000 for the first time allows respondents to indicate a multiracial identity and can be viewed as another step in racial formation. The 1990 Census and most earlier ones required people to indicate whether they were Black or White or American Indian or Asian and did not allow one to indicate multiple identities. There was great debate over this wording, as many felt it was unfair to ask people, especially the children of interracial marriages, to pick a single group. Some actually lobbied the government to include the category "multiracial," but instead a compromise was reached of allowing people to select several categories but while still working within the confines of traditionally used terms for racial groups. Sociologists and others are speculating on the likely outcome. How many tens of millions of people may identify themselves with multiple identities? The discussion over identifying people's race or ethnicity shows that race is socially defined. If it was relatively unambiguous, like age, such a debate would not occur. Later in this chapter we will give consideration to the issue of "Who am I?" in terms of racial and ethnic identity.

NOTE: Please answer BOTH Questions 5 and 6.

5 Is this person Spanish/Hispanic/Latino? Mark [X] *the* ***"No"*** *box if* ***not*** *Spanish/Hispanic/Latino.*

- ☐ **No**, not Spanish/Hispanic/Latino
- ☐ Yes, Mexican, Mexican Am., Chicano
- ☐ Yes, Puerto Rican
- ☐ Yes, Cuban
- ☐ Yes, other Spanish/Hispanic/Latino—*Print group.*

6 What is this person's race? ***Mark*** [X] ***one or more races*** *to indicate what this person considers himself/herself to be.*

- ☐ White
- ☐ Black, African Am., or Negro
- ☐ American Indian or Alaska Native—*Print name of enrolled or principal tribe.*
- ☐ Asian Indian
- ☐ Chinese
- ☐ Filipino
- ☐ Japanese
- ☐ Korean
- ☐ Vietnamese
- ☐ Other Asian—*Print race.*
- ☐ Native Hawaiian
- ☐ Guamanian or Chamorro
- ☐ Samoan
- ☐ Other Pacific Islander—*Print race.*
- ☐ Some other race—*Print race.*

Figure 1.2 Census 2000 Questions on Race and Ethnicity

Source: Bureau of the Census 1998a.

Sociology and the Study of Race and Ethnicity

Before proceeding further with our study of racial and ethnic groups, let us consider several sociological perspectives that provide insight into dominant–subordinate relationships. **Sociology** is the systematic study of social behavior and human groups and therefore is aptly suited to enlarge our understanding of intergroup relations. There is a long, valuable history of the study of race relations in sociology. Admittedly, it has not always been progressive and, indeed, it has at times reflected the prejudice and discrimination of society. There have been examples in the past where scholars who are members of racial, ethnic, and religious minorities, as well as women, have not been permitted to make the kind of contributions they are capable of to the field.

STRATIFICATION BY CLASS AND GENDER

All societies are characterized by members having unequal amounts of wealth, prestige, or power. Sociologists observe that entire groups may be assigned to have less or more of what a society values. The hierarchy that emerges is called stratification. **Stratification** is the structured ranking of entire groups of people that perpetuates unequal rewards and power in a society.

Much discussion of stratification identifies the **class**, or social ranking, of people who share similar wealth, according to sociologist Max Weber's classic definition. Mobility from one class to another is not necessarily easy. Movement into classes of greater wealth may be particularly difficult for subordinate-group members faced with life-long prejudice and discrimination (Gerth and Mills 1958).

Recall that the first property of subordinate group standing is unequal treatment by the dominant group in the form of prejudice, discrimination, and segregation. Stratification is intertwined with the subordination of racial, ethnic, religious, and gender groups. Race has implications for the way people are treated; so does class. One also has to add the effects of race and class together. For example, being poor and Black is not the same as being either one by itself. A wealthy Mexican American is not the same as an affluent Anglo or as Mexican Americans as a group.

The monumental 1992 south-central Los Angeles riots that followed the acquittal of four White police officers charged with beating African American Rodney King illustrated the power of both race and class. The most visible issue was White brutality against Blacks; yet during the riot, the concentrated attack on Korean American merchants, whose economic role placed them in a very vulnerable social position, underscored the role of race in defining how we see others. The multiracial character of the looting involving Hispanics and Whites was a response not only to the judicial system but also to poverty.

Frequently, public discussion of issues such as housing or public assistance is disguised as discussion of class issues when in fact the issues are based primarily on race. Similarly, some topics such as the poorest of poor or the working poor are addressed in terms of race, when the class component should be explicit. Nonetheless, the link between race and class in society is abundantly clear (H. Winant 1994).

Women are gradually moving into leadership positions in new areas. Carolyn Morris, assistant director of the Federal Bureau of Investigation, is the highest ranking African American in FBI history. She supervises 2,000 employees and a budget of more than $200 million.

Another stratification factor that we need to consider is gender. How different is the situation for women as contrasted with men? Returning again to that first property of minority groups—unequal treatment and less control—treatment for women is not equal to that received by men. Whether it is jobs or poverty, education or crime, the experience of women typically is more difficult. In addition, the situation faced by women in such areas as health care and welfare raise different concerns than it does for men. Just as we need to consider the role of social class to understand race and ethnicity better, we also need to consider the role of gender.

THEORETICAL PERSPECTIVES

Sociologists view society in different ways. Some see the world basically as a stable and ongoing entity. They are impressed by the endurance of a Chinatown, the relative sameness of male-female roles over time, and other aspects of intergroup relations. Some sociologists see society as composed of many groups in conflict, competing for scarce resources. Within this conflict, some people or even entire groups may be labeled or stigmatized in a way that blocks their access to what a society values. We will examine three theoretical perspectives that are widely used by sociologists today: the functionalist, conflict, and labeling perspectives.

Functionalist Perspective In the view of a functionalist, a society is like a living organism in which each part contributes to the survival of the whole. The **functionalist perspective** emphasizes how the parts of society are structured to maintain its stability. According to this approach, if an aspect of social life does not contribute to a society's stability or survival, it will not be passed on from one generation to the next.

It would seem reasonable to assume that bigotry between races offers no such positive function, and so, we ask, why does it persist? The functionalist, although agreeing that racial hostility is hardly to be admired, would point out that it does serve some positive functions from the perspective of the racists. We can identify five functions that racial beliefs have for the dominant group:

1. Racist ideologies provide a moral justification for maintaining a society that routinely deprives a group of its rights and privileges.
2. Racist beliefs discourage subordinate people from attempting to question their lowly status; to do so is to question the very foundations of the society.
3. Racial ideologies not only justify existing practices but serve as a rallying point for social movements, as seen in the rise of the Nazi Party.
4. Racist myths encourage support for the existing order. The argument is used that if there were any major societal change, the subordinate group would suffer even greater poverty and the dominant group would suffer lower living standards (Nash 1962).
5. Racist beliefs relieve the dominant group of the responsibility to address the economic and educational problems faced by subordinate groups.

As a result, racial ideology grows when a value system (for example, that underlying a colonial empire or slavery) is being threatened.

There are also definite dysfunctions caused by prejudice and discrimination. **Dysfunctions** are elements of society that may disrupt a social system or tend to decrease its stability. There are six ways in which racism is dysfunctional to a society, including to its dominant group:

1. A society that practices discrimination fails to use the resources of all individuals. Discrimination limits the search for talent and leadership to the dominant group.
2. Discrimination aggravates social problems such as poverty, delinquency, and crime and places the financial burden of alleviating these problems on the dominant group.
3. Society must invest a good deal of time and money to defend the barriers that prevent the full participation of all members.
4. Racial prejudice and discrimination undercut goodwill and friendly diplomatic relations between nations. They also negatively affect efforts to increase global trade.
5. Social change is inhibited, because change may contribute to assisting a subordinate group.
6. Discrimination promotes disrespect for law enforcement and for the peaceful settlement of disputes.

That racism has costs for the dominant group as well as the subordinate group reminds us that intergroup conflict is exceedingly complex (Bowser and Hunt 1996; Feagin and Vera 1995; A. Rose 1951).

Conflict Perspective In contrast to the functionalists' emphasis on stability, conflict sociologists see the social world as being in continual struggle. The **conflict perspective** assumes that the social structure is best understood in terms of conflict or tension among competing groups. Specifically, society is a struggle between the privileged (the dominant group) and the exploited (the subordinate groups). Such conflicts need not be physically violent and may take the form of immigration restrictions, real estate practices, or disputes over cuts in the federal budget.

The conflict model is often selected today when one is examining race and ethnicity because it readily accounts for the presence of tension between competing groups. The competition, according to the conflict perspective, takes place between groups with unequal amounts of economic and political power. The minorities are exploited or, at best, ignored by the dominant group. The conflict perspective is viewed as more radical and activist than functionalism because conflict theorists emphasize social change and the redistribution of resources. Functionalists are not necessarily in favor of such inequality; rather, their approach helps us to understand why such systems persist.

Those who follow the conflict approach to race and ethnicity have remarked repeatedly that the subordinate group is criticized for its low status. That the dominant group is responsible for the subordination is often ignored. William Ryan (1976) calls this an instance of "blaming the victim": portraying the problems of racial and ethnic minorities as their fault rather than recognizing society's responsibility. This idea is not new. Gunnar Myrdal, a Swedish social economist of international reputation, headed a project that produced the classic 1944 work on Blacks in the United States, ***The American Dilemma.*** Myrdal concluded that the plight of the subordinate group is the responsibility of the dominant majority. It is not a Black problem, but a White problem. Similarly, we can use the same approach and note it is not a Hispanic problem or a Haitian refugee problem, but a White problem. Myrdal and others since then have reminded the public and policy makers alike that the ultimate responsibility for society's problems must rest with those who possess the most authority and the most economic resources (D. Southern 1987; see also J. Hochschild 1995).

Labeling Approach Related to the conflict perspective and its concern over blaming the victim is labeling theory. **Labeling theory**, a concept introduced by sociologist Howard Becker, is an attempt to explain why certain people are viewed as different from or less worthy than others. Students of crime and deviance have relied heavily on labeling theory. A youth who misbehaves, according to labeling theory, may be considered and treated as a delinquent if she or he comes from the "wrong kind of family." Another youth, from a middle-class family, who commits the same sort of misbehavior might be given another chance before being punished.

The labeling perspective directs our attention to the role that negative stereotypes play in race and ethnicity. The image that prejudiced people maintain of a group toward which they hold ill feelings is called a stereotype. **Stereotypes** are exaggerated images of the characteristics of a particular group. The warrior image of American Indian people is perpetuated by the frequent use of tribal names or even terms like "Indians" and "Redskins" as sports team mascots. In Chapter 2, we will review some of the research on the stereotyping of minorities. This labeling is not limited to racial and ethnic groups, however. Age, for instance, can be used to exclude a person from an activity in which he or she is actually qualified to engage. Groups are subjected to stereotypes and discrimination in such a way that their treatment resembles that of social minorities. Social prejudice exists toward ex-convicts, gamblers, alcoholics, lesbians, gays, prostitutes, people with AIDS, and people with disabilities, to name a few.

The labeling approach points out that stereotypes, when applied by people in power, can have very negative consequences for people or groups identified falsely. A crucial aspect of the relationship between dominant and subordinate groups is the prerogative of the dominant group to define society's values. American sociologist William I. Thomas (1923), an early critic of racial and gender discrimination, saw that the "definition of the situation" could mold the personality of the individual. In other words, Thomas observed that people respond not only to the objective features of a situation (or person) but also to the meaning these features have for them. So, for example, a lone walker seeing a young Black male walking toward him may perceive the situation differently than if the oncoming person is an elderly woman. In this manner, we can create false images or stereotypes that become real in their consequences.

In certain situations, we may respond to negative stereotypes and act on them, with the result that false definitions become accurate. This is known as a **self-fulfilling prophecy**. A person or group described as having particular characteristics begins to display the very traits attributed to them. Thus, a child who is praised for being a natural comic may focus on learning to become funny to gain approval and attention.

Self-fulfilling prophecies can be devastating for minority groups (see Figure 1.3). Such groups often find that they are allowed to hold only low-paying jobs with

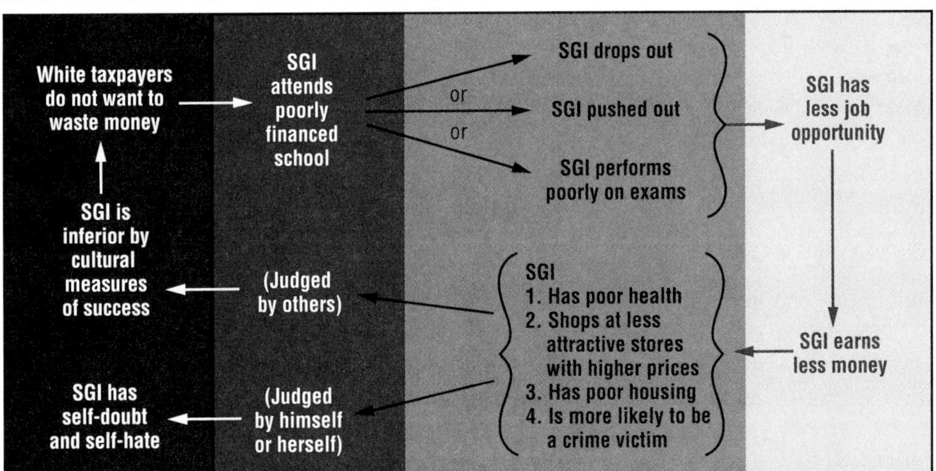

Figure 1.3 Self-fulfilling Prophecy
The self-validating effects of dominant-group definitions are shown in this figure. The subordinate-group individual (SGI) attends a poorly financed school and is left unequipped to perform jobs that offer high status and pay. He or she then gets a low-paying job and must settle for a standard of living far short of society's standards. Since the person shares these societal standards, he or she may begin to feel self-doubt and self-hatred.

little prestige or opportunity for advancement. The rationale of the dominant society is that these minority individuals lack the ability to perform in more important and lucrative positions. Training to become scientists, executives, or physicians is denied to many subordinate-group individuals, who are then locked into society's inferior jobs. As a result, the false definition becomes real. The subordinate group has become inferior because it was defined at the start as inferior and was therefore prevented from achieving the levels attained by the majority.

Because of this vicious circle, a talented subordinate-group individual may come to see the worlds of entertainment and professional sports as his or her only hope for achieving wealth and fame. Thus, it is no accident that successive waves of Irish, Jewish, Italian, African American, and Hispanic performers and athletes have made their mark on culture in the United States. Unfortunately, these very successes may convince the dominant group that its original stereotypes were valid—that these are the only areas of society in which subordinate-group members can excel. Furthermore, athletics and the arts are highly competitive areas. For every Michael Jordan and Gloria Estefan who makes it, many, many more will end up disappointed.

The Creation of Subordinate-Group Status

Three situations are likely to lead to the formation of a subordinate-group–dominant-group relationship. A subordinate group emerges through (1) migration, (2) annexation, and (3) colonialism.

MIGRATION

People who immigrate to a new country often find themselves a minority in that new country. Cultural or physical traits or religious affiliation may set the immigrant apart from the dominant group. Immigration from Europe, Asia, and Latin America has been a powerful force in shaping the fabric of life in the United States. **Migration** is the general term used to describe any transfer of population. **Emigration** (by emigrants) describes leaving a country to settle in another; **immigration** (by immigrants) denotes coming into the new country. From Vietnam's perspective, the "boat people" were emigrants from Vietnam to the United States, but in the United States they were counted among this nation's immigrants.

Although people may migrate because they want to, leaving the home country is not always voluntary. Conflict or war has displaced people throughout human history. In the twentieth century, we have seen huge population movements caused by two world wars; revolutions in Spain, Hungary, and Cuba; the partition of British India; conflicts in Southeast Asia, Korea, and Central America; and the confrontation between Arabs and Israelis.

In all types of movement, even the movement of an American family from Ohio to Florida, two sets of forces operate: push factors and pull factors. Push factors discourage a person from remaining where he or she lives. Religious persecution and economic factors such as dissatisfaction with employment opportunities are possible push factors. Pull factors, such as a better standard of living, friends and relatives who have already emigrated, and a promised job, attract an immigrant to a particular country.

While generally we think of migration as a voluntary process, much of the population transfer that has occurred in the world has been involuntary. The forced movement of people into another society guarantees a subordinate role. Involuntary migration is no longer common; although enslavement has a long history, all industrialized societies today prohibit such practices. Of course, many contemporary societies, including the United States, bear the legacy of slavery.

ANNEXATION

Nations, particularly during wars or as a result of war, incorporate or attach land. This new land is contiguous to the nation, as in the German annexation of Austria and Czechoslovakia in 1938 and 1939 and in the Louisiana Purchase of 1803. The Treaty of Guadalupe Hidalgo that ended the Mexican-American War in 1848 gave the United States California, Utah, Nevada, most of New Mexico, and parts of Arizona, Wyoming, and Colorado. The indigenous peoples in some of this huge territory were dominant in their society one day, only to become minority-group members the next.

When annexation occurs, the dominant power generally suppresses the language and culture of the minority. Such was the practice of Russia with the Ukrainians and Poles, and of Prussia with the Poles. Minorities try to maintain their cultural integrity despite annexation. Poles inhabited an area divided into territories ruled by three countries but maintained their own culture across political boundaries.

COLONIALISM

Colonialism has been the most frequent way for one group of people to dominate another. **Colonialism** is the maintenance of political, social, economic, and cultural domination over people by a foreign power for an extended period (W. Bell 1991). Colonialism is rule by outsiders but, unlike annexation, does not involve actual incorporation into the dominant people's nation. The long control exercised by the British Empire over much of North America, parts of Africa, and India is an example of colonial domination.

Societies gain power over a foreign land through military strength, sophisticated political organization, and the massive use of investment capital. The extent of power may also vary according to the dominant group's scope of settlement in the colonial land. Relations between the colonial nation and the colonized people are similar to those between a dominant group and exploited subordinate groups. The colonial subjects are generally limited to menial jobs and the wages from their labor. The natural resources of their land benefit the members of the ruling class.

By the 1980s colonialism, in the sense of political rule, had become largely a phenomenon of the past, yet industrial countries of North America and Europe still dominated the world economically and politically. Sociologist Immanuel Wallerstein (1974, 1979, 1996), drawing on the conflict perspective, views the global economic system today as much like the height of colonial days. Wallerstein has advanced the **world systems theory,** which views the global economic system as divided between nations that control wealth and those that provide natural resources and labor. Many of the ethnic, racial, and religious conflicts noted at the beginning of the chapter are exacerbated by the limited economic resources available in developing nations.

A significant exception to the end of foreign political rule is Puerto Rico, whose territorial or commonwealth status with the United States is basically that of a colony. The more than 2 million people on the island are U.S. citizens but are unable to vote in presidential elections unless they migrate to the mainland. In 1998, 58 percent of Puerto Ricans on the island voted for options favoring continuation of commonwealth status, 47 percent favored statehood, and less than 5 percent voted for independence. Despite their poor showing, pro-independence forces are very vocal and enjoy the sympathies of others concerned about the cultural and economic dominance of the U.S. mainland (L. Saad 1998; M. Navarro 1998).

Colonialism is domination by outsiders. Relations between the colonizer and the colony are similar to those between the dominant and subordinate peoples within the same country. This distinctive pattern of oppression is called **internal colonialism**. Among other cases, it has been applied to the plight of Blacks in the United States and Mexican Indians in Mexico, who are colonial peoples in their own country. Internal colonialism covers more than simple economic oppression. Nationalist movements in African colonies struggled to achieve political as well as economic independence from Europeans. Similarly, African Americans also call themselves nationalists in trying to gain more autonomy over their lives (R. Blauner 1969, 1972).

The Consequences of Subordinate-Group Status

There are several consequences for a group of subordinate status. These differ in their degree of harshness, ranging from physical annihilation to absorption into the dominant group. In this section, we will examine six consequences of subordinate-group status: extermination, expulsion, secession, segregation, fusion, and assimilation. Figure 1.4 illustrates how these consequences can be defined.

EXTERMINATION

The most extreme way of dealing with a subordinate group is to eliminate it. One historical example is the British destruction of the people of Tasmania, an island off the coast of Australia. There were 5,000 Tasmanians in 1800, but because they were attacked by settlers and forced to live on less habitable islands, the last full-blooded Tasmanian died in 1876. A human group had become extinct, totally eliminated.

Today the term **genocide** is used to describe the deliberate, systematic killing of an entire people or nation. This term is frequently used in reference to the Holocaust—Nazi Germany's extermination of 12 million European Jews and other ethnic minorities during World War II. The term **ethnic cleansing** was introduced into the world's vocabulary as ethnic Serbs instituted a policy intended to "cleanse"—

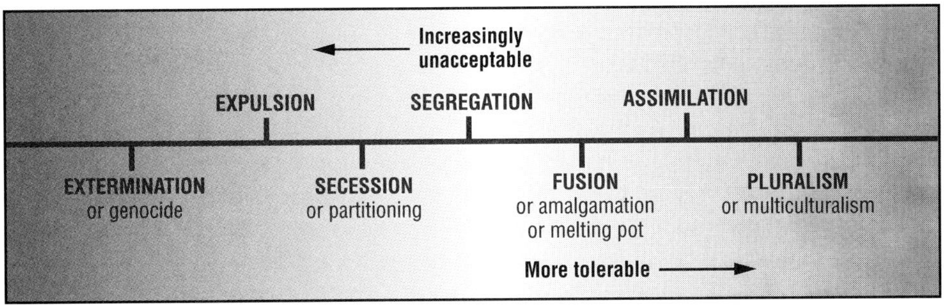

Figure 1.4 Intergroup Relations Continuum
The social consequences of being in a subordinate group can be viewed along a continuum ranging from extermination to forms of mutual acceptance such as pluralism.

eliminate—Muslims from parts of Bosnia. More recently, a genocidal war between the Hutu and Tutsi people in Rwanda left 300,000 school-age children orphaned.

Genocide, however, also appropriately describes White policies toward Native Americans in the nineteenth century. In 1800, the American Indian population in the United States was about 600,000; by 1850 it had been reduced to 250,000 through warfare with the U.S. Army, disease, and forced relocation to inhospitable environments.

EXPULSION

Dominant groups may choose to force a specific subordinate group to leave certain areas or even vacate a country. Expulsion is therefore another extreme consequence of minority-group status. European colonial powers in North America and eventually the U.S. government itself drove virtually all Native Americans out of their tribal lands into unfamiliar territory.

More recently, Vietnam in 1979 expelled nearly 1 million ethnic Chinese from the country, partly as a result of centuries of hostility between the two Asian neighbors. These "boat people" were abruptly eliminated as a minority within Vietnamese society. This expulsion meant, though, that they were now uprooted and became a new minority group in many nations, including Australia, France, the United States, and Canada. Thus expulsion may remove a minority group from one society; however, the expelled people merely go to another nation, where they are again a minority group.

SECESSION

A group ceases to be a subordinate group when it secedes to form a new nation or moves to an already established nation where it becomes dominant. After Great Britain withdrew from Palestine, Jewish people achieved a dominant position in 1948, attracting Jews from throughout the world to the new state of Israel. In a similar fashion, Pakistan was created in 1947 when India was partitioned. The predominantly Muslim areas in the north became Pakistan, making India predominantly Hindu.

Throughout this century, minorities have repudiated dominant customs. In this spirit, the Estonian, Latvian, Lithuanian, and Armenian peoples, for example, not content to be merely tolerated by the majority, all seceded to form independent states following the demise of the Soviet Union in 1991. In 1999, ethnic Albanians fought bitterly for their cultural and political recognition in the Kosovo region of Yugoslavia.

Some African Americans have called for secession. Suggestions dating back to the early 1700s supported the return of Blacks to Africa as a solution to racial problems. The settlement target of the American Colonization Society was Liberia, but proposals were also advanced to establish settlements in other areas. Territorial separatism and the emigrationist ideology were recurrent and interrelated themes among African Americans from the late nineteenth century well into the 1980s. The Black Muslims, or Nation of Islam, once expressed the desire for complete separation in their own state or territory within the present borders of the United States. Although a secession of Blacks from the United States has not taken place, it has been considered and even proposed in the past (Bracey, Meier, and Rudwick 1970; F. Butterfield 1986).

SEGREGATION

Segregation refers to the physical separation of two groups in residence, workplace, and social functions. Generally, the dominant group imposes segregation on a subordinate group. Segregation is rarely complete, however; intergroup contact inevitably occurs even in the most segregated societies.

The extent of racial and ethnic isolation in the United States is staggering. Two-thirds of all Blacks attend schools in which more than half of the students are either Black or Hispanic. Almost three-fourths of all Hispanics attend predominantly Hispanic and Black schools (G. Orfield 1993; see also Massey and Denton 1993).

While the word segregation usually evokes images of urban neighborhoods and schools, the isolation of reservations is yet another illustration of the legacy of past segregation. Shown here is the Hopi reservation in Arizona.

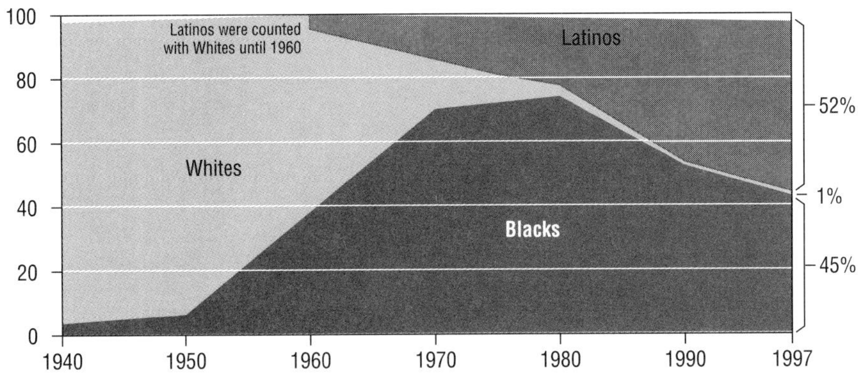

Figure 1.5 Segregation and Change, Compton, California, from 1940 to the Present

Source: Compton Department of Planning, Los Angeles County Department of Planning, Census Bureau, California Department of Finance, and interviews as prepared by L. Perlstein 1998

Residential segregation is also pervasive in the United States. Cities, suburbs, and even small towns have neighborhoods dominated by certain racial and ethnic groups. Residential patterns may change but segregation persists. In Figure 1.5, we consider the case of Compton, California, a city surrounded by Los Angeles. For much of its history it was all-White. This was not surprising since, until a Supreme Court decision in 1948, African Americans were barred from buying a home there. Blacks persevered despite both open and hidden White hostility, and by twenty years ago Compton was overwhelmingly Black. Gradually Blacks came to hold all the important governmental positions, and they boasted with pride that Compton was the largest Black city west of the Mississippi. Immigration contributed to increasing numbers of Latinos seeking affordable housing where they would not encounter the indifference of realtors and the hostility of local residents. Compton offered such a community. Eventually Latinos came to make up the largest segment of the population, and now they are looking to play a major role in all the community's institutions. The case of Compton shows how segregation patterns can change and may represent even an improvement for those moving in, but it also illustrates how residential housing is intertwined with government, public safety, medical services, and education.

This focus on metropolitan areas should not cause us to ignore the continuing legally sanctioned segregation of Native Americans on reservations. Although the majority of our nation's first inhabitants do live outside these tribal areas, the reservations play a prominent role in the identity of Native Americans. They face the difficult choice that, while it is easier to maintain tribal identity on the reservation, economic and educational opportunities are more limited in these areas segregated from the rest of society.

Residential segregation patterns are not unique to the United States. In Germany today, they speak of Ghettoisierung (or "ghettoization") as concentrations of Turkish immigrants are emerging. Social scientists in Sweden have used the segregation index to document the isolation of Greek, Chilean, and Turkish immigrants from the rest of the population. Segregation is present in virtually all multiracial societies.

FUSION

Fusion describes the result when a minority and a majority group combine to form a new group. This combining can be expressed as A+B+C→D, where A, B, and C represent the groups present in a society, and D signifies the result, a cultural-racial group unlike any of the initial groups. Theoretically, fusion does not require intermarriage, but it is very similar to **amalgamation**, or the cultural and physical synthesis of various groups into a new people. In everyday speech, the words fusion and amalgamation are rarely used, but the concept is expressed in the notion of a human **melting pot**, in which diverse racial or ethnic groups form a new creation, a new cultural entity (W. Newman 1973).

The analogy of the cauldron, the "melting pot," was first used to describe the United States by the French observer Crèvecoeur in 1782 (see P. Gleason 1980:33). The phrase dates back to the Middle Ages, when alchemists attempted to change less valuable metals into gold and silver. Similarly, the idea of the human melting pot implied that the new group would represent only the best qualities and attributes of the different cultures contributing to it. The belief in the United States as a melting pot became widespread in the first part of the twentieth century. This belief suggested that the United States had an almost divine mission to destroy artificial divisions and create a single kind of human. The dominant group, however, had indicated its unwillingness to welcome such groups as Native Americans, Blacks, Hispanics, Jews, Asians, and Irish Roman Catholics into the melting pot. It is a mistake to think of the United States as an ethnic mixing bowl. While there are superficial signs of fusion, as in a cuisine that includes sauerkraut and spaghetti, virtually all contributions of subordinate groups are ignored.

Marriage patterns indicate the resistance to fusion. People are unwilling, in varying degrees, to marry out of their own ethnic, religious, and racial groups. Surveys still show that 20 to 50 percent of various White ethnic groups report single ancestry. When White ethnics do cross boundaries, they tend to marry within their religion and social class. For example, Italians are more likely to marry Irish, who are still Roman Catholic, than they are to marry Protestant Swedes.

There is only modest evidence in the United States of a fusion of races. Racial intermarriage has been increasing, and the number of interracial couples immigrating to the United States has also grown. 1970 showed 678,000 interracial couples, but by 1995 the figure stood at over 3.2 million. Taken together, such marriages across racial lines represent about 3 percent of all couples. The growth of mixed marriages can be seen in the growing presence of children of biracial parentage (Bureau of the Census 1997:57; M. Lind 1998; Z. Naomi 1995; Z. Qian 1997).

ASSIMILATION

Assimilation is the process by which a subordinate individual or group takes on the characteristics of the dominant group and is eventually accepted as part of that group. Assimilation is a majority ideology in which A+B+C→A. The majority (A) dominates in such a way that the minorities (B and C) become indistinguishable from the dominant group. Assimilation dictates conformity to the dominant group, regardless of how many racial, ethnic, or religious groups are involved (H. Bash 1979;

Faced with new laws restricting rights of noncitizens, coupled with a desire to assimilate, 10,000 people representing 113 countries participate in naturalization ceremonies in Texas.

M. Gordon 1964, 1996; C. Hirschman 1983; W. Newman 1973:53).

To be complete, assimilation must entail an active effort by the minority-group individual to shed all distinguishing actions and beliefs and the total, unqualified acceptance of that individual by the dominant society. In the United States, dominant White society encourages assimilation. The assimilation perspective tends to devalue alien culture and to treasure the dominant. For example, assimilation assumes that whatever is admirable among Blacks was adapted from Whites and that whatever is bad is inherently Black. The assimilation solution to Black–White conflict is the development of a consensus around White American values (L. Broom 1965:23).

Assimilation is difficult. The individual must forsake his or her cultural tradition to become part of a different, often antagonistic, culture. Members of the subordinate group who choose not to assimilate look on those who do as deserters. Many Hindus in India complained of their compatriots who copied the traditions and customs of the British. Those who assimilate must break entirely with the past. Australian Aborigines who become part of dominant society conceal their origin by ignoring darker-skinned relatives, including their immediate family. As one assimilated Aborigine explained, "Why should I have anything to do with them? I haven't anything in common with them, and I don't even like most of them." These conflicting demands leave an individual torn between two value systems (Berndt and Berndt 1951; B. McCully 1940).

Assimilation does not occur at the same pace for all groups or for all individuals in the same group. Assimilation tends to take longer under the following conditions:

1. The differences between the minority and the majority are large.
2. The majority is not receptive, or the minority retains its own culture.
3. The minority group arrives in a short period of time.
4. The minority-group residents are concentrated rather than dispersed.
5. The arrival is recent, and the homeland is accessible.

Assimilation is not a smooth process (Warner and Srole 1945).

Assimilation is viewed by many as "unfair" or even "dictatorial." However, most see it as reasonable that people shed their distinctive cultural traditions. In public discussions today, assimilation is the ideology of the dominant group in forcing people how to act. Consequently, the social institutions in the United States, such as the educational system, economy, government, religion, and medicine, all push toward assimilation, with occasional references to the pluralist approach.

THE PLURALIST PERSPECTIVE

Thus far we have concentrated on how subordinate groups cease to exist (removal) or take on the characteristics of the dominant group (assimilation). The alternative to these relationships between the majority and the minority is pluralism. **Pluralism** implies that various groups in a society have mutual respect for one another's culture, a respect that allows minorities to express their own culture without suffering prejudice or hostility. Whereas the assimilationist or integrationist seeks the elimination of ethnic boundaries, the pluralist believes in maintaining many of them (see also R. Manning 1995).

There are limits to cultural freedom. A Romanian immigrant to the United States could not expect to avoid learning English and still move up the occupational ladder. In order to survive, a society must have a consensus among its members on basic ideals, values, and beliefs. Nevertheless, there is still plenty of room for variety. Earlier, fusion was described as A+B+C→D and assimilation as A+B+C→A. Using this same scheme, we can think of pluralism as A+B+C→A+B+C, where groups coexist in one society (W. Newman 1973; J. Simpson 1995.)

In the United States, cultural pluralism is more an ideal than a reality. Though there are vestiges of cultural pluralism—in the various ethnic neighborhoods in major cities, for instance—the rule has been for subordinate groups to assimilate. The cost of cultural integrity has been high. The various Native American tribes have succeeded to a large extent in maintaining their heritage, but the price has been bare subsistence on federal reservations.

In the United States, there is a reemergence of ethnic identification by groups that had previously expressed little interest in their heritage. Groups that make up the dominant majority are also reasserting their ethnic heritage. Various nationality groups are rekindling interest in almost forgotten languages, customs, festivals, and traditions. In some instances, this expression of the past has taken the form of a protest against exclusion from the dominant society. Chinese youths, for example, chastise their elders for forgetting the old ways and accepting White American influence and control.

The most visible controversy about pluralism is the debate surrounding bilingualism. **Bilingualism** is the use of two or more languages in places of work or education, with each language being treated as equally legitimate.

According to a report released by the U.S. Bureau of the Census, almost 32 million residents of the United States—or about one of every seven people—speak a native language other than English. Indeed, fifty different languages are spoken by at least 30,000 residents of this country. Over the period 1980–1990, there was a

38 percent increase in the number of people in the United States whose native language was not English (M. Usdansky 1993).

The passionate debate under way in the United States over bilingualism frequently acknowledges the large number of people who do not speak English at home. In education, bilingualism has seemed to be one way of assisting millions of people who want to learn English in order to function more efficiently within the United States.

In the 1990s, bilingualism became an increasingly controversial political issue. For example, a proposed Constitutional amendment has been introduced that designates English as the "official language of the nation." A major force behind the proposed amendment and other efforts to restrict bilingualism is "U.S. English," a nationwide organization that views the English language as the "social glue" that keeps the nation together. This organization supports assimilation. By contrast, Hispanic leaders see the U.S. English campaign as a veiled expression of racism.

Who Am I?

When Tiger Woods appeared on ***The Oprah Winfrey Show,*** he was asked if it bothered him, the only child of a Black American father and a Thai mother, to be called an African American, he replied, "It does. Growing up, I came up with this name: I'm a 'Cabalinasian'" (J. White 1997:34). This is a self-crafted acronym to reflect that Tiger Woods is one-eighth Caucasian, one-fourth Black, one-eighth American Indian, one-fourth Thai, and one-fourth Chinese roots. While we acknowledge his diversity in background, soon after he achieved professional stardom, another golfer was strongly criticized for making racist remarks based on seeing Woods only as African American. If Tiger Woods was not so famous, would most people upon meeting him see him as anything but an African American? Probably not. Tiger Woods's problem is really the problem of a diverse society that continues to try to place people in a few socially constructed racial and ethnic boxes.

The diversity of the United States today has made it more difficult for many people to view themselves clearly on the racial and ethnic landscape. It reminds us that racial formation continues to take place. Obviously, the racial and ethnic "landscape," as we have seen, is constructed not naturally but socially and is therefore subject to change and different interpretations. While our focus is on the United States, virtually every nation faces the same dilemmas.

Within little more than a generation, we have witnessed changes in labeling subordinate groups from Negroes to Blacks to African Americans, from American Indians to Native Americans or Native Peoples. However, more Native Americans prefer the use of their tribal name, such as Seminole, instead of a collective label. The old 1950s statistical term of people with a Spanish surname has long been discarded, yet there is disagreement over a new term: Latino or Hispanic. As with Native Americans, Hispanic Americans avoid such global terms and prefer the use of their native names, such as Puerto Ricans or Cubans. People of Mexican ancestry indicate preferences for a variety of names, such as Mexican American, Chicano, or simply Mexican.

Some advocates for racial and ethnic groups consider names a very important issue with great social significance. If nothing else, others argue, changes in names reflect that people are taking over the power to choose their name. Still others do not see this as an issue; as editor Anna Maria Arias of ***Hispanic*** magazine termed the debate, "It's stupid. There are more important issues we should be talking about" (P. Bennett 1993:A10; see also Portes and MacLeod 1996).

In the United States and other multiracial, multiethnic societies, panethnicity has emerged. **Panethnicity** is the development of solidarity among ethnic subgroups. The coalition of tribal groups as Native Americans or American Indians to confront outside forces, notably the federal government, is one example of panethnicity. Hispanic or Latinos and Asian Americans are other examples of panethnicity. While it is rarely recognized by dominant society, the very term Black or African American represents the descendants of many different ethnic or tribal groups, such as Akamba, Fulani, Hausa, Malinke, and Yoruba (Lopez and Espiritu 1990; Onishi 1996).

Is panethnicity a convenient label for "outsiders" or a term that reflects a mutual identity? Certainly, many people outside the group are unable or unwilling to recognize ethnic differences and prefer "umbrella" terms such as Asian Americans. For some small groups, combining with others is emerging as a useful way to make themselves heard, but there is always a fear that their own distinctive culture will become submerged. While many Hispanics share the Spanish language and many are united by Roman Catholicism, only one in four native-born people of Mexican, Puerto Rican, or Cuban descent prefers a panethnic label over nationality or ethnic identity. Yet the growth of a variety of panethnic associations among many groups, including Hispanics, continues in the 1990s (de la Garza et al. 1992; Y. Espirito 1992).

Children of biracial or multiracial couples face special challenges in the United States, where there is a strong desire to place everyone in just a few categories.

There is even less agreement about how to identify oneself in racially conscious America if one is of mixed ancestry. Roberto Chong, who immigrated to the United States, has a Chinese father and a Peruvian mother. He considers himself Hispanic, but others view him as Asian or Latino Asian American. As discussed earlier, there are relatively few intermarriages in America, and social attitudes discourage them, but such unions are on the increase. Interracial births doubled from 63,700 in 1978 to 133,200 in 1992. In a race-conscious society, how are we going to respond to these multiracial children? As the mother of one such child, Hannah Spangler, noted, how is she to complete the school form as Hannah starts first grade in Washington, D.C.? Hannah's father is White, and her mother is half Black and half Japanese. We may be slowly recognizing that the United States is a multiracial society, but we are not yet prepared to respond to such a society (S. Kalish 1995).

The Office of Management and Budget has established an Interagency Committee for the Review of the Racial and Ethnic Standards. This panel was created to address the effect of having a multiracial category among the list of races in the Census to be taken in the year 2000. While results showed that relatively few (1.5 percent) chose the multiracial category, it did mark a recognition that a segment of the population exists for whom old categories may not work. We are witnessing by such efforts the official recognition of the social construction of race and another phase of racial formation.

Add to this cultural mix the many peoples with clear social identities who are not yet generally recognized in the United States. Arabs are a rapidly growing segment whose identity is heavily subject to stereotypes or, at best, is still ambiguous. Haitians and Jamaicans affirm that they are Black but rarely accept the identity of African American. Brazilians, who speak Portuguese, often object to being called Hispanic, because of that term's association with Spain. Similarly, there are White Hispanics and non-White Hispanics, some of the latter being Black, and others, like Roberto Chong, Asian (P. Bennett 1993; Omi and Winant 1994:162).

Another challenge to identity is **marginality**, the status of being between two cultures, as in the case of an individual whose mother is a Jew and whose father is a Christian. Incomplete assimilation also results in marginality. While a Filipino woman migrating to the United States may take on the characteristics of her new host society, she may not be fully accepted and may therefore feel neither Filipino nor American. The marginal person finds himself or herself being perceived differently in different environments, with varying expectations (J. Billson 1988; R. Park 1928; E. Stonequist 1937).

As we seek to understand diversity in the United States, we must be mindful that ethnic and racial labels are just that: labels that have been socially constructed. Yet these social constructs can have a powerful impact, whether self-applied or applied by others.

Resistance and Change

By virtue of wielding power and influence, the dominant group may define the terms by which all members of society operate. This is particularly evident in a slave society, but even in contemporary industrialized nations, the dominant group has a disproportionate role in shaping immigration policy, the curriculum of the schools, and the content of the media. For example, ***Time***, in a 1996 cover story, proclaimed "back to segregation" and "the end of integration" over failed attempts in school busing to achieve racial balance. Such headlines suggest that the United States has never come close to being integrated or truly overcome segregation, whether in the schools, housing, health care, or religious worship. Yet the notion that we are giving up on integration is framed in such a way as to exaggerate the amount of change that has been accomplished, implying that we need only go a little further. Similarly, a book entitled ***Alien Nation*** attacked immigration and declared that the country is changing for the worse (P. Brimelow 1996; J. Kunen 1996).

Subordinate groups have not and do not merely accept the definitions and ideology proposed by the dominant group. A continuing theme in dominant–subordinate relations is the minority group's challenging their subordination. We will see throughout this book the resistance of subordinate groups as they seek to promote change that will bring them more rights and privileges, if not true equality (Moulder 1996).

Resistance can be seen in efforts by racial and ethnic groups to maintain their identity through newspapers, organizations, and, in today's technological age, cable stations and Internet sites. Resistance manifests itself in social movements such as the civil rights movement, the feminist movement, and gay rights efforts. The passage of such legislation as the Age Discrimination Act or the Americans with Disabilities Act marks the organization of the oppressed group to lobby on their behalf.

Resistance efforts may begin through small actions. For example, members of a reservation population question a second toxic waste dump being located on their land. While it may bring in money, they question the wisdom of such a move. Their concerns lead to further investigations of the extent to which American Indian lands are used disproportionately for the housing of dangerous materials. This action in turn leads to a broader investigation of the way that minority-group people often find themselves "hosting" dumps and incinerators. As we will discuss later, these local efforts led eventually to the Environmental Protection Agency monitoring the disproportionate placement of toxic facilities among or near racial and ethnic minority people's communities. There is little reason to expect that such reforms would have occurred if we had relied on traditional decision-making processes alone.

An even more basic form of resistance is to question societal values. In this book, we avoid the use of the term "American" to describe people of the United States, since in my geographical sense Brazilians, Canadians, and El Salvadorans are Americans as well. It is very easy to overlook how our understanding of today has been shaped by the way institutions and even the very telling of history has been presented by members of the dominant group. African-American studies scholar Molefi Kete Asante (1992, 1996) has called for an **Afrocentric perspective** that emphasizes the customs of African cultures and how they have pervaded the history, culture, and behavior of Blacks in the United States and around the world. Afrocentrism counters Eurocentrism and works toward a multiculturalist or pluralist orientation in which no viewpoint is suppressed. The Afrocentric approach could become part of our school curriculum, which has not adequately acknowledged the importance of this heritage.

The Afrocentric perspective has attracted considerable attention in colleges. Opponents view it as a separatist view of history and culture that distorts both past and present. Its supporters counter that African peoples everywhere can come to full self-determination only when they are able to overthrow "White" or Eurocentric intellectual interpretations (G. Early 1994).

In considering the inequalities present today, as we will in the chapters that follow, it is easy to forget how much change has taken place. Much of the resistance to prejudice and discrimination in the past, whether to slavery or to women's prohibition from voting, took the active support of members of the dominant group. The indignities still experienced by subordinate groups continue to be resisted as subordinate groups and their allies among the dominant group seek further change.

CONCLUSION

One hundred years ago sociologist and activist W. E. B. Du Bois took another famed Black activist, Booker T. Washington, to task for saying that the races could best work together apart, like fingers on a hand. Du Bois felt that Black people had to be a part of all social institutions and not create their own. Today among African Americans, Whites, and other groups, the debate persists as to what form society should take. Should we seek to bring everyone together into an integrated whole, considering the assimilation that will require? Or do we strive to maintain as much of our group identities as possible while working cooperatively as necessary?

In this first chapter, we have attempted to organize our approach to subordinate–dominant relations in the United States. We observed that subordinate groups do not necessarily contain fewer members than the dominant group. Subordinate groups are classified into racial, ethnic, religious, and gender groups. Racial classification has been of interest, but scientific findings do not explain contemporary race relations. Biological differences of race are not supported by scientific data. Yet as the continuing debate over The Bell Curve demonstrates, attempts to establish a biological meaning of race have not been swept entirely into the dustbin of history. The social meaning given to physical differences, however, is very significant. People have defined racial differences in such a way as to encourage or discourage the progress of certain groups.

The confinement of certain people to subordinate groups may function to serve some people's vested interests. This denial of opportunities or privileges to an entire group, however, only leads to conflict between dominant and subordinate groups. Societies such as the United States develop ideologies to justify privileges given to some and opportunities denied to others. These ideologies may be subtle, such as assimilation (that is, "You should be like us"), or overt, such as racist thought and behavior.

Subordinate groups generally emerge in one of three ways: migration, annexation, or colonialism. Once a group is given subordinate status, it does not necessarily keep it indefinitely. Extermination, expulsion, secession, segregation, fusion, and assimilation remove the status of subordination, although inequality may persist.

Subordinate-group members' reactions include the seeking of an alternate avenue to acceptance and success: "Why should we forsake what we are to be accepted by them?" In response to this question, there has been a resurgence of ethnic identification. Pluralism describes a society in which several different groups coexist, with no dominant or subordinate groups. The hope for such a society remains unfulfilled, except perhaps for isolated exceptions.

Subordinate groups have not and do not always accept their second-class status passively. They may protest, organize, revolt, and resist society as defined by the dominant group. Patterns of race and ethnic relations are changing, not stagnant. Furthermore, in many nations, including the United States, the nature of race and ethnicity changes through migration. Indicative of the changing landscape, biracial and multiracial children present us with new definitions of identity emerging through a process of racial formation, reminding us that race is socially constructed.

The two significant forces that are absent in a truly pluralistic society are prejudice and discrimination. In an assimilation society, prejudice disparages out-group differences, and discrimination financially rewards those who shed their past. In the next two chapters, we will explore the nature of prejudice and discrimination in the United States.

KEY TERMS

Afrocentric perspective 34
amalgamation 28
assimilation 28
bilingualism 30
biological race 12
class 17
colonialism 23
conflict perspective 19
dysfunction 19
emigration 22
ethnic cleansing 24
ethnic group 9
functionalist perspective 18
fusion 28
genocide 24
immigration 22
intelligence quotient 13
internal colonialism 24
labeling theory 20
marginality 33
melting pot 28
migration 22
minority group 6
panethnicity 32
pluralism 30
racial formation 15
racial group 8
racism 15
segregation 26
self-fulfilling prophecy 21
sociology 17
stereotypes 20
stratification 17
world systems theory 24

REVIEW QUESTIONS

1. In what ways have you seen issues of race and ethnicity emerge? Identify groups that have been subordinated for reasons other than race, ethnicity, or gender.
2. How can a significant political or social issue (such as bilingual education) be viewed in assimilationist and pluralistic terms?
3. How does the concept of racial formation relate to the issue of "Who Am I?"

CRITICAL THINKING

1. How diverse is your city? Can you see evidence that some group is being subordinated? What social construction of categories do you see that may be different in your community as compared to elsewhere?

2. In 1996 Denny Mendéz was crowned Miss Italy, but many people protested her selection because they said she did not reflect the appropriate physical image of the Italian people. Mendéz had moved to Italy from the Dominican Republic when her mother married an Italian and has since become a citizen. What does this controversy around a beauty pageant tell us about the social construction of race? What similar situations have you witnessed where it seems race and ethnicity can only be seen in their social context?
3. Identify some protest and resistance efforts by subordinated groups in your area. Have they been successful? Why are some people who say they favor equality uncomfortable with such efforts? How can people unconnected with such efforts either help or hinder such protests?

INTERNET EXERCISE

The Intergroup Relations Continuum displays the consequences of subordinate-group status to include extermination, expulsion, secession, segregation, fusion, and assimilation. Recent examples of these consequences can be found on the Anti-Defamation League's web page at (http://www.adl.org) and The American-Arab Anti-Discrimination Committee site (http://www.adc.org). Visit these sites to learn more about ADL and ADC, and to read the perspectives, stories, and on-line reports provided. What is the mission of each organization? Which of the consequences listed above have been faced by Jewish and Arab peoples, as detailed on the sites and in the chapter? What are the key goals and issues of the ADC's Action Alerts? What changes would ADL like to see with regard to religious accommodation in the workplace? What new legislation exists to combat hate crimes? Have you or your family ever experienced similar treatment?

FOR FURTHER INFORMATION

Spencie Love. ***One Blood: The Death and Resurrection of Charles R. Drew.*** Chapel Hill, NC: University of North Carolina Press, 1996.

A fascinating account of the rumors surrounding the death of the famed African-American physician Charles Drew serves as a poignant backdrop for an examination of the "one-drop" rule of creating the social definition of "Black" in the United States.

Michael Omi and Howard Winant. ***Racial Formation in the United States,*** 2d ed. New York: Routledge, 1994.

Presentation of the authors' concept of "racial formation" in light of political developments in the United States.

Patricia Williams. ***Seeing a Color-Blind Future.*** The Noonday Press/Farrar, Strauus & Giroux, 1998.

In a slim book (74 pages), this well-respected legal scholar offers insights into a world in which prejudice has been eradicated, and some of the barriers we may have reaching it.

2

Prejudice

CHAPTER OUTLINE

HIGHLIGHTS

Prejudice is a negative attitude that rejects an entire group; discrimination is behavior that deprives a group of certain rights or opportunities. Prejudice does not necessarily coincide with discrimination, as is made apparent by a typology developed by sociologist Robert Merton. Several theories have been advanced to explain prejudice. The explanations are scapegoating, authoritarian personality, exploitation, and normative. These explanations examine prejudice in terms of content (negative stereotypes) and extent. Prejudice is not limited to the dominant group; subordinate groups often dislike one another. The attitudes in the United States toward Arab Americans and American Muslims illustrate the development of stereotypes and scapegoating. The mass media seem to be of limited value in reducing prejudice and may even intensify ill feeling. Equal-status contact and the shared-coping approach may reduce hostility among groups.

Virtually the entire nation was stunned by events outside Jasper, Texas, in 1998. James Byrd, Jr., a 39-year-old African American, accepted a ride with three White men as he walked along a street. The next morning his mutilated body was found after he had been dragged behind the truck by his ankles for two miles. The three men's hatred for Blacks had been documented, and one sported tattoos reading "Aryan Pride" and displaying a Nazi SS symbol. Townspeople were shocked by such blatant racism within their midst, and within a week Whites and Blacks joined in a prayer vigil in front of the town's courthouse, singing "Amazing Grace."

In another case, the general public as well as law-enforcement officials were quick to accept the story when in 1994 a South Carolina White woman reported that a Black man had kidnapped her two children. Only later did we all learn that no Black man had been involved; in fact, the woman had killed her children by strapping them in their car seats and rolling the car into a lake.

In 1996 in Miami, a Palestinian American shot his Black employee during an argument. Although the assailant was quickly arrested, Black community members organized a boycott of all immigrant-owned stores, some of which were eventually looted.

Three men tied up two women on a Nebraska college campus, eventually raping them. Later the men bragged that they had been stalking them and had similarly attacked other women.

In California, a local AIDS activist received repeated telephone threats, including a bomb threat, at his home and at the store where he worked. One caller told the activist in very disparaging language that he did not want any gay people in town.

From a Web site on the Internet called Nazism Now, it is only a mouse click to reach I Hate Jews—The Anti-Semetic (misspelling the word "Semitic") Homepage, Knights of the Klux Klan, and the White Nationalist Resources Page.

These are just a few examples of the ill feelings and overt hostility expressed between groups in the United States. Sometimes the expression of prejudice may be explicit, as in these events, but it can also be found in a more subtle, indirect manner. In 1993, looking for a night's entertainment in the movie *Falling Down,* people cheered the Michael Douglas character of Bill "D-Fens" Foster as he went over the edge, assaulting a Korean-immigrant convenience store owner because of the owner's poor English and the price of a soda. We delivered "tomahawk chops" to cheer on the Atlanta Braves during the 1996 World Series. Subordinate groups rightly protest these indirect expressions of prejudice and try to bring about positive change. It took the combined effort of Native Americans and several large church groups to block the sale of a malt liquor named "Crazy Horse." It was argued that the name of the alcoholic beverage was offensive to the honored position that Crazy Horse has as a political and religious leader in Oglala Lakota history. And for those too young for liquor but not too old for video games, one finds that Asian characters appear in video games only in martial arts games, such as E. Honda in "Street Fighter" or Liu Kang in "Mortal Kombat II States" (Anti-Defamation League 1997; Jenness 1995; National Asian Pacific American Legal Consortium 1996; Robles and Casimir 1996).

Prejudice is so prevalent that it is tempting to consider it inevitable or, even more broadly, just part of human nature. Such a view ignores its variability from individual to individual and from society to society. People must learn prejudice as children before they exhibit it as adults. Therefore, prejudice is a social phenomenon, an acquired characteristic. A truly pluralistic society would lack unfavorable distinctions made through prejudicial attitudes among racial and ethnic groups.

Ill feeling among groups may result from ethnocentrism. **Ethnocentrism** is the tendency to assume that one's culture and way of life are superior to all others. The ethnocentric person judges other groups and other cultures by the standards

African American artist Jacob Lawrence portrays the separate facilities typical of the treatment received by Blacks in the earlier part of the twentieth century.

of his or her own group. This attitude leads people quite easily to view other cultures as inferior. As shown in Figure 2.1, in some cases people organize into groups with the express purpose of showing their hatred toward other groups of people.

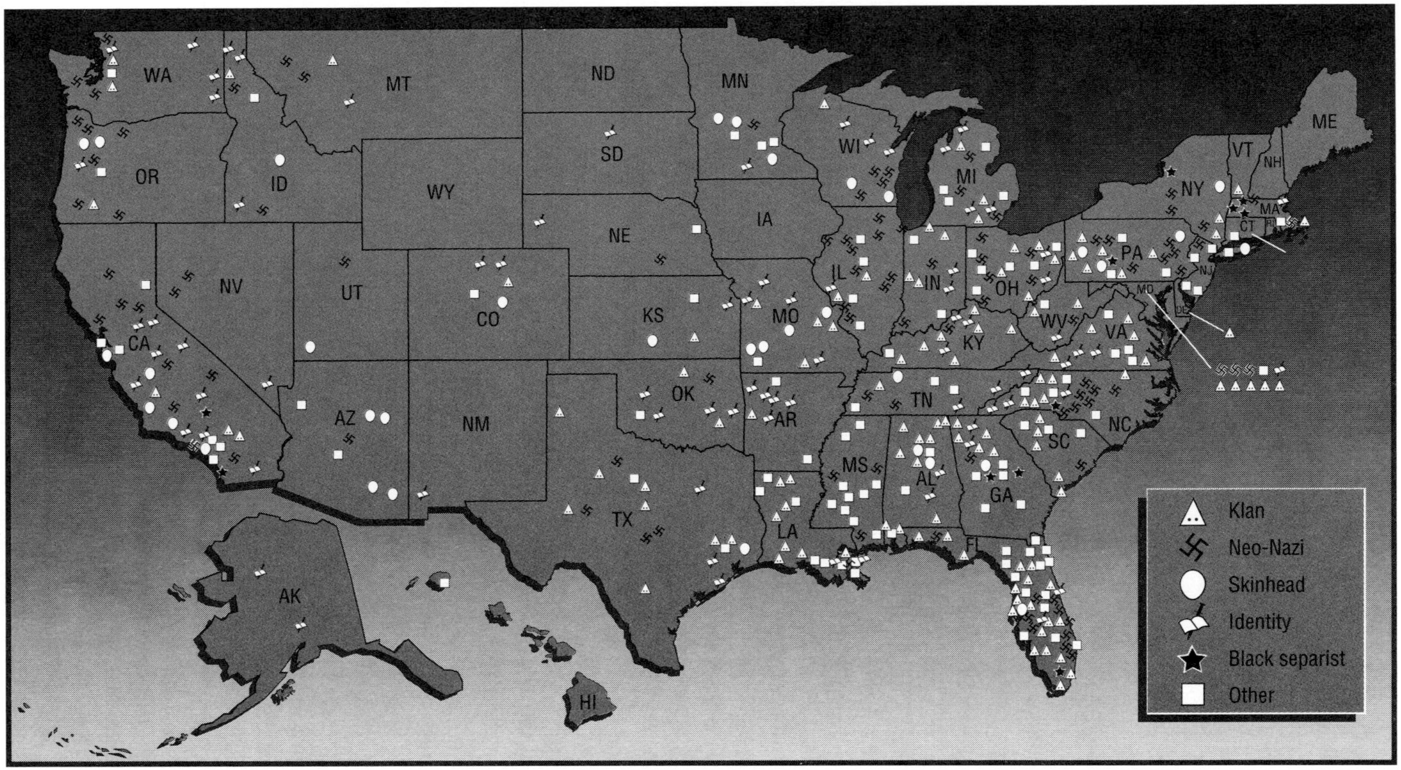

Figure 2.1 Racist Fringe Groups in 1997

No part of the nation is truly free of a variety of known fringe groups that espouse racial hatred and religious intolerance. "Identity" refers to the Christian Identity religion, which is fundamentally racist and anti-Semitic.

Source: From Southern Poverty Law Center's *Intelligence Report*, Winter 1999. Used by permission.

NOTE: Many organizations shown have numerous chapters in various states. However, only one symbol is shown per state for each separate organization. If a group has more than one chapter in a state, the group's state office is represented on the map, or, if that is not possible, a site is selected randomly.

Hate Crimes

While prejudice is certainly not new in the United States, it is receiving increased attention as it manifests itself in neighborhoods, at meetings, and on college campuses. The Hate Crime Statistics Act, which became law in 1990, directs the Department of Justice to gather data on hate or bias crimes. The government defines a hate crime as:

> *a criminal offense committed against a person, property, or society which is motivated, in whole or in part, by the offender's bias against a race, religion, ethnic/national origin group, or sexual-orientation group (Department of Justice 1997:57)*

This law created a national mandate to identify such crimes, whereas previously only twelve states had monitored hate crimes. In 1994, the act was amended to include disabilities, both physical and mental, as factors that could be considered a basis for hate crimes.

In 1998, law-enforcement agencies released hate crime data submitted by police agencies covering 83 percent of the United States. There were reports for 1997 of over 8,400 hate crimes and bias-motivated incidents. Race was the apparent motivation for the bias in 60 percent of the reports, and about 11 to 15 percent which were due to religion, sexual orientation, or ethnicity. While vandalism and intimidation were the most common, 31 percent of the incidents against people involved assault and even rape or murder (Department of Justice 1998:61–62).

National legislation and publicity have made *hate crime* a meaningful term, and we are beginning to recognize the victimization associated with such incidents. There is a proposal that would make a violent crime into a federal crime if it is motivated by racial or religious bias. While passage is uncertain, the serious consideration of the proposal indicates the willingness to consider a major expansion of federal jurisdiction. Currently, federal law prohibits crimes motivated by race, color, religion, or national origin only if they involve violation of a federally guaranteed right, such as voting (Jacobs and Potter 1998).

Victimized groups are not merely observing these events. Watchdog organizations play an important role in documenting bias-motivated violence—among such groups are the Anti-Defamation League (ADL), the National Institute Against Prejudice and Violence, the Southern Poverty Law Center, and the National Gay and Lesbian Task Force. Established hate groups have even set up propaganda sites on the World Wide Web. This also creates opportunities for previously unknown haters and hate groups to promote themselves. However, hate crimes legislation does not affect such outlets because of legal questions involving freedom of speech (ADL 1996; Jenness 1995).

What causes people to dislike entire groups of other people? Is it possible to change attitudes? This chapter tries to answer these questions about prejudice. Chapter 3 focuses on discrimination.

Prejudice and Discrimination

Prejudice and *discrimination* are related concepts but are not the same. **Prejudice** is a negative attitude toward an entire category of people. The two important components in this definition are *attitude* and *entire category*. Prejudice involves attitudes, thoughts, and beliefs, not actions. Frequently, prejudice is expressed through the use of **ethnophaulisms,** or ethnic slurs, which include derisive nicknames such as *honkie, gook,* or *wetback*. Ethnophaulisms also include speaking about or to members of a particular group in a condescending way—"José does well in school for a Mexican American"—or referring to a middle-aged woman as "one of the girls."

A prejudiced belief leads to categorical rejection. Prejudice is not disliking someone you meet because you find his or her behavior objectionable. It is disliking an entire racial or ethnic group, even if you have had little or no contact with that group. A college student who requests a room change after three weeks of enduring his roommate's sleeping all day, playing loud music all night, and piling garbage on his desk is not prejudiced. He is displaying prejudice, however, if he requests a change upon arriving at school and learning from his roommate's luggage tags that his new roommate is of a different nationality.

Prejudice is a belief or attitude; discrimination is action. **Discrimination** involves behavior that excludes all members of a group from certain rights, opportunities, or privileges. Like prejudice, it must be categorical. If an individual refuses to hire as a typist an Italian American who is illiterate, it is not discrimination. If an individual refuses to hire any Italian Americans because she thinks they are incompetent and does not make the effort to see if an applicant is qualified, it is discrimination.

Prejudice does not necessarily coincide with discriminatory behavior. Sociologist Robert Merton (1949, 1976), in exploring the relationship between negative attitudes and negative behavior, identified four major categories (see Figure 2.2). The label added to each of Merton's categories may more readily identify the type of individual being described. These are

1. The unprejudiced nondiscriminator: all-weather liberal
2. The unprejudiced discriminator: reluctant liberal
3. The prejudiced nondiscriminator: timid bigot
4. The prejudiced discriminator: all-weather bigot

Liberals, as the term is employed in types 1 and 2, are committed to equality among people. The all-weather liberal believes in equality and practices it. Merton was quick to observe that all-weather liberals may be far removed from any real competition with subordinate groups such as African Americans or women. Furthermore, such people may be content with their own behavior and may do little to change themselves. The reluctant liberal is not even this committed to equality among groups. Social pressure may cause such a person to discriminate. Fear of losing employees may lead a manager to avoid promoting women to supervisory capacities. Equal-opportunity legislation may be the best way to influence the reluctant liberals.

Types 3 and 4 do not believe in equal treatment for racial and ethnic groups, but they vary in their willingness to act. The timid bigot, type 3, will not discriminate if

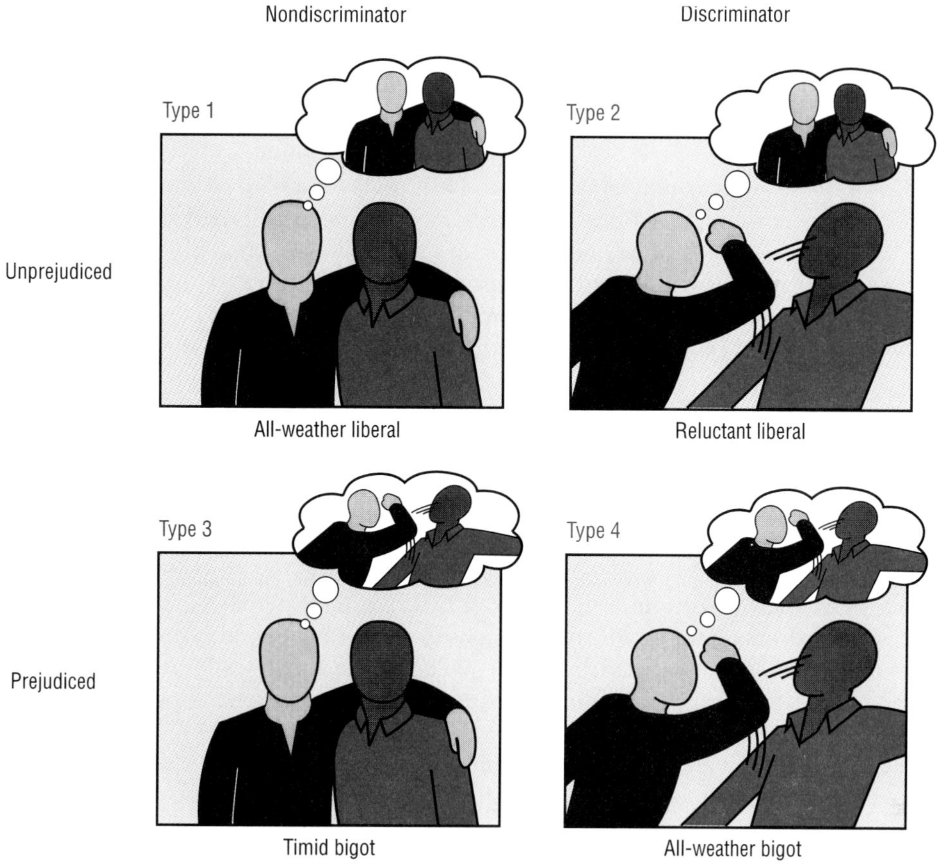

Figure 2.2 Prejudice and Discrimination
As sociologist Robert Merton's formulation shows, prejudice and discrimination are related to each other but are not the same.

discrimination costs money or reduces profits or if he or she is pressured not to by peers or the government. The all-weather bigot unhesitatingly acts on the prejudiced beliefs that he or she holds.

Merton's typology points out that attitudes should not be confused with behavior. People do not always act as they believe. More than half a century ago, Richard LaPiere (1934, 1969) exposed the relationship between racial attitudes and social conduct. From 1930 to 1932 LaPiere traveled throughout the United States with a Chinese couple. Despite an alleged climate of intolerance of Asians, LaPiere observed that the couple was treated courteously at hotels, motels, and restaurants. He was puzzled by the good reception they received; all the conventional attitude surveys showed extreme prejudice by Whites toward the Chinese.

Was it possible that LaPiere had been fortunate during his travels and consistently stopped at places operated by the tolerant members of the dominant group? To test this possibility, he sent questionnaires asking the very establishments at which they had been served if the owner would "accept members of the Chinese race as guests in your establishment." More than 90 percent responded no, even though LaPiere's Chinese couple had been treated politely at all the establishments. How can this inconsistency be explained? People who returned questionnaires reflecting prejudice were unwilling to act based on those asserted beliefs: they were timid bigots.

The LaPiere study is not without flaws. First, he had no way of knowing whether the respondent to the questionnaire was the same person who had served him and the Chinese couple. Second, he accompanied the couple, but the questionnaire suggested that the arrival would be unescorted (and in the minds of some, uncontrolled) and perhaps would consist of many Chinese individuals. Third, personnel may have changed between the time of the visit and the mailing of the questionnaire (Deutscher et al. 1993).

The LaPiere technique has been replicated with similar results. This technique raises the question of whether attitudes are important if they are not completely reflected in behavior. But if attitudes are not important in small matters, they are important in other ways: lawmakers legislate and courts may reach decisions based on what the public thinks.

This is not just a hypothetical possibility. Legislators in the United States are often persuaded to vote in a certain way by what they perceive as changed attitudes toward immigration, affirmative action, school busing, abortion, and prayer in public schools. Sociologists Jack and William C. Levin (1982) enumerated some of prejudice's functions. For the majority group, it serves to maintain privileged occupations and more power for its members. Levin and Levin go on to point out that prejudice may be viewed as having some functions even for subordinate groups. These functions include maintaining in-group solidarity and reducing competition in some areas of employment, admittedly those with lower status or smaller rewards.

The following sections examine the theories of why prejudice exists and discuss the content and extent of prejudice today.

Theories of Prejudice

Prejudice is learned. Friends, relatives, newspapers, books, movies, and television all teach it. Awareness begins at an early age that there are differences among people that society judges to be important. Several theories have been advanced to explain the rejection of certain groups in a society. We will examine four theoretical explanations—first, two (scapegoating and authoritarian personality) that tend to be psychological, emphasizing why a particular person harbors ill-feelings. Then we will turn to two that are more sociological (exploitation and normative), which view prejudice in the context of our interaction in larger society.

SCAPEGOATING THEORY

Scapegoating theory says that prejudiced people believe they are society's victims. Exploitation theory maintains that intolerant individuals abuse others, whereas scapegoaters feel they are being abused themselves. The term **scapegoat** comes from a

Many would regard this statue of colonist Hannah Duston in Massachusetts as perpetuating stereotypes about American Indians. She is honored for killing and scalping ten Abenaki Indians in 1697 while defending her family. Believed to be the first woman ever honored in the United States with a monument, it portrays her holding a hatchet.

biblical injunction telling the Hebrews to send a goat into the wilderness to symbolically carry away the people's sins. Similarly, the theory of scapegoating suggests that an individual, rather than accepting guilt for some failure, transfers the responsibility for failure to some vulnerable group. In the major tragic twentieth-century example, Adolf Hitler used the Jews as the scapegoat for all German social and economic ills in the 1930s. This premise led to the passage of laws restricting Jewish life in pre-World War II Germany and eventually escalated into the mass extermination of Europe's Jews.

Studies of prejudice in the United States have found that the downwardly economic mobile are usually more prejudiced. People who lose a job and are forced to accept a lower-status occupation experience increased tension and anxiety. Who is responsible, they ask, for their misfortune? At this time, a scapegoat, such as a racial, ethnic, or religious group, may enter the picture (Bettelheim and Janowitz 1964).

Like exploitation theory, scapegoating theory adds to our understanding of why prejudice exists but does not explain all its facets. For example, scapegoating theory offers little explanation of why a specific group is selected or why frustration is taken out on the real culprit when it is possible. Also, both the exploitation and the scapegoating theories suggest that every individual sharing the same general experiences in society would be equally prejudiced, but that is not the case. Prejudice varies among individuals who would seem to benefit equally from the exploitation of a subordinate group or who have experienced equal frustration. In an effort to explain these personality differences, social scientists developed the concept of the authoritarian personality.

AUTHORITARIAN PERSONALITY THEORY

A number of social scientists do not see prejudice as an isolated trait that anyone can have. Several efforts have been made to detail the prejudiced personality, but the most comprehensive effort culminated in a volume entitled *The Authoritarian Personality* (Adorno et al. 1950). Using a variety of tests and relying on more than 2,000 respondents, ranging from middle-class Whites to inmates of San Quentin (Calif.) State Prison, the authors claimed they had isolated the characteristics of the authoritarian personality.

In these authors' view, the basic characteristics of the **authoritarian personality** were adherence to conventional values, uncritical acceptance of authority, and concern with power and toughness. With obvious relevance to the development of intolerance, the authoritarian personality was also characterized by aggressiveness toward people who did not conform to conventional norms or obey authority. According to the authors, this personality type developed from an early childhood of harsh discipline. A child with an authoritarian upbringing obeyed and then later treated others as he or she had been raised.

This study has been widely criticized, but the very existence of such wide criticism indicates the influence of the study. Critics have attacked the study's equation of authoritarianism with right-wing politics (though liberals can also be rigid); its failure to see that prejudice is more closely related to other individual traits, such as social class, than to authoritarianism as it was defined; and the research methods employed. Graham Kinloch (1974), discussing personality research, added a fourth criticism: the authors concentrated on factors behind extreme racial prejudice, rather than on more common expressions of hostility.

EXPLOITATION THEORY

Racial prejudice is frequently used to justify keeping a group in a subordinate position, such as a lower social class. Conflict theorists in particular stress the role of racial and ethnic hostility as a way for the dominant group to keep intact its position of status and power. Indeed, this approach maintains that even the less affluent White working class uses prejudice to minimize competition from upwardly mobile minorities.

This **exploitation theory** is clearly part of the Marxist tradition in sociological thought. Karl Marx emphasized exploitation of the lower class as an integral part of capitalism. Similarly, the exploitation or conflict approach explains how racism can stigmatize a group as inferior so that the exploitation of that group can be justified. As developed by Oliver Cox (1942), exploitation theory saw prejudice against Blacks as an extension of the inequality faced by the entire lower class.

The exploitation theory of prejudice is persuasive. Japanese Americans were the object of little prejudice until they began to enter occupations that brought them into competition with Whites. The movement to keep Chinese out of the country became strongest during the latter half of the nineteenth century, when Chinese immigrants and Whites fought over dwindling numbers of jobs. Both the enslavement of African Americans and the removal westward of Native Americans were to a significant degree economically motivated.

Related to the exploitation theory is the **caste approach** to race relations in the United States. The term *caste* describes a system of social inequality in which status is inherited and people have little, if any, opportunity to change their social position. As we have seen through exploitation theory, economic subordination benefits the dominant group's financial interests. The caste approach, however, does not rely on Marxist theory for theoretical support. The caste explanation for racial subordination sees race and social class as closely related because Blacks and other non-Whites are destined by the social structure to occupy a castelike position. Membership in the subordinate group is inherited and permanent.

The caste approach is basically descriptive and not very analytical; for example, sociologists using it make less effort to explain why caste relations originated than do those working within the exploitation approach of Oliver C. Cox. The caste approach, although acknowledging the importance of social class, argues that race is more important, whereas Cox's general exploitation theory sees racial discrimination as merely an example of class differences. The caste explanation seems somewhat limited. In a caste system, as strictly defined, the lower castes accept the system and their low status. But the increased numbers of Blacks in high-paying occupations and the continuous struggle for equal rights indicate that African Americans have not and do not acquiesce (G. Berreman 1973).

Although some cases support the exploitation theory, it is too limited to explain prejudice in all its forms. First, not all minority groups are exploited economically to the same extent. Second, many groups that have been the victims of prejudice have not been persecuted for economic reasons—for example, the Quakers. Nevertheless, as Gordon Allport (1979) concludes, the exploitation theory correctly points a finger at one of the factors in prejudice, that is, the rationalized self-interest of the upper classes.

NORMATIVE APPROACH

Although personality factors are important contributors to prejudice, normative or situational factors must also be given serious consideration. The **normative approach** takes the view that prejudice is influenced by societal norms and situations that serve to encourage or discourage the tolerance of minorities.

Analysis reveals how societal influences shape a climate for tolerance or intolerance. Societies develop social norms that dictate not only what foods are desirable (or forbidden) but also what racial and ethnic groups are to be favored (or despised). Social forces operate in a society to encourage or discourage tolerance. The force may be widespread—for example, the pressure on White Southerners to oppose racial equality while there was slavery or segregation. The influence of social norms may be limited—for example, one male who finds himself becoming more sexist as he competes with three females for a position in a prestigious law firm.

Social psychologist Thomas Pettigrew (1958, 1959) collected data that substantiated the importance of such social norms in developing a social climate conducive to the expression of prejudice. Pettigrew found that Whites in the South were more anti-Black than Whites in the North, and that Whites in the United States were not as prejudiced as Whites in the Republic of South Africa.

Personality alone cannot account for such differences. Pettigrew's research revealed no significant variation between the two societies in the proportion of authoritarian individuals. This has been confirmed by research showing that as people moved from North to South and others moved from South to North during the 1980s and early 1990s, attitudes changed, adapting to the new social environment. This is particularly true when it comes to racial public policies such as fair housing, busing, and federal money aimed at assisting Blacks. We can conclude that structural factors explain differences in the levels of prejudice between these two regions (Glaser and Gilens 1997).

We should not view the four approaches to prejudice summarized in Table 2.1 as mutually exclusive. Social circumstances provide cues for a person's attitudes; personality determines the extent to which people follow social cues and the likelihood that they will encourage others to do the same. Societal norms may promote or deter tolerance; personality traits suggest the degree to which a person will conform to norms of intolerance.

The Content of Prejudice: Stereotypes

In 1993, the newly elected President attempted to remove the restrictions against homosexuals serving in the military and was met with strong opposition. Long-held stereotypes were invoked by some military leaders, and politicians predicted dire

Table 2.1 Theories of Prejudice

There is no one explanation of why prejudice exists, but several approaches taken together offer insight.

Theory	Proponent	Explanation	Example
Scapegoating	Bruno Bettelheim Morris Janowitz	People blame others for their own failures.	An unsuccessful applicant assumes that a minority member or a woman got "his" job.
Authoritarian personality	Adorno and associates	Childrearing leads one to develop intolerance as an adult.	The rigid personality type dislikes people who are "different."
Exploitation	Oliver C. Cox Marxist theory	People utilize others unfairly for economic advantage.	A minority member is hired at a lower wage level.
Normative	Thomas Pettigrew	Peer and social influences encourage tolerance or intolerance.	A person from an intolerant household is more likely to be openly prejudiced.

consequences if these citizens were allowed to wear a uniform. The irony, of course, is that, for generations, tens of thousands of gays and lesbians have been quietly and skillfully performing their patriotic duty in the armed forces without causing trouble (E. Aronson 1999).

In Chapter 1, we saw that stereotypes play a powerful role in how people come to view dominant and subordinate groups. Numerous scientific studies have been made of these exaggerated images. This research has shown the willingness of people to attribute positive and negative traits to entire groups of people, which are then used to generalize particular individuals. Stereotyping causes people to view Blacks as superstitious, Whites as uncaring, and Jews as shrewd. Over the last seventy years of such research, social scientists have found that people are less willing to express such views openly but, as we will see later, prejudice persists (Macrae et al. 1996).

The power of stereotypes is not confirmed only in research conducted by scholars. Many people recognize situations where they are the victims of stereotyping. In "Listen to Their Voices," *Newsweek* journalist Brent Staples recounts experiences where he has been viewed as a potential criminal merely because he is a male and Black.

If stereotypes are exaggerated generalizations, why are they so widely held, and why are some traits more often assigned than others? Evidence for traits may arise out of real conditions. For example, more Puerto Ricans live in poverty than Whites, and so the prejudiced mind associates Puerto Ricans with laziness. According to the New Testament, some Jews were responsible for the crucifixion of Jesus, and so, to the prejudiced mind, all Jews are Christ-killers. Some activists in the women's movement are lesbians, and so all feminists are lesbians. From a kernel of fact, faulty generalization creates a stereotype.

LISTEN TO THEIR VOICES

Just Walk On By

Brent Staples

My first victim was a woman—white, well dressed, probably in her early twenties. I came upon her late one evening on a deserted street in Hyde Park, a relatively affluent neighborhood in an otherwise mean, impoverished section of Chicago. As I swung onto the avenue behind her, there seemed to be a discreet, uninflammatory distance between us. Not so. She cast back a worried glance. To her, the youngish black man—a broad six feet two inches with a beard and billowing hair, both hands shoved into the pockets of a bulky military jacket—seemed menacingly close. After a few more quick glimpses, she picked up her pace and was soon running in earnest. Within seconds she disappeared into a cross street.

That was more than a decade ago. I was 22 years old, a graduate student newly arrived at the University of Chicago. It was in the echo of that terrified woman's footfalls that I first began to know the unwieldy inheritance I'd come into—the ability to alter public space in ugly ways. It was clear that she thought herself the quarry of a mugger, a rapist, or worse. Suffering a bout of insomnia, however, I was stalking sleep, not defenseless wayfarers. As a softy who is scarcely able to take a knife to a raw chicken—let alone hold it to a person's throat—I was surprised, embarrassed, and dismayed all at once. Her flight made me feel like an accomplice in tyranny. It also made it clear that I was indistinguishable from the muggers who occasionally seeped into the area from the surrounding ghetto. That first encounter, and those that followed, signified that a vast, unnerving gulf lay between nighttime pedestrians—particularly women—and me. And I soon gathered that being perceived as dangerous is a hazard in itself. I only needed to turn a corner into a dicey situation, or crowd some frightened, armed person in a foyer somewhere, or make an errant move after being pulled over by a policeman. Where fear and

Stereotyping of women and men is well documented, and we consider it in greater detail in Chapter 14. However, little research has been done on the stereotyping of women of color. Rose Weitz (1992), surveying White undergraduates, found a definite willingness to characterize African American women as "loud" and "argumentative," Mexican American women as "lazy" and "quick-tempered," and Jewish women as "spoiled" and "shrewd." "American white women" were seen as "intelligent," "materialistic," and "sophisticated"—quite a contrast to the labeling of women of color.

Labels take on such strong significance that people often ignore facts that contradict their previously held beliefs. People who believe many Italian Americans to be members of the Mafia disregard law-abiding Italian Americans. Muslims are regularly weapons meet—and they often do in urban America—there is always the possibility of death.

I often witness that "hunch posture," from women after dark on the warrenlike streets of Brooklyn where I live. They seem to set their faces on neutral and, with their purse straps strung across their chests bandolier style, they forge ahead as though bracing themselves against being tackled. I understand, of course, that the danger they perceive is not a hallucination. Women are particularly vulnerable to street violence, and young black males are drastically overrepresented among the perpetrators of that violence. Yet these truths are no solace against the kind of alienation that comes of being ever the suspect, against being set apart, a fearsome entity with whom pedestrians avoid making eye contact. . .

I began to take precautions to make myself less threatening. I move about with care, particularly late in the evening. I give a wide berth to nervous people on subway platforms during the wee hours, particularly when I have exchanged business clothes for jeans. If I happen to be entering a building behind some people who appear skittish, I may walk by, letting them clear the lobby before I return, so as not to seem to be following them. I have been calm and extremely congenial on those rare occasions when I've been pulled over by the police.

And on late-evening constitutionals along streets less traveled by, I employ what has proved to be an excellent tension-reducing measure: I whistle melodies from Beethoven and Vivaldi and the more popular classical composers. Even steely New Yorkers hunching toward nighttime destinations seem to relax, and occasionally they even join in the tune. Virtually everybody seems to sense that a mugger wouldn't be warbling bright, sunny selections from Vivaldi's *Four Seasons.* It is my equivalent of the cowbell that hikers wear when they know they are in bear country.

Source: Brent Staples. "Just Walk On By: A Black Man Ponders His Power to Alter Public Space." Reprinted by permission of the author. Brent Staples writes editorials for *The New York Times* and is the author of the prize-winning memoir "Parallel Time: Growing Up In Black and White."

portrayed in a violent, offensive manner that contributes to their being misunderstood and distrusted. We will consider later in the chapter how this stereotype has become widespread since the mid–1970s.

In the last 30 years, we have become more and more aware of the power of the mass media to introduce stereotypes into everyday life. Television is a prime example. Almost all television roles showing leadership feature Whites. Even urban-based programs such as *Seinfeld* and *Friends* prospered without any major Black or Hispanic or Asian American characters. A 1998 national survey of boys and girls aged 10 to 17 asked a very simple question and came up with some disturbing findings. The children were asked, "How often do you see your race on television?" The results showed that 71 percent of White children said "very often," compared to only

42 percent of African Americans, 22 percent of Latinos, and 16 percent of Asian Americans. Even more troubling is that generally the children view the White characters as affluent and well educated, while they see the minority characters as "breaking the law or rules," "being lazy," and "acting goofy." Later in this chapter we will consider the degree to which the media have changed in presenting stereotyped images (Children Now 1998).

The labeling of individuals has strong implications for the self-fulfilling prophecy besides fostering a negative racial climate. Studies show that people are all too aware of the negative images other people have of them. When asked to estimate the prevalence of hard-core racism among Whites, 1 in 4 Blacks agrees that more than half "personally share the attitudes of groups like the Ku Klux Klan toward Blacks"; only 1 Black in 10 says "only a few" share such views. Not only do stereotypes influence how people feel about themselves but, perhaps equally important, affect how people interact with others. If people feel that others hold incorrect, if not also extremely disparaging, attitudes, it undoubtedly will make it difficult to have harmonious relations (Sigelman and Tuch 1997).

Are stereotypes held only by dominant groups about subordinate groups? The answer is clearly no. White Americans even believe generalizations about themselves, although admittedly these are usually positive. Subordinate groups also hold exaggerated images of themselves. Studies before World War II showed a tendency for Blacks to assign to themselves many of the same negative traits assigned by Whites. Today stereotypes of themselves are largely rejected by African Americans, Jews, Asians, and other minority groups, although subordinate groups will to some degree stereotype each other. The nature of the subordinate group's self-image is explored later in this chapter. The subordinate group also develops stereotyped images of the dominant group. Anthony Dworkin (1965) surveyed Mexican Americans and found that the majority agreed that White non-Hispanics were prejudiced, snobbish, hypocritical, tense, anxious, and neurotic, and had little family loyalty. Stereotyping, like prejudice itself, is widespread.

The Extent of Prejudice

Interest in developing theories of prejudice or studying its concept has been exceeded only by interest in measuring it. From the outset, efforts to measure prejudice have suffered from disagreement over exactly what constitutes intolerance and whether there is such a phenomenon as no prejudice at all. Add to these uncertainties the methodological problems of attitude measurement, and the empirical study of prejudice becomes an undertaking fraught with difficulty.

The extent of prejudice can be measured only in relative, rather than absolute, differences. We cannot accurately say, for example, that prejudice toward Puerto Ricans is four times greater than that toward Portuguese Americans. We can conclude that prejudice is greater toward one group than toward the other; we just cannot quantify how much greater. The social distance scale is especially appropriate to assess differences in prejudice.

THE SOCIAL DISTANCE SCALE

Robert Park and Ernest Burgess first defined *social distance* as the tendency to approach or withdraw from a racial group (1921:440). A few years later, Emory Bogardus (1968) conceptualized a scale that could measure social distance empirically. His social distance scale is so widely used that it is frequently referred to as the **Bogardus scale.**

The scale asks people how willing they would be to interact with various racial and ethnic groups in specified social situations. The situations describe different degrees of social contact or social distance. The seven items used, with their corresponding distance scores, follow. People are asked if they would be willing to admit each group:

- To close kinship by marriage (1.00)
- To my club as personal chums (2.00)
- To my street as neighbors (3.00)
- To employment in my occupation (4.00)
- To citizenship in my country (5.00)

The Bogardus social-distance scale attempts to measure people's willingness to have social contact with people of different racial and ethnic backgrounds.

- As only visitors to my country (6.00)
- Would exclude from my country (7.00)

A score of 1.00 for any group would indicate no social distance and therefore no prejudice. The social distance scale has been administered to many different groups in other countries as well. Despite some minor flaws and certain refinements needed in the scale, the results of these studies are useful and can be compared.

The data in Table 2.2 summarize the results of studies using the social distance scale in the United States at three points in time over a sixty-five-year period. In the top third of the hierarchy are White Americans and northern Europeans. In the middle are eastern and southern Europeans, and generally near the bottom are racial minorities. This prestige hierarchy resembles the relative proportions of the various groups in the population.

The similarity in the hierarchy during the sixty-five years was not limited to White respondents. Several times, the scale was administered to Jewish, Mexican American, Asian, Puerto Rican, Black African, and Black American groups. These groups generally shared the same hierarchy, although they placed their own group at the top. The extent of prejudice as illustrated in the ranking of racial and ethnic groups seems to be widely shared. Studies have also been performed in other societies and show that they have a racial and ethnic hierarchy as well.

A tentative conclusion that we can draw from these studies is that the extent of prejudice is decreasing. At the bottom of Table 2.2 is the arithmetic mean of the racial reactions on a scale of 1.0 to 7.0. Although the change was slight from survey to survey, it is generally downward. Many specific nationalities and races, however, experienced little change. The spread in social distance (the difference between the top- and bottom-ranked groups) also decreased or held steady from 1926 to 1991, a finding indicating that fewer distinctions were being made. This result was also confirmed empirically in research on stereotypes (Crull and Bruton 1985; Owen et al. 1981).

ATTITUDE CHANGE

We hold certain images or stereotypes of each other, and we also may be more prejudiced toward some groups of people than others. However, is prejudice less than it used to be? The evidence we will see is mixed, with some indications of willingness to give up some old prejudices, while at the same time new negative attitudes emerge.

Over the years, nationwide surveys have consistently shown growing support by Whites for integration, even during the southern resistance and northern turmoil of the 1960s. National opinion surveys conducted from the 1950s through the 1990s, with few exceptions, show an increase in the number of Whites responding positively to hypothetical situations of increased contact with African Americans. For example, 30 percent of the Whites sampled in 1942 felt that Blacks should not attend separate schools, but by 1970, 74 percent supported integrated schools, and fully 93 percent responded in that manner in 1991 (Davis and Smith 1996).

Attitudes are still important, however, apart from behavior. A change of attitude may create a context in which legislative or behavioral change can occur. Such

Table 2.2 Changes in Social Distance

The social distance scale developed by Emory Bogardus has been a useful measure of people's feelings of hostility toward different racial and ethnic groups.

1926		1966		1991	
1. English	1.06	1. Americans (U.S.White)	1.07	1. Americans (U.S. White)	1.00
2. Americans (U.S. White)	1.10	2. English	1.14	2. English	1.08
3. Canadians	1.13	3. Canadians	1.15	3. French	1.16
4. Scots	1.13	4. French	1.36	4. Canadians	1.21
5. Irish	1.30	5. Irish	1.40	5. Italians	1.27
6. French	1.32	6. Swedish	1.42	6. Irish	1.30
7. Germans	1.46	7. Norwegians	1.50	7. Germans	1.36
8. Swedish	1.54	8. Italians	1.51	8. Swedish	1.38
9. Hollanders	1.56	9. Scots	1.53	9. Scots	1.50
10. Norwegians	1.59	10. Germans	1.54	10. Hollanders	1.56
11. Spanish	1.72	11. Hollanders	1.54	11. Norwegians	1.66
12. Finns	1.83	12. Finns	1.67	12. Native Americans	1.70
13. Russians	1.88	13. Greeks	1.82	13. Greeks	1.73
14. Italians	1.94	14. Spanish	1.93	14. Finns	1.73
15. Poles	2.01	15. Jews	1.97	15. Poles	1.74
16. Armenians	2.06	16. Poles	1.98	16. Russians	1.76
17. Czechs	2.08	17. Czechs	2.02	17. Spanish	1.77
18. Native Americans	2.38	18. Native Americans	2.12	18. Jews	1.84
19. Jews	2.39	19. Japanese Americans	2.14	19. Mexicans (U.S.)	1.84
20. Greeks	2.47	20. Armenians	2.18	20. Czechs	1.90
21. Mexicans	2.69	21. Filipinos	2.31	21. Americans (U.S. Black)	1.94
22. Mexican Americans	—	22. Chinese	2.34	22. Chinese	1.96
23. Japanese	2.80	23. Mexican Americans	2.37	23. Filipinos	2.04
24. Japanese Americans	—	24. Russians	2.38	24. Japanese (U.S.)	2.06
25. Filipinos	3.00	25. Japanese	2.41	25. Armenians	2.17
26. Negroes	3.28	26. Turks	2.48	26. Turks	2.23
27. Turks	3.30	27. Koreans	2.51	27. Koreans	2.24
28. Chinese	3.36	28. Mexicans	2.56	28. Mexicans	2.27
29. Koreans	3.60	29. Negroes	2.56	29. Japanese	2.37
30. Indians (from India)	3.91	30. Indians (from India)	2.62	30. Indians (from India)	2.39
Arithmetic mean	2.14	Arithmetic mean	1.92	Arithmetic mean	1.76
Spread in distance	2.85	Spread in distance	1.56	Spread in distance	1.39

Source: Emory S. Bogardus, "Comparing Racial Distance in Ethiopia, South Africa, and the United States," *Sociology and Social Research,* 52 (January 1968). and Tae-Hyon Song, "Social Contact and Ethnic Distance between Koreans and the U.S. Whites in the United States," paper, Macomb, Western Illinois University, 1991. Reprinted by permission.

attitude changes leading to behavior changes did, in fact, occur in some areas during the 1960s. Changes in intergroup behavior mandated by law in housing, schools, public places of accommodation, and the workplace appear to be responsible for making some new kinds of interracial contact a social reality. Attitudes translate into votes, peer pressure, and political clout, each of which can facilitate efforts to undo racial inequality. However, attitudes can work in the opposite direction. In the mid–1990s, surveys showed resistance to affirmative action and immigration. Policy makers quickly developed new measures to respond to these concerns voiced largely by Whites.

When surveying White attitudes toward African Americans, two conclusions are inescapable. First, attitudes are subject to change, and in periods of dramatic social upheaval, dramatic shifts can occur within one generation. Second, less progress has been made in the last part of the twentieth century than was made in the 1950s and 1960s. Researchers have variously termed these subtle forms of prejudice *symbolic racism, or modern racism, or laissez-faire racism.* People today may not be as openly racist or prejudiced as in the past in expressing the notion that they are inherently superior to others. Yet much of the opposition to policies related to eradicating poverty or immigration are often a smoke screen to dislike entire groups of racial and ethnic minorities (Bobo et al. 1997; McConahay and Hough 1976; Sears and Kinder 1971).

In the 1990s White attitudes hardened still further as issues such as affirmative action, immigration, and crime provoked strong emotions among members of this dominant group as well as members of subordinate groups. Economically less successful groups such as African Americans and Hispanics have been credited with negative traits to the point where issues such as welfare and crime are now viewed as "race issues." Besides making the resolution of very difficult social issues even harder, we have another instance of blaming the victim. These perceptions come at a time when the willingness of government to address domestic ills is limited by increasing opposition to new taxes. While there is some evidence that fewer Whites are consistently prejudiced on all issues from interracial marriage to school integration, it is also apparent that many Whites continue to endorse some anti-Black statements, and that negative images are widespread as they relate to the major domestic issues of the 1990s (M. Gilens 1996; M. Hughes 1997; Schaefer 1996).

The Mood of the Subordinate Group

Sociologist William E. B. Du Bois relates an experience from his youth in a largely White community in Massachusetts. He tells how, on one occasion, the boys and girls were exchanging cards, and everyone was having a lot of fun. One girl, a newcomer, refused his card as soon as she saw that Du Bois was Black. He wrote:

> *Then it dawned upon me with a certain suddenness that I was different from others . . . shut out from their world by a vast veil. I had therefore no desire to tear down that veil, to creep through; I held all beyond it in common contempt and lived above it in a region of blue sky and great wandering shadows (W. Du Bois 1903:2).*

In using the image of a "veil," Du Bois describes how members of subordinate groups learn they are being treated differently. In his case and that of many others, this leads to feelings of contempt toward all Whites that continue for a lifetime.

Opinion pollsters have been interested in White attitudes on racial issues longer than they have measured the views of subordinate groups. This neglect of minority attitudes reflects, in part, the bias of the White researchers. It also stems from the contention that the dominant group is more important to study because it is in a better position to act on its beliefs. The results of nationwide surveys conducted in the United States in 1997 offer insight into the sharply different attitudes of African Americans and Whites (see Table 2.3).

Racial attitudes were also reassessed in the aftermath of the 1992 Los Angeles riots, one of the worst civil disturbances in the twentieth century—possibly the worst. With fifty-three dead and 2,300 injured, this outbreak gave racism front-page attention. The riots were precipitated by a jury's failure to find four Los Angeles police officers guilty of beating a Black man, Rodney King. Since the beating had been videotaped and replayed numerous times on television, most people felt the police were guilty. In fact, a survey taken after the rioting began found that 100 percent of African Americans and 86 percent of Whites believed that the jury's verdict was wrong. Five years later, a survey showed that most Whites, Blacks, Hispanics, and Asians felt Los Angeles had remained about the same since the riots. Interestingly, all four groups also were likely to see Whites as getting more economic power and Blacks and Hispanics as experiencing the most discrimination. While the people of Los Angles, regardless of racial and ethnic group, generally felt the city was healing emotionally from the terrible violence, it did not seem that there was much feeling of positive change. However, there was somewhat more disagreement on other issues. Two-thirds of Whites, compared to four-fifths of Blacks, saw the Rodney King beating as evidence of widespread racism. Blacks definitely saw race relations worsening in the wake of the riots. Fully 43 percent felt relations were poor, compared to 17 percent of the Whites questioned (M. Baumann 1992, J. Merl 1997).

We have focused so far on what usually comes to mind when we think about prejudice: one group hating another group. But there is another form of prejudice: a group may come to hate itself. Members of groups held in low esteem by society may, as a result, have low self-esteem themselves. Many social scientists once believed that members of subordinate groups hated themselves or, at least, had low self-esteem. Similarly, they argued that Whites had high self-esteem. *High self-esteem* means that an individual has fundamental respect for himself or herself, appreciates his or her own merits, and is aware of personal faults and will strive to

Table 2.3 Views of the United States, 1997

Percentage answering "yes" to the question: Are blacks treated less fairly than whites?

	Blacks	Whites
On the job	45%	14%
On public transportation	25%	12%
In neighborhood shops	42%	18%
In stores downtown or in malls	46%	19%
In restaurants	42%	16%
By police	60%	30%

Source: Used by permission of the Gallup Organization.

overcome them. The research literature of the 1940s through the 1960s emphasized the low self-esteem of minorities. Usually, the subject was African Americans, but the argument has also been generalized to include any subordinate racial or ethnic group (J. Porter 1985; Rosenberg and Simmons 1971:9).

This view is no longer accepted. Leonard Bloom (1971:68–69) cautions against assuming that minority status influences personality traits in either a good or a bad way. First, Bloom says, such assumptions may create a stereotype. We cannot describe a Black personality any more accurately than we can a White personality. Second, characteristics of minority-group members are not entirely the result of subordinate racial status; they are also influenced by low incomes, poor neighborhoods, and so forth. Third, many studies of personality imply that certain values are normal or preferable, but the values chosen are those of dominant groups.

If, as Bloom suggests, assessments of a subordinate group's personality are so prone to misjudgments, why has the belief in low self-esteem been so widely held? Much of the research rests on studies with pre–school-age Black children asked to express preferences among dolls with different facial colors. Indeed, one such study, by psychologists Kenneth and Mamie Clark (1947), was cited in the arguments before the U.S. Supreme Court in the landmark 1954 case, *Brown* v. *Board of Education*. The Clarks' study showed that Black children preferred White dolls, a finding suggesting that the children had developed a negative self-image. While subsequent doll studies (Powell-Hopson and Hopson 1988) have sometimes shown Black children's preference for white-faced dolls, other social scientists contend that this shows a realization of what most commercially sold dolls look like rather than documenting low self-esteem.

Because African-American children, as well as other subordinate groups' children, can realistically see that Whites have more power and resources and therefore rate them higher does not mean that they personally feel inferior. Indeed, studies, even with children, show that when the self-images of middle-class or affluent African Americans are measured, their feelings of self-esteem are more positive than those of comparable Whites (W. Cross 1991; Hughes and Demo 1989; Martinez and Dukes 1991; C. Raymond 1991).

Intergroup Hostility

Prejudice is as diverse as the nation's population. It exists not only between dominant and subordinate peoples but also among specific subordinate groups. Unfortunately, until recently there was little research on this subject except for a few social distance scales administered to racial and ethnic minorities.

A 1993 national survey conducted for the National Conference of Christians and Jews (1994) revealed that, like Whites, many African Americans, Hispanic Americans, and Asian Americans held prejudiced and stereotypical views of other racial and ethnic minority groups. According to the survey:

- Majorities of Black, Hispanic, and Asian American respondents agreed that Whites are "bigoted, bossy, and unwilling to share power." Majorities of these non-White groups also believed that they had less opportunity than Whites to obtain a good education, a skilled job, or decent housing.

- Forty-six percent of Hispanic Americans and 42 percent of African Americans agreed that Asian Americans are "unscrupulous, crafty, and devious in business."
- Sixty-eight percent of Asian Americans and 49 percent of African Americans believed that Hispanic Americans "tend to have bigger families than they are able to support."
- Thirty-one percent of Asian Americans and 26 percent of Hispanic Americans agreed that African Americans "want to live on welfare."

Officials of the National Conference of Christians and Jews expressed concern about the extent to which subordinate-group members agreed with negative stereotypes about other subordinate groups. At the same time, the survey also revealed positive views of major racial and ethnic minorities:

- More than 80 percent of respondents admired Asian Americans for "placing a high value on intellectual and professional achievement" and "having strong family ties."
- A majority of all groups surveyed agreed that Hispanic Americans "take deep pride in their culture and work hard to achieve a better life."
- Large majorities from all groups stated that African Americans "have made a valuable contribution to American society and will work hard when given a chance."

Many people are surprised to see ill feelings expressed between subordinate groups. From the dominant-group perspective, these feelings can be very functional. For example, in the aftermath of the 1992 Los Angeles riots, much of the discussion focused on relations between Korean American merchants and their African American and Hispanic clientele. Also, attention was focused on economic competition between Hispanics and African Americans for jobs. In some respects, as these discussions continued, they served to direct attention away from the issues that precipitated the riots in the first place—the treatment by the criminal-justice system of Black people as displayed by the acquittal of four White police officers following the Rodney King beating (J. Merl 1997; J. Miles 1992).

The pattern of intergroup relations in the United States has changed over time as new groups have immigrated to the country. In the next section we focus on more groups that are a part of the nation's diverse mix of people. Unfortunately, this case study also reveals the presence of prejudice and hostility.

Arab Americans and American Muslims: A Case Study of Emerging Prejudice

The Arab American and Muslim American communities are among the most rapidly growing subordinate groups in the United States. Westerners often confuse the two groups. Actually, Arabs are an ethnic group, and Muslims are a religious group. Many Arabs are not Muslims, and most Muslims are not Arabs.

Arab immigration began in the late 1800s and then picked up dramatically in the 1960s. Initially, Arab immigrants were more likely to be Christian, and the first wave assimilated into many aspects of American culture. However, there are now an estimated 870,000 Arab Americans and their numbers are rising, leading to the development of small Arab retail centers in several cities. Many Arab Americans cling to the culture of their particular origin, which can vary considerably. Indeed, Arabs constitute an ethnic group found in twenty-two nations of North Africa and the Middle East, including Morocco, Syria, Iraq, Saudi Arabia, and Somalia. Obviously, to speak of Arabs (or Arab Americans) does not take into account the wide cultural differences and divisions within this group (El-Badry 1994; Siddiqi 1993).

Muslims are followers of Islam, the world's largest faith after Christianity. While they have some beliefs in common with Christians, such as belief in a common descent from Adam and Eve and reverence for the Virgin Mary, Islam is strongly influenced by the teachings of the Koran (or Al-Qur'an), the writings of the seventh-century prophet, Muhammed. Islamic believers are divided into a variety of faiths and sects, such as Sunnis and Shiites. These divisions sometimes result in antagonisms among the members, just as there are religious rivalries among Christian denominations. At present, there are about 4 million Muslims in the United States, of whom about 42 percent are African American, 24 percent are South Asian, 12 percent are Arab, and 22 percent are "other." By the year 2000, Muslims in the United States will outnumber Presbyterians and will be approaching Methodists, Lutherans, and Jews in number (Dart 1994; El-Badry 1994; S. Kloehn 1997).

A national 1993 survey found that over 40 percent of Americans view Muslims as supporting terrorism and the majority see them as suppressing women. Not coincidentally, these images have crystallized as the number of Arabs in the United States has increased. As marginal groups with virtually no power, Arab Americans and Muslim Americans are vulnerable to prejudice and discrimination (National Conference of Christians and Jews 1994).

News events have fueled the anti-Arab, anti-Muslim feeling. Major tragic activities carried out by Arabs or Muslims, including the 1972 terrorist raid at the Munich Olympics and the 1998 bombings of the U.S. embassies in Kenya and Tanzania, have contributed to the negative image. Media coverage of these events provided little insight into Arab cultures and Islamic religious practices. Contributing to this portrayal were stereotypical images in motion pictures such as *Cannonball Run* in 1979 and *The Siege* in 1998. The stereotyping of Arabs by Westerners is vivid and almost cartoon like—representing them as camel drivers or as wealthy, and treacherous. Even Disney's 1993 animated film *Aladdin* referred to Arabs as "barbaric" and depicted, contrary to Islamic law, a guard threatening to cut off a young girl's hand for stealing food. Like so many other groups, Arab Americans and American Muslims arriving in the United States have encountered simplistic views of their beliefs and behavior (*New York Times* 1994b; R. Niebuhr 1990; M. Siddiqi 1993).

The immediate aftermath of the 1995 bombing of the federal building in Oklahoma City showed the willingness of the public to accept stereotypes. Many television news reports indicated that Islamic fundamentalists or Arab terrorists were the prime suspects. A Jordanian American who lives in Oklahoma City was arrested in London but cleared of any involvement in the terrorist attack. Nevertheless, in the first three days after the bombing, there were at least 222 attacks against Muslims in the United States. In the end, two White American men were indicted in the bombing, but this hardly erased the pain felt by many Arab Americans and Muslim Americans about the way they had become scapegoats (Brooke 1995; Henneberger 1995).

In light of these feelings, some citizens have found themselves under special surveillance due to "profiling" at airports. Fearing terrorists, some airlines have established criteria involving people's appearance or ethnic-sounding names which has caused Arab Americans to be taken aside on domestic flights while they and their belongings are scrutinized. Muslim women who choose to don hair scarves or *hijab,* in keeping with their tradition to dress modestly, encounter harassment from strangers in the street and find many employers insisting they shed the covering if they wish to get a job or expect to be promoted. These citizens find it difficult to understand these attitudes in a nation of immigrants grounded in religious freedom.

Arab Americans and Muslim Americans, like other subordinate groups, have not responded passively to their treatment. Organizations have been created within these communities to counter negative stereotypes and to offer material to school curricula to respond to the labeling that has occurred. Perhaps more significantly, Arab Americans and Muslim Americans are beginning to become active in both major political parties in the United States (L. Sharn 1996).

Reducing Prejudice

Focusing on how to eliminate prejudice involves an explicit value judgment: prejudice is wrong and causes problems for those who are prejudiced and for their victims. The obvious way to eliminate prejudice is to eliminate its causes: the desire to exploit, the fear of being threatened, and the need to blame others for one's own failure. These might be eliminated by personal therapy, but therapy, even if it worked for every individual, is no solution for a society. Such a program would not be feasible because of its prohibitive cost and because it would have to be compulsory, which would violate civil rights. Furthermore, many of those in need of such therapy would not acknowledge their problem—the first step in effective therapy.

The answer appears to rest with programs directed at society as a whole. Prejudice is attacked indirectly when discrimination is attacked. Despite prevailing beliefs to the contrary, we can legislate against prejudice; statutes and decisions do affect attitudes. In the past, people firmly believed that laws could not overcome norms, especially racist ones. Recent history, especially after the civil rights movement began in 1954, has challenged that common wisdom. Laws and court rulings that have equalized the treatment of Blacks and Whites have led people to reevaluate their beliefs about what is right and wrong. The increasing tolerance by Whites during the civil rights period from 1954 to 1965 seems to support this conclusion.

Much research has been done to determine how to change negative attitudes toward groups of people. The most encouraging findings point to the mass media, education, and intergroup contact.

MASS MEDIA AND EDUCATION

The research on the mass media and education consists of two types: (1) research performed in artificially (experimentally) created situations and (2) studies examining the influence on attitudes of motion pictures, television, and advertisements.

Leaflets, radio commercials, comic books, billboards, and classroom posters bombard people with the message of racial harmony. Television audiences watch a public service message that for thirty seconds shows smiling White and African American infants reaching out toward each other. Law-enforcement and military personnel attend in-service training sessions that preach the value of a pluralistic society. Does this publicity do any good? Do these programs make any difference?

Most but not all studies show that well-constructed programs do have some positive effect in reducing prejudice, at least temporarily. The reduction is rarely as much as one might wish, however. The difficulty is that a single program is insufficient to change lifelong habits, especially if little is done to reinforce the program's message once it ends. Persuasion to respect other groups does not operate in a clear field because, in their ordinary environments, individuals are still subjected to situations that promote prejudicial feelings. Children and adults are encouraged to laugh at Polish jokes, or a Black adolescent may be discouraged by peers from befriending a White youth. All this serves to undermine the effectiveness of prejudice-reduction programs (G. Allport 1979).

Study results indicate the influence of educational programs designed specifically to reduce prejudice. For example, a special program in a small country town in Australia helped to reduce negative stereotypes of Aborigines, that nation's native people (Donovan and Levers 1993). However, studies consistently document that increased formal education, regardless of content, is associated with racial tolerance. Research data show that more highly educated people are more likely to indicate respect and liking for groups different from themselves. Why should more years of schooling have this effect? It could be that more education gives a broader outlook and makes a person less likely to endorse myths that sustain racial prejudice. Formal education teaches the importance of qualifying statements and the need at least to question rigid categorizations, if not reject them altogether. Another explanation is that education does not actually reduce intolerance but simply makes individuals more careful about revealing it. Formal education may simply instruct individuals in the appropriate responses, which in some settings could even be prejudiced views. Despite the lack of a clear-cut explanation, either theory suggests that the continued trend toward a better-educated population will contribute to a reduction in overt prejudice.

However, the education experience at the college level may not reduce prejudice uniformly. For example, some White students will come to hold the belief that minority students did not earn their admission into college. Students may feel threatened to see large groups of people of different racial and cultural backgrounds congregating together and forming their own groups. Racist confrontations do occur outside the classroom and, even if they do involve only a few, the events themselves will be followed by hundreds. Therefore, there are aspects of the college experience that may only foster the "we" and "they" (R. Schaefer 1986, 1996).

Education is not limited to formal schooling; increasingly, many forms of instruction are offered in the workplace. Remedies for intolerance can be taught there as well. With the entry of women and minority men into nontraditional work settings, training and support programs take on increased importance. Generally, when minorities enter an organization, they are thinly represented. Education programs have been introduced so that management does not treat these pioneers as golden (can do no wrong) or as hopeless cases doomed to failure (Pettigrew and Martin 1987).

The mass media, like schooling, may reduce prejudice without the need for specially designed programs. Television, radio, motion pictures, newspapers, and magazines present only a portion of real life, but what effect do they have on prejudice if the content is racist or antiracist, sexist or antisexist? As with measuring the influence of programs designed to reduce prejudice, coming to strong conclusions on the mass media's effect is hazardous, but the evidence points to a measurable effect. The 1915 movie *The Birth of a Nation* depicts African Americans unfavorably and glorifies the Ku Klux Klan. A study of Illinois schoolchildren has shown that watching the movie made them more unfavorably inclined toward African Americans than they had been, a negative effect that persisted even five months later when the children were retested. Conversely, the 1947 movie *Gentleman's Agreement,* which takes a strong stand against anti-Semitism, appears to have softened the anti-Semitic feelings of its audience (Commission on Civil Rights 1977, 1980a).

Recent research has examined the influence of television because it commands the widest viewing audience among children and adolescents. A 1988 study found that almost a third of high school students felt that television entertainment was "an accurate representation" of African American "real life" (Lichter and Lichter 1988). Many programs, such as *Amos n' Andy* or films with "dumb Injuns," which depict subordinate groups in stereotyped, demeaning roles, are no longer shown. Blacks and members of other subordinate groups are now more likely than before to appear in programs and commercials. As a result of the networks' greater sensitivity to the presentation of minority groups, people now see more balanced portrayals.

Television programs showing positive African American family life, as in *Family Matters, Living Single,* and *The Cosby Show,* have been quite a change from *Diff'rent Strokes* and *Webster,* which promoted the notion that African American orphans are best off in White homes. Yet even with these advances there is still evidence of the old ways. A study of the commentary on televised professional football games found that the commentators were much more likely to note the physical ability of Black players and the cognitive skills of White players (J. Rada 1995).

How far have the mass media really come? For one thing, we know that Whites and Blacks watch different programs. Of the top fifteen television programs watched in Black households during the 1994–1995 television season, only one was on the top fifteen list of all households—*NFL Monday Night Football.* Indeed, several of the top

Black-watched programs were canceled, leaving only two Black-cast programs, *Cosby* and *Family Matters,* on the three commercial networks. As Figure 2.3 shows, there have been modest increases in the presentation of African Americans over the last thirty years but no positive change for Hispanics. The overwhelming majority of Black actors on prime-time television are employed in comedic roles or as criminals; no Black dramatic series has lasted a season, and very few are even given a chance. Asians and Hispanics have an even greater image problem in contemporary television. The problem has been further complicated by the home video revolution, which has led videocassette marketers to exhume many of the most stereotypical films (BBDO 1996; H. Gates 1989).

The image of minorities in motion pictures is equally poor. The 1980s witnessed major movies such as *Fort Apache, the Bronx,* and *The Fiendish Plot of Dr. Fu Manchu,* distorting the image of minority groups. The 1996 Academy Awards was the subject of protests over its failure to recognize the few outstanding African American performers who appeared in big-budget pictures. Looking at the past, we do detect progress. Occasionally performers are cast against type, such as the African American actor Morgan Freeman as the President of the United States in the 1998 motion picture *Deep Impact.* Yet certainly the new mass media image of

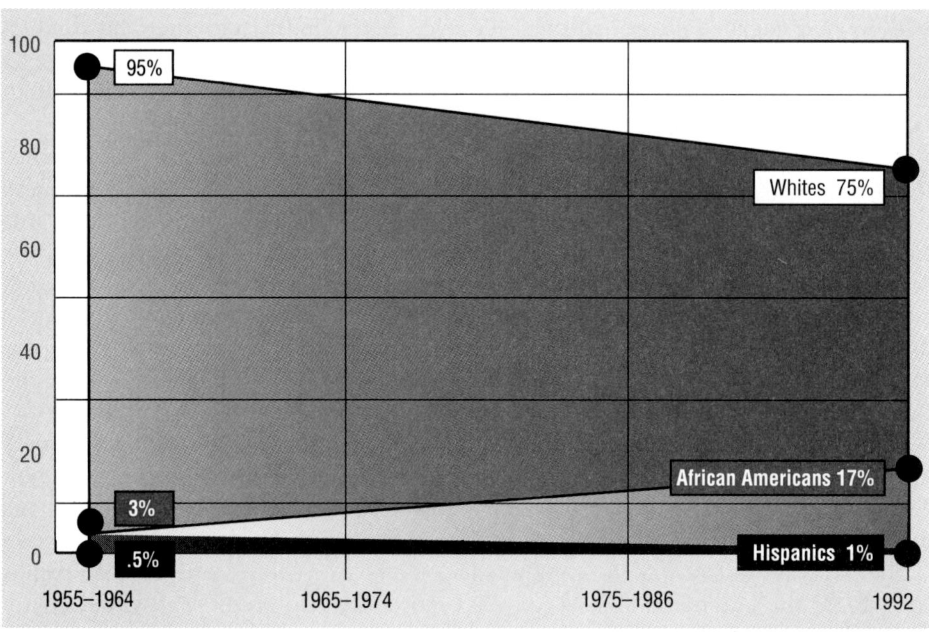

Figure 2.3 Television's Ethnic Portrayals
An analysis of prime-time entertainment (excluding reality-based syndicated series) shows an actual decline in the representation of Hispanics and an increase in the representation of African Americans.
Source: DuBrow 1994:5.

women and racial groups does not uniformly cause people to discard the old definitions, the old stereotypes.

Because prejudice is acquired from our social environment, it follows that the mass media and educational programs, as major elements of that environment, influence the level of prejudice. The movement to eliminate the stereotyping of minorities and the sexes in textbooks and on television recognizes this influence. Most of the effort has been to avoid contributing to racial hostility; less effort has been made

Prominent roles in motion pictures for members of subordinate groups are still relatively few. Thus, Morgan Freeman received considerable attention for his role as the President of the United States in the 1998 motion picture *Deep Impact*.

to attack prejudice actively, primarily because no one knows how to do that effectively. In looking for a way of attacking prejudice directly, many people advocate intergroup contact.

EQUAL-STATUS CONTACT

An impressive number of research studies have confirmed the **contact hypothesis,** a hypothesis that states that intergroup contact between people of equal status in harmonious circumstances will cause them to become less prejudiced and to abandon previously held stereotypes. Most studies indicate that such contact also improves the attitude of subordinate-group members. The importance of equal status in the interaction cannot be stressed enough. If a Puerto Rican is abused by his employer, little interracial harmony is promoted. Similarly, the situation in which contact occurs must be pleasant, making a positive evaluation likely for both individuals. Contact between two nurses, one Black and the other White, who are competing for one vacancy as a supervisor may lead to greater racial hostility (R. Schaefer 1976).

The key factor in reducing hostility in addition to equal-status contact is the presence of a common goal. If people are in competition, as already noted, contact may heighten tension. However, bringing people together to share a common task has been shown to reduce ill feeling when these people belong to different racial, ethnic, or religious groups. A 1994 study of Mexican and El Salvadoran immigrants in Houston found that contact with African Americans generally improved relations, and the absence of contact tended to foster ambivalent, even negative attitudes (McCollom 1996; Sherif and Sherif 1969; R. Slavin 1985).

In a 1992 study of housing integration, researchers examined the harassment, threats, and fears that Blacks face in White schools in which low-income Black students are in the minority. Did these African American youth experience acceptance, friendships, and positive interactions with their White classmates? The researchers interviewed youth who had moved to the suburbs and those who had relocated within the city of Chicago under the auspices of a federally funded program. In this program, low-income Black families received housing subsidies that allowed them to move from inner-city housing projects into apartment buildings occupied largely by middle-income Whites and located in middle-income, mostly White suburbs. The study found that these low-income Black youth did experience some harassment and some difficulty in gaining acceptance in the suburban schools, but the findings also suggested that they eventually experienced great success in social integration and felt they fit into their new environments (Rosenbaum and Meaden 1992).

As African Americans and other subordinate groups slowly gain access to better-paying and more responsible jobs, the contact hypothesis takes on greater significance. Usually, the availability of equal-status interaction is taken for granted, yet in everyday life intergroup contact does not conform to the equal-status idea of the contact hypothesis as often as we are assured by researchers who hope to see a lessening of tension. Furthermore, in a highly segregated society such as the United States, contact, especially between Whites and minorities, tends to be brief and superficial (W. Ford 1986; Sigelman et al. 1996).

CONCLUSION

This chapter has examined theories of prejudice and measurements of its extent. Prejudice should not be confused with discrimination. The two concepts are not the same: prejudice refers to negative attitudes and discrimination to negative behavior toward a group.

Several theories try to explain why prejudice exists. Some emphasize economic concerns (the exploitation and scapegoating theories), whereas other approaches stress personality or normative factors. No one explanation is sufficient. Surveys conducted in the United States over the past sixty years point to a reduction of prejudice as measured by the willingness to express stereotypes or maintain social distance. Survey data also show that many Whites and Blacks are still intolerant of each other. Prejudice involving Hispanic groups, Asian Americans, and relatively large recent immigrant groups such as Arab Americans and Muslim Americans is well documented. Issues such as immigration and affirmative action reemerge and cause bitter resentment. Furthermore, ill feelings exist among subordinate groups in schools, in the streets, and in the workplace.

Equal-status contact may reduce hostility among groups. However, in a highly segregated society defined by inequality, such opportunities are not typical. The mass media can be of value in reducing discrimination but has not done enough and may even intensify ill feeling by promoting stereotypical images. While strides are being made in increasing the appearance of minorities in positive roles in television and films, one would not realize how diverse our society is by sampling advertisements, programs, or movie theaters.

While we can be encouraged by the techniques available to reduce intergroup hostility, there are still sizable segments of the population who not want to live in integrated neighborhoods, do not want to work for or be lead by someone of a different race, and who certainly object to the idea of their relatives marrying outside their own group. People still harbor stereotypes toward one another, and this includes racial and ethnic minorities toward one another (Herring and Amissah 1997).

Chapter 3 outlines the effects of discrimination. Discrimination's costs are high to both dominant and subordinate groups. With that in mind, we will examine some techniques for reducing discrimination.

KEY TERMS

authoritarian personality 48
Bogardus scale 55
caste approach 49
contact hypothesis 68
discrimination 44
ethnocentrism 40
ethnophaulism 44
exploitation theory 49
normative approach 50
prejudice 44
scapegoat 46

REVIEW QUESTIONS

1. How are prejudice and discrimination both related and unrelated to each other?
2. How do theories of prejudice relate to different expressions of prejudice?
3. Besides Arab Americans and American Muslims, identify other groups recently subjected to prejudice, perhaps in your own community.
4. Why does prejudice develop even towards groups with whom people have little contact?

CRITICAL THINKING

1. Identify stereotypes associated with a group of people such as the elderly or people with physical handicaps.
2. What social issues do you think are most likely to engender hostility along racial and ethnic lines?
3. Consider the television programs you have watched the most. In terms of race and ethnicity, how well do the programs you watch tend to reflect the diversity of the population in the United States?

INTERNET EXERCISE

In this chapter, you learned about the definition, content, and extent of prejudice. The Gallup Organization conducts polls on the current attitudes people have on racial and social issues. Visit Gallup's "Special Report: Black/White Relations in the U.S." site (http://www.gallup.com/poll/socialaudits/sa970610.asp). Examine the data to find out how Blacks and Whites view educational opportunities, equality in the workplace, community relations, and the extent of prejudice in the U.S. What differences and similarities exist between Black and White attitudes? About which issues are Black and White Americans in most disagreement? Do people believe that there is more or less prejudice today in comparison to the past? How prejudiced does each group believe themselves and others to be? Can you apply the theories of prejudice from this chapter (exploitation, scapegoating, authoritarianism, and/or normative) to any of the findings on this web site?

FOR FURTHER INFORMATION

Ed Guerrero. *Framing Blackness: The African American Image in Film*. Philadelphia: Temple University Press, 1993.

Considers stereotyping in motion pictures from D. W. Griffiths' *The Birth of a Nation* through to Spike Lee's *Malcolm X*.

C. Neil Macrae, Charles Stangor, and Miles Hewstone, eds. *Stereotypes and Stereotyping*. New York: Guilford Press, 1996.
This collection of thirteen articles offers the latest insight among social psychologists into research on stereotypes, including the development of such images, their measurement, and theoretical explanations for the persistence of stereotypes.

Bart Schneider, ed. *An Anthology in the First Person*. New York: Crown Trade Books, 1997.
An excellent reader that brings a face to confronting prejudice, by such people as Henry Louis Gates, Jr., Richard Rodriguez, Peggy McIntosh, and Adrienne Rich.

Howard Schuman, Charlotte Steeh, Lawrence Bobo, and Maria Krysan. *Racial Attitudes in America: Trends and Interpretations,* rev. ed. Cambridge, MA: Harvard University Press, 1997.
A very detailed analysis of available data on White attitudes toward Blacks and some information on beliefs held by African Americans.

3

Discrimination

CHAPTER OUTLINE

HIGHLIGHTS

Just as social scientists have advanced theories to explain why prejudice exists, they have also presented explanations of why discrimination occurs. Social scientists look more and more at the manner in which institutions, not individuals, discriminate. Institutional discrimination describes a pattern in social institutions that produces or perpetuates inequalities, even if individuals in the society do not intend to be racist or sexist. Income data document that gaps do exist among racial and ethnic groups. Historically, attempts have been made to reduce discrimination, usually as a result of strong lobbying efforts by minorities themselves. Patterns of total discrimination make solutions particularly difficult for people in the informal economy or the underclass. Affirmative action was designed to equalize opportunity but has encountered significant resentment by those who charge that it constitutes reverse discrimination. Despite many efforts to end discrimination, glass ceilings and glass walls remain in the workplace.

Discrimination can take many forms. As the next two incidents indicate, discrimination can be direct or the result of a complex combination of factors. It can lead to indignities or to death.

Lawrence Otis Graham (1995) had "arrived" by the standards of most people in the United States. He was a graduate of Harvard Law School, married, and had become a well-regarded member of a Manhattan law firm. But he was also Black.

Despite his success in securing clients for himself and his firm, Graham had noticed that White attorneys seemed to get a jump on him because of their associations with corporate leaders at private clubs. By tradition, the clubs were exclusively White. Graham decided to take time out from his law firm and learn more about the workings of these private clubs that allowed some Whites to mingle in an informal atmosphere and so contributed to their establishing networks. These networks in turn allowed people to establish contacts that advanced their success in the business world. Rather than present himself as a successful Ivy League college graduate to become a member, he presented himself as a working-class African American seeking a job as a waiter. From the vantage point of a server, Graham figured he could observe the network of these predominantly White country-club members. This was not to be the case. He was not given a job at club after club. Despite all sorts of encouragement when he talked to employers over the phone, he was denied a job when he presented himself, and they saw that this articulate, well-mannered young man was Black. Eventually he obtained a job as a bus boy, clearing tables in a club where the White servers commented that he could do their job better than they could.

Cynthia Wiggins was also African American, but she lived in a different world from Lawrence Otis Graham. She was a seventeen-year-old single mother struggling to make a living. She had sought jobs near her home but had found no employment opportunities. Eventually she found employment as a cashier, but it was far from her home, and she could not afford a car. Still, she was optimistic and looked forward to marrying the man to whom she was engaged. In 1995, she made the fifty-minute bus ride from her predominantly Black neighborhood in Buffalo, New York, to her job at the Galleria, a fancy suburban shopping mall. Every day, charter buses unloaded shoppers from as far away as Canada, but city buses were not allowed on mall property. The bus Wiggins rode was forced to stop across the lot and across a seven-

Harvard-educated lawyer Lawrence Otis Graham sought a position as a waiter in exclusive clubs to learn more about contemporary discrimination.

lane highway without sidewalks. On a December day, with the roadway lined with mounds of snow, she tried to cross the highway, only to be struck by a dump truck. She died three weeks later. Later investigation showed that the bus company had been trying to arrange for the bus to stop in the mall parking lot, but the shopping center authorities had blocked the move. Prior to the incident, the mall said they would consider allowing in suburban buses but not public buses from the city. As one mall store owner put it, "You'll never see an inner-city bus on the mall premises" (Barnes 1996:33; Gladwell 1996).

Discrimination has a long history, right up to the present, of taking its toll on people. For some, like Lawrence Otis Graham, discrimination is being reminded that even when you do try to seek employment, you may be treated like a second-class citizen. For others, like Cynthia Williams, discrimination meant suffering for the unjust decisions made in a society that quietly discriminated. Williams lost her life not because anyone actually intended to kill her, but because decisions made it more likely that an inner-city resident would be an accident victim. Despite legislative and court efforts to eliminate discrimination, members of dominant and subordinate groups pay a price for continued intolerance.

Understanding Discrimination

Discrimination is the denial of opportunities and equal rights to individuals and groups because of prejudice or for other arbitrary reasons. Some people in the United States find it difficult to see discrimination as a widespread phenomenon. "After all," it is often said, "these minorities drive cars, hold jobs, own their homes, and even go to college." This does not mean that discrimination is rare. An understanding of discrimination in modern industrialized societies such as the United States must begin by distinguishing between relative and absolute deprivation.

RELATIVE VERSUS ABSOLUTE DEPRIVATION

Conflict theorists have said correctly that it is not absolute, unchanging standards that determine deprivation and oppression. It is crucial that, although minority groups may be viewed as having adequate or even good incomes, housing, health care, and educational opportunities, it is their position relative to some other group that offers evidence of discrimination.

The term **relative deprivation** is defined as the conscious feeling of a negative discrepancy between legitimate expectations and present actualities. After settling in the United States, immigrants often enjoy better material comforts and more political freedom than were possible in their old country. If they compare themselves to most other people in the United States, however, they will feel deprived because, while their standard has improved, the immigrants still perceive relative deprivation.

Absolute deprivation, on the other hand, implies a fixed standard based on a minimum level of subsistence below which families should not be expected to exist. Discrimination does not necessarily mean absolute deprivation. A Japanese American who is promoted to a management position may still be a victim of discrimination, if he or she had been passed over for years because of corporate reluctance to place an Asian American in a highly visible position.

Dissatisfaction is also likely to arise from feelings of relative deprivation. Those members of a society who feel most frustrated and disgruntled by the social and economic conditions of their lives are not necessarily worse off in an objective sense. Social scientists have long recognized that what is most significant is how people perceive their situations. Karl Marx pointed out that, although the misery of the workers was important in reflecting their oppressed state, so, too, was their position relative to the ruling class. In 1847, Marx wrote that

> *Although the enjoyment of the workers has risen, the social satisfaction that they have has fallen in comparison with the increased enjoyment of the capitalist. (Marx and Engels 1955:94)*

This statement explains why the groups or individuals who are most vocal and best organized against discrimination are not necessarily in the worst economic and social situation. They are likely, however, to be those who most strongly perceive that, relative to others, they are not receiving their fair share. Resistance to perceived discrimination, rather than the actual amount of absolute discrimination, is the key.

TOTAL DISCRIMINATION

Social scientists—and increasingly policy makers—have begun to use the concept of total discrimination. **Total discrimination,** as shown in Figure 3.1, refers to current discrimination operating in the labor market *and* past discrimination. Past discrimination experienced by an individual includes the relatively poorer education and job experience of racial and ethnic minorities compared to that of many White Americans. When considering discrimination, therefore, it is not enough to focus only on what is being done to people now. Sometimes a person may be dealt with fairly but may still be at a disadvantage because he or she suffered from poorer health care, inferior counseling in the school system, less access to books and other educational materials, or a poor job record resulting from absences to take care of brothers and sisters.

We find another variation of this past-in-present discrimination when apparently nondiscriminatory present practices have negative effects because of prior intentionally biased practices. Although unions that purposely discriminated against minority members in the past may no longer do so, some people are still prevented from achieving higher levels of seniority because of those past practices. Personnel records include a cumulative record that is vital in promotion and selection for desirable assignments. Blatantly discriminatory judgments and recommendations in the past, however, remain part of a person's record.

INSTITUTIONAL DISCRIMINATION

Individuals practice discrimination in one-to-one encounters, while institutions practice discrimination through their daily operations. Indeed, a consensus is growing today that this institutional discrimination is more significant than that committed by prejudiced individuals.

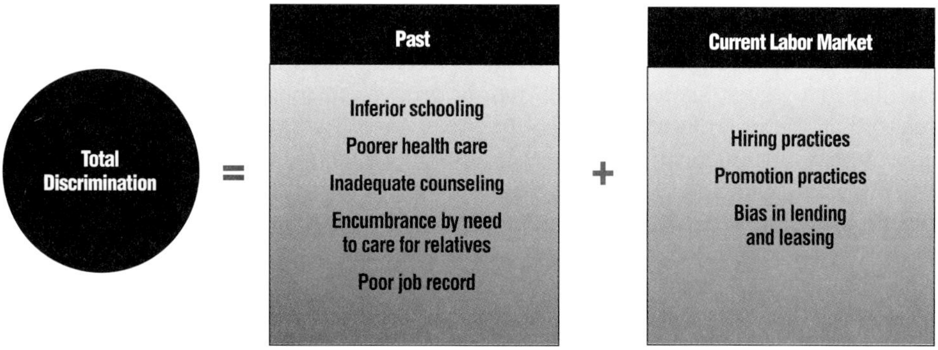

Figure 3.1 Total Discrimination

Social scientists are particularly concerned with the ways in which patterns of employment, education, criminal justice, housing, health care, and government operations maintain the social significance of race and ethnicity. **Institutional discrimination** refers to the denial of opportunities and equal rights to individuals and groups that results from the normal operations of a society.

Civil rights activist Stokely Carmichael and political scientist Charles Hamilton are credited with introducing the concept of *institutional racism*. Individual discrimination refers to overt acts of individual Whites against individual Blacks; Carmichael and Hamilton reserved the term *institutional racism* for covert acts committed collectively against an entire group. From this perspective, discrimination can take place without an individual's intending to deprive others of privileges and even without the individual's being aware that others are being deprived (Ture and Hamilton 1992).

How can discrimination be widespread and unconscious at the same time? The following represent a few documented examples of institutional discrimination:

1. Standards for assessing credit risks work against African Americans and Hispanics seeking to establish businesses because many lack conventional credit references. Businesses in low-income areas where these groups often reside also have much higher insurance costs.
2. IQ testing favors middle-class children, especially the White middle class, because of the types of questions included.
3. The entire criminal justice system, from the patrol officer to the judge and jury, is dominated by Whites who find it difficult to understand life in poverty areas.
4. Hiring practices often require several years experience at jobs only recently opened to members of subordinate groups

In some cases, even apparently neutral institutional standards can turn out to have discriminatory effects. In 1992, African American students at a Midwestern state university protested a policy under which fraternities and sororities that wished to use campus facilities for a dance were required to post a $150 security deposit to cover possible damage. The Black students complained that this policy had a discriminatory impact on minority student organizations. Campus police countered that the university's policy applied to *all* student groups interested in using these facilities. However, since overwhelmingly White fraternities and sororities at the school had their own houses, which they used for dances, the policy indeed affected only African American and other subordinate groups' organizations.

The U.S. population is becoming more diversified, and examples of institutional discrimination are confronting more different groups. Many Asian peoples have distinctive customs honoring their deceased family members. Among these traditions is the burning of incense at the grave site, placing food on the grave markers, and leaving fake money. These practices stem from ancestor worship but are often followed by Christian Chinese Americans who try to hold on to some of the "old ways." Cemetery proprietors maintain standards of what they regard as proper grave decoration in order to maintain a tidy appearance. Consequently, people of Asian descent find they are unable to bury their loved ones in the cemeteries most convenient to them and must travel to cemeteries that are more open to different ways of memorializing the dead. Cemeteries do not consciously seek to keep people out because they are Asian, but they develop policies, often with little thought, that fail to recognize the pluralistic nature of society (M. Eng 1998).

Institutional discrimination continuously imposes more hindrances on, and awards fewer benefits to, certain racial and ethnic groups than it does to others. This is the underlying and painful context of American intergroup relations.

The Informal Economy

The secondary labor market affecting many members of racial and ethnic minorities has come to be called the informal economy. The **informal economy** refers to transfers of money, goods, or services that are not reported to the government. This label describes much of the work in inner-city neighborhoods and poverty-stricken rural areas, in sharp contrast to the rest of the marketplace. Workers are employed in the informal economy seasonally or infrequently. The work they do may resemble the work of traditional occupations, such as mechanic, cook, or electrician, but these workers lack the formal credentials to enter such employment. Indeed, workers in the informal economy may work sporadically or may moonlight in the regular economy. The informal economy also includes unregulated child-care services, garage sales, and the unreported income of crafts people and street vendors.

The informal economy, sometimes referred to as the **irregular** or **underground economy**, exists worldwide. In 1996, wide publicity was given to the presence of sweatshops throughout the world and in urban America that supplied clothing for major retailers such as Kmart. Most of these employees were immigrants or non-Whites. Conflict sociologists in particular note that a significant level of commerce occurs outside traditional economies. Individually, the transactions are small, but they can be significant when taken together. Within the apparel industry, it has been estimated that perhaps half of all U.S.-produced garments in small shops are made

Many people work in the informal economy with little prospect of moving into the primary, better-paying economy. Pictured is a street vendor in New York City.

in businesses where two or more of the following laws are routinely violated: child labor, health and safety, minimum wage, and overtime. The informal economy taken in total makes up 10 to 20 percent of all economic activity in the United States (R. Ross 1998; D. Sontag 1993).

According to the **dual labor market model,** minorities have been relegated to the informal economy. While the informal economy may offer employment to the jobless, it provides few safeguards against fraud or malpractice that victimizes the workers. There are also few of the fringe benefits of health insurance and pension that are much more likely to be present in the conventional marketplace. Therefore informal economies are criticized for promoting highly unfair and dangerous working conditions. To be consigned to the informal economy is thus yet another example of social inequality.

Sociologist Edna Bonacich (1972, 1976) outlined the dual or split labor market that divides the economy into two realms of employment, the secondary one being populated primarily by minorities working at menial jobs. Labor, even when not manual, is still rewarded less when performed by minorities. In keeping with the conflict model, this dual-market model emphasizes that minorities fare unfavorably in the competition between dominant and subordinate groups.

The workers in the informal economy are ill prepared to enter the regular economy permanently or to take its better-paying jobs. Frequent changes in employment or lack of a specific supervisor leaves them without the kind of job résumé that employers in the regular economy expect before they hire. Some of the sources of employment in the informal economy are illegal, such as fencing stolen goods, narcotics peddling, pimping, and prostitution. More likely, the work is legal but not transferable to a more traditional job. An example is an "information broker," who receives cash in exchange for such information as where to find good buys or how to receive maximum benefits from public assistance programs (S. Pedder 1991).

Workers in the informal economy have not necessarily experienced direct discrimination. Because of past discrimination, they are unable to secure traditional employment. Working in the informal economy provides income but does not lead them into the primary labor market. A self-fulfilling cycle continues that allows past discrimination to create a separate work environment.

The Underclass

Many members of the informal economy, along with some employed in traditional jobs, compose what is called the underclass of American society.

The **underclass** consists of the long-term poor who lack training and skills. Conflict theorists, among others, have expressed alarm at the proportion of the nation's society living at this social stratum. Sociologist William Wilson (1987, 1988:15, 1996) drew attention to the growth of this varied grouping of families and individuals who are outside the mainstream of the occupational structure. While estimates vary depending on the definition, in 1990 the underclass included more than 3 million adults of working age, not counting children or the elderly. In the central city, about 49 percent of the underclass in 1990 comprised African Americans; 29 percent, Hispanics (or Latinos); 17 percent, Whites; and 5 percent, other (O'Hare and Curry-White 1992).

The discussion of the underclass has focused attention on society's inability to address the problems facing the truly disadvantaged—many of whom are Black or Hispanic. Some scholars have expressed concern that the portrait of the underclass seems to blame the victim, making the poor responsible. Wilson and others have stressed that it is not bad behavior but structural factors, such as the loss of manufacturing jobs, that have hit ghetto residents so hard. As the labor market has become tighter, the subordinate groups within the underclass are at a significant disadvantage. Associated with this structural problem is isolation from social services. The disadvantaged lack contact or sustained interaction with the individuals or institutions that represent the regular economy. It is the economy, not the poor, that needs reforming (J. DeParle 1991; W. Kornblum 1991; S. Wright 1993).

While the concept of underclass has been useful, its use reflects the division over issues involving race and poverty. Proponents of intervention use the underclass to show the need for a basic restructuring of the economy. Others use the term to describe a lifestyle whose practitioners refuse to try to move out of poverty and conclude that the poor reject responsibility for their plight. There is little evidence to support this pessimistic conclusion. Wilson (1996), in a 1978–1988 survey of African Americans living in poor neighborhoods, found that they believed in the work ethic and felt that plain hard work was important to getting ahead. The underclass, therefore, describes a segment of the population whose job prospects, as well as educational opportunities, are severely limited.

It is a commonly held notion that there are jobs available for the inner-city poor but they just do not seek them out. A study looked at jobs that were advertised in a help-wanted section of *The Washington Post*. The analysis showed that most of the jobs were beyond the reach of the underclass—perhaps 5 percent of all openings could even remotely be considered reasonable job prospects for people without skills or experience. During interviews with the employers, researchers found that an average of 21 people applied for each position, which typically was filled within three days of when the advertisement appeared. The mean hourly wage was $6.12 and 42 percent offered no fringe benefits, and the remaining positions offered "meager" fringe benefits after six months or one year of employment. The researchers concluded that this study, like others before it, counter the folk wisdom that there are plenty of jobs around for the underclass (Pease and Martin 1997).

Poverty is not new, yet the concept of an underclass describes a very chilling development: workers, whether employed in the informal economy or not, are beyond the reach of any safety net provided by existing social programs. Concern in the late 1990s about government spending and federal deficits have led to cutbacks of many public assistance programs and close scrutiny of those remaining. In addition, membership in the underclass is not an intermittent condition but a long-term attribute. The underclass is understandably alienated and engages sporadically in illegal behavior. This alienation and the illegal acts gain the underclass little support from the larger society to address the problem realistically.

The term *underclass* is often invoked to establish the superiority of the dominant group. Even if it is not stated explicitly, there is a notion that society and institutions have not failed the underclass but that somehow they are beyond hope. All too frequently, the underclass is treated as a homogeneous group, the object of scorn, fear, and embarrassment.

In "Listen to Their Voices" (on pp. 82–83), sociologist and former President of the American Sociological Association William Julius Wilson presents the findings of his research. In this selection Wilson shows how the poor are very aware of how larger society sees them, labels them, and stereotypes them.

Discrimination Today

Dateline NBC in August 1998 sent two young men—one African American and the other White—to shopping malls. They looked at merchandise in Eddie Bauer, Timberland, and other stores. Consistently, the Black shopper was tailed by in-store security. Often the guards, many of whom were themselves Black, left their assigned posts at the front of the store to follow the Black shopper. Confronted with the differential treatment of their customers, store executives indicated they gave

LISTEN TO THEIR VOICES

When Work Disappears

William Julius Wilson

It is interesting to note how the media perceptions of "underclass" values and attitudes contrast sharply with the views actually expressed by the residents of the inner-city ghetto. For example, a 28-year-old unmarried welfare mother of two children who lives in one of Chicago's large public housing projects described to one of the UPFLS (Urban Poverty and Family Life Study) interviewers how the media create the impression that the people who live in her housing project are all bad or are thugs and killers.

OK, I don't know where you live at, but you read the papers...they say, "Oh, Cabrini! Oh, they have gang killings... they have gang killings on the South Side! But the media and... and I guess the public, you know, they build it up so big. I mean, it's bad everywhere. Did anyone offend you when you came up here? My neighbor stopped you and gave you the message. You're white, you're white and they don't know you here, see, see, but you read the paper and your parents will say "don't go over there, girl!" I read where they said, you know, well, I read where there they kill blacks... whites, and they do this and they do that, and they, I mean, we're people, too. But it's... that's just the system. It makes us look like we're all the same, and we're all bad... . But that's not true.

A 28-year-old welfare mother from another South Side housing project raised a similar point:

no instructions to follow Black customers closely. White viewers were surprised by what they saw, while Black viewers generally saw little new to them in the report. Discrimination may take many forms and surface due to specific procedures or feelings of distrust (NBC News 1998).

Discrimination is widespread in the United States. It sometimes results from prejudices held by individuals. More significantly, it is found in institutional discrimination and the presence of the informal economy. The presence of an underclass is symptomatic of many social forces, and total discrimination—past and present discrimination taken together—is one of them.

Not so subtly, discrimination shows itself even when people are prepared to be customers. A 1990 study had Black and White men and women follow a script to buy new cars in the Chicago area. After 164 visits, the results showed that a White woman could be expected to pay \$142 more for a car than a White man, a Black man \$421 more, and a Black woman \$875 more. African Americans and women were perceived as less knowledgeable, and therefore were the victims of a higher markup in prices. A similar study in housing, nationwide in twenty-five metropolitan areas, showed that African Americans and Hispanics faced discrimination in a majority of their responses to advertisements. Housing agents showed fewer housing units to

'Cause a lot of people when they meet me, they say, "You live in a project?" I say "yeah." "Well, you don't look like the type of person." "How is a person supposed to look?" You know, like I tell them, the project don't make nobody, you make yourself. Now, if you want to get out there and carry that project name, be tough and rowdy and sloppy, disrespectful, well, shoot, that's lowlife. "You don't look like the type that lives in a project!" "Well, how am I supposed to look?" Just because I live in a project, that don't mean I have to come outside looking like a tramp, because I'm not. But they all, they like, "You too nice to be living in a project." You know, sometimes I get offended... . That just really gets on my nerves. You know, don't no building make you, you make yourself. You live in a home, you know. Look at all these people that's got Hollywood kids, busted for cocaine, o.d.'in' on it, you know, what's happened to them?

Our research reveals that the beliefs of inner-city residents bear little resemblance to the blanket media reports asserting that values have plummeted in impoverished inner-city neighborhoods or that people in the inner city have an entirely different value system. What is so striking is that despite the overwhelming joblessness and poverty, black residents in inner-city ghetto neighborhoods actually verbally endorse, rather than undermine, the basic American values concerning individual initiative.

Source: William Julius Wilson. From *When Work Disappears.*

Blacks and Hispanics, steered them to minority neighborhoods, and gave them far less assistance in finding housing that met their needs. Other recent studies reveal that lenders are 60 percent more likely to turn down a mortgage request from a minority applicant than from an equally qualified White and that lenders give minority applicants far less assistance in filling out their forms (I. Ayres 1991; J. Yinger 1995).

Discrimination also emerges when we look at data for groups other than Blacks and Hispanics. National studies have documented that White ethnics, such as Irish Catholics and Jewish Americans, are less likely to be in certain positions of power than White Protestants, despite equal educational levels (Alba and Moore 1982). The victims of discrimination are not limited to people of color.

MEASURING DISCRIMINATION

How much discrimination is there? As in measuring prejudice, problems arise in quantifying discrimination. Measuring prejudice is hampered by the difficulties in assessing attitudes and by the need to take many factors into account. It is further restrained by the initial challenge of identifying different treatment. A second difficulty of measuring discrimination is assigning a cost to the discrimination.

Some tentative conclusions about discrimination can be made, however. Figure 3.2 uses income data to show vividly the disparity in income between African Americans and Whites, men and women. The first comparison is of all workers. White men, with a median income of $36,118, earn almost 34 percent more than Black men and 89 percent more than Hispanic women, who earn only $19,676 in wages.

Clearly, White males earn most, followed by Black males, White females, Black females, Hispanic men, and Hispanic females. The sharpest drop is between White and Black males. Even worse, relatively speaking, is the plight of women. **Double jeopardy** refers to subordinate status twice, defined as experienced by women of color. This disparity between Black women and White men has remained unchanged over the more than fifty years during which such data have been tabulated. It illustrates yet another instance of the double jeopardy experienced by minority women. Also, Figure 3.2 includes only data for full-time, year-round workers, and therefore the figure excludes housewives and the unemployed. Even in this comparison, the deprivation of Blacks, Hispanics, and women is confirmed again.

Are these differences entirely the result of discrimination in employment? No, individuals within the four groups are not equally prepared to compete for high-paying jobs. Past discrimination is a significant factor in a person's present social position. As discussed previously and illustrated in Figure 3.1, past discrimination continues to take its toll on modern victims. Taxpayers, predominantly White, were unwilling to subsidize the public education of African Americans and Hispanics at the same levels as White pupils. Even as these actions have changed, today's schools show the continuing results of this uneven spending pattern from the past. Education is clearly an appropriate variable to control.

In Table 3.1, median income is compared, holding education constant, which means that we can compare Blacks and Whites and men and women with approximately

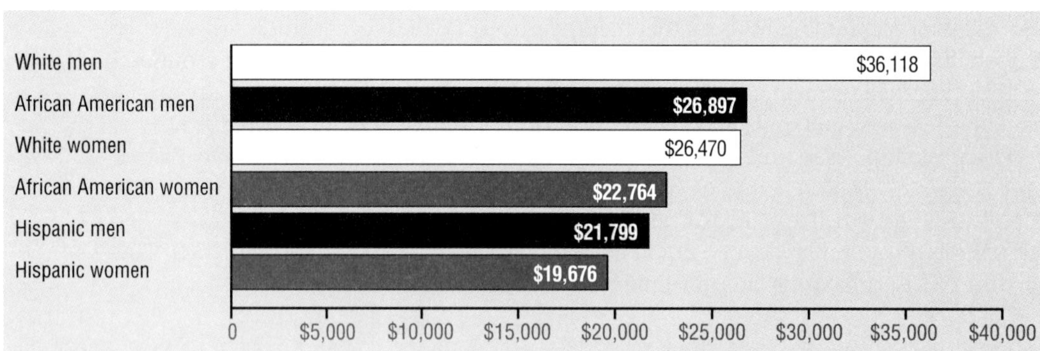

Figure 3.2 Median Income by Race, Ethnicity, and Gender, 1997
Even a brief analysis reveals striking differences in earning power between White men in the United States and other groups. Furthermore, the double jeopardy is apparent for African American and Hispanic women.
Note: Median income is from all sources and is limited to year-round, full-time workers over 15 years old.

Source: Bureau of the Census 1998b:28,29.

the same amount of formal schooling. More education means more money, but the disparity remains. The gap between races does narrow somewhat as education increases. However, both African American and women lag behind their more affluent counterparts. The contrast remains dramatic: women with a degree or graduate work ($29,781) earn less than men who fail to finish college ($30,536).

What do these individual differences look like if we consider them on a national level? Economist Andrew Brimmer (1995), citing numerous government studies, estimates that about 3 or 4 percent of the gross domestic product (GDP, or the value of goods and services) is lost annually by the failure to use African Americans' existing education. There had been little change in this economic cost from the mid–1960s to the mid–1990s. This estimate would be even higher, of course, if we took into account economic losses due to the underutilization of the academic talents of women and other minorities.

Now that education has been held constant, is the remaining gap caused by discrimination? No, not necessarily. Table 3.1 uses only the amount of schooling, not its quality. Racial minorities are more likely to attend inadequately financed schools. Some efforts have been made to eliminate disparities among school districts in the amount of wealth available to tax for school support, but with little success. In a 1973 case, *San Antonio Independent School District* v. *Rodriguez,* the U.S. Supreme Court ruled that attendance at an underfinanced school in a poor district does not constitute a violation of equal protection. The inequality of educational opportunity may seem less important in explaining sex discrimination. Even though women are usually not segregated from men, educational institutions encourage talented women

Table 3.1 Median Income by Race and Sex, Holding Education Constant

Even at the very highest levels of schooling, the income gap remains between Whites and Blacks. Education also has little apparent effect on the income gap between male and female workers.

	Race, 1996		Ratio	Sex, 1997		Ratio
	White	Black	Black to White	Male Workers	Female Workers	Women to Men
Total	$25,876	$20,262	.78	$28,919	$15,573	.54
High School						
1–3 years	15,135	13,054	.86	16,818	8,861	.53
4 years	21,307	17,285	.81	25,453	13,407	.53
College						
Some college	25,587	22,283	.87	30,356	17,153	.56
Bachelor's degree or more	36,941	31,639	.86	47,126	29,781	.63

Sources: Bureau of the Census 1998b: 26,27; 1998c.

Notes: Figures are median income from all sources except capital gain. Included are public assistance payments, dividends, pensions, unemployment compensation, and so on. Incomes are for all workers over twenty-five years of age. Data for Whites are for White non-Hispanics. "Some college" includes Associate Degree-holders for Race, excludes them for Sex data.

to enter fields that pay less (nursing or elementary education) than occupations requiring similar amounts of training.

ELIMINATING DISCRIMINATION

Two main agents of social change work to reduce discrimination: voluntary associations organized to solve racial and ethnic problems and the federal government including the courts. The two are closely related: most efforts initiated by the government were urged by associations or organizations representing minority groups, following vigorous protests against racism by African Americans. Resistance to social inequality by subordinate groups has been the key to change. Rarely has any government of its own initiative sought to end discrimination based on such criteria as race, ethnicity, and gender.

All racial and ethnic groups of any size are represented by private organizations that are to some degree trying to end discrimination. Some groups originated in the first half of the twentieth century, but most have either been founded since World War II or have become significant forces in bringing about change only since then. These include church organizations, fraternal social groups, minor political parties, and legal defense funds, as well as more militant organizations operating under the scrutiny of law-enforcement agencies. The purposes, membership, successes, and failures of these resistance organizations dedicated to eliminating discrimination are discussed throughout the balance of this book.

Government action toward eliminating discrimination is also relatively recent. Antidiscrimination actions have been taken by each branch of the government: the executive, the judicial, and the legislative.

The first antidiscrimination action at the executive level was President Franklin D. Roosevelt's 1943 creation of the Fair Employment Practices Commission (FEPC), which handled thousands of complaints of discrimination, mostly from African Americans, despite strong opposition by powerful economic and political leaders and many southern Whites. The FEPC had little actual power. It had no authority to compel employers to stop discriminating but could only ask for voluntary compliance. Its jurisdiction was limited to federal government employees, federal contractors, and labor unions. State and local governments and any business without a federal contract were not covered. Furthermore, the FEPC never enjoyed vigorous support from the White House, was denied adequate funds, and was part of larger agencies that were hostile to the commission's existence. This weak antidiscrimination agency was finally dropped in 1946, to be succeeded by an even weaker one in 1948. The judiciary, charged with interpreting laws and the U.S. Constitution, has a much longer history of involvement in the rights of racial, ethnic, and religious minorities. Its early decisions, however, protected the rights of the dominant group, as in the 1857 U.S. Supreme Court's *Dred Scott* decision, which ruled that slaves remained slaves even when living or traveling in states where slavery was illegal. Not until the 1940s did the Supreme Court revise earlier decisions and begin to grant African Americans the same rights as those held by Whites. The 1954 *Brown* v. *Board of Education* decision, which stated that "separate but equal" facilities, including education, was unconstitutional, heralded a new series of rulings, arguing, in effect, that to distinguish among races in order to segregate was inherently unconstitutional.

It was assumed incorrectly by many that *Brown* and other judicial actions would lead quickly to massive change. In fact, little change occurred initially, and resistance to racism continued. The immediate effect of many court rulings was minimal because the Executive branch and the Congress did not wish to violate the principle of **states' rights,** which holds that each state is sovereign in most of its affairs and has the right to order them without interference from the federal government. In other words, supporters of states' rights felt that the federal government had to allow state governments to determine how soon the rights of African Americans would be protected. Gradually, U.S. society became more committed to the rights of individuals. Legislation in the 1960s committed the federal government to protecting civil rights actively, rather than merely leaving action up to state and local officials.

The most important legislative effort to eradicate discrimination was the Civil Rights Act of 1964. This act led to the establishment of the Equal Employment Opportunity Commission (EEOC), which had the power to investigate complaints against employers and to recommend action to the Department of Justice. If the Justice Department sued and discrimination was found, the court could order appropriate compensation. The act covered employment practices of all businesses with more than twenty-five employees, as well as nearly all employment agencies and labor unions. A 1972 amendment broadened the coverage to employers with as few as fifteen employees.

The act also prohibited the application of different voting registration standards to White and Black voting applicants. It prohibited as well discrimination in public accommodations, that is, hotels, motels, restaurants, gasoline stations, and amusement parks. Publicly owned facilities, such as parks, stadiums, and swimming pools, were also prohibited from discriminating. Another important provision forbade discrimination in all federally supported programs and institutions, such as hospitals, colleges, and road construction projects.

The Civil Rights Act of 1964 covered discrimination based on race, color, creed, national origin, and sex. Although the inclusion of gender in employment criteria had been forbidden in the federal civil service since 1949, most laws and most groups pushing for change showed little concern about sex discrimination. There was little precedent for attention to sex discrimination even at the state level. Only Hawaii and Wisconsin had enacted laws against sex discrimination before 1964. As first proposed, the Civil Rights Act did not include mention of gender. One day before the final vote, opponents of the measure offered an amendment on gender bias in an effort to defeat the entire act. The act did pass with prohibition against sex bias included—an event that can only be regarded as a milestone for women seeking equal employment rights with men (Commission on Civil Rights 1975; E. Roth 1993).

The Civil Rights Act of 1964 was not perfect. Since 1964, several acts and amendments to the original act have been added to cover the many areas of discrimination it left untouched, such as criminal justice and housing. Even in those areas singled out for enforcement in the Civil Rights Act of 1964, discrimination still occurs. Federal agencies charged with its enforcement complain that they are underfunded or are denied wholehearted support by the White House. Also, regardless of how much the EEOC may want to act in a case, the individual who alleges discrimination has to pursue the complaint over a long time, marked by long periods of inaction.

Although civil rights laws have often established rights for other minorities, the Supreme Court made them explicit in two 1987 decisions involving groups other than African Americans. In the first of the two cases, an Iraqi American professor asserted that he had been denied tenure because of his Arab origins; in the second, a Jewish congregation brought suit for damages in response to the defacing of its synagogue with derogatory symbols. The Supreme Court ruled unanimously that, in effect, any member of an ethnic minority may sue under federal prohibitions against discrimination. These decisions paved the way for virtually all racial and ethnic groups to invoke the Civil Rights Act of 1964 (S. Taylor 1987a).

A particularly insulting form of discrimination seemed finally to be on its way out in the late 1980s. Many social clubs had limitations forbidding membership to minorities, Jews, and women. For years, exclusive clubs argued that they were merely selecting friends, but in fact, a principal function of these clubs has been providing a forum to transact business. Denial of membership meant more than the inability to attend a luncheon; it also seemed to exclude one from part of the marketplace, as Lawrence Otis Graham observed at the beginning of this chapter. The Supreme Court ruled unanimously in the 1988 case *New York State Clubs Association* v. *City of New York* that states and cities may ban sex discrimination by large private clubs where business lunches and similar activities take place. Although the ruling does not apply to all clubs and leaves the issue of racial and ethnic barriers unresolved, it did serve to chip away at the arbitrary exclusiveness of private groups (S. Taylor 1988).

Memberships and restrictive organizations remain perfectly legal. The rise to national attention in 1996 of the amateur champion and professional golfer Tiger Woods, of mixed Native American, African, and Asian ancestry, brought to public view that there were at least twenty-three golf courses he would be prohibited from playing by virtue of race (J. McCormick and S. Begley 1996; H. Yu 1996).

The inability of the Civil Rights Act, similar legislation, and court decisions to end discrimination is not due entirely to poor financial and political support, although they played a role. The number of federal employees assigned to investigate and prosecute bias cases declined in the 1990s. By 1996, the EEOC was looking at 121,230 unresolved complaints. Thus, even if the EEOC had been given top priority, discrimination would remain. The civil rights legislation attacked the most obvious forms of discrimination. Many discriminatory practices, such as those described as institutional discrimination, are seldom obvious (D. Price 1996).

Environmental Justice

Discrimination takes many forms and is not necessarily apparent even when its impact can be far-reaching. Take the example of Kennedy Heights, a well-kept working-class neighborhood nestled in the southeastern part of Houston. This community faces a real threat, and it is not from crime or drugs. The threat they fear is under their feet, in the form of three oil pits abandoned by Gulf Oil back in 1927. The residents, most of whom are African American, argue that they have suffered high rates of cancer, lupus, and other illnesses because the chemicals from the oil fields poison their water supply. The residents first sued Chevron USA back in 1985, and the case is still making its way through the courtrooms of no less than six states and the federal judiciary.

Lawyers and other representatives for the residents say that the oil company is guilty of *environmental racism* because it knowingly allowed a predominantly Black housing development to be built on the contaminated land. They are able to support this charge based on documents, including a 1954 memorandum from an appraiser who suggested that the oil pits be drained of any toxic substances and the land filled for "low-cost houses for White occupancy." When the land did not sell right away, an oil company official in a 1967 memorandum suggested a tax-free land exchange with a developer who intended to use the land for "Negro residents and commercial development." For this latter intended use by African Americans, there was no mention of environmental cleanup of the land. The oil

The location of health hazards near minority and low-income neighborhoods is regarded as a concern of environmental justice. Pictured is an old refinery adjacent to homes in Richmond, California.

company counters that it just assumed the developer would do the necessary cleanup of the pits (A. Manning 1997; S. Verhovek 1997).

The conflict perspective sees the case of the Houston suburb as one where pollution harms minority groups disproportionately. **Environmental justice** refers to the efforts to ensure that hazardous substances are controlled so that all communities receive protection regardless of race or socioeconomic circumstance. Following Environmental Protection Agency and other organization reports documenting discrimination in the locating of hazardous waste sites, an Executive Order was issued in 1994 that requires all federal agencies to ensure that low-income and minority communities have access to better information about their environment and have an opportunity to participate in shaping government policies that affect their community's health. Initial efforts to implement the policy have met widespread opposition, including criticism from some proponents of economic development who argue that to conform to guidelines unnecessarily delays or blocks altogether locating new industrial sites. Effort by the EPA to further clarify environmental justice guidelines in 1998 created more problems when the agency proceeded without sufficient consultation with states, cities, and industry (J. Cushman 1998).

Sociologist Robert Bullard (1990) has shown that low-income communities and areas with significant minority populations are more likely to be adjacent to waste sites than are affluent White communities. Similarly, undergraduate student researchers at Occidental College in California found in 1995 that the poor, African Americans, Hispanics, Asian Americans, and Native Americans were especially likely to be living near Los Angeles County's 82 potential environmental hazards (Moffat 1995). Issues of environmental justice are not restricted to metropolitan areas. Another continuing problem is abuse of Native American reservation land. Many American Indian leaders are concerned that tribal lands are too often regarded as "dumping grounds" for toxic waste that go to the highest bidder. We will return to this aspect of environmental justice in Chapter 6.

As with other aspects of discrimination, experts disagree. There is controversy within the scientific community over the potential hazards of some of the problems, and there is even some opposition within the subordinate communities being affected. This complexity of the issues in terms of social class and race is apparent, as some observers question the wisdom of an Executive Order that slows economic development coming to areas in dire need of employment opportunities. On the other hand, some counter that such businesses typically employ few less-skilled workers and only make the environment less livable for those left behind. Despite such varying viewpoints, environmental justice offers an excellent example of resistance and change in the 1990s that could not have been foreseen by the civil rights workers of the 1950s.

Affirmative Action

Affirmative action is the positive effort to recruit subordinate-group members including women for jobs, promotions, and educational opportunities. The phrase *affirmative action* first appeared in an Executive Order issued by President Kennedy in 1961. The order called for contractors to "take affirmative action to ensure that applicants are employed, and that employees are treated during employment, without regard to their race, creed, color, or national origin." However, at this early time no enforcement procedures were specified. Six years later, the order was amended to prohibit discrimination on the basis of sex, but affirmative action was still defined vaguely.

Today *affirmative action* has become a catch-all term for racial-preference programs and goals. It has also become a lightning rod for opposition to any programs that suggest special consideration of women or racial minorities.

AFFIRMATIVE ACTION EXPLAINED

Affirmative action has been viewed as an important tool for reducing institutional discrimination. Whereas previous efforts had been aimed at eliminating individual acts of discrimination, federal measures under the heading of affirmative action have been aimed at procedures that deny equal opportunities even if they are not intended to be overtly discriminatory. This policy has been implemented to deal with both the current discrimination and the past discrimination outlined earlier in this chapter.

The Commission on Civil Rights (1981:9–10) gave some examples of areas where affirmative action had been aimed at institutional discrimination:

- Height and weight requirements that are unnecessarily geared to the physical proportions of White males without regard to the actual requirements needed to perform the job and therefore exclude females and some minorities.
- Seniority rules, when applied to jobs historically held only by White males, that make more recently hired minorities and females more subject to layoff—the "last hired, first fired" employee—and less eligible for advancement.
- Nepotism-based membership policies of some unions that exclude those who are not relatives of members, who, because of past employment practices, are usually White.
- Restrictive employment-leave policies, coupled with prohibitions on part-time work or denials of fringe benefits to part-time workers, which make it difficult for the heads of single-parent families, most of whom are women, to get and keep jobs and also meet the needs of their families.
- Rules requiring that only English be spoken at the workplace, even when not a business necessity, which result in discriminatory employment practices toward individuals whose primary language is not English.
- Standardized academic tests or criteria, geared to the cultural and educational norms of middle-class or White males, when these are not relevant predictors of successful job performance.
- Preferences shown by law and medical schools in the admission of children of wealthy and influential alumni, nearly all of whom are White.

- Credit policies of banks and lending institutions that prevent the granting of mortgages and loans in minority neighborhoods or prevent the granting of credit to married women and others who have previously been denied the opportunity to build good credit histories in their own names.

Employers have also been cautioned against asking leading questions in interviews, such as "Did you know you would be the first Black to supervise all Whites in that factory?" or "Does your husband mind your working on weekends?" Furthermore, the lack of minority-group (Blacks, Asians, Native Americans, and Hispanics) or female employees may in itself represent evidence for a case of unlawful exclusion (Commission on Civil Rights 1981).

THE DEBATE

How far can an employer go in encouraging women and minorities to apply for a job before it becomes unlawful discrimination against White males? Since the late 1970s, a number of bitterly debated cases on this difficult aspect of affirmative action have reached the U.S. Supreme Court. The most significant cases are summarized in Table 3.2. Furthermore, as we will see, the debate has moved into party politics.

In the 1978 *Bakke* case (*Regents of the University of California* v. *Bakke*), by a narrow 5–4 vote, the Court ordered the medical school of the University of California at Davis to admit Allan Bakke, a qualified White engineer who had originally been denied admission solely on the basis of his race. The justices ruled that the school had violated Bakke's constitutional rights by establishing a fixed quota system for minority students. The Court added, however, that it was constitutional for universities to adopt flexible admissions programs that use race as one factor in making decisions.

Colleges and universities responded with new policies designed to meet the *Bakke* ruling while broadening opportunities for traditionally underrepresented minority students. However, in 1996, the Supreme Court allowed a lower court decision to stand that affirmative action programs for African American and Mexican American students at the University of Texas law school were unconstitutional. The ruling effectively prohibited schools in the lower court's jurisdiction of Louisiana, Mississippi, and Texas from taking race into account in admissions. Given this action, further challenges to affirmative action can be expected in higher education (Lederman and Burd 1996).

Even if the public in the United States acknowledges the disparity in earnings between White males and others, growing numbers of people doubt that everything done in the name of affirmative action is desirable. In 1991, national surveys showed that 24 percent of respondents agreed that "affirmative action programs designed to help minorities get better jobs and education go too far these days." Further analysis of the survey data reveals sharp racial division. In 1995, 46 percent of Whites and only 8 percent of African Americans indicated that affirmative action had gone too far (D. Lauter 1995).

Beginning in the 1980s, the Supreme Court, increasingly influenced by conservative justices, has issued many critical rulings concerning affirmative action programs.

Table 3.2 Key Decisions on Affirmative Action

In a series of split and often very close decisions, the Supreme Court has expressed a variety of reservations in specific situations.

Year	Favorable/ Unfavorable to Policy	Case	Vote	Ruling
1971	+	*Griggs* v. *Duke Power Co.*	9–0	Private employers must provide a remedy where minorities were denied opportunities even if unintentional
1978	–	*Regents of the University of California* v. *Bakke*	5–4	Prohibited specific number of places for minorities in college admissions
1979	+	*United Steelworkers of America* v. *Weber*	5–2	OK for union to favor minorities in special training programs
1984	–	*Firefighters Local Union No. 1784 (Memphis, TN)* v. *Stotts*	6–1	Seniority means recently hired minorities may be laid off first in staff reductions
1986	+	*International Association of Firefighters* v. *City of Cleveland*	6–3	May promote minorities over more senior Whites
1986	+	*New York City* v. *Sheet Metal*	5–4	Approved specific quota of minority workers for union
1987	+	*United States* v. *Paradise*	5–4	Endorsed quotas for promotions of state troopers
1987	+	*Johnson* v. *Transportation Agency, Santa Clara, CA*	6–3	Approved preference in hiring for minorities and women over better-qualified men and Whites
1989	–	*Richmond* v. *Croson Company*	6–3	Ruled a 30 percent set-aside program for minority contractors unconstitutional
1989	–	*Martin* v. *Wilks*	5–4	Ruled Whites may bring reverse discrimination claims against court-approved affirmative action plans
1990	+	*Metro Broadcasting* v. *FCC*	5–4	Supported federal programs aimed at increasing minority ownership of broadcast licenses
1995	–	*Adarand Constructors Inc.* v. *Peña*	5–4	Benefits based on race are constitutional only if narrowly defined to accomplish a compelling interest
1996	–	*Texas* v. *Hopwood*	*	Let stand a lower court decision covering Louisiana, Mississippi, and Texas, that race could not be used in college admissions

* 5th U.S. Circuit Court of Appeals decision.

In a key case in 1989 the Court invalidated, by a 6–3 vote, a Richmond, Virginia, law that had guaranteed 30 percent of public works funds to construction companies owned by minorities. In ruling that the Richmond statute violated the constitutional right of White contractors to equal protection under the law, the Court held that affirmative action programs are constitutional only when they serve the "compelling state interest" of redressing "identified discrimination" by the government or private parties. More recently, in 1994, a divided Supreme Court, by a 5–4 vote in *Adarand* v. *Peña,* held that federal programs that award benefits on the basis of race are constitutional only if they are "narrowly tailored" to accomplish a "compelling governmental interest." The Court's ruling was expected to encourage further legal challenges to federal affirmative action programs (Commission on Civil Rights 1995; L. Greenhouse 1989).

Has affirmative action actually helped to alleviate employment inequality on the basis of race and gender? This is a difficult question to answer given the complexity of the labor market and the fact that there are other antidiscrimination measures, but it does appear that affirmative action has had significant impact in the sectors where it has been applied. Sociologist Barbara Reskin (1998) studied available studies looking at workforce composition in terms of race and gender in light of affirmative action policies. She found that gains in minority employment can be attributed to affirmative action policies. This includes both firms mandated to follow affirmative action guidelines and those that took them on voluntarily. There is also evidence that some earnings gains can be attributed to affirmative action. Economists M. V. Lee Badgett and Heidi Hartmann (1995), reviewing twenty-six other research studies, came to similar conclusions: affirmative action and other federal compliance programs have modest impact, but it is difficult to assess, given larger economic changes such as recessions or the massive increase in women in the paid labor force.

Sometimes the impact of affirmative action is clear, such as during the 1970s and 1980s—a period during which courts ordered about 40 percent of the nation's police departments to engage in affirmative action because they had systematically discriminated against minorities and women. Another 42 percent of police departments adopted voluntary plans, leaving over 80 percent of the nation's law enforcement departments working ambitiously to improve representation. The result is dramatic in that minority representation among police officers increased from 7 percent to 22.5 percent, and women's presence rose from 2 percent to 9 percent (Martin 1991).

REVERSE DISCRIMINATION

While researchers debated the merit of affirmative action, the general public—particularly Whites but also some affluent African Americans and Hispanics—questioned the wisdom of the program. Particularly vocal were the charges of **reverse discrimination:** that government actions cause better-qualified White males to be bypassed in favor of women and minority men. Reverse discrimination is an emotional term because it conjures up the notion that somehow women and minorities will subject White males in the United States to the same treatment received by

The national debate over affirmative action provoked vocal demonstrations, including this rally at the state capitol in Olympia, Washington.

minorities during the last three centuries. Increasingly, critics of affirmative action called for color-blind policies, which would end affirmative action and, they argue, allow all people to be judged fairly. Of major significance, often overlooked in public debates, is that a color-blind policy implies a very limited role for the state in addressing social inequality between racial and ethnic groups (A. Kahng 1978; D. Skrentny 1996; H. Winant 1994).

Is it possible to have color-blind policies in the United States as we move into the twenty-first century? Supporters of affirmative action contend that as long as businesses rely on informal social networks, personal recommendations, and family ties, White men will have a distinct advantage built upon generations of being in positions of power. Furthermore, an end to affirmative action should also mean an end to the many programs that give advantages to certain businesses, homeowners, veterans, farmers, and others. The vast majority of these preference-holders are White (M. Kilson 1995; R. Mack 1996).

Consequently, by the 1990s, affirmative action had emerged as an increasingly important issue in state and national political campaigns. Generally, discussion focused on the use of quotas in hiring practices. Supporters of affirmative action argue that hiring goals establish "floors" for minority inclusion but do not exclude

Gary Markstein: ©Milwaukee Journal Sentinel/Copley News Service

truly qualified candidates from any group. Opponents insist that these "targets" are, in fact, quotas that lead to reverse discrimination. However, according to the U.S. Department of Labor, affirmative action has caused very few claims of reverse discrimination by White people. Fewer than 100 of the more than 3,000 discrimination opinions in federal courts from 1990 to 1994 even raised the issue of reverse discrimination, and reverse discrimination was actually established in only six cases (Joint Center for Political and Economic Studies 1996).

The state of California, in particular, was a battleground over this controversial issue. The California Civil Rights Initiative was placed on the ballot in 1996 as a referendum to amend the state constitution and prohibit any programs that give preference to women and minorities for college admission, employment, promotion, or government contracts. Overall, 54 percent of the voters backed the state proposition, with 61 percent of men in favor compared to only 48 percent of women. Whites, who represented 74 percent of the voters, voted in favor of the measure overwhelmingly, with 63 percent backing Proposition 209. This compares to 26 percent of African Americans, 24 percent of Hispanics, and 39 percent of Asian Americans favoring the end of affirmative action in state-operated institutions. Obviously, those voters—Whites and men—who perceived themselves as least likely to benefit from affirmative action overwhelmingly favored Proposition 209.

Legal challenges continue concerning Proposition 209, which is being implemented unevenly throughout the state. Much of the attention has focused on the impact that reducing racial preference programs will have in law and medical schools, where competition for admission is very high. Initial evidence is that there has been a significant decline at elite institutions, particularly at UCLA and the University of California at Berkeley, but that less impact is being experienced at most institutions. These charges come just as a study in the prestigious *Journal of the American Medical Association* showed that while giving preference to ethnicity yields "powerful effects on the diversity of the student population," there is "no evidence of diluting the quality of the graduates" (Davidson and Lewis 1997:1153).

Ironically, just as supporters of Proposition 209 were cheering its passage, national attention was riveted on a scandal involving alleged discrimination at the highest levels of Texaco—the nation's fourteenth largest corporation. Audio tapes were released that showed senior company executives plotting to destroy documents demanded in a discrimination suit and using racial epithets in discussing Black employees. Texaco, facing a threatened nationwide boycott, agreed to pay $176 million in compensation for outstanding grievances and complaints concerning racial discrimination. The company agreed to give about 11,000 African American employees an 11 percent pay hike, spend millions more on programs designed to wipe out discrimination, and let outsiders come inside to monitor progress (Roberts and White 1998).

The Glass Ceiling

We have been talking primarily about racial and ethnic groups as if they have uniformly failed to keep pace with Whites. While that is accurate, there are tens of thousands of people of color who have matched and even exceeded Whites in terms of income. For example, in 1991 there were more than 133,000 Black households and over 134,000 Hispanic households that earned over $100,000. What can we say about affluent members of subordinate groups in the United States?

Prejudice does not necessarily end with wealth. Black newspaper columnist De Wayne Wickham (1993) wrote of the subtle racism he had experienced. He had witnessed a White clerk in a supermarket ask a White customer if she knew the price of an item the computer would not scan; when the problem occurred while the clerk was ringing up Wickham's groceries, she called for a price check. Affluent subordinate-group members routinely report being blocked as they move toward the first-class section aboard airplanes or seek service in upscale stores. Another journalist, Ellis Cose (1993), has termed these insults the soul-destroying slights to affluent minorities that lead to the "rage of a privileged class."

Discrimination persists for even the educated and qualified from the best family backgrounds. As subordinate-group members are able to compete successfully, they sometimes encounter attitudinal or organizational bias that prevents them from reaching their full potential. They have confronted what has come to be called the **glass ceiling.** This refers to the barrier that blocks the promotion of a qualified worker because of gender or minority membership (see Figure 3.3 on p. 98). Often people entering nontraditional areas of employment become *marginalized* and made to feel uncomfortable, much like the situation of immigrants who feel a part of two cultures, as we discussed in Chapter 1.

The reasons for glass ceilings are as many as the occurrences. It may be that one Black or one woman vice-president is regarded as enough, so the second potential candidate faces a block to movement up through management. Decision makers may be concerned that their clientele will not trust them if they have too many people of color or may worry that a talented woman could become overwhelmed with her duties as a mother and wife and thus perform poorly in the workplace.

Concern about women and minorities climbing a broken ladder led to the formation in 1991 of the Glass Ceiling Commission, with the U.S. Secretary of Labor chairing the twenty-one-member group. Initially, it regarded some of the glass ceiling barriers as:

- Lack of management commitment to establishing systems, policies, and practices for achieving workplace diversity and upward mobility
- Pay inequities for work of equal or comparable value

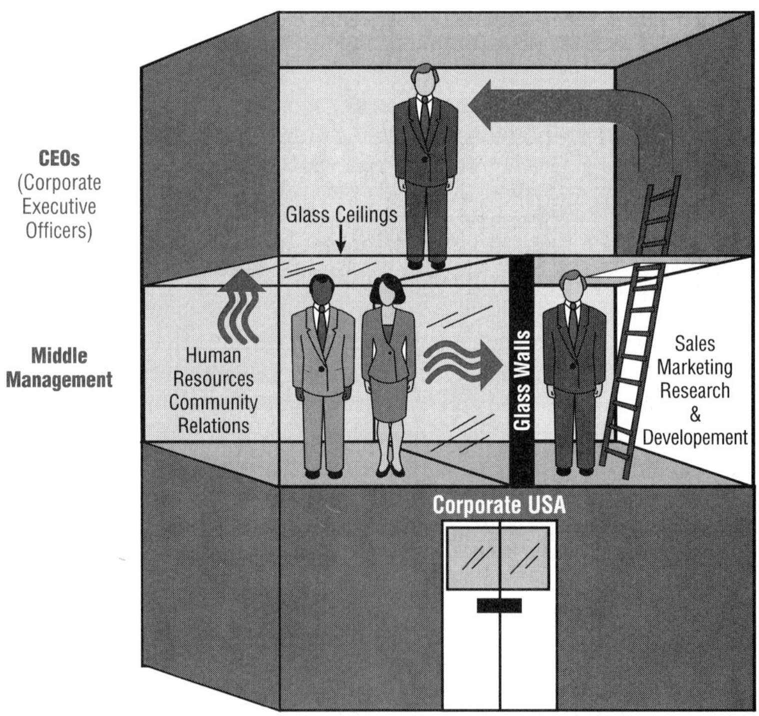

Figure 3.3 Glass Ceilings and Glass Walls
Women and minority men are moving up in corporations but encounter glass ceilings that block entry to top positions. In addition, they face glass walls that block lateral moves to areas from which executives are promoted.

- Sex-, race-, and ethnic-based stereotyping and harassment
- Unfair recruitment practices
- Lack of family-friendly workplace policies
- "Parent-track" policies
- Limited opportunities for advancement to decision-making positions

The commission report documented that the underrepresentation of women in managerial positions is due in large part to the presence of glass ceilings. As the commission noted, 97 percent of the senior managers of Fortune 1000 industrial and Fortune 500 service companies are White, and about 96 percent are male. A follow-up study in 1996 found little change, with only 2 percent or 50 of the top 2,500 executives women in the Fortune 500 companies (Department of Labor 1993, 1995; S. Silverstein 1996).

While glass ceilings have been widely described and condemned in business during the 1990s, this does not necessarily mean that there has been a dramatic move to remove them. A 1998 survey of Chicago's top 100 companies found only modest representation by women (7.5 percent) and minorities (5.8) among boards of directors. Yet 53 percent of the Chicago-area CEOs declared that they were satisfied with the makeup of their board of directors (Chandler 1998).

Glass ceilings are not the only barrier. Catalyst, a nonprofit research organization, conducted interviews in 1992 with senior and middle managers from larger corporations. The study found that, even before glass ceilings are encountered, women

Court decisions, steps by government, and public opinion against affirmative action accompanied by charges of "reverse discrimination" have made it unclear what future actions, if any, may be taken to end racism.

By Peters for the Dayton Daily News, Ohio

and racial and ethnic minorities face **glass walls** that keep them from moving laterally. Specifically, the study found that women tend to be placed in staff or support positions in areas such as public relations and human resources and are often directed away from jobs in core areas such as marketing, production, and sales. Women are assigned, and therefore trapped, in jobs that reflect their stereotypical helping nature and encounter glass walls that cut off access to jobs that might lead to broader experience and advancement (J. Lopez 1992).

How do members of subordinate groups respond to glass walls and glass ceilings? Some endure them, but others take their potential and begin their own businesses. Susan Crowe Chamberlain, past president of Women in Management, summarized it succinctly by saying that for many women and minority men, the real way to get to the top is to get out. Instead of fighting the ceiling, they form their own companies (R. Richman 1992: sec. 6, 11).

Focusing on the employed and even the relatively affluent should not lead us to ignore the underclass people employed in the informal economy or Native Americans without economic opportunities on isolated reservations. Surveying the past ten years, Urban League President John Jacob said in 1994 that Blacks can do only so much themselves; self-development cannot succeed without an "opportunity environment." He called on President Clinton to endorse a "Marshall Plan for America" that would focus on job creation and job training (*USA Today* 1994). Yet even the affluent subordinate-group person is reminded of her or his second-class status through subtle racism or a glass ceiling.

CONCLUSION

Discrimination takes its toll, whether a person who is discriminated against is part of the informal economy or not. Even members of minority groups who are not today being overtly discriminated against continue to fall victim to past discrimination. We have also identified the costs of discrimination to members of the privileged group. The attitudes of Whites and even members of minority groups themselves are influenced by the images they have of racial and ethnic groups. These images come from what has been termed statistical discrimination, which causes people to act based on stereotypes they hold and the actions of a few subordinate-group members.

From the conflict perspective, it is not surprising to find the widespread presence of the informal economy proposed by the dual labor-market model and even an underclass. Derrick Bell (1994), an African American law professor, has made the sobering assertion that "racism is permanent." He contends that the attitudes of dominant Whites prevail, and society is willing to advance programs on behalf of subordinate groups only when they coincide with needs as perceived by those Whites. Bell observes that the criticism of the affirmative action program in the 1990s exceeded any concern over corporate downsizing, which led to a loss of 1.6 million manufacturing jobs from 1989 to 1993 alone.

Women are a particularly vulnerable group, for whether the comparisons are within or across racial and ethnic groupings, they face significant social disparities. This inequality will be a recurring theme throughout this book, but we can observe that it is present even in developing fields such as computer science. In 1990, women accounted for 35 percent of computer systems analysts and programmers, but data for 1997 shows the proportion to be down to 29 percent. Is computer science openly discriminating against women? There is little evidence of blatant discrimination, but increasing numbers of women drop out of the field claiming they are not taken seriously, have few role models, and face a family-unfriendly environment. So, is the industry taking steps to address this need? Actually, the major initiative has been for the computer industry to lobby the federal government to increase the number of legal immigrants with the desired computer skills who are allowed to enter the country (Piller 1998).

The surveys presented in Chapter 3 show gradual acceptance of the earliest efforts to eliminate discrimination but that support is failing, especially as it relates to affirmative action. Indeed, concerns about doing something about alleged reverse discrimination are as likely to be voiced as racial or gender discrimination or penetrating glass ceilings and concrete walls.

Institutional discrimination remains a formidable challenge in the United States. Attempts to reduce discrimination by attacking institutional discrimination have met with staunch resistance. Partly as a result of this outcry from some of the public, especially White Americans, the federal government gradually deemphasized its efforts in affirmative action during the 1980s and 1990s. Yet resistance continues. States and the federal government have not been as quick to jump on the anti-affirmative action bandwagon as many had predicted in the wake of the passage of Proposition 209. Indeed, even in California the resistance has been clear (Bobo 1998).

As we turn to examine the various groups that make up the American people, through generations of immigration and religious diversity, look for the types of programs designed to reduce prejudice and discrimination that were discussed here. Most of the material in this chapter has been about racial groups, especially Black and White Americans. It would be easy to see intergroup hostility as a racial phenomenon, but that would be incorrect. Throughout the history of the United States, relations among some White groups have been characterized by resentment and violence. The next two chapters examine the nature and relations of White ethnic groups.

KEY TERMS

absolute deprivation 75
affirmative action 90
discrimination 75
double jeopardy 84
dual labor market 79
environmental justice 90
glass ceiling 97
glass wall 100
informal economy 78
institutional discrimination 77
irregular or underground economy 78
relative deprivation 75
reverse discrimination 94
states' rights 87
total discrimination 76
underclass 80

REVIEW QUESTIONS

1. Why might people still feel disadvantaged even though their incomes are rising and their housing circumstances have improved?
2. Why does institutional discrimination sometimes seem less objectionable than individual discrimination?
3. In what way does an industrial society operate on several economic levels?
4. Why are questions raised about affirmative action while inequality persists?
5. Distinguish between glass ceilings and wall. How do they differ from more obvious forms of discrimination in employment?

CRITICAL THINKING

1. Discrimination can take many forms. Consider the college you attend. Select a case of discrimination that you think just about everyone would agree is wrong. Then describe another incident in which the alleged discrimination was of a more subtle form. Who is likely to condemn and who is likely to overlook such situations?
2. Resistance is a continuing theme of intergroup race relations. Discrimination implies the oppression of a group, but how may discrimination also serve to unify the oppressed group to resist such unequal treatment? How can acceptance, or integration for example, weaken the sense of solidarity within a group?
3. Voluntary associations like the NAACP and government units such as the courts have been important vehicles for bringing about a measure of social justice. In what ways can the private sector, corporations and businesses, also work to bring about an end to discrimination?

INTERNET EXERCISE

One way that people have tried to reduce institutional discrimination is through the use of affirmative action programs, yet changing attitudes, legal decisions, and current events are frequently reshaping the definition and quality of affirmative action. Log on to (http://headlines.yahoo.com/Full_Coverage/US/Affirmative_Action) in order to check the latest information. What recent legal decisions have been made regarding affirmative action? What are individual states and corporations doing to ensure that equal opportunities exist? Are there examples or stories on the site of how affirmative action has helped someone? Are there examples or stories of reverse discrimination? After reading the most recent news, do you think that affirmative action programs will survive? Why or why not? What is best about the current state/condition of affirmative action? In your opinion, what changes need to be made to the way we define and implement affirmative action today?

FOR FURTHER INFORMATION

William G. Bowen and Derek Bok. *The Shape of the River: Long-Term Consequences of Considering Race in College and University Admissions.* Princeton, NJ: Princeton University Press, 1998.
A thorough statistical analysis of data (grades, SAT scores, and so forth) gathered on 93,000 students of all races at 34 elite colleges and universities. The authors conclude that eliminating affirmative action would not do much to help Whites who are rejected for admission.

Sharon M. Collins-Lowry. *Black Corporate Executives: The Making and Breaking of a Black Middle Class.* Philadelphia, PA: Temple University Press, 1997.
Based on extensive interviews with African American executives in Chicago concerning their success and barriers to further advancement.

Barbara F. Reskin. *The Realities of Affirmative Action in Employment.* Washington, DC: American Sociological Association, 1998.
Offers a concise (121 pages) but comprehensive look at affirmative action in the labor market.

John Yinger. *Closed Doors, Opportunities Lost. The Continuing Costs of Housing Discrimination.* New York: Russell Sage Foundation, 1995.
Economist Yinger provides a history of fair housing and fair lending enforcement and examines the underlying causes of discrimination present.

STATISTICAL SOURCES

Hundreds of federal government publications provide statistical data comparing racial and ethnic groups to each other and women to men. The *Current Population Report Series* P–20 and P–60 and the annual *Statistical Abstract of the United States* are among the best. Increasing numbers of data sets are first available, and sometimes only available, on the Bureau of the Census WEB site at http//www.census.gov.sources.

4

Immigration and the United States

HIGHLIGHTS

The diversity of the American people is unmistakable evidence of the variety of places from which immigrants have come. The different new arrivals did not necessarily welcome one another. Instead they brought their European rivalries to the Americas. The Chinese were the first to be singled out for restriction, with the passage of the 1882 Exclusion Act. The initial Chinese immigrants became, in effect, scapegoats for America's sagging economy in the last half of the nineteenth century. Growing fears that too many non-American types were immigrating motivated the creation of the national origins system and the quota acts of the 1920s. These acts gave preference to certain nationalities, until the passage of the Immigration and Naturalization Act in 1965 ended that practice. Concern about illegal immigration—legal, too—has continued through the 1990s, leading to the 1994 passage of the controversial Proposition 187 in California. Restrictionist sentiment has grown, and debates rage over whether immigrants, even legal ones, should receive services such as education, government-subsidized health care, and welfare. Controversy also continues to surround the policy of the United States toward refugees.

Eduardo Román García, age 29, works for $260 a week in a car body shop in southern California. His situation is both similar and different from that of many new arrivals in the United States. The similarities lie in his desire for a better life. He works to send as much money as possible back to his wife and two children in Veracruz, Mexico. He hopes he can remain in the United States because he knows there is little chance to find employment back home. Even if he found a job, Mexican factory wages start at $2.90 a day. He found his job and a place to live through a network of Mexican Americans. Indeed, his place of employment is owned by a man who entered the United States illegally twenty years ago but later became a citizen and now operates a business with ten employees. Román expected to work hard when he came. "Others told me it would be difficult in this country," he said, "but they said it was worth it [to come here] because you could live a little better" (E. Boyer 1996:B8; S. Dillon 1996).

Román's situation is different because his face was seen on national television in 1996. In April of that year, Román, along with eighteen others, was being transported illegally by truck into the United States when it was stopped by police. News crews covered the long chase and videotaped the beating of two unarmed suspects. If it had not been for the national attention, Román and the others would soon have been deported, but instead they were granted temporary work permits while they waited to testify at the trials of the police deputies. Meanwhile, the Mexican government expressed outrage at their citizens' treatment here, just as the United States many times has condemned treatment of Americans abroad (B. Shuster 1996).

This drama being played out in both an auto body shop and on a California freeway illustrates the themes in immigration today. Immigrants come to the United States trying to get ahead. In doing so, many come legally, applying for immigrant visas, while others enter illegally. In the United States we do not like lawbreakers, but often we seek the services and low-priced products made by people who come here illegally. How do we control this immigration without violating the principles that we uphold of relatively free movement within the nation? How do we decide who enters? And how do we treat those who come here illegally?

The diversity of ethnic and racial backgrounds of Americans today is the living legacy of immigration. Except for descendants of Native Americans or of Africans brought here enslaved, today's population is entirely the product of individuals who chose to leave familiar places to come to a new country.

The social forces that cause people to emigrate are complex. The most important have been economic: financial failure in the old country and expectations of higher incomes and standards of living in the new land. Other factors include dislike of new regimes in their native lands, racial or religious bigotry, and a desire to reunite families. All these factors push individuals from their homelands and pull them to other nations such as the United States. Immigration into the United States in particular has at times been facilitated by cheap ocean transportation and by other countries' removal of restrictions on emigration.

The reception given to immigrants in this country, however, has not always been friendly. Open bloodshed, restrictive laws, and the eventual return of close to one-third of the immigrants and their children to their home countries attest to the uneasy feeling toward strangers who wish to settle here. Nevertheless, vast numbers of immigrants have still come. Figure 4.1 indicates the high but fluctuating number of immigrants that have arrived during every decade from the 1820s through the 1990s. We can anticipate the largest number of legal immigrants during the 1990s but, of course, in the period from 1900 through 1910, the country was much smaller, so the numerical impact was even greater.

Opinion polls in the United States from 1946 through the present never show more than 13 percent of the public in favor of more immigration, and usually about 50 percent want less. Even a special 1995 survey of immigrants themselves found that only 15 percent wanted immigration increased, 44 percent wanted it left as is, and a sizable 30 percent advocated having immigration levels decreased. We want the door open until we get through, and then we want to close it (L. Saad 1995).

Early Immigration

European explorers of North America were soon followed by settlers, the first immigrants to the Western Hemisphere. The Spanish founded St. Augustine in Florida in 1565, and the English, Jamestown, Virginia, in 1607. Protestants from England emerged from the colonial period as the dominant force numerically, politically, and socially. The English accounted for 60 percent of the 3 million White Americans in 1790. Although exact statistics are lacking for the early years of the United States, the English

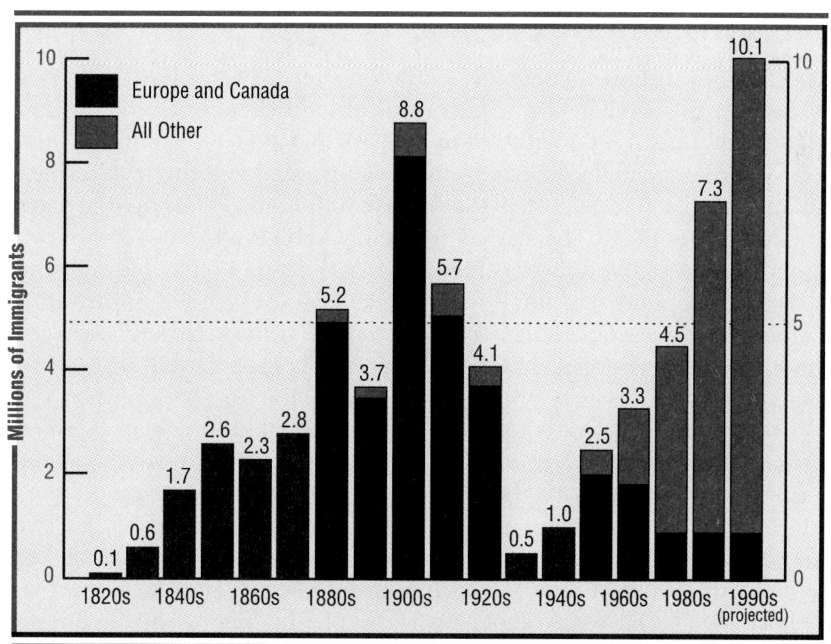

Figure 4.1 Immigration in the United States, 1820s through 1990s

Source: Immigration and Naturalization Service, 1997:26–29. Projection for the 1990s by the author based on Immigration and Naturalization data.

were soon outnumbered by other nationalities, as the numbers of Scotch-Irish and Germans, in particular, swelled. The English colonists, however, maintained their dominant position, as Chapter 5 will examine.

Throughout American history, immigration policy has been politically controversial. The policies of the English king, George III, were criticized in the U.S. Declaration of Independence for obstructing immigration to the colonies. Toward the end of the nineteenth century, the American republic itself was criticized for enacting immigration restrictions. In the beginning, however, the country encouraged immigration. At first, legislation fixed the residence requirement for naturalization at five years, although briefly, under the Alien Act of 1798, it was fourteen years, and "dangerous" people could be expelled. Despite this brief harshness, immigration was unregulated through most of the 1800s, and naturalization was easily available.

Besides holding the mistaken belief that concerns about immigration are something new, we also assume that immigrants to the United States rarely reconsider their change of country. Detailed analysis of available records beginning in the early 1900s suggests that about 35 percent of all immigrants to the United States eventually emigrated back to their home country. The proportion varies, with the figures for some countries being much higher, but the overall pattern is clear: about one in three immigrants to this nation eventually chooses to return home (Wyman 1990).

THE ANTI-CATHOLIC CRUSADE

The relative absence of federal legislation from 1790 to 1881 does not mean that all new arrivals were welcomed. **Xenophobia** (the fear or hatred of strangers or foreigners) led naturally to **nativism** (beliefs and policies favoring native-born citizens over immigrants). Roman Catholics in general and the Irish in particular were among the first Europeans to be ill treated. Anti-Catholic feeling originated in Europe and was brought by the early Protestant immigrants. The Catholics of colonial America, although few, were subject to limits on their civil and religious rights.

From independence until around 1820, little evidence appeared of the anti-Catholic sentiment of colonial days, but the cry against "popery" grew as Irish immigration increased. Prominent Americans encouraged hatred of these new arrivals. Samuel F. B. Morse, inventor of the telegraph and an accomplished painter, wrote a strongly worded anti-Catholic work in 1834 entitled *A Foreign Conspiracy Against the Liberties of the United States.* Morse felt that the Irish were "shamefully illiterate and without opinions of their own" (1835: 61). In the mind of the prejudiced American, the Irish were particularly unwelcome because they were Roman Catholics. Many Americans readily believed Morse's warning that the Pope planned to move the Vatican to the Mississippi River Valley (J. Duff 1971:34). Even poet and philosopher Ralph Waldo Emerson wrote of "the wild Irish . . . who sympathized, of course, with despotism" (J. Kennedy 1964:70).

This antagonism was not limited to harsh words. From 1834 to 1854, mob violence against Catholics across the country led to death, the burning of a Boston convent, the destruction of a Catholic church and the homes of Catholics, and the use of Marines and state militia to bring peace to American cities as far west as St. Louis.

A frequent pattern saw minorities striking out against each other rather than at the dominant class. Irish Americans opposed the Emancipation Proclamation and the freeing of the slaves because they feared Blacks would compete for the unskilled work open to them. This fear was confirmed when free Blacks were used to break a longshoremen's strike in New York. Hence, much of the Irish violence during the 1863 riot was directed against Blacks, not against the Whites who were most responsible for the conditions in which the immigrants found themselves (J. Duff 1971; S. Warner 1968).

In retrospect, the reception given to the Irish is not difficult to understand. Many immigrated following the 1845–1848 potato crop failure and famine in Ireland. They fled not so much to a better life as from almost certain death. The Irish Catholics brought with them a celibate clergy, who struck the New England aristocracy as strange and reawakened old religious hatreds. The Irish were worse than Blacks, according to the dominant Whites, because unlike the slaves and even the freed Blacks, who "knew their place," the Irish did not suffer their maltreatment in silence. Employers balanced minorities by judiciously mixing immigrant groups to prevent unified action by the laborers. For the most part, nativist efforts only led the foreign-born to emphasize their ties to Europe.

By the 1850s, nativism became an open political movement pledged to vote only for "native" Americans, to fight Roman Catholicism, and to demand a twenty-one-year naturalization period. Party members were instructed to divulge nothing about their program and to say that they knew nothing about it. As a result, they came to be called the Know-Nothings. Although the Know-Nothings soon vanished, the anti-alien mentality survived and occasionally became formally organized into such societies as the Ku Klux Klan in the 1860s and the anti-Catholic American Protective Association in the 1890s. Revivals of anti-Catholicism continued well into the twentieth century. The most dramatic outbreak of nativism in the nineteenth century, however, was aimed at the Chinese. If there had been any doubt by the mid–1800s that the United States could harmoniously accommodate all, debate on the Chinese Exclusion Act would negatively settle the question once and for all (D. Gerber 1993; R. Wernick 1996).

THE ANTI-CHINESE MOVEMENT

Before 1851, official records show that only forty-six Chinese had immigrated to the United States. Over the next thirty years, more than 200,000 came to this country, lured by the discovery of gold and the opening of job opportunities in the West. Overcrowding, drought, and warfare in China also encouraged them to take a chance in the United States. Another important factor was improved oceanic transportation: it was actually cheaper to travel from Hong Kong to San Francisco than from Chicago to San Francisco. The frontier communities of the West, particularly in California, looked on the Chinese as a valuable resource to fill manual jobs. As early as 1854, so many Chinese desired to emigrate that ships had difficulty handling the volume.

Chinese workers, such as these pictured in 1844, played a major role in building the railroads in the West.

During the 1860s, railroad work provided the greatest demand for Chinese labor, until the Union Pacific and Central Pacific railroads were joined at Promontory, Utah, in 1869. The Union Pacific relied primarily on Irish laborers, but 90 percent of the Central Pacific labor force was Chinese because Whites generally refused the back-breaking work over the western terrain. Despite the contribution of the Chinese, White workers physically prevented even their presence when the golden spike was driven to mark the joining of the two railroads.

With the dangerous railroad work largely completed, people began to rethink the wisdom of encouraging Chinese to immigrate to do the work no one else would do. Reflecting their xenophobia, White settlers found the Chinese immigrants and their customs and religion difficult to understand. Indeed, relatively few people actually tried to understand these immigrants from Asia. Easterners and legislators, although they had had no first-hand contact with Chinese Americans, were soon on the anti-Chinese bandwagon as they read sensationalized accounts of the lifestyle of the new arrivals.

Even before the Chinese immigrated, stereotypes of them and their customs were prevalent. American traders returning from China, European diplomats, and Protestant missionaries consistently emphasized the exotic and sinister aspects of life in China. The **sinophobes**, people with a fear of anything associated with China, appealed to the racist theory developed during the slavery controversy that non-Europeans were subhuman. Similarly, Americans were beginning to be more conscious of biological inheritance and disease, and so it was not hard to conjure up fears of alien genes and germs. The only real challenge the anti-Chinese movement had was to convince people that the negative consequences of unrestricted Chinese immigration outweighed any possible economic gain. Perhaps briefly, racial prejudice had earlier been subordinated to industrial dependence on Chinese labor for the work that Whites shunned, but acceptance of Chinese was short-lived. The fear of the "yellow peril" overwhelmed any desire to know more about Asian people and their customs (R. Takaki 1989).

Another nativist fear of Chinese immigrants was based on the threat they posed as laborers. Californians, whose labor force felt the effects of the Chinese immigration first, found support throughout the nation as organized labor feared that the Chinese would be used as strikebreakers. By 1870, Chinese workers had been used for that purpose as far east as Massachusetts. When Chinese workers did unionize, they were not recognized by major labor organizations. Samuel Gompers, founder of the American Federation of Labor (AFL), consistently opposed any effort to assist Chinese workers and refused to consider having a union of Chinese restaurant employees admitted into the AFL (H. Hill 1967). Gompers worked effectively to see future Chinese immigration ended and produced a pamphlet entitled "Chinese Exclusion: Meat vs. Rice, American Manhood Against Asiatic Coolieism—Which Shall Survive?" (Gompers and Gustadt 1908). Although employers were glad to pay the Chinese low wages, laborers came to direct their resentment against the Chinese rather than against their compatriots' willingness to exploit the Chinese. Only a generation earlier, the same concerns had been felt about the Irish, but with the Chinese, the hostility was to reach new heights because of another factor.

While many arguments were voiced, racial fears motivated the anti-Chinese movement. Race was the critical issue. The labor-market fears were largely unfounded, and most advocates of restrictions at the time knew that. There was no possibility that Chinese would immigrate in numbers that would match those of Europeans at the time, so it is difficult to find an explanation other than racism for their fears (H. Winant 1994).

From the sociological perspective of conflict theory, we can explain how the Chinese immigrants were welcomed only when their labor was necessary to fuel growth in the United States. When that labor was no longer necessary, the welcome mat for the immigrants was withdrawn. Further, as conflict theorists would point out, restrictions were not applied evenly; Americans focused on a specific nationality group—the Chinese—in order to reduce the overall number of foreign workers in the nation. Because decision making at that time rested in the hands of the descendants of European immigrants, the steps to be taken were most likely to be directed against those least powerful: immigrants from China who, unlike Europeans seeking entry, had few allies among legislators and other policy makers.

In 1882, Congress enacted the Chinese Exclusion Act, which outlawed Chinese immigration for ten years. It also explicitly denied naturalization rights to those Chinese in the United States; that is, they were not allowed to become citizens.

There was little debate in Congress, and discussion concentrated on how suspension of Chinese immigration could best be handled. No allowance was made for spouses and children to be reunited with their husbands and fathers in the United States. Only brief visits of Chinese government officials, teachers, tourists, and merchants were exempted.

The balance of the nineteenth century saw the remaining loopholes allowing Chinese immigration closed. Beginning in 1884, Chinese laborers were not allowed to enter the United States from any foreign place, a ban that lasted ten years. Two years later, the Statue of Liberty was dedicated, with the poem by Emma Lazarus inscribed on its base. To the Chinese, the poem welcoming the tired, the poor, the huddled masses must have seemed a hollow mockery.

In 1892, Congress extended the Exclusion Act for another ten years and added that Chinese laborers had to obtain certificates of residence within a year or face deportation. After the turn of the century, the Exclusion Act was extended again. Two decades later, the Chinese were not alone; the list of people restricted by immigration policy expanded many times.

Restrictionist Sentiment Increases

As Congress closed the door to Chinese immigration, the debate on restricting immigration turned in new directions. Prodded by growing anti-Japanese feelings, the United States entered into the so-called Gentlemen's Agreement, completed in 1908. Japan agreed to halt further immigration to the United States, and the United States agreed to end discrimination against those Japanese who had already arrived. The immigration ended, but anti-Japanese feelings continued. Americans were growing uneasy that the "new immigrants" would overwhelm the culture established by the "old immigrants." The earlier immigrants, if not Anglo-Saxon, were from similar groups such as the Scandinavians, the Swiss, and the French Huguenots. These were more experienced in democratic political practices and had a greater affinity with the dominant Anglo-Saxon culture. By the end of the nineteenth century, however, more and more immigrants were neither English speaking nor Protestant and came from dramatically different cultures.

For four years, the United States Immigration Commission, known popularly as the Dillingham Commission, exhaustively studied the effects of immigration. The findings, presented in 1911, were determined by the commission's assumption that there were types of immigrants. The two types were the old immigrants, mostly Anglo-Saxons, who were characterized as hard-working pioneers, and the new immigrants from southern Europe, who were branded as opportunists. Not surprising, pressure for a more restrictive immigration policy became insurmountable. A literacy test was one of the results of hostility against the new immigrants (L. Fermi 1971; O. Handlin 1957).

In 1917, Congress finally overrode President Wilson's veto and enacted an immigration bill that included the controversial literacy test. Critics of the bill, including Wilson, argued that illiteracy does not signify inherent incompetence but reflects lack of opportunity for instruction (*New York Times* 1917a). Such arguments were not heeded, however. The act seemed innocent at first glance—it merely required immigrants to read thirty words in any language—but it was the first attempt to restrict immigration from western Europe. The act also prohibited immigration from the South Sea islands and other parts of Asia not already excluded. Curiously, this law that closed the door on non-Anglo-Saxons permitted waiver of the test if the immigrants came because of their home government's discrimination against their race (*New York Times* 1917b).

THE NATIONAL ORIGINS SYSTEM

Beginning in 1921, a series of measures was enacted that marked a new era in American immigration policy. Whatever the legal language, the measures were drawn up to block the growing immigration from southern Europe, such as from Italy and Greece.

Anti-immigration sentiment, combined with the isolationism that followed World War I, caused Congress to restrict severely entry privileges not only to the Chinese and Japanese but to Europeans as well. The national origins system was begun in 1921 and remained the basis of immigration policy until 1965. This system used the country of birth to determine whether an individual could enter as a legal alien, and the number of previous immigrants and their descendants was used to set the quota of how many from a country could enter annually.

Italian Americans aboard a ship arrive at Ellis Island.

To understand the effect that the national origins had on immigration, it is necessary to clarify the quota system. The quotas were deliberately weighted in favor of immigration from northern Europe. Because of the ethnic composition of the country in 1920, the quotas placed severe restrictions on immigration from the rest of Europe and from other parts of the world. Immigration from the Western Hemisphere (that is, Canada, Mexico, Central and South America, and the Caribbean) continued unrestricted. The quota for each nation was set at 3 percent of the number of people descended from each nationality recorded in the 1920 census. Once the statistical manipulations were completed, almost 70 percent of the quota for the Eastern Hemisphere went to just three countries: Great Britain, Ireland, and Germany.

The absurdities of the system soon became obvious, but it was nevertheless continued. British immigration had fallen sharply and so most of its quota of 65,000 went unfilled. The openings, however, could not be transferred, even though countries such as Italy, with a quota of only 6,000, had 200,000 people who wished to enter (F. Belair 1970). However one rationalizes the purpose behind the act, the result was obvious: any English person, regardless of skill and whether related to anyone already here, could enter the country more easily than, say, a Greek doctor whose children were American citizens. The quota for Greece was 305, with the backlog of people wishing to come reaching 100,000.

By the end of the 1920s, annual immigration had dropped to one-fourth of its pre-World War I level. The worldwide economic depression of the 1930s decreased immigration still further. A brief upsurge in immigration just before World War II reflected the flight of Europeans from the oppression of expanding Nazi Germany. The war virtually ended transatlantic immigration. The era of the great European migration to the United States had been legislated out of existence.

It is important to recall the living legacy of the great immigration. Millions of people in the Untied States are descended from these immigrants, and many maintain close ties to the old traditions. In "Listen to Their Voices," Raffi Ishkanian, now a high school social studies teacher, describes what it is like to be not only a college student but also an Armenian American. His father's parents immigrated during the first years of the National Origins System from Armenia—a nation between Turkey and Iran that became part of the Soviet Union and since has become politically independent of Russia. While a college student he has had a summer internship with an Armenian community service organization.

THE 1965 IMMIGRATION AND NATURALIZATION ACT

The national origins system was abandoned with the passage of the 1965 Immigration and Naturalization Act, signed into law by President Lyndon B. Johnson at the foot of the Statue of Liberty. The primary goals of the act were reuniting families and protecting the American labor market. The act also initiated restrictions on immigration from Latin America. After the act, immigration increased by one-third, but the act's influence was primarily on the composition rather than the size of immigration. The sources of immigrants now included Italy, Greece, Portugal, Mexico, the Philippines, the West Indies, and South America. The effect is apparent when we compare the changing sources of immigration over the last hundred years, as in Figure 4.2. The most recent period shows that Asian and Latin American immigrants combined to account for 82 percent of the people who were permitted entry. This contrasts sharply with early immigration, which was dominated by arrivals from Europe.

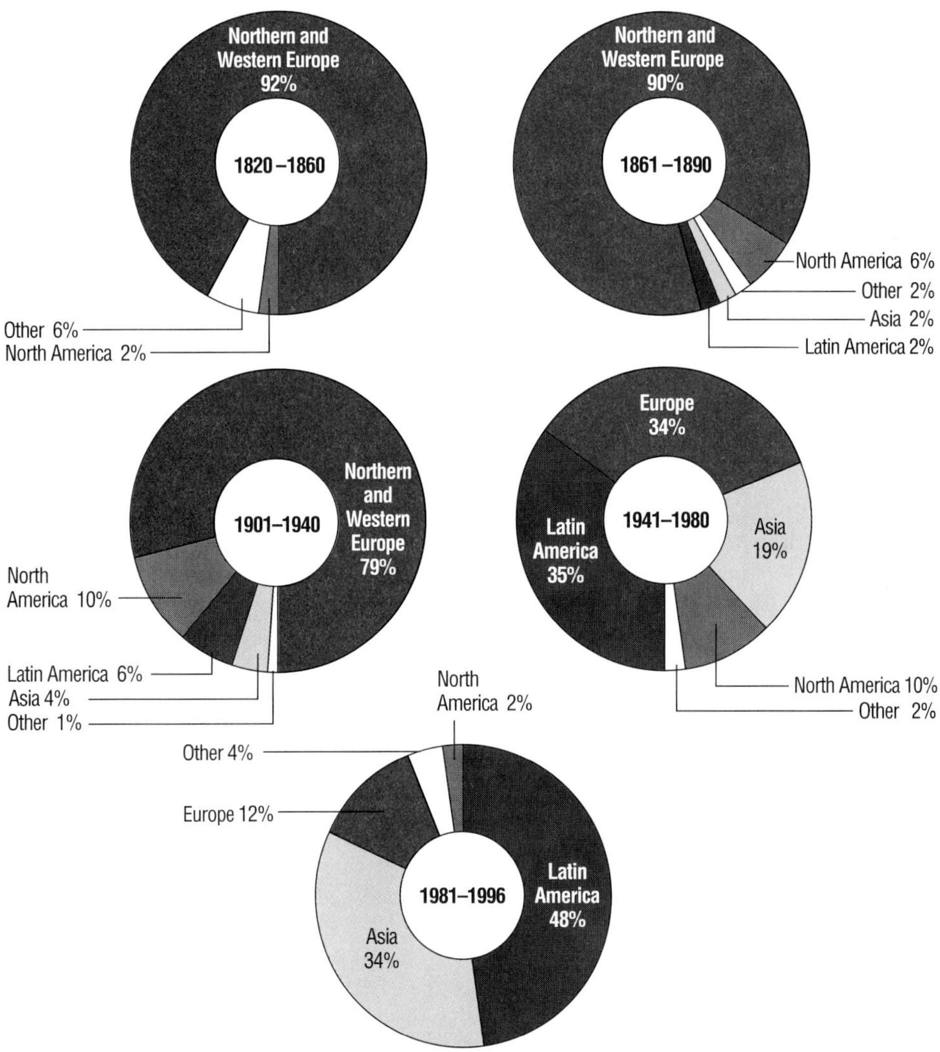

Figure 4.2 Legal Immigrants Admitted to the United States by Region of Last Residence, 1820–1996

Source: Immigration and Naturalization Service 1997:26–29.

LISTEN TO THEIR VOICES

Roots

Raffi Ishkanian

Ethnicity has had a definite impact on my life. My mother, although an "odar" (Armenian for non-Armenian), has adopted the culture entirely, with a great deal of enthusiasm. She is active in the church choir (which sings only in Armenian), is part of an Armenian Dance group, and has learned to cook most of the dishes. As a result, although I am genetically only half Armenian, I feel 100 percent Armenian. I attended the Armenian church and Armenian language school throughout my childhood. I live in the suburbs and did not have the benefit of having a lot of Armenians in my neighborhood. So like my father, I ended up with mostly non-Armenian friends. I always resented that I had to go to Armenian school on Fridays. My complaints found a deaf ear everywhere except amongst my Korean friends who had to go to Korean school and Korean church. I wanted to go to Catholic church. I hated that every time a substitute teacher would read off attendance and botch up my name, everyone was on the floor. I hated that whenever I got a trophy, my name was spelled wrong. I hated that whenever my name was in the paper for soccer, even when I got all-county honors, they spelled it wrong.

Yet, at the same time, I relished the tightness of my Armenian family. I loved how on holidays, and particularly Thanksgiving, we all got together. And as much as I hated that my church was different, I loved it. I loved the church picnics, the bazaars, the fact that almost all my parents' friends were there. I loved how it seemed like anywhere we went, if we found an Armenian, an instant friend was found. That ethnic bond was so strong. If we were in Canada, and ran into an Armenian, chances are we would find out that they were either a relative of a friend in church, or a good

The nature of immigration laws is exceedingly complex and is subjected to frequent, although often minor adjustments. Generally, in the latter 1990s approximately 700,000 people were legally admitted annually, for the following reasons:

Family unification	
Relatives of citizens	18%
Relatives of legal residents	32
Employment-based	23
Refugees/people seeking political asylum	24
Other	3

The liberalization of eligibility rules also brought a backlog of applications from relatives of American citizens who had earlier failed to qualify under the more restric-

friend of so-and-so's in our church, or even from the same village back in Armenia. All I needed was people around me, in my immediate area, to appreciate it with me, to let me know it was okay to like these things that were so culturally different.

Like my father, in college I find myself liking more and more about my ethnicity and disliking less and less. I think that this is more than mere coincidence. The more education a person receives, the easier it becomes to see the value of one's ethnic identity. Children are uneducated as to the values of individuality. Childhood is one nonstop battle to fit in. Whether a kid is too smart, too slow, too unathletic, or too different, the kid is teased. In turn, the kid winds up hating that difference and perhaps education, combined with time, allows him or her to view that difference—that which makes him or her an individual—as an asset, rather than a handicap. I have become very proud of who I am. There are very few Armenians on this campus, yet rather than view that fact as a negative, I thrive on it. I jump at every chance I can get to talk about being Armenian, Armenia, or the genocide. It seems that today whenever an ethnic group gets together, the majority jumps on it as an excuse to say the group does not want to assimilate. These groups are needed because ethnicity is a vital part of a person's identity. For Armenians in particular, this struggle for recognition and distinction is vital. The genocide shattered the Armenian community into fragmented populations worldwide. The remembrance of these events, as for the victims of the Nazi Holocaust, is critical to the survival of the Armenian people. As long as my name is Raffi Ara Ishkanian, whether I want to be part of the Armenian ethnic community or not, my name will associate me with it, be it good or bad. And I am proud.

Source: Excerpted and reprinted from "Roots Paper" by Raffi Ishkanian, included in *Becoming American, Becoming Ethnic: College Students Explore Their Roots* edited by Thomas Dublin, by permission of Temple University Press.

tive national origins scheme. Backlogs of applicants still existed throughout the world, but the equal treatment for all underlying the 1965 legislation gave them greater hope of eventually entering the United States.

Overall, half of the immigrants come to join their relatives, a quarter are admitted for their special skills, and another quarter enter because of special refugees status (Immigration and Naturalization Service 1997:16, 20).

Contemporary Concerns

While our current immigration policies are less restrictive than other nations' restrictions, they are the subject of great debate. In Table 4.1 we summarize the benefits and concerns regarding immigration to the United States. We will consider three

Table 4.1 Immigration Benefits and Concerns

Potential Benefits	Areas of Concern
Provide needed skills	Drain needed resources from home country
Contribute to taxes	Send remittances (or migradollars) home
May come with substantial capital to start business	Less skilled immigrants compete with those already disadvantaged
Diversify the population—intangible gain	Population growth
Serve to maintain ties with countries throughout the world	May complicate foreign policy through lobbying the government
	Illegal immigration

continuing criticisms of our immigration policy: the brain drain, population growth, and illegal immigration. All three, but particularly illegal immigration, have provoked heated debates and continuing efforts to resolve them with new policies. We will then consider the economic impact of immigration, followed by the nation's policy toward refugees, a group distinct from immigrants.

THE BRAIN DRAIN

How often have you identified your science or mathematics teacher or even your physician as someone who was not born in the United States? This nation has clearly benefited from attracting human resources from throughout the world, but this phenomenon has had its price for the nation of origin.

The term **brain drain** refers to the immigration to the United States of skilled workers, professionals, and technicians who are desperately needed by their home countries. During the mid-twentieth century many scientists and other professionals from industrial nations, principally Germany and Great Britain, came to the United States. More recently, however, the brain drain has pulled emigrants from developing nations, including India, Pakistan, Philippines, and several African nations. Earlier in the chapter we heard Raffi Ishkanian speak of his Armenian roots. Thousands of skilled, educated Armenians now seek to enter the United States, pulled by the economic opportunity here but also pushed by difficult times in a country where earnings rarely exceed $50 a month (V. Bennett 1998).

The brain drain controversy was evident long before the passage of the 1965 Immigration Act. The 1965 act seemed, though, to encourage such immigration by placing the professions in one of the categories of preference. Various corporations, including Motorola and Intel, now find that one-third of their high-tech jobs are held by people born abroad, although many received their advanced education in the United States. Furthermore, these immigrants have links to their old countries and are boosting U.S. exports to the fast-growing economic regions of Asia and Latin America (H. Bloch 1996).

Conflict theorists see the current brain drain as yet another symptom of the unequal distribution of world resources. In their view, it is ironic that the United States gives foreign aid to improve the technical resources of African and Asian countries while simultaneously maintaining an immigration policy that encourages professionals in such nations to migrate to our shores. These are the very countries that have unacceptable public health conditions and need native scientists, educators, technicians, and other professionals. In addition, by relying on foreign talent, the United States does not need to take the steps necessary to encourage native members of subordinate groups to enter these desirable fields of employment.

Some of the effects of the brain drain have been lessened since 1982, when the entry of foreign-born and foreign-educated physicians was greatly restricted. Yet the United States continues to beckon to foreign professionals and to retain highly motivated foreign students, who remain in the United States after completing their education. A National Science Foundation study of Asian doctoral recipients found that 60 percent of the engineers and 85 percent of the scientists planned to stay in the United States (*Journal of Blacks in Higher Education* 1994c).

While many people in the United States express concern with immigration, in actuality, many immigrants bring skills needed here, which contributes to the brain drain in their home country.

By Sharpnack/Washington Post National Weekly Edition

One proposed solution to continuing international concern over the brain drain is to limit the number of professionals from a nation who may enter the United States in a year as students. Such legislation has not received widespread support with Congress. Furthermore, many industries wish to recruit from a global talent pool and voice their opposition to limits on skilled workers. Thus, the brain drain from developing countries continues.

POPULATION GROWTH

The United States, like a few other industrial nations, continues to accept large numbers of permanent immigrants and refugees. Although such immigration has increased since the passage of the 1965 Immigration and Naturalization Act, the nation's birthrate has decreased. Consequently, the contribution of immigration to population growth has become more significant. Legal immigration accounted for one-fourth of the nation's growth in the 1990s. The respected environmentalist group Sierra Club debated for over a year taking an official position favoring restricting immigration, recognizing that more people puts greater strain on the nation's natural resources. Finally, in 1998, 60 percent of the members voted to keep a neutral position rather than enter the politically charged immigration debate (M. Cone 1998).

It is projected that immigrants who come to the United States in the period 1990–2080 and their descendants will add 72 million more people, or 25 percent of today's total, to the population. Assuming that native-born Americans maintain a low birthrate, and that the immigrant contribution to the population of the United States is just 50 percent higher than at present, the contribution could run as high as 37 percent. By contrast, however, many other countries are currently receiving a much higher proportion of immigrants. Over the last ten years, more than 80 percent of population growth in Greece and Austria and more than 40 percent in Canada and Australia have come from immigration (Bouvier and Grant 1994; Martin and Widgren 1996:7).

The patterns of uneven settlement in the United States are expected to continue so that future immigrants' impact on population growth will be felt much more in certain areas—California and New York rather than Iowa or Massachusetts. For example, California, which is the most extreme case, is expected to grow from 32 million people in 1995 to over 49 million people by the year 2025. Of this increase of 17 million people, nearly half will be new immigrants to the United States, and a sizable proportion of the remaining will be the children of recent immigrants. While immigration and population growth may be viewed as a national concern, its impact is localized in certain areas such as southern California and large urban centers nationwide (El Nasser 1996).

ILLEGAL IMMIGRATION

The most bitterly debated aspect of U.S. immigration policy has been the control of illegal or undocumented immigrants. These immigrants and their families come to the United States in search of higher-paying jobs than their home countries can provide. As we noted at the beginning of the chapter, people like Eduardo Román García, who left his home in Veracruz, Mexico, seek employment in the United States even if they are not able to enter legally.

Immigrants are pulled here by the lure of prosperity and better lives for their children, while they are pushed out of their native lands by unemployment and poverty. Despite fears to the contrary, immigrants—whether legal or illegal—have had only a slight impact on the employment prospects of longtime U.S. citizens. While some immigrants enter professional jobs, in general, immigrants are employed in jobs that employers find difficult to fill and that many residents do not want (G. Borjas 1990).

Illegal immigrants, and even legal immigrants, have become tied by the public to virtually every social problem in the nation. They become the scapegoats for unemployment; they are labeled as "drug runners" and even "terrorists." Yet their vital economic and cultural contribution to the United States is generally overlooked, as it has been for over a hundred years.

There were over 5 million illegal immigrants in the United States in 1998, and that number is increasing by about 275,000 annually. While Mexican nationals make up about 54 percent of this total, undocumented aliens are here from throughout the world (Gallo 1998; Immigration and Naturalization Service 1997:197).

The cost of the federal government's attempt to police the nation's borders and locate illegal immigrants is sizable. There are significant costs for aliens, that is, foreign-born noncitizens, and for other citizens as well. Civil rights advocates have expressed concern that the procedures used to apprehend and deport people are discriminatory and deprive many aliens of their legal rights. American citizens of Hispanic or Asian origin, some of whom were born in the United States, may be greeted with prejudice and distrust, as if their names automatically imply that they are illegal immigrants. Furthermore, these citizens and legal residents of the United States may be unable to find work because employers wrongly believe that their documents are forged (Domestic Council Committee on Illegal Aliens 1976; M. Farber 1975).

In the context of this illegal immigration, Congress approved the Immigration Reform and Control Act of 1986, after debating it for nearly a decade. The act marked a historic change in immigration policy compared to earlier laws, as summarized in Table 4.2. For the first time, hiring illegal aliens became illegal, so that employers are subject to fines and even prison sentences. It appears that the act has had mixed results in terms of illegal immigration. According to data compiled by the U.S. Border Patrol, arrests along the border declined substantially in the first three years after the law took effect. However, illegal immigration eventually returned to the levels of the early 1980s.

Although the Immigration Reform and Control Act prohibited employers from discriminating against legal aliens because they were not United States citizens, a 1990 report by the General Accounting Office revealed that the law had produced a "widespread pattern of discrimination" against people who looked or sounded like foreigners. The report estimated that some 890,000 employers had initiated one or more discriminatory practices in response to the 1986 immigration law. Although

Table 4.2 Major Immigration Policies

Policy	Target Group	Impact
Chinese Exclusion Act, 1882	Chinese	Effectively ended all Chinese immigration for over 60 years
National Origins System, 1921	Southern Europeans	Reduced overall immigration and significantly reduced likely immigration from Greece and Italy
Immigration and Naturalization Act, 1965	Western Hemisphere and the less skilled	Facilitated entry of skilled workers and relatives of U.S. residents
Immigration Reform and Control Act of 1986	Illegal Immigration	Modest reduction of illegal immigration

these firms employed nearly 7 million workers, fewer than 1,000 complaints of discrimination had been filed with government agencies—in good part because most employees were unaware of the protections included in the Immigration Reform and Control Act. A 1996 law weakened the ability of the government to sue employers who use immigration laws to discriminate against individuals (C. Brown 1990; D. Carney 1996).

Many illegal immigrants continue to live in fear and hiding, subject to even more severe harassment and discrimination than before. From a conflict perspective, these immigrants—primarily poor and Hispanic or Asian—are being firmly lodged at the bottom of the nation's social and economic hierarchies. However, from a functionalist perspective, employers, by paying low wages, are able to produce goods and services that are profitable for industry and more affordable to consumers. Despite the poor working conditions often experienced by illegal immigrants here, they continue to come because it is still in their best economic interest to work here in disadvantaged positions rather than to seek wage labor unsuccessfully in their home country.

The public in the United States does occasionally notice that the pattern of taking advantage of immigrant workers has gone too far. In the 1960s there were significant protests over the working conditions of migrant farm workers, many of whom came from Latin America and the Philippines. More recently, in 1996, national attention was drawn to several urban sweatshops, where illegal immigrants were discovered working under slave-like conditions. The garments they produced were sold in a number of national retail outlets such as Wal-Mart. While laws exist to prevent such situations, enforcement rarely occurs (Branigin 1995; C. Dugger 1996).

In the 1996 presidential campaign, immigration became an issue both in terms of the number of immigrants to be allowed to enter and the benefits they should receive. Congress proposed measures that would have restricted benefits such as schooling or public assistance to immigrants, even legal arrivals. Eventually a compromise passed, called the Illegal Immigration Reform and Immigrant Responsibility Act of 1996, which emphasized more effort to keep immigrants from entering the

Rex Rabin/Times Union

country illegally. Illegal immigrants will not have access to such benefit programs as Social Security and welfare, although enforcement of this measure appears to be weak. Legal immigrants, for now, will be entitled to such benefits, although welfare reform measures enacted at about the same time would likely restrict these benefits (D. Carney 1996).

One unintended consequence of all this debate about restricting government benefits to new arrivals has been a surge in the number of immigrants seeking to become citizens. In 1997, over 1.5 million people successfully sought citizenship, compared to 300,000 annually in the early 1990s. These new citizens will have an impact on the political scene if they choose to exercise their right to vote. However, it remains unclear whether these newest citizens will necessarily be much different politically from the voting electorate they are now joining (M. Ojito 1998).

Policy makers continue to avoid the only real way to stop illegal immigration, and that is to discourage employment opportunities. The public often thinks in terms of greater surveillance at the border. A 1995 Gallup poll showed that 35 percent of the public favored erecting a Berlin-like wall along the border with Mexico. Actually, about half of the illegal immigrants come into the United States legally as students or as workers on visas but then overstay. Therefore, the solution lies in preventing illegal immigrants from obtaining employment. This solution would involve employee verification procedures, tougher penalties on employers, and perhaps national identity cards. Numerous government commissions have continued to support such measures in recent years. Conservatives, while favoring a crackdown on illegal immigration, oppose interfering further with employers' autonomy, and liberals are concerned about infringing upon people's civil rights through greater workplace surveillance (D. Carney 1996; W. Cornelius 1996; M. Puente 1996b).

The Economic Impact of Immigration

There is considerable public and scholarly debate about the economic effects of immigration, both legal and illegal. Varied, conflicting conclusions have resulted from research ranging from case studies of Korean immigrants' dominance among New York City greengrocers to mobility studies charting the progress of all immigrants and their children. The confusion is due in part to the different methods of analysis. For example, the studies do not always include political refugees, who generally are less prepared than other refugees to become assimilated. Sometimes the research focuses only on economic effects, such as whether people are employed or on welfare; in other cases it also considers cultural factors such as knowledge of English.

Perhaps the most significant factor is whether a study examines the national impact of immigration or only its effects on a local area. Overall, we can conclude from the research that immigrants adapt rather well and are an asset to the local economy. In some areas, heavy immigration may drain a community's resources. However, it can also revitalize a local economy.

According to survey data, many people in the United States hold the stereotypical belief that immigrants often end up on welfare and thereby cause increases in taxes. Economist David Card studied the 1980 "Mariel" boatlift that brought 125,000 Cubans into Miami and found that even this substantial addition of mainly low-skilled workers had no measurable impact on the wages or unemployment rates of low-skilled White and African American workers in the Miami area (D. Card et al. 1998; R. Wright 1995).

Social science studies generally contradict many of the negative stereotypes about the economic impact of immigration. Both a 1997 National Research Council report and a 1998 Cato Institute and National Immigration Reform report found that immigrants are a net economic gain for the population. However, as stated above, national gains do not preclude that in some areas and for some groups, immigration may be an economic burden or create unwanted competition for jobs. Overall, however, at this time no evidence suggests that the most recent wave of immigrants to the United States will join the nation's permanent underclass (Borjas and Freeman 1997; S. Moore 1998; R. Rumbaut 1998, Smith and Edmonston 1997).

Even more intense is the controversy over illegal immigrants' receipt of welfare and health benefits. Immigrants generally pay more in taxes than they receive in benefits, even if they live in major cities such as Los Angeles that have a large population of immigrants. However, because most of the taxes go to the federal government and do not generally relieve local burdens, some states and municipalities are paying these costs themselves. For example, the state of California spends about $2.35 billion on illegal immigrants' education, health care, and other services. These workers generate $2.4 billion a year in taxes, or more than the costs. However, $1.3 billion of this revenue goes to the federal government, leaving California with a large bill while benefiting the nation overall. Studies in other states have shown a similar pattern (*Harvard Law Review* 1995; Martin and Midgley 1994; Paral 1996; Passel et al. 1996).

One economic aspect of immigration that has received increasing attention is the effort to measure remittances. **Remittances (or migradollars)** are the monies that immigrants return to their country of origin. The amounts are significant and measure in the tens of millions of dollars flowing from the United States to a number of countries where they are a very substantial source of support for families and even venture capital for new businesses. While some observers express concern over this outflow of money, others counter that it probably represents a small price to pay for the human capital that the United States is able to utilize in the form of the immigrants themselves.

These recent immigrants near Calexico, California, are harvesting broccoli. Such immigrants working at low wages help keep produce prices low.

States have sought legal redress because the federal government has not seriously considered granting impact aid to heavily burdened states. In 1994, Florida joined California in suing the U.S. government to secure strict enforcement of immigration laws and reimbursement for services rendered to illegal immigrants. As frustration mounted, California voters considered a 1994 referendum banning illegal immigrants from public schools, public assistance programs, and all but emergency medical care. Although the constitutionality of the proposal was doubtful, voters heavily favored the referendum, which we discuss in greater detail later. Surveys show that such a measure would pass nationwide (D. Carney 1996a).

This California referendum, Proposition 187, symbolized the revolt against immigration, especially illegal immigration. Although 59 percent of California voters approved the measure in 1994, the vote showed significant ethnic differences: 65 percent of Whites, 47 percent of African and Asian Americans, and 33 percent of Hispanics favored this proposition. The so-called "Save Our State" (SOS) proposition denied illegal immigrants education, welfare, and nonemergency health care. Public employees, including teachers, were to report illegal immigrants to authorities.

Immediately after its approval, opponents of Proposition 187 filed lawsuits posing constitutional challenges to implementation. A federal appeals court struck down the anti-immigrant measure as unconstitutional, but appeals are expected. Supporters

Tens of thousands of Hispanics gathered in Washington, D.C., in October 1996 to march for full participation in U.S. society, demanding expansion of health services, affirmative action, and streamlined citizenship programs.

hoped the success of the proposition would lead to similar movements in other states, but none have materialized so far (D. Anderson 1998).

The concern about immigration in the 1990s is both understandable and perplexing. The nation has always been uneasy about new arrivals, especially those who are different from the more affluent and the policy makers. Yet the 1990s have been marked by relatively low unemployment, low inflation, and much-diminished anxiety about our economic future. This paradoxical situation—a strong economy and concerns about immigration framed in economic arguments—suggests that other concerns, such as ethnic and racial tension, are more important in explaining current attitudes toward immigration in the United States (W. Cornelius 1996).

Refugees

Refugees are people living outside their country of citizenship for fear of political or religious persecution. Enough refugees exist to populate an entire nation. There are approximately 15 million refugees worldwide. That makes the nation of refugees larger than Belgium, Sweden, or Cuba. The United States has touted itself as a haven for political refugees. However, as we shall see, the welcome to political refugees has not always been unqualified.

The United States makes the largest financial contribution of any nation to worldwide assistance programs and serves as the host to over 150,000 refugees. Many nations much smaller than the United States have many more refugees than that, with Jordan, Iran, and Zaire hosting over a million refugees each (U.S. Committee for Refugees 1996a).

The United States, insulated by distance from wars and famines in Europe and Asia, has been able to be selective about which and how many refugees are welcomed. Since the arrival of refugees uprooted by World War II, the United States has allowed three groups of refugees to enter in numbers greater than regulations would ordinarily permit: Hungarians, Cubans, and Southeast Asians. Compared to the other two groups, the nearly 40,000 Hungarians who arrived following the unsuccessful revolt against the Soviet Union of November 1956 were few indeed. At the time, however, theirs was the fastest mass immigration to this country since before 1922. With little delay, the United States amended the laws so that the Hungarian refugees could enter. Because of their small numbers and their dispersion throughout this country, the Hungarians are little in evidence four decades later. The much larger and longer period of movement of Cuban and Southeast Asian refugees into the United States continues to have a profound social and economic impact.

Despite periodic public opposition, the U.S. government is officially committed to accepting refugees from other nations. According to the United Nations treaty on refugees, which our government ratified in 1968, countries are obliged to refrain from forcibly returning people to territories where their lives or liberty might be endangered. It is not always clear, though, whether an individual is fleeing for his or her personal safety or to escape poverty. Although people in the latter category may be of humanitarian interest, they do not meet the official definition of refugees and are subject to deportation.

It is the practice of deporting people fleeing poverty that has been the subject of criticism. There is a long tradition in the United States of facilitating the arrival of people leaving Communist nations. Mexicans who are refugees from poverty, Liberians fleeing civil war, and Haitians running from despotic rule are not similarly welcomed. The plight of Haitians has become of particular concern.

Haitians fled their country, often on small boats, from the time of the military coup in 1991 that overthrew the elected government of President Jean-Bertrand Aristide until he was restored to power in October 1994. The U.S. Coast Guard intercepted many Haitians at sea, saving some of these boat people from death in their rickety and overcrowded wooden vessels.

The Haitians said they feared detentions, torture, and execution if they remained in Haiti. However, the Bush administration viewed most of the Haitian exiles as economic migrants rather than political refugees and opposed granting them asylum and permission to enter the United States. During the 1992 presidential campaign, candidate Bill Clinton denounced the policy of interdiction as "cruel" and illegal; yet after assuming the Presidency in 1993, he kept in place the policy of keeping Haitians from entering. In 1993, the U.S. Supreme Court, by an 8–1 vote, upheld the government's right to intercept Haitian refugees at sea and return them to their homeland without asylum hearings. Steven Forester, an attorney at the Haitian Refugee Center in Miami, wondered how the justices could uphold a policy of forcibly returning Haitian refugees to "their military persecutors, . . . who the State Department condemns for their horrendous human rights practices" (L. Greenhouse 1993b; L. Rohter 1993b:18).

In 1996, 130,000 people overseas sought to enter the United States as refugees, but only slightly more than 19,000 were granted refugee status within the year. The Immigration and Naturalization Service attempts to deal with the huge backlog of more than 455,000 residents who are waiting for hearings regarding their petitions. A massive bureaucracy that includes 325 asylum officers and 179 immigration judges has been developed to deal with the refugees. Currently most of the refugees seeking to enter the United States are from Central America, the former Soviet Union, Haiti, and China. Refugees are a worldwide challenge to all nations, and the United States is no exception (U.S. Committee for Refugees 1996a, 1996b).

CONCLUSION

For its first hundred years, the United States allowed all immigrants to enter and become permanent residents. The federal policy of welcome did not mean, however, that immigrants would not encounter discrimination and prejudice. With the passage of the Chinese Exclusion Act, discrimination against one group of potential immigrants became law. The Chinese were soon joined by the Japanese as peoples forbidden by law to enter and prohibited from becoming naturalized citizens. The development of the national origins system in the 1920s created a hierarchy of nationalities, with people from northern Europe encouraged to enter while other Europeans and Asians encountered long delays. The possibility of a melting pot, which had always been a fiction, was legislated out of existence.

In the 1960s and again in 1990, the policy was liberalized so that the importance of nationality was minimized, and a person's work skills and relationship to an American were emphasized. This liberalization came at a time when most Europeans no longer desired to immigrate into the United States. The legacy of the arrival of the over 64 million immigrants since 1820 is apparent today in their descendants, such as Raffi Ishkanian.

Throughout the history of the United States, as we have seen, there has been intense debate over the nation's immigration and refugee policies. In a sense, this debate reflects the deep value conflicts in the culture of the United States and parallels the "American dilemma" identified by Swedish social economist Gunnar Myrdal (1944). One strand of our culture—well epitomized by the words "Give us your tired, your poor, your huddled masses"—has emphasized egalitarian principles and a desire to help people in their time of need. At the same time, however, hostility to potential immigrants and refugees—whether the Chinese in the 1880s, European Jews in the 1930s and 1940s, or Mexicans, Haitians, and Arabs today—reflects not only racial, ethnic, and religious prejudice, but also a desire to maintain the dominant culture of the in-group by keeping out those viewed as outsiders. The conflict between these cultural values is central to the American dilemma of the 1990s.

At present the debate about immigration is highly charged and emotional. Some people see it in economic terms, while others see the new arrivals as a challenge to the very culture of our society. Clearly, the general perception is that immigration presents a problem rather than offers a promise for the future. A 1997 national survey found the majority of respondents convinced that immigration would overburden the welfare system, take jobs away from people already here, and even lead to increased conflict between racial and ethnic groups (Princeton Research Survey Associates 1997).

Today's concern about immigrants follows generations of people coming to settle in the United States. This immigration in the past produced a very diverse country in terms of both nationality and religion even before the immigration of the last fifty years. Therefore, the majority of Americans today are not descended from the English, and Protestants are little over half of all worshipers. This diversity of religious and ethnic groups will be examined next.

KEY TERMS

brain drain 118
nativism 108
refugees 127
remittances (or migradollars) 125
sinophobes 110
xenophobia 108

REVIEW QUESTIONS

1. Why are nationality and religion used to oppose immigration?
2. What were the social and economic issues when public opinion mounted against Chinese immigration into the United States?
3. Ultimately, what do you think is the major concern people have about contemporary immigration to the United States—the numbers of immigrants or their nationality?
4. What are the principles that appear to guide the refugee policy?

CRITICAL THINKING

1. What is the immigrant root story of your family? Consider how your ancestors arrived in the United States, and also how your family's past has been shaped by other immigrant groups.
2. Can you find evidence of the brain drain in terms of the professionals with whom you come in contact? Do you regard this as a benefit? What groups in the United States may have been not encouraged to fill such positions by the availability of such professionals?

INTERNET EXERCISE

The U.S. Immigration and Naturalization Service maintains an official homepage at (http://www.ins.usdoj.gov). Log on to the site and click the "statistics" section to explore the information for the most recent year available. How many immigrants admitted to the United States were women? According to the data, immigrants come from which kinds of occupational groups? Are most immigrants younger or older? From which three countries do most immigrants come? What sociological reasons can you offer to explain some of these findings? Which statistic from the site or the chapter did you find the most surprising? Why?

Return to the main homepage, and click on the "naturalization" section. Next, select the "Am I Eligible?" section. Once there, make a list of the requirements for naturalization. What is your opinion of these? Should there be more or fewer requirements? Why? Review the 100 sample questions and answers to see how you would fare if you were an immigrant seeking citizenship. Would you have passed the test and become a citizen?

FOR FURTHER INFORMATION

Peter Brimelow. *The Alien Nation*. New York: Random House, 1996.
A strong critique of present-day immigration and its impact on life in the United States.

Barry R. Chiswick, ed. *Immigration, Language, and Ethnicity: Canada and the United States*. Washington, D.C.: AEI Press, 1992.
The contributions are organized around the topics of immigration history and policy, demographic characteristics and earnings, language, and women and minorities.

Thomas Dublin, ed. *Becoming American, Becoming Ethnic: College Students Explore Their Roots*. Philadelphia: Temple University Press, 1996.
A collection of thirty-one essays written by college students reflecting on their immigrant ancestors and their current cultural experience in the United States.

Kevin Kenny. *Making Sense of the Molly Maquires*. New York: Oxford University Press, 1998.
Historian considers a chapter in U.S. history characterized by both anti-Irish and anti-Roman Catholic feelings.

PERIODICALS

Both the *International Migration Review* (formerly the *International Migration Digest*), begun in 1966, and *Migration Today,* begun in 1972, are published by the Center for Migration Studies. The *Journal of Refugee Resettlement* (1981), the *Journal of Refugee Studies* (1988), and *Refugee Reports* (1979) reflect the renewed interest in refugees. The monthly *Migration News* is available on-line at http://migration.ucdavis.edu.

5

Ethnicity and Religion

CHAPTER OUTLINE

HIGHLIGHTS

The United States includes a multitude of ethnic and religious groups. Do they coexist in harmony or in conflict? How significant are they as sources of identity for their members? There was a resurgence of interest in their ethnicity among Whites in the 1960s and well into the 1970s, partly in response to the renewed pride in the ethnicity of Blacks, Hispanics, and Native Americans. We have an ethnicity paradox where White ethnics seem to enjoy their heritage while at the same time seeking to assimilate into larger society. White ethnics are the victims of humor (or respectable bigotry) that some still consider socially acceptable, and they find themselves with little power in big business. Religious minorities have also experienced intolerance in the present as well as the past. Constitutional issues such as school prayer, secessionist minorities, creationism, and public religious displays are regularly taken to the Supreme Court. Italian Americans and the Amish are presented as case studies of the experiences of specific ethnic and religious groups in the United States.

Betty O'Keefe is a 60-year-old Californian who is a fifth-generation Irish American—that would mean her grandmother's grandmother came to the United States from Ireland. Sociologist Mary Waters (1990:97) asked her what it was like growing up in the United States.

> *When I was in high school my maiden name was Tynan. This was 1940. I was dating some boys from school, and two different*

times when the parents found out I was an Irish Catholic, they told him he couldn't go out with me. The Protestants were like that. . . . One of his brothers later married someone named O'Flannery and I was so thrilled. I said I hope your mother is turning in her grave. So I am happy that my children have the name O'Keefe. So that people know right away what their background is. I think it is better. They would never be put in the position I was in.

Do you think something like that could happen now?

I don't think so openly. But I think it is definitely still there. You are not as bad (being an Irish Catholic) as a Black, but you are not Protestant. You are not Jewish either, which would be worse, but still you are not of their church.

Their names may be Badovich, Hoggarty, Jablonski, Reggio, or Williams. They may follow any one of thousands of faiths and gather at any of the 360,000 churches, mosques, synagogues, and temples. Our nation's motto is *E Pluribus Unum,* and while there may be doubt that we are truly united into one common culture following a single ideology, there is little doubt about our continuing diversity as a nation of peoples.

Indeed, the very complexity of relations between dominant and subordinate groups in the United States today is partly the result of its heterogeneous population. No one ethnic origin or religious faith encompasses all the inhabitants of the United States. Even though its largest period of sustained immigration is two generations past, an American today is surrounded by remnants of cultures and practitioners of religions whose origins are foreign to this country. Religion and ethnicity continue to be significant in defining an individual's identity.

Ethnic Diversity

The ethnic diversity of the United States in the 1990s is apparent to almost everyone. Passersby in New York City were undoubtedly surprised once when two street festivals met head to head. The procession of San Gennaro, the patron saint of Naples, marched through Little Italy, only to run directly into a Chinese festival originating in Chinatown. Teachers in many public schools frequently face students who speak only one language, and it is not English. Students in Chicago are taught in Spanish, Greek, Italian, Polish, German, Creole, Japanese, Cantonese, or the language of a Native American tribe. In the Detroit metropolitan area, classroom instruction is conveyed in twenty-one languages, including Arabic, Portuguese, Ukrainian, Latvian, Lithuanian, and Serbian. In many areas of the United States, you can refer to a special Yellow Pages and find a driving instructor who speaks Portuguese or a psychotherapist who will talk to you in Hebrew.

Germans are the largest ancestral group; the 1990 Census showed almost one-fourth of Americans saying they had at least some German ancestry. While most German Americans are assimilated, it is possible to see the ethnic tradition in some areas, particularly in Milwaukee, whose population has 48 percent German ancestry. There, three Saturday schools teach German, and one can affiliate with thirty-four German-American clubs and visit a German library that operates within the public library system (D. Carvajal 1995; K. Johnson 1992; M. Usdansky 1992a).

As shown in Table 5.1, Germany is one of twenty-one European nations from which at least 1 million people claim to have ancestry. The numbers are striking when one considers the size of some of the sending countries. For example, there are almost 39 million Irish Americans, and the Republic of Ireland had a population of 3.7 million in 1998. Similarly, nearly 5 million people claim Swedish ancestry, and there are 8.9 million people living in Sweden today. Now, of course, many Irish and Swedish Americans are of mixed ancestry, but not everyone in Ireland is Irish nor is everyone in Sweden Swedish.

Why Don't We Study Whiteness?

Race is socially constructed, as we learned in Chapter 1. Sometimes, we come to define race in a clear-cut manner—a descendant of a Pilgrim is White, for example. But sometimes race is more ambiguous—people who are the children of an African American and Vietnamese American union are biracial or "mixed," or whatever they come to be seen by others. Our recognition that race is socially constructed has sparked a renewed interest in what it means to be White in the United States. Two aspects of White as a race are useful to consider: the historical creation of whiteness, and how contemporary White people reflect on their racial identity.

Table 5.1 Population by European Ancestry, 1990

The major sources of European ancestry in the present population in the United States are Germany, Ireland, England, Italy, and France.

Ancestry Group	Total (1,000)	Ancestry Group	Total (1,000)
Austrian	865	Lithuanian	812
British	1,119	Norwegian	3,869
Croatian	944	Polish	9,366
Czech	1,296	Portuguese	1,153
Danish	1,635	Russian	2,953
Dutch	6,227	Scandinavian	679
English	32,652	Scotch-Irish	5,618
European	467	Scottish	5,394
Finnish	659	Slovak	1,883
French	10,321	Swedish	4,681
German	57,947	Swiss	1,045
Greek	1,110	Ukrainian	741
Hungarian	1,582	Welsh	2,034
Irish	38,736	Yugoslavian	258
Italian	14,665		

Source: Bureau of the Census, 1996: 53.

LISTEN TO THEIR VOICES

When the Boats Arrived

Diane Glancy

Some of my ancestors came from Europe on boats. Others were already here when the boats arrived. I have done a lot of my writing examining the Indian part of my heritage, which came through my father. The white part didn't seem to need definition. It just was. Is. And shall be. But what does it mean be part white? What does whiteness look like viewed from the other, especially when that other is also within oneself?

I can say whiteness is the dominant culture, for now anyway. Or I can say I was taught that whiteness gives definition instead of receiving it. It is the upright. The unblemished. The milk or new snow. It is the measure by which others are measured. There's nothing off center in it to make it aware of itself as outside or other. It doesn't need examination or explanation, but is the center around which others orbit. It is the plumb line. Other races/cultures/ethnicities are looked at in terms of their distance from whiteness.

Whiteness is a heritage I can almost enter, but I have *unwhiteness* in me. There is something that is not milk or new snow. I am a person of part color. I can feel my distance from whiteness. There is a dividing line into it I cannot cross. But neither can I cross fully into the Indian, because I am of mixed heritage.

When I look at my white heritage, it is as fragmented and hard to pinpoint as the native side. My mother's family came from England and Germany. They settled in Pennsylvania, then Virginia, and finally on the Missouri-Kansas border. What do I

When the English immigrants established themselves as the political founders of the United States, they also came to define what it meant to be White. Other groups that today are regarded as White, such as Irish, German, Norwegian, or Swedish, were not always considered White in the eyes of the English. Differences in language and religious worship, as well as past allegiance to a king in Europe different from the English, all caused these groups to be seen not as Whites in the Western Hemisphere but more as nationals of their home country who happened to be residing in North America. The old distrust in Europe, where, for example, the Irish were viewed by the English as socially and culturally inferior, continued on this side of the Atlantic Ocean. Karl Marx, writing from England, reported that the average English worker looked down on the Irish the way poor Whites in the American South looked down on Black people (N. Ignatiev 1994, 1995; D. Roediger 1994).

In "Listen to Their Voices," Diane Glancy, Macalester College professor of Native American literature and creative writing, draws on both "insider" and "outsider" know of them any more than of my father's family? The European part of the family were practical, middle-of-the-road people. They got their work done. They didn't say a lot about it. They were fair-minded and tenacious. They were church-goers and voters who migrated from the farm to the city in my parents' generation. They educated their children and died without much ceremony.

As for the white culture I saw in my mother's family—every Christmas Eve, they served Canadian bacon, which my father brought from the stockyards where he worked. I received an Easter basket on Easter. I got a sparkler on the Fourth of July. But that hardly defines culture.

I can look at the whiteness in my mother's family and say there was a determination, a punctuality, a dependability. There was a sense of Manifest Destiny, which was another tool for dominance. There was a need for maintenance and responsibility. A sense of a Judeo-Christian God. A holding to one's own. There was a need to be goal-oriented. To make use of resources.

There also was opportunity to do all these things.

Who can say what will happen to whiteness as the people of color become the majority in the new century? Who can say what will happen as the cultures of the minorities deepen, as the white is mixed with others and gets harder to define? Can the white culture continue to be defined by its lack of ceremonies, its Elvises and White Castles, its harbor of ideas? Will it continue to invent its inventiveness? Will it continue to thrive?

I guess I would define white American culture as industriousness without overwhelming tradition. It doesn't seem to have anchors, but slides past others into port. Into the port it created, after all.

Source: Diane Glancy. "When the Boats Arrived." First appeared in *The Hungry Mind Review,* Spring 1998.

perspectives on being White in the United States. As she describes, she is descended from Native Americans (American Indians) as well as English and Germans. As this chapter continues we will consider in a variety of ways what it means to be White in the United Sates at the beginning of the twentieth century.

As European immigrants and their descendants assimilated to the English and distanced themselves from other oppressed groups such American Indians and African Americans, they came to be viewed as White rather than part of a particular culture. Writer Noel Ignatiev (1994:84), contrasting being White with being Polish, argues that "Whiteness is nothing but an expression of race privilege." This strong statement argues that being White, as opposed to being Black or Asian, is characterized by being a member of the dominant group.

Contemporary White Americans generally give little thought to "being White." Hence there is little interest in studying "whiteness" or considering "being White" except that it is "not being Black." White people are occasionally reminded when filling out a form that asks for race, or when they hear White people in general accused of being racist. Unlike non-Whites, who are much more likely to interact with Whites, take orders from Whites, see Whites as the leading figures in the mass media, Whites enjoy the privilege of not being reminded of their Whiteness.

There is a new interest in the 1990s that seeks to look at whiteness but not from the vantage point of a White supremacist. Rather, focusing on White people as a race or what it means today to be White goes beyond any definition that implies superiority over non-Whites. This is still a relatively new field of inquiry, even in academic fields, so the area is still in the process of being defined. However, as we will discuss later, as African Americans, Hispanics, and Native Americans (American Indian) celebrated their roots, many Whites felt left out. In response, while they did not celebrate being White, they sought out their ethnic roots, such as being Polish American or Irish American. As sociologist Mary Waters (1990) reports in her book, *Ethnic Options*, this is not difficult because White people are well aware of their ancestry. They are more likely to know about their ancestors' birthplaces than they do about their religion, occupation, education, or year of birth.

Religious Pluralism

In popular speech, the term "pluralism" has often been used in the United States to refer explicitly to religion. Although certain faiths figure more prominently in the worship scene, there has been a history of religious tolerance in the United States compared to most nations. Today there are over 1,500 religious bodies in the United States, ranging from the more than 60 million members of the Roman Catholic Church to sects with fewer than 1,000 adherents.

There is an increasingly non-Christian presence in the United States. In 1900, an estimated 96 percent of the nation was Christian, just over 1 percent nonreligious, and about 3 percent all other faiths. Today, it is estimated that the nation is 85 percent Christian, nearly 8 percent nonreligious, and about 6 percent all other faiths. The United States has a long Jewish tradition, and Muslims number close to 5 million. A smaller but also growing number of people adhere to such Eastern faiths as Hinduism, Buddhism, Confucianism, and Taoism (Barret and Johnson 1998).

The diversity of religious life in the United States is apparent from Figure 5.1, which shows the Christian faiths that dominate various areas of the country numerically. For many nations of the world, a map of religions would hardly be useful, because one faith accounts for almost all religious followers in the country. The diversity of beliefs, rituals, and experiences that characterizes religious life in the United States reflects both the nation's immigrant heritage and the First Amendment prohibition against establishing a state religion (ACLU 1996a).

Sociologists use the word **denomination** for a large, organized religion that is not linked officially with the state or government. By far the largest denomination in the United States is Roman Catholicism, yet at least twenty-three other religious denominations have 1 million or more members (see Table 5.2). Protestants collectively accounted for about 58 percent of the nation's adult population in 1998, compared with 25 percent for Roman Catholics and about 2 percent for Jews (Gallup Poll Monthly 1998:40).

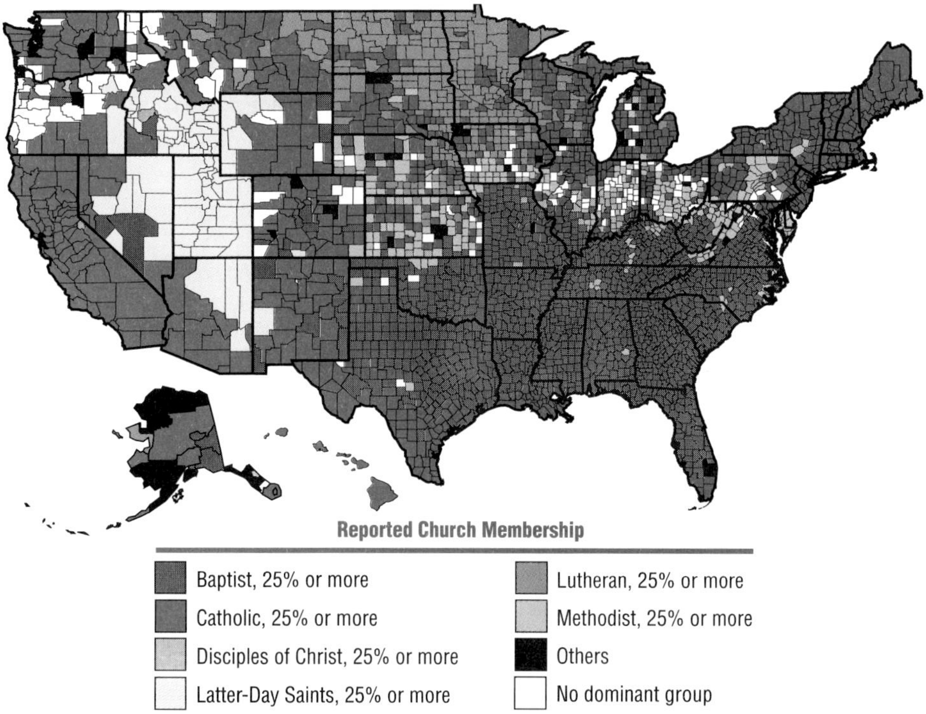

Figure 5.1 Predominant Christian Denominations by Counties, 1990
The diversity of Christian religious life in the United States is apparent in the figure. Many Christian denominations account for 25 percent or more of the church members in a county. Among non-Christian faiths, only Judaism may figure so significantly—in New York County (Manhattan) of New York City and in Dade County, Florida (which includes Miami Beach).
Source: M. Bradley, et al. 1992.

One notable characteristic of religious practice in the United States is the almost completely separate worship practices of Blacks and Whites. During the 1976 presidential campaign, an unusual amount of attention was directed to the segregation practiced by churches in the United States. The church attended by Jimmy Carter in Plains, Georgia, captured headlines when it closed its doors to a Black civil rights activist seeking membership. The Plains church later opened its membership to African Americans at Carter's urging. Such formal racial restrictions are unusual, but today the church hour on Sunday mornings still fits the description "the most segregated hour of the week." Of all major Protestant denominations, the United Methodist Church boasts the largest Black constituency, but that is only 3 percent. Overall, no more than 10 percent of Black Christians belong to predominantly White denominations, usually attending all-Black congregations. At the local or church level, it is estimated that only 1 percent of Black Christians belong to White churches (K. Briggs 1976; R. Stark 1987).

Table 5.2 Churches with More Than a Million Members, 1998

Denomination	Membership
The Roman Catholic Church	61,207,914
Southern Baptist Convention	15,691,964
The United Methodist Church	8,495,378
National Baptist Convention, USA, Inc.	8,200,000
The Church of God in Christ	5,499,875
Evangelical Lutheran Church in America	5,180,910
The Church of Jesus Christ of Latter-Day Saints	4,800,000
Presbyterian Church (U.S.A.)	3,637,375
National Baptist Convention of America, Inc.	3,500,000
African Methodist Episcopal Church	3,500,000
The Lutheran Church—Missouri Synod	2,601,144
Episcopal Church	2,536,550
Progressive National Baptist Convention, Inc.	2,500,000
National Missionary Baptist Convention of America	2,500,000
Assemblies of God	2,467,588
Churches of Christ	2,250,000
The Orthodox Church in America	2,000,000
Greek Orthodox Archdiocese	1,950,000
American Baptist Churches in the U.S.A.	1,503,267
Baptist Bible Fellowship International	1,500,000
United Church of Christ	1,452,565
African Methodist Episcopal Zion Church	1,252,369
Christian Churches and Churches of Christ	1,071,616
Pentecostal Assemblies of the World	1,000,000

Source: "Churches with More Than 1 Million Members" *Yearbook of American and Canadian Churches,* edited by Eileen W. Lindner.

About seven in ten Americans (69 percent) are counted as church members, but it is difficult to assess the strength of their religious commitment. A persuasive case can be made that religious institutions continue to grow stronger through an influx of new members despite mounting secularism in society. Some observers think that, after reaching a low in the 1960s, religion is becoming important to people again. The past upheavals in American religious life are reflected on the covers of *Time* magazine, which have cried out variously, "Is God Dead?" (April 8, 1966), "Is God Coming Back to Life?" (December 26, 1969), and "The Jesus Revolution" (June 21, 1971). Much more recently, *Newsweek* proclaimed "Science Finds God" (July 20, 1998). At present, there is little statistical support for the view that the influence of religion on society is diminishing (*Gallup Poll Monthly* 1998:38).

In reviewing data on church attendance and feelings about organized religion, however, we surmise that religion is not uniformly on the upswing. There is a great deal of switching of denominations and, as in the past, considerable interest in new ways of expressing spirituality. Some new groups encounter hostility from organized, established faiths that question the tactics used to attract members and financial support. It would be incorrect to conclude either that religion is slowly being abandoned or that Americans are turning to religion with the zeal of new converts. The future may bring not only periods of religious revivalism but also times of decline in religious fervor.

It would also be incorrect to focus only on older religious organizations. Local churches which developed into national faiths during the 1990s, such as the Calvary Chapel, Vineyard, and Hope Chapel, have created a following among Pentecostal believers, who embrace a more charismatic form of worship devoid of many traditional ornaments, with pastors and congregations alike favoring informal attire. New faiths develop with increasing rapidity in what can only be termed a very competitive market for individual religious faith. In addition, people, with or without religious affiliation, become fascinated with spiritual concepts such as angels or become a part of loose-knit fellowships such as the Promise Keepers, an all-male movement of evangelical Christians founded in 1990. Religion in the United States is an ever-changing social phenomenon (D. Miller 1997; Miller and Schaefer 1998).

Throughout our discussion we have considered how the media distort, if not stereotype, racial and ethnic groups. This distortion also appears to be true in media depiction of the role of religion in our daily lives. While a 1998 national survey showed that 59 percent considered religion very important to them, one would not know that by watching motion pictures or television. Religion rarely appears as a subject except at times of scandal or to offer an inside look at some satanic cult. An analysis of the top-grossing films shows religion and religious characters increasingly depicted in negative light and less likely to reach their goals than are nonreligious characters. Religion is relatively absent from television: only 5 percent of television characters are shown as practicing religion in any way. Historically, spirituality appeared routinely on such shows as *M*A*S*H* (Father Francis Mulcahy), *The Waltons, Little House on the Prairie,* and *Highway to Heaven*. However, since 1991, among hundreds of programs, only *Dr. Quinn: Medicine Woman, Northern Exposure, Picket Fences, Good News, Soul Man, Touched by an Angel*, and *Promised Land* have occasionally had religion-oriented story lines. Reverend Billy Graham views the lack of prime-time religion as a "cultural breakdown" and, recognizing how important religion is to people, has called on like-minded viewers to let the television "industry know how much it means to us when programs depict our Judeo-Christian values" (D. Gable, 1993; *Gallup Poll Monthly* 1998:37; Goldstein 1997; S. Rothman 1996; Saad and McAneny 1994).

The Rediscovery of Ethnicity

Robert Park (1950:205), a prominent early sociologist, wrote in 1913 that "a Pole, Lithuanian, or Norwegian cannot be distinguished, in the second generation, from an American, born of native parents." At one time, sociologists saw the end of ethnicity as nearly a foregone conclusion. W. Lloyd Warner and Leo Srole (1945) wrote in their often-cited Yankee City series that the future of ethnic groups seemed to be limited in the United States and that they would be quickly absorbed. Oscar

Handlin's *Uprooted* (1951) told of the destruction of immigrant values and their replacement by American culture. Although Handlin was among the pioneers in investigating ethnicity, assimilation was the dominant theme in his work.

Many writers have shown almost a fervent hope that ethnicity would vanish. The persistence of ethnicity was for some time treated by sociologists as dysfunctional because it meant a continuation of old values that interfered with the allegedly superior new values. For example, to hold on to one's language delayed entry into the larger labor market and the upward social mobility it afforded. Ethnicity was expected to disappear not only because of assimilation, but also because aspirations to higher social class and status demanded that it vanish. Somehow, it was assumed that one could not be ethnic and middle class, much less affluent.

THE THIRD-GENERATION PRINCIPLE

Historian Marcus Hansen's (1952) **principle of third-generation interest** was an early exception to the assimilationist approach to White ethnic groups. Simply stated, Hansen maintained that in the third generation—the grandchildren of the original immigrants—ethnic interest and awareness would actually increase. According to Hansen, "What the son wishes to forget the grandson wishes to remember." Hansen's principle has been tested several times since it was first put forth. John Goering (1971), in interviewing Irish and Italian Catholics, found that ethnicity was more important to members of the third generation than it was to the immigrants themselves. Similarly, Mary Waters (1990), in her interviews of White ethnics living in suburban San Jose, California, and suburban Philadelphia, Pennsylvania, observed many grandchildren wishing to study their ancestors' language even though it would be a foreign language to them. They also expressed interest in learning more of their ethnic group's history and a desire to visit the homeland.

Social scientists in the past were quick to minimize the ethnic awareness of blue-collar workers. In fact, ethnicity was viewed as merely another aspect of White ethnics' alleged racist nature, an allegation that will be examined later in this chapter. Curiously, the very same intellectuals and journalists who bent over backward to understand the growing solidarity of Blacks, Hispanics, and Native Americans refused to give White ethnics the academic attention they deserved (D. Wrong 1972).

The new assertiveness of Blacks and other non-Whites of their rights in the 1960s unquestionably presented White ethnics with the opportunity to reexamine their own position. "If solidarity and unapologetic self-consciousness might hasten Blacks' upward mobility, why not ours?" asked the White ethnics, who were often only half a step above Blacks in social status. The African American movement pushed other groups to reflect on their past. The increased consciousness of Blacks and their positive attitude toward African culture and the contributions worldwide of African Americans are embraced in what we termed earlier (Chapter 1) the Afrocentric perspective. The mood, therefore, was set in the 1960s for the country to be receptive to ethnicity. By legitimizing Black cultural differences from White culture, along with those of Native Americans and Hispanics, the country's opinion leaders legitimized other types of cultural diversity.

SYMBOLIC ETHNICITY

Observers comment both on the evidence of assimilation and, at the same time, the signs of ethnic identity that seem to support a pluralistic view of society. How can both be possible?

First, we have the very visible evidence of **symbolic ethnicity,** which may lead us to exaggerate the persistence of ethnic ties among White Americans. According to sociologist Herbert Gans (1979), ethnicity today increasingly involves the symbols of ethnicity, such as eating ethnic food, acknowledging ceremonial holidays such as St. Patrick's Day, and supporting specific political issues or the issues confronting the old country. A recent example was the push in 1998 by Irish Americans to convince state legislatures to make it compulsory in public schools to teach about the Irish potato famine, which was a significant factor in immigration to the United States. This symbolic ethnicity may be more visible, but this type of ethnic heritage does not interfere with what people do, read, or say, or even whom they befriend or marry. Richard Alba (1990) surveyed Whites in the Albany, New York, area in the mid–1980s and found that while there had been a decline in distinctions among ethnic groups, ethnic identity was still acknowledged. Heritage may not have disappeared, and indeed, the past, however defined, may even be important in today's frantic world.

The ethnicity of the 1990s embraced by English-speaking Whites is typically symbolic. It does not include active involvement in ethnic activities or participation in ethnic-related organizations. In fact, sizable proportions of White ethnics have gained large-scale entry into almost all clubs, cliques, and fraternal groups. Such acceptance is a key indicator of assimilation. Ethnicity has become increasingly peripheral to the lives of the members of the ethnic group. Although they may not relinquish their ethnic identity, other identities become more important (M. Gordon 1964).

Second, the ethnicity that does exist may be more a result of living in the United States than actual importing of practices from the past or the old country. Many so-called ethnic foods or celebrations, for example, began in the United States. The persistence of ethnic consciousness, then, may not depend on foreign birth, a distinctive language, and a unique way of life. Instead, it may reflect the experiences in the United States of a unique group that developed a cultural tradition distinct from that of the mainstream. For example, in Poland the *szlachta,* or landed gentry, rarely mixed socially with the peasant class. In the United States, however, even with those associations still fresh, they interacted together in social organizations as they settled in relatively concentrated communities segregated physically and socially from others (N. Glazer 1971; Glazer and Moynihan 1970; Lopata 1993).

Third, maintaining ethnicity can be a critical step toward successful assimilation. This **ethnicity paradox** facilitates full entry into the dominant culture. The ethnic community may give its members not only a useful financial boost, but also the psychological strength and positive self-esteem that will allow them to compete effectively in larger society. Thus, we may witness people participating actively in their

Immigrants and their descendants often prosper by serving their ethnic community. In a Chicago deli, a clerk serves up a plate of olives.

ethnic enclave while at the same time trying to cross the bridge into the wider community (Lal 1995).

Ethnicity, therefore, gives continuity with the past, in the form of an affective or emotional tie. The significance of this sense of belonging cannot be emphasized enough. Whether reinforced by distinctive behavior or by what Milton Gordon (1964) called a sense of "peoplehood," ethnicity is an effective, functional source of cohesion. Proximity to fellow ethnics is not necessary for a person to maintain social cohesion and in-group identity. Fraternal organizations or sports-related groups can preserve associations among ethnics who are separated geographically. Members of ethnic groups may even maintain their feelings of in-group solidarity after leaving ethnic communities in the central cities for the suburban fringe.

The Price Paid by White Ethnics

Many White ethnics shed their past and wish only to be Americans, with no ancestral ties to another country. Boris Shlapak, who played forward on a professional soccer team, changed his name to Ian Stone because "American kids need to identify with soccer players as Americans" (C. Terry 1975). Stone, who by his own admission "never felt ethnic," was not concerned about being a figure to whom Slavic

Americans would look as a hero. Some ethnics do not wish to abandon their heritage, but to retain their past as a part of their present, they must pay a price because of prejudice and discrimination.

PREJUDICE TOWARD WHITE ETHNIC GROUPS

Our examination of immigration to the United States in Chapter 4 pointed out the mixed feelings that have greeted European immigrants. They are apparently still not well received. In 1944, well after most immigration from Poland had ended, the Polish-American Congress, an umbrella organization of forty Polish fraternities, was founded to defend the image of Polish Americans. Young Polish Americans are made to feel ashamed of their ethnic origin when teachers find their names unpronounceable and when they hear Polish jokes bandied about in a way that anti-Black or anti-Semitic humor is not. One survey found that half of second-generation Polish Americans encounter prejudice. Curiously, it was socially proper to condemn the White working class as racist but quite improper to question the negative attitude of middle-class people toward White ethnics. Michael Lerner (1969) called this hostility toward White ethnics **respectable bigotry.** Polish jokes are acceptable, whereas anti-Black humor is considered to be in poor taste.

An important component of Lerner's respectable bigotry is not ethnic prejudice but class prejudice. In 1973, researchers surveyed Whites living in areas of Florida that had undergone school desegregation. After identifying whether or not a respondent had protested against school desegregation, the researchers sought to determine if the opposition had been caused by racial prejudice. The affluent and well educated, the researchers found, were more disturbed by the possibility of interacting more with working-class people, regardless of race. Although not conclusive, the study suggests that, even if affluent Whites are more tolerant of racial minorities, they may be less accepting of class differences (Giles et al. 1976).

White ethnics in the early 1970s felt that the mass media unfairly ridiculed them and their culture while celebrating Black Power and African culture. Italian Americans, for instance, remain concerned that their image is overwhelmed by stereotypes of organized crime, spaghetti, overweight mothers, and sexy women. Even television's Italian police seem to conform to the old stereotypes. In response to such stereotyping, the Columbian Coalition, founded in 1971, employs lawyers to handle cases of Italian Americans who claim they are victims of bigotry. Italian Americans are also not pleased by their conspicuous absence from the Roman Catholic Church hierarchy in the United States and from high political office. The Italians are well aware that another ethnic group, the Irish, dominates the American Catholic hierarchy, with 57 percent of the bishops in the country, although it has only 17 percent of the Catholic population. Not all Italian Americans are convinced that such self-help organizations as the Columbian Coalition, the Italian American Civil Rights League, or the Americans of Italian Descent are the answer. Despite disagreement over methods, most would agree that attitudes need changing. Italian Americans are just one example, however. Across the country and among all ethnic groups, appreciation of ethnic heritage is increasing (R. Gambino 1974a, 1974b; Glazer and Moynihan 1970; M. Novak 1996; N. Pileggi 1971; R. Severo 1970).

THE PREJUDICE OF ETHNICS

In the 1960s, as the civil rights movement moved north, White ethnics replaced the southern White as the typical bigot portrayed in the mass media. The chanting of protesters resulted in ugly incidents that made White ethnics and bigots synonymous. This stereotype of the prejudiced White ethnic has rarely been questioned. The danger of this and any stereotype is that it becomes indistinguishable from fact. David Matza (1964) referred to these mental pictures, which "tend to remain beyond the reach of such intellectual correctives as argument, criticism and scrutiny. . . . Left unattended, they return to haunt us by shaping or bending theories that purport to explain major social phenomena" (p. 1). This 1964 picture of ethnics and the degree of truth behind it needs to be examined.

The first issue to resolve is whether White ethnic groups are more prejudiced than other Whites. Sociologist Andrew Greeley (1974a, 1977; Nie et al. 1974) examined attitudes toward race, social welfare, and American involvement in Vietnam. The evidence pointed to minimal differences between ethnics and others. Some of the differences actually showed greater tolerance and liberalism among White ethnics. White ethnics, for example, were more in favor of welfare programs and more opposed to this country's participation in the Vietnam war.

Even when more sophisticated statistical analysis is introduced, the overall finding remains unchanged. No evidence supports the image of White ethnics as bigots. Greeley (1974a) concludes, "Our argument is not that ethnics are the last bastion of liberalism in America today, but rather that it is a misrepresentation of the facts to picture them as a vanguard of conservatism" (p. 202). Working-class ethnic neighborhoods, however, have undeniably been the scene of ugly racial confrontations. If ethnics are no more bigoted than others, how have such incidents come to occur, and how has this reputation developed? For that answer, the unique relationship between White ethnic groups and African Americans must be understood.

In retrospect, it should be no surprise that one group that has been antagonistic to African Americans is the White ethnics. For many citizens, including White ethnics, the United States they remembered from the 1950s seemed to change. When politicians told people in the 1960s, "We must fight poverty and discrimination," this translated to White ethnics as, "Share your job, share your neighborhood, but pay more taxes." Whites recalled how in several generations they had moved from membership in a poor immigrant group to becoming a prosperous part of the working class. Government assistance to the poor was virtually nonexistent then, public education was more restricted, and subsidized training programs were absent. Why was it different now? Many White ethnics found it difficult to understand why African Americans seemed to be singled out as a cause for concern in the 1960s when they perceived that they too had real needs (Glazer and Moynihan 1970; M. Novak 1996; Sanders and Morawska 1975; G. Tyler 1972).

White ethnics went so far as to turn their backs on federal aid offered them, because they did not wish to have their neighborhoods marked as "poverty pockets," nor did they wish to be associated with Black-oriented programs. In Newark, New Jersey, Italians successfully prevented an antipoverty office from being established and thereby cut off the jobs its programs would have created (F. Barbaro 1974). This ethnic opposition to publicly sponsored programs was not new. James Wilson and Edward Banfield (1964) studied elections in seven major cities between 1956 and 1963 for referenda to build new hospitals, parks, and schools. The results indicated that the least support came from White ethnics, who would have paid the least and benefited the most.

The prevailing conception of urban America has been that the city is Black and the suburbs are White. Although the latter was almost true, the former was definitely not. Along with poor African Americans and Hispanics in the big city were many White ethnics who were "economically unmonied and geographically immobile." White ethnics thought they were being made to pay for past injustices to Black Americans and others even though they were not in key decision-making roles. White ethnics found it difficult to be happy with minority-group gains (J. Conforti 1974; G. Tyler 1972).

White ethnics have not only separated themselves from African Americans, they have chosen to distinguish themselves from WASPs (White Anglo-Saxon Protestants) as well, as the next section indicates. White ethnics have learned that they are not considered part of the dominant group and that in order to achieve a larger slice of government benefits, they must now function as a self-interest group, just as racially subordinate groups have.

Case Example: The Italian Americans

While each European country's immigration to the United States has created its own social history, the case of Italians, while not typical of every nationality, offers insight into the White ethnic experience. Italians immigrated even during the colonial period, and they played prominent roles during the American Revolution and the early days of the republic. Mass immigration, however, began in the 1880s, peaking in the first twenty years of the twentieth century, when Italians accounted for one-fourth of European immigration.

Italian immigration was concentrated not only in time but also geographically. The majority of the immigrants were landless peasants from rural southern Italy, the Mezzogiorno. This is not just a trivial bit of information. While many people in the United States may assume that Italians are a nationality with a single culture, that is not true either culturally or economically. The Italian people recognize multiple geographic divisions reflecting sharp cultural distinctions. Indeed, today there is an observable movement in Padania, the region of northern Italians, to establish its own parliament and secede from Italy.

Many Italians, especially in the early years of mass immigration in the nineteenth century, received their jobs through an ethnic labor contractor, the *padrone*. Similar

Italian Americans gather in Massachusetts to celebrate a cultural festival.

arrangements have been used by Asian, Hispanic, and Greek immigrants, where the labor contractors, most often immigrants, have mastered sufficient English to mediate for their compatriots. Exploitation was common within the *padrone* system through kickbacks, provision of inadequate housing, and withholding of wages. By World War I, 90 percent of Italian girls and 99 percent of Italian boys in New York City were leaving school at the age of fourteen to work, but by that time Italian Americans were sufficiently fluent in English to seek out work on their own, and the *padrone* system had disappeared.

Along with manual labor, the Roman Catholic Church was a very important part of the Italian Americans' life at this time. Yet they found little comfort in a Catholic church dominated by an earlier immigrant group: the Irish. The traditions were different; weekly attendance for Italian Americans was overshadowed by the religious aspects of the *feste* (or festivals) held throughout the year in honor of saints (the Irish viewed the *feste* as practically a form of paganism). These initial adjustment problems were overcome with the establishment of ethnic parishes—a pattern repeated by other non-Irish immigrant groups. Thus, parishes would be staffed by Italian priests, sometimes imported for that purpose. While the hierarchy of the church would adjust more slowly, Italian Americans were increasingly able to feel at home in their local parish church. Today, over 70 percent of Italian Americans identify themselves as Roman Catholics (R. Alba 1985; Kosmin and Lachman 1993; A. Rolle 1972).

A controversial aspect of the Italian American experience involves organized crime, as typified by Al Capone (1899–1947). Arriving in U.S. society in the bottom layers, Italians lived in decaying, crime-ridden neighborhoods that became known as Little Italies. For a small segment of these immigrants, crime did serve as a significant means of upward social mobility. In effect, entering and leading criminal activity were one aspect of assimilation—admittedly not a positive one. Complaints linking ethnicity and crime actually began in colonial times with talk about the criminally inclined Irish and Germans, and it continues with contemporary stereotyping about such groups as Colombian drug dealers and Vietnamese street gangs. Yet the image of Italians as criminals has persisted from Prohibition Era gangsters to the view of mob families today. As noted earlier, it is not at all surprising that groups such as the Columbian Coalition have been organized to counter such negative images.

The fact that Italians are often characterized as criminal, even in the mass media, is another example of what we have termed respectable bigotry toward White ethnics. The persistence of linking Italians, or any other minority group, with crime is probably attributable to attempts to explain a problem by citing a single, naive cause: the presence of perceived undesirables (R. Alba 1985; D. Bell 1953; R. Daniels 1990; R. Gambino 1974a; P. Lupsha 1981; J. O'Kane 1992).

The immigration of Italians was slowed by the national origins system, described in the previous chapter. As Italian Americans settled permanently, the mutual-aid societies that had grown up in the 1920s to provide basic social services began to dissolve. More slowly, education came to be valued by Italian Americans as a means of upward mobility. Even becoming more educated, however, did not ward off prejudice. In 1930, for example, President Herbert Hoover rebuked Fiorello La Guardia, then an Italian American member of Congress from New York City, stating that "the Italians are predominantly our murderers and bootleggers" and recommending that La Guardia "go back to where you belong" because, "like a lot of other foreign spawn, you do not appreciate this country which supports you and tolerates you" (E. Baltzell 1964:30).

While U.S. troops, including 500,000 Italian Americans, battled Italy during World War II, some hatred and sporadic violence emerged against Italian Americans and their property. However, the actions were not limited to individual actions. They were even confined by the federal government in specific areas of California by virtue of their ethnicity alone, while 10,000 were relocated from coastal areas. In addition, 1,800 Italian Americans who were citizens of Italy were actually placed in an internment camp in Montana. The internees were eventually freed on Columbus Day 1942 as President Roosevelt lobbied the Italian American community to gain full support for the impending land invasion of Italy (B. Beyette 1995; J. Brooke 1997; S. Fox 1990).

In politics, Italian Americans have been quite a bit more successful, at least at the local level, where family and community ties can be translated into votes. However, political success did not come easily, because many Italian immigrants anticipated returning to their homeland and did not always take neighborhood politics seriously. It was even more difficult for Italian Americans to break into national politics: not until 1962 was an Italian American named to a cabinet-level position. Geraldine Ferraro's being named the Democratic vice-presidential candidate in 1984 was every bit as much an achievement for Italian Americans as it was for women (Cornacchia and Nelson 1992).

In 1990, people of Italian ancestry accounted for about 6 percent of the population, although less than 1 percent of them had actually been born in Italy. Italian Americans still remain the seventh-largest immigrant group. Just how ethnically conscious is the Italian American community? While the number is declining, 1.3 million Americans speak Italian at home; only Spanish, French, and German are spoken more within the family. For another 10 million Italian Americans, however, the language tie to their culture is absent, and depending on their degree of assimilation, only traces of symbolic ethnicity may remain.

Ethnicity, Religion, and Social Class

Generally, several social factors influence a person's identity and life chances. Pioneer sociologist Max Weber described **life chances** as people's opportunities to provide themselves with material goods, positive living conditions, and favorable life experiences. Religion, ethnicity, or both may affect life chances.

Religion and ethnicity do not necessarily operate together. Sometimes, they have been studied as if they were synonymous. Groups have been described as Irish Catholic, Swedish Lutheran, or Russian Jewish, as if religion and ethnicity had been merged into some type of national church. In the 1990s, the religion–ethnic tie took on new meaning as Latin American immigration invigorated the Roman Catholic Church nationwide, and West Indian immigration, particularly to New York City, brought new life to the Episcopal Church.

In the 1960s, sociologists felt that religion was more important than ethnicity in explaining behavior (Glazer and Moynihan 1963; W. Herberg 1983). They based this conclusion not on data, but on the apparently higher visibility of religion in society. Using survey data collected between 1963 and 1972, Andrew Greeley came to different conclusions (1974a; 1974b). He attempted to clarify the relative importance of religion and ethnicity by measuring four areas:

1. Personality characteristics, such as authoritarianism, anxiety, and conformity
2. Political participation, such as voting and civic activity
3. Civil liberties and civil rights, such as support for legislation
4. Family structure, such as the role of women, marital happiness, and sexual adjustment

The sample consisted of German and Irish Americans, both Protestant and Catholic. If religion was more significant than ethnicity, Protestants, whether of German or Irish ancestry, and Catholics, regardless of ethnicity, would have been similar in outlook. Conversely, if ethnicity was the key, then the similarities would be among the Germans of either faith or among the Irish as a distinct group.

On seventeen of the twenty-four items that made up the four areas measured, the differences were greater between German Catholics and Irish Catholics than between German Catholics and Protestants or between Irish Catholics and Protestants. Ethnicity was a stronger predictor of attitudes and beliefs than religion. In one area, political party allegiance, religion was more important, but this was the exception rather than the rule. (The significance of religion will be examined later in this chapter.)

In sum, Greeley found ethnicity to be generally more important than religion in predicting behavior. In reality, it is very difficult to separate the influences of religion and ethnicity on any one individual, but Greeley's research cautions against discounting the influence of ethnicity in favor of religion.

In addition, as already noted several times, social class is yet another significant factor. Sociologist Milton Gordon (1978) developed the term **ethclass** (ethnicity

Celebrating Eid al-Adha, a three-day feast of charity commemorating Abraham's willingness to sacrifice his son, worshipers at a neighborhood mosque in New York spill onto the sidewalk.

and class) to denote the importance of both factors. All three factors—religion, ethnicity, and class—combine to form one's identity, determine one's social behavior, and limit one's life chances. For example, in certain ethnic communities, friendships are limited, to a degree, to people who share the same ethnic background and social class. In other words, neither race and ethnicity nor religion nor class alone places one socially. One must consider several elements together as reflected in ethclass.

Religion in the United States

Divisive conflicts along religious lines are relatively muted in the United States compared with those in, say, Northern Ireland or the Middle East. Although not entirely absent, conflicts about religion in the United States seem to be overshadowed by civil religion. **Civil religion** refers to the religious dimension in American life that merges the state with sacred beliefs.

Sociologist Robert Bellah (1967) borrowed the phrase "civil religion" from the eighteenth-century French philosopher Jean-Jacques Rousseau to describe a significant phenomenon in the contemporary United States. Civil religion exists alongside established religious faiths and embodies a belief system incorporating all religions but not associated specifically with any one. It is the type of faith to which Presidents refer in inaugural speeches and to which American Legion posts and Girl Scout troops swear allegiance. In 1954, Congress added the phrase "under God" to the Pledge of Allegiance as a legislative recognition of religion's significance. Presidents of the United States beginning with Ronald Reagan and continuing through Bill Clinton typically conclude even their most straightforward speech with "God Bless the United States of America," which, in effect, evokes the civil religion of the nation.

Functionalists see civil religion as reinforcing central American values which may be more expressly patriotic than sacred in nature. Frequently, the mass media following major societal upheavals, from the 1995 Oklahoma City bombing to the 1998 issuance of the Starr Report listing impeachable offenses of President Clinton, shows church services with clergy praying and asking for national healing. Bellah sees no sign that the importance of civil religion has diminished in promoting collective identity, but he does acknowledge that it is more conservative than during the 1970s (see also R. Bellah 1968, 1970, 1989; M. Marty 1976, 1985; J. Mathisen 1989).

In the following section we will explore the diversity among the major Christian groups in the United States, such as Roman Catholics and Protestants. However, as already noted, significant numbers of people in the United States practice religions long established in other parts of the world, such as Islam, Hinduism, and Buddhism, to name the three major ones, in addition to Judaism, which is discussed in Chapter 13. The greater visibility of religious diversity in the United States is primarily the result of immigrants' bringing their religious faith with them and not assimilating to the dominant Christian rituals.

While courts have consistently ruled against prayer in public schools, the practice continues in the United States.

DIVERSITY AMONG ROMAN CATHOLICS

Social scientists have persistently tended to ignore the diversity within the Roman Catholic Church in the United States. Recent research has not sustained the conclusions that Roman Catholics are melding into a single group, following the traditions of the American Irish Catholic model, or all attending English-language churches. A recent finding of special interest is that religious behavior has been different for each ethnic group within the Roman Catholic Church. The Irish and the French Canadians left societies that were highly competitive both culturally and socially. Their religious involvement in the United States is more relaxed than it was in Ireland and Quebec. The influence of life in the United States, however, has increased German and Polish involvement in the Roman Catholic Church, while Italians have remained relatively inactive. Variations by ethnic background continue to emerge in studies of contemporary religious involvement in the Roman Catholic Church.

Since the mid–1970s, the Roman Catholic Church in America has received a significant number of new members from the Philippines, Southeast Asia, and particularly Latin America. While these new members have been a stabilizing force offsetting the loss of White ethnics, they have also challenged a church that for generations was dominated by Irish, Italian, and Polish parishes. Perhaps the most prominent subgroup in the Roman Catholic Church is the Hispanics, who now account for one-third of all Roman Catholic parishioners. Some Los Angeles churches in or near Hispanic neighborhoods must now schedule fourteen Masses each Sunday to accommodate the crowds of worshipers. According to a conservative estimate, Hispanics will constitute the majority of Roman Catholics nationwide by 2050 (J. Bonfante 1995).

The Roman Catholic Church, despite its ethnic diversity, has clearly been a powerful force in reducing the ethnic ties of its members, making it also a significant assimilating force. The irony in this role of Catholicism is that so many nineteenth-century Americans heaped abuse on Catholics in this country for allegedly being un-American and having a dual allegiance. The history of the Catholic church in the United States may be portrayed as a struggle within the membership between the Americanizers and the anti-Americanizers, with the former ultimately winning (A. Greeley 1977). Unlike the various Protestant churches that accommodated immigrants of a single nationality, the Roman Catholic Church had to Americanize a variety of linguistic and ethnic groups. The Catholic Church may have been the most potent assimilating force after the public school system (Fishman et al. 1966). Comparing the assimilationist goal of the Catholic Church and the present diversity in it leads us to the conclusion that ethnic diversity has continued in the Roman Catholic Church in spite of, and not because of, this religious institution.

DIVERSITY AMONG PROTESTANTS

Protestantism, like Catholicism, is often portrayed as a monolithic entity. Little attention is given to the doctrinal and attitudinal differences that sharply divide the various denominations, in both laity and clergy. Several studies, however, document the diversity. Unfortunately, many opinion polls and surveys are content to learn if a respondent is a Catholic or a Protestant or a Jew. Stark and Glock (1968), in their massive undertaking, found sharp differences in religious attitudes within Protestant churches. For example, 99 percent of Southern Baptists had no doubt that Jesus was the divine Son of God, as contrasted to only 40 percent of Congregationalists. Based on the data, Glock and Stark (1965) identified four "generic theological camps" among Protestants:

1. Liberals: Congregationalists, Methodists, and Episcopalians
2. Moderates: Disciples of Christ and Presbyterians
3. Conservatives: American Lutherans and American Baptists
4. Fundamentalists: Missouri Synod Lutherans, Southern Baptists, and various small sects

Roman Catholics generally hold religious beliefs similar to those of conservative Protestants, except on essentially Catholic issues such as papal infallibility (the authority of the spiritual role in all decisions regarding faith and morals). Whether or not there are four distinct camps is not important: the point is that the familiar practice of contrasting Roman Catholics and Protestants is clearly not productive. Some differences between Catholics and Protestants are inconsequential compared with the differences among Protestant sects.

Religious faiths may be distinguished by secular criteria as well as doctrinal issues. Research has consistently shown that denominations can be arranged in a hierarchy based on social class. As Figure 5.2 reveals, certain faiths, such as Episcopalian, Judaism, and Presbyterian, have a higher proportion of affluent members. Members of other faiths, including Baptists and Evangelicals, are comparatively poor. Of course, all Protestant groups draw members from each social stratum. Nonetheless, the social significance of these class differences is that religion becomes a mechanism for signaling social mobility. A person who is moving up in wealth and power may seek out a faith associated with a higher social ranking. Similar contrasts are shown in formal schooling in Figure 5.3.

Protestant faiths have been diversifying, and many of their members have been leaving them for churches that follow strict codes of behavior or fundamental interpretations of Biblical teachings. This trend is reflected in the decline of the five "mainline" churches: Baptist, Episcopalian, Lutheran, Methodist, and Presbyterian. In 1998, these faiths accounted for about 20 percent of total church membership, compared to 51 percent 25 years earlier. With a broader acceptance of new faiths and continuing immigration, it is unlikely that these mainline churches will regain their dominance (Gallup 1995; *Gallup Poll Monthly* 1998:41).

While Protestants may seem to define the civil religion and the "accepted" dominant orientation, some Christian faiths feel they too experience the discrimination usually associated with non-Christians such as Jews and Muslims. For example, the leadership of the military's chaplain corps is dominated by representatives of the liberal and moderate faiths even though 41 percent of the military are conservatives

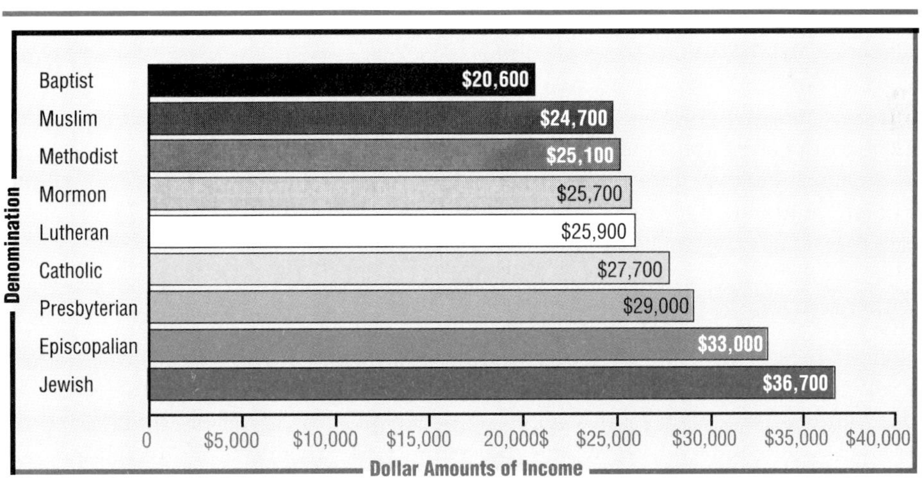

Figure 5.2 Income and Denominations

Denominations attract different income groups. All groups have both affluent and poor members, yet some have a higher proportion of members with high incomes, and others are comparatively poor.

Source: Barry Kosmin and Seymour P. Lachman, *One Nation Under God*. Copyright © 1993 by Barry Kosmin and Seymour P. Lachman. Reprinted by permission of Harmony Books, a division of Crown Publishers, Inc.

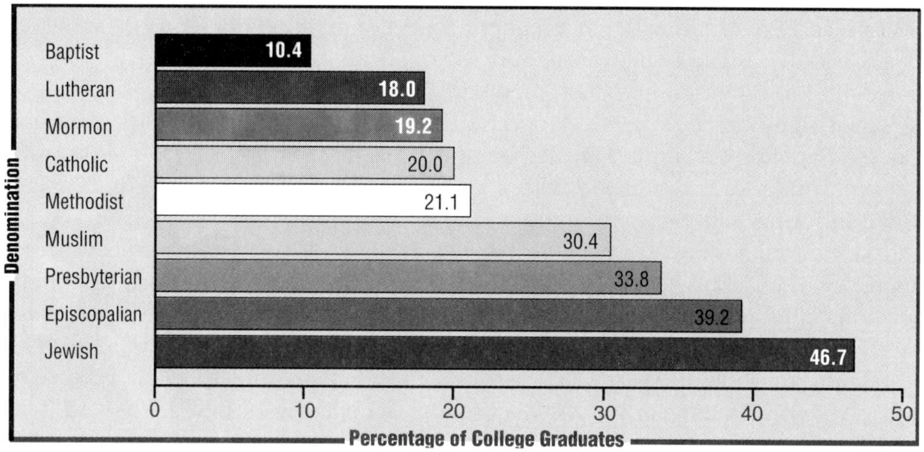

Figure 5.3 Education and Denominations
There are sharp differences in the proportion of college graduates by denomination.

Source: Barry Kosmin and Seymour P. Lachman, *One Nation Under God.* Copyright © 1993 by Barry Kosmin and Seymour P. Lachman. Reprinted by permission of Harmony Books, a division of Crown Publishers, Inc.

and fundamentalists. As another example of denominational discrimination, in 1998 the Southern Baptist Convention amended its basic theological statements of beliefs to include a strong statement on family life. However, the statement included a declaration that a woman should "submit herself graciously" to her husband's leadership. There were widespread attacks on this position, which many Baptists felt was inappropriate since they were offering guidance for their denomination's members. In some respects, Baptists felt this was a form of respectable bigotry. It was acceptable to attack them for their views on social issues even though such criticism would be much more muted for many more liberal faiths, which seem free to endorse abortion (T. Bowman 1998; G. Niebuhr 1998).

WOMEN AND RELIGION

Religious beliefs have often placed women in an exalted, but protected, position. As religions are practiced, this position has often meant being "protected" from becoming leaders. Perhaps the only major exception in the United States is the Christian Science church, in which the majority of practitioners and readers are women. Women may be evangelists, prophets, and even saints, but they find it difficult to enter the clergy within their own congregations.

Even today, the largest denomination in the United States, Roman Catholicism, does not permit women to be priests. A 1996 Gallup survey found that 65 percent of Roman Catholics in this country favor the ordination of women, compared to only 29 percent in 1974, but the church hierarchy has continued to maintain its long-standing requirement that priests be male (D. Briggs 1996).

The largest Protestant denomination, the Southern Baptist Convention, has voted against ordaining women (although some of its autonomous churches have women ministers). Other religious faiths that do not allow women clergy include the Lutheran Church—Missouri Synod, the Greek Orthodox Archdiocese of North and South America, the Orthodox Church in America, the Church of God in Christ, the Church of Jesus Christ of Latter-day Saints, and Orthodox Judaism.

Despite these restrictions, there has been a notable rise in female clergy in the last twenty years. The Bureau of the Census (1996a) shows that 6 percent of clergy were women in 1983, but that figure had increased to 11 percent in 1995. Increasingly, some branches of Protestantism and Judaism have been convinced that women have the right to become spiritual leaders. Yet a lingering question remains: once ordained, are these female ministers and rabbis necessarily accepted by congregations? Will they advance in their calling as easily as their male counterparts, or will they face blatant or subtle discrimination in their efforts to secure desirable posts within their faiths?

It is too early to offer any definitive answers to these questions, but thus far, women clearly continue to face lingering sexism after ordination. Evidence to date indicates that women find it more difficult than men to secure jobs in larger, more prestigious congregations. Although they may be accepted as junior clergy or as co-pastors, women may fail to receive senior clergy appointments. In both Reform and Conservative Judaism, women rabbis are rarely hired by the largest and best-known congregations. Consequently, women clergy in many denominations appear to be gathered at the low end of the pay scale and the hierarchy (*Religion Watch* 1995a).

Women clergy are aware that their struggle for equality is far from over. Reverend Joan Forsberg, an administrator at the Yale Divinity School, tells women graduates that they must view their efforts as part of a larger, long-term process of change. "Even if you don't see change overnight," she notes, "you must remind yourself that you are making a difference for future generations" (U. King 1995; E. Lehman 1993; W. Swatos 1994).

RELIGION AND THE U.S. SUPREME COURT

Religious pluralism owes its existence in the United States to the First Amendment declaration that: "Congress shall make no law respecting an establishment of religion, or prohibiting the free exercise thereof." The U.S. Supreme Court has consistently interpreted this wording to mean not that government should ignore religion but that it should follow a policy of neutrality to maximize religious freedom. For example, the government may not help religion by financing a new church building, but it also cannot obstruct religion by denying a church adequate police and fire protection. We will examine four issues that continue to require clarification: school prayer, secessionist minorities, creationism, and the public display of religious symbols.

Among the most controversial and continuing disputes has been whether prayer has a role in the schools. Many people were disturbed by the 1962 Supreme Court decision in *Engel* v. *Vitale* that disallowed an allegedly nondenominational prayer

SIGNE
PHILADELPHIA DAILY NEWS
Philadelphia
USA

drafted for use in the New York public schools. The prayer was: "Almighty God, we acknowledge our dependence upon Thee, and we beg Thy blessings upon us, our parents, our teachers, and our country." Subsequent decisions overturned state laws requiring Bible reading in public schools, laws requiring recitation of the Lord's Prayer, and laws permitting a daily one-minute period of silent meditation or prayer.

What about prayers at public gatherings? In 1992, the Supreme Court ruled 5-4 in *Lee* v. *Weisman* that prayer at a junior high school graduation in Providence, Rhode Island, violated the U.S. Constitution's mandate of separation of church and state. A rabbi had given thanks to God in his invocation. The district court suggested that the invocation would have been acceptable without that reference. The Supreme Court did not agree with the school board that a prayer at a graduation was not coercive. The Court did say in its opinion that it was acceptable for a student speaker voluntarily to say a prayer at such a program.

Despite such judicial pronouncements, children in many public schools in the United States are led in regular prayer recitation or Bible reading. Many communities believe that schools should transmit this aspect of the dominant culture of the United States by encouraging prayer. In a 1985 survey (the most recent available), 15 percent of public school administrators (including 42 percent of school administrators in the South) reported that prayers were said in at least one of their schools. Moreover, according to a 1995 survey, 71 percent of adults in the United States favored a constitutional amendment that would permit organized prayer in public schools (J. Bacon 1987; Gallup and Moore 1995).

Among religious groups are several that have been in legal and social conflict with the rest of society. Some can be called **secessionist minorities,** in that they reject both assimilation and coexistence in some form of cultural pluralism. The Amish are one such group that comes into conflict with outside society because of their beliefs and way of life. The Old Order Amish shun most modern conveniences, and later in this chapter we will consider them as a case study of maintaining a lifestyle dramatically different from that of larger society.

Are there limits to the free exercise of religious rituals by secessionist minorities? Today, tens of thousands of members of Native American religions believe that the ingestion of the powerful drug peyote is a sacrament and that those who partake of peyote will enter into direct contact with God. In 1990, the Supreme Court ruled that prosecuting people who use illegal drugs as part of a religious ritual is not a violation of the First Amendment guarantee of religious freedom. The case arose because Native Americans were dismissed from their jobs for the religious use of peyote and were then refused unemployment benefits by the State of Oregon's employment division. In 1991, however, Oregon enacted a new law permitting the sacramental use of peyote by Native Americans (*New York Times* 1991).

In another ruling on religious rituals, in 1993, the Supreme Court unanimously overturned a local ordinance in Florida that banned ritual animal sacrifice. The high court held that this law violated the free-exercise rights of adherents of the Santeria religion, in which the sacrifice of animals (including goats, chickens, and other birds) plays a central role. The same year Congress passed the Religious Freedom Restoration Act that said the government may not enforce laws that "substantially burden" the exercise of religion. Presumably this action will give religious groups more flexibility in practicing their faith. However, many local and state officials are concerned that the law has led to unintended consequences, such as forcing states to accommodate prisoner's requests for questionable religious activities or to permit a church to expand into a historic district in defiance of local laws. A Supreme Court clarification is expected to try to unravel these complex issues (L. Greenhouse 1993a, 1996b).

The third area of contention has been whether the Biblical account of creation should be or must be present in school curricula and whether this account should receive the same emphasis as scientific theories. In the famous "monkey trial" of 1925, Tennessee schoolteacher John Scopes was found guilty of teaching the scientific theory of evolution in public schools. Since then, however, Darwin's evolutionary theories have been presented in public schools with little reference to the Biblical account in Genesis. People who support the literal interpretation of the Bible, commonly known as **creationists**, have formed various organizations to crusade for creationist treatment in American public schools and universities.

In a 1987 Louisiana case, *Edwards* v. *Aguillard,* the Supreme Court ruled that states may not require the teaching of creationism alongside evolution in public schools if the primary purpose of such legislation is to promote a religious viewpoint.

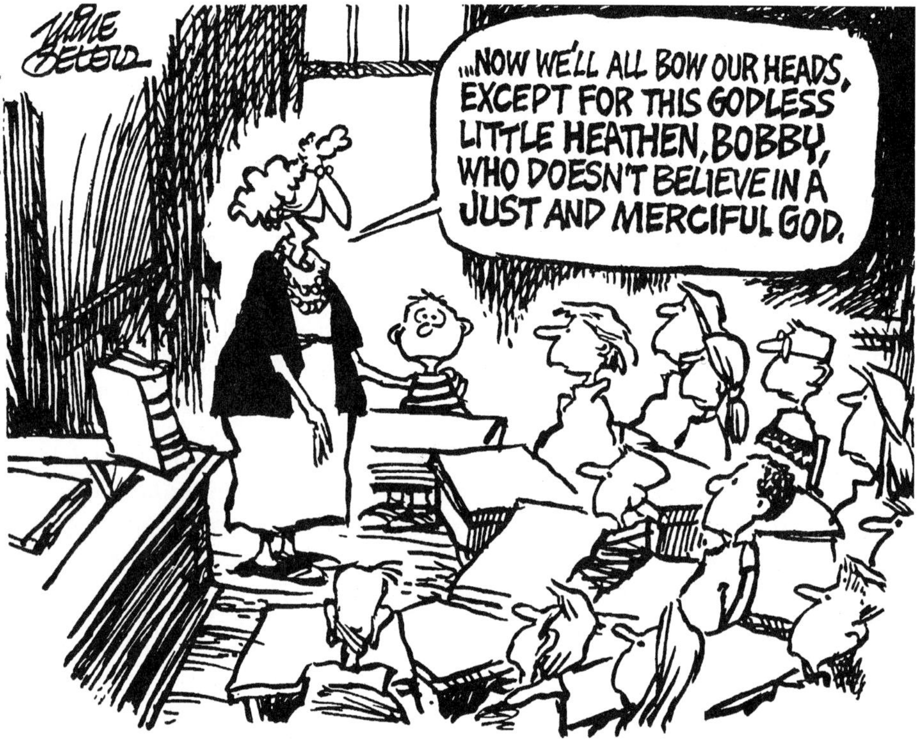

Nevertheless, the teaching of evolution and creationism has remained a controversial issue in many communities across the United States (P. Applebome 1996; Chalfant et al. 1994; S. Taylor 1987).

The fourth area of contention has been a battle over public displays that depict symbols or seem associated with a religion. Can manger scenes be erected on public property? Do people have a right to be protected from large displays such as a cross or a star atop a water tower overlooking an entire town? In a series of decisions in the 1980s through to 1995, the Supreme Court ruled that tax-supported religious displays on public government property may be successfully challenged but are not permissible if they are made more secular. Displays that combine a crèche, the Christmas manger scene depicting the birth of Jesus, or the Hanukkah menorah and also include Frosty the Snowman or even Christmas trees have been ruled secular. These decisions have been dubbed "the plastic reindeer rules." In 1995, the Court clarified the issue by stating that privately sponsored religious displays may be allowed on public property if other forms of expression are permitted in the same location. The final judicial word has not been heard, and all these rulings should be viewed as tentative because the Court cases have been decided by close votes and changes in the Supreme Court composition may alter the outcome of future cases (R. Bork 1995; M. Hirsley 1991; T. Mauro 1995).

Limits of Religious Freedom: The Amish

The Amish offer an interesting case study of a religious group that has endured despite challenges from both within and outside the close-knit community. They are members of a conservative Christian group in North America, primarily members of the Old Order Amish Mennonite Church. They originated in Europe as followers of Jakob Ammann, a seventeenth-century Mennonite elder whose teachings caused controversy and internal splits during the years 1693–1697 among the Mennonites in Switzerland, Alsace, and south Germany.

The Amish began migrating to North America early in the eighteenth century and settled first in eastern Pennsylvania, where a large settlement is still found. Those who continued the characteristic lifestyle of the Amish are primarily members of the Old Order Amish Mennonite Church. In the late twentieth century there were about fifty Old Order Amish settlements in the United States and Canada; the largest were located in Pennsylvania, Ohio, Indiana, Iowa, Illinois, and Kansas. Estimates place their number at about 80,000, with approximately 75 percent living in three states—Ohio, Pennsylvania, and Indiana.

Amish practice self-segregation, living in settlements divided into church districts that are autonomous congregations composed of about seventy-five baptized members. If the district becomes much larger it is again divided, because the members meet in each other's homes. There are no church buildings. Amish homes are large, with the main floor often having removable walls so a household can take their periodic turn hosting the Sunday service (Linder 1998).

Each Amish district has a bishop, two to four preachers, and an elder; but there are no general conferences, mission groups, or cooperative agencies. The Amish differ little from the Mennonites in formal religious doctrine. Holy Communion is celebrated twice each year, and both groups practice washing of feet. Adults are baptized when they are admitted to formal membership in the church at about age 17 to 20. Old Order Amish services are conducted in German with a mixture of English, commonly known as Pennsylvania Dutch (from *Deutsch,* the German word for "German").

The Amish are best known for their severely plain clothing and their nonconformist way of life. Sociologists sometimes use the term "secessionist minorities" to refer to groups like the Amish who reject assimilation and practice coexistence or pluralism with the rest of society primarily on their own terms. While Jakob Amman is not a central figure among the Amish today, the practice of *Meidung*, or shunning, persists. Sociologists view it as central to the Amish system of social control. The social norms of this secessionist minority that have evolved over the years are known as the *Ordnung*. These "understandings" specify the color and style of clothing, color and style of buggies, the use of horses for fieldwork, the use of the Pennsylvania Dutch dialect, worship services in the homes, unison singing without instruments, and marriage within the church, to name a few.

Amish people are distinctive in their appearance. Clothing serves as an important source of group identity. The men wear broad-brimmed black hats, beards—but not mustaches—and home-made plain clothes fastened with hooks and eyes instead of buttons. The women wear bonnets, long full dresses with capes over the shoulders, shawls, and black shoes and stockings. No jewelry of any kind (except for wedding rings) is worn, and no cosmetics are used. Such personal items are viewed as not functional and thus encourage a needless focusing on oneself rather than the larger Amish community and especially on God. This cultural nonconformity is thought by the Amish to be obedience to Biblical strictures, but it is primarily the continuance of seventeenth-century European rural costume. The Amish also shun telephones and electric lights and drive horses and buggies rather than automobiles. The *Ordnung* also prohibits filing a lawsuit, entering military service, divorce, using air transportation, and even wall-to-wall carpeting. They are generally considered excellent farmers, but they often refuse to use modern farm machinery. Concessions have been made but do vary from one Amish settlement to another. Among common exceptions to the *Ordnung* is the use of chemical fertilizers, insecticides, and pesticides, the use of indoor bathroom facilities, and modern medical and dental practice.

Conversely, larger society has made concessions to the Amish to facilitate their lifestyle. For example, the 1972 United States Supreme Court, in *Yoder* v. *Wisconsin,* allowed Wisconsin Amish to escape prosecution from laws that required parents to send their children to school to age 18. Amish education ends at about the age of 13, since the community feels their members have received all the schooling necessary to prosper as Amish people. Associated with this, states waive for the Amish certification requirements for their teaching staff (who are other Amish people), minimum wage requirements for the teachers, and school building requirements.

The Amish do not totally reject social change. For example, until the late 1960s, church members could be excommunicated for being employed in other than agricultural pursuits. While you will not find Amish computer programmers, there are Amish engaged as blacksmiths, harness makers, buggy repairers, and carpenters. Non-Amish often make use of these craftsmen as well.

The movement by the Amish into other occupations is sometimes a source of tension with larger society, or the "English," as the Amish refer to non-Amish people. Conflict theorists observe that as long as the Amish remained totally apart from dominant society in the United States, they experienced relatively little hostility. As they entered the larger economic sector, however, intergroup tensions developed in the form of growing prejudice. The Amish today may underbid their competitors. The Amish entry into the commercial marketplace has also strained the church's traditional teaching on litigation and insurance—both of which are to be avoided. Mutual assistance has been the historical path taken, but that does not always mesh well with the "modern" businessperson. Following legal action taken on their behalf, Amish businesses typically have been allowed to be exempt from paying Social Security and workers' compensation—another sore point with "English" competitors.

The Amish entrepreneur represents an interesting variation of the typical ethnic businessperson one might encounter in a Chinatown, for example. Research on ethnic businesses often cites discrimination against minorities and immigrants as a prime force prodding the development of minority enterprises. The Amish represent a very different case, because it is their own restrictions on education, factory work, and certain occupations that have propelled them into becoming small business owners. However, stratification is virtually absent among the Old Order Amish. The notion of ethclass would have no meaning, as the Amish truly regard one another as equal.

Children are not sent to high schools. This practice had caused the Amish some difficulty because of compulsory school attendance laws, and some Amish parents have gone to jail rather than allow their children to go to high school. Eventually, as noted earlier, the Supreme Court, in *Yoder* v. *Wisconsin*, upheld a lower court's decision that a Wisconsin compulsory-education law violated the Amish right to religious freedom. Not all court rulings have been friendly to Amish efforts to avoid the practices and customs of the English. In another court case, the effort by the Amish to avoid using the legally mandated orange triangles for marking slow-moving vehicles (such as their buggies) was rejected. If you travel through Amish areas, you can now see their horse-drawn buggies displaying this one symbol of modernity.

A growing area of Amish–English legal clashes is over the custom of young Amish children working as laborers. Amish families in western and central Pennsylvania in 1998 protested the federal government's enforcement of labor laws that are intended to protect children from workplace hazards. The Amish are turning to new businesses, such as sawmills and wood shops, as their available farmland begins to disappear. That means more children on the shop floor. The Amish contend that their religious and cultural traditions hold that children should work, but the U.S. Labor Department takes a different view. From 1996 to 1998, the government leveled tens of thousands of dollars in fines against Amish companies for using underage workers. The Department of Labor's view is that there is no basis in the law for different treatment of people based on race, gender, ethnic origin, religion, or cultural background. The Amish counter that letting children work alongside their fathers instills core values of hard work, diligence, cooperation, and responsibility, values they say are central to their faith. English businesses see this underage employment as another form of unfair competition by the Amish. The Amish are hoping to work with the Labor Department to hammer out a legislative compromise to the child labor issue, perhaps allowing some children on the shop floor doing limited work away from dangerous tools.

The Old Order Amish have developed a pluralistic position that has become increasingly difficult to maintain as their numbers grow and as they enter the economy in competition with the English or non-Amish (B. Dart 1998; D. Kraybill 1989; Kraybill and Nolt 1995; Public Broadcasting System 1998).

CONCLUSION

Considering ethnicity and religion reinforces our understanding of the patterns of intergroup relations first presented in Chapter 1. Figure 5.4 shows the rich variety of relationships as defined by people's ethnic and religious identity.

Any study of life in the United States, but especially one focusing on dominant and subordinate groups, cannot ignore religion and ethnicity. The two are closely related, as certain religious faiths predominate in certain nationalities. Both religious activity and

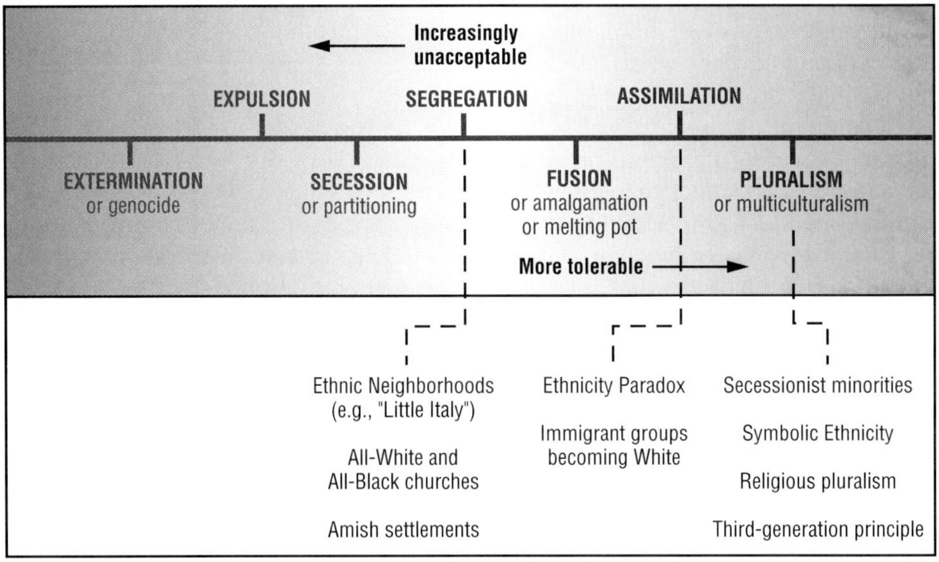

Figure 5.4 Intergroup Relations Continuum

interest by White ethnics into their past heritage continue to be prominent features of the contemporary scene. People have been and continue to be ridiculed or deprived of opportunities solely because of their ethnic or religious affiliation. To get a true picture of a person's place in society, we need to consider both ethnicity and social class (or what has been termed ethclass) in association with their religious identification.

The issue of the persistence of ethnicity is an intriguing one. Some people may only casually exhibit their ethnicity and practice what has been termed *symbolic ethnicity*. However, can people immerse themselves in their ethnic culture without having society punishing them for their will to be different? The tendency to put down White ethnics through respectable bigotry continues. Despite this intolerance, ethnicity remains a viable source of identity for many citizens today. There is also the ethnicity paradox, which finds that practicing one's ethnic heritage often strengthens people and allows them to move successfully into the larger society.

The issue of religious expression also raises a variety of intriguing questions. Women, in particular, are at a disadvantage in organized religion. How might this change in decades ahead? How will the courts and society resolve the issues of religious freedom? This is a particularly important issue in such areas as school prayer, secessionist minorities, creationism, and public religious displays. Some examination of religious ties is fundamental to completing an accurate picture of a person's social identity.

Ethnicity and religion are a basic part of today's social reality and of each individual's identity. The emotions, disputes, and debate over religion and ethnicity in the United States are powerful indeed.

KEY TERMS

civil religion 152
creationists 159
denomination 138
ethclass 152
ethnicity paradox 143
life chances 150
principle of third-generation interest 142
respectable bigotry 145
secessionist minority 159
symbolic ethnicity 143

REVIEW QUESTIONS

1. In what respect are the ethnic and religious diversity of the United States related to each other?
2. Is assimilation automatic within any given ethnic group?
3. Can "blaming the victims" be applied to White ethnic groups?
4. To what extent has a non-Christian tradition been developing in the United States?
5. How have court rulings affected religion?

CRITICAL THINKING

1. When do you see ethnicity become more apparent? When does it appear to occur only in response to other people advancing their own ethnicity? From these situations, how can ethnic identity be both positive and perhaps counterproductive or even destructive?
2. Why do you think we are so often reluctant to show our religion to others?
3. How does religion reflect the conservative–liberal position on social issues? Consider how religious groups actually provide services for the homeless, the need for child care, acceptance or rejection of gays and lesbians, and a woman's right to terminate a pregnancy versus the fetus's right to survive?

INTERNET EXERCISES

1. The experiences of Italian Americans highlight many of the points made in Chapter 5 regarding prejudice toward ethnic groups. Visit *Una Storia Segreta: When Italian-Americans Were "Enemy Aliens,"* at (http://www.io.com/~segreta) for more information on the treatment of this group during World War II. What restrictions and exclusions did Italian Americans face? What was internment and forced relocation like? In what other ways were the everyday lives and rights of Italian Americans violated during the war? Which other ethnic

groups also faced such challenges during wartime? Which of the personal stories presented on the homepage affected you the most? Why?

2. The connection between religion, ethnicity, history, and constitutional freedoms can be found at *First Amendment Cyber-Tribune: Religious Liberty* (http://w3.trib.com/FACT/1st.relig.liberty.html). Here you will find links to government documents, presidential memorandums, and social commentary on freedom of religious expression for people of different faiths and ethnicities. In what ways are Native Americans' religious freedoms protected? What are the President's views on the freedom of religion, and what are some of the guidelines, laws, and executive orders enacted to protect our rights? What connections do all these documents help you make regarding ethnic background and religious membership? Be sure to read some of the historical writings provided, such as those by John Locke, James Madison, and Thomas Jefferson. Which of the concerns and issues raised back then are still important today? Why?

FOR FURTHER INFORMATION

Richard D. Alba. *Ethnic Identity: The Transformation of White America*. New Haven, CT: Yale University Press, 1990.

An overview of the changing role of ethnicity among European Americans, with particular attention to Italian Americans.

Donna R. Gabaccia. *We Are What We Eat. Ethnic Food and the Making of America*. Cambridge, MA: Harvard University Press, 1998.

An insightful look at how food defines ethnic groups and how ethnicity defines food. Also looks at the important role of ethnic entrepreneurs.

William M. Kephart and William M. Zellner. *Extraordinary Groups: The Sociology of Unconventional Life-Styles*, 6th ed. New York: St. Martin's Press, 1999.

Kephart and Zellner bring together for the first time in a sociological treatment the Romani (commonly known as the Gypsies), the Amish, the Oneida community, Hasidic Jews, the Church of Christ, Scientist, the Father Divine Movement, the Jehovah's Witnesses, and the Mormons.

Barry A. Kosmin and Seymour P. Lachman. *One Nation Under God: Religion in Contemporary American Society*. New York: Harmony Books, 1993.

An overview of religion in the United States that draws upon the National Survey of Religious Identification.

Annalee Newitz and Matt Wray, eds. *White Trash: Race and Class in America*. London: Routledge, 1997.

This collection is devoted to exploring stereotypes of poor Whites and compares these images with the realities of life under conditions of economic hardship.

David R. Roediger, ed. *Black on White: Black Writers on What It Means to Be White*. New York: Schocken Books, 1998.

This anthology includes both historical and more contemporary essays including writings by W. E. B. DuBois, Amiri Baraka, Toni Morrison, Bell Hooks, and Ralph Ellison.

JOURNALS

Among the journals that focus on issues of race and ethnicity is *Ethnic and Racial Studies* (1978). The sociological study of religion is reflected in the *Journal for the Scientific Study of Religion* (founded in 1961), *Religion Watch* (1986), *Review of Religious Research* (1958), *Social Compass* (1954), and *Sociology of Religion* (formerly *Sociological Analysis,* 1940). The monthly newsletter *Emerging Trends,* first published by the Princeton Religion Research Center in 1979, provides the latest data on religious life.

6

The Native Americans

CHAPTER OUTLINE

HIGHLIGHTS

The original inhabitants of North America were the first to be subordinated by Europeans. Those Native Americans who survived contact with the White people were usually removed, often far away, from their ancestral homes. The U.S. government weakened tribal institutions through a succession of acts, beginning with the Allotment Act of 1884. Even efforts to strengthen tribal autonomy, such as the 1934 Reorganization Act, did so by encouraging Native Americans to adopt White society's way of life. The modern period of Native American–White relations is much the same, as shown by such measures as the Termination Act and the Employment Assistance Program. Today, the pan-Indian movements speak for a diverse Native American people with many needs: settlement of treaty violations, economic development, improved educational programs, effective health care, religious and spiritual freedom, control over natural resources, and greater self-rule.

The computer says "Zik" followed by "Cax sep." This is not the latest space adventure from the local arcade but the words for "squirrel" and "eagle" as spoken by a Ho-chunk elder. Preschoolers gather around the computer at a Head Start program in Wisconsin, where Ho-chunk children learn the language of their tribe. The Ho-chunk, formerly known as the Winnebago tribe, are using modern technology to keep their language and therefore their culture alive. The challenge is immense, as Two Bears, an anthropologist who works at the tribe's cultural center, observes:

> *There was a whole generation by the 1980s that didn't know a word. Turning that around will be a long process—we figure it'll take two years to advance our language curriculum up one grade level in the schools that Ho-chunk kids attend. (P. Salopek 1995:2)*

The concern of the Ho-chunk tribal elders is faced by most of the tribes in the United States. It is estimated that children are actively learning only 20 of the surviving 175 Native American languages. While much of the country debates the need for a larger percentage of new immigrants to master English, the first Americans' major concern is maintaining the tie to their linguistic past and making it a viable part of the present. In Chicago, adult students gather to learn the languages of their tribes—Kalota and Ojibwee—while in Window Rock, Arizona, the 1996 Super Bowl was broadcast in Navajo for the first time. All these efforts and many more are aimed at maintaining tribal identity while being members of American society (J. Brooke 1998; G. Mitchel 1996).

Although our focus in this chapter is on the Native American experience in the United States, the pattern of land seizure, subjugation, some assimilation, and significant resistance to domination has been repeated with indigenous people in nations throughout the world. Indeed, in Chapter 15 we will consider the experiences of the tribal people in Mexico and Canada. Another native people, Hawaiians, that fell under political, economic, and cultural control of the United States is considered in Chapter 12. Indigenous peoples on almost every continent are familiar with the patterns of subjugation and the pressure to assimilate. So widespread is this oppression that the United Nations (1997), and even its precursor organization the League of Nations, has repeatedly considered this issue.

Native American preschool children are taught their tribal language in the Ho-chunk Preschool Head Start program in Wisconsin.

The common-use term *American Indians* tells us more about the Europeans who explored North America than it does about the native people. The label reflects the initial explorers' confusion in believing that they had arrived in "the Indies" of the Asian continent. However, reference to the diversity of tribal groups either by *American Indians* or *Native Americans* comes as a result of the forced subordination to the dominant group (Rakow and Wickwitz 1998:105).

The Census Bureau estimated in 1997 that there were about 2.3 million Native Americans (including the Inuit and Aleut), 22 percent of them living on reservations. Over twenty cities have at least 10,000 American Indians, with the largest numbers in Los Angeles, Tulsa, New York City, Oklahoma City, and San Francisco. The Cherokee, followed by the Navajo, Chippewa, and Sioux, are the largest tribes today. Nationally, the most, 13 percent, are in Oklahoma, followed by Arizona, California, New Mexico, and Alaska. The present Native American population reflects a significant growth in the last ten to twenty years, primarily because of Native Americans' increased willingness to claim their heritage (Bureau of the Census 1997i; M. Snipp 1997).

Early European Contacts

The Native Americans have been misunderstood and ill treated by their conquerors for several centuries. Assuming that he had reached the Indies, Christopher Columbus called them "people of India." The European immigrants who followed Columbus did not understand them any more than the Native Americans comprehended their invaders. But the Europeans had superior weaponry and the diseases they brought wiped out huge numbers of indigenous people. Thus, it was the mistakes and misunderstandings of the English, French, Spanish, and Portuguese that prevailed.

The first explorers of the Western Hemisphere came long before Columbus and Leif Ericsson. The ancestors of today's Native Americans were hunters in search of wild game, including mammoths and long-horned bison. For thousands of years, these people spread through the Western Hemisphere, adapting to its many physical environments. Hundreds of cultures evolved, including the complex societies of the Maya, Inca, and Aztec (V. Deloria 1995).

It is beyond the scope of this book to describe the many tribal cultures of North America, let alone the ways of life of Native Americans in Central and South America and the islands of the Caribbean. We must appreciate that the term *Indian culture* is a convenient way of glossing over the diversity of cultures, languages, religions, kinship systems, and political organizations that existed—and in many instances, remain—among the peoples referred to collectively as Native Americans or American Indians. For example, in 1500, an estimated 700 distinct languages were spoken in the area north of Mexico. For simplicity's sake we will refer to these many cultures as Native American, but we must be always mindful of the differences this term conceals. Similarly, we will refer to non-Native Americans as White people, although in this context, this term encompasses many groups, including African Americans and Hispanics in some instances (J. Schwartz 1994; W. Swagerty 1983).

Columbus commented in his diary, "It appears to me that the people [of the New World] are ingenious and would be good servants. . . . These people are very unskilled in arms. . . . With fifty men they could all be subjected to do all that one wishes" (*Akwesasne Notes* 1972:22). The words of the first European explorer were prophetic. The period between initial European contact and the formation of the United States was characterized by cultural and physical conflict between Native Americans and Whites.

The number of Native Americans north of the Rio Grande, estimated at about 10 million in 1500, gradually decreased as their food sources disappeared or they fell victim to diseases such as measles, smallpox, and influenza. By 1800 the Native American population was about 600,000, and by 1900 it had been reduced to less than 250,000. This loss of human life can only be judged as catastrophic. The United States does not bear total responsibility. The pattern had been well established by the early Spaniards in the Southwest and by the French and English colonists who sought to gain control of the eastern seaboard. As Figure 6.1 reminds us, there were many tribal nations here before European contact (R. Edmunds 1995).

Native Americans did have warfare among tribes, which presumably reduces the guilt for European-initiated warfare. However, their conflicts differed significantly from those of the conquerors. The Europeans launched large campaigns against the tribes, resulting in mass mortality. In contrast, in the Americas, the tribes restricted warfare to specific campaigns designed for very specific purposes, such as recapturing some resource or avenging some loss.

Not all the initial contacts led to deliberate loss of life. Some missionaries traveled well in advance of settlements in efforts to Christianize the Native Americans before they came into contact with other, less "Christian" Europeans. Fur trappers, vastly outnumbered by Native Americans, were forced to learn their customs, but these trappers established routes of commerce that more and more Whites were to follow (C. Snipp 1989; W. Swagerty 1983; R. Thornton 1991).

Gradually, the policies directed from Europe toward the indigenous peoples of North America resembled the approach described in the world systems theory. As introduced in Chapter 1, the **world systems theory** takes the view that the global economic system is divided between nations that control wealth and those that provide natural resources and labor. The indigenous peoples and, more important to the Europeans, the land they occupied were regarded as targets of exploitation by Spain, England, France, Portugal, and other nations with experience as colonizers in Africa and Asia (Chase-Dunn and Hall 1998).

Treaties and Warfare

The United States formulated a policy during the nineteenth century toward Native Americans that followed the precedents established during the colonial period. The government policy was not to antagonize the Native Americans unnecessarily. Yet, if the needs of tribes interfered with the needs, or even the whims, of Whites, Whites were to have precedence. For example, the exploits of the Forty-Niners, the nineteenth-century gold miners in northern California, have been long glorified.

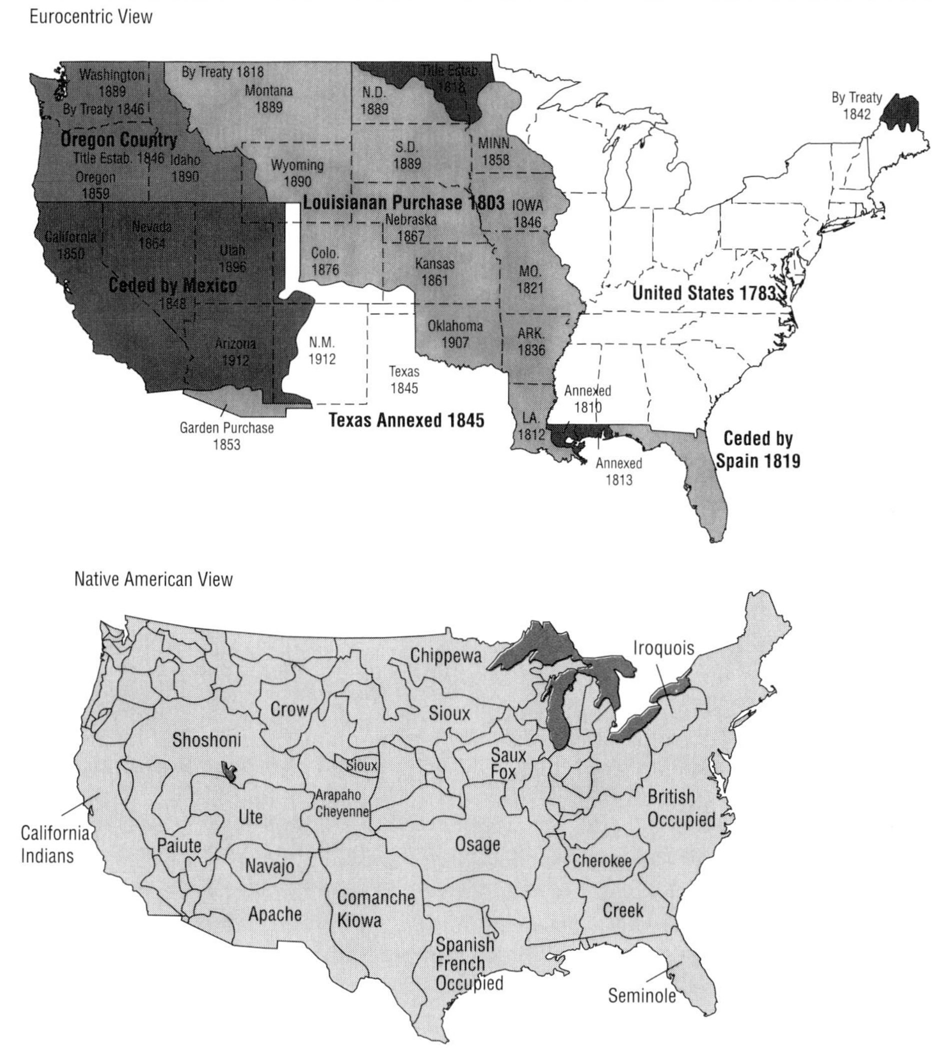

Figure 6.1 Eurocentric and Native American Views of Expansionism
Students are typically presented with a view that the United States gained its lands through settlement and from Mexico, Spain, France, and Great Britain. This depiction glosses over the land held by tribal groups.
Source: From Atlas of American History, 1993. Maps © by Rand McNally R.L. #99–S72.

However, the areas they entered near Sacramento were inhabited by 150,000 native people. Authorities offered bounties to the settlers for the heads of American Indians, and the state spent about $1 million to reimburse individuals for the bullets used to shoot them. Within twenty-five years, the native population had plummeted to about 30,000 (Ybarra 1996).

By this time, the tribes were viewed as separate nations, to be dealt with by treaties arrived at through negotiations with the federal government. Fair-minded as that policy might seem, it was clear from the very beginning that the White people's government would deal harshly with the tribal groups that refused to agree to treaties. Federal relations with the Native Americans were the responsibility of the secretary of war. Consequently, when the Bureau of Indian Affairs was created in 1824 to coordinate the government's relations with the tribes, it was placed in the War Department. The government's primary emphasis was on maintaining peace and friendly relations along the frontier. Nevertheless, as settlers moved the frontier westward, they encroached more and more on land that Native Americans had inhabited for centuries.

The Indian Removal Act, passed in 1830, called for the relocation of all eastern tribes across the Mississippi River. The act was very popular with Whites because it opened more land to settlement through annexation of tribal land. Almost all Whites felt that the Native Americans had no right to block progress, defining *progress* as movement by White society. Among the largest groups relocated were the five tribes of the Creek, Choctaw, Chickasaw, Cherokee, and Seminole, who were resettled in what is now Oklahoma. The movement, lasting more than a decade, has been called the Trail of Tears because the tribes left their ancestral lands under the harshest conditions. Poor planning, corrupt officials, little attention to those ill from a variety of epidemics, and inadequate supplies characterized the forced migration (Deloria and Lytle 1983).

The Removal Act not only totally disrupted Native American culture, it didn't move the tribes far enough or fast enough to stay out of the path of the ever-advancing White settlers. Following the Civil War, settlers moved westward at an unprecedented pace. The federal government negotiated with the many tribes but primarily enacted legislation that affected them with minimal consultation. The government's first priority was almost always to allow the settlers to live and work regardless of Native American claims.

THE CASE OF THE SIOUX

The nineteenth century was devastating for every Native American tribe in the areas claimed by the United States. No tribe was the same after federal policy touched it. The treatment of the Great Sioux Nation was especially cruel and remains fresh in the minds of tribal members even today.

In an effort to safeguard White settlers, the United States signed the Fort Laramie Treaty of 1868 with the Sioux, then under the leadership of Red Cloud. The government agreed to keep Whites from hunting or settling on the newly established Great Sioux Reservation, which included all of the land that is now South Dakota west of the Missouri River. In exchange, the Sioux relinquished most of the remaining land they occupied at that time. The first few years saw relative peace, except for some raids by warrior bands under the leadership of the medicine man Sitting Bull. Red Cloud even made a much-publicized trip to Washington and New York in 1870.

A flood of White people eventually entered the Sioux territory, spurred on by Colonel George Custer's exaggerated 1874 reports of gold in the Black Hills. Hostilities followed, and bands of Native Americans were ordered to move during the winter, when travel was impossible. When the Sioux failed to move, Custer moved in to pacify them and the neighboring Cheyenne. Relying on Crow scouts, Custer underestimated the strength of the Sioux warriors under the leadership of Crazy Horse. The ensuing Battle of the Little Big Horn in 1876 was the last great Sioux victory. After the battle, the large encampment of warriors scattered throughout the plains into small bands, which were defeated one by one by a Congress and an Army more determined than ever to subdue the Sioux.

In 1876, the Sioux reluctantly sold the Black Hills and agreed to the reduction of the Great Sioux Reservation to five much smaller ones. The Sioux, unable to hunt game as they traditionally had, found life unbearable on the reservation. They sought escape through the supernatural—the Ghost Dance. The Ghost Dance was a religion that included dances and songs proclaiming the return of the buffalo and the resurrection of dead ancestors in a land free of the White people. The religion soon became what social scientists call a **millenarian movement**—a movement founded on the belief that a cataclysmic upheaval would occur in the immediate future, followed by collective salvation. The movement originated among the Paiutes of Nevada and, ironically, spread northward to the Plains Indians via the cornerstone of the government's assimilationist policy: the schools. The English that Native Americans learned in the mission or government schools gave them the means to overcome the barriers of tribal languages and communicate with one another. By 1890, about 65 percent of the tribes in the West, according to sociologist Russell Thornton (1981), were involved in this movement.

A U.S. Army photograph shows the burial of the Sioux dead at Wounded Knee, South Dakota, in 1890.

From a functionalist perspective, this millenarian movement can be viewed as a means of coping with the domination of White intruders. Although the Ghost Dance was essentially harmless to Whites, they nevertheless feared that the new tribal solidarity encouraged by the movement would lead to renewed warfare. As a result, more troops were summoned to areas where the Ghost Dance had become popular.

In late December 1890, anticipating that a massive Ghost Dance would be staged, a cavalry division arrived at an encampment of Teton Sioux at Wounded Knee Creek on the Pine Ridge, South Dakota, reservation. When the soldiers began to disarm the warriors, a random shot was fired at the soldiers, touching off a close-range battle. The cavalry then turned its artillery on men, women, and children. Approximately 300 Sioux and 25 government soldiers were killed in the ensuing fighting, which is now referred to as the Battle of Wounded Knee. One Sioux witness later recalled, "We tried to run, but they shot us like we were a buffalo. I know there are some good white people, but the soldiers must be mean to shoot children and women" (D. Brown 1971:417).

For the federal government, what it considered the Indian problem remained. Despite the effects of disease and warfare, nearly 250,000 Indians still lived, according to the 1890 census. The reservation system constructed in the last decades of the nineteenth century to provide settlements for Native American peoples has formed the basis of the relationship of Native Americans to the government from then until the present.

Ruling the Native Americans

Along with the military defeat of the tribes, the federal government tried to limit the functions of tribal leaders. If tribal institutions were weakened, it was felt, the Native Americans would assimilate more rapidly. The government's intention to merge the various tribes into White society was unmistakably demonstrated in the 1887 Dawes, or General Allotment, Act. This failure to assist Native American people was followed by a somewhat more admirable effort—the Indian Reorganization Act of 1934. The Allotment Act and the Reorganization Act established the government's paternalistic approach.

These early policies also reflect the oppression of internal colonialism. As we presented in Chapter 1, **internal colonialism** is the treatment of subordinate groups like colonial subjects by those in power. Native Americans found themselves to be the subordinate group on land that once they occupied alone. Now they were being treated like a colonized people by the newly formed government, which itself had successfully broken from the colonial hold of Great Britain. Ironically, the former colony was now itself practicing internal colonialism toward the indigenous people of the new land.

THE ALLOTMENT ACT

The Allotment Act bypassed tribal leaders and proposed to make individual landowners of tribal members. Each family was given up to 160 acres under the government's assumption that, with land, they would become more like the White homesteaders who were then flooding the not-yet-settled areas of the West.

The effect of the Allotment Act on the Native Americans was disastrous. In order to guarantee that they would remain homesteaders, the act prohibited their selling the land for twenty-five years. Yet no effort was made to acquaint them with the skills necessary to make the land productive. Because many tribes were not accustomed to cultivating land and, if anything, considered such labor undignified, assistance to the new homesteaders would have been needed for them to adapt to homesteading. None was forthcoming.

Much of the land initially deeded under the Allotment Act eventually came into the possession of White landowners. The land could not be sold legally, but it could be leased and was subsequently transferred through fraudulent procedures. Whites would even go so far as to arrange to become legal guardians of Native American youths who had received allotments. The Bureau of Indian Affairs (BIA) tried to close such loopholes, but unscrupulous Whites and their Native American allies inevitably discovered new loopholes. For those Native Americans who managed to retain the land, the BIA required that, upon the death of the owner, the land be divided equally among all descendants, regardless of tribal inheritance customs. In documented cases, this division resulted in as many as thirty individuals trying to live off an 80-acre plot of worthless land. By 1934, Native Americans had lost approximately 90 million of the 138 million acres in their possession before the Allotment Act. The land left was generally considered worthless for farming and marginal even for ranching (Deloria and Lytle 1983; W. Hagan 1961; D. Holford 1975; S. Tyler 1973; M. Wax 1971; S. Witt 1970).

THE REORGANIZATION ACT

The assumptions behind the Allotment Act and the missionary activities of the nineteenth century were that (1) it was best for Native Americans to assimilate into the White society, and (2) each individual was best considered apart from his or her tribal identity. Very gradually, in the twentieth century, government officials have accepted the importance of tribal identity. The Indian Reorganization Act of 1934, known as the Wheeler-Howard Act, recognized the need to use, rather than ignore, tribal identity. But assimilation, rather than movement toward a pluralistic society, was still the goal.

Many provisions of the Reorganization Act, including revocation of the Allotment Act, benefited Native Americans. Still, given the legacy of broken treaties, many tribes at first distrusted the new policy. Under the Reorganization Act, tribes could adopt a written constitution and elect a tribal council with a head. This system imposed foreign values and structures. Under it, the elected tribal leader actually represented an entire reservation, which might include several tribes, some hostile to one another. Furthermore, the leader had to be elected by majority rule, a concept alien to many tribes. Many full-blooded Native Americans resented the provision that mixed-bloods were to have full voting rights. The Indian Reorganization Act did facilitate tribal dealings with government agencies, but the dictating to Native Americans of certain procedures common to White society alien to the tribes was another sign of forced assimilation.

As had been true of earlier government reforms, the Reorganization Act sought to assimilate Native Americans into the dominant society on the dominant group's terms. In this case, the tribes were absorbed within the political and economic structure of the larger society. Apart from the provision about tribal chairmen who were to oversee reservations with several tribes, the Reorganization Act served to solidify tribal identity. Unlike the Allotment Act, it recognized the right of Native Americans to approve or reject some actions taken on their behalf. The act still maintained substantial non-Native American control over the reservations. As institutions, the tribal governments owed their existence not to their people but to the BIA. These tribal governments rested at the bottom of a large administrative hierarchy (S. Cornell 1984; V. Deloria 1971; D. McNickle 1973; W. Washburn 1984; Wax and Buchanan 1975).

Reservation Life and Federal Policies

Today, over 437,000 Native Americans live on 314 reservations and trust lands, which account for a bit more than 2 percent of the land throughout the United States. While the majority of the entire Native American population lives outside these tribal areas, the reservations nevertheless play a prominent role in the identity of the Native American peoples (see Figure 6.1).

More than any other segment of the population, with the exception of the military, the reservation Native American finds his or her life determined by the federal government. From the condition of the roads to the level of fire protection to the quality of the schools, reservation life is effectively controlled by the federal government through such agencies as the Bureau of Indian Affairs and the Public Health Service. Tribes and their leaders are now consulted more than in the past, but the ultimate decisions rest in Washington, D.C., to a degree that is not true for the rest of the civilian population.

As early as April 1954, an editorial in the *Washington Post* expressed sympathy with efforts of the federal government to "get out of the Indian business." Many of the policies instituted by the BIA during the twentieth century have been designed with this purpose in mind. Most Native Americans and their organizations do not quarrel with this goal. They may only wish that the government and the White people had never gotten into Indian business in the first place. Disagreement between the BIA and the tribes and among Native Americans themselves has focused on how to reduce federal control and subsidies, not on whether they should be reduced. The government has taken three steps in this direction since World War II. Two of these measures have been the formation of the Indian Claims Commission and the passage of the Termination Act, examined second. The following section shows how the third step, the Employment Assistance Program, has created a new meeting place for Native Americans in cities, far from either their native homelands or the reservations (S. Tyler 1973).

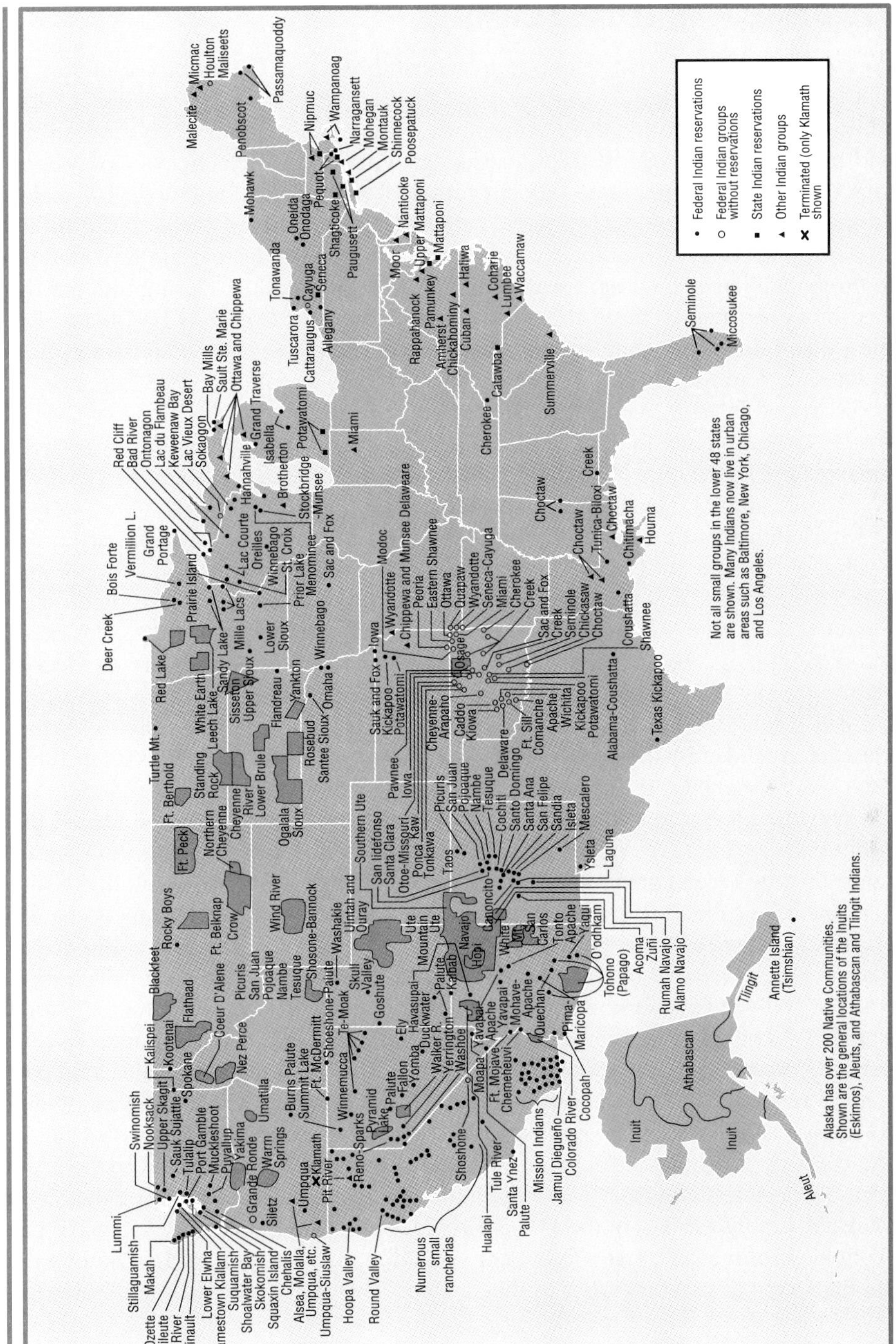

Figure 6.2 Native American Lands and Communities

Source: Bureau of Indian Affairs (1986:12–13).

NATIVE AMERICAN LEGAL CLAIMS

Native Americans have had a unique relationship with the federal government. As might be expected, little provision was ever made for them as individuals or tribes to bring grievances against the government. From 1863 to 1946, Native Americans could bring no claim against the government without a special act of Congress, a policy that effectively prevented most charges of treaty violations. Only 142 claims were heard during those eighty-three years. In 1946, Congress created the Indian Claims Commission, with authority to hear all tribal cases against the government. The three-member commission was given a five-year deadline. During the first five years, however, nearly three times as many claims were filed as had been filed during the eighty-three years of the old system. Therefore, the commission's term was extended and extended again, and its size was expanded. The Commission was disbanded in 1978, with its cases now being heard by the U.S. Court of Claims. As of 1997, the Commission and Court, over the period of more than fifty years, paid claims totaling an average of $1,000 for each American Indian for all treaty violations and related claims (D. Drabellle 1997; J. Nagel 1996).

If legal judgments are made in favor of the Native Americans, courts then determine the value of the land at the time it was illegally seized. Native Americans do not usually receive payment based on present value, nor do they usually receive interest on the money due. Value at time of loss, perhaps a few pennies an acre, is considered "just compensation." Payments are then decreased by setoffs. **Setoffs** are deductions from the money due that are equal to the cost of federal services provided to the tribe. It is not unusual to have a case decided in favor of the tribe, only to have its settlement exceeded by the setoffs (V. Deloria 1971; R. Ellis 1972; G. Wilkinson 1966).

The U.S. Supreme Court has begun to consider more tribe-related cases and to find in favor of the tribes. Other courts have reasserted the following basic principles: that the tribes are separate governments; that the states have no jurisdiction over the reservations; that the federal government has a responsibility to the tribes; and that Native Americans have substantial rights to the resources on their land. Native American legal groups have organized to protect these and other legal rights, while various anti–Native American groups have organized to oppose what they regard as special privileges to tribes. The anti–Native American groups, linked openly to conservative extremist groups, argue that recognition of the tribes is a violation of the U.S. Constitution. Native Americans express concern about these groups, which have formed alliances on specific legal cases with such established groups as the National Wildlife Federation and the National Rifle Association (*Akwesasne Notes* 1988; W. Schmidt 1988).

Native Americans increasingly express a desire to recover their land, rather than accept financial settlements. Following numerous legal decisions favoring the Sioux Indians, including a ruling of the U.S. Supreme Court, Congress finally agreed to pay $106 million for the land that was illegally seized in the aftermath of the Battle of the Little Big Horn, described earlier in this chapter. The Sioux rejected the money and lobbied for measures such as the 1987 Black Hills Sioux Nation Act in Congress, to return the land to the tribe. No positive action has yet been taken on these measures. In the meantime, however, the original settlement, the subsequent unaccepted payments, and the interest brought the 1991 total of funds being held for the Sioux to over $330 million. Despite the desperate need for housing, food, health care,

Most reservations today have a measure of self-government through an elected tribal council. Pictured is the Apache tribal council at work.

and education, the Sioux still prefer regaining the land lost in the 1868 Fort Laramie Treaty and, as of 1996, have not accepted payment.

THE TERMINATION ACT

The most controversial government policy toward reservation Native Americans during the twentieth century was initiated by the Termination Act of 1953. As with many such policies, the act originated in ideas that were meant to benefit Native Americans. The BIA commissioner, John Collier, had expressed concern in the 1930s over extensive governmental control of tribal affairs. In 1947, congressional hearings were held to determine which tribes had the economic resources to be relieved of federal control and assistance. The policy proposed at that time was an admirable attempt to give Native Americans greater autonomy and at the same time to reduce federal expenditures, a goal popular among taxpayers.

The services the tribes received, such as subsidized medical care and college scholarships, should not have been viewed as special and deserving to be discontinued. These services were not the result of favoritism but merely fulfilled treaty obligations. The termination of the Native Americans' relationship to the government then came to be viewed by Native Americans as a threat to reduce services rather than a release from arbitrary authority. Native Americans might be gaining greater self-governance, but at a high price.

Unfortunately, the Termination Act as finally passed in 1953 emphasized reducing costs and ignored individual needs. Recommendations for a period of tax immunity were dropped. According to the act, federal services such as medical care, schools, and road equipment were supposed to be withdrawn gradually. Instead, when the

Termination Act's provisions began to go into effect, federal services were stopped immediately, with minimal coordination between local government agencies and the tribes themselves to determine whether the services could be continued by other means. The effect of the government orders on the Native Americans was disastrous, with major economic upheaval on the affected tribes, who were unable to establish some of the most basic services—such as road repair and fire protection—that the federal government had previously provided. The federal government resumed these services in 1975 with congressional action that signaled the end of another misguided policy intended to be good for tribal peoples (V. Deloria 1969; D. Fixico 1988; S. Tyler 1973; Wax and Buchanan 1975).

EMPLOYMENT ASSISTANCE PROGRAM

The depressed economic conditions of reservation life might lead one to expect government initiatives to attract business and industry to locate on or near reservations. The government could provide tax incentives that would eventually pay for themselves. Such proposals, however, have not been advanced. Rather than take jobs to the Native Americans, the federal government decided to lead the more highly motivated away from the reservation. This policy has further devastated the reservations' economic potential.

In 1952, the BIA began programs to relocate young Native Americans. One of these programs, after 1962, was called the Employment Assistance Program (EAP). Assistance centers were created in Chicago, Cleveland, Dallas, Denver, Los Angeles, Oakland, San Jose, Oklahoma City, Tulsa, and Seattle. In some cities the Native American population increased as much as fivefold in the 1950s, primarily because of the EAP. By 1968, more than 100,000 individuals had participated in the program, and 200,000, or one-fourth of the Native American population, had moved to urban areas. They have tended not to spread throughout urban areas but to remain somewhat segregated. Though not as segregated as African Americans or Hispanics, Native Americans often experience moderate segregation, similar to that of European ethnic groups (J. Bohland 1982).

Menominee tribe member Ada Deer is sworn in to head the BIA in 1993. It is very unusual for Native Americans to have leadership positions in government.

The EAP's primary provision was for relocation, individually or in families, at government expense, to urban areas where job opportunities were greater than those on the reservations. The BIA stressed that the EAP was voluntary, but as Howard

Bahr (1972) correctly states, this voluntary aspect was "a fiction to the extent that the white man has structured the alternatives in such a way that economic pressures force the Indian to relocate" (p. 408). The program was not a success for the many Native Americans who found the urban experience unsuitable or unbearable. By 1965, one-fourth to one-third of the people in the EAP had returned to their home reservation. So great was the rate of return that in 1959 the BIA actually stopped releasing data on the percentage of returnees, fearing that these would give too much ammunition to critics of the EAP.

The movement of Native Americans into urban areas has had many unintended consequences. It has further reduced the labor force on the reservation. Because those who leave tend to be better educated, it is the Native American version of the brain drain described in Chapter 4. Urbanization unquestionably contributed to the development of an intertribal network or pan-Indian movement, described in the next section of this chapter. The city became the new meeting place of Native Americans, who learned of their common predicament both in the city and on the federally administered reservations. Government agencies also had to develop a policy of continued assistance to nonreservation Native Americans; despite such efforts, the problems of Native Americans in cities persist.

New programs have emerged to meet the needs of city-dwelling Native Americans. Founded in 1975, the Native American Education Service College in Chicago is an independent, accredited college trying to partially provide for the education of that city's 16,000 Native Americans, who represent 100 tribes. It offers college degrees, with specialized courses in Native American language and history. The college emphasizes small classes and individualized instruction. This institution is not only unusual in higher education but also in offering urban Native Americans a pluralistic solution to being an American Indian in White America (C. Lauerman 1993).

Pan-Indianism

The growth of pan-Indian activism is an example of both panethnicity and social protest. As we noted in Chapter 1, the panethnic development of solidarity among ethnic subgroups has been reflected in terms such as *Hispanic*, *Latino*, and *Asian American*. **Pan-Indianism** refers to the intertribal social movements in which several tribes, joined by culture but not by kinship, unite in a common identity. Today, these pan-Indian efforts are most vividly seen in cultural efforts or in political protests of government policies (S. Cornell 1996).

Proponents of this movement see the tribes as captive nations or internal colonies. They generally see the enemy as the federal government. Until recently, pan-Indian efforts have usually failed to overcome the cultural differences and distrust among tribal groups. However, some efforts to unite have succeeded even in the past. The Iroquois make up a six-tribe confederation dating back to the seventeenth century. The Ghost Dance briefly united the Plains tribes during the 1880s, some of which had earlier combined to resist the U.S. Army. But these were the exceptions. It took nearly a century and a half of BIA policies to accomplish a significant level of unification.

The National Congress of American Indians (NCAI), founded in 1944 in Denver, Colorado, was the first national organization representing Native Americans. The

NCAI registered itself as a lobby in Washington, D.C., hoping to make the Native American perspective heard in the aftermath of the Reorganization Act described earlier. Concern about "White people's meddling" is reflected in the NCAI requirement that White members pay twice as much in dues. The NCAI has had its successes. Early in its history, it played an important role in creating the Indian Claims Commission, and it later pressured the BIA to abandon the practice of termination. It is still the most important civil rights organization for Native Americans and uses tactics similar to those of the NAACP, although the problems facing African Americans and Native Americans are legally and constitutionally different.

A more recent arrival is the more radical American Indian Movement (AIM), the most visible pan-Indian group. The AIM was founded in 1968 by Clyde Bellecourt (of the White Earth Chippewa) and Dennis Banks (of the Pine Ridge Oglala Sioux), both of whom then lived in Minneapolis. Initially, AIM created a patrol to monitor police actions in order to document charges of police brutality. Eventually, it promoted programs for alcohol rehabilitation and school reform. By 1972, AIM was nationally known not for its neighborhood-based reforms but for its aggressive confrontations with the BIA and law enforcement agencies.

FISH-INS AND ALCATRAZ

Fish-ins began in 1964 to protest interference by Washington State officials with Native Americans who were fishing, as they argued, in accordance with the 1854 Treaty of Medicine Creek and were not subject to fine or imprisonment, even if they did violate White society's law. The **fish-ins** had protesters fishing *en masse* in restricted waterways. This protest was initially hampered by disunity and apathy, but several hundred Native Americans were convinced that civil disobedience was the only way to bring attention to their grievances with the government. Legal battles followed, and the U.S. Supreme Court confirmed the treaty rights in 1968. Other tribes continued to fight in the courts, but the fish-ins brought increased public awareness of the deprivations of Native Americans. One of the longest battles continues to the present: the Chippewas have rights to 50 percent of the fish, timber, and wildlife across the upper third of Wisconsin. In 1991, Wisconsin agreed with this long-standing treaty right, but Whites continue to demonstrate against what they feel is the unfair advantage extended to the Native Americans (L. Jolidon 1991; S. Steiner 1968).

The fish-ins were only the beginning. After the favorable Supreme Court decision in 1968, other events followed in quick succession. In 1969, members of the San Francisco Indian Center seized Alcatraz Island in San Francisco Bay. The 13-acre island was an abandoned maximum-security federal prison, and the federal government was undecided about how to use it. The Native Americans claimed "the excess property" in exchange for $24 in glass beads and cloth, following the precedent set in the sale of Manhattan more than three centuries earlier. With no federal response and the loss of public interest in the demonstration, the protesters left the island more than a year later. The activists' desire to transform it into a Native American cultural center was ignored. Despite the outcome, the event gained international publicity for their cause. Red Power was born, and those Native Americans who sympathized with the BIA were branded either "Uncle Tomahawks" or "apples" (red on the outside, white on the inside).

The federal government did not totally ignore calls for a new policy that involved Native Americans in its formulation. Nevertheless, no major breakthroughs came in the 1960s. One significant step, however, was passage of the Alaska Native Settlement Act of 1971. Alaskan Native American people—the Inuits and Aleuts—have maintained their claim to the land since Alaska was purchased from Russia in 1867. The federal government had allowed the natives to settle on about one-third of the land they claimed but had not even granted them title to that land. The discovery of huge oil reserves in 1969 made the issue more explosive, as the state of Alaska auctioned off mineral rights, ignoring Inuit occupation of the land. The Alaskan Federation of Natives (AFN), the major native Alaskan group, which had been organized in 1967, moved quickly to stop "the biggest land grab in the history of the U.S.," as the AFN termed it. An AFN-sponsored bill was revised, and a compromise—the Native Claims Settlement Act—was passed in late 1971. The final act, which fell short of the requests by the AFN, granted control and ownership of 44 million acres to Alaska's 53,000 Inuits, Aleuts, and other peoples and gave them a cash settlement of nearly $1 billion. Given the enormous pressures from oil companies and conservationists, the Native Claims Settlement Act can be regarded as one of the more reasonable agreements reached between distinctive tribal groups of Native Americans and the government. Further reforms in 1988 helped to safeguard the original act, but as a major trade-off the Alaskan Native Americans surrendered future claims to all aboriginal lands (A. Ervin 1987; P. Iverson 1993; S. Langdon 1982; D, Morrow 1996; S. Nickerson 1971).

PROTEST EFFORTS

The federal government, by closing the door to those presenting grievances and by the lack of positive movement, ensured that it would be only a matter of time before Native Americans took new steps to be heard. Thus, the 1970s were marked by increasingly militant protests by Native Americans. One moderate group organized a summer-long caravan to reach the nation's capital just when the presidential election was being held in 1972. The Nixon administration, increasingly distrustful of protesting Native Americans, refused to meet with them. The militant AIM then emerged as the leader of those frustrated by government unresponsiveness.

The most dramatic confrontation between Native Americans and the government came early the next year in the battle of Wounded Knee II. In January 1973, AIM leader Russell Means led an unsuccessful drive to impeach Richard Wilson as tribal chairman of the Oglala Sioux tribe on the Pine Ridge Reservation. In the next month, Means, accompanied by some 300 supporters, started a seventy-day occupation of Wounded Knee, South Dakota, site of the infamous cavalry assault in 1890 and now part of the Pine Ridge Reservation. The occupation received tremendous press coverage.

The coverage, however, did not affect the outcome. Negotiations between AIM and the federal government on the occupation itself brought no tangible results. Federal prosecutions were initiated against most participants. AIM leaders Russell Means and Dennis Banks eventually faced prosecution on a number of felony charges and both men were imprisoned. AIM had less visibility as an organization then. Russell Means wryly remarked in 1984, "We're not chic now. We're just Indians, and we have to help ourselves" (N. Hentoff 1984:23; also see J. Nagel 1988, 1996; Smith and Warrior 1996; T. Johnson 1996).

The most visible recent AIM activity has been its efforts to gain clemency for one of its leaders, Leonard Peltier. Imprisoned since 1976, Peltier was given two life sentences for murdering two FBI agents the year before on the embattled Sioux reservation of Pine Ridge, South Dakota. Fellow AIM leaders such as Dennis Banks organized a 1994 Walk for Justice to bring attention in Washington, D.C., to the view that Peltier is innocent. This view had been supported in two 1992 movie releases: the documentary, *Incident at Oglala,* produced by Robert Redford, and the more entertaining, fictionalized *Thunderheart.* To date, clemency appeals to the President to lift the federal sentence have gone unheeded, but this issue remains the rallying point for today's remnants of AIM (P. Matthiessen 1991).

In 1994, a symbolic show of support for Native Americans took place in the nation's capital; only time will tell whether significant reforms will result. President Bill Clinton issued invitations to all 547 federally recognized tribal leaders—their largest meeting ever with a U.S. President. On the lengthy agenda were issues such as:

- Tribal sovereignty
- Law enforcement and juvenile delinquency
- Casinos and the gaming industry
- Religious freedom
- Natural resources protection

Ada Deer, director of BIA from 1992 to 1997 and earlier leader of the Menominee anti-Termination effort, declared that the historic meetings should erase the "vanishing Indian" image of an old warrior riding a horse alone down the last trail: "We have an opportunity, a moment in history now, to address many of these long-standing issues and problems. This is not just a show" (L. Kanamine 1994:A2).

Clinton issued federal directives to accommodate Native Americans' need for eagle feathers (whose use was banned under the Endangered Species Act) for spiritual purposes and to consult with tribes over the use of their natural resources. Yet leaders expressed dismay that programs directed at Native Americans have been subject to significant budget cuts as a part of general budget tightening (M. Cooper 1996).

PAN-INDIANISM: AN OVERVIEW

Pan-Indianism, an example of panethnicity, has created a greater solidarity among Native Americans as they seek solutions to common grievances with government agencies. Whether through moderate groups like the NCAI or the more activist AIM, these developments have awakened Whites to the real grievances of Native Americans and have garnered the begrudging acceptance of even the most conservative tribal members, who are more willing to cooperate with governmental action.

The results of pan-Indianism, however, have not all been productive, even when viewed from a perspective sympathetic to Native American self-determination. The national organizations are dominated by Plains tribes, not only politically but culturally as well. Powwow styles of dancing, singing, and costuming derived from the Plains tradition are spreading nationwide as common cultural traits.

The growing visibility of powwows is symbolic of Native Americans in the 1990s. The phrase *pau wau* referred to the medicine man or spiritual leader of the Algonquian tribes, but Europeans who watched medicine men dance thought that the word referred to entire events. Over the last hundred years, **powwows** have evolved into gatherings in which Native Americans of many tribes come to dance, sing, play music, and visit. More recently, they have become organized events featuring competitions and prizes at over 1,000 locations. The general public sees them as entertainment, but for Native Americans, they are a celebration of their culture (M. Parfit 1994).

Native Americans Today

The United States has taken most of the land originally occupied or deeded to Native Americans, has restricted their movement, has unilaterally severed agreements, has created a special legal status for them, and after World War II attempted to move them again. After all this ill treatment, how well are they doing today?

A very public insult is the continuing use of American Indian names as mascots for athletic teams of schools including colleges and many professional sports teams in the United States. Virtually all American Indian organizations including AIM members have brought attention to the use of Native Americans as the mascots of sports teams, such as the Washington Redskins, as well as to such spectator practices as the "Tomahawk chop" associated with the Atlanta Braves.

Many sports fans and college alumni find it difficult to understand why Native Americans take offense to a name like "Braves" or even "Redskins" if it is meant to represent a team about which they have positive feelings. For Native Americans, however, the use of such mascots trivializes their past and their presence today. In "Listen to Their Voices" (on pp. 188–189), journalist and Lakota Sioux tribe member Tim Giago's sharp editorial expresses his disapproval over the fascination in using American Indian names as mascots.

There is no easy answer for native peoples, who face a variety of challenges. Any discussion of Native American socioeconomic status today must begin with an emphasis on the diversity of the people. Besides the variety of tribal heritages already noted, the contemporary Native American population is split between those on and off reservations and those living in small towns and in central cities. Life in these contrasting social environments is quite different, but enough similarities exist to warrant some broad generalizations on the status of Native Americans in the United States today.

The sections that follow summarize the status of contemporary Native Americans in economic development, education, health care, religious and spiritual expression, and the environment.

ECONOMIC DEVELOPMENT

The Native Americans are an impoverished people. To even the most casual observer of a reservation, the poverty is a living reality, not merely numbers and percentages. Some visitors seem unconcerned, arguing that because Native Americans are used to hardship and lived a simple life before the Europeans arrived, poverty is a familiar and traditional way of life. In an absolute sense of dollars earned or quality of housing, Native Americans are no worse off now. But in a relative sense that compares their position to that of Whites, they are dismally behind on all standards of income and occupational status. A 1995 national survey showed that overall

LISTEN TO THEIR VOICES

Honor Another Race of People as Mascots

Tim Giago
(*Nawica Keijio*)

Nearly every Lakota (Sioux) man and woman knew the basketball team from Utah would lose in the finals of the NCAA Tournament.

How did we know? Because Utah calls themselves the Utes (named for an Indian tribe in Utah) and all of the major athletic teams in America that used Indians as mascots in 1997 lost in the big games.

The Atlanta Braves, Cleveland Indians, Washington Redskins, the Fighting Illini of the University of Illinois and the Florida State Seminoles all bit the dust last year and we are happy that Utah started 1998 by joining their brethren. The lesson: Indians are human beings, not mascots for America's fun and games.

The Standing Rock High School Warriors of the Standing Rock Sioux Indian Reservation won the North Dakota State "B" Championship last week, but the team is made up of real Indians, not non-Indians making themselves up as Indians.

You will notice that the two new big league baseball teams have chosen the Devil Rays and the Diamond Backs as their mascots. There was no thought of either team using the American Indians as their mascots. I wonder why. Could it be that the protests of the Indian people and the column I have been writing about this disgraceful habit for the past 16 years has finally reached a few sensitive ears?

I would ask John Kent Cooke, the new owner of the Washington, D.C., professional football team to stand tall and change the name of his mascot to the Washington Blackskins. Since D.C. has a population nearly 75 percent African American, this would be the right thing to do. The American Indian is tired of this

unemployment is more than 30 percent. Among those who do have jobs, a third earned less than $10,000.

In 1997, the federal government introduced a welfare program that limited how long people can receive public assistance. This clearly will have impact on many tribal reservations, where high proportions of people depend on public assistance because of the lack of any training or job oportunities. For example, in South Dakota, American Indians make up 7 percent of the population but account for 53 percent of the welfare recipients. State officials declared they could give five tribes a one-time infusion of start-up money, but after that they would be on their own (P. Belluck 1997; T. Egan 1998).

Given the lower incomes and higher poverty rates, it is not surprising that the occupational distribution of Native Americans is similarly bleak. Those who are employed are less likely to be managers, professionals, technicians, salespeople, or administrators. This pattern of low-wage employment is typical of many of the honor bestowed upon us and we believe it is only proper to honor another race of people as mascots.

This way the Washington fans can put away their tomahawks, war bonnets, facial paint and other items made of turkey feathers, for good. They can prepare for the Sunday football games by painting their faces black, wearing Afro wigs, selecting some appropriate African attire and creating some new African war chants. Just think, we could see a football stadium filled with modern versions of Al Jolsen. Wouldn't most African-Americans consider this to be a real honor?

I mean the white man and the black man have been honoring American Indians for 100 years. Don't you think it is time to honor another ethnic group? Why shouldn't the Dallas Cowboys change their name to the Dallas Caballeros? Think of the honor their fans could bring to the Mexican-Americans if they filled the stands with people wearing sombreros and serapes. I'm sure they could come up with a real Mexican chant to egg on their team.

Why should all of this honor be reserved for American Indians? We're not selfish. We wouldn't mind a bit if it was spread around a little bit.

Lordy, Lordy: I almost forgot the dominant society. What about the white people? I realize this includes Germans, Irish, Italians, French, Danes, etc., but they all have one thing in common: white faces. Just as the Washington football team rolls all Indians into one group perhaps the Cleveland Indians could change their name to the Cleveland Honkies. This takes in the whole group. All of the fans could paint their faces white and imitate the things they believe the white folks do. What an honor.

John Kent Cooke and Ted Turner: are you reading this? If so, please spread this honoring thing around. It's getting a little old to the American Indian.

Source: Tim Giago. "Honor Another Group of People as Mascots." Reprinted by permission of *Indian Country Today.*

racial and ethnic minorities in the United States, but Native Americans differ in three areas: their roles in tourism, casino gambling, and government employment.

Tourism Tourism is an important source of employment for many reservation residents, who either serve the needs of visitors directly or sell souvenirs and craft items. Generally, such enterprises do not achieve the kind of success that improves the tribal economy significantly. Even if they did, sociologist Murray Wax (1971) argues, "It requires a special type of person to tolerate exposing himself and his family life to the gaze of tourists who are often boorish and sometimes offensively condescending in their attitudes" (p. 69).

Anthropologist Joan Laxson (1991) interviewed tourists visiting museums and reservations and found that, regardless of the presentation, the visitors interpreted their brief experiences to be consistent with their previously held stereotypes of and prejudices toward Native Americans.

Craft work rarely realizes the profits most Native Americans desire and need. Most Whites are interested in trinkets, not the more expensive and profitable items. The trading-post business has also taken its toll on Native American cultures. Many craftworkers have been manipulated by other Native Americans and Whites to produce what the tourists want. Creativity and authenticity have frequently been replaced by mechanical duplication of "genuine Indian" curios. There is a growing concern and controversy surrounding art such as paintings and pottery that may not be produced by real Native Americans fetching high prices. The price of economic survival is very high (National Public Radio 1992; M. Smith 1982; C. Snipp 1980; S. Steiner 1976; J. Sweet 1990).

Casino Gambling A more recent source of significant income and some employment has been the introduction of gambling on reservations. Forms of gambling, originally part of tribal ceremonies or celebrations, existed long before Europeans arrived in the Western Hemisphere. Today, however, commercial gambling is the only viable source of employment and revenue available to several tribes.

Under the 1988 Indian Gaming Regulatory Act, states must negotiate gambling agreements with reservations and cannot prohibit any gambling already allowed under state law. By 1996, in twenty states and with approval to begin in three more, 200 tribes were operating a variety of gambling operations, including off-track betting, casino tables such as blackjack and roulette, lotteries, sports betting, video games of chance, telephone betting, slot machines, and high-stakes bingo. The gamblers, almost all non–Native Americans, sometimes travel long distances for the opportunity to wager money. The actual casinos are a form of tribal government enterprise as opposed to private business operations.

The economic impact on some reservations has been enormous, and nationwide receipts amounted to $4.9 billion in 1996 from reservation casino operations. Some successful casinos have led to staggering windfalls, such as to the 493 members of the Connecticut Mashantucket Pequot Indians, whose Foxwoods Resort Casino provides generous benefits to anyone who can establish that they are at least one-sixteenth Pequot. However, the more typical picture is of moderately successful gambling operations associated with tribes whose social and economic needs are overwhelming. Tribes that have opened casinos had 24 percent higher unemployment than nongaming tribes in 1989, but by 1995 enjoyed 13 percent lower unemployment. However, the impact is limited. The tribes that make substantial revenue from gambling are less than 1 percent of the total Native American people (Cambridge Economic Group 1998; M. Goozner 1997; Harrah's Entertainment 1996).

Criticism is not hard to find, even among Native Americans, some of whom oppose gambling both on moral grounds and because it is marketed in a form that is incompatible with Native American culture. Opponents are concerned about the appearance of compulsive gambling among tribal members. The majority of the gamblers are not Native Americans, and virtually all of the reservation casinos, while owned by the tribes, are operated by White-owned businesses. Some tribal members feel that the casinos trivialize and cheapen their heritage. The issue of who shares in gambling profits also has led to heated debates in some tribal communities as to who is a member of the tribe. In addition, established White gaming interests in Nevada and Atlantic City, New Jersey, are beginning to lobby Congress to restrict the tribes, even though

The Meskwaki Casino in Iowa is open 24 hours a day. The Meskwaki were an indigenous tribe to the area successfully obtaining their land from the government in 1856.

Native Americans generate only 9 percent of the nation's gambling revenue (Cozzetto and Larocque 1996; National Indian Gaming Association 1995, 1996).

While income from gambling has not dramatically changed the lifestyle of the vast majority of Native Americans, it has been a magnet of criticism from outsiders. Critics question the special status being afforded to Native Americans and contend that there should be an even playing field. This view certainly would have been endorsed by tribal members, because most of what passed for government policies over the last 200 years placed tribes at a major disadvantage. In the latter 1990s, attention was drawn to some tribes that had made contributions to politicians involved in policies concerning gambling laws. While some of these contributions may have been illegal, the national media attention was far more intense than was warranted in the messy area of campaign financing. It is another example of how the notion that Native Americans are now playing the White man's game of capitalism "too well" becomes big news (S. Faiman-Silva 1997).

Government Employment Another major source of employment for Native Americans is the government, principally the BIA, but also other federal agencies, the military, and state and local governments. In 1970, one of every four employed Native Americans worked for the federal government. More than half the BIA's employees have tribal ancestry. In fact, since 1854, the BIA has had a policy of giving employment preference to Native Americans over Whites. This policy has been questioned, but the U.S. Supreme Court (*Morton* v. *Mancari*) upheld it in 1974. Although this is a significant source of employment opportunity, other tribe members have leveled many criticisms at Native American government workers, especially federal employees.

These government employees form a subculture in Native American communities. They tend to be Christians, educated in BIA schools, and sometimes the third generation born into government service. Discrimination against Native Americans in private industry makes government work attractive, and once a person is employed and has seniority, he or she is virtually guaranteed security. Of course, this security may lead some individuals (whether Native Americans or Whites) to do less-than-efficient work. (Bureau of Indian Affairs 1970; C. Rachlin 1970).

We have examined the sources of economic development, such as tourism, government service, and legalized gambling, but the dominant feature of reservation life is nevertheless unemployment. A government report issued by the Full Employment Action Council opened with the statement that such words as *severe*, *massive*, and *horrendous* are appropriate to describe unemployment among Native Americans. Official unemployment figures for reservations range from 23 percent to 90 percent. It is little wonder that the 1990 Census showed that the poorest county in the nation was wholly on tribal lands: Shannon County, South Dakota, of the Pine Ridge Reservation, had a 63 percent poverty rate. Unemployment rates for urban-based Indians are also very high; Los Angeles reports more than 40 percent and Minneapolis 49 percent (Cornell and Kalt 1990; L. Kanamine 1992; T. Knudson 1987; C. Sullivan 1986).

The economic outlook for Native Americans need not be bleak. A single program is not the solution; the diversity of both Native Americans and their problems demands a multifaceted approach. The solutions need not be unduly expensive; indeed, because the Native American population is exceedingly small compared to the total population, programs with major influence may be financed without significant federal

Many issues confront Native Americans, including the use of the gaming industry in economic development and whether their children should be eligible for adoption by Whites. Both issues raise concerns about maintaining their cultural identity.

Source: TK

expenditures. Murray Wax (1971) observed that reformers viewing the economically depressed position of Native Americans often seize on education as the key to success. As the next section shows, improving educational programs for Native Americans would be a good place to start.

EDUCATION

Government involvement in the education of Native Americans dates as far back as a 1794 treaty with the Oneida Indians. In the 1840s, the federal government and missionary groups combined to start the first school for American Indians. By 1860, the government was operating schools that were free of missionary involvement. Today, laws prohibit federal funds for Native American education from going to sectarian schools. Also, since the passage of the Johnson-O'Malley Act in 1934, the federal government has reimbursed public school districts that include Native American children.

Federal control of the education of Native American children has had mixed results from the beginning. Several tribes started their own school systems at the beginning of the nineteenth century, financing the schools themselves. The Cherokee tribe developed an extensive school system that taught both English and Cherokee, the latter using an alphabet developed by the famed leader Sequoyah. Literacy for the Cherokees was estimated by the mid–1800s at 90 percent, and they even published a bilingual newspaper. The Creek, Chickasaw, and Seminole also maintained school systems. But by the end of the nineteenth century, all these schools had been closed by federal order. Not until the 1930s did the federal government become committed to ensuring an education for Native American children. Despite the push for educational participation, by 1948 only a quarter of the children on the Navajo reservation, the nation's largest, were attending school (D. Adams 1995; C. Pewewardy 1998).

Educational Attainment A serious problem in Native American education has been the unusually high level of underenrollment. Many children never attend school, or they leave while in elementary school and never return. Enrollment rates are as low as 30 percent for Alaska Eskimos (or Inuits). This high dropout rate is at least 50 percent higher than that of Blacks or Hispanics and nearly three times that of Whites. The term *dropout* is misleading, because many tribal American schoolchildren have found their educational experience so hostile that they had no choice but to leave (K. James et al. 1995).

Rosalie Wax (1967) conducted a detailed study of the education among the Sioux on the Pine Ridge Reservation of South Dakota. She concluded that terms like **kick-out** or **pushout** are more appropriate. The children are not so much hostile toward school as they are set apart from it; they are socialized by their parents to be independent and not to embarrass their peers, but teachers reward docile acceptance and expect schoolchildren to correct one another in public. Socialization is not all that separates home from school. Teachers are often happy to find parents not "interfering" with their job. Parents do not visit the school, and teachers avoid the homes, a pattern that only furthers the isolation of school from home. This lack of interaction is due partly to the predominance of non-Native American teachers, although the situation is improving.

Quality of Schooling The quality of Native American education is more difficult to measure than is the quantity. How does one measure excellence? And excellence for what? White society? Tribal life? Both? Chapter 1 discussed the disagreement over measuring intellectual achievement (how much a person has learned) and the greater hazards in measuring intellectual aptitude (how much a person is able to learn). Studies of reservation children, using tests of intelligence that do not require a knowledge of English, consistently show scores at or above the levels of intellectual middle-class urban children. Yet in the upper grades, a **crossover effect** appears, when tests used assume lifelong familiarity with English. Native American students drop behind their White peers and so would be classified by the dominant society as underachievers (Bureau of Indian Affairs 1988; Coleman et al. 1966: 450; Fuchs and Havighurst 1972).

Preoccupation with such test results perhaps avoids the more important question: Educational excellence for what? It would be a mistake to assume that the tribal peoples have reached a consensus. They do wish, however, to see a curriculum that, at the very least, considers the unique aspects of their heritage. Charles Silberman (1971:173) reported visiting a sixth-grade English class in a school on a Chippewa reservation where the students were all busily at work writing a composition for Thanksgiving: "Why We Are Happy the Pilgrims Came." A 1991 Department of Education report entitled "Indian Nations at Risk" still found the curriculum presented from a European perspective. It is little wonder when a 1990 national survey found that at 48 percent of all schools Native American children attend, there is not a single Native American teacher.

Some positive changes are occurring in education. At the beginning of the chapter, we noted the example of the Ho-chunk preschoolers learning their native language. About 23 percent of the students in BIA-funded schools receive bilingual education, but as yet no coordinator exists in the BIA for this important activity. There is growing recognition of the need to move away from past policies that suppressed or ignored the native language and to acknowledge that educational results may be maximized when the native language is included (Bureau of Indian Affairs 1988; K. James et al. 1995; D. Reese 1996; R. Wells 1991).

Higher Education The picture for Native Americans in higher education is decidedly mixed, with some progress and some promise. Enrollment in college increased steadily from the mid–1970s through the mid–1990s, but degree completion, especially the completion of professional degrees, may actually be declining. The economic and educational background of Native American students, especially reservation residents, makes considering entering a predominantly White college a very difficult decision. Native American students may soon feel isolated and discouraged, particularly if the college does not help them understand the alien world of American-style higher education. Even at campuses with large numbers of Native Americans in their student bodies, few Native American faculty or advisors are present to serve as role models. About 53 percent of the students leave at the end of their first year (Carnegie Foundation for the Advancement of Teaching 1990; R. Wells 1989).

The most encouraging development in higher education in recent years has been the creation of tribally controlled colleges—usually two-year community colleges. The Navajo Community College, the first such institution, was established in 1968, and by 1996 there were twenty-nine nationwide. Besides serving in some rural areas as the only educational institution for many miles, tribal colleges also provide services such as counseling and child care. Tribal colleges enable the students to maintain their cultural identity while training them to succeed outside the reservation. Only 10 percent of Native American students who leave the reservation for traditional college complete bachelor's degrees, but 35 percent entering tribal colleges go on to complete their bachelor's degree, and of these another 53 percent find jobs after leaving tribal college.

Funding for tribal colleges is a major problem. When Congress passed the Tribally Controlled Community College Assistance Act in 1978, it proposed $5,280 per year in federal funds for every full-time student. Over the years, the assistance has been under $3,000, jeopardizing the school's ability to maintain adequate educational programming (B. Campbell 1992; J. Kleinhuizen 1991b; L. McMillen 1991).

At higher levels, Native Americans virtually disappear from the educational scene. In 1992, of the 25,759 doctorates awarded to U.S. citizens, 148 went to Native Americans, compared to the over 13,000 that went to citizens of foreign countries (Carter and Wilson 1993).

Summary *"Dine bizaad beeyashti!"* Unfortunately, this declaration, "I speak Navajo!" is not commonly heard from educators. Gradually, schools have begun to encourage the preservation of native cultures. Until the 1960s, BIA and mission schools forbade speaking in the native languages, so it will take time to produce an educated teacher corps knowledgeable in and conversant with native cultures (L. Linthicum 1993).

As we have seen, there are many failures in our effort to educate, not just assimilate, the first Americans. The problems include:

1. Underenrollment at all levels, from the primary grades through college
2. The need to adjust to a school with values sometimes dramatically different from those of the home
3. The need to make the curriculum more relevant
4. The underfinancing of tribal community colleges
5. The unique hardships encountered by reservation-born Native Americans who later live in and attend schools in large cities
6. The language barrier faced by the many children who have little or no knowledge of English.

Other problems include lack of educational innovation (the BIA had no kindergartens until 1967) and a failure to provide special education to children who need it.

HEALTH CARE

For Native Americans, "health care" is a misnomer, another broken promise in the array of unmet pledges the government has made. Native Americans are more likely to die before age forty-five than any other racial or ethnic group. Even more frustrating: In 1994 they died of treatable diseases such as tuberculosis at rates 700 percent higher than White Americans. This dramatic difference is a result of their poverty and also of the lack of health services. There are only 96 doctors per 100,000 Native Americans, compared to 208 per 100,000 of the general population. Similarly, there are 251 nurses per 100,000 Native Americans, contrasted to 672 per 100,000 for the nation as a whole (R. Coddington 1991; Indian Health Service 1995; L. Kanamine 1992, 1994; G. Sandefur et al. 1996).

In 1955, the responsibility for health care for Native Americans was transferred from the BIA to the Public Health Service (PHS). Although their health has improved markedly since the mid–1960s, serious problems remain. As is true of industrial development and education, advances in health care are hampered by the poverty and geographic isolation of the reservations. Also, as in the educational and economic sectors, health policies, in effect, initiate a cultural war in which Native Americans must reject their traditions to secure better medical treatment (S. Kunitz 1996).

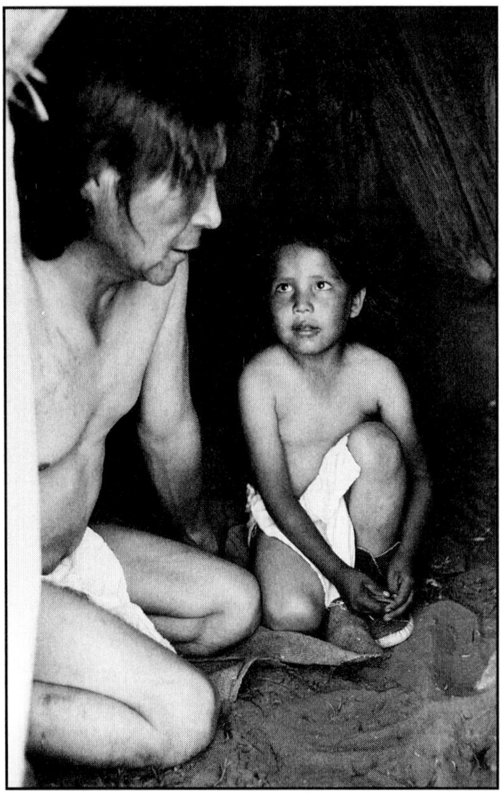

Traditional healing techniques are often used instead of and sometimes along with "modern medicine." A Navajo medicine man accompanies his 6-year-old son in a sweat lodge to purify their bodies.

With the pressure to assimilate Native Americans in all aspects of their lives, there has been little willingness to recognize their traditions of healing and treating illnesses. Native treatments tend to be noninvasive, with the patient encouraged to contribute actively to the healing benefits and prevent future recurrence. In the 1990s, a pluralistic effort was slowly emerging to recognize alternative forms of medicine, including those practiced by Native Americans. In addition, reservation health-care workers began to accommodate traditional belief systems as they administered the White culture's medicine (N. Angier 1993; E. Fox 1992).

It is not merely that Native Americans have more diseases and shorter life spans than the rest of the population; they also have acute problems in such areas as mental health, nutrition, the needs of the elderly, and alcoholism, which have been documented for generations but have only recently been addressed through innovative programs. Further improvement can be expected, but it will be some time before the gains make health care for Native Americans comparable to that for the general population (Carrese and Rhodes 1995; J. Cohen 1998).

RELIGIOUS AND SPIRITUAL EXPRESSION

Like other aspects of Native American culture, the expression of religion is diverse, reflecting the variety of tribal traditions and the assimilationist pressure of the Europeans. Initially, missionaries and settlers expected Native Americans simply to forsake their traditions for European Christianity, and, as in the case of the repression of the Ghost Dance, sometimes force was used to do so. Today, many Protestant churches and Roman Catholic parishes with large tribal congregations incorporate customs such as the sacred pipe ceremony, native incenses, ceremonies affirming care for the Earth, as well as services and hymns in native languages (Associated Press 1997; R. Loar 1997).

Following generations of formal and informal pressure to adopt Christian faiths and their rituals, in 1978 Congress enacted the American Indian Religious Freedom Act, which declares that it is the government's policy to "protect and preserve the inherent right of American Indians to believe, express, and practice their traditional religions." However, the act contains no penalties or enforcement mechanisms. For this reason, Hopi leader Vernon Masayesva (1994) refers to it as "the law with no teeth" (p. 93). Therefore, Native Americans are lobbying to strengthen this 1978 legislation. They are seeking protection for religious worship services for military personnel and incarcerated Native Americans, as well as better access to religious relics, such as eagle feathers, and better safeguards against the exploitation of sacred lands (M. Burgess 1992; V. Deloria 1992; Friends Committee on National Legislation 1993).

In recent years, significant publicity has been given to an old expression of religion: the ritual use of peyote, which dates back thousands of years. The sacramental use of peyote was first observed by Europeans in the 1640s. In 1918, the religious use of peyote, a plant that creates mild psychedelic effects, was organized as the Native American Church (NAC). At first a Southwest-based religion, the NAC has spread since World War II among northern tribes. The use of the substances is a relatively small part of a long and moving ritual. The exact nature of NAC rituals varies widely. Clearly, the church maintains the tradition of ritual curing and the seeking of individual visions. However, practitioners also embrace elements of Christianity, representing a type of religious pluralism of Indian and European identities.

Peyote is a hallucinogen, however, and the government has been concerned about NAC use of it. Several states passed laws in the 1920s and 1930s prohibiting the use of peyote. In the 1980s, several court cases involved the prosecution of Native Americans who were using peyote for religious purposes. Finally, in 1994, Congress amended the American Indian Religious Freedom Act to allow Native Americans the right to use, transport, and possess peyote for religious purposes (Hirschfelder and Molin 1992; T. Wilson 1996).

Another area of spiritual concern is the stockpiling of Native American relics, including burial remains. Contemporary Native Americans are increasingly seeking the return of their ancestors' remains and artifacts, a demand that alarms museums and archeologists. The Native American Graves Protection and Repatriation Act of 1990 requires an inventory of such collections and provides for the return of materials if a claim can be substantiated. Many scholars believe the ancient bones and burial artifacts to be valuable clues to humanity's past. In part, however, this belief reflects a difference in cultural traditions. Western scientists have been dissecting cadavers for hundreds of years, but many tribes believe that disturbing the graves of ancestors will bring spiritual sickness to the living.

Today's Native Americans are asking that their traditions be recognized as an expression of pluralist rather than assimilationist coexistence. These traditions are also closely tied to religion. The sacred sites of Native Americans have been under attack as well as their religious practices. In the last section, looking at contemporary Native Americans, we will focus on aspects of environmental disputes that are anchored in the spiritualism of Native Americans (G. Johnson 1996; S. Russell 1995).

ENVIRONMENT

Environmental issues bring together many of the concerns that we have previously considered surrounding Native Americans—stereotyping, land rights, social inequality, economic development, and spiritualism. First, we can find in some of today's environmental literature the stereotypes that creates the image of the native peoples as the last defense against the encroachment of "civilization." This image tends to trivialize native cultures, making them into what one author called a "New Age savage" (D. Waller 1996).

Second, many of the environmental issues are rooted in continuing land disputes arising from treaties and agreements over a century old. Reservations contain a wealth of natural resources and scenic beauty. In the past, Native Americans often lacked the technical knowledge to negotiate beneficial agreements with private corporations, and when they did have this ability, the federal government often stepped in and made the final agreements more beneficial to the non-Native Americans than to the residents of the reservations. The native peoples have always been rooted in their land. It was their land that became the first source of tension and conflict with the Europeans. As the twenty-first century approaches, it is not surprising that land and the natural resources it holds continue to be major concerns. In 1976, the Council of Energy Resource Tribes (CERT) was formed by the leaders of twenty-five of the West's largest tribes. This new council reasoned that by organizing together, it could ensure more revenue from the tribes' vast mineral resources. CERT, which in 1998 represented forty-five tribes in the United States and four in Canada, has provided numerous services to tribes. CERT, together with consultants, assists them to develop their resources by marketing natural gas more effectively and dealing with deregulation of utilities (Archuleta 1998; CERT 1991).

Third, environmental issues reinforce the tendency to treat the first inhabitants of the Americas as inferior. This is manifested in **environmental justice**—a term introduced in Chapter 3 describing efforts to ensure that hazardous substances are controlled so that all communities receive protection regardless of race or socioeconomic circumstances. Reservation representatives often express concern about how their lands are literally used as dumping grounds. For example, the Navajo reservation is home to almost 1,100 abandoned uranium mines. Following legal action, the federal government finally provided assistance to Navajos who had worked in the mines and were showing ill effects from radiation exposure. While compensation has been less than was felt necessary, the Navajos continue to monitor closely new proposals to use their land. Few reservations have escaped negative environmental impact, as some observers contend that Native American lands are targeted for nuclear waste storage. Critics see this as a de facto policy of "nuclear colonialism," whereby reservation land is forced to accept all the hazards of nuclear energy while the Native American people have seen few of its benefits over the last fifty years (V. Kuletz 1998:110, also see Brugge and Benally 1998; A. Gedicks 1993).

Fourth, environmental concerns by American Indians are often balanced against economic needs, just as they are in the larger society. On some reservations, authorization by timber companies to access hardwood forests lead to very conflicted feelings among American Indians. However, often such arrangements are the only realistic source of needed revenue. Even on the Navajo reservation, a proposed new uranium mine has its supporters—those who consider the promises of royalty payments coupled with alleged safety measures, compared to the past half-century of radiation problems (F. Clifford 1998).

Fifth, spiritual needs have to be balanced against demands on the environment. For example, numerous sacred sites lie in such public areas as the Grand Canyon, Zion, and Canyonlands National Parks that, while not publicized, are accessible to outsiders. Tribal groups have sought vainly to restrict entry to such sites. Similarly, Plains Indians have sought to ban tourists from climbing of Devils Tower—long the site of religious visions, where prayer bundles of tobacco and sage were left behind by native peoples (*News from Indian Country* 1995).

CONCLUSION

Do Native Americans have to choose between assimilating to the dominant White culture and maintaining their identity? In Figure 6.3, we revisit the continuum of intergroup relations as it relates to Native Americans. Recently there is evidence of pluralism, but aspirations to improve themselves economically usually drives them toward assimilation.

It is not easy to maintain one's tribal identity outside a reservation. One has to consciously seek out one's cultural heritage amid the pressure to assimilate. Even on a reservation, it is not easy to integrate being Native American with elements of contemporary society. The dominant society needs innovative approaches to facilitate pluralism.

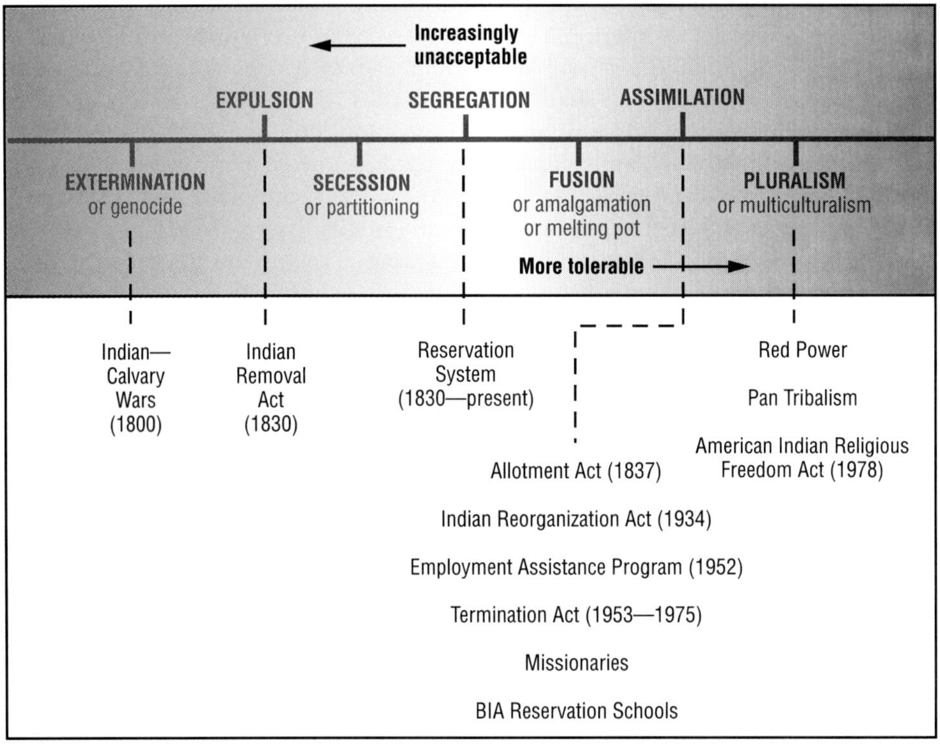

Figure 6.3 Intergroup Relations Continuum

The reservations are economically depressed, but they are also the home of the Native American people ideologically, if not always physically. Furthermore, the reservation's isolation means that the frustrations of reservation life and the violent outbursts against them do not alarm large numbers of Whites, as do disturbances in urban centers. Native Americans today, except in motion pictures, are out of sight and out of mind. The federal government, since the BIA was created in 1824, has had much greater control over Native Americans than over any other civilian group in the nation. For Native Americans, the federal government and White people are virtually synonymous. The typical White, however, tends to be more sympathetic, if not paternalistic, toward Native Americans than toward African Americans.

Subordinate groups in the United States, including Native Americans, have made tremendous gains and will continue to do so in the years to come. But the rest of the population is not standing still. As Native American income rises, so, too, does White income. As Native American children stay in school longer, so, too, do White children. American Indian health care improves, but so, too, does White health care. Advances have been made, but the gap remains between the descendants of the first Americans and those of later arrivals. Low incomes, inadequate education, and poor health care spurred relations between Native Americans and Whites to take a dramatic turn in the 1960s and 1970s, when Native Americans demanded a better life in America.

As Chapter 7 will show, African Americans have achieved a measure of recognition in Washington, D.C., that Native Americans have not. Only 5 percent as numerous as the Black population, the Native Americans' collective voice is weaker. Only a handful of Native Americans have ever served in Congress, and many of the Whites representing states with large numbers of Native Americans have emerged as their biggest foes, rather than their advocates.

The greatest challenge to and asset of the descendants of the first Americans is their land. Although it is only a small slice of what they once occupied, the land they still possess is a rich natural resource. It is barren and largely unproductive agriculturally, but some of it is unspoiled and often rich in natural resources. No wonder many large businesses, land developers, environmentalists, and casino managers covet their land for their own purposes. For Native Americans, the land they still occupy, as well as much of that occupied by other Americans, represents their roots, their homeland.

One Thanksgiving Day, a scholar noted that, according to tradition, at the first Thanksgiving in 1621, the Pilgrims and the Wampanoag ate together. The descendants of these celebrants increasingly sit at distant tables with equally distant thoughts of equality. Today's Native Americans are the "most undernourished, most short-lived, least educated, least healthy." For them, "That long ago Thanksgiving was not a milestone, not a promise. It was the last full meal" (M. Dorris 1988).

KEY TERMS

crossover effect 194
environmental justice 199
fish-ins 184
internal colonialism 176
kickouts or pushouts 193
millenarian movements 175
pan-Indianism 183
powwows 187
setoffs 180
world systems theory 172

REVIEW QUESTIONS

1. Why are sports team mascots such a burning issue for many Native Americans?
2. How have land rights been a continuing theme in White-Native American contact?
3. How much are Native Americans expected to shed their cultural heritage to become a part of contemporary society?
4. Do casinos and other gaming outlets represent a positive force for Native American tribes today?
5. What challenges are there to reservation residents receiving effective health care?

CRITICAL THINKING

1. Consider these two national holidays, Independence Day and Thanksgiving. How do these events remind Native Americans today of their marginal status?
2. Chronicle how aspects of leisure time from schoolyard games to Halloween costumes to team mascots trivialize Native Americans. What experience have you had with such episodes or seen in the mass media?
3. Why do you think that many people in the United States hold more benevolent attitudes toward Native Americans than they do such other subordinate groups as African Americans and Latinos?

INTERNET EXERCISE

Figure 6.2 in the chapter details the location and names of Native American lands and communities. To learn more about some of the people who live/lived there, visit the following web address: (http://www.yahoo.com/Society_and_Culture/Cultures_and_Groups/Cultures/Native_American/). Once there, click on the selection "Tribes, Nations, and Bands." Choose one of the Native American groups and link to the site provided. In which geographic area did this group originally reside? What are some of the religious/spiritual practices described on the Web page? If the site contains pictures, be sure to examine the clothing, symbols, and tools used by the group in the past. What social challenges exist for members of this tribe, nation, or band today? What did you find most surprising about the group you researched? How does the information you found compare to the media's representation of Native Americans?

FOR FURTHER INFORMATION

Vine Deloria, Jr. *Red Earth, White Lies.* New York: Scribner's 1995.
Born on the Pine Ridge Indian Reservation, Deloria examines the bias in the treatment of issues related to Native Americans, including widely accepted scientific views.

Andrew Garrod and Colleen Larimore, eds. *First Person First Peoples: Native American College Graduates Tell Their Life Stories.* Ithaca, NY: Cornell University Press, 1998.
These contributions are all written by Native American alumni reflecting on their experiences of struggle and adjustment in attending Dartmouth College after growing up on a reservation.

Valerie L. Kuletz. *The Tainted Desert: Environmental and Social Ruin in the American West.* New York: Routledge, 1998.
A sociologist offers a compelling account of nuclear testing, uranium mining, and disposition of nuclear waste and its impact on people in the Southwest and, in particular, tribal people.

Russell Thornton, ed. *Studying Native America: Problems and Prospects.* Madison: University of Wisconsin Press, 1998.
The fourteen essays provide contemporary information on Native American Studies, linguistics, identity issues, rituals and beliefs, and the recovery of cultural artifacts.

PERIODICALS

Many tribes publish regular newspapers, and there are also national papers: *Akwesasne Notes,* founded in 1969, and *News from Indian Country,* founded in 1986. Journals include the *American Indian Culture and Research Journal* (1977), *American Indian Religions: An Interdisciplinary Journal* (1994), *Indian Historian* (1967), *Journal of American Indian Education* (1961), and *Tribal College* (1989). In terms of indigenous peoples worldwide, Amnesty International publishes numerous reports, and *Covert Action Information Bulletin* (1983) appears quarterly.

7

The Making of African Americans in a White America

CHAPTER OUTLINE

HIGHLIGHTS

The African presence in the United States began almost simultaneously with permanent White settlement. Unlike most Europeans, however, the African people were brought involuntarily and in bondage. The end of slavery heralded new political rights during Reconstruction, but this was a short-lived era of dignity. Despite advocacy of nonviolence by leaders such as the Reverend Martin Luther King, Jr., the civil rights movement met violent resistance throughout the South. In the mid–1960s, the nation's attention was diverted to urban violence in the North and the West. Blacks responded to their relative deprivation and rising expectations by advocating Black Power, which, in turn, met with White resistance. Religion was and continues to be a major force in the African American community.

Back in 1962, Camden, Alabama, like a number of communities in the South, was the site of civil rights protests. The protesters came from the neighboring town of Gee's Bend, just across the Alabama River. They came by ferry, about a ten-minute trip. The people of predominantly White Camden did not like the marchers, so the county closed down the ferry. For over three decades, the ferry remained closed, requiring the 400 residents of all-Black Gee's Bend to drive more than 80 miles each way to get to their jobs, schools, or the hospital. Finally, in 1996, the isolation ended when ferry service was reinstated.

Two residents noted the significance of this event. "This is the first time there has been a concerted effort on the part of blacks and whites to do something positive," said Perry Hale, a Black high school teacher. Newspaper publisher Hollis Curl, who is White, remarked, "It's hard for people in other parts of the country to realize what a coming together this has been" (R. Tyson 1996).

Relationships between Whites and Blacks in the United States have been marked by many episodes like those along the Alabama River—sometimes a step backward and occasionally a step forward.

The United States, with more than 33 million Blacks (or African Americans), has the sixth-largest Black population in the world; only Brazil, Ethiopia, Nigeria, South Africa, and Zaire have larger Black populations. Despite their large numbers, Blacks in this country have had virtually no role in major national and political decisions and have been allowed only a peripheral role in many crucial decisions that influenced their own destiny.

The history of African Americans is, to a significant degree, the history of the United States. Black people accompanied the first explorers, and a Black man was among the first to die in the American Revolution. The enslavement of Africans was responsible for the South's wealth in the nineteenth century and led to the country's most violent domestic strife. After they were freed from slavery, their continued subordination led to sporadic outbreaks of violence in the rural South and throughout urban America. This chapter concentrates on the history of African Americans into the 1990s. Their contemporary situation is the subject of Chapter 8.

As with European immigrants described in Chapter 4, Black Africans brought with them a variety of cultural traditions. As illustrated in Figure 7.1, while most of the people brought forcibly to North America from Africa to be enslaved came from a limited geographic area of the African continent, they represented diverse cultural experiences. Today, we rarely remember these tribal or ethnic variations among the descendants of the Africans in the way we customarily do among Europeans.

The Black experience in what came to be the United States began as something less than citizenship, yet slightly better than slavery. In 1619, twenty Africans arrived in Jamestown as indentured servants. Their children were born free people. These Blacks in the British colonies were not the first in the New World, however; some Blacks had accompanied European explorers, perhaps even Columbus. But all this is a historical footnote. By the 1660s, the British colonies had passed laws making Africans slaves for life, forbidding interracial marriages, and making children of slaves bear the status of their mother regardless of their father's race. Slavery had begun in North America; more than three centuries later we still live with its legacy.

Slavery

Slavery seems far removed from the debates over issues that divide Whites and Blacks today. Both contemporary institutional and individual racism, however, which are central to today's conflicts, have their origins in the institution of slavery. Slavery was not merely a single aspect of American society for three centuries; it has been an essential part of our country's life. For nearly half of this country's history, slavery was not only tolerated but legally protected by the U.S. Constitution as interpreted by the U.S. Supreme Court.

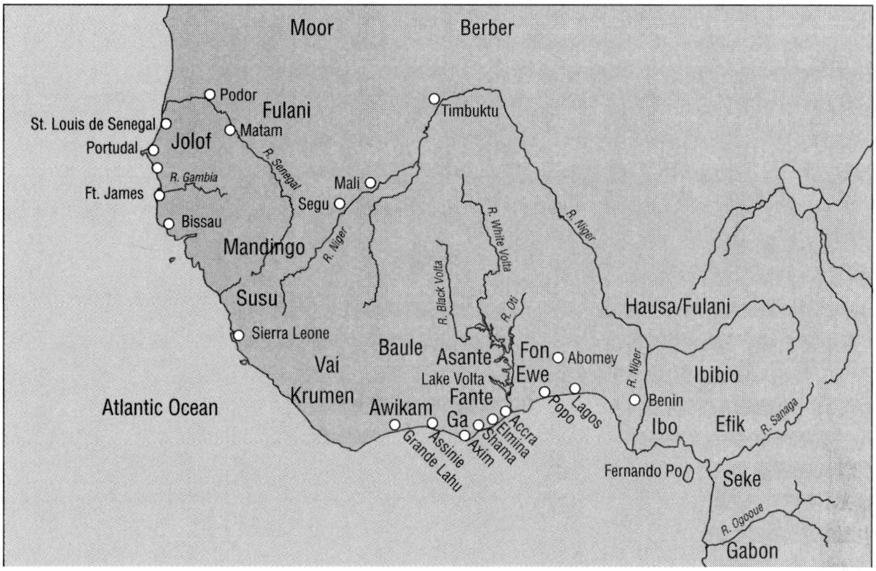

Figure 7.1 West African Tribal Groups During Slave Trade
Most Africans who were forcibly brought to the United States came from a relatively limited area of Africa but brought with them a rich variety of cultural traditions, as reflected on this map.

Source: Reprinted with the permission of Macmillan Library Reference USA, a division of Ahsuog, Inc. From *The Historical and Cultural Atlas of African Americans* by Molefi K. Asante and Mark T. Mattson. Copyright ©1992 by Molefi Kete Asante and Mark Mattson.

In sharp contrast to the basic rights and privileges enjoyed by White Americans, Black people in bondage lived under a system of repression and terror. Because the institution of slavery was so fundamental to our culture, it continues to influence Black-White relations as we begin the twenty-first century (ACLU 1996b).

SLAVE CODES

Slavery in the United States rested on five central conditions: first, slavery was for life; second, the status was inherited; third, slaves were considered mere property; fourth, slaves were denied rights; and fifth, coercion was used to maintain the system (D. Noel 1972). As slavery developed in colonial America and the United States, so did **slave codes,** laws that defined the low position of slaves in the United States. Although the rules varied from state to state and from time to time and were not always enforced, the more common features demonstrate how completely subjugated the Africans were.

1. A slave could not marry or even meet with a free Black.
2. Marriage between slaves was not legally recognized.

Table 7.1 Black Population, 1790–2050

Blacks accounted for a decreasing proportion of the total population until the 1940s, primarily because White immigration to the United States far outdistanced population growth by Blacks.

Census	Black Population (in Thousands)	Black Percentage of Total Population
1790	757	19.3
1810	1,378	19.0
1830	2,329	18.1
1850	3,639	15.7
1870	4,880	12.7
1890	7,489	11.9
1910	9,828	10.7
1930	11,891	9.7
1950	15,042	10.0
1970	22,581	11.1
1990	29,986	12.1
1997	34,200	12.8
2000 (projection)	35,454	12.9
2050 (projection)	62,592	15.4

Source: Bureau of the Census 1975: 9; J. Day, 1996: 16; DeBarros and Bennett, 1998.

3. A slave could not legally buy or sell anything except by special arrangement.
4. A slave could not possess weapons or liquor.
5. A slave could not quarrel with or use abusive language toward Whites.
6. A slave could not possess property (including money), except as allowed by his or her owner.
7. A slave could make no will, nor could he or she inherit anything.
8. A slave could not make a contract or hire himself or herself out.
9. A slave could not leave a plantation without a pass noting his or her destination and time of return.
10. No one, including Whites, was to teach a slave (and in some areas even a free Black) to read or write or to give a slave a book, including the Bible.
11. A slave could not gamble.
12. A slave had to obey established curfews.
13. A slave could not testify in court except against another slave.

Violations of these rules were dealt with in a variety of ways. Mutilation and branding were not unknown. Imprisonment was rare; most violators were whipped. An owner was virtually immune from prosecution for any physical abuse of slaves. Because slaves could not testify in court, a White's actions toward enslaved African Americans were practically above the law (ACLU 1996b; S. Elkins 1959; Franklin and Moss 1994; K. Stampp 1956).

Slavery, as enforced through the slave codes, controlled and determined all facets of the lives of the enslaved Africans. The organization of family life and religious worship were no exceptions. Naturally, the Africans had brought to America their own cultural traditions. In Africa, people had been accustomed to a closely regulated family life and a rigidly enforced moral code. Slavery rendered it impossible for them to retain these family ties in the New World. The demand for male Africans created an extreme imbalance in the sexes in the slave population. It was not until 1840, two centuries after African slave labor had begun, that the number of Black women equaled the number of Black men in America. Religious life in Africa was rich with rituals and beliefs, but like family structures, the religious practices of the slaves underwent a major transformation in the New World (W. Du Bois 1970; K. Stampp 1956).

The slave family had no standing in law. Marriages among slaves were not legally recognized, and masters rarely respected them in selling adults or children. Slave breeding—deliberate efforts to maximize the number of offspring—was practiced with little attention to the emotional needs of the slaves themselves. The slaveholder, not the parents, decided at what age children should begin working in the fields. The slave family could not offer its children shelter or security, rewards or punishments. The man's only recognized family role was that of siring offspring, being the sex partner of a woman. In fact, slave men were often identified as if they were the woman's possession, for example, as "Nancy's Tom." Southern law consistently ruled that "the father of a slave is unknown to our law." This does not imply that the male slave did not occupy an important economic role. Men held virtually all the managerial positions open to slaves.

By permission of Mike Luckovich and Creators Syndicate

Unlike the family structure, to which slavery dealt near-mortal blows, a strong religious tradition survived. In fact, a slaveholder wishing to do "God's work on earth" would encourage the slave church, finding it functional in dominating the slaves. Of course, African religions were forbidden, and the White people's Christianity flourished, but Blacks still used West African concepts in the totally new way of life that slavery brought. The preacher maintained an intense relationship with the congregation, similar to the role played by the elder in West Africa. The Christianity to which the slaves were introduced stressed obeying their owner. Complete surrender to Whites meant salvation and eternal happiness in the hereafter. In contrast, to question God's will, to fight slavery, caused everlasting damnation. Obviously, this twisted version of Christianity was intended to make slaves acquiesce in their holders' wishes in return for reward after death. To some degree, however, religion did keep the desire for freedom alive in slaves, and to some extent it formed the basis of their struggle for freedom: nightly prayer meetings and singing gave them a sense of unity and common destiny necessary for that struggle. On a more personal level, religion made the slaves' daily lives more bearable (E. Frazier 1964; G. Rawick 1972; K. Stampp 1956).

AFRICAN AMERICANS AND AFRICA

The importance of Africa to Black Americans can be seen in the aspects of African culture that became integral parts of Blacks' lives in the United States. This importance was recognized long before the emergence of the Afrocentric perspective in the 1990s. Black scholars W. E. B. Du Bois (1939) and Carter Woodson (1968), along with respected White anthropologist Melville Herskovits (1930, 1941), have all argued persuasively for the continued influence of the African heritage.

Scholars debate to what degree African culture was able to persist despite efforts by slaveholders to replace any vestige of African tradition. The survival of African culture can be most easily documented in folklore, religion, language, and music. It is difficult to clarify the degree of survival, however, because Africans came from many different cultures. When we think of ethnic origins, our thoughts turn to European groups such as Poles or Greeks, but within Africa are the Ibos, Gas, and Yorubas, to name a few of the sources of slaves from Africa (refer back to Figure 7.1). Thus, to speak of a single source of African culture ignores the complexity of social life on that continent. Furthermore, as the Afrocentric perspective argues, some aspects of African culture, such as certain art forms, have so permeated Western culture that we mistakenly believe their origins are European.

Africa has had and will always have an importance to Blacks that many Blacks and most Whites do not appreciate, and this importance is unlikely to be changed by the continued debate over which aspects of Black life today can be traced back to African culture. The significance of Africa to Black Americans is one of the most easily identifiable themes in the Black experience. During certain periods (the 1920s and the late 1960s), the Black cultural tradition was the rallying point of many Blacks, especially those living in the cities. Studies continue to document the survival of African culture in North America. Research has identified remnants of grammar and sentence construction in the speech patterns of low-income and rural Blacks. **Ebonics** refers to the distinctive dialect, with a complex language structure, that is found among Black Americans. Although the term *Ebonics* (*ebony* and *phonics*) was coined in the 1970s, there has long been a recognition of a distinctive language pattern, sometimes called "Black English," which includes some vocabulary and grammar rules that reflect the West African origins of Black Americans. In 1996, Ebonics became a national issue following the Oakland, California, school board's recognition of it as the primary language of schoolchildren who were then learning mainstream American English. This debate aside, there is consensus that, a century after slavery, remnants of African cultural traditions survive (P. Applebone 1997).

THE ATTACK ON SLAVERY

Although the slave was vulnerable to his or her owner's wishes, slavery as an institution was vulnerable to outside opinion. For a generation after the American Revolution, restrictions on slaves increased as Southerners accepted slavery as permanent. Slave revolts and antislavery propaganda only accelerated the intensity of

Kwanzaa is a nonreligious cultural celebration of African American values developed in the United States in 1966. It has its roots in the African cultural principles of sharing, unity, and community. The annual event, which starts December 26, is gaining popularity and, to the concern of its proponents, is becoming more commercialized.

oppression. This change led to the ironic situation that as slavery was attacked from within and without, its conditions became harsher and its defenders became more outspoken in asserting what they saw as its benefits.

The antislavery, or **abolitionist,** movement involved both Whites and free Blacks. Many Whites who opposed slavery, such as Abraham Lincoln, did not also believe in racial equality. In their minds, even though slavery was a moral evil, racial equality was still unimaginable. This apparent inconsistency did not lessen the emotional fervor of the efforts to end slavery. Antislavery societies had been founded even before the American Revolution, but the Constitution dealt the antislavery movement a blow. In order to appease the South, the framers of the Constitution recognized and legitimized slavery's existence. The Constitution even allowed slavery to increase Southern political power. A slave was counted as three-fifths of a person in determining population representation in the House of Representatives.

Abolitionists, both Black and White, continued to speak out against slavery and the harm it was doing not only to the slaves but to the entire nation, which had become economically dependent on bondage. Frederick Douglass and Sojourner Truth, both freed slaves, became very visible in the fight against slavery through their eloquent speeches and publications related to their remarks. Harriet Tubman, along with other Blacks and sympathetic Whites, developed the Underground Railroad to convey escaping slaves to freedom in the North and Canada (Franklin and Moss 1994).

Another aspect of Black enslavement was the slaves' own resistance to servitude. Slaves did revolt, and between 40,000 and 100,000 actually escaped from the South and slavery. Yet fugitive-slave acts provided for the return even of slaves who had reached free states. Enslaved Blacks who did not attempt escape, at least in part because failure often led to death, resisted slavery through such means as passive resistance. Slaves feigned clumsiness or illness; pretended not to understand, see, or hear; ridiculed Whites with a mocking, subtle humor that their owners did not comprehend; and destroyed farm implements and committed similar acts of sabotage (Bauer and Bauer 1942; L. Bennett 1966; J. Oakes 1993).

SLAVERY'S AFTERMATH

On January 1, 1863, President Lincoln issued the Emancipation Proclamation. The document created hope in slaves in the South, but many Union soldiers resigned rather than participate in a struggle to free slaves. The proclamation freed slaves only in the Confederacy, over which the President had no control. The 800,000 slaves in the border states were unaffected. Nonetheless, 179,000 Black men served in the Union Army, and 37,300 of them died. Six months after the surrender of the Confederacy in 1865, abolition became law when the Thirteenth Amendment abolished slavery throughout the nation.

From 1867 to 1877, during the period called Reconstruction, Black–White relations in the South were unlike anything they had ever been. The Reconstruction Act of 1867 put each Southern state under a military governor until a new state constitution could be written, with Blacks participating fully in the process. Whites and Blacks married each other, went to public schools and state universities together, and rode side by side on trains and streetcars. The most conspicuous evidence of the new position of Blacks was their presence in elected office. In 1870, the Fifteenth Amendment was ratified, prohibiting the denial of the right to vote on grounds of race, color, or previous condition of servitude. Black men put their vote to good use; Blacks were elected as six lieutenant governors, sixteen major state officials, twenty members of the House of Representatives, and two U.S. Senators. Despite accusations that they were corrupt, Black officials and Black-dominated legislatures created new and progressive state constitutions. Black political organizations, such as the Union League and the Loyal League, rivaled the church as the focus of community organization (I. Berlin 1998, Berlin et al. 1998; W. Du Bois 1969b).

Reconstruction was ended as part of a political compromise in the election of 1876 and, consequently, segregation became entrenched in the South. Evidence of Jim Crow's reign was apparent by the close of the nineteenth century. The term **Jim Crow** appears to have its origin in a dance tune, but by the 1890s it was synonymous with segregation and referred to the statutes that kept African Americans in an inferior position. Segregation often preceded laws and in practice often went beyond their provisions. The institutionalization of segregation gave White supremacy its ultimate authority. In 1896, the U.S. Supreme Court ruled in *Plessy* v. *Ferguson* that state laws requiring "separate but equal" accommodations for Blacks were a "reasonable" use of state government power (L. Bennett 1966; C. Woodward 1974).

It was in the political sphere that Jim Crow exacted its price soonest. In 1898, the Court's decision in *Williams* v. *Mississippi* declared constitutional the use of poll taxes, literacy tests, and residential requirements to discourage Blacks from voting. In Louisiana that year, 130,000 Blacks were registered to vote. Eight years later only 1,342 were. Even all these measures did not deprive all African Americans of the vote, and so White supremacists erected a final obstacle—the **White primary,** which forbade Black voting in election primaries. By the turn of the century, the South had a one-party system, making the primary the significant contest and the general election a mere rubber stamp. Beginning with South Carolina in 1896 and spreading to twelve other states within twenty years, statewide Democratic Party primaries were adopted. The party explicitly excluded Blacks from voting, an exclusion that was constitutional because the party was defined as a private organization that was free to define its own membership qualifications. The White primary brought a virtual end to the political gains of Reconstruction (D. Lacy 1972; P. Lewinson 1965; C. Woodward 1974).

The Challenge of Black Leadership

The institutionalization of White supremacy precipitated different responses from African Americans, just as slavery had. In the late 1800s and early 1900s, a number of articulate Blacks attempted to lead the first generation of freeborn Black Americans. Most prominent were Booker T. Washington and W. E. B. Du Bois. The personalities as well as the ideas of these two men contrasted with one another. Washington was born a slave in 1856 on a Virginia plantation. He worked in coal mines after emancipation and attended elementary school. Through hard work and driving ambition, Washington became the head of an educational institute for Blacks in Tuskegee, Alabama. Within fifteen years, his leadership brought the Tuskegee Institute national recognition and made him a national figure. Du Bois, on the other hand, was born in 1868 of a free family in Massachusetts. He attended Fisk University and the University of Berlin and became the first Black to receive a doctorate from Harvard. Washington died in 1915, while Du Bois died in self-imposed exile in Africa in 1963.

THE POLITICS OF ACCOMMODATION

Booker T. Washington's approach to White supremacy is referred to as the *politics of accommodation*. He was willing to forego social equality until White people saw Blacks as deserving of it. Perhaps his most famous speech was made in Atlanta on September 18, 1895, to an audience that was mostly White and mostly wealthy. Introduced by the governor of Georgia as "a representative of Negro enterprise and Negro civilization," Washington (1900) gave a five-minute speech in which he pledged the continued dedication of Blacks to Whites:

> *As we have proved our loyalty to you in the past, in nursing your children, watching by the sick-bed of your mothers and fathers, and often following them with tear-dimmed eyes to their graves, so in the future, in our humble way, we shall stand by you with a*

A 1935 lynching in Ft. Lauderdale of an African American who had been charged with "threatening and frightening" a White woman. Note the reaction of some of the onlookers. Over 3,000 Blacks were executed by lynching between 1889 and 1938.

devotion that no foreigner can approach, ready to lay down our lives, if need be, in defense of yours (p. 221).

The speech catapulted Washington into the public forum, and he became the anointed spokesperson for Blacks for the next twenty years. President Grover Cleveland congratulated Washington for the "new hope" he gave Blacks. Washington's essential theme was compromise. Unlike Frederick Douglass, who had demanded the same rights for Blacks as for Whites, Washington asked that Blacks be educated because it would be a wise investment for Whites. Racial hatred he referred to as "the great and intricate problem which God has laid at the doors of the South." The Blacks' goal should be economic respectability. Washington's accommodating attitude ensured his popularity with Whites. His recognition by Whites contributed to his large following of Blacks, who were not used to seeing their leaders achieve fame among Whites (H. Hawkins 1962; R. Logan 1954; A. Pinkney 1994).

It is easy in retrospect to be critical of Washington and to write him off as simply a product of his times. Booker T. Washington entered the public arena when the more militant proposals of Douglass had been buried. Black politicians were losing political contests and influence. To become influential as a Black, Washington reasoned, required White acceptance. His image as an accommodator allowed him to fight discrimination covertly. He assisted Presidents Roosevelt and Taft in appointing Blacks to patronage positions. Washington's goal was for African Americans eventually to have the same rights and opportunities as Whites. Just as people disagree with leaders today, some Blacks disagreed over the means that Washington chose to reach that goal. No African American was more outspoken in his criticism of the politics of accommodation than W. E. B. Du Bois (J. Conyers 1996; L. Harlan 1972; H. Hawkins 1962; Meier and Rudwick 1966).

THE NIAGARA MOVEMENT

The rivalry between Washington and Du Bois has been exaggerated. Actually, they enjoyed fairly cordial relations for some time. In 1900, Washington recommended Du Bois, at his request, for superintendent of Black schools in Washington, D.C. By 1905, however, relations between the two had cooled. Du Bois spoke critically of Washington's influence, arguing that his power was being used to stifle African Americans such as himself who spoke out against the politics of accommodation. He also charged that Washington had caused the transfer of funds from academic programs to vocational education. Du Bois's greatest objection to Washington's statements was that they encouraged Whites to place the burden of the Blacks' problems on the Blacks themselves (W. Du Bois 1961; see also H. Hawkins 1962).

As an alternative to Washington's program, Du Bois (1903) advocated the theory of the *talented tenth,* which reflected his atypical educational background. Unlike Washington, Du Bois was not at home with both intellectuals and sharecroppers. Although the very words *talented tenth* have an elitist ring to them, Du Bois argued that these privileged Blacks must serve the other nine-tenths. This argument was also Du Bois's way of criticizing Washington's emphasis on vocational education. He thought education for African Americans should emphasize academics, which would be more likely to improve their position. Drawing on the talented tenth, Du Bois invited twenty-nine Blacks to participate in a strategy session near Niagara Falls in 1905. Out of a series of meetings came several demands that unmistakably placed the responsibility for the problems facing African Americans on the shoulders of Whites.

The Niagara Movement, as it came to be called, was closely monitored by Booker T. Washington. Du Bois encountered difficulty gaining financial support and recruiting prominent people, and Du Bois (1968) himself was to write, "My leadership was solely of ideas. I never was, nor ever will be, personally popular" (p. 303). The movement's legacy was the education of a new generation of African Americans in the politics of protest. After 1910, the Niagara Movement ceased to hold annual conventions. In 1909, however, the National Association for the Advancement of Colored People (NAACP), with White and Black members, was founded by the Niagara Movement leaders. It was through the work of the NAACP that the Niagara Movement accomplished most of the goals set forth in 1905. The NAACP also marked the merging of White liberalism and Black militancy, a coalition unknown since the end of the abolition movement and Reconstruction (L. Bennett 1966; J. Conyers 1996; E. Rudwick 1957).

The Exodus Northward

The most significant event for African Americans during the first half of the twentieth century was not in the realm of legal or social rights, but in the demographic

In this classic Margaret Bourke-White photograph, a line of Black Americans awaits food handouts in 1937 in Louisville, Kentucky.

change in the distribution of Black people. In 1900, 90 percent of African Americans lived in the South. As shown in Figure 7.2, Blacks moved out of the South and into the West and North, especially the urban areas in those regions, during the post-Civil War period and continued to migrate through the 1950s and 1960s. However, most African Americans still live in the South in the 1990s.

Life in the North was generally better than it had been in the South, where agricultural conditions had worsened considerably. Although the migrants entered the job market at the bottom and lived in the worst housing the North offered, they were still better off than in the rural South. The principal reason for Black migration out of the South was similar to the motivation for the many millions of Europeans who came to the United States: the search for better economic opportunities.

The pattern of violence, with Blacks usually the victims, started in the South during Reconstruction and continued into the twentieth century, when it also spread northward. In 1917, a riot in East St. Louis, Illinois, claimed the lives of thirty-nine Blacks and nine Whites. The several days of violence resulted from White fear of social and economic gains made by Blacks. The summer of 1919 saw so much violence that it is commonly referred to as the "red summer." Twenty-six riots broke out

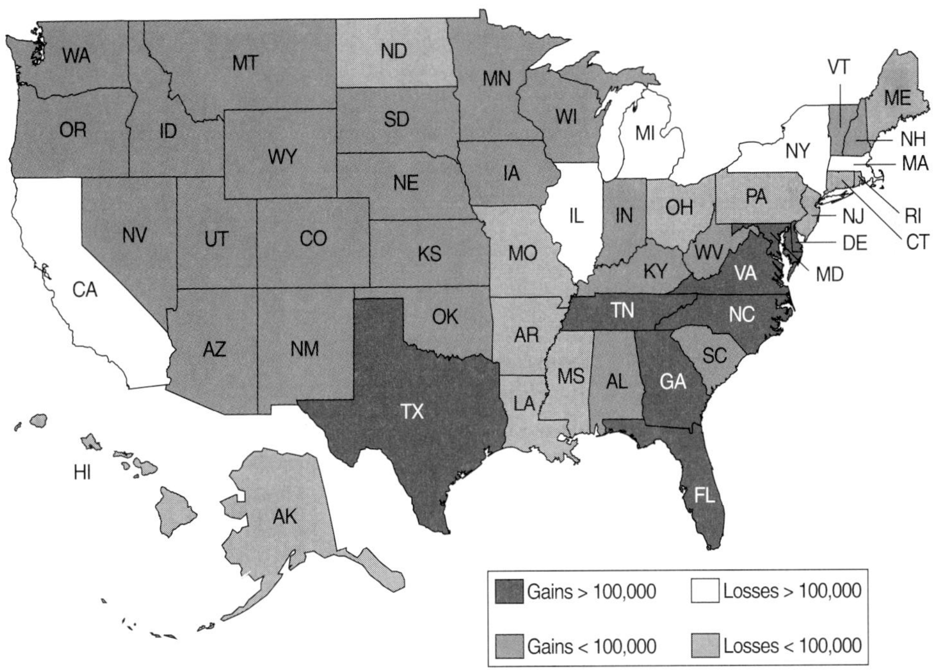

Figure 7.2 Projected Black Net Migration, 1995 to 2025

Although the early part of the twentieth century was characterized by migration from the South to the North and West, predicting migration patterns in the future is a bit more complicated. The biggest gains, however, are expected to be in the South, reflecting anticipated economic growth in that part of the country.

Source: William H. Frey. Analysis of U.S. Census Data, 1998.

throughout the country as White soldiers returned from World War I fearing the new competition that Blacks represented. This period of violence against African Americans also saw a resurgence of the Ku Klux Klan, which at its height had nearly 9 million members (E. Bonacich 1976; A. Grimshaw 1969; R. Schaefer 1971, 1980).

The competition between African Americans and Whites for jobs was short-lived. The unionization of industrial plants by the all-White American Federation of Labor (AFL) generally meant the expulsion of all Blacks, regardless of their skills or seniority. The National Urban League, founded in 1911 by Blacks and Whites allied with Booker T. Washington, wrestled unsuccessfully with the mass unemployment of Blacks. The NAACP did not involve itself at this time with job discrimination. Basically, the needs and frustrations of African Americans in the growing ghettos of the North were unmet by the government and the existing organizations (L. Bennett 1966; Franklin and Moss 1994; D. Lacy 1972; Meier and Rudwick 1966).

Reemergence of Black Protest

American involvement in World War II signaled prosperity for both Whites and Blacks. Nearly a million African Americans served in the military in rigidly segregated units. Generally, more Blacks could participate in the armed services in World War II than in previous military engagements, but efforts by Blacks to contribute to the war effort at home were hampered by discriminatory practices in defense plants. A. Philip Randolph, president of the Brotherhood of Sleeping Car Porters, threatened to lead 100,000 Blacks in a march on Washington in 1941 to ensure their employment. Randolph's proposed tactic was nonviolent direct action, which he modeled on Mahatma Gandhi's practices in India. Randolph made it clear that he intended the march to be an all-Black event because he saw it as neither necessary nor desirable for Whites to lead Blacks to their own liberation. President Franklin Roosevelt responded to the pressure and agreed to issue an executive order prohibiting discrimination if Randolph would call off the march. Although the order and the Fair Employment Practices Commission (FEPC) it set up did not fulfill the original promises, a precedent had been established for federal intervention in job discrimination (H. Garfinkel 1959).

Racial turmoil during World War II was not limited to threatened marches. Racial disturbances occurred in cities throughout the country, the worst riot occurring in Detroit in June 1943. In that case, President Roosevelt sent in 6,000 soldiers to quell the violence, which left twenty-five Blacks and nine Whites dead. The racial disorders were paralleled by a growth in civil disobedience as a means to achieve equality for Blacks. The Congress of Racial Equality (CORE) was founded in 1942 to fight discrimination with nonviolent direct action. This interracial group used sit-ins to open restaurants to Black patrons in Chicago, Baltimore, and Los Angeles. In 1947, CORE sent "freedom riders" to test a court ruling that prohibited segregation in interstate bus travel. In contrast to the red summer of 1919, the end of World War II was not followed by widespread racial violence, in part because the continued expansion of the postwar economy reduced competition between Whites and Blacks for employment (A. Grimshaw 1969; Meier and Rudwick 1966).

The war years and the period following saw several U.S. Supreme Court decisions that suggested the High Court was moving away from tolerating racial inequities. The White primary elections endorsed in Jim Crow's formative period were finally challenged in the 1944 *Smith* v. *Allwright* decision. The effectiveness of the victory was limited; many states simply passed statutes that used new devices to frustrate African American voters.

A particularly repugnant legal device for relegating African Americans to second-class status was restrictive covenants. A **restrictive covenant** was a private contract entered into by neighborhood property owners stipulating that property could not be sold or rented to certain minority groups, thus ensuring that they could not live in the area. In 1948, the Supreme Court finally declared in *Shelley v. Kramer* that restrictive covenants were not constitutional, although it did not actually attack their discriminatory nature. The victory was in many ways less substantial than it was symbolic of the new willingness by the Supreme Court to uphold the rights of Black citizens.

The Democratic administrations of the late 1940s and early 1950s made a number of promises to Black Americans. The party adopted a strong civil rights platform in 1948, but its provisions were not enacted. Once again, union president Randolph threatened Washington, D.C., with a massive march. This time he insisted that, as long as Blacks were subjected to a peacetime draft, the military must be desegregated. President Truman responded by issuing an executive order on July 26, 1948, desegregating the armed forces. The U.S. Army abolished its quota system in 1950, and training camps for the Korean War were integrated. Desegregation was not complete, however, especially in the reserves and the National Guard, and even today charges of racial favoritism confront the armed forces. Whatever its shortcomings, the desegregation order offered African Americans an alternative to segregated civilian life (C. Moskos 1966).

The Civil Rights Movement

It is difficult to say exactly when a social movement begins or ends. Usually, a movement's ideas or tactics precede the actual mobilization of people and continue long after the movement's driving force has been replaced by new ideals and techniques. This description applies to the civil rights movement and its successor, the continuing struggle for African American freedom. Prior to 1954, there were some confrontations of White supremacy: the CORE sit-ins of 1942 and efforts to desegregate buses in Baton Rouge, Louisiana, in 1953. The civil rights movement gained momentum with a Supreme Court decision in 1954 that eventually desegregated the public schools, and it ended as a major force in Black America with the civil disorders of 1965 through 1968. However, beginning in 1954, toppling the traditional barriers to full rights for Blacks was the rule, not the exception.

STRUGGLE TO DESEGREGATE THE SCHOOLS

For the majority of Black children, public school education meant attending segregated schools. Southern school districts assigned children to school by race, rather than by neighborhood, a practice that constituted de jure segregation. **De jure segregation** refers to segregation that results from children being assigned to schools specifically to maintain racially separate schools. It was this form of legal humiliation that was attacked in the landmark decree of *Linda Brown et al.* v. *Board of Education of Topeka, Kansas.*

Seven-year-old Linda Brown was not permitted to enroll in the grade school four blocks from her home in Topeka, Kansas. Rather, school board policy dictated that she attend the Black school almost two miles away. This denial led the NAACP Legal Defense and Educational Fund to bring suit on behalf of Linda Brown and twelve other Black children. The NAACP argued that the Fourteenth Amendment was intended to rule out segregation in public schools. Chief Justice Earl Warren of the Supreme Court wrote the unanimous opinion that "in the field of public education the doctrine of 'separate but equal' has no place. Separate educational facilities are inherently unequal."

The freedom that African Americans saw in their grasp at the time of the *Brown* decision essentially amounted to a reaffirmation of American values. What Blacks sought was assimilation into White American society. The motivation for the *Brown* suit came not merely because Black schools were inferior, although they were. Blacks were assigned to poorly ventilated and dilapidated buildings, with overcrowded classrooms and unqualified teachers. Less money was spent on Black schools than on White schools throughout the South in both rural and metropolitan areas. The issue was not such tangible factors, however, but the intangible effect of not being allowed to go to school with Whites. All-Black schools could not be equal to all-White schools. Even in this victory, Blacks were reaffirming White society and the importance of an integrated educational experience.

Linda Brown, of *Brown* v. *Board of Education*, standing in front of the school near her home, which she could not attend because the schools of Topeka, Kansas, were segregated.

Although *Brown* marked the beginning of the civil rights movement, the reaction to it showed just how deeply prejudice was held in the South. Resistance to court-ordered desegregation took many forms: some people called for impeachment of all the Supreme

Court justices, others petitioned Congress (to declare the Fourteenth Amendment unconstitutional), cities closed schools rather than comply, and the governor of Arkansas even used the state's National Guard to block Black students from entering a previously all-White high school in Little Rock.

The issue of school desegregation was extended to higher education, and Mississippi state troopers and the state's National Guard confronted each other over the 1962 admission of James Meredith, the first African American accepted by the University of Mississippi. Scores were injured, and two were killed in this clash between segregationists and the law. A similar defiant stand was taken a year later by Governor George Wallace, who "stood in the schoolhouse door" to block two Blacks from enrolling in the University of Alabama. President Kennedy federalized the Alabama National Guard to guarantee admission of the students. *Brown* did not resolve the school controversy, and many questions remain unanswered. More recently, the issue of school segregation resulting from neighborhood segregation has been debated. In the next chapter, another form of segregation, called *de facto* segregation, is examined more closely (J. Butler 1996).

CIVIL DISOBEDIENCE

The success of a year-long boycott of city buses in Montgomery, Alabama, dealt Jim Crow another setback. On December 1, 1955, Rosa Parks defied the law and refused to give her seat on a crowded bus to a White man. Her defiance led to the organization of the Montgomery Improvement Association, headed by 26-year-old Martin Luther King, Jr., a Baptist minister with a Ph.D. from Boston University. The bus boycott was the first of many instances in which nonviolent direct action was employed as a means that Blacks used to obtain the rights that Whites already enjoyed. Initially, the boycott protested discourtesies to Blacks and asked that Black drivers be hired for bus routes in predominantly Black areas. Eventually, the demands included the outright end of segregated seating. The *Brown* decision woke up all of America to racial injustice, but the Montgomery boycott marked a significant shift away from the historical reliance on NAACP court battles (L. Killian 1975).

Civil disobedience is based on the belief that individuals have the right to disobey the law under certain circumstances. This tactic was not new; it had been used before in India and also by Blacks in the United States. Under King's leadership, however, civil disobedience became a widely used technique and even gained a measure of acceptability among some prominent Whites. King distinguished clearly between the laws to be obeyed and those to be disobeyed: "A just law is a man-made law of God. An unjust law is a code that is out of harmony with the moral law" (1963:82). In disobeying unjust laws, King developed this strategy.

1. Active nonviolent resistance to evil
2. Not seeking to defeat or humiliate opponents, but to win their friendship and understanding
3. Attacking the forces of evil rather than the people who happen to be doing the evil

4. Willingness to accept suffering without retaliating
5. Refusing to hate the opponent
6. Acting with the conviction that the universe is on the side of justice. (1958:101–107)

King, like other Blacks before him and since, made it clear that passive acceptance of injustice was intolerable. He hoped that by emphasizing nonviolence, southern Blacks would display their hostility to racism in a way that would undercut violent reaction by Whites.

The pattern had now been established and a method devised to confront racism. But civil disobedience did not work quickly. The struggle to desegregate buses in the South, for example, took seven years. Civil disobedience was also not spontaneous. The success of the civil rights movement rested on a dense network of local efforts. People were spontaneously attracted to the efforts, but organized tactics and targets were crucial to dismantling racist institutions that had existed for generations (A. Morris 1993; C. Payne 1995).

Beginning in April 1963, the Southern Christian Leadership Conference (SCLC), founded by King, began a series of marches in Birmingham to demand fair employment opportunities, desegregation of public facilities, and the release of 3,000 people arrested for participating in the marches. King, himself arrested, tells in "Listen to Their Voices" (pp. 200–201) why civil disobedience and the confrontation that followed were necessary. In May, the Birmingham police used dogs and water from high-pressure hoses on the marchers, who included many schoolchildren.

Congress had still failed to enact any sweeping federal barrier to discrimination. Following the example of A. Philip Randolph in 1941, Blacks organized the March on Washington for Jobs and Freedom on August 28, 1963. With more than 200,000 people participating, the march was the high point of the civil rights movement. The mass of people, middle-class Whites and Blacks looking to the federal government for support, symbolized the struggle. However, a public opinion poll conducted shortly before the march documented the continuing resentment of the majority of Whites: 63 percent were opposed to the rally (G. Gallup 1972:1836).

King (1971) delivered his famous "I Have a Dream" speech before the large crowd; he looked forward to a time when all Americans "will be able to join hands and sing in the words of the old Negro spiritual, 'Free at last! free at last! Thank God almighty, we are free at last!'" (p. 351). Just eighteen days later, a bomb exploded in a Black church in Birmingham, killing four little girls and injuring twenty others.

Despair only increased as the November 1963 elections saw segregationists successful in their bid for office. Most distressing was the assassination of President Kennedy on November 22. As President, Kennedy had appealed to Blacks despite his previously mediocre legislative record in the U.S. Senate. His death left doubt as to the direction and pace of future actions on civil rights by the executive branch under President Lyndon Baines Johnson. Two months later, the Twenty-fourth Amendment was ratified, outlawing the poll tax that had long prevented Blacks from voting. The enactment of the Civil Rights Act on July 2, 1964, was hailed as a major

LISTEN TO THEIR VOICES

Letter from Birmingham Jail

Martin Luther King, Jr.

You may well ask: "Why direct action? Why sit-ins, marches and so forth? Isn't negotiation a better path?" You are quite right in calling for negotiation. Indeed, this is the very purpose of direct action. Nonviolent direct action seeks to create such a crisis and foster such a tension that a community which has constantly refused to negotiate is forced to confront the issue. It seeks so to dramatize the issue that it can no longer be ignored. My citing the creation of tension as part of the work of the nonviolent-resister may sound rather shocking. But I must confess that I am not afraid of the word "tension." I have earnestly opposed violent tension, but there is a type of constructive, nonviolent tension which is necessary for growth. Just as Socrates felt that it was necessary to create a tension in the mind so that individuals could rise from the bondage of myths and half-truths to the unfettered realm of creative analysis and objective appraisal, so must we see the need for nonviolent gadflies to create the kind of tension in society that will help men rise from the dark depths of prejudice and racism to the majestic heights of understanding and brotherhood.

The purpose of our direct-action program is to create a situation so crisis-packed that it will inevitably open the door to negotiation. I therefore concur with you in your call for negotiation. Too long has our beloved Southland been bogged down in a tragic effort to live in monologue rather than dialogue....

You express a great deal of anxiety over our willingness to break laws. This is certainly a legitimate concern. Since we so diligently urge people to obey the Supreme Court's decision of 1954 outlawing segregation in the public schools, at first glance it may seem rather paradoxical for us consciously to break laws. One may well ask: "How can you advocate breaking some laws and obeying others?" The answer lies in the fact that there are two types of laws: just and unjust. I would be the first to advocate obeying just laws. One has not only a legal but a moral responsibility to obey just laws. Conversely, one has a moral responsibility to disobey unjust laws. I would agree with St. Augustine that "an unjust law is no law at all."

victory and provided at least for a while what historian John Hope Franklin called "the illusion of equality" (Franklin and Moss 1994).

In the months that followed the passage of the act, the pace of the movement to end racial injustice slowed. The violence continued, however, from the Bedford-Stuyvesant section of Brooklyn to Selma, Alabama. Southern state courts still found White murderers of Blacks innocent, and they had to be tried and convicted in federal civil, rather than criminal, court cases on the charge that by killing a person one violates that person's civil rights. Government records, which did not become public until 1973, revealed a systematic campaign by the FBI to infiltrate civil rights groups in an effort to discredit them, in the belief that such activist groups were subversive. It was in such an atmosphere that the Voting Rights Act was passed in August 1965, but this significant, positive event was somewhat overshadowed by violence in the Watts section of Los Angeles in the same week (N. Blackstock 1976).

Explaining Urban Violence

Riots involving Whites and Blacks did not begin in the 1960s. As we saw earlier in this chapter, urban violence occurred after World War I and even during World War II, and violence against Blacks in the United States is nearly 350 years old. But the urban riots of the 1960s influenced Blacks and Whites in the United States and throughout the world so extensively that they deserve special attention. We must remember, however, that most violence between Whites and Blacks has not been large-scale collective action but has involved only a relatively small number of people.

The summers of 1963 and 1964 were a prelude to riots that gripped the country's attention. Although most people knew of the civil rights efforts in the South and legislative victories in Washington, everyone realized that the racial problem was national after several cities outside the South experienced violent disorders. The riot in Los Angeles in August 1965 first shocked those who thought that racial harmony had been achieved. Thirty-four were killed in the Black ghetto of Watts in the worst riot since Detroit in 1943. Americans were used to tension between Whites and Blacks in the South, but not in the North, and certainly not in California (R. Blauner 1972; R. Conot 1967; C. Degler 1969; A. Oberschall 1968).

The next two years saw major riots in Cleveland, Newark, and Detroit. Violence was not limited to a few urban ghettos, however. One estimate for 1967 alone identifies 257 disorders in 173 cities that claimed 87 lives, injured 2,500, and led to 19,200 arrests. In April 1968, after the assassination of Martin Luther King, more cities exploded than had in all of 1967. Even before the summer of 1968 began, there were 369 civil disorders. Communities of all sizes were hit. More than one-fourth of race-related disturbances occurred in cities with populations of less than 25,000. Most of the civil disorders were relatively minor and probably would have received no publicity if the major riots had not created increased awareness (Baskin et al. 1971, 1972).

As the violence continued and embraced many ghettos, a popular explanation was that riot participants were mostly unemployed youths who had criminal records, often involving narcotics, and who were vastly outnumbered by the African Americans who repudiated the looting and arson. This explanation was called the **riff-raff theory** or the rotten-apple theory because it discredited the rioters and left the barrel of apples, White society, untouched. On the contrary, research shows that the Black community expressed sympathetic understanding toward the rioters and that the rioters were not merely the poor and uneducated but included middle-class, working-class, and educated residents (Sears and McConahay 1969, 1973; T. Tomlinson 1969; R. Turner 1994).

Several alternatives to the riff-raff theory explain why Black violent protest increased in the United States at a time when the nation was seemingly committed to civil rights for all. Two explanations stand out. One ascribes the problem to Black frustration with rising expectations in the face of continued deprivation relative to Whites. The other explanation points to increased national consciousness.

RELATIVE DEPRIVATION AND RISING EXPECTATIONS

The standard of living of African Americans improved remarkably after World War II, and it continued to do so during the civil rights movement. White income and occupation levels, however, also improved, so the gap between the groups remained. Chapter 3 showed that feelings of relative deprivation are often the basis for perceived discrimination. **Relative deprivation** is the conscious feeling of a negative discrepancy between legitimate expectations and present actualities (J. Wilson 1973:69).

It is of little comfort to African Americans that their earning power matches that of Whites eight to ten years earlier. As shown in Figure 7.3, Black family income has increased significantly, but so has that of White families, leaving the gap between the two virtually unchanged. Relative to Whites, most Blacks made no tangible gains in housing, education, jobs, or economic security. African Americans were doing better in absolute numbers, but not relative to Whites.

As we consider the effect of this situation on African Americans, we must determine what group they select as an appropriate reference or comparison group. Frustration comes not from a group's absolute level of attainment, but from its position relative to the appropriate comparison group. David Matza (1971:607) wrote that "profound degradation in an absolute sense may be tolerable or even pass unnoticed if others close at hand fare no better or if one never had any reason to expect better." The Blacks' situation was thus intolerable in both ways, because the continued greater affluence of Whites was apparent to Blacks at the same time that Blacks were consistently being promised equality with the dominant group.

At the same time that African Americans were feeling relative deprivation, they were also experiencing growing discontent. **Rising expectations** refers to the increasing sense of frustration that legitimate needs are being blocked. Blacks felt that they had legitimate aspirations to equality, and the civil rights movement reaffirmed that discrimination had blocked upward mobility. As the horizons of African Americans broadened, they were more likely to make comparisons with Whites and feel discontented. The civil rights movement gave higher aspirations to Black America; yet for the majority, life remained basically unchanged. Not only were their lives unchanged, the feeling was widespread that the existing social structure held no prospect for improvement (R. Garner 1996; Sears and McConahay 1970:133; Thomas and Thomas 1984).

DEVELOPING A NATIONAL CONSCIOUSNESS

After the smoke had cleared, the first riots in the 1960s were examined in an effort to find causes in the community. Had the chief of police misjudged the situation? Had it been crucial that the governor was vacationing out of the country? Would the riot have occurred if the unemployment rate had been slightly lower? As rioting became a national phenomenon, such localized explanations were replaced by statistical efforts to find similarities among riot cities that contrasted them to cities without riots.

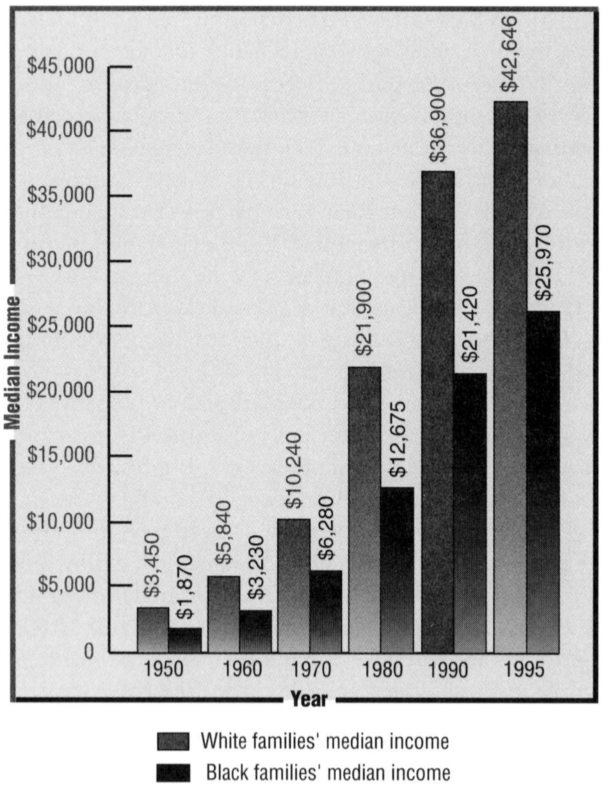

Figure 7.3 Black-White Income Gap
For the more than 40 years of available data, median Black family income has been only about half that of White family income.
Source: Bureau of the Census 1975:297; 1998c.

What social scientists concluded was that the nature of the community was not important in explaining the outbreak of racial conflict, both because the federal government played a pivotal role and because the influence of the mass media had transformed local issues into national ones: the federal government was responsible for promoting or failing to promote racial equality. Blacks in Jacksonville and Boston were in many respects more affected by decisions made in the nation's capital than by those made in their own city halls. In addition, coverage of civil rights in the mass media, especially national television newscasts, created national interest and a national racial identity that transcended community boundaries. The mass media were criticized for emphasizing the emotional side of the riots, but the Kerner Commission, established to investigate the riots and their causes, found reporting to be calm and factual.

There is no question that through the media, and particularly television, the civil rights movements created a national agenda for the rising expectations of African Americans. Before the riots, mass media coverage of sit-ins, marches, and angry confrontations with government officials had served to develop a national consciousness. Blacks had become aware not only of deprivation unique to their own neighborhood but also of the deprivation common to all ghettos. Given this increased awareness of their low status despite years of promises, almost any Black community could explode (National Advisory Commission on Civil Disorders 1968).

Black Power

The riots in the northern ghettos captured the attention of Whites, and Black Power was what they heard. Appropriately enough, Black Power was born not of Black but of White violence. On June 6, 1966, James Meredith was carrying out a one-person march from Memphis to Jackson, Mississippi, to encourage fellow African Americans to overcome their own fears and vote, following the passage into law of the Voting Rights Act. During that march, an unidentified assailant shot and wounded Meredith. Blacks from throughout the country immediately continued the march. During the march, Stokely Carmichael of the Student Nonviolent Coordinating Committee (SNCC) proclaimed to a cheering Black crowd, "What we need is Black Power." King and others later urged "Freedom Now" as the slogan for the march. A compromise dictated that no slogan would be used, but the mood of Black America said otherwise (M. King 1967; L. Lomax 1971).

In retrospect, it may be puzzling that the phrase *Black Power* frightened Whites and offended so many Blacks. It was not really new. The National Advisory Commission on Civil Disorders (1968:234–235) correctly identified it as *old wine in new bottles*: Black consciousness was not new, even if the phrase was. Furthermore, it was the type of umbrella term that could mean everything or nothing. A survey of Detroit Blacks in the following year showed many respondents confused or vague about the meaning of the concept. To many Whites, however, the meaning was clear enough. Set against the backdrop of riots in the North, Black Power signaled to many that the civil rights movement was no longer the sole focus for overcoming social inequality. Indeed, they were right (Aberbach and Walker 1973).

By advocating Black Power, Carmichael was distanced himself from the assimilationism of King. Carmichael rejected the goal of assimilation into White middle-class society. Instead, he said, Blacks must create new institutions. To succeed in this endeavor, Carmichael argued that Blacks must follow the same path as the Italians, Irish, and other White ethnic groups. "Before a group can enter the open society, it must first close ranks. . . . Group solidarity is necessary before a group can operate effectively from a bargaining position of strength in a pluralistic society" (Ture and Hamilton 1992:44). Prominent Black leaders opposed the concept; many feared that Whites would retaliate even more violently. King (1967) saw Black Power as a "cry of disappointment" but acknowledged that it had a "positive meaning."

Eventually Black Power gained wide acceptance among Blacks and even many Whites. Although it came to be defined differently by nearly every new proponent, support of Black Power generally implied endorsing Black control of the political, economic, and social institutions in Black communities. One reason for its popularity among African Americans was that it gave them a viable option for surviving in a segregated society (J. Ladner 1967; A. Pinkney 1994). The civil rights movement strove to end segregation, but the White response showed how committed White society was to maintaining it. Black Power presented restructuring society as the priority item on the Black agenda.

One aspect of Black Power clearly operated outside the conventional system. The Black Panther Party was organized in October 1966 in Oakland, California, by Huey Newton, age twenty-four, and Bobby Seale, age thirty, to represent urban Blacks in a political climate that the Panthers felt was unresponsive. The Panthers were controversial from the beginning, charging police brutality and corruption among government officials. They engaged in violent confrontations with law enforcement officers. From 1969 to 1972, internal weaknesses, a long series of trials involving most of the leaders, intraparty strife, and several shoot-outs with police combined to bring the organization to a standstill. The Panthers, although they were frequently portrayed as the most separatist of the Black militant movements, were willing to form alliances with non-Black organizations, including Students for a Democratic Society (SDS), the Peace and Freedom Party, the Young Lords, the Young Patriots, and the Communist Party of the United States. Despite, or perhaps because of, such coalitions, the Panthers were not a prominent force in shaping contemporary Black America. Newton himself admitted in 1973 that the party had alienated Blacks and had become "too radical" to be accepted by the Black community (J. Abron 1986; K. Cleaver 1982; C. Woodward 1974).

The militant Black Panthers encountered severe difficulties during the 1970s and fell victim to both internal political problems and external surveillance. Finally, their formerly outspoken leaders moved in new directions. Eldridge Cleaver became a born-again Christian and confined himself to lecturing on the virtues of his evangelical faith. Cofounder Bobby Seale ran unsuccessfully for mayor of Oakland, California, in the kind of traditional campaign he had formerly denounced as unproductive. Following that unsuccessful bid, Seale became an organizer of moderate community groups. Former Panther defense minister Bobby Rush became deputy chairman of the Illinois State Democratic Party, was elected to the U.S. Congress in 1992, and was reelected to two more terms. The role of spokesperson for a minority group in the United States is exhausting, and people who have assumed that role for a time often turn to more conventional, less personally demanding roles, especially if public support for their programs wanes.

The Religious Force

It is not possible to overstate the role religion has played, good and bad, in the social history of African Americans. Historically, Black leaders have emerged from the pulpits to seek out rights on behalf of all Blacks. Churches have served as the basis for community organization in neighborhoods abandoned by businesses and even government. Religion has been a source of antagonism as well. For example, at least 93 southern Black churches were bombed or burned because they were leading the way in voter registration and in the promotion of community integration. As recently as 1996, a rash of 318 mysterious church bombings and fires created new anxiousness in the African American community (Fields and Price 1996; Kosmin and Lachman 1993).

As we saw earlier in this chapter, because the Africans who were brought involuntarily to the Western Hemisphere were non-Christian, they were seen as heathens and barbarians. To "civilize" the slaves in the period before the Civil War, southern slaveholders encouraged and often required their slaves to attend church and embrace Christianity. The Christian churches to which Blacks were introduced in the United States encouraged them to accept the inferior status enforced by Whites, and the religious teaching that the slaves received equated whiteness with salvation, presenting whiteness as an acceptable, if not preferred, object of reverence.

Despite being imposed in the past by Whites, the Christian faiths are embraced by most African Americans today. As shown in Figure 7.4, African Americans are overwhelmingly Protestant, with half being Baptist. The Methodists and Roman Catholics account for another 9 percent each. Therefore, almost seven out of ten African Americans are members of these three faiths, compared to less than half of Whites.

However, a variety of non-Christian groups have exerted a much greater influence on African Americans than the reported numbers of their followers suggest. The Nation of Islam, for example, which became known as the Black Muslims, has attracted a large number of followers and received the most attention. The Muslim religion was first introduced to Black Americans in 1930 with the arrival of Wali D. Fard, later called W. Fard Muhammad, in Detroit.

Under the leadership of Elijah Muhammad, Fard's most trusted follower and his successor, the Nation of Islam became a well-known, controversial organization. While Black Muslims were preaching racial hatred and suffering internal violence, they built a financial empire. At the same time, many members of White society respected the Nation of Islam for its impressive use of capitalism to the

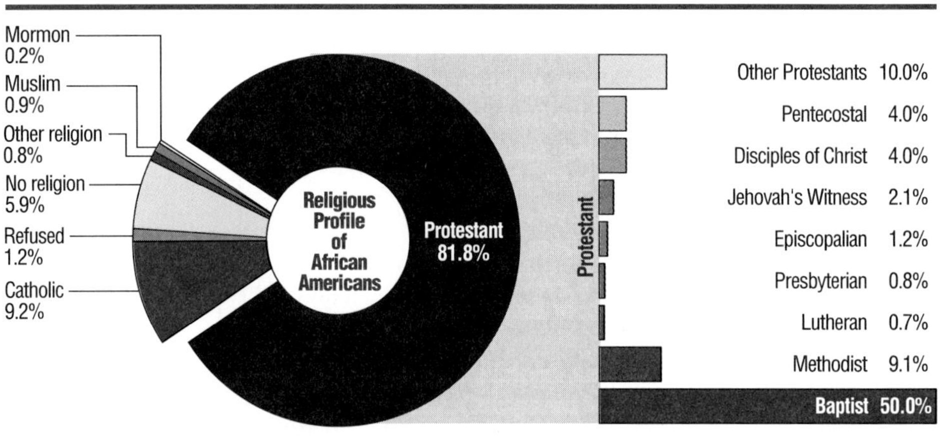

Figure 7.4 Religious Profile of African Americans

Based on a 1990 national sample, most African Americans are Baptist, Roman Catholic, or Methodist.

Source: Barry Kosmin and Seymour P. Lachman, *One Nation Under God.* Copyright © 1993 by Barry Kosmin and Seymour P. Lachman. Reprinted by permission of Harmony Books, a division of Crown Publishers, Inc.

organization's advantage and for the strict moral code its members followed. The membership of the group, then officially called the American Muslim Mission, dropped from 250,000 in the mid–1970s to 100,000 a decade later. W. Deen Muhammad, successor and son of Elijah Muhammad, opened the faith to people of all races, although he acknowledged that it was basically an African American organization. In 1985, Muhammad dissolved the sect, leaving the 200 mosques and worship centers to operate independently.

Malcolm X, originally a member of the Nation of Islam, became the most powerful and brilliant voice of Black self-determination in the 1960s. He was an authentic folk hero to his sympathizers. Besides his own followers, he commanded an international audience and is still referred to in a manner befitting a prophet. Indeed, Spike Lee's 1993 movie based on the *Autobiography of Malcolm X* reintroduced him to another generation. Malcolm X was highly critical of the civil rights movement in general and of Martin Luther King, Jr., in particular.

Malcolm X is not remembered for his stiff attacks on other Black leaders, for his break with the Nation of Islam, or even for his apparent shift to support the formation of coalitions with progressive Whites. Rather, he is remembered for teaching Blacks lessons that came to haunt the champions of nonviolent direct action—among them, that Blacks must resist violence "by any means necessary." During his last year, Malcolm X (by then known as Malik El-Shabazz) created the secular Organization of Afro-American Unity, which was meant to internationalize the civil rights movement. Malcolm X's life was ended by three assassins in 1964. "His philosophy can be summarized as pride in Blackness, the necessity of knowing Black history, Black autonomy, Black unity, and self-determination for the Black community" (A. Pinkney 1975:213; 1993; see also M. Dyson 1995; G. Kieh 1995).

In recent years, Minister Louis Farrakhan has been the most visible spokesperson among the various Muslim groups in the African American community. Farrakhan broke with W. Deen Muhammad in 1977 and named his group Nation of Islam, adopting, along with the name used by the earlier group, the more orthodox ideals of Elijah Muhammad, such as Black moral superiority. Farrakhan's endorsement of the candidacy of Rev. Jesse Jackson for both the 1984 and 1988 Democratic nominations for the Presidency propelled Farrakhan into the limelight, although his public statements about Jews and Israel gave an anti-Semitic taint to his teachings. The split between Farrakhan and Muhammad is not new to the Black followers of Islam, as Malcolm X's life indicates (W. Henry 1994; C. Lincoln 1994).

Martin Luther King, Jr., and Malcolm X in March 1964 at the only time they met. They had gathered along with other Black leaders to listen to the debate at the Capitol on the civil rights bill. King was assassinated in 1968, and Malcolm X was assassinated less than a year after this picture was taken.

While Farrakhan's statements against Whites—Jews in particular—as well as his anti-Israel foreign policy, have attracted the media's attention, many of his speeches and writings reflect the basic early tenets of the Nation of Islam. Abortion, drugs, and homosexuality are condemned. Self-help, bootstrap capitalism, and strict punishment are endorsed. Farrakhan is not pessimistic about the future of race relations in the United States. As leader of the 1995 Million Man March, he encouraged those present and African Americans nationwide to register to vote and work for positive change. While it is impossible to assess Farrakhan's effect independent of other efforts, the Black male vote did increase by 5 percent in 1996 over 1992 (D. Bositis 1996; E. Cose 1996b; G. Loury 1996).

Minister Louis Farrakhan speaking at the Million Man March in Washington, D.C., on October 16, 1995.

CONCLUSION

The dramatic events affecting African Americans today have their roots in the forcible bringing of their ancestors to the United States as slaves. In the South, whether as slaves or later as victims of Jim Crow, Blacks were not a real threat to any but the poorest Whites, although even affluent Whites feared the perceived potential threat that Blacks posed. During their entire history here, Blacks have been criticized when they rebelled and praised when they went along with the system. During the time of slavery, revolts were met with increased suppression; after emancipation, leaders calling for accommodation were applauded.

The Black migration to the urban North helped to define a new social order. Whites found it more difficult to ignore Blacks as residents of the ghetto than as sharecroppers in the rural South. No longer excluded by the "White primary" as in the South, the Black urban voter had potential power. The federal government and city halls slowly began to acknowledge the presence of Blacks. From the Black community came voices that spoke of pride and self-help: Douglass, Tubman, Washington, Du Bois, King, and Malcolm X.

Respected African American scholar John Hope Franklin headed up the 1998 President's Initiative on Race and reflected on his experiences:

> *When you talk about the role of slavery, ask why do people look at me and think that I'm their servant? What the hell is that all about? If they haven't somehow come to the conclusion that I'm here to serve them the way my ancestors 150*

years ago were there to serve theirs. Imagine asking an 82-year-old man to fetch for them? Or to serve them, to get their coat or their car or to call me "boy." That's the shadow that's over this whole thing (K. Breslau 1997:61).

In confronting this "shadow," Blacks in their resistance have understandably differed in their willingness to form coalitions with Whites. Resisting African Americans, in the days of either slavery or the civil rights meovement, would have concurred with Du Bois's (1903:3–4) comment that a Black person "simply wishes to make it possible to be both a Negro and an American, without being cursed and spit upon by his fellows, without having the door of opportunity closed roughly in his face." The object of Black protest seems simple enough, but on many, including Presidents, the point was lost.

How much progress has been made? When covering several hundred years, beginning with slavery and ending with rights recognized constitutionally, it is easy to be impressed. Yet let us consider Topeka, Kansas, the site of the 1954 *Brown* v. *Board of Education* case. Linda Brown, one of the original plaintiffs, was recently touched by another segregation case. In 1992, the courts held that Oliver Brown, her grandchild, was being victimized because the Topeka schools were still segregated, now for reasons of residential segregation. The remedy to separate schools in this Kansas city is still unresolved (K. Hays 1994).

Chapter 8 assesses the status of African Americans today. Recall the events chronicled in this chapter as you consider the advances that have been made. These events are a reminder that any progress has followed years—indeed, generations—of struggle by African Americans, enlisting the support of Whites sympathetic to the removal of second-class status for African Americans in the United States.

KEY TERMS

abolitionists 212
civil disobedience 221
de jure segregation 220
Ebonics 211
Jim Crow 213
relative deprivation 225
restrictive covenants 219
riff-raff theory 225
rising expectations 225
slave codes 207
White primary 213

REVIEW QUESTIONS

1. In what ways were slaves defined as property?
2. How did slavery provide a foundation for both White and Black America today?
3. If civil disobedience is nonviolent, why is so much violence associated with it?
4. How does the research on the 1960s urban riots help us to understand better more recent disturbances such as those in Los Angeles in 1992?
5. Why has religion proved to be a force for both unity and disunity among African Americans?

CRITICAL THINKING

1. How much time do you recall spent in school thus far learning about the history of Europe? How about Africa? What do you think this says about the way education is delivered or what we choose to learn?
2. What would you consider the three most important achievements in civil rights for African Americans since 1900? What roles did Whites and Blacks play in making these events happen?
3. Growing numbers of Blacks are immigrating to the United States (especially to the eastern U.S.) from the Caribbean. What impact may this have on what it means to be Black or African American in the United States? What would the social construction of race say about this development?

INTERNET EXERCISE

This chapter details the importance of civil disobedience in the civil rights movement. To learn more about the concept, its ties to antislavery ideals, and its historical advocate Henry David Thoreau, direct your Internet browser to http://www.geocities.com/Athens/7687/1thorea.html. Who is Henry David Thoreau? When did he live, and what are some of his most influential writings? Read his works, *On Civil Disobedience* and *Slavery in Massachusetts*. What were his views on slavery? In what ways are his ideas similar to those espoused by Dr. Martin Luther King? In what ways are they different? Are the writings of Thoreau applicable to the modern racial and social climate in the United States? Why or why not?

FOR FURTHER INFORMATION

Molefi Kete Asante. *The Afrocentric Idea*. Philadelphia: Temple University Press, 1987.
Historians, philosophers, and others are taken to task for promoting a Eurocentric view of life so rigid that it ignores the experience and the contributions of African Americans.

W. E. B. Du Bois. *The Philadelphia Negro: A Social Study*. Philadelphia: University of Pennsylvania Press, 1996.
This, the first important sociological study of a Black community, was originally published in 1899 and is worth reading today with its introduction by sociologist Elijah Anderson. Du Bois discusses family life, interracial relations, education, occupations, and other aspects of the North's largest Black community just three decades after the end of slavery.

C. Eric Lincoln and Lawrence H. Mamiya. *The Black Church in the African American Experience*. Durham, NC: Duke University Press, 1990.
An overview of the role of organized religion from the days of slavery through the challenges experienced today in the United States.

Malcolm X. *The Autobiography of Malcolm X*. New York: Grove Press, 1964.
Just before his assassination, Malcolm X related his experiences that led to his leadership in the Nation of Islam and his subsequent disenchantment with that organization.

Nathan McCall. *What's Going On*. New York: Random House, 1997.
In this collection of essays, McCall considers topics ranging from the Black middle class, to illegitimacy, gangsta rap, and White attitudes with a blend of humor and sharp commentary.

PERIODICALS

Numerous mass-circulation magazines deal primarily with African Americans, including *American Legacy, Black Collegiate, Black Enterprise, Ebony, Essence, Emerge,* and *Jet*. Journals include *Black Politics* (first issued in 1969), *Black Scholar* (1969), *Journal of African American Men* (1991), *Journal of Negro Education* (1931), *Journal of Negro History* (1916), *Negro History Bulletin* (1946), and *Black Issues in Higher Education* (1884).

8

African Americans Today

CHAPTER OUTLINE

HIGHLIGHTS

African Americans have made significant progress in many areas, but they have not kept pace relative to White Americans in any sectors. African Americans have advanced in formal schooling to a remarkable degree, although in most areas residential patterns have left many public schools predominantly Black or White. Higher education also reflects the legacy of a nation that has operated two schooling systems: one for Blacks and another for Whites. Gains in earning power have barely kept pace with inflation, and the gap between Whites and Blacks has remained relatively unchanged. African American families are susceptible to the problems associated with a low-income group that also faces discrimination and prejudice. Housing in many areas remains segregated, despite growing numbers of Blacks in suburban areas. African Americans are more likely to be victims of crimes as well as to be arrested for violent crimes. The subordination of Blacks is also apparent in the delivery of health care. African Americans have made substantial gains in elective office but still are underrepresented compared to their numbers in the general population.

John and Glenn are alike in almost every way—about the same age, Big Ten college graduates, similar jobs, and active sports enthusiasts. But they find that they have very dissimilar experiences in such everyday activities as walking into a shopping mall to buy shoes or look over the latest CDs. John typically receives instant attention when he walks even near the shoe department, while the same salesperson fails to acknowledge Glenn even though he has been waiting five minutes. A little later John casually picks up some CDs in a record store. At the very same time, Glenn is engaged in exactly the same behavior in the same store, but he is closely shadowed by a store employee, who observes Glenn's every move.

John is White and Glenn is Black, which makes all the difference even in this everyday shopping behavior. They were part of an experiment conducted by the television newsmagazine *Primetime Live* in St. Louis to assess the impact of race on the day-to-day lives of average African Americans and Whites. Over a period of three weeks, the program closely monitored the two researchers, who had been trained to present themselves in an identical manner in a variety of situations.

In a televised report on this experiment, *Primetime Live* host Diane Sawyer acknowledged that, at times, the two men were treated equally. However, Sawyer added that not once or twice but "every single day," there were instances of differential treatment. At an employment agency, Glenn was lectured on laziness and told that he would be monitored "real close." John, by contrast, was encouraged to pursue job leads, and staff members made it clear that he could expect to find a suitable position (ABC News 1992).

Despite the publicity given to obvious discrimination that has persisted well into the present, a superficial sense of complacency about the position of African Americans in the United States is evident as the twenty-first century begins. Uninformed, casual observers see that more African Americans are inside city halls and Congress rather than marching outside, and conclude that equality has been achieved. From time to time, however, this sense that everything was going well has been interrupted. For example, the 1992 Los Angeles riots led to short-lived expressions of concern over police brutality and insufficient government policies. By 1995, however, complacency had returned. Plans to address inner-city problems were low on the nation's list of priorities. Instead, the dismantling of affirmative action emerged as the major race issue of the 1996 elections.

As you read this chapter, try to keep in perspective the profile of African Americans in the United States today. This chapter will assess education, the economy, family life, housing, criminal justice, health care, and politics among the nation's African Americans. Progress has occurred, and some of the advances are nothing short of remarkable. The deprivation of the African American people relative to Whites remains, however, even if absolute deprivation has been softened. A significant gap remains between African Americans and the dominant group, and to this gap a price is assigned: the price of being African Americans in the United States.

Education

The African American population in the United States has placed special importance on acquiring education, beginning with its emphasis in the home of the slave family and continuing through the creation of separate, inferior schools for Black children because the regular schools were closed to them by custom or law. Today, long after the old civil rights coalition has disbanded, education remains a controversial issue. Since racial and ethnic groups realize that formal schooling is the key to social mobility, they wish to maximize this opportunity for upward mobility and therefore want better schooling. White Americans also appreciate the value of formal schooling and do not wish to do anything that they perceive will jeopardize their own position.

QUALITY AND QUANTITY OF EDUCATION

Several measures document the inadequate education received by African Americans, starting with the quantity of formal education. The gap in educational attainment between Blacks as a group and Whites as a group has always been present. Despite programs directed at the poor, such as Head Start, White children are still more likely to have a prekindergarten experience than are African American children. Later, Black children generally drop out of school sooner and are therefore less likely to receive high school diplomas, let alone college degrees. Table 8.1 shows the gap in the amount of schooling African Americans receive compared to Whites. It also illustrates progress in reducing this gap in recent years. Despite this progress, however, the gap remains substantial, with twice the proportion of Whites holding a college degree compared with Blacks in 1998. Indeed, the level of college completion for Blacks today is comparable to that of Whites in about 1970. As sociologist Christopher Jencks described the situation, "This may be a case of running fast to stand still" (S. Holmes 1996b:A8).

Table 8.1 Years of School Completed (Percentages of Persons 25 years Old and Over)

	1960	1980	1998
Completing high school			
Black			
Male	18.2%	51.1%	75.2%
Female	21.7	51.3	76.7
White			
Male	41.6	71.0	83.6
Female	44.7	70.1	83.8
Completing college			
Black			
Male	2.8	7.7	13.9
Female	3.3	8.1	15.4
White			
Male	10.3	22.1	27.3
Female	6.0	14.0	22.8

Source: Bureau of the Census 1998c:167; Day and Curry 1998: 4–5.

A second aspect of inadequate schooling, many educators argue, is that many students would not drop out of school were it not for the combined inadequacies of their education. Among the deficiencies noted have been:

1. Insensitive teachers
2. Poor counseling
3. Unresponsive administrators
4. Overcrowded classes
5. Irrelevant curricula
6. Dilapidated school facilities

While several of these problems can be addressed with more adequate funding, some are stalemated by what changes would lead to the best outcome. For example, there is significant debate among educators and African Americans in general over the content of curriculum that is best for minority students. Some schools have developed academic programs that take an Afrocentric perspective and immerse students in African American history and culture. Yet a few of these programs have been targeted as ignoring fundamentals such as the debate in Oakland, California, noted in the previous chapter, over recognizing Ebonics as a language in the classroom. On other occasions, Afrocentric curriculum has even been viewed as racist against Whites. The debates over a few controversial programs attract a lot of attention,

Most African American parents, according to recent surveys, would still like to see their children attend integrated schools.

clouding the widespread need to reassess the content of curriculum for racial and ethnic minorities.

Middle- and upper-class children occasionally face these barriers to a high-quality education, but they are more likely than the poor to have a home environment that is favorable to learning. Even African American schoolchildren who stay in school are not guaranteed equal opportunities in life. Many high schools do not prepare these students who are interested in college for advanced schooling. The problem is that schools are failing to meet the needs of students, not that students are failing in schools. Therefore, the problems with schooling were properly noted as a part of the past discrimination component of total discrimination illustrated in Figure 3.1.

SCHOOL SEGREGATION

It has been over forty years since the U.S. Supreme Court issued its unanimous ruling in *Brown* v. *Board of Education of Topeka, Kansas,* that "separate educational facilities are inherently unequal." What has been the legacy of that decision? Initially, the courts, with the support of the federal government, ordered southern school districts to end racial separation. But as attention turned to larger school districts, especially in the north, the challenge was to have integrated schools even though the neighborhoods were segregated. In addition, some city school districts were predominantly African American and Hispanic, surrounded by suburban school districts that were predominantly White. This type of school segregation that results from residential patterns is referred to as **de facto segregation.**

Initially, courts sought to overcome de facto segregation just as they had with the de jure school segregation dealt with in the *Brown* case. Typically, students were bused within a school district to achieve racial balance, but in a few cases Black students were bused to predominantly White suburban schools while White children were bused into the city. In 1974, however, the Supreme Court ruled in *Millikin* v. *Bradley* that it was improper to order Detroit and the suburbs to have a joint metropolitan busing solution. These and other Supreme Court decisions have effectively ended initiatives to overcome residential segregation, once again creating racial isolation in the schools. Indeed, even in Topeka, one-third of the schools are segregated today (J. Kozol 1994; G. Orfield et al. 1996).

Even as the courts debated the merits of busing, there was a great deal of controversy about it within the Black and White communities. Initially, it was bitterly opposed by some White students and their parents, who objected both to their children's being bused to previously Black schools and to African Americans being bused into their local schools. While research has shown the positive outcomes of desegregated classrooms, some African American parents have come to question sending their children into what may be hostile environments, preferring to take control of their own schools, even within large, troubled urban school districts. They contend that in the absence of racial equality outside the educational system, significant integration in education has become impossible. At least, African Americans argue, let us have the same degree of influence over our children's education as White parents do.

In some urban areas, the response by African Americans has been to create all-Black or even all-Black, all-male schools, with the expectation that separate classes will foster positive self-images and role models. However, a 1998 national survey of Black parents shows continued support for integrated schools. Nearly eight in ten African American parents say it is important that their children's schools be racially integrated, either through redrawing district lines or through a magnet school system, which draws students nationwide (Public Agenda 1998).

Although studies have shown positive effects of integration, a diverse student population does not guarantee an integrated, equal schooling environment. For example, tracking in schools, especially middle and high schools, serves to intensify segregation at the classroom level. **Tracking** is the practice of placing students in specific curriculum groups on the basis of test scores and other criteria. It also has the effect of decreasing White–Black classroom interaction as African American children are disproportionately assigned to general classes, while more White children are placed in college-preparatory classes. Some studies indicate that African American students are more likely than White students to be classified as learning disabled or emotionally disturbed. Although there are successes in public education, integration is clearly not one of them (J. Oakes 1995; Serwatka, Deering, and Grant 1995).

HIGHER EDUCATION

Higher education for Blacks reflects the same pattern—the overall picture of African American higher education is not promising. While strides were made in the period following the civil rights movement, a plateau was reached in the mid–1970s. African Americans, compared to Whites, are more likely to be part-time students and in need of financial aid, which began to be severely cut in the 1980s. They are also finding the social climate on predominantly White campuses less than positive. As a result, the historically Black colleges and universities (HBCU) are once again playing a significant role in educating African Americans. For a century, they were the only real source of college degrees for Blacks. Then, in the 1970s, predominantly White colleges began to recruit African Americans. In 1998, however, the 105 HBCUs still accounted for about one-quarter of all Black college students (S. Fulwood 1998).

As shown in Table 8.1, while African Americans are more likely today to be college graduates, the upward trend has declined. Several factors account for this reversal in progress:

1. A reduction in financial aid and more reliance on loans than on grants-in-aid, coupled with rising costs, have tended to discourage students who would be the first members of their families to attend college.
2. Pushing for "higher standards" and "excellence" in educational achievement without providing remedial courses has locked out many minority students.
3. Employment opportunities, though slight for African Americans without some college, have continued to lure young people who must contribute to their family's income and who otherwise might have gone to college.

4. Negative publicity about affirmative action may have discouraged some African Americans from even considering college.
5. Increasing attention to what appears to be a growing number of racial incidents on predominantly White college campuses has also been a discouraging factor.

Colleges and universities seem uneasy about these problems; publicly, the schools appear committed to addressing them.

There is little question that special challenges face the African American student at a college with an overwhelmingly White student body, faculty, advisors, coaches, and administrators. The campus culture may be neutral at best, and it is often hostile to the presence of members of racial minorities. The high attrition rate of African American students on predominantly White college campuses confirms the need for a positive environment (H. Edwards 1970; R. Schaefer 1996; R. Sidel 1994).

As noted above, a growing number of widely publicized racial incidents have occurred on college campuses. These have included cross burnings, overt discrimination, distribution of racist literature, physical attacks, derogatory behavior, and racist remarks. Beyond these are more subtle practices, such as campus bars that discourage minority-student patronage by not including minority-oriented music in their selections and local law-enforcement officials who more closely monitor the activities of African American students than of Whites.

Because fewer African Americans complete their higher education, relatively fewer are available to fill faculty and administrative positions. This means that despite increases in the numbers of Blacks who enter college, there are no more, and perhaps fewer, role models standing in the fronts of college classrooms for students from subordinate groups to see.

The disparity in schooling becomes even more pronounced at the highest levels, and the gap is not closing. Only 3.8 percent of all doctorates awarded in 1995 were to African Americans; that proportion was about the same in 1981. Since the early 1980s, the proportion of African Americans receiving medical degrees has remained steady at 5–6 percent. Despite the prevailing view that financial assistance is widely available to subordinate-group students, data released in 1993 showed that only 47 percent of Black doctoral students were receiving any aid, compared to 56 percent of Whites. Blacks were also less likely than White graduate students to receive grants (Bureau of the Census 1998c:202; K. Manzo 1994).

In Chapter 1, we said that one of the consequences of subordinate-group status is segregation. This is certainly true in education. De facto segregation is present in the public schools, and indeed, some state university systems, such as Mississippi's, are accused of promoting segregation. African Americans who attend predominantly White colleges often encounter a chilly climate that isolates them from their classmates and even their teachers. The apparent gains of the 1970s in educational advancement have not continued.

The Economic Picture

The general economic picture for African Americans has been gradual improvement over the last forty years, but this improvement is modest compared to Whites, whose standard of living has also increased. Therefore, in terms of absolute deprivation, African Americans are much better off today but have experienced much less significant improvement with respect to their relative deprivation to Whites on virtually all economic indicators. We will consider income and wealth, employment, and African American-owned businesses.

INCOME AND WEALTH

There are two useful measures of the overall economic situation of an individual or a household—income and wealth. **Income** refers to salaries, wages, and other money received; while **wealth** is a more inclusive term encompassing all of a person's material assets, including land and other types of property.

There is a significant gap between the incomes of Black and White families in the United States. As we saw in Figure 7.2, Black income has been steadily increasing, but so has that of Whites. In 1997, the median income of Black families was $28,602, compared to $46,254 for White families. Another way to consider the gap is that Black family income resembles that of White families ten years ago. This ten-year lag has been present since World War II. In Figure 8.1, we look at the overall composition of Black and White income today and can readily see that most Black families have incomes under $29,000 a year, while most Whites have incomes of $46,000 or more.

The underside of the income picture is those people trapped in poverty. In 1996, about 26 percent of Black people lived below the poverty level, compared to about 9 percent of Whites. The proportion of African Americans who live below the poverty level has not changed significantly in the last quarter-century. Low incomes are counterbalanced to some extent by Medicare, Medicaid, public assistance, and food stamps. That an African American family is three times more likely to be poor shows that social inequality is staggering (Bureau of the Census 1998c:473).

Wealth is more difficult to measure because it takes more effort to determine accurately how much people own and owe as opposed to how much they earn in a given year. Yet wealth is very important in that it protects one against financial hardship and may offer a means of passing amounts of money or property to future generations, giving them a good start. On the other hand, the lack of wealth or even the presence of debt can place young people at a severe disadvantage as they seek to become independent.

The wealth picture in the United States shows even greater disparity between Whites and Blacks than does income. Sociologists Melvin Oliver and Thomas Shapiro (1995) drew on data from over 12,000 households and conducted in-depth interviews with a range of Black and White families. There is clearly a significant difference in wealth patterns because the generations of social inequality have left African Americans, as a group, unable to accumulate the kind of wealth that Whites, as a group, have. This is particularly true in the area of being able to own a home—most people's biggest asset. The inability of Blacks typically to own a home and develop this asset is due not only to lower incomes but also to discriminatory lending practices, which we will consider later in this chapter. There are, of course,

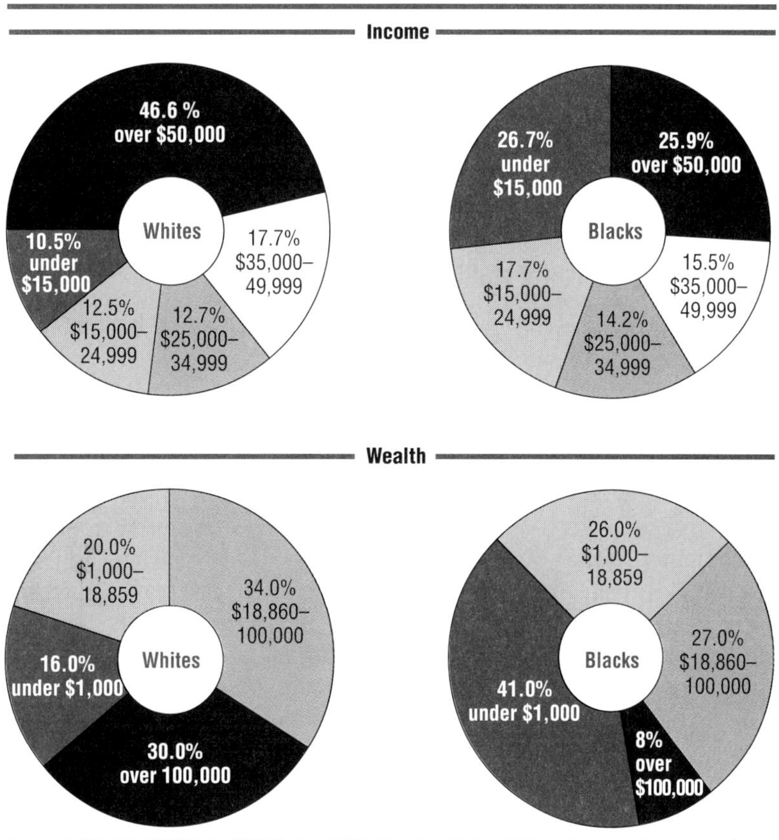

Figure 8.1 Comparing Income and Wealth

Note: Income data for 1997 were reported in 1998. The wealth data for 1988 were reported in 1996.

Source: Bureau of the Census 1998b: 5; and Melvin Oliver and Thomas Shapiro, *Black Wealth/White Wealth: A New Perspective on Racial Equality.* Copyright © 1996. Reprinted by permission of Routledge.

poor Whites and very rich Blacks, but the group differences that the researchers documented are unmistakable. The most striking differences are there when we compare Blacks and Whites in their thirties and also when we compare the most educated Blacks with the most educated Whites. Both the young adults and the more educated African Americans would have benefited the most from efforts to reduce inequality, but the gap remains.

As shown in Figure 8.1, most Whites are not in debt in terms of assets, and 30 percent have a net worth over $100,000. In contrast, over 40 percent of African Americans have a net worth of less than $1,000, with only 6 percent showing assets over $100,000. Assets are valuable as a means to protect people from falling into poverty if all sources of income are interrupted. About 57 percent of all Whites can stay out of poverty for at least six months if all income ends, but only 17 percent of African Americans are in a similar positive situation.

Assets are important both to insulate households against short-term crisis but also to help other family members. Wealth has significance not only for the present generation but for the next generation as well. The typical White household is able to establish itself without the kind of debt often experienced by Black households. Furthermore, White families are more likely to be subsidized by assistance from the previous generation, whether it comes as help with furthering their education, paying insurance premiums, buying an automobile, or even starting to furnish their first home.

EMPLOYMENT

This precarious situation for African Americans—the lack of dependable assets—is particularly relevant as we consider their employment picture. Higher unemployment rates for Blacks have persisted since the 1940s, when they were first documented. Since 1960, the national unemployment rate for Whites has ranged from 4.2 percent to 6.6 percent, while for Blacks it has ranged from 9.4 percent to 15.1 percent. This means that even in the best economic times, the Black unemployment rate is still significantly higher than it is for Whites during recessions. Obviously, when there is a national economic downturn, the results for the African American community are disastrous. Recessions take a heavy toll on African Americans. Reverend Joseph Lowery, former aide to Martin Luther King, Jr., said appropriately that "when America catches a cold, the black community gets pneumonia" (Bureau of the Census 1998c:423).

The employment picture is especially grim for African American workers aged 16–24. Many live in the central cities and fall victim to the unrecorded, irregular—perhaps illegal—economy outlined in Chapter 3. Many factors have been cited by social scientists to explain why official unemployment rates for young African Americans exceed 30 percent:

1. Many African Americans live in the depressed economy of the central cities.
2. Immigrants and illegal aliens present increased competition.
3. White middle-class women have entered the labor force.
4. Illegal activities at which youths find they can make more money have become more prevalent.

None of these factors is likely to change soon, so depression-like levels of unemployment will probably persist (R. Farley 1993; Massey and Gross 1993).

The picture grows even more somber when we realize that we are considering only official unemployment. The federal government's Bureau of Labor Statistics counts as unemployed only those people who are actively seeking employment. Thus, in order to be counted as unemployed, a person must not hold a full-time job, must be registered with a government employment agency, and must be engaged in writing job applications and seeking interviews.

Quite simply, the official unemployment rate leaves out millions of Americans—Black and White—who are effectively unemployed. It does not count persons so discouraged that they have temporarily given up looking for employment. The problem of unemployment is further compounded by underemployment. The term **underemployment** refers to working at a job for which one is overqualified, involuntarily working part-time, or being employed only intermittently.

The official unemployment rate for African American teenagers in a central city is about 40–45 percent, well above the 25 percent jobless rate for the nation as a whole during the Depression of the 1930s. Again, such official statistics do not include youths who have dropped out of the system: those who are not at school, not at work, and not looking for a legitimate job. If we add to the official figures the discouraged job seeker, the rate of unemployment and underemployment of African American teenagers in central-city areas climbs to 90 percent. As discouraging as these data are, the picture becomes even grimmer as we consider studies showing that underemployment remains high for young African Americans.

African American-owned businesses are on the rise in the United States. Terri Gardner, head of Soft Sheen, and her parents, Edward and Bettiann Gardner, who built Soft Sheen into an $80 million company, one of the largest ethnic hair products makers in the United States.

Although relatively few African Americans have crashed through the glass ceiling and made it into the top echelons of business or government, more have entered a wider variety of jobs. The taboo against putting them in jobs in which they would supervise Whites has weakened, and the percentage of African Americans in professional and managerial occupations rose from 4 percent in 1949 to 7.3 percent in 1997, a remarkable improvement. However, most of this advancement came prior to 1980. Little advancement has occurred since then.

As shown in Table 8.2, African Americans, who constitute 10–11 percent of the labor force, are underrepresented in high-status, high-paying occupations. Less than 5 percent of lawyers, judges, physicians, financial managers, public relations specialists, architects, pharmacists, and dentists are African American. On the other hand, they account for over 15 percent of cooks, health aides, hospital orderlies, maids, janitors, and stock handlers.

AFRICAN AMERICAN BUSINESSES

Many people aspire to run their own businesses, but this possibility is more attractive to subordinate groups, including African Americans. Frustrated by the difficulty of moving up in conventional businesses, members of minority groups often seek to begin their own businesses. Going into business themselves offers the opportunity to make it into the middle class. It is also a way to avoid some of the racism in business: the glass ceilings that block the promotion of a qualified worker and the tensions of a multiracial work environment.

Table 8.2 Percentage of African American Employees in Selected Occupations, 1972 and 1997

Occupation	1972	1997
Professional workers	6%	8%
Engineers	2	4
Lawyers and judges	2	4
Physicians	3	4
Registered nurses	6	8
College teachers	4	7
Other teachers	8	10
Social workers	16	22
Managers	3	7
Sales workers	3	8
Service workers	17	18
Cleaners and servants	64	18
Firefighters	4	12
Police and detectives	8	18

Source: Bureau of the Census 1982: 419–420; 1998c: 417–419.

Historically, the first Black-owned businesses developed behind the wall of segregation. African Americans provided other African Americans with services that Whites would not provide, such as insurance, hairdressing, legal assistance, and medical help. Although this is less true today, African American entrepreneurs usually cater first to the market demand within their own community in such areas as music and mass media. However, if these new ventures become profitable, the entrepreneur usually faces stiff competition from outside the African American community. A very visible example is the rhythm-and-blues music industry and more recently the rap music business, which began as small Black-owned businesses but which, as they became profitable, were often taken into larger White-owned corporations.

The future for Black-owned businesses is uncertain. Among the factors creating new obstacles are the following:

1. Continuing backlash against affirmative action programs
2. Difficulty in obtaining loans and other capital
3. A changing definition of minority that allows women, veterans, and people with disabilities to qualify for special small-business-assistance programs
4. A reduction in the number and scope of set-aside programs

The last item requires further explanation. **Set-asides** are stipulations that government contracts must be awarded in a minimum proportion, usually 10–30 percent, to minority-owned businesses. However, in 1989, the U.S. Supreme Court determined that the city of Richmond, Virginia, had acted illegally in its set-aside programs (see Table 3.2). Since *City of Richmond* v. *Croson,* cities and government have abandoned programs with specific quotas for minority-owned enterprises, thus jeopardizing already fragile African American businesses. Then, in 1995, amid criticism of affirmative action, set-aside programs at the federal level also came under attack (D. Savage 1995).

In the aftermath of the 1992 South-Central Los Angeles riots, President George Bush advanced his policy of creating enterprise zones in urban areas. Although it was not aimed directly at minority-owned businesses, the policy intended to use tax breaks to encourage employment and investment in blighted neighborhoods. A business building in such zones would be taxed at a lower rate than if it had been built in a less economically depressed area. Following Bush's lead, in 1993 President Bill Clinton proposed the creation of empowerment zones, with a total of fifty by 1997. The idea of offering tax incentives to attract investment is not new and has been used by thirty states with varying degrees of success. In Los Angeles, successful African American business leaders began to develop their own strategies to create business opportunities in the ghetto. Ironically, Los Angeles was passed over when the first group of zones was named. Critics contend that this approach is just the latest of many half-hearted attempts at community development that stretch back to urban renewal in 1949 and the Model Cities program in 1966 (J. Sterngold 1998).

Even if programs that stress increasing the number of African American businesses succeeded, most ghetto Blacks would still be left poor. Writing more than a generation ago, W. E. B. Du Bois (1968) mentioned this potentially negative effect of Black

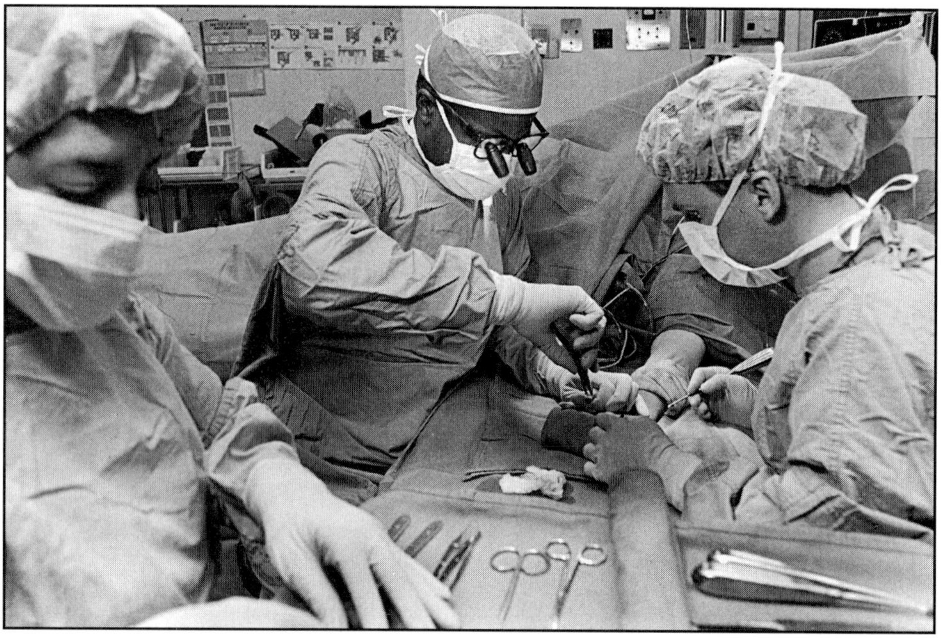

The proportion of African Americans engaged in professional occupations has increased but still lags well behind White Americans.

capitalism. Encouraging a few African Americans to move up the capitalistic ladder, he said, "will have inserted into the ranks of the Negro race a new cause of division, a new attempt to subject the masses of the race to an exploiting capitalist class of their own people" (p. 208). Du Bois's alternative was a program that would substantially improve the economic conditions of all African Americans, not just a few.

In summary, the economic differences between Whites and Blacks remain striking. The same generalizations made before the civil rights movement are still accurate as the twenty-first century begins. African Americans still have lower incomes, significantly fewer assets, a higher unemployment rate, lower-paying jobs, and a greater rate of business failures relative to Whites. As might be expected, this weak economic picture takes a toll on family life.

Family Life

In its role as a social institution providing for the socialization of children, the family is crucial to its members' life satisfaction. The family also reflects the influence, positive or negative, of income, housing, education, and other social factors. For African Americans, the family reflects both amazing stability and the legacy of racism and low income across many generations.

CHALLENGES TO FAMILY STABILITY

It is the conventional view that the typical African American family is headed by a female. Yet it is only since about 1989 that the majority of African American families have not been two-parent households. In 1998, about 5.6 million African American families with children lived in the United States. In more than 2.1 million of them, both a father and a mother were present. In the remaining 3.5 million, however, a single parent was raising children under age 18 (see Figure 8.2). So, while single-parent African American families are common, they are not universal. In comparison, such single-parent arrangements were also present among about one in four White families in 1998.

It is as inaccurate to assume that a single-parent family is necessarily "deprived" as it is to assume that a two-parent family is always secure and happy. Nevertheless, life in a single-parent family can be extremely stressful for all single parents and their children, and not just those who are members of subordinate groups. Since the absent parent is most often the father, lack of the male presence almost always means the lack of a male income. This monetary impact of a single-parent household is not to be minimized (A. Hacker 1995; Tucker and Mitchell-Kernan 1995).

Looming behind the issue of woman-headed families is the plight of the African American man. Simply stated, the economic status of Black men is deteriorating. Historically, this has not always been a significant economic problem. Despite the absence of legal protection for the slave family, African Americans were nevertheless able to establish significant kinship relationships with the sharing of economic resources, meager as they might be. After emancipation, males preferred that their wives remain at home because a working woman was considered a mark of slavery. But it was hard for many Black men to find work as anything other than strikebreakers, and so women were the more important source of wages *anyway*. In 1900, about 41 percent of Black women were employed, compared to only 16 percent of White women. The twentieth-century movement from the rural South to the ghettos of the North increased employment opportunities for Black men, but Black women found job opportunities as well, including relatively highly paid positions in nursing and teaching.

Ever since labor statistics on African Americans were first collected in 1890, Black men have had more jobs than Black women, but when Blacks are compared to Whites, Black women come closer to the earning power of their White women counterparts than do Black men to White men. As we saw in Chapter 3, the employment gap is narrower between Black and White women than it is between Black and White men. In the 1990s, the unfavorable stereotype of African American males, especially young men, in terms of work ethic, follows them virtually wherever they go in society (B. Baker 1992; R. Mincy 1994; W. Wilson 1996).

For many single African American women living in poverty, having a child is an added burden. However, the tradition of extended family among African Americans eases this burden somewhat. The absence of a husband does not mean that no one shares in child care: 85 percent of the out-of-wedlock children born to Black teenage mothers live with their grandparents and form three-generation

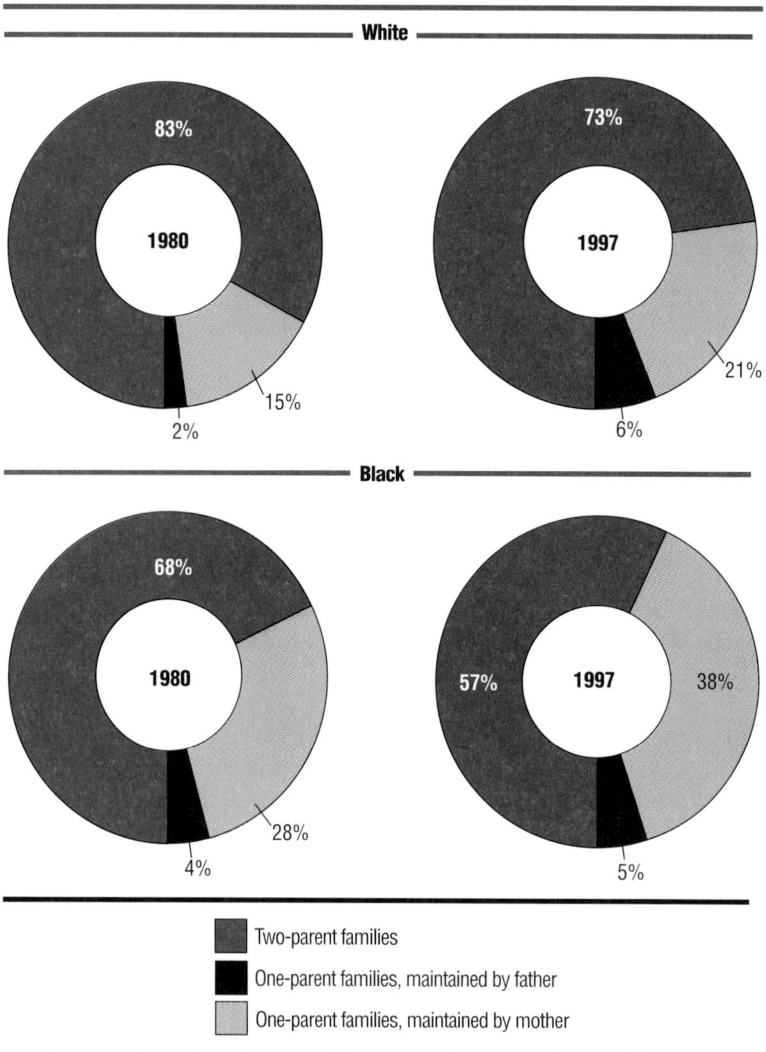

Figure 8.2 Family Groups with Children Under Eighteen Years Old by Race

Source: Bureau of the Census 1998c:65; Casper and Bryson 1998:96, 100.

households. Stronger religious beliefs contribute to teenage Blacks' being only half as likely as Whites to terminate a pregnancy by abortion (C. Billingsley 1992; Staples and Johnson 1993).

No one explanation accounts for the rise in single-parent households. Sociologists attribute the rapid expansion in the number of such households primarily to shifts in the economy that have kept Black men, especially in urban areas, out of work.

The phenomenon certainly is not limited to African Americans. Increasingly, both unmarried White and Black women bear children. More and more parents, both White and Black, divorce, so even children born into a two-parent family end up living with only one parent.

STRENGTHS OF AFRICAN AMERICAN FAMILIES

In the midst of ever-increasing single parenting, another picture of African American family life becomes visible: success despite discrimination and economic hardship. Robert Hill (1972, 1987), of the National Urban League, listed five strengths of African American families that allow them to function effectively in a hostile (racist) society.

1. Strong kinship bonds. Blacks are more likely than Whites to care for children and the elderly in an extended family network.
2. A strong work orientation. Poor Blacks are more likely to be working, and poor Black families often include more than one wage earner.
3. Adaptability of family roles. In two-parent families, the egalitarian pattern of decision making is the most common. The self-reliance of Black women who are the primary wage earners best illustrates this adaptability.
4. A high achievement orientation. Working-class Blacks indicate a greater desire for their children to attend college than do working-class Whites. Even a majority of low-income African Americans desire to attend college.
5. A strong religious orientation. Since the time of slavery, Black churches have been the impetus behind many significant grass-roots organizations.

Social workers and sociologists have confirmed through social research these strengths that Hill noted (J. Hudgins 1992). Within the African American community, these are the sources of family strength. While poverty fosters instability, the African American family remains a resilient and adaptive social institution (A. Billingsley 1992).

Increasingly, social scientists are learning to look at both aspects of African American family life: the weaknesses and strengths. Expressions of alarm about instability date back to 1965, when the Department of Labor issued the report, *The Negro Family: The Case for National Action*. The document, commonly known as the *Moynihan Report,* after its principal author, sociologist Daniel Patrick Moynihan, outlined a "tangle of pathology" with the Black family at its core. More recently, two studies, the Stable Black Families Project and the National Survey of Black Americans, sought to learn how Black families encounter problems and resolve them successfully with internal resources such as those that Hill outlined in his highly regarded work (F. Chideya 1993; Department of Labor 1965; Gary et al. 1983; Hatchett, Cochran, and Jackson 1991).

The most consistently documented strength of African American families is the presence of an extended family household—the first strength listed above. The most common feature is having grandparents residing in the home. Extended living arrangements are twice as common among Black as among White households. These arrangements are recognized as having the important economic benefit of pooling limited economic resources. Because of the generally lower earnings of African American heads-of-household, income from second, third, and even fourth wage earners is required to achieve a desired standard of living or, in all too many cases, simply to meet daily needs (Farley and Allen 1987; Taylor et al. 1990).

THE AFRICAN AMERICAN MIDDLE CLASS

Many characterizations of African American family life have been attacked because they overemphasize the poorest segment of the African American community. An opposite error is the exaggeration of the success that African Americans have achieved. Social scientists face the challenge of avoiding a selective, one-sided picture of Black society. The problem is similar to viewing a partially filled glass of water. Does one describe it as half-empty and emphasize the need for assistance? Or does one describe the glass as half-full to give attention to what has been accomplished? The most complete description would acknowledge both perspectives (A. Gouldner 1970).

A clearly defined African American middle class has emerged. In 1997, nearly one-third of African Americans earned more than the median income for Whites. At least 29 percent of Blacks, then, are middle class or more. Many have debated the character of this middle class. E. Franklin Frazier (1957), a Black sociologist, wrote an often-critical study of the African American middle class, in which he identified its overriding goal as achieving petty social values and becoming acceptable to White society (Bureau of the Census 1998c:475).

African Americans are still aware of their racial subordination even when they have achieved economic equality. The Black middle class may not be militant, but neither do its newest members forget their roots. They are more likely than Whites to be first-generation middle class, dependent on two or more sources of income, and precariously close to the lower class both financially and residentially. Yet with their relative success has come a desire to live in better surroundings. The migration of middle-class African Americans out of the ghetto in the 1970s and 1980s has left a vacuum. They may still care about the problems of the Black poor, but they are no longer present as role models (Durant and Louden 1986; B. Landry 1987; N. Lemann 1986a, 1986b).

Members of the African American middle class do not automatically accept all aspects of the White middle class. For years, for example, Whites have relied on books and magazines on infant and child care; such materials treated African American children as if they did not exist. To counter this neglect, James Comer and Alvin Poussaint wrote *Raising Black Children* (1992), in which the authors advise parents on how to deal with questions like "What is Black?, a child's first encounter with prejudice, and a teenage girl's being watched by store security.

Directing attention to the Black middle class also requires that we consider the relative importance of the two components in ethclass, Milton Gordon's concept introduced in Chapter 5. The degree to which relatively affluent Blacks identify themselves in class terms or racial terms is an important ideological question. W. E. B. Du Bois (1952) argued that, when racism decreases, class issues become more important. As Du Bois saw it, exploitation would remain, and many of the same people would continue to be subordinate. Black elites might become economically successful, either as entrepreneurs (Black capitalists) or professionals (Black white-collar workers), but they would continue to identify with and serve the dominant group's interest.

Social scientists have long recognized the importance of class. **Class** is a term that was used by sociologist Max Weber to refer to persons who share a similar level of wealth and income. The significance of class in people's lives is apparent to all. In the United States today, roughly half the lower-class population suffers from chronic health conditions that limit their activity, compared with only one in eleven among the affluent. The poor are more likely to become victims of crime, and they are only about half as likely as the affluent to send their children to colleges or vocational schools (Schaefer and Lamm 1998).

The complexity of the relative influence of race and class was apparent in the controversy surrounding the publication of sociologist William J. Wilson's *The Declining Significance of Race* (1980). Pointing to the increasing affluence of African Americans, Wilson concluded that "class has become more important than race in determining black life-chances in the modern world" (p. 150). The policy implications of his conclusion are that programs must be developed to confront class subordination rather than ethnic and racial discrimination. Wilson did not deny the legacy of discrimination reflected in the disproportionate number of African Americans who are poor, less educated, and living in inadequate and overcrowded housing. He pointed, however, to "compelling evidence" that young Blacks were competing successfully with young Whites.

Critics of Wilson comment that focusing attention on this small educated elite ignores vast numbers of African Americans relegated to the lower class (A. Pinkney 1984; C. Willie 1978, 1979). Wilson himself was not guilty of such an oversimplification and indeed expressed concern over lower-class, inner-city African Americans' seemingly falling even further behind, like those who become a part of the irregular economy discussed in Chapter 3. He pointed out that the poor are socially isolated and have shrinking economic opportunities (1987, 1996). It is easy to conclude superficially, however, that because educated Blacks are entering the middle class, race has ceased to be of concern.

As many African Americans have learned, prejudice and discrimination do not end with professional status and scholarship. Glenn encountered discrimination as described in the chapter-opening example that could be experienced by any Black person. In "Listen to Their Voices," respected law professor Patricia J. Williams, an African American, describes her inability to secure a mortgage despite initial approval after an analysis of her financial status but before the bank realized she was Black. Her recent experience is not unusual and helps to explain the housing patterns still found in the United States that we consider next.

LISTEN TO THEIR VOICES

Of Race and Risk

Patricia J. Williams

Several years ago, at a moment when I was particularly tired of the unstable lifestyle that academic careers sometimes require, I surprised myself and bought a real house. Because the house was in a state other than the one where I was living at the time, I obtained my mortgage by telephone. I am a prudent little squirrel when it comes to things financial, always tucking away stores of nuts for the winter, and so I meet the criteria of a quite good credit risk. My loan was approved almost immediately.

A little while later, the contract came in the mail. Among the papers the bank forwarded were forms documenting compliance with the Fair Housing Act, which outlaws racial discrimination in the housing market. The act monitors lending practices to prevent banks from redlining—redlining being the phenomenon whereby banks circle certain neighborhoods on the map and refuse to lend in those areas. It is a practice for which the bank with which I was dealing, unbeknownst to me, had been cited previously—as well as since. In any event, the act tracks the race of all banking customers to prevent such discrimination. Unfortunately, and with the creative variability of all illegality, some banks also use the racial information disclosed on the fair housing forms to engage in precisely the discrimination the law seeks to prevent.

I should repeat that to this point my entire mortgage transaction had been conducted by telephone. I should also note that I speak a Received Standard English, regionally marked as Northeastern perhaps, but not easily identifiable as black. With my credit history, my job as a law professor and, no doubt, with my accent, I am not only middle class but apparently match the cultural stereotype of a good white person. It is thus, perhaps, that the loan officer of the bank, whom I had never met, had checked off the box on the fair housing form indicating that I was white.

Race shouldn't matter, I suppose, but it seemed to in this case, so I took a deep breath, crossed out "white" and sent the contract back. That will teach them to presume too much, I thought. A done deal, I assumed. But suddenly the transaction came to a screeching halt. The bank wanted more money, more points, a higher rate of interest. Suddenly I found myself facing great resistance and much more debt. To make a long story short, I threatened to sue under the act in question, the bank quickly backed down and I procured the loan on the original terms.

Housing

Housing plays a major role in determining the quality of a person's life. For African Americans, as for Whites, housing is the result of personal preferences and amount of income. African Americans differ from Whites, however, in that their housing has been restricted through discrimination in a manner that it has not for Whites.

What was interesting about all this was that the reason the bank gave for its newfound recalcitrance was not race, heaven forbid. No, it was all about economics and increased risk: The reason they gave was that property values in that neighborhood were suddenly falling. They wanted more money to buffer themselves against the snappy winds of projected misfortune.

Initially, I was surprised, confused. The house was in a neighborhood that was extremely stable. I am an extremely careful shopper; I had uncovered absolutely nothing to indicate that prices were falling. It took my realtor to make me see the light. "Don't you get it," he sighed. "This is what always happens." And even though I suppose it was a little thick of me, I really hadn't gotten it: For of course, I was the reason the prices were in peril....

In retrospect, what has remained so fascinating to me about this experience was the way it so exemplified the problems of the new rhetoric of racism. For starters, the new rhetoric of race never mentions race. It wasn't race but risk with which the bank was so concerned....

By this measure of mortgage-worthiness, the ingredient of blackness is cast not just as a social toll but as an actual tax. A fee, an extra contribution at the door, an admission charge for the high costs of handling my dangerous propensities, my inherently unsavory properties. I was not judged based on my independent attributes or financial worth; not even was I judged by statistical profiles of what my group actually does. (For in fact, anxiety-stricken, middle-class black people make grovelingly good cake-baking neighbors when not made to feel defensive by the unfortunate historical strategies of bombs, burnings or abandonment.) Rather, I was being evaluated based on what an abstraction of White Society writ large thinks we—or I—do, and that imagined "doing" was treated and thus established as a self-fulfilling prophecy. It is a dispiriting message: that some in society apparently not only devalue black people but devalue themselves and their homes just for having us as part of their landscape.

"I bet you'll keep your mouth shut the next time they plug you into the computer as white," laughed a friend when he heard my story. It took me aback, this postmodern pressure to "pass," even as it highlighted the intolerable logic of it all. For by these "rational" economic measures, an investment in my property suggests the selling of myself.

Source: Patricia J. Williams. "Of Race and Risk." Reprinted from the December 29, 1997 issue of *The Nation*.

While Black housing has improved, as indicated by statistics on home ownership, new construction, density of living units, and quality as measured by plumbing facilities, African Americans remain behind Whites on all these standards. The quality of Black housing is inferior to that of Whites at all income levels; yet Blacks pay a larger proportion of their income for shelter.

Housing was the last major area to be covered by civil rights legislation. The delay was not due to its insignificance; quite the contrary, it was precisely because housing touches so many parts of the American economy and relates to private property rights that legislators were slow to act. After an executive order by President Kennedy, the government required nondiscrimination in federally assisted housing, but this ruling included only 7 percent of the housing market. In 1968, the Federal Fair Housing Law (Title VIII of the 1968 Civil Rights Act) and the U.S. Supreme Court decision in *Jones* v. *Mayer* combined to outlaw all racial discrimination in housing. Enforcement has remained weak, however, and many aspects of housing, real estate customs, and lending practices remain untouched.

RESIDENTIAL SEGREGATION

Typically in the United States, as noted, White children attend predominantly White schools, Black children attend predominantly Black schools, and Hispanic children attend predominantly Hispanic schools. This school segregation is not only the result of the failure to accept busing but also the effect of residential segregation. In their studies on segregation, Douglas Massey and Nancy Denton (1993) concluded that racial separation "continues to exist because white America has not had the political will or desire to dismantle it" (p. 8). In Chapter 1, we noted the persuasiveness of residential segregation. This racial isolation in neighborhoods has not improved since the beginnings of the civil rights movement in the 1950s.

What are the factors that create residential segregation in the United States? Among the primary factors are that:

1. Because of private prejudice and discrimination, people refuse to sell or rent to people of the "wrong" race, ethnicity, or religion.
2. The prejudicial policies of real estate companies steer people to the "correct" neighborhoods.
3. Government policies enforce antibias legislation ineffectively.
4. Public housing policies today, as well as past construction patterns, reinforce housing for the poor in inner-city neighborhoods.
5. Policies of banks and other lenders create barriers based on race to financing home purchasing.

This last issue of racial-basis financing deserves further explanation. In the 1990s, new attention was given to the persistence of **redlining,** the practice of discrimination against people trying to buy homes in minority and racially changing neighborhoods. It has been repeatedly documented that financial lenders designated minority and racially changing neighborhoods as poor investments for home and commercial loans. Research results showed that, in many cities, including Atlanta, Baltimore, Boston, Chicago, New York City, Philadelphia, and Washington, D.C., the neighborhoods of subordinate groups received fewer and smaller loans than did White neighborhoods, even when economic factors were taken into account. The race of the prospective buyers further affected their chances of getting a loan. White borrowers with the lowest incomes were approved for mortgages more often than Black borrowers with median incomes over $66,000 per year. The disparity continued whether mortgages were sought from local banks, the Federal Housing Administration, or the Veteran's Administration. Redlining exists primarily because of continued residential segregation (P. Passell 1996; J. Yinger 1995).

It is important to recall the implications of this discrimination in home financing for the African American community. Earlier in the chapter, we noted the great disparity between Black and White family wealth and the implications this had for both the present and future generations. The key factor in this inequality was the failure of African Americans to accumulate wealth through home buying. Now we see that discrimination plays a documented role in this barrier to what is possible; in 1990, 43 percent of Blacks were homeowners, compared to 68 percent of Whites. Indeed, in the 1980s, home ownership among Whites increased slightly, while for Blacks it decreased slightly (Bureau of the Census 1996a:719; Oliver and Shapiro 1995).

Although the African American concentration in the central cities has increased, a small but growing number of Blacks have moved into suburban areas. By 1990, 32 percent of the nation's metropolitan African Americans lived in suburban areas. Yet the most significant growth in the percentage of suburban African Americans has come from movement into suburbs that are predominantly Black or are adjacent to predominantly Black areas. In many instances, therefore, it represents further ghettoization and spillover from city slums. It is not necessarily a signal of two cars and a backyard pool. In many instances, the suburbs with large Black populations are isolated from surrounding White communities and have less satisfactory housing and municipal services but, ironically, pay higher taxes (De Witt 1996; Massey and Denton 1993; Phelan and Schneider 1996).

A dual housing market is part of today's reality, although attacks continue against the remaining legal barriers to fair housing. **Zoning laws,** in theory, are enacted to ensure that specific standards of housing construction will be satisfied. These regulations can also separate industrial and commercial enterprises from residential areas. Some zoning laws in suburbs, though, have seemed to curb the development of low- and moderate-income housing that would attract African Americans who want to move out of the central cities.

For years, the construction of low-income public housing in the ghetto has furthered racial segregation. The courts have not ruled consistently in this matter in recent years so, as with affirmative action and busing, public officials lack clear guidance. In the suburban Chicago community of Arlington Heights, the courts decided in 1977 that a community could refuse to rezone to allow low-income housing, a policy that effectively kept out African Americans. In 1988, however, the courts fined Yonkers, a city adjoining New York City, for failing to build public housing for low- and middle-income households in a way that would foster integration.

Even if court decisions continue to dismantle exclusionary housing practices, the rapid growth of integrated neighborhoods is unlikely. In the future, African American housing will likely (1) continue to improve, (2) remain primarily in all-Black neighborhoods, and (3) remain inferior in quality to White housing. This gap is greater than can be explained by differences in social class.

Criminal Justice

A complex, sensitive topic affecting African Americans is their role in criminal justice. It was reported in 1997 that Blacks constitute less than 3 percent of judges and lawyers, 18 percent of police detectives, and 27 percent of correction institutional officers, but 43 percent of jail inmates (Bureau of the Census 1998c:229, 419).

Data collected annually in the FBI's *Uniform Crime Report* show that Blacks account for 31 percent of arrests, even though they represent only about 12 percent of the nation's population. Conflict theorists point out that the higher arrest rate is not surprising for a group that is disproportionately poor and therefore much less able to afford private attorneys, who might be able to prevent formal arrests from taking place. Even more significantly, the *Uniform Crime Report* focuses on index crimes (mainly property crimes), which are the type of crimes most often committed by low-income people (Bureau of the Census 1998c:219).

President Bill Clinton stated matter of factly in 1995 that "Violence for white people too often comes with a black face" (E. Hutchinson 1995:M5). Yet 70 percent of all violent crimes against Whites are perpetrated by Whites, according to the FBI. In contrast to popular misconceptions about crime, African Americans and the poor are especially likely to be the victims of serious crimes. This fact is documented in **victimization surveys,** which are systematic interviews of ordinary people carried out annually to reveal how much crime occurs. These Department of Justice (1996b) statistics show that African Americans are 25 percent more likely to be victims of violent crimes and are 13 percent more likely to be victims of property crimes than are Whites.

The videotaped beating of Rodney King and the subsequent initial not-guilty verdict given four Los Angeles police officers touched off the 1992 South-Central Los Angeles riots. These events gave very different messages to the public. For Blacks, many minorities, and sympathetic Whites, the events called for renewed attention to police procedures and the handling of citizen complaints. For others, the televised looting and arson pointed to the need for a stronger law-enforcement presence in the inner city.

Central to the concern that minorities often express about the criminal justice system is **differential justice**; that is, Whites are dealt with more leniently than are Blacks, whether at time of arrest, indictment, conviction, sentencing, or parole. Several studies demonstrate that police often deal with African American youths more harshly than with White youngsters. For example, sociologists George Bridges and Sara Stern (1998) found that probation officers were more likely to evaluate Black youth negatively and to describe them as potentially dangerous in their recommendations to judges than White youths who committed comparable violent offenses and who had similar records of prior convictions.

In the 1990s, the concerns within the African American community over the devastating impact of crime became more visible. One concern was that the growth of Black-on-Black crime was not being dealt with as seriously as when Whites were victimized. Researchers on crime have come to call this **victim discounting,** that is, society's tendency to view crimes as less socially significant if the victim is viewed as less worthy. African American men aged 12–24 are especially likely to be victimized—at a rate double that of Whites. Young African American men are also more likely to be victimized by violent crimes (robberies and assaults). In 1992, one of every six Black males aged 16–19 sustained a violent crime, compared to 1 of 11 in 1973 (Bastian and Taylor 1994; T. Gibbons 1985).

Perhaps the most extreme form of victim discounting comes in homicide cases. Although half of all homicide victims in the United States from 1977 to 1992 were African American, 85 percent of prisoners executed were convicted of killing Whites. Viewed from a conflict perspective, such data suggest that, in applying the death penalty, the judicial system in the United States considers Black lives less valuable than White lives. Prosecutors are less likely to argue for a death sentence—and juries and judges less likely to impose it—when the murder victim is Black (E. Zorn 1995).

The second community concern revolves around the impact that crime is having on the quality of life of African Americans. Housing, health, education, and employment opportunities are all being adversely affected by the presence of crime. A Bureau of Justice Statistics report released in 1998 showed that Black central-city dwellers were much more likely than Whites to view crime as a neighborhood problem and also to report having been victimized. C. Deloris Tucker, of the National Political Congress of Black Women, declared, "Our great fear is not from hurricanes or earthquakes, not from disease or war, but from violence against one another" (T. McNulty 1994:7, also see DeFrances and Smith 1998).

There is also a reluctant acceptance that the government cannot be counted on to address inner-city problems. There has been less action than talk about private enterprise becoming involved, and empowerment zones have not really been given a chance. The solution will not be simple. As one writer noted, "There is no magic bullet to reduce youth violence" (K. McFate 1994:4).

Pat Earthly, 29, is employed at a church in Beverly Hills, often working at night. He has joined four other Black Beverly Hills male residents in charging that they have been regularly stopped and illegally searched by the local police, who are unprepared to see anyone other than Whites walking in residential areas and thus suspect Blacks of criminal intent.

Health Care

The price of being an African American took on new importance with the release in 1996 of a shocking study in a prestigious medical journal that revealed that two-thirds of boys in Harlem, a predominantly Black neighborhood in New York City, can expect to die in young or mid-adulthood—that is, before they reach the age of 65. In fact, they have less chance to survive even to 45 than their White counterparts nationwide have of reaching 65. The medical researchers noted that it is not the stereotyped images of AIDS and violence that explain the staggering difference. Black men are much more likely to fall victim to unrelenting stress, heart disease, and cancer (J. Fing et al. 1996).

The morbidity and mortality rates for African Americans as a group, and not just Harlem men, are equally distressing. Compared with Whites, Blacks have higher death rates from diseases of the heart, pneumonia, diabetes, and cancer. The death rate from strokes was twice as high among African Americans as it was among Whites. Such epidemiological findings reflect in part the higher proportion of Blacks found among the nation's lower classes. White Americans can expect to live 79.0 years. By contrast, life expectancy for African Americans is only 70.3 years (Bureau of the Census 1998c:94). Drawing on the conflict perspective, sociologist Howard Waitzkin (1986) suggests that racial tensions contribute to the medical problems of African Americans. In his view, the stress resulting from racial prejudice and discrimination helps to explain the higher rates of hypertension found among African Americans (and Hispanics) than among Whites. Hypertension is twice as common in Blacks as in Whites; it is believed to be a critical factor in Blacks' high mortality rates from heart disease, kidney disease, and stroke. Although medical experts disagree, some argue that the stress resulting from racism and suppressed hostility exacerbates hypertension among African Americans (D. Goleman 1990).

The health problems facing African Americans are complicated by the evidence that they receive less medical care than do Whites with similar medical conditions. Studies presented by the American Medical Association in 1994 reported that African Americans and Whites receive different levels of health care. In addition, two separate studies of Medicare patients found that African Americans and low-income people of all races received less care than affluent Whites, regardless of the type of hospital (rural hospital, urban nonteaching hospital, or urban teaching hospital) (Gornick 1996; Health Care Financing Administration 1995; Kahn et al. 1994; Peterson et al. 1994).

The previous section noted that African Americans are underrepresented among lawyers in the criminal justice system. A similar phenomenon is visible in health care. Blacks represent less than 5 percent of practicing physicians. This is especially significant given that communities with a high proportion of African American residents are four times more likely to have a physician shortage than are White neighborhoods. There is little reason to expect this to improve soon. Applications by Blacks to medical schools and subsequent acceptances declined beginning in 1997. There is also evidence that there is a declining presence of minorities among medical school faculty members, reflecting disenchantment with rolling back of affirmative action in many professional schools (Bowen and Bok 1998; H. Noble 1998).

Related to the health care dilemma is the problem of environmental racism, which was introduced in Chapter 6 with reference to Native Americans. Problems associated with toxic pollution and hazardous garbage dumps are more likely to be faced by low-income Black communities than their affluent counterparts. This disproportionate exposure to environmental hazards can be viewed as part of the complex cycle of discrimination faced by African Americans and other subordinate groups in the United States (R. Pinderhughes 1996).

Just how significant is the impact of poorer health on the lives of the nation's less educated people, less affluent classes, and subordinate groups? Drawing on a variety of research studies, population specialist Evelyn Kitagawa (1972) estimated the "excess mortality rate" to be 20 percent. In other words, 20 percent more people were dying than otherwise might have because of poor health linked to race and class. Using Kitagawa's model, we can calculate that, if every African American in the United States were White and had at least one year of college education, some 56,000 fewer Blacks would have died in 1996 and in each succeeding year (Bureau of the Census 1998c:96).

Politics

African Americans have never received an equal share of the political pie. After Reconstruction, it was not until 1928 that a Black was again elected to Congress. Now, over nearly seventy years and several civil rights acts later, there are still only thirty-eight African American congressional representatives. Recent years have brought some improvement. In fact, between 1972 and 1996, the number of Black elected officials more than tripled (see Table 8.3).

While African Americans have a long way to go to reach equality in the political arena, two events show the beginnings of their full-scale entry. First, in 1973, Councilman Tom Bradley, a Black sharecropper's son, defeated the incumbent to become mayor of Los Angeles at a time when the city was only 15 percent African American. Bradley served in that capacity for almost twenty years. Second, in 1983, Bobby Rush was elected to Chicago's City Council, in 1992, elected to the U.S. House of Representatives, and, in 1999, ran for mayor of Chicago. This elected official began his public career as the defense minister of the Black Panther Party. The political landscape is definitely changing.

Reverend Jesse Jackson is the most visible African American political figure today, even though he has never been elected to public office. Well known for his civil rights activity, Jackson campaigned for the 1984 Democratic Party nomination for President. His expressed goal was to create a "Rainbow Coalition" of disenfranchised Americans, including African Americans, Hispanics, Asian Americans, women, and gay people. Aided by a dramatic turnout of Black voters across the

Table 8.3 Black Elected Officials, 1972–1996

Although the rate of increase has leveled off, the number of Black elected officials has continued to increase.

Year	Number	Percentage Change During Preceding 4 Years	Percentage Increase Since 1972
1972	2,264	—	—
1976	3,979	58	58
1980	4,912	23	117
1984	5,700	16	152
1988	7,225	27	219
1992	7,552	5	234
1996	8,395	11	271

Source: From Data in National Roster of Black Elected Officials, 1998. Reprinted by permisison of the Joint Center for Political and Economic Studies.

country, Jackson made a strong showing, winning 18 percent of the votes cast in Democratic presidential primaries. His success appeared to encourage more African Americans to run for national and statewide offices. Jackson ran for President again in 1988 and won 29 percent of the votes in Democratic primaries, second only to the 43 percent won by Massachusetts governor Michael Dukakis (*Congressional Quarterly* 1984; E. Dionne 1988).

African Americans continue to hold a disproportionately small share of elective and appointive offices in the United States. They usually serve in predominantly Black areas and rarely represent mixed constituencies. White political leaders, however, continue to represent many areas populated by racial minorities. As they have since passage of the Voting Rights Act of 1965, African Americans continue to grow as a political force (A. Pinkney 1994).

The political gains by African Americans, as well as Hispanics, have been placed in jeopardy by legal actions that questioned several race-based districts. Especially beginning with the 1992 presidential election, states drew boundaries for congressional districts so that African American residential areas were grouped together to virtually guarantee the success of a minority candidate.

Some of these new minority districts were redrawn in such a way as to raise cries of gerrymandering. A practice dating from 1810, **gerrymandering** refers to the bizarre outlining of districts to create politically advantageous outcomes. One such example is the 11th Congressional District of Georgia. Initially this district was drawn to be a majority Black district, to increase the likelihood of an African American being elected. Indeed, Cynthia McKinney was elected in 1992. In 1995, however, the Supreme Court declared unconstitutional a strangely shaped Georgia district, calling into question race-based districts in other states. The district was redrawn for the 1996 election when, despite a majority White electorate, Repre-

Georgia Congresswoman Cynthia McKinney (right) celebrates victory in 1996 even though the district had been redrawn to significantly reduce the proportion of it that was African American.

sentative McKinney was reelected. Despite her success, she and others staunchly defended race-based districts, and further Supreme Court action is anticipated (J. Greenburg 1996).

The conflict view in sociology would note that such attacks on race-based minority districts fail to acknowledge that these districts have routinely been drawn based on a commonality of interests, such as rural versus urban interests, or to maximize the likelihood of electing a representative from a certain political party. The use of race-based districts and the subsequent legal attacks demonstrate the vulnerability of racial and ethnic groups' role in the U.S. political system (K. Cooper 1994; D. Kaplan 1993).

CONCLUSION

Black and White Americans have dealt with the continued disparity between the two groups by endorsing several ideologies, as shown in Figure 8.3. Assimilation was the driving force behind the civil rights movement, which sought to integrate Whites and Blacks into one society. People who rejected contact with the other group endorsed separatism. Both Whites and Blacks, as Chapter 2 showed, generally lent little support to separatism. In the latter 1960s, the government and various Black organizations

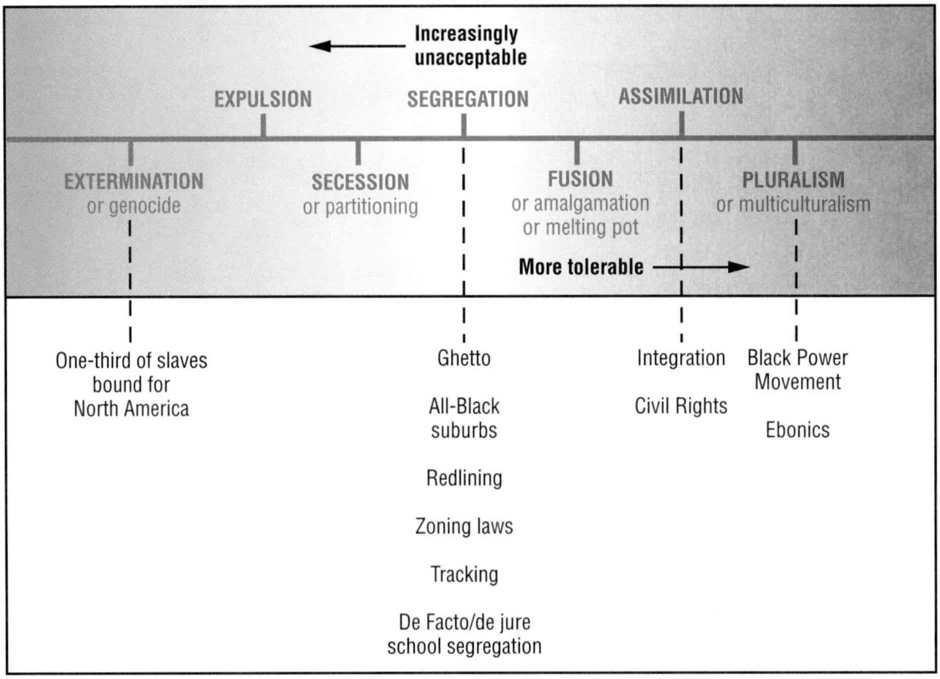

Figure 8.3 Intergroup Relations Continuum

began to recognize cultural pluralism as a goal, at least paying lip service to the desire of many African Americans to exercise cultural and economic autonomy. Perhaps on no other issue is this condition more evident than in the schools.

As the future of African American people in the United States unfolds, one element of the population generally unnoticed thus far may move into prominence. An ever-growing proportion of the Black population consists of people of foreign birth. In the 1980 census, 816,000 foreign-born Blacks were counted, or 3.1 percent of the Black population, the highest ever recorded. By 1994 the number had nearly doubled to 1,596,000, which constituted 5.1 percent of the Black population. Fully 20 percent of the foreign-born Black population arrived in the preceding four years, with the primary source of the immigration being the island nations of the Caribbean. The immigration numbers are expected to increase, as is the proportion of the African American population that is foreign born. Diversity exists in a significant degree with the Black community today (Farley and Allen 1987; Hansen and Bachu 1995; J. Reid 1986).

Twice in this nation's history, African Americans have received significant attention from the federal government and, to some degree, from the larger White society. The first period extended from the Civil War to the end of Reconstruction. The second period was during the civil rights movement of the 1960s. In both periods, the government acknowledged that race was a major issue, and society made commitments to eliminate inequality (R. Farley 1993). As we noted in the previous chapter, Reconstruction was followed by decades of neglect, and on

In South Carolina, a Klan museum opened in 1996 featuring displays of old photographs and Klan robes. The museum's gift shop sold Klan miniatures and offered T-shirts that read, "It's a White Thing. You Wouldn't Understand."

several measures, the position of Blacks deteriorated in the United States. While the 1980s and 1990s have not been without their successes, race is clearly not a major issue on today's national agenda. Even riots in Miami and Los Angeles only divert our attention, while attacks on school integration and affirmative action persist.

The gains that have been made are substantial, but will the momentum continue? Improvement has occurred in a generation inspired and spurred on to bring about change. If the resolve to continue toward that goal lessens in the United States, the picture may become bleaker, and the rate of positive change may decline further.

KEY TERMS

class 255
de facto segregation 241
differential justice 260
gerrymandering 264
income 244
redlining 258
set-asides 249
tracking 242
underemployment 247
victim discounting 260
victimization surveys 260
wealth 244
zoning laws 259

REVIEW QUESTIONS

1. To what degree have the civil rights movement initiatives in education been realized, or do they remain unmet?
2. What challenges face the middle class within the African American community?
3. What are the biggest assets and problems facing African American families?
4. How are differential justice and victim discounting related?
5. How is race-based gerrymandering related to affirmative action?

CRITICAL THINKING

1. Without the comparison to John, Glenn might have taken the shoe salesman to be merely incompetent at his job rather than purposefully avoiding selling to African Americans. Drawing on the case of John and Glenn, what are other types of situations in which people may be victims of discrimination but be unaware of it?
2. What has been the ethnic and racial composition of the neighborhoods you have lived in and the schools you have attended? Consider how the composition of one may have influenced the other. What steps would have been necessary to ensure more diversity?
3. How are the problems in crime, housing, and health interrelated with one another?

INTERNET EXERCISE

The site *The Black World Today* (http://www.tbwt.com/) offers commentary and research on modern issues facing African Americans. Visit the site and read the headline ticker and top stories. What are some of the important personal and social issues mentioned? Click on the "Commentaries and Opions" area. What is the perspective of the featured columnist on current events? Do you agree or disagree with his or her views? Also, be sure to explore the "Black History" area and take the on-line quiz. How many questions about historical facts and persons did you answer correctly? How do you think historical forces have shaped modern experiences for African Americans? What does the future hold?

FOR FURTHER INFORMATION

Andrew Billingsley. *Climbing Jacob's Ladder: The Enduring Legacy of African American Families.* New York: Simon & Schuster, 1992.
Sociologist Billingsley considers the strengths of African American families and relates them to studies of the underclass.

William G. Bowen and Derek Bok. *The Shape of the River: Long-Term Consequences of Considering Race in College and University Admissions.* Princeton, NJ: Princeton University Press, 1998.
Two distinguished educators describe a study of the records and experiences of tens of thousands of students over 20 years at the nation's elite colleges that concludes affirmative action policies created the backbone of the Black middle class and taught White classmates the value of integration.

Alphonso Pinkney. *Black Americans,* 4th ed. Englewood Cliffs, NJ: Prentice-Hall, 1994.
Pinkney presents an excellent profile of African Americans and devotes a chapter to Black nationalism, although that subject is described in even greater detail in the author's 1976 work. He evaluates Milton Gordon's seven assimilation variables in the context of contemporary Black life.

Brent Staples. *Parallel Time: Growing Up Black and White.* New York: Pantheon Press, 1994.
Staples, an editorial writer for *The New York Times*, reflects on his life and that of his younger brother, who was murdered by a rival drug dealer.

9

Hispanic Americans

CHAPTER OUTLINE

HIGHLIGHTS

The group label *Hispanic* or *Latino American* links a diverse population that shares a common language heritage but otherwise has many significant differences. The language barrier in an assimilation-oriented society has been of major significance to Hispanics. For generations, schools made it difficult for Spanish-speaking children to succeed. The United States has only recently recognized its bilingual, bicultural heritage and allowed those whose native language is not English to use it as an asset rather than a liability. The strength of resistance even to elements of pluralism has been exhibited by the language purity movement. Hispanics include several major groups, of which Mexican Americans, Puerto Ricans, and Cubans are the largest. Cuban Americans constitute a significant presence in southern Florida. Increasingly, immigrants and refugees from Central and South America have also established communities throughout the United States.

Air travel and professional sports offer examples of how the United States is gradually adjusting to an increasing number of Latinos. Beginning in 1998, the Anaheim Angels baseball team began to use not only Spanish broadcasters but hired Spanish-speaking ushers and printed everything from team schedules to beverage cups in both Spanish and English. On game days now, spectators can make their way to *la Tienda del Euipo* (Team Store). The year before, American Airlines was roundly criticized for the content of its manual for pilots flying between the United States and Latin America. A section called "Surviving in Latin America" included guidelines concerning mountainous areas near some local airports but also declared that Latin American fliers like to drink alcohol before a flight, and "Unruly and/or intoxicated passengers are not infrequent." It is certainly reasonable to ask why these changes did not occur sooner, but the fact that these and other changes are indeed happening indicates recognition that Latinos represent a substantial economic presence in the United States (K. Baxter 1998; UPI 1997).

More than one of ten people in the U.S. population are of Spanish or Latin American origin. Collectively this group is referred to today as Hispanics or Latinos, two terms that we will use interchangeably in this book. The Census Bureau estimates that by the year 2050, Hispanics will constitute about one-quarter of the U.S. population and that by 2005, they will outnumber African Americans. In fact, in 1997, the number of Hispanics age nineteen and under surpassed the number of nineteen-and-under non-Hispanic Blacks in the United States. The Latino population is very diverse. Today, 19 million, or the majority of Hispanics in the United States, are Mexican Americans, or Chicanos. Puerto Ricans and Cuban Americans account for the largest segment of the remaining 11 million Hispanics. The diversity of Hispanics and their distribution in the United States is shown in Figures 9.1 and 9.2 (Bureau of Census 1997; Day 1996).

The Latino influence is everywhere. Motion pictures such as *La Bamba, Born in East L.A., Stand and Deliver, Salsa, The Mambo Kings,* and *My Family/Mi Familia* did not cater only to Hispanic audiences. The historic Radio City Music Hall now features Spanish-speaking music groups for up to 50 percent of its yearly music productions. They range from the successful Gloria Estefan to newer groups such as Shakira and Jaquares. MTV has begun to offer a new channel, MTV Ritmo, featuring all-Latin music. The number-one radio stations in Los Angeles and Miami broadcast in Spanish. In their speeches, politicians address the needs and desires of Latino Americans. Are these significant signs of acceptance or tokens of tolerant curiosity? In this chapter and the two that follow, we will examine the vibrant, growing group of Hispanic residents in the United States (P. Watrous 1996).

Some images of Hispanic settlements that still prevail in the United States are in reality no longer accurate. Latinos do not live in rural areas. They are generally urban dwellers: 86 percent live in metropolitan areas, in contrast to 73 percent of the general population. In addition, some Hispanics have moved away from their traditional areas of settlement. Many Mexican Americans have left the southwest, and many Puerto Ricans have left New York City. In 1940, 88 percent of Puerto Ricans residing in the United States lived in New York City, but by the 1980 Census the proportion had already dropped to less than half.

Hispanic Identity

Is there a common identity among Latinos? Is a panethnic identity emerging? **Panethnicity** refers to the development of solidarity among ethnic subgroups. We

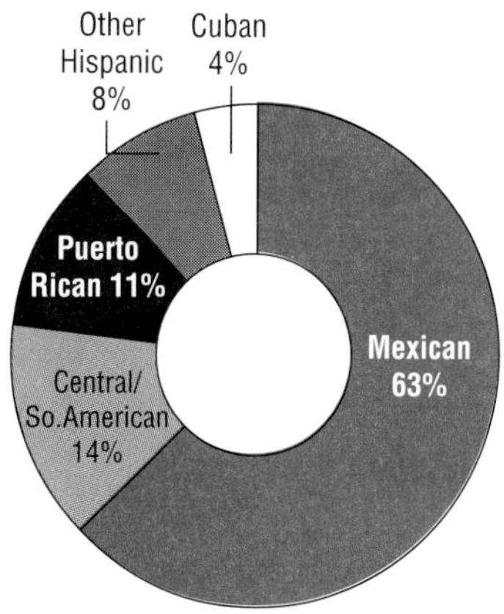

Figure 9.1 Hispanic Population in the United States by Origin, 1997

Source: Bureau of the Census 1998c:54.

noted in Chapter 1 that ethnic identity is not self-evident in the United States and may lead to heated debates even among those who share the same ethnic heritage. Non-Hispanics often give a single label to the diverse group of native-born Latino Americans and immigrants. This labeling by the out-group is similar to the dominant group's way of viewing "American Indians" or "Asian Americans" as one collective group. For example, sociologist Clara Rodriguez has noted that Puerto Ricans, who are American citizens, are viewed as an immigrant group and lumped with all Latinos or Hispanics. She observes that, to most Anglos, "All Hispanics look alike. It's the tendency to see all Latinos as the same. It's an unfortunate lack of attention to U.S. history" (R. Rodríguez 1994:32).

Are Hispanics or Latinos themselves developing a common identity? Indicators vary. The collective term itself is subject to debate with regional variations—*Latino*, for example, is more common in the west, while *Hispanic* is more frequently used in the east and by the federal government. Whatever the term, the actions of the dominant group have an impact to some degree in defining cultural identity. Latinos are brought together through language, national cable TV stations such as Univision and Telemundo, and periodicals aimed at them both in English and in Spanish. These trends are significant because they counter the Anglo-dominated media. For example, in 1994 a survey reported that only 11 of the 800 prime-time television parts were Hispanic roles (N. Kanellos 1994; H. Waters 1994).

However, sharp divisions remain among Hispanics on the identity issue. Only a minority, one out of four (see Chapter 1), prefers to use panethnic names such as

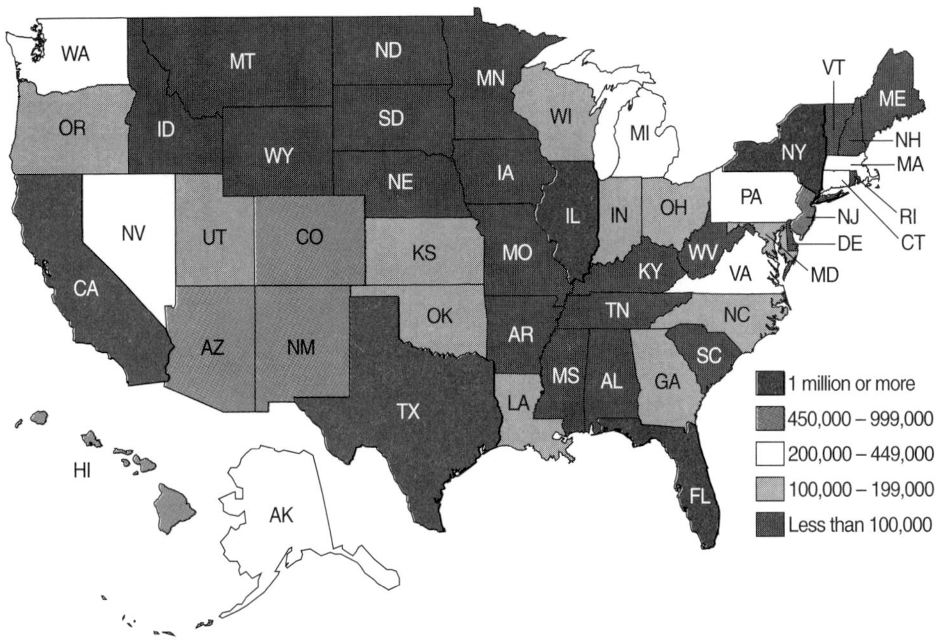

Figure 9.2 Where Most Hispanic Americans Lived, 1997
Source: Bureau of the Census 1998c:34.

Hispanic or *Latino* or *Spanish American*. Even among those born in the United States, fewer than one-third use such names, the majority preferring to identify themselves by nationality—*Mexicans, Mexican Americans, Chicanos, Puerto Ricans, Cubans,* and *Dominicans*. Indeed, in Miami, one can see bumper stickers proclaiming "*No soy Hispano, soy Cubano*"—"I am not Hispanic, I am Cuban" (D. Gonzalez 1992). Such "name issues" or "language battles," as they have been termed, are not inconsequential, but they do distract these groups' attention from working together for common concerns. For example, bridging differences is important in politics, where the diverse Latino or Hispanic groups meet to support candidates or legislative initiatives (G. Fox 1996:12–15).

The Language Divide

Hispanics, wherever they reside in the United States, share the heritage of the Spanish language. They do not all speak Spanish all the time; some, despite their heritage, do not know the language at all. About one-third speak Spanish at work, and over 60 percent speak Spanish at home. Three-quarters listen to Spanish-language television and radio stations. Cubans, Mexican Americans (or Chicanos), Puerto Ricans, Dominicans, and other Hispanic groups can instantly identify their own forms of Spanish, but others, in particular Anglos, note more similarities than differences (P. Braus 1993; N. Kanellos 1994).

The myth of Anglo superiority has rested in part on language differences. (The term *Anglo* in the following text is used to mean all non-Hispanics, but primarily Whites.) First, the criteria for economic and social achievement usually include proficiency in English. By such standards, Spanish-speaking pupils are judged less able to compete until they learn English. Second, many Anglos believe that Spanish is not an asset occupationally. Only recently, as government agencies have belatedly begun to serve Latino people and as businesses recognize the growing Latino consumer market, have Anglos recognized that knowing Spanish is not only useful but necessary to carry out certain tasks. However, as we see in education, voting, and language practices, many people in the United States are concerned and suspicious about the public use of any language other than English.

The need for bilingual workers is obvious in many areas, such as the situation shown here of a bilingual 911 emergency operator in Los Angeles.

BILINGUAL EDUCATION

Until the last twenty or thirty years, there was a conscious effort to devalue the Spanish language and to discourage Hispanics from using it in schools. This practice was built upon a pattern of segregating Hispanic schoolchildren from Anglos. In the recent past in the southwest, Mexican Americans were assigned to Mexican schools to keep Anglo schools all-White. These Mexican schools, created through *de jure* school segregation, were substantially underfunded compared to the regular public schools. Legal action against such schools dates back to 1945, but it was not until 1970 that the U.S. Supreme Court ruled, in *Cisneros* v. *Corpus Christi Independent School District,* that the de jure segregation of Mexican Americans was unconstitutional. Appeals delayed implementation of that decision, and not until September 1975 was the de jure plan forcibly overturned in Corpus Christi, Texas (Commission on Civil Rights 1976a).

Even in integrated schools, Latino children were given separate, unequal treatment. "No Spanish" was a rule enforced throughout the southwest, Florida, and New York City by school boards in the 1960s. Children speaking Spanish on school grounds, even on the playground, might be punished with detention after school, fines, physical reprimands, and even expulsion for repeated violations. From 1855 to as recently as 1968, teaching in any language other than English was illegal in California. Such laws existed despite a provision in the 1848 Treaty of Guadalupe Hidalgo between the United States and Mexico that guaranteed the right of Mexicans to maintain their culture. All official publications were to be bilingual, but "English only" became the social norm.

Language is not only inseparable from culture, but also from identity. In "Listen to Their Voices," Adela de la Torre, an economist at the University of Arizona, reflects on the importance of language to her life.

Is it essential that English be the sole language of instruction in schools in the United States? **Bilingualism** is the use of two or more languages in places of work or educational facilities, according each language equal legitimacy. Thus, a program of **bilingual education** may instruct children in their native language (such as Spanish) while gradually introducing them to the language of the dominant society (English). If such a program is also bicultural, it will teach children about the culture of both linguistic groups. Bilingual education allows students to learn academic material in their own language while they are simultaneously learning a second language. Proponents believe that ideally, bilingual education programs should also allow English-speaking pupils to be bilingual, but generally they are directed only to making non–English speakers proficient in more than one language.

Programs to teach English as a second language (ESL) have been the cornerstone of bilingual education, but they are limited in approach. For example, ESL programs tend to emphasize bilingual, but not bicultural, education. As a result, the method can unintentionally contribute to ethnocentric attitudes, especially if it seems to imply that a minority group is not really worthy of attention. As conflict theorists are quick to note, the interests of the less powerful—in this case, millions of non–English-speaking children—are those least likely to be recognized and

LISTEN TO THEIR VOICES

"Language Is a Bridge to Culture"

Adela de la Torre

I remember well the magic of knowing two languages as a child. My maternal grandmother, an immigrant from the heart of central Mexico, raised me with the certainty that mastering the language of her adopted country would only bring greater opportunities. Although I rarely quibbled with my grandmother, I knew that with the warmth of our home language—our *dichos* (sayings) and *canciones* (songs)—I could begin to understand who I was and who I would become.

Over time, I learned to weave my home language into my new life. I chose never to abandon my home language; rather, I learned that Spanish allowed me to stay rooted to my grandmother's vision as I transformed myself into a new *mestiza.*

Although I never attained the level of Spanish fluency that I desired, I continued my grandmother's tradition of maintaining our home language with my own daughters. My goal was less focused on the notion of fluency than on ensuring that they would maintain some semblance of a distinct Mexican cultural identity. Understanding Spanish would provide them not only with a link to our roots, but also with an entry point to traversing more than one culture. How they will view my efforts as adult women is hard to tell. Yet like many Latinas, I tried, at least symbolically, to maintain our language as well as our customs....

In many ways, maintaining our language is a final act of resistance—a resistance that increasingly is fueled by the racism that is manifest in popular culture as well as popular initiatives like Proposition 187 and more recently in Proposition 227, the so-called Unz initiative. Language never will be a simple binary issue for most Latinos. This becomes even more apparent when opponents of bilingual education code their message in racial terms. Despite attempts to make bilingual education a more general issue, it is viewed by many Latinos as a language rights issue. This inevitably strikes at the heart of how we view ourselves. Across generations, we struggle to maintain some continuity with our roots, and those roots are deeply embedded in our language.

Source: Adela de la Torre. "Language as a Bridge to Culture." Originally appeared in *The Los Angeles Times.* Reprinted by permission of the author.

respected. One alternative to the ESL approach, viewed with much less favor by advocates of bilingualism, is **English immersion,** in which students are taught primarily in English, using their native languages only when they do not understand their lessons. In practice, such instruction usually becomes an English-only "crash program" (F. Hechinger 1987).

Since its introduction into U.S. schools, bilingual education has been beset by problems. Its early supporters were disillusioned by the small number of English-speaking children participating and by the absence of a bicultural component in most programs. However, the frustration has been most clearly visible in the lack of consensus among educators on how best to implement bilingual programs. Even when a school district decides what methods it prefers, superintendents find it difficult to hire qualified instructors, although this varies depending on the language and the part of the country. The problem is further complicated by the presence of children speaking languages other than the predominant second language, so that superintendents must mount bilingual programs in many languages. Indeed, federally supported programs now serve nearly 3 million schoolchildren and operate in an estimated 125 languages (National Clearinghouse for Bilingual Education 1995).

Do bilingual programs help children to learn English? It is difficult to reach firm conclusions on the effectiveness of the bilingual programs in general because they vary so widely in their approach to non–English-speaking children. The programs differ in the length of the transition to English and how long they allow students to remain in bilingual classrooms. However, according to the largest study conducted on bilingual education, comparing the performance of 42,000 non–English-speaking students over thirteen years, the researchers found that children who had six years of bilingual education in well-designed programs performed far better on standardized English tests in eleventh grade than did those without the benefits of a bilingual education. Children who are plunged into an English environment before they are fluent show unnecessary long-term academic difficulties. Despite such studies, bilingual programs are a cost that many communities and states are unwilling to pay and are quick to cut back despite the long-term price of poorly educated students (Portes and Schauffler 1996; Thomas and Collier 1996).

Drawing on the perspective of conflict theory, we can understand some of the attacks on bilingual programs. The criticisms do not necessarily result from careful educational research. Rather, they stem from the effort to assimilate children and to deprive them of language pluralism. This view that any deviation from the majority is bad is expressed by those who wish to stamp out foreigners wherever it occurs, especially in our schools. Research findings have little influence on those who, holding such ethnocentric views, try to persuade policy makers to follow their thinking. This perspective does not take into account that success in bilingual education may begin to address the problem of high school dropouts and the paucity of Hispanics in colleges and universities.

VOTING RIGHTS AND THE LATINO POLITICAL PRESENCE

In 1975, Congress moved toward recognizing the multilingual background of the U.S. population. Federal law now requires bilingual or even multilingual ballots in voting districts where at least 5 percent of the population belong to a single minority group. Even before Congress acted, the federal courts had been ordering cities such as Chicago, Miami, and New York City to provide bilingual ballots where necessary (J. Crawford 1992).

Bilingual voting, like bilingual education, is designed to compensate for decades of inequality when the goal of equality could not be achieved through strictly "equal treatment." Merely banning literacy tests was insufficient to restore rights to linguistic minorities; yet twenty years of voting reforms did not have the impact that many of their advocates had hoped. The poor turnout was not because Hispanics were not interested in voting. Many were ineligible under the U.S. Constitution because they were noncitizens. Ironically, this pattern began to change as the result of attacks on granting services to legal immigrants. In the mid–1990s, legislators in states such as California and Florida that have a large immigrant presence proposed restricting certain health services to citizens only. Such initiatives, coupled with federal welfare reform in 1996 that considered denying assistance to noncitizens, led to massive increases in naturalization applications. Typical of the feelings expressed by newly eligible voters were those of Jesse Henriquez, a forty-eight-year-old office assistant who had emigrated from El Salvador sixteen years before and voted for the first time in 1996. He observed, "The only way we can tell the people that we are working

Proposition 227, passed by California voters in 1997, called for an end to bilingual education in public schools.

Philadelphia Business Journal/John Spencer

hard and that Latinos should not be blamed for all the country's problems is to register and vote" (W. Claiborne 1996:14).

The prospect for a greater Latino political presence is strong. Anticipating the greater turnout, political parties are advancing more Hispanics for candidates. Generally, the Democrats have been more successful in garnering the Hispanic vote—Clinton garnered 71 percent of the Hispanic vote in 1996. However, observers agree that this is not as much a pro-Democrat vote as a stand against the Republicans, who favor reducing legal immigration, limiting welfare benefits to legal immigrants, and eliminating bilingual education. In fact, Latinos as a group are not nearly as pro-Democrat as, for example, African Americans. Indeed, evidence shows that younger Hispanics are becoming more conservative and more likely to consider Republican candidates. All these factors among Hispanics—rapidly growing population, higher proportions of voter registration, higher participation in elections, less commitment to a single political party—will increase efforts by politicians to elicit their support. (G. Rodriguez 1998).

OFFICIAL LANGUAGE MOVEMENT

Attacks on bilingualism both in voting and in education have taken several forms and have even broadened to question the appropriateness of U.S. residents using any language other than English. Federal policy has become more restrictive. Local schools have been given more authority to determine appropriate methods of instruction; they have also been forced to provide more of their own funding for bilingual education. Early in 1981 the federal government decided to scrap new proposals requiring school districts to offer bilingual education to non–English-speaking children. The government's action was bitterly protested by Representative Robert García, a Puerto Rican congressman from New York City, who stated, "This is a signal to the rest of the country that does not want civil rights for Latinos that school districts can say, 'The hell with it, why should we bother?' It will be back to business as usual, which in many states is back to bigotry" (Barrett and Cooper 1981:24).

The congressman's warnings were not heeded. Beginning in 1985, federal funds for bilingual education could also be used for alternative programs, which included the immersion of Spanish-speaking children in English-language programs. A 1988 law further stipulates that no student can be in a federally funded transitional bilingual program for more than three years unless special requirements are met.

Attacks on bilingualism have come on a number of fronts, but most seek to declare English a state's official language. By 1996, twenty-three states, by law or constitutional amendment, had established English as the official language. The measures range from simple declarations to actually preventing state business from being conveyed in any language other than English. However, generally such measures are mostly symbolic, having little impact on bilingual publications, for example. On the national level, measures have been introduced in Congress for a constitutional amendment, most recently in 1995, forbidding the federal government from conducting its business in anything but English. This amendment would end, for example, the printing of income tax preparation information in Spanish. Debates around such measures stir emotions on both sides, but there has been little concrete success in declaring English the official language nationally (M. Dorning 1996; T. Mauro 1996).

Challenges to bilingualism continue. In 1997, California voters supported Proposition 227, calling for the end of bilingual education in its public schools. Implementation has been uneven, with some districts taking advantage of a provision for parents to keep their children out of English-immersion classes if they fill out a form declaring they have an "educational need" to remain in bilingual classes (Puente and Morello 1998).

The lack of movement toward bilingualism in the United States makes this country unusual. Switzerland has four official languages and India more than twenty, and most nations elevate more than one language to some kind of official status. It is depressing to see businesses recognize the marketing potential; they are reaching out to a language-rich public while English speakers resist recognizing more than one language. While public sentiment favors the dominance of English, the economic reality is quite different. Even in Miami, with its large Latino population, businesses are forced to rely on recent immigrants to transact business with Latin Americans because the second and third generation of Cuban and Latin Americans lack practical knowledge of Spanish. Even though half the children in Miami are of Hispanic descent, only about 2 percent of high school students graduate fully fluent in Spanish—that is, able to read, write, and converse in it (M. Navarro 1996). Again, conflict sociologists would see this condition as an instance of the interests of the powerful being given primacy.

McDonald's touts its "hamburguesas," and Anheuser-Busch insists that "Budweiser es para usted" (is for you). Perhaps at some time in the future teachers and poll watchers will more often offer the greeting, "*Se habla inglés y español* (English and Spanish spoken)."

The Borderlands

Language is an invisible barrier. National borders, on the other hand, are visible divides that sometimes can be very easily breached. The term **borderlands** here refers to the area of a common culture along the border between Mexico and the United States. While particularly relevant to Mexicans and Mexican Americans, the growing Mexican influence is relevant to the other Latino groups that we will discuss (Heyck 1994).

Legal and illegal emigration from Mexico to the United States, day laborers crossing the border regularly to go to jobs in the United States, the implementation of the North American Free Trade Agreement (NAFTA), and the exchange of media across the border all make the notion of separate Mexican and U.S. cultures obsolete in the borderlands.

The economic position of the borderlands is complex, in terms of both businesses and workers. Very visible is the presence of **maquiladoras** on the Mexican side. These are foreign-owned companies that establish operations in Mexico, yet are

Maguiladoras are foreign-owned manufacturers located in Mexico along the U.S. border. A worker packages seat belt components for export to the U.S. at a plant in Reynosa, Mexico.

exempt from Mexican taxes and are not required to provide insurance or benefits for their workers. By the year 2000, an estimated 1.5 Mexican people were employed in 5,000 maquiladoras. The emergence of factories has been criticized in the United States as contributing to the flight of manufacturing jobs from other parts of North America to Mexico (Bissio 1995; *Migration News* 1998a; Russell 1996).

Immigrant workers have significant economic impact on their home country while employed in the United States. Many Mexicans, as well as other Hispanic groups we will be discussing, send some part of their earnings back across the border to family members remaining in their native country. This substantial flow of money, sometimes referred to as **remittances (or migradollars),** is estimated at a minimum of $2 billion annually and accounts for 3 percent of Mexico's gross domestic product (Durand et al. 1996).

The closeness culturally and economically of the home country found in the borderlands is applicable to other Latino groups. We will see the continuing prominent role that the events, economic and political, have on the immigrants and their children, and even grandchildren, in the United States.

As we have noted several times already, the Latino or Hispanic community is comprised of several nationalities. The Mexican Americans, the people of the borderlands and beyond, and the Puerto Ricans are by far the two largest and will be considered separately in the next chapter. We will continue in this chapter by considering the other Latino groups—first considering the largest of the remaining Hispanic groups.

Cuban Americans

Third in numbers only to Mexican Americans and Puerto Ricans, Cuban Americans represent a significant ethnic Hispanic minority in the United States. Their presence in this country is a relatively long one, with Cuban settlements in Florida dating back to as early as 1831. These settlements tended to be small, close-knit communities organized around a single enterprise, such as a cigar-manufacturing firm.

Until recently, however, the number of Cuban Americans was very modest. The 1960 Census showed that 79,000 people who had been born in Cuba lived in the United States. By 1995, over 1.1 million people of Cuban birth or descent lived in the United States. This tremendous increase followed Fidel Castro's assumption of power after the 1959 Cuban Revolution.

IMMIGRATION

Cuban immigration to the United States since the 1959 revolution has been continuous, but there have been four significant influxes of large numbers of immigrants. First, the initial exodus of about 200,000 Cubans following Castro's assumption of power lasted about three years. Regular commercial air traffic continued despite the U.S. severing diplomatic relations with Cuba. This first wave stopped with the missile crisis of October 1962, when all legal movement between the two nations was halted. An agreement between the United States and Cuba in 1965 produced the second wave through a program of "freedom flights"—specially arranged charter flights from Havana to Miami. Through these, more than 340,000 refugees arrived between 1965 and 1973. Despite efforts to encourage these arrivals to disperse into other parts of the United States, most settled in the Miami area (M. Abrahamson 1996).

The third major migration, the 1980 Mariel boatlift, has been the most controversial. In 1980 more than 124,000 refugees fled Cuba in the "freedom flotilla." In May of that year, a few boats from Cuba began to arrive in Key West, Florida, with people seeking asylum in the United States. President Carter, reflecting the nation's hostility toward Cuba's communist government, told the new arrivals and anyone else who might be listening in Cuba that they were welcome "with open arms and an open heart." As the number of arrivals escalated, it became apparent that Castro had used the invitation as an opportunity to send prison inmates, patients from mental hospitals, and addicts. The majority of the refugees, though, were neither marginal to the Cuban economy nor social deviants.

The most recent influx of 20,000 Cuban refugees came in 1994, as Cuba's social and economic problems mounted.

The Cuban refugees of this migration were soon given by other Cubans the name **Marielitos.** The word, which implies that these refugees were undesirable, refers to Mariel, the fishing port west of Havana from which the boats departed, where Cuban authorities herded people into boats. The term *Marielitos* remains a stigma in the media and in Florida. The immigrants also became an embarrassment to the Carter administration, which first welcomed them. Because of their negative reception by longer-established Cuban immigrants, as well as the group's relatively modest skills and little formal education, this group had a great deal of difficulty in adjusting to their new life in the United States.

The difficult transition for many members of this "freedom flotilla" is linked with other factors as well. Unlike the earlier waves, they grew up in a country bombarded with anti-American images. Despite these problems, their eventual acceptance by the Hispanic community has been impressive, and many members of this third significant wave have found employment. Most have applied for permanent resident status. Government assistance to these immigrants was limited, but help from some groups of Cuban Americans in the Miami area was substantial. However, for a small core group of 3,700, adjustment was impossible. The legal status of a few of these detainees (that is, arrivals who were held by the government pending clarification of their refugee or immigrant status) was ambiguous because of alleged offenses committed either in Cuba or the United States or both. Major prison riots in Louisiana and Georgia by some of these detainees also brought attention to their situation (Boswell and Curtis 1984; Hufker and Cavender 1990; J. LeMoyne 1990; Portes and Stepick 1985; H. Silva 1985).

A smaller, but also controversial, fourth wave of immigration occurred in 1994, when Cuba faced particularly harsh economic conditions and social unrest created when the Russians ended their long-standing aid to Cuba, without which Cuba experienced severe shortages. Castro encouraged migration, and the Clinton administration acquiesced at first by picking up the refugees at sea and transporting them to the U.S. mainland. However, opposition grew to this welcome, particularly in Florida, where the governor expressed the need for vast amounts of assistance to help with the influx of Cubans. President Clinton then revised the policy, relocating the refugees temporarily to the U.S. Navy base at Guantánamo, Cuba, as well as to other nations, such as Panama. An estimated 20,000 arrived at the base during this migration. Overall, since the assumption of power by Fidel Castro, one-tenth of the island's population of 11 million people has fled to the United States (M. Clary 1997; F. Masud-Piloto 1996; T. Post 1994).

THE PRESENT PICTURE

Compared to other recent immigrant groups and to Latinos as a whole, Cuban Americans are doing well. As shown in Table 9.1, Cuban Americans have college completion rates twice those of other Latinos. In this and all other social measures, the pattern is similar. Cuban Americans in 1995 compared favorably to other Hispanics, although recent arrivals as a group trail behind White Americans.

The presence of Cubans has been felt in urban centers throughout the United States, but most notably in the Miami, Florida, area. Throughout their various immigration phases, Cubans have been encouraged to move out of southern Florida, but many have returned to Dade County (metropolitan Miami), with its warm climate and proximity to other Cubans and Cuba itself. As of 1990, 53 percent of all Cuban Americans lived in Miami; another 15 percent lived in New York City, and 5 percent lived in Los Angeles. Metropolitan Miami itself now has a Hispanic majority, compared to a Hispanic presence of only 4 percent in 1950 (M. Winsberg 1994).

Table 9.1 Selected Social and Economic Characteristics of Cubans and South Americans, 1997

	Total White	Total Hispanic	Cuban	Central and South Americans
Percent completing college, 25 years and over	24.6	10.3	19.7	14.8
Percent unemployed	4.2	5.3	4.2	5.1
Percent of families with a single parent	22.7	31.8	23.1	34.8
Percent living below poverty level	7.8	26.4	12.5	19.0
Median income (year-round workers)	$58,904	$26,179	$35,616	$29,960

Source: Bureau of the Census 1998c: 51, 54.

Probably no ethnic group has had more influence on the fortunes of a city in a relatively short period of time than have the Cubans on Miami. Most consider the Cubans' economic influence positive. The Cuban and other Latin American immigrants have transformed Miami from a quiet resort to a boomtown. To a large degree they have re-created the Cuba they left behind. Today, the population of metropolitan Miami is 35 percent foreign born—more than any other city. Residents like to joke that one of the reasons they like living in Miami is that it is close to the United States (M. Clary 1997).

The relations between Miami's Cuban Americans and other groups have not been perfect. For example, Miami's other Hispanics, including Venezuelans, Ecuadorians, and Colombians, resent being mistaken for Cubans and feel that their own distinctive nationalities are being submerged. Perhaps the primary criticism heard in Miami's Anglo community is that the Cubans invest their profits in other Cuban-owned businesses and have little to do with Anglos and Blacks. Non-Cuban Americans feel that the economic resurgence of Miami is bypassing them. Disadvantaged African Americans resented Cuban Americans who seek public assistance because, as a group, they are better off than other immigrant groups. A 1996 metropolitan Miami mayoral contest put the friction out in the open as Cubans crossed party lines to elect

Relations are strained between Cubans and African Americans in Miami, primarily as the result of economic competition. In 1990, Cuban Americans protested the visit of South African leader Nelson Mandela following his favorable comments about Cuba's Fidel Castro.

as mayor Republican Cuban American Alex Penelas rather than vote for the Black Democratic candidate (M. Abrahamson 1996; D. Wickham 1996).

All Cuban immigrants have had much to adjust to, and they have not been able to immediately establish the kind of life they sought. Although those who fled Cuba were sometimes forced to give up their life's savings, the early immigrants of the first wave were generally well educated, had professional or managerial backgrounds, and therefore met with greater economic success than later immigrants. However, regardless of the occupations the immigrants were able to enter, there was tremendous adjustment for the family. Women who typically did not work outside the home now often had to seek employment. Immigrant parents found their children being exposed to a foreign culture. All the challenges typically faced by immigrant households were complicated by uncertainty surrounding those they left behind in Cuba (Portes and Stepick 1993; Z. Suárez 1998).

The long-range prospects for Cubans in the United States depend on several factors. Of obvious importance are events in Cuba, for many Cuban refugees publicly proclaim their desire to return if the communist government is overturned. A powerful force in politics in Miami is the Cuban-American National Foundation, which takes a strong anti-Castro position. They have actively opposed any proposals that the United States develop a more flexible policy toward Cuba. More moderate voices in the Cuban exile community have not been encouraged to speak out. Indeed, sporadic violence has even occurred within the community over United States–Cuban relations. In addition, artists or speakers who come from Cuba receive a cold reception in Miami unless they are outspoken critics of Fidel Castro (L. Martin 1996).

As the years pass and as the refugees' prosperity increases, however, fewer and fewer are likely to return even if a political reversal occurs. A 1996 survey of Miami's Cuban community found that the majority still favor the trade embargo with Cuba, but 48 percent favor negotiations with the Cuban government. Assimilation may not be dampening their anti-Castro feelings, but it is deepening their roots in the United States (M. Navarro 1997).

Not surprisingly, Miami has become the most bilingual of any city in the United States that is not on the Mexican border. In spite of this, or perhaps because of it, bilingualism became an emotional issue in southern Florida. In a 1980 election, the electorate, by a three-fifths majority vote, reversed a 1978 resolution designating Dade County a bilingual county. This vote ended the practice of translating county legal documents into Spanish, although bilingual education programs continue. This 1980 vote was a statement by the overwhelming majority of non-Cubans that they were uncomfortable with the Latinization of their area. However, it was for the most part an ideological statement; it has had little practical effect. Just as Cuban Americans are at a clear disadvantage if they cannot communicate effectively in English, Anglo business people have increasingly realized the value, as reflected in profit statements, of being able to communicate in Spanish as well as English (R. Mohl 1986).

Cuban Americans have selectively accepted Anglo culture. But Cuban culture has been tenacious; the Cuban immigrants do not feel that they need to forget

Spanish while establishing fluency in English, the way other immigrant children have shunned their linguistic past. Still, a split between the original exiles and their children is evident. Young people are more concerned about the Miami Dolphins football team than they are about what is happening in Havana. They are more open to reestablishing relations with a Castro-led Cuba. However, the latest wave of immigrants in 1994, the *recién llegados* (recently arrived) have again introduced more openly anti-Castro feelings (M. Clary 1997; Hill and Moreno 1996; L. Martin 1996.

Central and South Americans

The immigrants that have come from Central and South America are a diverse population that has not been closely studied. Indeed, most government statistics treat its members collectively as "other" and rarely differentiate among them by nationality. Yet people from Chile and Costa Rica have little in common other than their hemisphere of origin and the Spanish language, if that. Not all Central and South Americans have Spanish as their native tongue; for example, immigrants from Brazil speak Portuguese, immigrants from French Guyana speak French, and those from Surinam speak Dutch.

Many of the nations of Central and South America have a complex system of placing people into a myriad of racial groups. African slaves were brought to almost all of these countries, and these people of African descent, in varying degrees, have intermarried with each other or with indigenous peoples, as well as with the European colonists. Rather than placing people in two or three distinct racial groupings, these societies describe skin color in a continuum from light to dark in what is referred to as a color gradient. A **color gradient** is the placement of people along a continuum from light to dark skin color rather than in distinct racial groupings by skin color. The presence of color gradients is yet another reminder of the social construction of race. Terms such as *mestizo Hondurans*, *mulatto Colombians*, or *African Panamanians* reflect this continuum of a color gradient.

Added to language diversity and the color gradient are social class distinctions, religious differences, urban-versus-rural backgrounds, and differences in dialect even among those speaking the same language. We can understand historians Ann Orlov and Reed Ueda's (1980) conclusion that "social relations among Central and South American ethnic groups in the United States defy generalization" (p. 212). Central and South Americans do not form, nor should they be expected to form, a cohesive group, nor do they naturally form coalitions with Cuban Americans or Mexican Americans or Puerto Ricans.

IMMIGRATION

Immigration from the various Central and South American nations has been sporadic—influenced by both our immigration laws and social forces operating in the home country. Perceived economic opportunities escalated the northward movement in the 1960s. By 1970, Panamanians and Hondurans represented the largest national groupings, most of them being identified in the Census as "nonwhite."

Since the mid–1970s, increasing numbers of Central and South Americans have fled unrest. While Latinos as a whole are a fast-growing minority, Central and South Americans increased in numbers even faster than Mexicans or any other group during the 1980s. In particular, from about 1978, war and economic chaos in El Salvador, Nicaragua, and Guatemala prompted many to seek refuge in the United States. Not at all a homogeneous group, they range from Guatemalan Indian peasants to wealthy Nicaraguan exiles. These latest arrivals probably had some economic motivation for migration, but this concern was overshadowed or at least matched by their fear of being killed or hurt if they remained in their home country (A. Camarillo 1993).

The immigrants who fled violence and poverty often have difficulty in adjusting initially because they received little preparation for their movement to a foreign culture. Mario fled to the United States from Nicaragua when he was sixteen. As he writes, the initial years were trying:

> *At first it was difficult to adjust. People are very materialistic in the U.S. I was starting from zero. I had nothing. They made fun of my clothes. They treated me differently. They pushed me out of their circle. Luckily, I met a friend from school back home who had been in the U.S. eight years. He took care of me. (K. Cerar 1995: 57)*

Eventually Mario felt comfortable enough to help immigrants and to serve as a tutor at the local community college. His experience has been played out before in the United States and undoubtedly will be many times again.

Central and South Americans are a newly emerging group—as of 1996, 87 percent of the adults in this Latino group were foreign-born of foreign-born parents. El Salvador is a major source of immigrants from this part of Latin America. It is estimated that there are almost as many illegal El Salvadorans in the United States

The civil unrest that has occurred in some Latin American countries such as El Salvador spurred immigration to the United States in the 1980s and 1990s.

as there are those who have entered with proper documentation. Many of the illegal immigrants are seeking political asylum, but few receive it—an issue of concern within the Latino community (Pinal and Singer 1997).

THE PRESENT PICTURE

The recent settlement of Central and South Americans has been clouded by two issues. First, many of the arrivals are illegal immigrants. Among those uncovered as undocumented workers, citizens from El Salvador, Guatemala, and Colombia are outnumbered only by Mexican nationals. Second, significant numbers of highly trained and skilled people have left these countries, which are in great need of professional workers. We noted in Chapter 4 how often immigration produces a **brain drain**—immigration to the United States of skilled workers, professionals, and technicians.

Economically, as a group, Central and South Americans experience high unemployment levels compared to other Latinos; yet they are better educated, as shown in Table 9.1. This disparity reflects the plight that frequently faces recent immigrants. Upon relocating in a new country, they initially experience downward mobility in terms of occupational status.

The challenges to immigrants from Latin America are reflected in the experience of Colombians. The initial arrivals from this South American nation after World War I were educated middle-class people who quickly assimilated to life in the United States. Rural unrest in Colombia during the 1980s triggered large-scale movement to the United States, where the Colombian immigrants had to adapt to a new culture and to urban life. The adaptation of this later group has been much more difficult. Some have found success through catering to other Colombians. For example, enterprising immigrants have opened *bodegas* (grocery stores) to supply traditional, familiar foodstuffs. Similarly, Colombians have established restaurants, travel agencies, and real estate firms that serve other Colombians. However, many find themselves obliged to take menial jobs and to combine the income of several family members to meet the high cost of urban life. Colombians of mixed African descent face racial as well as ethnic and language barriers (Orlov and Ueda 1980).

In 1991, violence broke out in the Hispanic Mount Pleasant area of Washington, D.C., heavily populated by Central American immigrants. El Salvadorans figured prominently among those arrested during the several days of rioting that followed the police shooting of a Salvadoran man being arrested. In the aftermath, many concerns were raised similar to those after the riots in African American neighborhoods in the 1960s: no jobs, police brutality, an unresponsive city government, exploitative employers, and uncaring teachers. One difference between Blacks and these immigrants were their expectations of a better, fairer government; many neighborhood residents had come to our nation's capital fleeing violent warfare in their home countries (W. Raspberry 1991; S. Sanchez 1991).

What is likely to be the future of Central and South Americans in the United States? Although much will depend on future immigration, they could assimilate over the course of generations. One alternative is that they will become trapped with Mexican

Americans as a segment of the dual labor market of the urban areas where they have taken residence. A more encouraging possibility is that they will retain an independent identity, like the Cubans, while also establishing an economic base. An examination of the urban economy of the San Francisco metropolitan area in the 1980s seemed to show that they were entering the same irregular economy and poverty populated by the Mexican Americans there. Little evidence of the establishment of a local economic base was found. Whether this initial assessment has continued to be valid and can be generalized to other cities will await subsequent analysis (S. Wallace 1989).

CONCLUSION

The signals are mixed. Many movies and television programs and much music have a Hispanic flavor. Candidates for political office seek Latino votes and sometimes even speak Spanish to do so. Yet the poverty rate of Latino families reported in 1995 was almost 31 percent, compared to less than 11 percent for White Americans.

The successes are there. Texas Tech University President Lauro Cavazos was named by Ronald Reagan in 1988 to head the Department of Education—the first Hispanic cabinet appointee in this nation's history. George Bush subsequently asked him to continue in that position. President Bill Clinton named Federico Peña secretary of transportation, and later Peña headed the Department of Energy. Yet our system has failures as well. In 1995, a Texas woman seeking custody of her five-year-old was accused by the judge of "abusing" her child and causing her to be "ignorant" by speaking Spanish to her at home in her effort to make the child bilingual (S. Verhovek 1995).

This mixture of positive and negative trends is visible in other areas. Ballots are printed in Spanish and other languages. Bilingual education at taxpayer expense is available throughout the United States. Yet more and more states are declaring English their official language, and even Congress from time to time considers a constitutional amendment to that effect. Many Hispanics feel that to be bilingual is not to be less a part of the United States. Espousing pluralism rather than assimilation is not un-American. This contrast of images and substance will be evident again in the chapters that follow, on Mexican Americans and Puerto Ricans. "In World War II, more Latinos won Medals of Honor than any other ethnic group," said Democratic Representative Matthew Martinez, a former U.S. Marine who represented part of Los Angeles. "How much blood do you have to spill before you prove you are a part of something?" (D. Whitman 1987: 49).

KEY TERMS

bilingual education 276
bilingualism 276
borderlands 281
brain drain 290
color gradient 288
English immersion 277
maquiladoras 281
Marielitos 284
panethnicity 272
remittances (or migradollars) 282

REVIEW QUESTIONS

1. What different factors seem to unite and to divide the Hispanic community in the United States?
2. How do Hispanics view themselves as a group? How are they viewed by others?
3. Why have language and bilingualism become almost ideological issues in the United States?
4. To what extent has the Cuban migration been positive, and to what degree do significant challenges remain?
5. How have Central and South Americans contributed to the diversity of the Hispanic peoples in the United States?

CRITICAL THINKING

1. Language and culture are almost inseparable. How might you anticipate your life would change if you were not permitted to speak your native language? Or how has it been affected if you have been expected to speak some other language?
2. How have you witnessed the presence of a different culture in the United States? At what times have you found it to be interesting and intriguing? Are there times you felt threatened by it or felt its presence to be unfair?
3. Why do you think the borderlands of the US–Mexico border region have been the subject of such close scrutiny, while there is little attention relatively speaking to similar areas along the US–Canada border?

INTERNET EXERCISE

This chapter outlines "The Language Divide" and the debate over bilingual education in U.S. schools. The Office of Bilingual Education and Minority Languages Affairs (http://www.ed.gov/offices/OBEMLA) maintains a site that offers information, statistics, and government services. What is the mission of OBEMLA? What is the most recent news regarding the status of bilingual education programs? According to the literature on the site, why is bilingual education necessary? Why is this an issue of importance for Hispanic Americans? Which of the statistics offered about education surprised you the most? Why? What is your position on bilingual education? Defend your opinion.

FOR FURTHER INFORMATION

William V. Flores and Rina Benmajor (eds.). *Latino Cultural Citizenship: Claiming Identity, Space, and Rights*. Boston: Beacon Press, 1997.

Looking at the role of citizenship as an expression of cultural and national identity.

Nicolás Kanellos. *The Hispanic Almanac: From Columbus to Corporate America*. Detroit: Visible Ink, 1994.

A compendium of history and cultural events, including sections on the media, the performing arts, Hispanic literature, and sports.

Felix Masud-Piloto. *From Welcomed Exiles to Illegal Immigrants*. Lanham, MD: Rowman and LittleField, 1996.

A historian and Latino studies scholar looks at the changing position of the U.S. on Cuban migration from 1959 to 1995.

Clara E. Rodríguez (ed.). *Latin Looks: Images of Latinas and Latinos in the U.S. Media*. Boulder, CO: Westview Press: 1997.

A collection of essays on how Latinos have been portrayed in movies, television, and other media since the early years of the twentieth century and how those images have changed over time.

Victor Andres Triay. *Fleeing Castro: Operation Pedro Pan and the Cuban Children's Program*. Gainesville, FL: University of Florida Press, 1998.

A stirring account of airlifting of Cuban children in the early 1960s to the United States and their subsequent experiences in the United States.

PERIODICALS

Journals devoted exclusively to the Hispanic experience are *Aztlán* (founded in 1969), *Crítica: A Journal of Puerto Rican Policy and Politics* (1994), *Hispanic Outlook on Higher Education* (1990), and the *Hispanic Journal of Behavioral Sciences* (1979). *Latina* and *Hispanic* are among the popular periodicals oriented to the Hispanic audience.

10

Mexican Americans and Puerto Ricans

CHAPTER OUTLINE

HIGHLIGHTS

The history of Mexican Americans is closely tied to immigration, which has been encouraged (the Bracero program) when Mexican labor is in demand or discouraged (repatriation and Operation Wetback) when Mexican workers are unwanted. The Puerto Rican people are divided between those who live in the island commonwealth and those who live on the mainland. Puerto Ricans who migrate to the mainland most often come in search of better jobs and housing. Both Mexican Americans and Puerto Ricans, as groups, have lower incomes, less formal education, and greater health problems compared to White Americans. Both the family and religion are sources of strength for the typical Puerto Rican or Mexican American.

Citizenship is the basic requirement for receiving one's legal rights and privileges in the United States. However, for both Mexican Americans and Puerto Ricans, citizenship has been an ambiguous concept at best. Mexican Americans (or Chicanos) have a long history in the United States, stretching back before the nation was even formed, to the early days of European exploration. Santa Fe, New Mexico, was founded more than a decade before the Pilgrims landed at Plymouth. The Mexican American people trace their ancestry to the merging of Spanish settlers with the Native Americans of Central America and Mexico. This ancestry reaches back to the brilliant Mayan and Aztec civilizations, which attained their height about A.D. 700 and 1500, respectively. However, roots in the land do not guarantee a group dominance over it. Over several centuries, the Spaniards conquered the land and merged with the Native Americans to form the Mexican people. In 1821, Mexico obtained its independence, but this independence was short-lived, for domination from the north began less than a generation later (Meier and Rivera 1972).

Today, Mexican Americans are creating their own destiny in the United States, while functioning in a society that is often concerned about immigration, legal and illegal. In the eyes of some, including a few in positions of authority, to be Mexican American is to be suspected of being in the country illegally or, at least, of knowingly harboring illegal aliens.

For no other minority group in the United States is citizenship so ambiguous as it is for Puerto Ricans. Even Native Americans, who are subject to some unique laws and are exempt from others because of past treaties, have a future firmly dominated by the United States. This description does not necessarily fit Puerto Ricans. They and their island home are the last major U.S. colonial territories and, for that matter, one of the few colonial areas remaining in the world. Besides assessing the situation of Puerto Ricans on the mainland, we will also need to consider the relationship of the United States to Puerto Rico.

Mexican Americans

Wars play a prominent part in any nation's history. The United States was created as a result of the colonies' war with England to win their independence. During the 1800s, the United States acquired significant neighboring territory in two different wars. The legacy of these wars and the annexation that resulted was to create the two largest Hispanic minorities in the United States—Mexican Americans and Puerto Ricans.

A large number of Mexicans became aliens in the United States without ever crossing any border. These people first became Mexican Americans with the conclusion of the Mexican-American War. In the Treaty of Guadalupe Hidalgo, signed February 2, 1848, Mexico acknowledged the annexation of Texas by the United States and ceded California and most of Arizona and New Mexico to the United States for $15 million. In exchange, the United States granted citizenship to the 75,000 Mexican nationals who remained on the annexed land after one year. With citizenship, the United States was to guarantee religious freedom, property rights, and cultural integrity—that is, the right to continue Mexican and Spanish cultural traditions and to use the Spanish language.

The beginnings of the Mexican experience in the United States were as varied as the people themselves. Some Mexican Americans were affluent, with large land holdings. Others were poor peasants barely able to survive. Along such rivers as the Rio Grande, commercial towns grew up around the increasing river traffic. In New Mexico and Arizona, many Mexican American people welcomed the protection that the U.S. government offered against several Native American tribes. In California, life was quickly dominated by the gold miners, and Anglos controlled the new-found wealth. One generalization can be made about the many segments of the Mexican American population in the nineteenth century: they were regarded as a conquered people. In fact, even before the war, many Whites who traveled into the West were already prejudiced against people of mixed blood (in this instance, against Mexicans). Whenever Mexican American and Anglo interests conflicted, Anglo interests won (M. Servin 1974).

A pattern of second-class treatment for Mexican Americans emerged well before the twentieth century. Gradually, the Anglo system of property ownership replaced the Native American and Hispanic systems. Mexican Americans who inherited land proved no match for Anglo lawyers. Court battles provided no protection for poor Spanish-speaking landowners. Unscrupulous lawyers occasionally defended Mexican Americans successfully, only to demand half the land as their fee. Anglo cattle ranchers gradually pushed out Mexican American ranchers. By 1892, the federal government was granting grazing privileges on public grasslands and forests to anyone except Mexican Americans. Wayne Moquin and Charles Van Doren (1971) called this the period of Anglo American conquest, when the Mexican Americans "became outsiders in their own homeland" (p. 251). The ground was laid for the social structure of the Southwest in the twentieth century, an area of growing productivity in which minority groups have increased in size but remain largely subordinate.

THE IMMIGRANT EXPERIENCE

Nowhere else in the world do two countries with such different standards of living and wage scales share a relatively open border. Immigration from Mexico is unique in several respects. First, it has been a continuous large-scale movement for most of this century. The United States did not restrict immigration from Mexico through legislation until 1965. Second, the proximity of Mexico encourages past immigrants to maintain strong cultural and language ties with the homeland through friends and relatives. Return visits to the old country are only one- or two-day bus rides for Mexican Americans, not once-in-a-lifetime voyages, as they were for most European immigrants. The third point of uniqueness is the aura of *illegality* that has surrounded Mexican migrants. Throughout the twentieth century, the suspicion in which Anglos have held Mexican Americans has contributed to mutual distrust between the two groups.

The years preceding World War I brought large numbers of Mexicans into the expanding agricultural industry of the Southwest. The Mexican revolution of 1909–1922 thrust refugees into the United States, and World War I curtailed the flow of people from Europe, leaving the labor market open to the Mexican Americans. After the war, continued political turmoil in Mexico and more prosperity in the Southwest brought still more Mexicans across the border.

Simultaneously, corporations in the United States, led by agribusinesses, invested in Mexico in such a way as to maximize their profits but minimize the amount of money remaining in Mexico to provide needed employment. Conflict theorists view this investment as part of the continuing process in which American businesses—with the support and cooperation of affluent Mexicans—have used Mexican people when it has been in corporate leaders' best interests. The Mexican workers are used either as cheap laborers in their own country by their fellow Mexicans

Mexican laborers on a Texas cotton field in 1919. These workers were imported for work when there was an insufficient number of laborers in the United States available for such work.

and by Americans or as undocumented workers here who are dismissed when they are no longer judged to be useful (C. Guerin-Gonzales 1994).

Beginning in the 1930s, the United States embarked on a series of measures aimed specifically at Mexicans. The Depression brought pressure on local governments to care for the growing number of unemployed and impoverished. Government officials developed a quick way to reduce welfare rolls and eliminate people seeking jobs: ship Mexicans back to Mexico. This program of deporting Mexicans during the 1930s was referred to as **repatriation.** As officially stated, the program was constitutional because only illegal aliens were to be repatriated. Actually, it was much more complex. Border records were incomplete because, before 1930, the United States had shown little interest in whether Mexicans entered with all the proper credentials. Also, many Mexicans who could be classified as illegal aliens had resided in the United States for decades. Because they had children who were citizens by birth, they could not legally be deported. The legal process of fighting a deportation order was overwhelming, however, especially for a poor Spanish-speaking family. The Anglo community virtually ignored this outrage against the civil rights of those deported, nor did it show interest in assisting repatriates to ease the transition (Meier and Rivera 1972).

When the Depression ended, Mexican laborers again became attractive to industry. In 1942, when World War II was depleting the labor pool, the United States and Mexico agreed to a program allowing migration across the border by contracted laborers, or ***braceros.*** Within a year of the initiation of the bracero program, more than 80,000 Mexican nationals had been brought in; they made up one-eleventh of the farm workers on the Pacific Coast. The program continued with some interruptions until 1964. It was devised to recruit labor from poor Mexican areas for U.S. farms. In a program that was supposed to be supervised jointly by Mexico and the United States, minimum standards were to be maintained for the transportation, housing, wages, and health care of the braceros. Ironically, these safeguards placed the braceros in a better economic situation than Mexican Americans, who often worked alongside the protected Mexican nationals. The Mexicans were still regarded as a positive presence by Anglos only when useful, and the Mexican American people were merely tolerated (E. Galarza 1964; R. Scott 1974; E. Stoddard 1973).

Another crackdown on illegal aliens was to be the third step in dealing with the perceived Mexican problem. Alternately called Operation Wetback and Special Force

Operation, it was fully inaugurated by 1954. The term *wetbacks*, or ***mojados***, the derisive slang for Mexicans who enter illegally, refers to those who secretly swim across the Rio Grande. Like other roundups, this effort failed to stop the illegal flow of workers. For several years, some Mexicans were brought in under the bracero program while other Mexicans were being deported. With the end of the bracero program in 1964 and stricter immigration quotas for Mexicans, illegal border crossings increased because legal crossings became more difficult (W. Gordon 1975; E. Stoddard 1973, 1976a, 1976b).

More dramatic than the negative influence that continued immigration has had on employment conditions in the Southwest is the effect on the Mexican and Mexican American people themselves. Routinely, the rights of Mexicans, even the rights to which they are entitled as illegal aliens, are ignored. Of those illegal immigrants deported, relatively few have been expelled through formal proceedings. The Mexican American Legal Defense and Education Fund (MALDEF) has repeatedly expressed concern over the government's handling of illegal aliens.

Against this backdrop of legal maneuvers is the tie that the Mexican people have to the land both in today's Mexico and in the parts of the United States that formerly belonged to Mexico. *Assimilation* may be the key word in the history of many immigrant groups, but for Mexican Americans the key term is ***La Raza.*** *La Raza* literally means the people, but among contemporary Mexican Americans the term connotes pride in a pluralistic Spanish, Native American, and Mexican heritage. Mexican Americans cherish their legacy and, as we shall see, strive to regain some of the economic and social glory that once was theirs.

Despite passage of various measures designed to prevent illegal immigration, neither the immigration nor the apprehension of illegal aliens is likely to end. Mexican Americans will continue to be more closely scrutinized by law enforcement officials because their Mexican descent makes them more suspect as potential illegal aliens. In the United States, Mexican Americans have mixed feelings toward the illegal Mexican immigrants. Many are their kin, and Mexican Americans realize that entry into the United States brings Mexicans better economic opportunities. Massive deportations, however, only perpetuate the Anglo stereotype of Mexican and Mexican American alike as surplus labor. Mexican Americans, largely the product of past immigration, find that the continued controversy over illegal immigration places them in the ambivalent role of citizen and relative. Mexican American organizations opposing illegal immigration must confront people to whom they are closely linked by culture and kinship, and they must cooperate with government agencies they deeply distrust (W. Graham 1996).

THE ECONOMIC PICTURE

As shown in Table 10.1, both Mexican Americans and Puerto Ricans have higher unemployment rates, higher rates of poverty, and significantly lower incomes than White Americans. In 1995, little more than 4 percent of all managerial and professional positions were held by Latinos. When considering their economic situation, three topics deserve special attention—the debate over what has been termed the culture of poverty and the effort to improve the status of migrant workers.

Table 10.1 Selected Social and Economic Characteristics of Mexican Americans and Puerto Ricans, 1997

	Total White	Total Hispanic	Mexican Americans	Puerto Ricans
Percent completing college, 25 years and over	24.6	10.3	7.4	10.8
Percent unemployed	4.2	5.3	7.7	9.8
Percent of families with a single parent	22.7	31.8	27.9	45.7
Percent living below poverty level	7.8	26.4	27.7	33.1
Median income (year-round workers)	$58,904	$26,179	$25,347	$23,646

Source: Bureau of the Census 1998c: 51, 54.

The Culture of Poverty Like the African American families described in Chapter 8, Mexican American families are labeled as having traits that, in fact, describe poor families rather than specifically Mexican American families. Indeed, as long ago as 1980, a report of the Commission on Civil Rights (1980b:8) stated that the two most prevalent stereotypical themes appearing in works on Hispanics showed them as (1) exclusively poor and (2) prone to commit violence.

Social scientists have also relied excessively on the traits of the poor to describe an entire subordinate group such as Mexican Americans. Anthropologist Oscar Lewis (1959, 1965, 1966), in several publications based on research conducted among Mexicans and Puerto Ricans, identified the "culture of poverty." According to its theorists, the **culture of poverty** embraces a deviant way of life that involves no future planning, no enduring commitment to marriage, and absence of the work ethic. This culture supposedly follows the poor, even when they move out of the slums or the *barrio*.

The culture-of-poverty view is another way of blaming the victim (W. Ryan 1976): the affluent are not responsible for social inequality, nor are the policy makers; it is the poor who are to blame for their own problems. This stance allows government and society to attribute the failure of antipoverty and welfare programs on Mexican Americans and other poor people, rather than on the programs themselves. These are programs designed and too often staffed by middle-class, English-speaking Anglo professionals. Conflict theorists, noting a similar misuse of the more recent term *underclass*, argue that it is unfair to blame the poor for their lack of money, low education, poor health, and low-paying jobs.

Lewis's hypothesis about the culture of poverty came to be used indiscriminately to explain continued poverty. Critics argue that Lewis sought out exotic, pathological behavior, ignoring the fact that, even among the poor, most people live fairly conventionally and strive to achieve goals similar to those of the middle class. A second criticism challenges the use of the term *culture of poverty* to describe an entire ethnic group. Because Lewis's data were on poor people, social scientists have increasingly stressed that his conclusions may be correct as far as the data permit, but the data cannot be generalized to all Latinos because the sample was not a representative cross section drawn from different economic and educational levels (H. Gans 1995; C. Valentine 1968).

More recent social science research, unlike Lewis's, does sample Mexican American families across a broad range of socioeconomic levels. This research shows that, when Anglo and Mexican American families of the same social class are compared, they differ little in family organization and attitudes toward child rearing. In addition, comparisons of work ethics find no significant differences between Mexican Americans and Anglos. Poverty is present among Mexican Americans; there is no doubt about that. However, that does not mean there is a culture of poverty or a permanent underclass. Institutions such as the family and the church seem viable, although the schools are in disrepair, and the picture on businesses is mixed. However, to question the label of culture of poverty does not deny the poor life chances facing many Mexican Americans (R. Aponte 1991; Moore and Pinderhughes 1993; K. Winkler 1990).

Chávez and the Farm Laborers The best-known Hispanic labor leader for economic empowerment was César Chávez, the Mexican American who crusaded to organize migrant farm workers. Efforts to organize agricultural laborers date back to the turn of the century, but Chávez was the first to enjoy any success. These laborers had never won collective bargaining rights, partly because their mobility made it difficult for them to organize into a unified group.

In 1962, Chávez, then thirty-five years old, formed the National Farm Workers Association, later to become the United Farm Workers union (UFW). Organizing migrant farm workers was not easy, for they had no savings to pay for organizing or to live on while striking. Growers could rely on a virtually limitless supply of Mexican laborers to replace the Mexican Americans and Filipinos who struck for higher wages and better working conditions.

Chávez's first success was the grape boycott launched in 1965, which carried the struggle into the kitchens of families throughout the country. The UFW launched the boycott with the aim of damaging growers economically until they accepted the union and improved working conditions. It took five years for the grape growers to sign three-year contracts with Chávez's union, which had affiliated with the AFL-CIO. This victory signaled a new era in labor relations and made Chávez a national folk hero (J. Levy 1975; R. McVeigh 1993; Majka and Majka 1996).

César Chávez, in his role as president of the United Farm Workers, leads the picketing of a supermarket in the 1960s, urging shoppers not to buy nonunion grapes or lettuce.

Despite their success, Chávez and the United Farm Workers were plagued with the continual opposition of agribusiness. Problems resurfaced in the 1980s as California's governor and lawmakers, many of whom had been elected with the strong support of agribusiness, became less supportive of Chávez. This was about the time the UFW was also trying to heighten public consciousness of the pesticides used in the fields worked by laborers. Research into the long-term effects of pesticides had only begun. Although Chávez's 1988 fast to bring attention to this issue was widely publicized, his efforts did not gain the support he had hoped for.

Chávez had difficulty fulfilling his objectives. By 1993, union membership had dwindled from a high of 80,000 in 1970 to 21,000. Nevertheless, what he and the UFW accomplished was considerable. First, they succeeded in making federal and state governments more aware of the exploitation of migrant laborers. Second, the migrant workers, or at least those organized in California, developed a sense of their own power and worth that will make it extremely difficult for growers to abuse them in the future as they had in the past. Third, working conditions improved. California agricultural workers were paid an average of less than $2 an hour in the mid–1960s. By 1987 they were being paid an average of about $5.85 an hour, but by 1994, as the entire California economy suffered, wages had dropped to $4.75 an hour. Regardless of the set wage, a 1998 report found half of the contractors were paying California grape pickers less than the minimum wage (R. Sanchez 1998).

Recently, farm workers have protested their working conditions and the pesticide use that may threaten their lives.

Migrant workers still face a very harsh life. Under pressure to reduce government spending in general, the federal government in the 1980s reduced its enforcement of migrant worker laws. Tuberculosis, alcoholism, and malnutrition remain common among migrant farm workers. Their children receive inadequate education because they move many times during the school year. As of 1998, 32 percent of the nation's 2.5 million farm workers had inadequate housing (S. Greenhouse 1998b).

Cesar Chávez died in 1993. A year later, hundreds of supporters of the UFW arrived in Sacramento, California, to commemorate his death and to acknowledge the full agenda that remains. By the end of the 1990s the primary challenge came from efforts to permit more foreign workers—primarily from Mexico and Central America—to enter the United States temporarily at even lower wages. The problems of migrant farm workers are inextricably tied to the lives of both Latinos and Latin Americans (Griego and Jiménez 1998).

POLITICAL ORGANIZATIONS

As noted in Chapter 9, Latinos are becoming more involved in party politics in the United States. While tending to support Democratic candidates (with the exception of Cuban Americans, who typically back Republicans), Latinos are showing a willingness to be more independent voters. As one might expect, given their growing numbers and greater voting power, more Latinos are successfully seeking elective office. This has not always been the case. Frustrated by the lack of responsiveness of established politicians, Mexican Americans for a brief period created their own independent party in Texas. *La Raza Unida* (LRU) was a third party, supporting candidates who offered alternatives to the Democratic and Republican Parties (R. Hero 1995; F. Rosales 1996).

The social protests that characterized much of the political activity in the United States of the mid–1960s touched the Mexican American community as well. In Southern California in 1966, young Chicanos in college were attracted to the ideology of ***Chicanismo*** (or *Chicanozaje*) and joined what is popularly called the Chicano movement. Like Black Power, Chicanismo has taken on a variety of meanings, but all definitions stress a positive self-image and place little reliance on conventional forms of political activity. Followers of Chicanismo, unlike the more assimilation-oriented older generations, have been less likely to accept the standard claim that the United States is equally just to all.

Besides a positive self-image, Chicanismo and the movement of La Raza include renewed awareness of the plight of Chicanos at the hands of Anglos. Mexican Americans are a colonial minority, as Joan Moore (1970) wrote, because their relationship with Anglos was originally involuntary. Mexican culture in the United States has been either transformed or destroyed by Anglos, and the Mexican American people themselves have been victims of racism. The colonial model points out the ways in which societal institutions have failed Mexican Americans and perpetuated their problems. Militant Mexican Americans refer to assimilationists, who they say would sell out to the White people, as *vendidos*, or traitors. The ultimate insult is the term *Malinche,* the name of the Mexican American woman who became the mistress of the Spanish conqueror, Cortés. Many in the Chicano movement believe that, if one does not work actively in the struggle, one is working against it (F. Rosales 1996; see also Barrera et al. 1972; Moore and Pachon 1985).

Perhaps as well as any recent Mexican American, Reies Lopéz Tijerina captures the spirit of Chicanismo. Born in a cotton field worked by migrant farmers, Tijerina became a Pentecostal preacher and in the late 1950s took an interest in old Spanish land grants. From research in Mexico, Spain, and the Southwest, he concluded that the Mexican Americans—and (more specifically, the Hispanos)—had lost significant tracts of land through quasi-legal and other questionable practices. In 1963, he formed the *Alianza Federal de Mercedes* (Federal Alliance of Land Grants), whose purpose is to recover the lost land. To publicize his purpose when few Anglos would pay attention, he seized part of the Kit Carson National Forest in New Mexico. Tijerina spent the next few years either in jail or awaiting trial. Tijerina's quest for restoration of land rights has been accompanied by violence, even though he advocates civil disobedience. The violence, nonetheless, led him to be criticized by some Hispanics, as well as Anglos (P. Nabokov 1970; F. Rosales 1996).

Thirty years later, Tijerina's arguments, which had seemed outrageous to most, were beginning to be endorsed by politicians. In 1997, Republican members of Congress introduced the Guadalupe-Hidalgo Treaty Claims Act to review Latino land claims especially as they relate to government-held forest land. Clearly, the Republicans are trying to identify an issue that can garner them support from Hispanic voters, but most important, this action shows that the goals of Tijerina and his followers are finally being considered seriously (J. Brooke 1998).

Organized in 1967, the Mexican American Legal Defense and Education Fund (MALDEF) has emerged as a potent force to protect Mexican Americans' constitutional rights. Although it does not endorse candidates, it has made itself felt in the political arena, much as the NAACP has for African Americans. On the education side, it has addressed segregation, biased testing, inequities in school financing, and failure to promote bilingualism. MALDEF has been involved in litigation concerning employment practices, immigration reform, and voting rights. It has emerged as the primary civil rights group for Mexican Americans and other Latinos (M. Vigil 1990).

The latter 1990s saw the Mexican community in the United States faced with a new political challenge. Beginning in 1998, Mexicans in the United States could acquire rights as Mexican nationals under Mexico's new dual nationality law. Their children, even if U.S.-born, are also eligible for Mexican nationality. The United States does not prohibit dual nationality, and it is estimated that anywhere from 5 to 10 million Mexican Americans are eligible for such dual nationality. While much of this second nationality will not be allowed to vote in Mexico's elections, it is likely to further their interest in political life south of the border. As we will now see with Puerto Rico, Latinos in the United States find political issues of importance outside the fifty states (*Migration News* 1998b).

Puerto Ricans

Puerto Ricans' current association with the United States, like that of the Mexican people, began as the result of the outcome of a war. The island of Borinquén, subsequently called Puerto Rico, was claimed by Spain in 1493. The native inhabitants, the Táino Indians, were promptly wiped out by conquest, slavery, and genocide. After it had been ruled by Spain for four centuries, the island was seized by the United States in 1898 during the Spanish-American War. Spain relinquished control of it in the Treaty of Paris. The value of Puerto Rico for the United States, as it had been for Spain, was mainly its strategic location, which was advantageous for maritime trade (see Figure 10.1).

The beginnings of rule by the United States quickly destroyed any hope that Puerto Ricans—or *Boricas*, as Puerto Ricans call themselves—had for self-rule. All power was given to officials appointed by the President, and any act of the island's legislature could be overruled by Congress. Even the spelling was changed briefly to *Porto Rico* to suit North American pronunciation. English, previously unknown on the island, became the only language permitted in the school systems. The people were colonized—first politically, then culturally, and finally economically (Aran et al. 1973; D. Christopulos 1974).

Citizenship was extended to Puerto Ricans by the Jones Act of 1917, but Puerto Rico remained a colony. This political dependence altered in 1948, when Puerto Rico

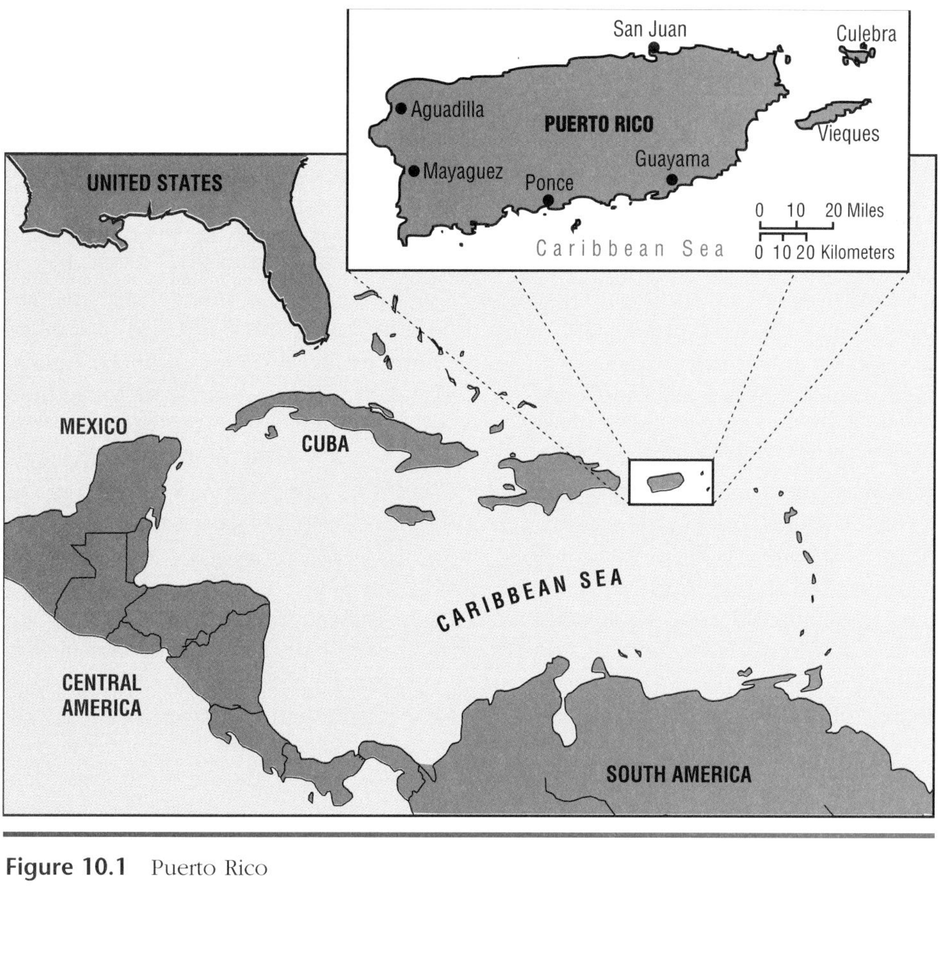

Figure 10.1 Puerto Rico

elected its own governor and became a commonwealth. This status, officially *Estado Libre Asociado,* or Associated Free State, extends to Puerto Rico and its people privileges and rights different from those of people on the mainland. Although Puerto Ricans are U.S. citizens and elect their own governor, they may not vote in presidential elections and have no voting representation in Congress. They are subject to military service, Selective Service registration, and all federal laws. Puerto Ricans have a homeland that is and at the same time is not a part of the Untied States.

THE BRIDGE BETWEEN THE ISLAND AND THE MAINLAND

Despite their citizenship, Puerto Ricans are occasionally challenged by immigration officials. Because other Latin Americans attempt to enter the country posing as Puerto Ricans, Puerto Ricans find their papers scrutinized more closely than do other U.S. citizens.

Puerto Ricans came to the mainland in relatively small numbers during the first half of the century, often encouraged by farm labor contracts similar to those extended to Mexican *braceros*. During World War II, the government recruited hundreds of Puerto Ricans to work on the railroads, in food manufacturing plants, and in copper mines on the mainland. But migration has been largely a post-World War II phenomenon. The 1940 Census showed fewer than 70,000 Puerto Ricans on the mainland, compared to nearly 3 million today. Among the factors that have contributed to migration are (1) the economic pull away from the underdeveloped and overpopulated island, (2) the absence of legal restrictions against travel, and (3) the growth of relatively cheap air transportation. As the migration continues, the mainland offers the added attraction of a large Puerto Rican community in New York City, which makes adjustment easier for new arrivals.

New York City still has a formidable population of Puerto Ricans, larger than metropolitan San Juan's, but significant changes have taken place. First, Puerto Ricans no longer dominate the Latino scene in New York City, comprising perhaps half of the city's Hispanic population. Second, Puerto Ricans are now more dispersed throughout the mainland's cities, with sizable numbers in New Jersey, Illinois, Florida, California, Pennsylvania, and Connecticut. The Puerto Ricans who have moved out of the large ethnic communities in cities such as New York City, Chicago, and Philadelphia, are as a group more familiar with U.S. culture and the English language. This movement from the major settlements has been hastened as well by the loss of manufacturing jobs in these cities, a loss that hits Puerto Rican men especially hard (M. Jones-Correa 1998; L. Stains 1994).

As the U.S. economy underwent recession in the 1970s and 1980s, unemployment among mainland Puerto Ricans, always high, increased dramatically. This increase shows in migration. In the 1950s, Puerto Ricans were half of the Latino arrivals. By the 1970s, they accounted for only 3 percent. Indeed, in some years during the 1980s, more Puerto Ricans went from mainland to the island than the other way around.

Puerto Ricans returning to the island have become a significant force. Indeed, they have come to be given the name ***Neoricans*** (or *Nuyoricans*)—a term the islanders also use for Puerto Ricans in New York. Longtime islanders direct a modest amount of hostility toward these *Neoricans*. They usually return from the mainland with more formal schooling, more money, and a better command of English than native Puerto Ricans have. Not too surprisingly, *Neoricans* compete very well with islanders for jobs and land (C. Muschkin 1993).

THE ISLAND OF PUERTO RICO

Puerto Rico, located about a thousand miles from Miami, has never been the same since Columbus discovered it in 1493. The original inhabitants of the island were wiped out in a couple of generations by disease, tribal warfare, hard labor, unsuccessful rebellions against the Spanish, and fusion with their conquerors. These social processes are highlighted in the Intergroup Relations continuum that summarizes the experience of Latinos in the United States (Figure 10.2).

Among the institutions imported to Puerto Rico by Spain was slavery. Although slavery in Puerto Rico was not as harsh as in the southern United States, the legacy of the transfer of Africans is present in the appearance of Puerto Ricans today, many of whom are seen by people on the mainland as Black.

The commonwealth period that began in 1948 has been a most significant one for Puerto Rico. Change has been dramatic, though whether it has all been progress is debatable. On the positive side, Spanish has been reintroduced as the language of classroom instruction, but the study of English is also required. The popularity in the 1980s of groups such as the rock singers Menudo shows that Puerto Rican young

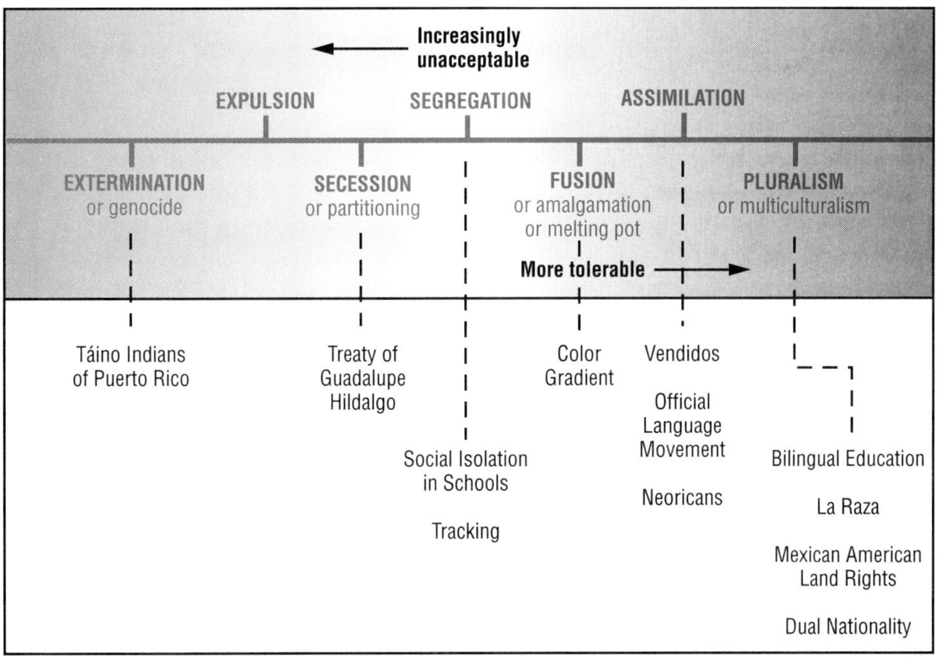

Figure 10.2 Intergroup Relations Continuum

people wish to maintain ties with their ethnicity. Such success is a challenge because Puerto Rican music is almost never aired on non-Hispanic radio stations. The Puerto Rican people have had a vibrant and distinctive cultural tradition, as seen clearly in their folk heros, holidays, sports, and contemporary literature and drama. Dominance by the culture of the United States makes it difficult to maintain the culture on the mainland and even on the island itself.

Puerto Rico and its people reflect a phenomenon called **neocolonialism,** which refers to continuing dependence of former colonies on foreign countries. Initially this term was introduced to refer to African nations that, even after gaining their political independence from Great Britain, France, and other European nations, continued to find their destiny in the hands of the former colonial powers. While most Puerto Ricans today are staunchly proud of their American citizenship, they also wish to have their own national identity, independent of the United States. This has not and continues not to be easy.

Novelist and Puerto Rican Rosario Ferré reflects in "Listen to Their Voices" (on pp. 310–311) on what it means to be a Puerto Rican today amidst forces of neocolonialism, pride in the USA, and a strong sense of Puerto Rican identity.

From 1902, English was the official language of the island but Spanish was the language of the people, serving to reaffirm the island's cultural identity independent of the United States. In 1992, however, Puerto Rico also established Spanish as an official language.

In reality, the language issue is related more to ideology than to substance. While English is once again required in primary and secondary schools, textbooks may be written in English while the classes are conducted in Spanish. Indeed, Spanish remains the language of the island; only 20 percent of the islanders speak English, and another 10 percent are fully bilingual (D. Heyck 1994; R. Rodriquez 1993; Third World Journalists 1994).

Issues of Statehood and Self-Rule Puerto Ricans have periodically argued and fought for independence for most of the 500 years since Columbus landed. They continued to do so in the 1990s. The contemporary commonwealth arrangement is popular with many Puerto Ricans, but others prefer statehood, while some call for complete independence from the United States.

The arguments for continuation of commonwealth status include both the serious and the trivial. Among some island residents, the idea of statehood invokes the fear of higher taxes and an erosion of their cultural heritage. Some even fear the end of separate Puerto Rican participation in the Olympics and the Miss Universe pageant. On the other hand, while independence may be attractive, commonwealth supporters argue that it includes too many unknown costs, and therefore they embrace the status quo. Others view statehood as a key to increased economic development and expansion for tourism.

Proponents of independence have a long, vocal history insisting on the need for Puerto Rico to regain its cultural and political autonomy. Some of the supporters of independence have even been militant. In 1950, nationalists attempted to assassinate President Truman, killing a White House guard in the process. Four years later, another band of nationalists opened fire in the gallery of the U.S. House of

Representatives, wounding five members of Congress. Beginning in 1974, a group calling itself the Armed Forces of National Liberation (FALN, for *Fuerzas Armadas de Liberación Nacional*) took responsibility for more than 100 explosions that continued through 1987. The FALN is not alone; at least four other militant groups advocating independence were identified as having been at work in the 1980s. The island itself is occasionally beset by violent demonstrations, often reacting to U.S. military installations there—a symbol of U.S. control (G. Marx 1995).

The issue of Puerto Rico's political destiny is in part ideological. Independence is the easiest way for the island to retain and strengthen its cultural as well as political identity. Some nationalists express the desire that an autonomous Puerto Rico develop close political ties with communist Cuba. The crucial arguments for and against independence are probably economic. An independent Puerto Rico would no longer be required to use U.S. shipping lines, which are more expensive than those of foreign competitors. However, an independent Puerto Rico might be faced by a tariff wall when trading with its largest current customer, the mainland United States. Also, Puerto Rican migration to the mainland could be restricted.

Puerto Rico's future status most recently faced a vote in 1998. In the latest nonbinding referendum, 50 percent favored options that favor continuing commonwealth status, and 47 percent backed statehood. Less than 3 percent favored independence. Interestingly, a 1998 survey of people on the mainland found the

A demonstration in San Juan urging voters to participate in a referendum on Puerto Rico's future relationship with the United States.

LISTEN TO THEIR VOICES

"Puerto Rico, U.S.A."

Rosario Ferré

The Senate may soon be debating a bill that would permit Puerto Ricans living on the island to vote for statehood or independence or to become an enhanced commonwealth that would eventually evolve toward sovereignty. Feeling on the island is divided almost equally between statehood and commonwealth, with independence favored by less than 4 percent of the voters.

But if Puerto Ricans living on the mainland are allowed to participate in the proposed referendum, as some have recommended, they could sway the vote, because many of them favor independence. This could mean that the next generation of Puerto Ricans would be deprived of the right to American citizenship.

As a Puerto Rican writer, I constantly face the problem of identity. When I travel to the States I feel as Latina as Chita Rivera. But in Latin America, I feel more American than John Wayne. To be Puerto Rican is to be a hybrid. Our two halves are inseparable; we cannot give up either without feeling maimed.

For many years, my concern was to keep my Hispanic self from being stifled. Now I discover it's my American self that's being threatened.

I recently was on a book tour in the United States. Wherever I went, people who knew about the plebiscite asked, "Why do you want to be American?"

The question was unsettling. Puerto Ricans have been Americans for almost a hundred years. At least 6,000 Puerto Ricans have died fighting for the United States, and many thousands more served in Korea and Vietnam. My son led a platoon of Puerto Rican soldiers in the Persian Gulf war. At the time, no one asked if he wanted to be an American. He simply did his duty.

Puerto Ricans living on the mainland think of the island in much the same way as African-Americans think of Africa—as an almost mythical place inhabited by ancestral gods. For those Puerto Ricans, the homeland is a place of origin, proof of a vital "difference" that sets them apart from what can seem the vast sameness of the United States.

Puerto Ricans living in the United States also point out that crime, drugs, AIDS and other ills are the result of too much American-style progress. They want us on the island to preserve the bucolic paradise they left behind, a place where one could drive lazily down half-deserted avenues, walk in the streets at night without feeling terrified, go for a drive in mountains still covered with lush vegetation.

But this paradise exists only in their minds. Puerto Ricans have already joined the first world, deeply involved with American interests.

Puerto Ricans have contributed more than $500,000 to political campaigns in the United States. We have our reasons.

The outcome of the Senate vote could have a great impact. Since we have practically no natural resources, independence would be sure to hurt Puerto Rico's economy. It would mean poverty, deteriorated health care and education, a disintegrating infrastructure and, worst of all, the disappearance of the Puerto Rican middle class.

In 1976 I lived in Mexico for a year and learned what it was like to live in a country that called itself a democracy, but where a small class of the wealthy dominates the vast majority, which is poor. Puerto Rico is different. Its strong middle class sets it apart. Our average income per household is $27,000; our annual per-capita income is $8,500, compared with $4,000 for most of Latin America.

The majority of Puerto Ricans prize their American citizenship. It represents for us economic stability and the assurance of civil liberties and democracy. On the other hand, we also cherish our language and culture. Thus, Puerto Rico's situation has historically been a paradox.

Living on the island, I've witnessed our Catch-22 situation from up close. I've lived through two plebiscites, both of them nonbinding, and have voted for independence. It was the only honorable solution, because losing our language and culture would have been a form of spiritual suicide.

But conditions have changed. Latinos are the fastest growing minority in the United States; by 2010 their numbers are expected to reach 39 million—more than the population of most Latin American republics. Bilingualism and multiculturalism are vital aspects of American society. Florida's Dade County is about 60 percent Hispanic. New York City, Los Angeles, Houston and Chicago all have large Hispanic populations. The reality is that we can no longer "be disappeared."

President Clinton recently declared, in no uncertain terms, that in order to become a state, Puerto Rico should not be forced to adopt English as its only official language and thereby abandon, possibly, its Hispanic culture. The decision on language, he said, should be left to Puerto Ricans, just as it was in the case of Hawaii, where both English and the Hawaiian dialect were made official tongues. Mr. Clinton's remark acknowledged that ethnic diversity has become a fundamental value in the United States.

Puerto Ricans have been Americans since 1898, and our culture and language remain as healthy as ever. We are no longer poor, undernourished or anemic. We are mulatto-mestizo, bilingual and proud of it. We no longer need fear that "el otro," the other, will swallow us up.

We have become the other. As a Puerto Rican and an American, I believe our future as a community is inseparable from our culture and language, but I'm also passionately committed to the modern world. That's why I'm going to support statehood in the next plebiscite.

Source: Rosario Ferré. "Puerto Rico, USA." First appeared in *The New York Times,* March 19, 1998. Vol. CXLVII, No. 51, 101.

population evenly split—a third favored each: statehood, independence, and continued territorial status. Given the lack of overwhelming feelings for statehood on the island, it is unlikely that there will be sufficient support in Congress to move toward statehood. Yet with half the island population expressing a preference for a change, it is clear that discontent with the current arrangement prevails and remains a "colonial dilemma" (L. Saad 1998; M. Navarro 1998).

The Social Construction of Race Puerto Rican migrants to the mainland must make adjustments in language, housing, and employment. These changes are required of most immigrants, but Puerto Ricans must also adapt to different social construction of race—new racial identities. Racism does exist in Puerto Rico. People are arbitrarily denied opportunities merely because of their skin color. The racism, however, is not the same as on the mainland. As we noted in Chapter 1, race is a social concept that changes with time and culture. In Puerto Rico, slavery was not as significant as it was in the U.S. South, and Puerto Rico has had a long history of accepting interracial marriages. Puerto Rico did not experience the mainland practices of segregation, laws against intermarriage, and Jim Crow. More recently, however, Puerto Rico has started to resemble the mainland in taking on rigid racial attitudes.

The most significant difference between the meaning of race on Puerto Rico and on the mainland is that Puerto Rico, like so many other Caribbean societies, has a color gradient. The phrase **color gradient** describes distinctions based on skin color made on a continuum, rather than by sharp categorical separations. The presence of a color gradient reflects past fusion between different groups (refer to Figure 10.2). Rather than being either "black" or "white," people are judged in such societies as "lighter" or "darker" than others. Rather than seeing people as either black or white in skin color, Puerto Ricans perceive people as ranging from pale white to very black. Puerto Ricans are more sensitive to degrees of difference and make less effort to pigeonhole a person in one of two categories.

The presence of a color gradient rather than two or three racial categories does not necessarily mean that prejudice is less. Generally, however, societies with a color gradient permit more flexibility and are therefore less likely to impose specific sanctions against a group of people based on skin color alone. Puerto Rico has not suffered interracial conflict or violence; its people are conscious of the different racial heritages. Studies disagree on the amount of prejudice in Puerto Rico, but all concur that race is not as clear-cut an issue on the island as it is on the mainland.

Racial identification in Puerto Rico depends a great deal on the attitude of the individual making the judgment. If one thinks highly of a person, he or she may be seen as a member of a more acceptable racial group. A variety of terms are used in the color gradient to describe people racially: *blanco* (white), *prieto, moreno,* or *de color* (dark-skinned), and *negro* (black) are a few of these. Factors such as social class and social position determine race, but on the mainland race is more likely to determine social class. This situation may puzzle people from the mainland, but racial etiquette on the mainland may be just as difficult for Puerto Ricans to comprehend and accept. Puerto Ricans arriving in the United States may find a new identity thrust on them by the dominant society (Comas-Díaz et al. 1998; J. Egerton 1971; Omi and Winant 1994; C. Rodríguez 1989; J. Russell 1996).

THE ISLAND ECONOMY

The United States's role in Puerto Rico has produced an overall economy that, while strong by Caribbean standards, remains well below that of the poorest areas of the United States. For many years the federal government exempted U.S. industries locating in Puerto Rico from taxes on profits for at least ten years. By 1993, this amount was over $11 billion in profits, subject only to modest taxation. In addition, the federal government's program of enterprise zones, which grants tax incentives to promote private investment in inner cities, has been extended to Puerto Rico. Unquestionably, Puerto Rico has become attractive to mainland-based corporations. Skeptics point out that, as a result, the island's agriculture has been virtually ignored. Furthermore, the economic benefits to the island are limited. Businesses have spent the profits gained on Puerto Rico back on the mainland.

Puerto Rico's economy is in severe trouble compared to that of the mainland. Its unemployment rate has been about three times that of the mainland. In addition, the per-capita income is less than half that of Mississippi, the poorest state. Efforts to raise the wages of Puerto Rican workers only make the island less attractive to labor-intensive businesses, that is, those employing larger numbers of unskilled people. Capital-intensive companies, such as the petrochemical industries, have found Puerto Rico attractive, but they have not created jobs for the semiskilled. A growing problem is that Puerto Rico is emerging as a major gateway to the United States for illegal drugs from South America, which has led the island to experience waves of violence and the social ills associated with the drug trade (J. Castañeda 1996; D. Hemlock 1995; M. Navarro 1995).

Puerto Rico is an example of the world systems theory as initially presented in Chapter 1. **World systems theory** is the view of the global economic system as divided between certain industrialized nations that control wealth and developing countries that are controlled and exploited. While Puerto Rico may be relatively well off compared to many other Caribbean nations, it clearly is at the mercy of economic forces in the United States and, to a much lesser extent, other industrial nations. Puerto Rico continues to struggle

The row of upscale hotels and condominium complexes catering to vacationers masks the poverty experienced by many people on the island of Puerto Rico.

with the advantages of citizenship and the detriment of playing a peripheral role to the economy of the United States.

Another major factor in Puerto Rico's economy is tourism. Government subsidies have encouraged the construction of luxury hotels. After U.S. citizens' travel to Cuba was cut off in 1962, tourists discovered Puerto Rico's beaches and warm climate. Critics complain that the major economic beneficiaries of tourism are not local but are primarily investors from the mainland, and that high prices prevent the less affluent from visiting, thus unnecessarily restricting tourism. As has been true of other aspects of the island's economic development, the tourist boom has had little positive effect on most Puerto Ricans.

Puerto Rico continues to face new challenges. First, with congressional approval in 1994 of NAFTA (the North American Free Trade Agreement), Mexico, Canada, and the United States became integrated into a single economic market. The reduction of trade barriers with Mexico, coupled with that nation's lower wages, may combine to undercut Puerto Rico's commonwealth advantage. Second, many more island nations now offer the sun-bound tourist from the mainland alternatives to Puerto Rico. In addition, cruise ships present another attractive option for tourists. Given the economic problems of the island, it is not surprising that many Puerto Ricans migrate to the mainland (Rivera-Batz and Santiago 1996; L. Rohter 1993).

For years, migration to the mainland has served as a safety valve for Puerto Rico's population, which has grown annually at a rate 50 percent faster than that of the rest of the United States. Typically, migrants from Puerto Rico represent a broad range of occupations. There are seasonal fluctuations, as Puerto Rican farm workers leave the island in search of seasonal employment. Puerto Ricans, particularly agricultural workers, earn higher wages on the mainland. Yet a significant proportion return despite their relatively higher wages (E. Meléndez 1994).

The Contemporary Picture of Mexican Americans and Puerto Ricans

We will now consider the major social institutions of education, the family, health care, and religion, noting the similarities in their organization between Puerto Ricans and Mexican Americans.

EDUCATION

Both Mexican Americans and Puerto Ricans, as groups, have experienced gains in formal schooling but still lag behind White Americans in many standards of educational attainment. As is apparent in Table 10.1, Mexican Americans and Puerto Ricans lag well behind other Latinos, and even further behind Anglos. While bilingual education is still endorsed in the United States, the implementation of effective, quality programs has been difficult, as the previous chapter showed. In addition, attacks on the funding of bilingual education continued into the 1990s.

Latinos, including Mexican Americans and Puerto Ricans, have become increasingly isolated from non-Latinos. In 1968, 54.8 percent of all Hispanics attended predominantly minority schools, that is, schools where at least half of the students were members of minorities. Twenty-five years later, this rate was 73.6 percent—a level of segregation higher than even that for Black students. Significantly, the schools in certain states with large numbers of Hispanics, such as Illinois, New York, and Texas, are more segregated than in the national averages. In a parallel development, between 1970 and 1985, the percentage of Whites in the typical Mexican American student's school in Los Angeles County dropped from 45 percent to 17 percent. The trend toward the growing isolation of Latinos is found in virtually all parts of the nation and, since 1968, has prevailed in almost every period in which national data have been collected (G. Orfield 1993).

Three factors explain this increasing social isolation of Mexican Americans and Puerto Ricans from other students in school. First, Hispanics are increasingly concentrated in the largest cities, where minorities dominate. Second, the numbers of Hispanics have increased dramatically since the 1970s, when efforts to desegregate schools began to lose momentum. Third, schools once desegregated have become resegregated as the numbers of school-aged Mexican Americans in an area have increased and as the determination to maintain balances in schools has lessened (Moore and Iadicola 1981).

Even where Anglos and Latinos live in the same school district, the problem of social isolation in the classroom is often furthered through tracking. **Tracking** is the practice of placing students in specific classes or curriculum groups on the basis of test scores and other criteria. Tracking begins very early in the classroom, often in reading groups during first grade. These tracks may reinforce the disadvantages of Hispanic children from less affluent families and non-English-speaking households who have not been exposed to English reading materials in their homes during early childhood (C. Rodríguez 1989; Schaefer and Lamm 2000). .

Students see few teachers and administrators like themselves because relatively few Latino university students have been prepared to serve as teachers and administrators. In 1997, only 49 percent of Mexican Americans and 61 percent of Puerto Ricans aged twenty-five or over had completed high school, compared to 83 percent of Whites. Mexican Americans and Puerto Ricans who do choose to continue their education beyond high school are more likely to select a proprietary, or technical, school or community college, in order to acquire work-related skills.

Mexican Americans and Puerto Ricans are almost entirely missing from higher education—in all roles. Recent reports have documented the absence of Hispanics among college teachers and administrators—less than 4 percent of all college teachers were Latino in 1997. The situation is similar in this respect to that of Blacks; however, there are no Latino counterparts to historic Black colleges, such as Tuskegee Institute, to provide a source of leaders (Bureau of the Census 1998c:51, 54, 407).

Motivation does not appear to be the barrier to school achievement, at least among Mexican immigrants. A Harvard University study of the attitudes of Mexican immigrant adolescents showed that 84 percent felt that school was the most important thing, compared to 40 percent of White teenagers. Again, 68 percent of immigrant children felt that doing their homework was more important than helping a friend, compared to only 20 percent of White adolescents who held the same priorities.

There is evidence, however, that as these children assimilate, they begin to take on the prevailing White views. The same survey showed second-generation Mexican Americans still giving education a higher priority, but not as high as their immigrant counterparts (E. Woo 1996).

With respect to higher education, Latinos face challenges similar to those Black students meet on predominantly White campuses. Given the social isolation of Latino high schools, Mexican Americans are likely to have to adjust for the first time to an educational environment almost totally populated by Anglos. They may experience racism for the first time, just as they are trying to accommodate to a heavier academic load. Mexican Americans at more selective universities report that classmates accuse them of having benefited from affirmative-action admissions policies and of not really belonging (E. Fiske 1988a, 1988b).

The plight of Hispanics sometimes leads to innovative responses. The University of Texas at El Paso, for example, has allowed Mexicans to commute over the border since 1989 and, if they demonstrate financial need, to pay in-state tuition. In 1992, there were 927 Mexican students, of whom 84 percent qualified for the lower tuition rate. Since many of the commuters are not fluent in English, the university provides an array of support services for non-English-speaking students (K. Manigan 1991).

The admissions policy of the University of Texas at El Paso reflects the growing recognition of the borderlands and their social reality, described in the previous chapter. The growing immigration, legal and illegal, the exchange of media, workers crossing on a daily basis, and the passage in 1994 of the North American Free Trade Agreement (NAFTA) all make the notion of separate Mexican and U.S. cultures increasingly obsolete along the border. Gradually, social institutions such as universities are recognizing the social reality of the borderlands.

FAMILY LIFE

The most important organization or social institution among Latinos, or for that matter any group, is the family. The structure of the Mexican American family differs little from that of all families in the United States, a statement remarkable in itself given the impoverishment of a significant number of Mexican Americans. In 1997, most White families (81 percent) and most Hispanic families (68 percent) were headed by both a husband and a wife (Bureau of the Census 1998c:48, 54).

Latino households are described as laudably more familistic than others in the United States. By **familism** is meant pride and closeness in the family, which results in family obligation and loyalty coming before individual needs. The family, therefore, is the primary source of both social interaction and care giving.

Familism has been viewed as both a positive and a negative influence on individual Mexican Americans and Puerto Ricans. It may have the negative effect of discouraging youths with a bright future from taking advantage of opportunities that would separate them from their family. Familism is generally regarded as good, however, because an extended family provides emotional strength in times of crisis. Close family ties maintain the mental and social well-being of the elderly. Most

Latinos, therefore, see the intact, extended family as a norm and as a nurturing unit that provides support throughout the individual's lifetime. The many significant aspects of familism include (1) the importance of *compadrazgo* (the godparent–godchild relationship); (2) the benefits of the financial dependency of kin; (3) the availability of relatives as a source of advice; and (4) the active involvement of the elderly within the family.

This traditional value of familism, whether judged good or bad, is expected to decline in importance with urbanization, industrialization, and the acquisition of middle-class status. It will also mean taking on some practices more common in the United States, such as divorce. Characteristics that marked differences between Latino and Anglo family life were sharper in the past. Even among past generations, the differences were of degree, not of kind; that is, Hispanic families tended to exhibit some traits more than Anglos, not different traits altogether. A comparison between similar Anglo and Mexican American families in San Diego found no significant differences in family life between the two groups. The Mexican American and Puerto Rican families, in summary, display all the variety of American families in general, while, also in general, still suffering higher levels of poverty (O. Alárcon 1995; N. Kanellos 1994; Landale and Ogena 1995; Vega et al. 1986; R. Zambrana 1995).

HEALTH CARE

Earlier, in Chapter 5, we introduced the concept of **life chances,** which are people's opportunities to provide themselves with material goods, positive living conditions, and favorable life experiences. We have consistently seen Latino groups as having more limited life chances. Perhaps in no other area does this apply so much as in the health care system.

Hispanics as a group are locked out of the health care system more often than any other racial or ethnic group. A third have no health insurance (or other coverage such as Medicaid) compared to 14 percent of Whites and 20 percent of Blacks. Predictably, the uninsured are less likely to have a regular source of medical care. This means that they wait for a crisis before seeking care. Fewer are immunized, and rates of preventable diseases such as lead poisoning are higher. Noncoverage is increasing, a circumstance that may reflect a further breakdown in health care delivery or may be a result of continuing immigration (Bureau of the Census 1994).

The health care dilemma facing Mexican Americans and other Hispanic groups is complicated by the lack of Hispanic health professionals. In 1997, Hispanics accounted for 7 percent or less of dentists, nurses, pharmacists, and physicians, yet are more than 11 percent of the population. Less than 5 percent of students in medical school are Hispanic, so the situation will not change soon. Obviously, one does not need to be administered health care by someone in one's own ethnic group, but the paucity of Hispanic professionals increases the likelihood that the group will be underserved (Bureau of the Census 1998c:417).

Given the high proportion of uninsured individuals and the low number of Latino health care personnel, it is not surprising to learn of the poor status of Latinos' health care as a group. They are at increased risk for certain medical conditions, including diabetes, hypertension, tuberculosis, AIDS, alcoholism, and specific cancers. The situation begins to deteriorate at the start of life. Only about 60 percent of Mexican Americans and Puerto Ricans initiate prenatal care in the first trimester, compared to 80 percent of Whites. Interestingly, however, infant mortality rates are generally lower for Mexican American children than for Whites. Experts suggest that familism may account for the surprising advantage in infants' health, in that infants receive more help even if it is not professional. However, this is less true of Latinos born in the United States to parents who show signs of assimilating to some U.S. habits such as poor diet and smoking. Women's health has not received sufficient attention, and this is especially true of minority women. The American Medical Association acknowledges, for example, that not enough is known about why Latino women are especially vulnerable to cervical cancer and AIDS. The challenge is to develop a health care system that can respond to these needs (Becerra et al. 1991; Council on Scientific Affairs 1991; J. Kleinhuizen 1991a; Novello et al. 1991).

Some Mexican Americans and many other Latinos have cultural beliefs that make them less likely to use the medical system. They may interpret their illnesses according to folk practices or ***curanderismo***—Latino folk medicine, a form of holistic health care and healing. This orientation influences how one approaches health care and even how one defines illness. Most Hispanics probably use folk healers, or *curanderos,* infrequently, but perhaps 20 percent rely on home remedies. While these are not necessarily without value, especially if a dual system of folk and establishment medicine is followed, reliance on natural beliefs may be counterproductive. Another aspect of folk beliefs is the identification of folk-defined illnesses such as *susto* (or fright sickness) and *atague* (or fighting attack). While these complaints, alien by these names to Anglos, often have biological bases, they need to be dealt with carefully by sensitive medical professionals who can diagnose and treat illnesses accurately (Council on Scientific Affairs 1991; G. Rivera 1988).

RELIGION

The most important formal organization in the Hispanic community is the church. Most Puerto Ricans and Mexican Americans express a religious preference for the Roman Catholic Church. In 1994, about 70 percent of Hispanics were Roman Catholic, as shown in Figure 10.3.

The Roman Catholic Church basically took an assimilationist role in the past, whether with Hispanic Catholics or with other minority Catholics. The church has only sporadically involved itself in the Chicano movement, and rarely in the past did the upper levels of the church hierarchy support *Chicanismo.* For example, only with some prodding did the Roman Catholic Church support the United Farm Workers, a group whose membership was predominantly Catholic. Recently the Roman Catholic Church has become more community oriented, seeking to identify Latino, or at least Spanish-speaking, clergy and staff to serve Latino parishes (F. Rosales 1996).

Not only is the Roman Catholic Church important to Hispanics, but Hispanics also play a significant role for the church. The population growth of Mexican

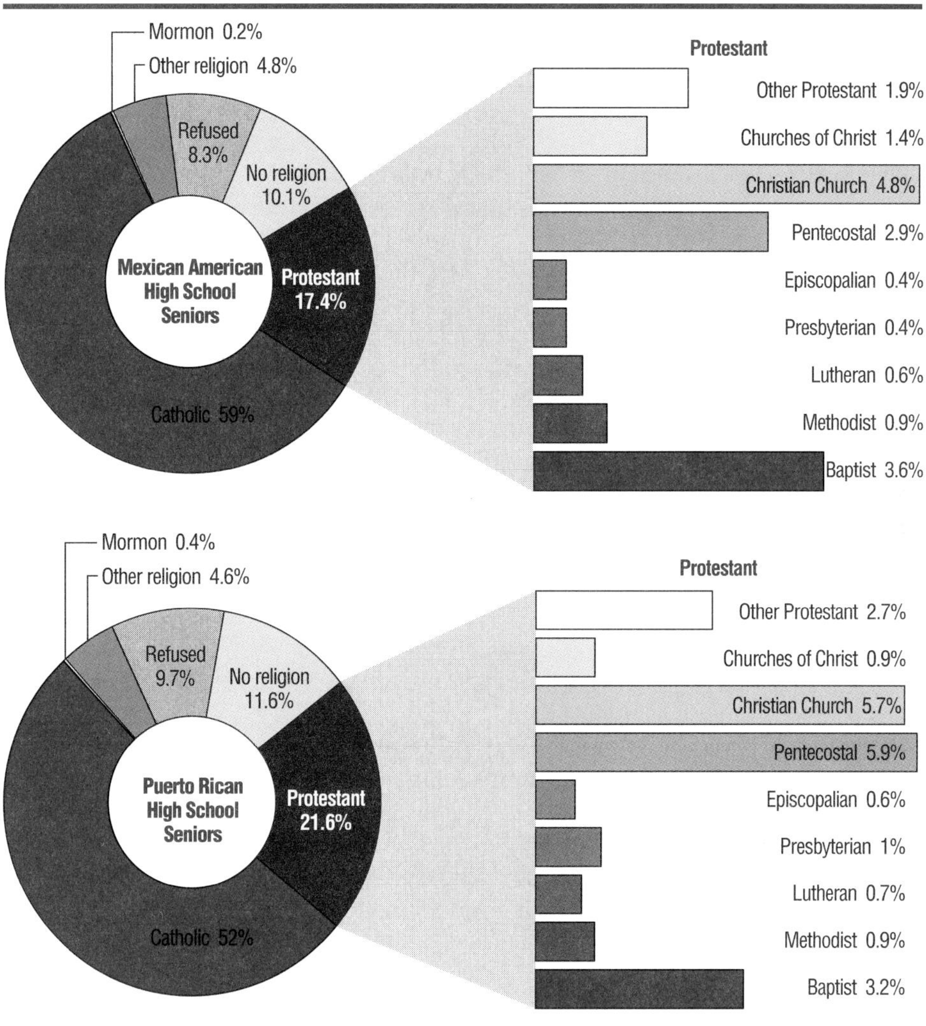

Figure 10.3 Religious Preferences, 1990
Using national data, we see that the majority of both Mexican Americans and Puerto Ricans expressed a preference for the Roman Catholic Church.

Source: Barry Kosmin and Seymour P. Lachman, *One Nation Under God.* Copyright © 1993 by Barry Kosmin and Seymour P. Lachman. Reprinted by permission of Harmony Books, a division of Crown Publishers, Inc.

Americans and other Hispanics has been responsible for the Roman Catholic Church's continued growth in recent years, while mainstream Protestant faiths have declined in size. Hispanics account for over a third of Roman Catholics in the United States. The church is trying to adjust to Hispanics' more expressive manifestation of religious faith, with frequent reliance on their own patron saints and the presence of special altars in their homes. Roman Catholic churches in some parts of the United States are even starting to accommodate observances of the *Mexican Dia de los Muertos*—"Day of the Dead." Such practices are a tradition from rural Mexico, where religion was followed without the benefit of any trained clergy. Yet even today in the United States, Hispanics continue to be underrepresented among priests, with only 4.4 percent nationwide being Hispanic (A. O'Connor 1998).

Dia De Los Muertos—"Day of the Dead"—is a popular annual practice among Mexican Americans honoring one's ancestors.

While Latinos are predominantly Roman Catholic, their membership in Protestant and other Christian faiths is growing. **Pentecostalism,** a type of evangelical Christianity, is growing in Latin America and is clearly making a significant impact on Latinos in the United States. Adherents to Pentecostal faiths hold beliefs similar to those of the evangelicals but, in addition, believe in the infusion of the Holy Spirit into services and in religious experiences such as faith healing. Pentecostalism and similar faiths are attractive to many because they offer followers the opportunity to express their religious fervor openly. Furthermore, many of the churches are small and thus offer a sense of community, often with Spanish-speaking leadership. Gradually, the more established faiths are recognizing the desirability of offering Latino parishioners a greater sense of belonging (R. Martinez 1998).

CONCLUSION

David Gomez (1971) described Mexican Americans as "strangers in their own land." The Puerto Ricans, on the other hand, are still debating what should be the political destiny of their island nation. All of this makes nationality a very real part of the destiny of Mexican Americans and Puerto Ricans. Can they also preserve their culture along with a sense of national fervor, or will these be a casualty of assimilation?

As we have seen, even when we concentrate on just Mexican Americans or Puerto Ricans out of the larger collective group of Hispanics or Latinos, diversity remains. Mexican Americans are divided among the Hispanos and the descendants of earlier

Mexican immigrants, and the more recent arrivals from Mexico. Puerto Ricans can be divided, too, by virtue of residency and the extent to which they identify with the island culture. For many Puerto Ricans, the identity dilemma is never truly resolved—*No soy de aquí ni de allá* (I am not from here nor from there) (Comas-Díaz et al. 1998).

Economic change is also apparent. Poverty and unemployment rates are high, and new arrivals from Mexico and Puerto Rico are particularly likely to enter the lower class, or working class at best, upon arrival. There is, however, a growing middle class within the Hispanic community—perhaps half of the Hispanic population can now be regarded as on parity with the White middle class (G. Rodriquez 1996).

Mexican culture is alive and well within the Mexican American community. Some cultural practices that have become more popular than in Mexico here are now being imported back to Mexico with their distinctive Mexican American flavor. All this is occurring in the midst of a reluctance to expand bilingual education and a popular move to make English the official language. In 1998, Puerto Rico observed its five-hundredth anniversary as a colony—four centuries under Spain and another century under the United States. Its dual status as a colony and as a developing nation has been the defining issue for Puerto Ricans, even those who have migrated to the mainland (R. Perusse 1990).

Mexican Americans and Puerto Ricans are still among the groups who find themselves economically on the outside despite Latinos' long history of immigration to the United States. Another group with such a history that has also met problems of racial prejudice and economic discrimination, the Asian Americans, will be the subject of the next chapter.

KEY TERMS

bracero 298
Chicanismo 303
color gradient 312
culture of poverty 300
curanderismo 318
familism 316
La Raza 299
life chances 317
mojados 299
neocolonialism 308
Neoricans 306
Pentecostalism 320
repatriation 298
tracking 315
world systems theory 313

REVIEW QUESTIONS

1. In what respects has Mexico been viewed as a source of workers and a place to leave unwanted laborers?
2. In what respects are Hispanic families similar to and different from Anglo households?
3. How does *Chicanismo* relate to the issue of Hispanic identity?
4. How does the case of Puerto Rico support the notion of race as a social concept?
5. What role does religion play in the Latino community?

CRITICAL THINKING

1. Consider what it means to be "patriotic" and "loyal" in terms of being a citizen of the United States. How do the concerns that Puerto Ricans have for the island's future and the Mexican concept of dual nationality affect those notions of patriotism and loyalty?
2. The phrase "territorial minorities" has been used to apply to subordinate groups who have special ties to their land, such as Native American tribes. How would you apply this to Mexican Americans?
3. The family is often regarded by observers as a real strength within the Latino community. How can this strength be harnessed to address some of the challenges that Mexican Americans and Puerto Ricans face in the United States?
4. Evaluate the statement, "the United States is the last great colonial power and does not even realize it." How might your response change if we substitute the term neocolonialism for colonialism?

INTERNET EXERCISES

1. To learn more about the cause that César Chávez dedicated himself to, visit "Si Se Puede! César E. Chvez and His Legacy" (http://clnet.ucr.edu/research/chavez/). Click on and read the "Biography" and "Themes" sections. What were some of the major challenges and social problems faced by farm workers that Chávez sought to change? In what ways do Chvez's philosophies and strategies compare to those used by Dr. Martin Luther King? Who were Nan Freeman, Rene Lopez, and Rufino Contreras, and what roles did they play in the struggle to improve the lives of farm workers? Be sure to visit the "Housing Photos" within the "Museum" section for a view of what living conditions were like for workers. What feelings and thoughts do these pictures invoke?
2. "The Puerto Rican Hall of Fame" (http://www.angelfire.com/biz/chago/puertorros.html) offers a multitude of resources and information about Puerto Rican history, culture, and influence. Link to the section on "Famous Puerto Ricans" and select three individuals who interest you. For each person, answer the following questions: When did the person live? What is he or she famous for? In what ways has that person influenced Puerto Ricans and other groups? At this site, you can also take a cybertour of Puerto Rico, listen to Puerto Rican music, and view the work of Puerto Rican artists and chefs. After exploring such links, how has your view of Puerto Rico changed? What new facts did you learn? What is your view on the issues of statehood and self-rule? Defend your position.

FOR FURTHER INFORMATION

Roberto M. De Anda. *Chicanas and Chicanos in Contemporary Society.* Boston: Allyn & Bacon, 1996.
This anthology of fifteen articles provides an overview of the major social institutions.

José Trias Monge. *Puerto Rico: The Trials of the Oldest Country in the World.* New Haven, CT: Yale University Press, 1997.
The former Chief Justice of Puerto Rico provides an account of the island's dubious political status and makes a case for "decolonizing" Puerto Rico.

F. Arturo Rosales. *Chicano! The History of the Mexican American Civil Rights Movement.* Houston, TX: Arte Público Press, 1996.
This well-illustrated book is based on the Public Broadcasting System's series chronicling the effort to achieve equal rights for Mexican Americans.

James W. Russell. *After the Fifth Sun. Class and Race in North America.* Englewood Cliffs, NJ: Prentice-Hall, 1996.
A sociologist looks at the social construction of race and its relationship to social class from the days of the Aztecs to the present.

11

Asian Americans: Growth and Diversity

©*Los Angeles Times* Photo/Al Seib

CHAPTER OUTLINE

HIGHLIGHTS

Asian Americans are a diverse group that is one of the fastest-growing segments of the U.S. population. Asian Americans are often viewed as a model minority that has successfully overcome discrimination. This inaccurate image disguises lingering maltreatment and anti-Asian American violence. Further, it denies Asian Americans the special treatment afforded other racial minorities. Immigration is the primary source of growth among Filipinos, Asian Indians, Southeast Asians, and Koreans. All Asian groups, along with Blacks and Whites (or Haoles, as they are known) coexist in Hawaii.

The scene seems ordinary enough—a group of young club goers are piled into a small room furnished with two big couches, a disco ball, colored lights, two microphones, and a large TV with a videodisk player. It is time to do some karaoke. However, there are signs that something is a bit different—the refreshments include a plate of dried squid and sliced oranges along with a six-pack of beer. We are witnessing a scene found in several cities in the United States—nightclubs that cater to the growing number of young U.S.-born Korean Americans looking for a good time. Korean pop songs are more likely to give way to Grease's "Summer Nights" or ZZ Top's "Sharp Dressed Man" and English is more the language heard than Korean. *Norebang,* the Korean version of karaoke, is very popular in Koreatown night-life in cities such as Chicago and Los Angeles (M. Eng 1998).

As is true of all the minority groups discussed so far, Asians in the United States who want to be accepted have been pressured to assimilate. The effects of this pressure vary. For recent refugees from Asia, assimilation is a new experience; the grandchildren of Japanese immigrants, in contrast, may be culturally indistinguishable from Whites. Figure 11.1 shows how Asian Americans combine with other groups to form the diversity typical of an American metropolitan area such as Los Angeles.

Young people having a night out reminds us that the legacy of immigration to the United States is not merely quaint turn-of-the-century black-and-white photos

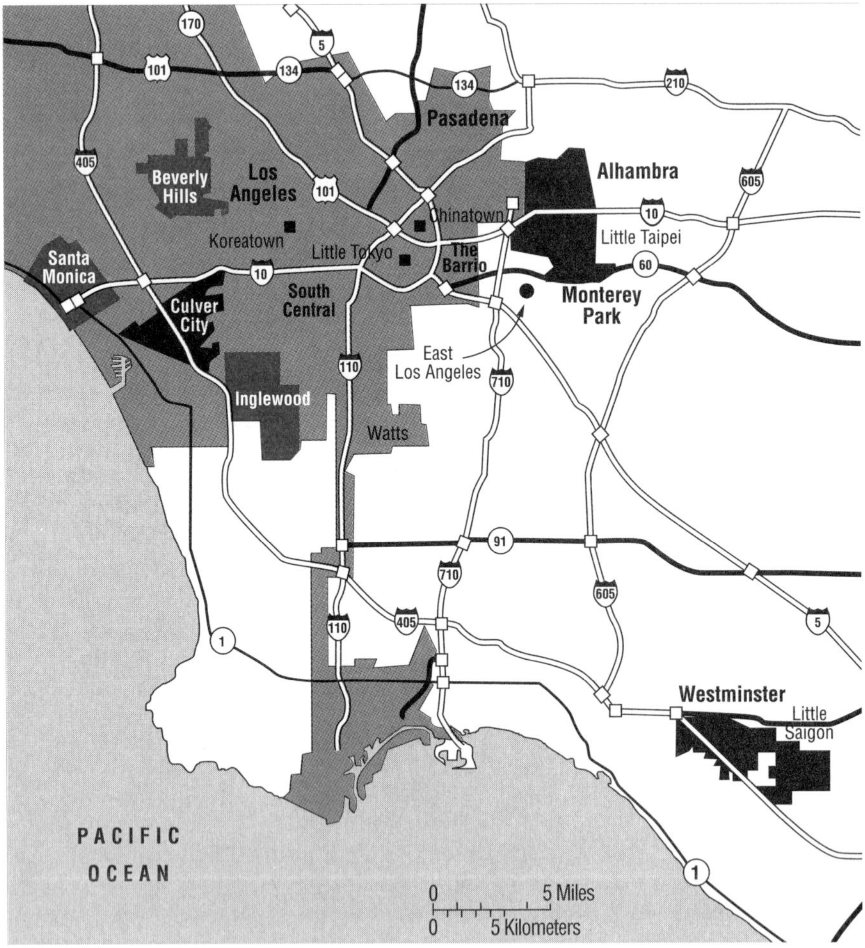

Figure 11.1 Ethnic Diversity in Los Angeles
The diversity of life in Los Angeles, the second-largest city in the United States, reflects migration from Mexico (East L.A. or the *barrio*), Korea (Koreatown), China and Hong Kong (Chinatown), Taiwan (Monterey Park and Alhambra), Vietnam (Little Saigon in Westminister), and Japan (Little Tokyo). Also noted on the map are the locations of the 1965 riots (Watts) and 1992 riots (south-central Los Angeles).

posed at Ellis Island. It is not merely a thickly accented elderly person telling of the "old country." Immigration, race, and ethnicity are being lived out among people of all ages, and for no collective groups is this more true than Asian Americans. Asian Americans in 1997 numbered 9.7 million—a 276 percent increase over 1980, compared to an overall population increase of 117 percent (S. Lee 1998).

To comprehend better the collective picture of Asian Americans, we will first consider a powerful image that many people have of Asian Americans—that they constitute some kind of perfect, model minority. We will then turn our attention to the role they play politically in the United States.

We will then consider four of the larger groups—Filipinos, Asian Indians, Southeast Asians, and Koreans—in greater depth. The chapter will conclude by examining the coexistence of a uniquely mixed group of peoples—Hawaiians—among whom Asian Americans form the numerical majority. Chapter 12 will concentrate on the Chinese and the Japanese, the two Asian groups with the longest historical tradition in the United States.

The "Model-Minority" Image Explored

"Asian Americans are a success! They achieve! They succeed! There are no protests, no demands. They just do it!" This is the general image that people in the United States so often hold of Asian Americans as a group. They constitute a **model** or **ideal minority** because, although they have experienced prejudice and discrimination, they seem nevertheless to have succeeded economically, socially, and educationally without resorting to political or violent confrontations with Whites. Some observers point to the existence of a model minority as a reaffirmation that anyone can get ahead in the United States. Proponents of the model-minority view declare that because Asian Americans have achieved success, they have ceased to be subordinate and are no longer disadvantaged. This is only a variation of "blaming the victim"; with Asian Americans, it is "praising the victim." An examination of aspects of their socioeconomic status will allow a more thorough exploration of this view (Hurh and Kim 1989).

THE PICTURE IN EDUCATION AND THE ECONOMY

Asian Americans as a group do have impressive school enrollment rates in comparison to the total population. In 1997, half of Asian Americans twenty-five years or older held bachelor's degrees, compared to 29 percent of the White population. These rates vary among Asian American groups, with Asian Indians, Chinese Americans, and Japanese Americans having higher levels of educational achievement (Bureau of the Census 1998g).

This encouraging picture does have some qualifications, however, which call into question the optimistic model-minority view. According to a study of California's state university system that was released in 1991, while Asian Americans are often viewed as successful overachievers, they have unrecognized and overlooked needs and experience discomfort and harassment on campus. As a group, they also lack Asian faculty and staff members to whom they can turn for support. They confront many identity issues and have to do a sort of "cultural balancing act" along with all the usual pressures faced by college students. The report noted that an "alarming number" of Asian American students appear to be experiencing intense stress and alienation, problems that have often been "exacerbated by racial *harassment*" (K. Ohnuma 1991:5; D. Takagi 1992; J. Tamaki 1998).

Even the positive stereotype of Asian American students as "academic stars" can be dysfunctional or counterproductive to people so labeled. Asian Americans who do only modestly well in school may face criticism from their parents or teachers for their failure to conform to the "whiz kid" image. In fact, despite the model-minority label, the high school dropout rate for Asian Americans is increasing rapidly. California's special program for low-income, academically disadvantaged students has a 30 percent Asian American clientele, and the proportion of Asian students in the programs is on the rise (F. Lee 1991; J. Tachibana 1990).

That Asian Americans as a group work in the same occupations as Whites suggests that they have been successful, and many have. The pattern, however, shows some differences. Asian immigrants, like other minorities and immigrants before them, are found disproportionately in the low-paying service occupations. At the same time, they are also concentrated at the top in professional and managerial positions. Yet, as we will see, they rarely reach the very top. They hit the "glass ceiling" (as described in Chapter 3) or, as some others say, try to "climb a broken ladder," before they reach management. In 1998, there were only 65 Asian Americans on any of the boards of the nation's 1,000 largest corporations—that amounts to less than 1 percent. In California, where the Asian American presence is very visible, the situation is a bit

Students at Cal Poly-Pomona proudly gaze on a mural depicting the contributions of Asian Americans during Asian-Pacific Heritage Month (annually March nationwide).

better. An analysis found that Asian Americans, who make up 10 percent of the state's workforce, hold about that share of administrative and managerial jobs, but remain underrepresented in top levels of management (D. Lee 1998; E. Lee 1993).

The absence of Asian Americans as top executives also indicates that their success is not complete. Asian Americans have become middlemen in the economy, doing well in small businesses and modest agricultural ventures. While self-employed and managing their own businesses, Asian Americans have had very modest-sized operations. Because of the long hours, the income from such a business may be below prevailing wage standards, so even when they are business owners, they may still constitute cheap labor—although they also get the profits. Chinese restaurants, Korean American cleaning businesses and fruit and vegetable stores, and motels, gasoline stations, and newspaper-vending businesses operated by Asian Indians fall into this category.

Asian Americans are therefore typical of what sociologists refer to as **middlemen minorities**—groups that occupy middle positions rather than positions at the bottom of the social scale, where many racial and ethnic minorities are typically located at least in the early years of residence here. Asian Americans involved in small businesses tend to maintain closer ties with other Asian Americans than do individuals who join larger corporations. These ethnic owners generally hire other ethnics, who are paid low wages in exchange for paternalistic benefits such as on-the-job training or even assistance in creating their own middleman businesses. The present high proportion of Asian Americans as middlemen, however, is often the result of exclusion from other work, not of success (E. Bonacich 1988; Bonacich and Modell 1981; Kim and Kim 1998).

Another sign of the apparent "success" of Asian Americans is their high incomes as a group. Like other elements of the image, however, this deserves closer inspection. Asian American family income approaches parity with that of Whites because of their greater achievement than Whites in formal schooling. If we look at specific educational levels, Whites earn more than their Asian counterparts of the same age. Asian Americans' average earnings increased by at least $2,300 for each additional year of schooling, while Whites gained almost $3,000 (O'Hare and Felt 1991; Zhou and Kamo 1994).

There are striking contrasts among Asian Americans. Asian Americans have the lowest divorce rate of any racial group in the United States (3 percent), the lowest unemployment rate (3.5 percent), the lowest rate of teen pregnancy (6 percent), and the highest household family income ($35,000). Nevertheless, for every Asian American family with an annual income of $75,000 or more, another earns less than $10,000 a year. In New York City's Chinatown neighborhood, about one-quarter of all families live below the poverty level. In San Diego, dropout rates were close to 60 percent among Southeast Asians in 1997. Even relatively successful Asian Americans continue to face obstacles because of their racial heritage. According to a study of three major public hospitals in Los Angeles, Asian Americans account for 34 percent of all physicians and nurses but fill only 11 percent of management positions at these hospitals (Bureau of the Census 1998h; A. Dunn 1994; S. Sengupta 1997).

At first glance, one might be puzzled to see criticism of a positive generalization such as "model minority." Why should the stereotype of adjusting without problems be a disservice to Asian Americans? The answer is that this incorrect view helps to exclude Asian

Asian Americans are subject to stereotypes, one of which, "straight-A student," reflects the model-minority image.
©Oliver Chin

Americans from social programs and conceals unemployment and other social ills. When representatives of Asian groups do seek assistance for those in need, they are resented by those who are convinced of the model-minority view. If a minority group is viewed as successful, it is unlikely that its members will be included in programs designed to alleviate the problems they encounter as minorities. The positive stereotype reaffirms the American system of mobility: new immigrants as well as established subordinate groups ought to achieve more merely by working within the system. At the same time, viewed from the conflict perspective outlined in Chapter 1, this becomes yet another instance of "blaming the victim"; if Asian Americans have succeeded, Blacks and Hispanics must be responsible for their own low status (W. Ryan 1976).

THE DOOR HALF OPEN

Despite the widespread belief that they constitute a "model minority," Asian Americans are victims of both prejudice and violence. A forty-eight-page report released in 1997 by the National Asian Pacific American Legal Consortium chronicled 534 incidents of suspected and proven anti-Asian American incidents that occurred in 1996. Assaults and aggravated assaults motivated by bigotry increased by over 17 percent over the previous year (A. Yip 1997).

This anti-Asian American feeling is built on a long cultural tradition. The term "yellow peril" dates back to the view of Asian immigration, particularly from China, as unwelcome. **Yellow peril** came to refer to the generalized prejudice toward Asian people and their customs. The immigrants were characterized as heathen, morally inferior, drug-addicted, savage, or lustful. Although the term was first used around the turn-of-the-century, this anti-Asian sentiment is very much alive today. Many contemporary Asian Americans find this intolerance very unsettling given their conscientious efforts to extend their education, seek employment, and conform to the norms of society (W. Hurh 1994).

What explains the increase in violence against Asian Americans? Prejudice against Asian Americans is fueled by how they are represented in the media. The Asian American Journalists Association (1991, 1993, 1994) initiated Project Zinger to identify how mainstream news media use ethnic slurs and stereotypes, demonstrate insensitivity, and otherwise exhibit bias in reporting. We can identify several ways in which this occurs—some subtle, some more overt:

- *Inappropriate use of clichés.* News reports use "Asian invasion" even when referring to a small number of Asian Americans. For example, a 1994 *Sports Illustrated* article about Asians trying out for Major League baseball teams was billed "Orient Express" and "Asian invasion," yet the story noted a total of only two Asians as examples.
- *Mistaken identity.* Not only are Asians identified by the wrong nationality, but American citizens of Asian descent are presented as if they were foreigners.
- *Overgeneralization.* Inappropriate assumptions are made and too widely applied. For example, a newspaper article discussing the growth of Chinatown was headlined "There Goes the Neighborhood," implying that any increase in the number of Chinese Americans was undesirable.
- *Ethnic slurs.* While the print media generally take great pains to avoid racially derogatory terms, radio talk shows offer frequent examples of racism. U.S. Senator Alfonse D'Amato engaged in a pidgin-English mockery of Judge Lance Ito of the O. J. Simpson trial (B. Frankel 1995b) during a morning radio broadcast.
- *Inflammatory reporting.* Unbalanced coverage of such events as World War II or Asian investment in the United States can needlessly contribute to ill feelings.
- *Japan bashing.* News accounts may unfairly blame Asian nations for economic problems in the United States. For example, as Japan-based automakers gained a foothold in the United States, much of the coverage failed to note that U.S. carmakers had not maintained their own competitive advantage.
- *Media invisibility.* News reports may ignore Asian Americans and rarely seek their views on issues related to Asia.
- *Model minority.* This positive portrayal can also have a negative effect.

In its own way, each of these biases contributes to the unbalanced view we have developed of the large, diverse Asian American population.

The resentment against Asian Americans is not limited to these overt incidents of violence. Like other subordinate groups, Asian Americans are subject to institutional discrimination. For example, some Asian American groups have large families and find themselves subject to zoning laws stipulating the number of people per room, which make it difficult to live together. Kinfolk are unable to take family members in legally. While we may regard these family members as distant relatives, many Asian cultures view cousins, uncles, and aunts as relatives to whom they have a great deal of familial responsibility.

Furthermore, the success of Asian Americans in some areas such as academic achievement has led to charges that schools and universities establish higher performance standards for admission, seeking to prevent high numbers of Asian Americans from enrolling. Although these charges are hard to prove and universally denied, some independent studies have supported the charges (Commission on Civil Rights 1992; D. Takagi 1992; Nakanishi 1986; E. Yu 1980).

For young Asian Americans, life in the United States is often a struggle for one's identity. Sometimes it means finding a role in White America, other times finding a place among Asian Americans collectively and then locating oneself within one's own racial or ethnic community. In Listen to Their Voices, we become acquainted with Shanlon Wu, a Chinese American who literally searched the United States for Chinese American heroes.

Political Activity

Against this backdrop of prejudice, discrimination, and searching for one's identity, it would not be surprising to see Asian Americans seeking to recognize themselves. Historically, Asian Americans have followed the pattern of other immigrant groups: they bring organizations from the homeland and later develop groups to respond to the special needs identified in the United States. Most recently, during the expressions of anti-immigrant sentiment in 1996, Asian Americans sought to stage demonstrations in several cities seeking to persuade people to become citizens and register to vote. These efforts, similar to the recent steps taken by Hispanic groups discussed in the previous chapters, have also met with mixed success.

For newly arrived Asians, grass-roots organization and political parties are a new concept. With the exception of Asian Indians, the immigrants come from nations where political participation was unheard of or looked upon with skepticism and sometimes fear. Using the sizable Chinese American community as an example, we can see why Asian Americans have been slow to achieve political mobilization. At least six factors have been identified that explain why Chinese Americans—and to a large extent, Asian Americans in general—have not been more active in politics:

1. To become a candidate means to take risks, invite criticism, be assertive, and be willing to extol one's virtues. These traits are alien to Chinese culture.
2. Older people remember when discrimination was blatant, and they tell others to "be quiet" and not attract attention.
3. As noted earlier, many recent immigrants have no experience with democracy and arrive with a general distrust of government.
4. Like many new immigrant groups, Chinese Americans have concentrated on getting ahead economically and educating their children rather than thinking in terms of the larger community.
5. The careers that the brightest students pursue tend to be in business and science rather than law or public administration and therefore do not provide preparation for politics.
6. Chinatowns notwithstanding, Chinese and other Asian American groups are dispersed and cannot control the election even of local candidates.

On the other hand, Asian Americans are increasingly being regarded by both Democrats and Republicans as a future political force in the United States (J. Gross 1989; S. Holmes 1996a).

Many political observers have expected Asian Americans to favor Democratic candidates, like most Latinos and especially African Americans. Indeed, in the 1998 elections, 56 percent of Asian Americans favored Democratic candidates, compared to 43 percent of Whites. However, the Republicans, nationally and locally, continue to try to cut into this Democratic preference among these voters. A major test of this effort occurred in California in 1998, when U.S. Senate incumbent Barbara Boxer faced Republican challenger Matt Fong. Boxer was reelected, but Chinese American Fong garnered the support of the majority of Asian American voters. For them, it apparently was easier to follow ethnic loyalty and momentarily forget the Republican party's opposition to affirmative action and bilingual education in California (M. Connelly 1998; J. Sooc 1998).

Diversity Among Asian Americans

The political activity of Asian Americans occurs within a complex segment of the population—Asian Americans who reflect the diversity of their native lands. Asia is a vast region, holding more than half the world's population. The successive waves of immigrants to the United States from that continent have been composed of a large number of nationalities and cultures. In addition to the six groups listed in Figure 11.2, the Census Bureau enumerates the Bangladeshi, Bhutanese, Bornean, Burmese, Cambodian, Celebesian, Cernan, Indochinese, Iwo-Jiman, Laotian, Malayan, Maldivean, Nepali, Okinawan, Sikkimese, Singaporean, Sri Lankan, and Vietnamese. Given this variety among Asian people, we can apply to Asian Americans several generalizations made

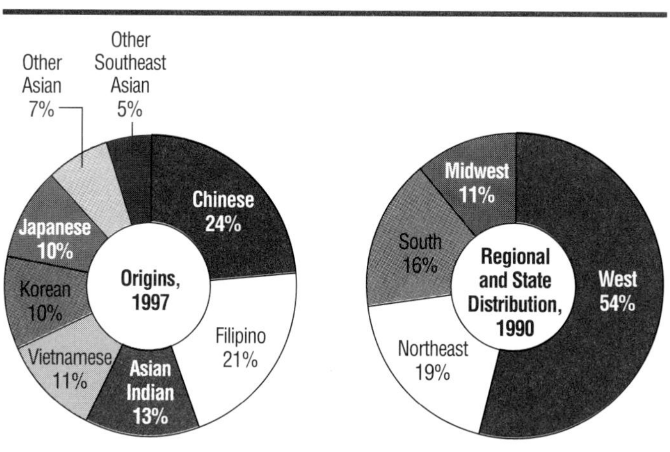

Figure 11.2 Asian Americans
Note: "Other Southeast Asian" includes Cambodian, Hmong, and Laotian.
Source: Sharon M. Lee. "Asian Americans: Diverse and Growing." *Population Bulletin,* 53, (June 1998).

LISTEN TO THEIR VOICES

In Search of Bruce Lee's Grave

Shanlon Wu

It's Saturday morning in Seattle, and I am driving to visit Bruce Lee's grave. I have been in the city for only a couple of weeks and so drive two blocks past the cemetery before realizing that I've passed it. I double back and turn through the large wrought-iron gate, past a sign that reads: "Open to 9 p.m. or dusk, whichever comes first."

It's a sprawling cemetery, with winding roads leading in all directions. I feel silly trying to find his grave with no guidance. I think that my search for his grave is similar to my search for Asian heroes in America.

I was born in 1959, an Asian-American in Westchester County, N.Y. During my childhood there were no Asian sports stars. On television I can recall only that most pathetic of Asian characters, Hop Sing, the Cartwright family houseboy on "Bonanza." But in my adolescence there was Bruce.

I was 14 years old when I first saw "Enter the Dragon," the granddaddy of martial-arts movies. Bruce had died suddenly at the age of 32 of cerebral edema, an excess of fluid in the brain, just weeks before the release of the film. Between the ages of 14 and 17, I saw "Enter the Dragon" 22 times before I stopped counting. During those years I collected Bruce Lee posters, putting them up at all angles in my bedroom. I took up Chinese martial arts and spent hours comparing my physique with his....

My parents, who immigrated to America and had become professors at Hunter College, tolerated my behavior, but seemed puzzled at my admiration of an "entertainer." My father jokingly tried to compare my obsession with Bruce to his boyhood worship of Chinese folk-tale heroes.

"I read them just like you read American comic books," he said.

But my father's heroes could not be mine; they came from an ancient literary tradition, not comic books. He and my mother had grown up in a land where they belonged to the majority. I could not adopt their childhood and they were wise enough not to impose it upon me.

Although I never again experienced the kind of blind hero worship I felt for Bruce, my need to find heroes remained strong.

In college, I discovered the men of the 442d Regimental Combat Team, a United States Army all-Japanese unit in World War II. Allowed to fight only against Europeans, they suffered heavy casualties while their families were put in internment camps. Their motto was "Go for Broke."

I saw them as Asians in a Homeric epic, the protagonists of a Shakespearean tragedy;

earlier about Native Americans. Both groups are a collection of diverse peoples with distinct linguistic, social, and geographic backgrounds.

Asian Americans, like Native Americans, are not evenly distributed across the United States (refer again to Figure 11.2). To lump these people together ignores the sharp differences among them. Any examination of Asian Americans quickly reveals their diversity, which will be apparent as we focus on individual Asian American groups, beginning with Filipinos.

I knew no Eastern myths to infuse them with. They embodied my own need to prove myself in the Caucasian world. I imagined how their American-born flesh and muscle must have resembled mine: epicanthic folds set in strong faces nourished on milk and beef. I thought how much they had proved where there was so little to prove.

After college, I competed as an amateur boxer in an attempt to find my self-image in the ring. It didn't work. My fighting was only an attempt to copy Bruce's movies. What I needed was instruction on how to live. I quit boxing after a year and went to law school.

I was an anomaly there: a would-be Asian litigator. I had always liked to argue and found I liked doing it in front of people even more. When I won the first-year moot court competition in law school, I asked an Asian classmate if he thought I was the first Asian to win. He laughed and told me I was probably the only Asian to even compete.

The law-firm interviewers always seemed surprised that I wanted to litigate.

"Aren't you interested in Pacific Rim trade?" they asked.

"My Chinese isn't good enough," I quipped.

My pat response seemed to please them. It certainly pleased me. I thought I'd found a place of my own—a place where the law would insulate me from the pressure of defining my Asian maleness. I sensed the possibility of merely being myself....

The hunger is eased this gray morning in Seattle. After asking directions from a policeman—Japanese—I easily locate Bruce's grave. The headstone is red granite with a small picture etched into it. The picture is very Hollywood—Bruce wears dark glasses—and I think the calligraphy looks a bit sloppy. Two tourists stop but leave quickly after glancing at me.

I realize I am crying. Bruce's grave seems very small in comparison to his place in my boyhood. So small in comparison to my need for heroes. Seeing his grave, I understand how large the hole in my life has been, and how desperately I'd sought to fill it.

I had sought an Asian hero to emulate. But none of my choices quite fit me. Their lives were defined through heroic tasks—they had villains to defeat and wars to fight—while my life seemed merely a struggle to define myself.

But now I see how that very struggle has defined me. I must be my own hero even as I learn to treasure those who have gone before.

Source: Shanlon Wu. *New York Times Magazine,* April 15, 1990.

Filipino Americans

Relatively little has been written about the Filipinos (also spelled Philipinos), although they are the second-largest Asian American group in the United States, with more than a million now living here. Social science literature considers them Asians for geographic reasons, but physically and culturally, they also reflect centuries of Spanish rule.

IMMIGRATION PATTERNS

The earliest Filipino immigrants came as American nationals, when, in 1899, the United States gained possession of the Philippine Islands at the conclusion of the Spanish-American War. In 1934, the islands gained commonwealth status. The Philippines gained their independence in 1948 and with it lost their unrestricted immigration rights. Despite the close ties that remained, immigration was sharply restricted to only 50 to 100 persons annually until the 1965 Immigration Act lifted these quotas. Before the restrictions were removed, pineapple growers in Hawaii lobbied successfully to import Filipino workers to the islands. Another exception was the U.S. Navy, which put Filipino citizens to work in kitchens. Filipino veterans of World War II had believed their U.S. citizenship would be expedited. This proved untrue; the problem was only partially resolved by a 1994 federal court ruling. Similarly, many of the 14,000 Filipinos employed as mess stewards by the Navy later settled in the United States. However, many of these workers felt they were not welcomed as former Navy employees but as unwanted immigrants (P. Calica 1995; Y. Espiritu 1996).

Filipino immigration can be divided into four distinct periods:

1. The first generation, immigrating in the 1920s, was mostly male and employed in agricultural labor.
2. A second group, also arriving in the early twentieth century, immigrated into Hawaii to serve as contract workers on Hawaii's sugar plantations.
3. The post-World War II arrivals included many war veterans and brides of U.S. servicemen.
4. The newest immigrants, who include many professionals (physicians, nurses, and others), arrived under the 1965 Immigration Act (H. Kitano 1997; P. Min 1995; A. Pido 1986).

As within other Asian groups, the people are diverse. Besides these stages of immigration, the Filipinos can also be defined by various states of immigration—different languages, regions of origin, and religions—distinctions that sharply separate people in their homeland as well. In the Philippines and among Filipino immigrants to the United States, eight distinct languages with 200 dialects are spoken. Yet assimilation is underway; a 1995 survey showed that 47 percent of younger Filipino Americans speak only English and do not speak Tagalog, the primary language of the Philippine people (K. Kang 1996; A. Pido 1986).

THE PRESENT PICTURE

The Filipino population increased dramatically when restrictions on immigration were eased in 1965. More than two-thirds of the new arrivals qualified for entry as professional and technical workers, but like Koreans, they have often worked at jobs below those they left in the Philippines. Surprisingly, U.S.-born Filipinos often have less formal schooling and lower job status than the newer arrivals. They come from poorer families that are unable to afford higher education, and they have been relegated to unskilled work, including migrant farm work. Their relatively poor economic background means that they have little start-up capital for businesses. Therefore, unlike other Asian American groups, Filipinos have not developed small-business bases such as retail or service outlets that capitalize on their ethnic culture.

The volume of Philippine exports to the United States is low—less than one-third of South Korean exports. The Filipino exports are mostly agricultural, and so their volume and the content of the products do not provide an opening for small businesses. Filipinos, therefore, have been absorbed into primarily low-wage, private-sector jobs. Prospects for immediate economic advancement for Filipino Americans as a group seem dim (Bureau of the Census 1998c:803–804; P. Min 1987, 1995; Nee and Sanders 1985).

Despite their numbers, no significant Filipino social organization has formed, for several reasons. First, Filipinos' strong loyalty to family and church, particularly Roman Catholicism, works against time-consuming efforts to create organizations that include a broad spectrum of the Filipino community. Second, the people's diversity makes forming ties here problematic. A 1995 survey of Filipino Americans revealed that 72 percent agreed that rivalries within the Filipino community make it difficult for the community to have one strong voice. Third, though Filipinos have organized many groups, these tend to be clublike or fraternal. They do not seek to represent the general Filipino population and therefore remain invisible to Anglos. Fourth, although Filipinos initially stayed close to events in their homeland, they show every sign of seeking involvement in broader non-Filipino organizations and avoiding group exclusiveness. The election of Filipino-American Benjamin Cayetano as governor of Hawaii in 1994 is an example of such involvement in mainstream political organization (Y. Espiritu 1996; K. Kang 1996; Lin and Arguelles 1995; H. Melendy 1980).

Asian Indians

Among the four largest Asian American groups are the immigrants from India and their descendants. Sometimes the immigrants from Pakistan, Bangladesh, and Sri Lanka are also included in this group.

IMMIGRATION

Like several other Asian immigrant groups, Asian Indians (or East Indians) are relatively recent immigrants. Only 17,000 total came from 1820 to 1965, with the majority of those arriving before 1917. These pioneers were subjected to some of the same anti-Asian measures passed to restrict Chinese immigration. In the ten years following the Immigration and Naturalization Act, which eliminated national quotas, over 110,000 arrived (R. Takaki 1989).

Immigration law, while dropping nationality preferences, gave priority to the skilled, so the Asian Indians arriving in the 1960s through the 1980s tended to be urban, educated, and English-speaking. Three times the proportion of Asian Indians aged twenty-five and over had a college degree compared to the general population. These families experienced a relatively smooth transition from life in India to life in the United States. They usually settled here in urban areas or located

Reflecting the growth of the Indian American population, the landscape is changing. A Hindu priest makes his way toward the entrance to the largest Hindu temple in the United States, which is located outside Chicago.

near universities or medical centers. Initially they flocked to the northeast, but by 1990, California had edged out New York as the state with the largest concentration of Asian Indians (M. Mogelonsky 1995).

The transition for the new arrivals from India was not without the costs familiar to many immigrant groups. Asian Indians often worked much longer hours than did their U.S. counterparts and sought even more education to facilitate their acquiring desired employment (J. Jensen 1980).

More recent immigrants, sponsored by earlier immigrant relatives, are displaying less facility with English, and the training they have tends to be less easily adapted to the U.S. workplace. They are more likely to work in service industries, usually with members of their extended families. They are often in positions that many Americans reject because of the long hours, the seven-day workweek, and vulnerability to crime. Consequently, Asian Indians are employed as frequently as cab drivers or managers of motels or convenience stores as they are as physicians or college teachers. Asian Indians see the service industries as transitional jobs to acclimatize them to the United States and to give them the money they need to become more economically self-reliant (M. Mogelonsky 1995; C. Woodyard 1995).

THE PRESENT PICTURE

It is difficult to generalize about Asian Indians because, like all Asian Americans, they reflect a diverse population. With 950 million people in 1996, India is the second most populous nation in the world. Diversity governs every area. The Indian government recognizes fifteen official languages, each with its own cultural heritage. Some can be written in more than one type of script. While Hindus are the majority in India and among the immigrants to the United States, significant religious minorities include Sikhs, Muslims, and Zoroastrians.

Religion among Asian Indians presents an interesting picture. Among the initial immigrants, religious orthodoxy is often stronger than it is in India. Immigrants make concerted efforts to practice the Hindu and Muslim faiths true to their practices in India, rather than joining the Caribbean versions of these major faiths already established in the United States by other immigrant groups. While other Indian traditions are maintained, older immigrants see challenges not only from U.S. culture, but also from pop culture from India, which is imported through motion pictures and magazines. It is a very dynamic situation that is likely to undergo change as the Asian Indian population moves into the twenty-first century (J. Lessinger 1995).

Maintaining traditions within the family household is a major challenge for Indian immigrants to the United States. Parents are concerned about the erosion of traditional family authority. Children, dressed like their peers, go to fast-food restaurants and eat hamburgers while out on their own—yet both Hindus and Muslims are vegetarian by practice. Sons do not feel the responsibility to the family that tradition dictates. Daughters, whose occupation and marriage could, in India, be closely controlled by the family, assert their right to choose work and select a husband or, in an even more dramatic breech with tradition, remain single (Jain and Belsky 1997; J. Jensen 1980).

Arranged marriage is a custom at variance with U.S. customs. Marriages arranged by one's parents and other relatives are the subject of endless discussion among second-generation Indian immigrants. One study showed that at least one-third of Asian Indian young people in California seemed still to accept the custom, but the balance rejected it in varying degrees. Sometimes feeling pressure, a young person may allow his parents to introduce him to "eligible" mates, but the event may be more simply tolerated than regarded as a step toward marriage. Many people may find it difficult to understand how a young man or woman growing up in the United States, attending high school dances, and joining a sorority or fraternity in college could accept an arranged or even a semi-arranged marriage. Many Asian Indian young people, however, see the involvement of their parents as a possible improvement over potential rejection and failure, as well as the sexual pressure that is integral to the contemporary dating scene. However, it would be incorrect to assume that arranged marriages, like other family customs, are not changing significantly because of the practices of the host society (J. Lessinger 1995; R. Segall 1998).

Southeast Asian Americans

The people of Southeast Asia—Vietnamese, Cambodians, and Laotians—were part of the former French Indochinese Union. Indochinese is an umbrella term used for convenience; the peoples of these areas are ethnically and linguistically diverse. Ethnic Laotians constitute only half of the Laotian people, for example; a significant number of Mon-Khmer, Yao, and Hmong form minorities (Kitano and Daniels 1988; M. Wright 1980).

THE REFUGEES

The problem of U.S. involvement in Indochina did not end when all U.S. personnel were withdrawn from South Vietnam in 1975. The final tragedy was the reluctant welcome given to the refugees from Vietnam, Cambodia, and Laos by Americans and people of other nations. One week after the evacuation of Vietnam in April 1975, a Gallup poll reported that 54 percent of Americans were against giving sanctuary to the Asian refugees, with 36 percent in favor and 11 percent undecided. The primary objection to Vietnamese immigration was that it would further increase unemployment (Schaefer and Schaefer 1975).

Many Americans offered to house refugees in their homes, but others declared that the United States had too many Asians already and was in danger of losing its "national character." This attitude toward the Indochinese has been characteristic of the feeling that Harvard sociologist David Riesman termed the **gook syndrome.** Gook is a derogatory term for an Asian, and the syndrome refers to the tendency to stereotype these people in the worst possible light. Riesman believed that the American news media created an unflattering image of the South Vietnamese and their government, leading the American people to believe they were not worth saving (C. Luce 1975:E19).

The initial 135,000 Vietnamese refugees who fled in 1975 were joined by more than a million running from the later fighting and religious persecution that plagued Indochina. The United States accepted about half of the refugees, some of them the so-called boat people, primarily Vietnamese of ethnic Chinese background, who took to the ocean in overcrowded vessels, hoping that some ship would pick them up and offer sanctuary. Hundreds of thousands were placed in other nations or remain in overcrowded refugee camps administered by the United Nations.

As immigration to the United States continued, so, too, did mixed feelings among people in the United States. Surveys in the 1980s showed that 30 to 50 percent of Americans still worried that the refugees would be an economic drain. Furthermore, some critics argued that the movement that began as a genuine refugee flow had clearly shifted to a migratory flow composed of some refugees, a growing number of people seeking family reunification, and an even larger economic migrant component (B. Gwertzman 1985; Starr and Roberts 1981).

THE PRESENT PICTURE

Like other immigrants, the refugees from Vietnam, Laos, and Cambodia face a difficult adjustment. Few expect to return to their homeland for visits, and fewer expect ever to return there permanently. Therefore, many look to the United States as their permanent home and the home of their children. The adult immigrants still, however, accept jobs well below their occupational positions in Southeast Asia; geographic mobility has been accompanied by downward social mobility. For example, only a small fraction of refugees employed as managers in Vietnam have been employed in similar positions in the United States. Language is also a factor; a person trained as a manager cannot hold that position in the United States until his English is fairly fluent. The available data indicate that refugees from Vietnam have increased their earnings at a relatively fast rate, often by working long hours. Partly because Southeast Asian people comprise significantly different subgroups, assimilation as well as acceptance is not likely to occur at the same rate for all (J. Freeman 1995).

Even though most refugee children spoke no English upon their arrival here, they have done extremely well in school. Studies indicate that immigrant parents place great emphasis on education and are pleased by the prospect of their children going to college—something very rare in their homelands. The children do very well with this encouragement, which is not unlike that offered by Mexican immigrants to their children, as we discussed in Chapter 10. It remains to be seen whether this motivation will decline as the next young generation looks more to their American peers as role models (J. Freeman 1995; Zhous and Bankston 1998).

The picture for young Southeast Asians in the United States is not completely pleasant. Crime is present in virtually all ethnic groups, but some fear that in this case it has two very ugly aspects. Some of this crime may represent reprisals for the war: anticommunists and communist sympathizers who continue their conflicts here. At the same time, gangs are emerging, as young people seek the support of close-knit groups even if they engage in illegal and violent activities. This pattern is, of course, very similar to that followed by all groups in the United States. Indeed, defiance of authority can be regarded as a sign of assimilation. Another unpleasant but

The Eden shopping center in Falls Church, Virginia, during a busy Sunday. First opened in 1984 to serve the growing Vietnamese American population, the center underwent an expansion in 1996.

well-documented aspect of the present picture is the series of violent episodes directed at Southeast Asians by Whites and others expressing resentment over their employment or even their mere presence (P. Long 1996; National Asian Pacific American Legal Consortium 1996; S. St. Pierre 1995; Zhou and Bankston 1998).

In contrast to its inaction concerning earlier immigrant groups, the federal government involved itself conspicuously in locating homes for the refugees from Vietnam, Cambodia, and Laos. Pressured by many communities afraid of being overwhelmed by immigrants, government agencies attempted to disperse the refugees throughout the nation. Such efforts failed, though, mostly because the refugees, like European immigrants before them, sought out their compatriots. As a result, Southeast Asian communities and neighborhoods have become visible, especially in California and Texas. In such areas, where immigrants from Asia have reestablished some cultural practices from their homeland, a more pluralistic solution to their adjustment seems a possible alternative to complete assimilation. Also, Southeast Asians living outside of metropolitan areas may make frequent trips to urban areas such as Chicago, where they can stock up on food, books, and even videotapes in their native language (Aguillar-San Juan 1998).

In 1995, the United States initiated normal diplomatic relations with Vietnam, which is leading to more movement between the nations. Gradually, Vietnamese Americans are returning to visit, but generally not to take up permanent residence. **Viet Kieu,** Vietnamese living abroad, are making the return—some 270,000 in 1996 compared to only 80,000 four years earlier. While data are unavailable for how many are coming from the United States, it is the country with the largest Viet Kieu community. Such movement back and forth will help to keep Vietnamese culture alive in the United States (D. Lamb 1997).

CASE STUDY: A HMONG COMMUNITY

Wausau (population 37,000) is a community located in rural Wisconsin, best known, perhaps, for the insurance company bearing its name. To sociologists, it is distinctive for its sizable Hmong (pronounced "Mong") population. Wausau finds itself with the greatest percentage of Hmong of any city in Wisconsin. These Southeast Asians account for 10 percent of the city's population and 22 percent of its kindergarten pupils. But because the Hmong are concentrated in the more affordable downtown area of Wausau, they constitute as much as 62 percent of the students in some schools. The Hmong immigrated to the United States from Laos and Vietnam following the April 1975 end of the U.S. involvement in Vietnam. Coming from a very rural, peasant society, the immigrants faced dramatic adjustment upon arrival in the United States (N. Teijesen 1998).

Wausau school officials believed that progress in teaching the Hmong English was stymied because the newcomers continued to associate with each other and spoke only their native tongue. In the fall of 1993, the Wausau school board decided to distribute the Hmong and other poor students more evenly by restructuring its elementary schools in a scheme that requires two-way busing.

The desegregation has divided the city, and its residents voted in a 1993 special election to decide whether to recall the five school board members who had backed the plan. "People feel this decision was just stuffed down their throats," said Peter Beltz, the director of Families Approve Neighborhood Schools (FANS), which fielded candidates and gathered the signatures for the recall (R. Worthington 1993).

Wausau school officials said that their plan, which is not federally mandated, is aimed less at integration and more at achieving an equitable socioeconomic balance and learning environment. The busing, they say, had began as a convenience for parents, whose children now travel an average of 2 miles farther than before.

Pictured displaying their traditional dress, the Hmong are one of several distinctive groups that are part of the larger Asian American population in the United States.

Recalls of elected officials are rare in the United States, but in December 1993 opponents of the busing plan organized a special election that led to the removal of the five board members. This left the Wausau board with a majority who opposed the busing plan that had integrated Asian American youngsters into mostly White elementary schools. "Busing and partner schools as envisioned is [sic] over," declared Don Langlois, one of the winners, after the votes were counted on a Tuesday night. "We plan to have a neighborhood school plan for the fall 1994 school year," Langlois said (*Chicago Tribune* 1993).

How events will unfold in Wausau are unclear. However, positive signs are identifiable in Wausau and other centers of Hmong life in the United States. While many struggle to make a go of it economically, large numbers are able to move off public assistance. Welfare dependency dropped from 77 percent to 12 percent between 1987 and 1997 in Wisconsin. Language barriers and lack of formal schooling still are barriers encountered by older Hmong residents, but soon a younger generation will be emerging to face some of the same identity and assimilation questions experienced by other Asian American groups (L. Feldman 1998; W. Smith 1997).

Korean Americans

The population of Korean Americans is now nearly as large as that of Japanese Americans, yet Korean Americans are often overlooked in studies in favor of groups such as Chinese Americans and Japanese Americans who have a longer historical tradition.

HISTORICAL BACKGROUND

Today's Korean American community is the result of three waves of immigration. The initial wave of a little more than 7,000 immigrants came to the United States between 1903 and 1910, when laborers migrated to Hawaii. Under Japanese colonial rule (1910–1945), Korean migration was halted except for a few hundred "picture brides" allowed to join their prospective husbands.

The second wave took place during and after the Korean War, accounting for about 14,000 immigrants from 1951 through 1964. Most of these immigrants were war orphans and wives of American servicemen. Relatively little research has been done on these first two periods of immigration.

The third wave was initiated by the passage of the 1965 Immigration Act, which made it much easier for Koreans to immigrate. During the four years before passage of the act, Koreans accounted for only 7 of every 1,000 immigrants. In the first four years after the act's passage, 38 of every 1,000 immigrants to the United States were Korean. This third wave, which continues today, reflects the admission priorities set up in the 1965 immigration law. These immigrants have been well educated and have arrived in the United States with professional skills (P. Min 1995).

Many of the most recent immigrants, though, must at least initially settle for positions of lower responsibility than those they held in Korea and must pass through a period of "exigency" or disenchantment, as described in Chapter 2. The problems documented reflect the pain of adjustment—stress, loneliness, alcoholism, family strife, and mental disorders. Korean American immigrants who accompanied their parents to the United States when young now occupy a middle, marginal position between the cultures of Korea and the United States. They have also been termed the **ilchomose,** or "1.5 generation": today, they are middle-aged, remain bilingual and bicultural, and tend to form the professional class in the Korean American community (W. Hurh 1990, 1998; Hurh and Kim 1988; M. Quintanila 1996).

THE PRESENT PICTURE

Today's young Korean Americans face many of the cultural conflicts common to any initial generation born in a new country. The parents may speak the native tongue, but the signs on the road to opportunity are in the English language, and the road itself runs through U.S. culture. It is very difficult to maintain a sense of Korean culture in the United States; the host society is not particularly helpful. Although the United States fought a war there and U.S. troops remain in South Korea, Korean culture is very foreign to contemporary Americans. In the few studies of attitudes toward Koreans, White Americans respond with vague, negative attitudes or simply lump Korean Americans with other Asian groups.

Studies by social scientists indicate that Korean Americans face many problems typical for immigrants, such as difficulties with language. In Los Angeles, home to the largest concentration, more than 100 churches have only Korean-language services, and local television stations feature several hours of Korean programs. The Korean immigrants' high level of education should help them cope with the challenge. While Korean Americans stress conventional schooling as a means to success, Korean schools have also been established in major cities. Typically operated on

Saturday afternoons, they offer classes in Korean history, customs, music, and language to help students maintain their cultural identity (Abelman and Lie 1995; Hurh and Kim 1982, 1984; D. Lee 1992).

Korean American women commonly participate in the labor force, as do many other Asian American women. About 60 percent of U.S.-born Korean American women and half the women born abroad work in the labor force. These figures may not seem striking compared with the data for White women, but the cultural differences make the figures more significant. Korean women come here from a family system with established, well-defined marital roles: the woman is expected to serve as homemaker and mother only. Although these roles are carried over to the United States, women are pressed, because of their husbands' struggles to establish themselves, to help support their families financially as well.

Many Korean American men begin small service or retail businesses and gradually involve their wives in the business. Wages do not matter as the household mobilizes to make a profitable enterprise out of a marginal business. Under economic pressure, Korean American women must move away from traditional cultural roles. The move, however, is only partial; studies show that despite the high rate of participation in the labor force by Korean immigrant wives, first-generation immigrant couples continue in sharply divided gender roles in other aspects of daily living (Kim and Hurh 1984, 1985a, 1985b; P. Min 1995).

Korean American businesses are seldom major operations—most are relatively small. They do benefit from a special form of development capital (or cash) used to subsidize businesses, called a **kye** (pronounced "kay"). Korean Americans pool their money through the kye—an association that grants members money on a rotating basis to allow them to gain access to additional capital. Kyes depend on trust and are not protected by laws or insurance, as bank loans are. Kyes work as follows. Say, for example, that twelve people agree to contribute $500 a month. Then, once a year, one of these individuals receives $6,000. Few records are kept because the entire system is built on trust and friendship. Rotating credit associations are not unique to Korean Americans; they have, for example, been used in the United States by West Indians and Ethiopians. Not all Korean business entrepreneurs use the kye, but it does represent a significant source of capital. A 1984 Chicago survey revealed that 34 percent of Korean merchants relied on a kye (M. Goozner 1987; I. Light 1996; Light and Bonacich 1988; L. Sun 1995).

In the early 1990s, nationwide attention was given to the friction between Korean Americans and other subordinate groups, primarily African Americans, but also Hispanics. In New York City, Los Angeles, and Chicago, Korean American merchants confronted African Americans allegedly robbing them. The African American neighborhood sometimes responded with hostility to what they perceived as the disrespect and arrogance of the Korean American entrepreneurs toward their Black customers. Such friction is not new; earlier generations of Jewish, Italian, and Arab merchants encountered similar hostility from what to outsiders seems an unlikely source, another oppressed subordinate group. The contemporary conflict was dramatized in Spike Lee's 1989 movie, *Do the Right Thing,* in which African Americans and Korean Americans clashed. The situation arose because Korean Americans are the latest immigrant group prepared to cater to the needs of the inner city that has been abandoned by those who have moved up the economic ladder (Weitzer 1997).

The tension that can arise between subordinate groups gained national attention during the 1992 riots in south-central Los Angeles. In that city's poor areas, the only shops in which to buy groceries, liquor, or gasoline are owned by Korean immigrants. They have largely replaced the White business owners who left the ghetto area after the 1965 Watts riot. African Americans were well aware of the dominant role Korean Americans played in their local retail market. Some Blacks' resentment of the Koreans had previously been fueled by the 1991 fatal shooting of a fifteen-year-old Black girl by a Korean grocer in a dispute over a payment for orange juice. The resentment grew when the grocer, convicted of manslaughter, had her prison sentence waived by a judge in favor of a five-year probation period.

The 1992 riots focused in part on retailers in south-central Los Angeles and therefore on Korean Americans. During the unrest, 2,000 Korean businesses valued at $350 million were destroyed. In a postriot survey of those African Americans arrested, 80 percent felt that Korean Americans had been disrespectful to African Americans, compared to 56 percent who felt similarly about Whites. Desire to succeed had led Korean Americans to the inner city, where they did not face competition from Whites. But it also meant that they had to deal on a daily basis with the frustration of another minority group. As a direct outgrowth of the violence and tension, numerous cross-ethnic groups have been organized in Los Angeles

Kibook Yoo, whose liquor store was ruined in the Los Angeles riots, learned that her insurance did not cover the loss. About 2,000 other Korean American businesses were also destroyed.

and other cities, such as Chicago and New York City, to improve relations between Korean Americans and subordinate groups (Commission on Civil Rights 1992; Diaz-Veizades and Chang 1996; D. Fears 1998; Kim and Kim 1998).

Among Korean Americans, the church is the most visible organization holding the group together. Half the immigrants had been affiliated with Christian churches prior to immigrating. One study of Koreans in Chicago and Los Angeles found that 70 percent were affiliated with Korean ethnic churches, mostly Presbyterian, with small numbers of Roman Catholics and Methodists. Korean ethnic churches are the fastest-growing segment of the Presbyterian and Methodist faiths. The church performs an important function, apart from its religious one, in giving Korean Americans a sense of attachment and a practical way to meet other Korean Americans. The churches are much more than simply sites for religious services; they assume multiple secular roles for the Korean community. As the second generation seeks a church with which to affiliate as adults, they may find the ethnic church and its Korean-language services less attractive, but for now, the fellowship in which Korean Americans participate is both spiritual and ethnic (Kim and Kim 1995).

Hawaii and Its People

The entire state of Hawaii (or Hawai'i) appears to be the complete embodiment of cultural diversity. Nevertheless, despite a dramatic blending of different races living together, prejudice, discrimination, and pressure to assimilate are very much present in Hawaii. As we will see, life on the island is much closer to that in the rest of the country than to the ideal of a pluralistic society. Hawaii's population is unquestionably diverse, as shown in Table 11.1. To grasp contemporary social relationships, we must first understand the historical circumstances that brought races together on the islands—the various Asian peoples plus the **Haoles** (pronounced "hah-oh-lehs"), the term frequently used to refer to Whites in Hawaii.

Table 11.1 Hawaii: Racial Composition, 1950 and 1990

	1950		1990	
Racial Group	Percent	Total	Percent	Total
White	23.0	114,793	33.4	369,616
Japanese	36.9	184,598	22.3	247,486
Filipino	12.2	61,062	15.2	168,682
Hawaiian	17.2	86,090	11.7	129,663
Chinese	6.5	32,376	6.2	68,804
Black	.5	2,651	2.4	27,195
Korean	1.4	7,030	2.2	24,454
All other	2.2	11,169	6.6	72,329
Total	99.9	499,769	100.0	1,108,229

Sources: A. Lind 1969: 47; Bureau of the Census 1991a; J. Ng, 1991. Hawaiian 1990 count is the author's estimate.

HISTORICAL BACKGROUND

Geographically remote, Hawaii was initially populated by Polynesian people who had their first contact with Europeans in 1778, when English explorer Captain James Cook arrived. The Hawaiians (who killed Cook) tolerated the subsequent arrival of plantation operators and missionaries. Fortunately, the Hawaiian people were united under a monarchy and received respect from the European immigrants, a respect that developed into a spirit of goodwill. Slavery was never introduced, even during the colonial period, as it was in so many areas of the Western Hemisphere. Nevertheless, the effect of the White arrival on the Hawaiians themselves was disastrous. Civil warfare and disease had reduced the number of full-blooded natives to fewer than 30,000 by 1900, and the number is probably well under 10,000 now. Meanwhile, large sugarcane plantations imported laborers from China, Portugal, Japan, and, in the early 1900s, the Philippines, Korea, and Puerto Rico.

In 1893, a revolution encouraged by foreign commercial interests overthrew the monarchy. During the revolution, the United States landed troops, and five years later, Hawaii was annexed as a territory to the United States. The 1900 Organic Act guaranteed racial equality, but foreign rule dealt a devastating psychological blow to the proud Hawaiian people. American rule had mixed effects on relations among the races. Citizenship laws granted civil rights to all those born on the islands, not just the wealthy Haoles. However, the anti-Asian laws still applied, excluding the Chinese and Japanese from political participation.

The twentieth century witnessed Hawaii's transition from a plantation frontier to the fiftieth state and an integral part of the national economy. During that transition, Hawaii became a strategic military outpost, although that role has had only a limited effect on race relations. Even the attack on Pearl Harbor had relatively little influence on Japanese Americans in Hawaii.

THE PRESENT PICTURE

Hawaii has achieved some fame for its good race relations. Tourists, who are predominantly White, have come from the mainland and have seen and generally accepted the racial harmony. Admittedly, Waikiki Beach, where large numbers of tourists congregate, is atypical of the islands, but even there tourists cannot ignore the differences in intergroup relations.

One clear indication of the multicultural nature of the islands is the degree of exogamy—marrying outside one's own group. The out-group marriage rate varies annually but seems to be stabilizing; about 45 percent of all marriages performed in the state involving residents are exogamous. The rate varies by group from a low of 34 to 39 percent among Koreans and Haoles to 58 percent among Chinese and Blacks (Hawaii 1994).

A closer look shows that equality among the people is not absolute, let alone among the races as groups. The pineapple and sugarcane plantation legacy persists. A 1972 estimate placed 97 percent of Hawaiian workers in the employ of forty landholders. One estate alone owned nearly one-tenth of the state's territory. Native Hawaiians tend to be least well off, working land they do not own. The economy is dominated by Japanese Americans and Haoles. The **AJAs** (Americans of Japanese ancestry, as they are called in Hawaii) are especially important in education, where they account for nearly 58 percent of teachers, and in politics, where they dominate. The political activity of the AJAs certainly contrasts to that of mainland Japanese Americans. The majority of the state legislators are AJAs. Chinese Americans have been successful in business in Hawaii, but top positions are almost all filled by Haoles. Recent immigrants from Asia and, more significantly, even long-term residents of Filipino and Hawaiian descent, showed little evidence of sharing in Hawaii's overall picture of affluence (T. Kaser 1977; W. Turner 1972; Wright and Gardner 1983).

Prejudice and discrimination are not alien to Hawaii. Attitudinal surveys show definite racial preferences and sensitivity to color differences. Housing surveys taken before the passage of civil rights legislation showed that many people were committed to nondiscrimination, but racial preferences were still present. Residential neighborhoods are sometimes dominated by certain groups, but there are no racial ghettos. As shown in Figure 11.3, the various racial groups are not distributed uniformly among the islands, but they are clustered rather than segregated. All civilian census tracts in Honolulu have residents of the five largest groups: Haoles, Japanese, Chinese, Hawaiian, and Filipino.

Discrimination by exclusive social clubs exists but is diminishing. Groups such as the Rotary and Lions' clubs opened their doors to Asians in Hawaii before they did on the mainland. Undoubtedly, Hawaii has gradually absorbed the mainland's racial consciousness, but a contrast between the islands and the rest of the nation remains. Evidence of racial harmony is much more abundant. Hawaii has never known forced school segregation, Jim Crow laws, slavery, or laws prohibiting racial intermarriage.

The multiracial character of the islands will not change quickly, but the identity of the native Hawaiians has already been overwhelmed. While rich in cultural heritage, they tend to be very poor and often view the U.S. occupation as the beginning of their cultural and economic downfall. The organization *Ka Lahui Hawaii,* or Hawaiian Nation, is seeking to have Hawaiian native people receive federal recognition similar to that accorded mainland tribes; to date, that recognition has not occurred. This growing effort, often referred to as the pro-sovereignty movement, has also sought restoration of the native Hawaiian land that has been lost to Anglos over the last century, or compensation for it.

Sol Kaho'ohalahala, chair of the Hawaiian sovereignty councils, speaks in favor of sovereignty being extended to native Hawaiians.

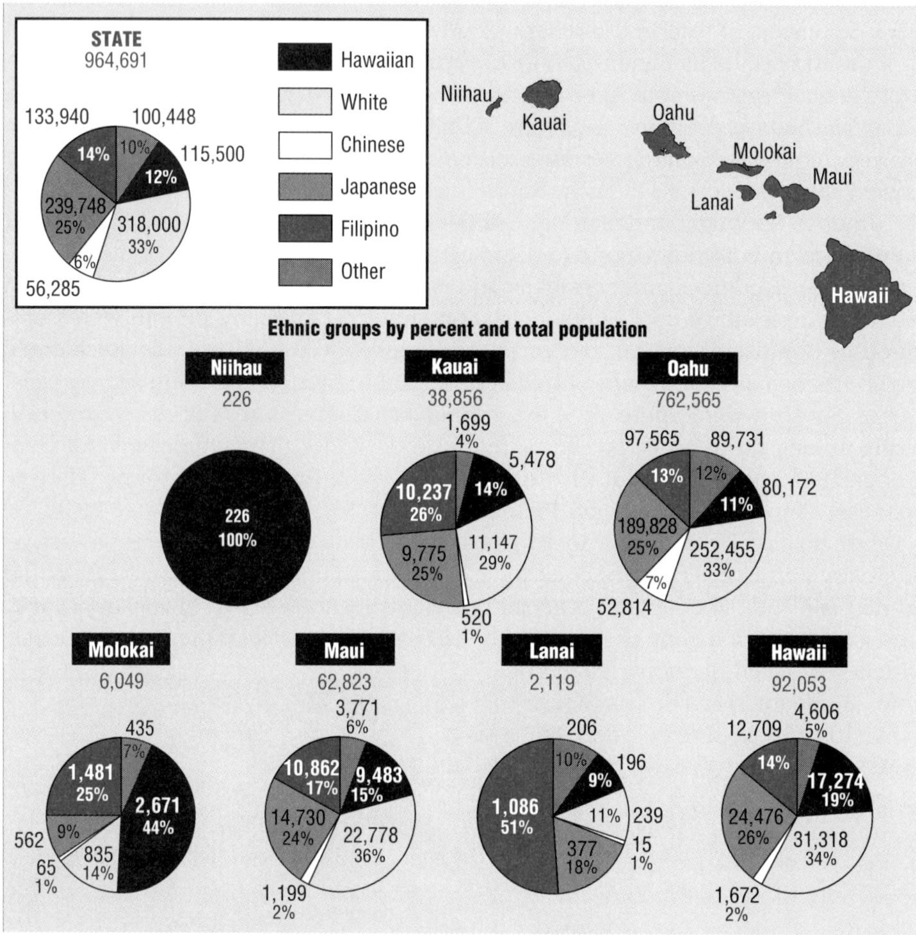

Figure 11.3 Racial Distribution in the Hawaiian Islands
There are few racial enclaves in Hawaii. The best known is Niihau, a privately owned island on which only Hawaiians are permitted to live.

Source: Department of Geography, University of Hawaii, *Atlas of Hawaii,* 2d ed. Honolulu: University of Hawaii Press, 1983:113.

Sometimes, the native Hawaiians successfully form alliances with environmental groups that wish to halt further commercial development on the islands. In 1996, a native Hawaiian vote was held seeking a response to the question, "Shall the Hawaiian people elect delegates to propose a native Hawaiian government?" The results indicated 73 percent voting were in favor of such a government structure (E. Nakashima 1996; J. Morín 1997; D. Ward 1996).

In an absolute sense, Hawaii is not a racial paradise. Certain occupations and even social classes tend to be dominated by a single racial group. Hawaii is not immune to intolerance, and it is expected that the people will not totally resist prejudice as the island's isolation is reduced. On the other hand, newcomers to the islands do set aside some of their old stereotypes and prejudices. The future of race relations in Hawaii is uncertain, but relative to the mainland and much of the world, Hawaii's race relations are characterized more by harmony than discord.

CONCLUSION

Despite the diversity among groups of Asian Americans, they have spent generations being treated as a monolithic group. Out of similar experiences have come panethnic identities in which people share a self-image, as do African Americans or Whites of European descent. As we noted in Chapter 1, **panethnicity** is the development of solidarity among ethnic subgroups. Are Asian Americans finding a panethnic identity? It is true that, in the United States, extremely different Asian nationalities have been lumped together in past discrimination and present stereotyping. Asian Americans now see the need to unify their diverse subgroups. After centuries of animosity between ethnic groups in Asia, any feelings of community among Asian Americans must develop anew here; they bring none with them (E. Lie 1998; Ong and Umemoto 1994; N. Onishi 1996).

Asian Americans are a rapidly growing group, with well over 7 million now living in the United States. Despite striking differences among them, they are frequently viewed as if they arrived all at once and from one culture. They are often characterized, too, as a successful or model minority. Individual cases of success and some impressive group data do not imply, however, that the diverse group of peoples who make up the Asian American community are uniformly successful. Indeed, despite significantly high levels of formal schooling, Asian Americans earn far less than Whites with comparable education and continue to be victims of discriminatory employment practices.

The diversity within the Asian American community belies the similarity suggested by the panethnic label of Asian American. Chinese and Japanese Americans share a history of several generations in the United States. Filipinos are veterans of a half-century of direct U.S. colonization and a cooperative role with the military. In contrast, Vietnamese, Koreans, and Japanese are associated in a negative way with three wars. Korean Americans come from a nation that still has a major U.S. military presence and a persisting "cold war" mentality. Korean Americans and Chinese Americans have taken on middleman roles, while Filipinos, Asian Indians, and Japanese Americans tend to avoid the ethnic enclave pattern.

Who are the Asian Americans? This chapter has begun to answer that question by focusing on four of the larger groups: Filipino Americans, Asian Indians, Southeast Asian Americans, and Korean Americans. Hawaii is a useful model because its relatively harmonious social relationships cross racial lines. Though it is not an interracial paradise, Hawaii does illustrate that, given proper historical and economic conditions, continuing conflict is not inevitable. Chinese and Japanese Americans, the subjects of Chapter 12, have experienced problems in American society despite striving to achieve economic and social equality with the dominant majority.

KEY TERMS

AJAs 348
gook syndrome 340
Haoles 347
ilchomose 344
kye 345
middlemen minorities 329
model or ideal minority 327
panethnicity 351
Viet Kieu 342
yellow peril 320

REVIEW QUESTIONS

1. In what respects has the mass media image of Asian Americans been both undifferentiated and negative?
2. How is the model-minority image a disservice to both Asian Americans and other subordinate racial and ethnic groups?
3. How has the tendency of many Korean Americans to help each other been an asset but is also viewed with suspicion by those outside their community?
4. What critical events or legislative acts increased each Asian American group's immigration into the United States?
5. To what degree do race relations in Hawaii offer both promise and a chilling dose of reality to the future of race and ethnicity on the mainland?

CRITICAL THINKING

1. How is the model-minority image reinforced by images in the media?
2. Coming of age is difficult for anyone given the ambiguities of adolescence in the United States. How is it doubly difficult for the children of immigrants? How do you think the immigrants themselves, such as those from Asia, view this process?
3. "American Indians," "Hispanics," and "Asian Americans" are all convenient terms to refer to diverse groups of people. Do you see these broad umbrella terms as being more appropriate for one group than the others?

INTERNET EXERCISE

The WWW Hmong Homepage (http://www.stolaf.edu/people/cdr/hmong/) catalogs current events, cultural information, community resources, history, and research regarding the Hmong. Visit the site and explore some of the areas that interest you. Be sure to view the following sections specifically: "Teen Feedback," "Hmong Frequently-Asked Questions," and "Hmong Pictures/Images." What does the word "Hmong" mean? What is the debate surrounding its meaning? What influence did the Vietnam War have on the Hmong people? What would it be like to live as a Hmong teenager in the United States? Would you feel connected to the wider American culture? Why or why not? In what ways does a Hmong funeral differ from ones you have experienced or heard about? What challenges do the Hmong face today?

FOR FURTHER INFORMATION

Yen Le Espiritu. *Asian American Women and Men: Labor, Laws, and Love.* Thousand Oaks, CA: Sage, 1997.
A sociological examination of differences in gender roles among various Asian American groups.

Sharon M. Lee. *Asian Americans: Diverse and Growing.* Population Bulletin 53 (June 1998).
This brief (40 pages) issue of a Population Reference Bureau publication provides a fine demographic overview of the Asian American community.

Stacy J. Lee. *Unraveling the "Model Minority" Stereotype: Listening to Asian American Youth.* New York: Teachers College Press, 1996.
A study of Asian American high school students showing how they have developed their identity and how they relate to the model-minority image.

Min Zhou and Carl L. Bankston III. *Growing Up American: How Vietnamese Children Adapt to Life in the United States.* Washington, DC: Russell Sage Foundation, 1998.
An overview of the contemporary status of Asian Americans.

PERIODICALS

Amerasia Journal (1971) is an interdisciplinary journal focusing on Asian Americans. Periodicals presenting contemporary coverage of Asian Americans include *A. Magazine: Inside Asian America* (founded in 1991), *Asian American Review* (1972), *Bridge* (1971), *Jade* (1974), and *Viet Now* (1995). The *Aloha Aina* is a newspaper that represents the interests of native Hawaiians. *AsianWeek,* published in San Francisco, stresses concerns and events in the Chinese American, Filipino American, Japanese American, and Korean American communities.

12

Chinese Americans and Japanese Americans

CHAPTER OUTLINE

HIGHLIGHTS

Present-day Chinese Americans are descendants of both pre-Exclusion Act immigrants and of those who immigrated after World War II. While Chinese Americans are associated with Chinatown and its glitter of tourism, this facade hides the poverty of the newly arrived Chinese and the discontent of the U.S.-born Chinese Americans. Japanese Americans encountered discrimination and ill treatment during the early twentieth century. The involuntary wartime internment of 113,000 Japanese Americans was the result of sentencing without charge or trial. During wartime, merely to be of Japanese ancestry was reason enough to be suspected of treason. A little more than a generation later, Japanese Americans did very well, with high educational and occupational attainment. Today, Chinese Americans and Japanese Americans experience both prejudice and discrimination despite a measure of economic success.

It was another one of those summer festivals intended to bring tourists to a community and allow local residents to show off their best. Each year in June, Macomb, Illinois, a rural college town of about 20,000 people, holds a Heritage Days weekend, complete with plays about local history, a flea market, and, of course, a parade. In 1995, however, a local manufacturer that employed 600 people decided to sponsor a float. Although the company had been welcomed into the community years earlier when manufacturing jobs that paid well were scarce, a problem arose when some local residents learned that the float would display the U.S. flag, a corporate flag, and a flag of Japan, because the company is Japanese-owned. The local Veterans of Foreign Wars refused to participate in the parade. Initially, the local American Legion Post joined the boycott, only later agreeing to participate. Eventually the company decided to display neither the U.S. nor Japanese flag, and applause greeted the float as it moved by the crowd, with only a handful of protesters present. A half-century after World War II, bitter feelings are still being played out in rural Illinois, with the target an important source of jobs and income (J. Berry 1995).

Another Illinois community has regarded Asians negatively for even longer. Pekin High School called its athletic teams the "Chinks" and featured a student dressed up as a "Chinaman," who paraded at half-time at football games and struck a gong when the team scored. Despite pressure in 1974 from the Organization of Chinese Americans and the Illinois Department of Human Relations and brief consideration of more neutral nicknames, the school retained the "Chinks" nickname until 1980, when the teams finally became the Dragons. Set against these events, it is not difficult to understand the prejudice and discrimination that have been the experience for Japanese and Chinese Americans and, for that matter, all Asian people in the United States (D. Holmberg 1974; G. Sloan 1980).

Many people in the United States find it difficult to distinguish between Japanese Americans and Chinese Americans physically, culturally, and historically. As we will see in this chapter, the two groups differ in some ways but also share similar patterns in their experiences in the United States.

Chinese Americans

China, the most populous country in the world, has been a source of immigrants for centuries. Many nations have a sizable Chinese population whose history there may be traced back more than five generations. The United States is such a nation. Even before the great migration from Europe began in the 1880s, more than 100,000 Chinese already lived in the United States. Today, Chinese Americans number over 2.2 million (see Table 12.1).

From the beginning of Chinese immigration, Americans have held conflicting views about it. In one sense, Chinese immigration was welcome because it brought to these shores needed hard-working laborers. At the same time, it was unwelcome because the Chinese brought with them an alien culture that the European settlers were unwilling to tolerate. There was also a perception of economic competition by people in the western United States, and the Chinese newcomers proved to be very convenient and powerless scapegoats. As detailed in Chapter 4, the anti-Chinese mood led to the passage of the Exclusion Act in 1882, which was not repealed until 1943. Even then, the group that lobbied for repeal, the Citizens Committee to Repeal Chinese Exclusion, encountered the old racist arguments against Chinese immigration.

Very gradually, the Chinese were permitted to enter the United States after 1943. Initially, the annual limit was 105; then several thousand wives of servicemen were admitted, and later, college students were allowed to remain after finishing their

Table 12.1 Chinese American and Japanese American Population, 1860–1997

U.S. population until Chinese immigration escalated in the 1980s.

Year	Chinese Americans	Japanese Americans
1860	34,933	—
1880	105,465	148
1900	89,863	24,326
1930	74,954	138,834
1950	117,629	141,768
1960	237,292	464,332
1970	435,062	591,290
1980	806,027	700,747
1990	1,640,000	848,000
1998	2,268,000	925,000

Source: J. Ng 1991; S. Lee 1998:15.

Data beginning with 1960 include Alaska and Hawaii

education. Not until after the 1965 Immigration Act did Chinese immigrants arrive again in large numbers, almost doubling the Chinese American community. Immigration continues to exert a major influence on the growth of the Chinese American population. It has approached 100,000 annually. The influx was so great during the 1990s that the number of new arrivals in the 1990s exceeded the total number of Chinese Americans present in 1980.

The underside of immigration, illegal immigration, is also functioning in the Chinese American community. The lure of perceived better jobs and a better life lead overseas Chinese to seek alternative routes to immigration if legal procedures are unavilable to them. The impact in some areas of the country of illegal entry can be significant. For example, a 1998 estimate placed at 12,000 the number of legal arrivals that year in New York City alone, and another 12,000 *illegal* immigrants (J. Swerdlow 1998).

OCCUPATIONAL PROFILE OF CHINESE AMERICANS

Asian Americans are employed in all aspects of the economy, and the Chinese are no exception. Superficially, they appear to do very well. They have lower unemployment rates and are better represented in professional occupations than the population as a whole. In 1990, 36 percent of Chinese Americans were employed in managerial and professional positions, compared to 26 percent of people in the United States as a whole (Bureau of the Census 1993a).

The background of the contemporary Chinese American labor force lies in Chinatown. For generations, Chinese Americans were virtually barred from working elsewhere. The Chinese Exclusion Act was only one example of discriminatory legislation. Many laws were passed that made it difficult or more expensive for

With the growth of the Chinese American population in the United States, businesses develop to cater to their needs. Bo Bo Poultry Market, located in upstate New York, produces "Buddhist-style" chicken—referring to birds sold with their heads and feet still attached and killed and prepared to precise specifications.

Chinese Americans to enter certain occupations. Whites did not object to Chinese in domestic service occupations or in the laundry trade, because most White males were uninterested in such menial, low-paying work. When given the chance to enter better jobs, as they were in wartime, Chinese Americans jumped at the opportunities. Without those opportunities, however, many Chinese Americans sought the relative safety of Chinatown. The tourist industry and the restaurants dependent on it grew out of the need for employment of the growing numbers of idle workers in Chinatown (R. Lee 1960; I. Light 1973, 1974).

New immigration has added to Chinatown's economic dependence on tourism. First, new immigrants have difficulty finding employment outside Chinatown. Potential employers who are not Asian American are reluctant to hire Chinese Americans because they believe that many are illegal aliens. Language may also be a barrier. Instead, they hire a White applicant to avoid the issue.

Second, because many new immigrants do speak little English, they flock to Chinatowns, where they are frequently employed as restaurant workers. Women may end up in the sweatshops, as we will discuss later.

CHINATOWNS TODAY

Chinatowns represent a paradox. The casual observer or tourist sees them as thriving areas of business and amusement, bright in color and lights, exotic in sounds and sights. Behind this facade, however, they have large poor populations and face the problems associated with all slums. Most Chinatowns are in older, deteriorating sections of cities. There are exceptions, such as Monterey Park outside Los Angeles, where Chinese Americans dominate the economy. However, in the older enclaves, the problems of Chinatowns include the entire range of the social ills that infest low-income areas but with even greater difficulties because the glitter sometimes conceals the problems from both outsiders and even social planners. A unique characteristic of Chinatowns, one that distinguishes them from other ethnic enclaves, is the variety of social organizations they encompass.

Organizational Life The Chinese in this country have a rich history of organizational membership, much of it carried over from China. Chief among such associations are the clans, or *tsu;* the benevolent associations, or *hui kuan;* and the secret societies, or *tongs.*

The clans, or **tsu,** that operate in Chinatown have their origins in the Chinese practice in which families with common ancestors unite. At first, immigrant Chinese continued to affiliate themselves with those sharing a family name, even if a blood relationship was absent. Social scientists agree that the influence of clans is declining as young Chinese become increasingly acculturated. The clans in the past provided mutual assistance, a function increasingly taken on by government agencies. The strength of the clans, although diminished today, still points to the extended family's important role for Chinese Americans. Social scientists have found parent-child relationships stronger and more harmonious than those among non-Chinese Americans. Just as the clans have become less significant, however, so has the family structure changed. The differences between family life in Chinese and in non-Chinese homes are narrowing with each new generation (W. Li 1976; S. Lyman 1986; B. Sung 1967).

The benevolent associations, or **hui kuan,** help their members adjust to a new life. Rather than being organized along kinship ties like the clans, *hui kuan* membership is based on the person's district of origin in China. Besides extending help with adjustment, the *hui kuan* loan money to and settle disputes among their members. They have thereby exercised wide control over their members. The various *hui kuan* are traditionally, in turn, part of an unofficial government in each city called the Chinese Six Companies, later changed to the Chinese Consolidated Benevolent Association (CCBA). The president of the CCBA is sometimes called the mayor of a Chinatown. The CCBA often protects newly arrived immigrants from the effects of racism. The organization works actively to promote political involvement among Chinese Americans and to support the democracy movement within the People's Republic of China. Some members of the Chinese community have resented, and still resent, the CCBA's authoritarian ways and its attempt to speak as the sole voice of Chinatown.

The Chinese have also organized in **tongs,** or secret societies. The secret societies' membership has been determined not by family or locale but by interest. Some have been political, attempting to resolve the dispute over which China (the People's Republic of China or the Republic of China) is the legitimate government, and others have protested the exploitation of Chinese workers. Other *tongs* provide illegal goods and services, such as drugs, gambling, and prostitution. Because they are secret, it is difficult to determine accurately the power of *tongs* today. Most observers concur that their influence has dwindled over the last fifty years and that their functions, even the illegal ones, have been taken over by elements less closely tied to Chinatown.

Some conclusions can be reached about these various social organizations. First, all have followed patterns created in traditional China. Even the secret societies had antecedents, organizationally and historically, in China. Second, all three types have performed similar functions, providing mutual assistance and representing their members' interests to a sometimes hostile dominant group. Third, because all these groups have had similar purposes and have operated in the same locale, conflict among them has been inevitable. Such conflicts were very violent in the nineteenth century, but in the twentieth century, they tended to be political. Fourth, the old associations have declined in significance, notably since the mid-1970s, as new arrivals from Asian metropolises bring little respect for the old rural ways to which such organizations were important. Fifth, when communicating with the dominant society, all these groups have downplayed the problems that afflict Chinatowns. Only recently has the magnitude of social problems become known (H. Lai 1980; S. Lyman 1974, 1986; L. Sherry 1992; W. Wei 1993; D. Ziegler 1992).

Social Problems It is a myth that Chinese Americans and Chinatowns have no problems. This false impression grows out of our tendency to stereotype groups as being all one way or the other, as well as the Chinese people's tendency to keep their problems within their community. The false image is also reinforced by the desire to maintain tourism. The tourist industry is a double-edged sword. It does provide needed jobs, even if some do pay substandard wages. But it also forces Chinatown to keep its problems quiet and not seek outside assistance, lest tourists hear of social problems and stop coming. Slums do not attract tourists. This parallel between Chinese Americans and Native Americans finds both groups depending on the tourist industry even at the cost of hiding problems (Light et al. 1994).

In the late 1960s, White society became aware that all was not right in the Chinatowns. This awareness grew not because living conditions suddenly deteriorated in Chinese American settlements but because the various community organizations could no longer maintain the facade that hid Chinatowns' social ills. Despite Chinese Americans' remarkable achievements as a group, the inhabitants suffered by most socioeconomic measures. Poor health, high suicide rates, rundown housing, rising crime rates, poor working conditions, inadequate care for the elderly, and the weak union representation of laborers were a few of the documented problems.

These problems have grown more critical as Chinese immigration has increased. For example, the population density of San Francisco's Chinatown in the late 1980s was ten times that of the city as a whole. The problems faced by elderly Chinese are also exacerbated by the immigration wave, because the proportion of older Chinese immigrants is more than twice that of older people among immigrants in general. The economic gap between Chinatown residents and outsiders is growing. As Chinese Americans become more affluent, they move out of Chinatowns. Census data for 1990 showed the household income for San Francisco's Chinatown to be under $23,000, compared to over $45,000 for the rest of the city (M. Wong 1995; A. Yip 1996).

Chinatowns such as this one in New York City represent a study of contrasts—the glitter of tourism versus the bleakness of deep pockets of poverty.

Life in Chinatown has been and still is particularly dreary for many Chinese American women. Dozens of women labor over sewing machines ten hours a day, often above a restaurant. Chinatown in New York City remained a prime site of sweatshops in the 1990s. These small businesses, often in the garment industry, consist of workers sewing twelve hours a day, six and seven days a week, and earning about $200 weekly—well below minimum wage. The workers—most of whom are women—can be victimized because they are either illegal immigrants, who may owe labor to the smugglers who brought them into the United States, or legal residents unable to find better employment (A. Finder 1995; P. Kwong 1994).

Chinatown communities continue to diversify and grow in population. Ethnic Chinese from Vietnam and other Asian countries are both revitalizing cultural traditions and bringing new ones. For example, Toysanese, Cantonese, and Fuzhounese are just a few of the languages spoken. Several dialects of Chinese are now found, thus dividing somewhat an enclave that was once more cohesive. The diversity has also led new Chinese firms to appeal to more varied preferences in cuisine, reading material, and so forth. Although outsiders may view Chinatowns as untouched by time, they are not (M. Abrahamson 1996; V. Torres 1996).

Not all Chinese live in Chinatowns; most have escaped them or never experienced their social ills. Chinatown remains important for many of those who now live outside its borders, although it is less important than in the past. For many Chinese, movement out of Chinatown is itself a sign of success. Upon moving out, however, they soon encounter discriminatory real estate practices and White parents' fears about their children playing with Chinese American youths.

Many Chinese Americans who have advanced economically have moved into new, middle-class Chinese communities. Because the suburban Los Angeles community of Monterey Park has a distinct presence of Chinese Americans, new arrivals from Taiwan have caused it to be referred to as "Little Taipei" (see Figure 11.1).

As recently as 1960, Monterey Park's population was 85 percent White, 12 percent of Spanish surname, and only 3 percent Asian and other minorities. Ten years later, Japanese represented 9 percent and Chinese 4 percent of the city's 49,166 residents. Since then, the Chinese have become the largest ethnic group, totaling over 50 percent of the 61,000 residents in 1988. During the early 1980s, the city elected its first Chinese American mayor, Lilly Chen. Not everyone has welcomed the new Chinese presence. In 1986 a sign at a gas station near the city limits, for example, displayed two slanted eyes with the inscription, "Will the last American to leave Monterey Park please bring the flag?" (T. Fong 1994; Horton et al. 1995).

The movement of Chinese Americans out of Chinatowns parallels the movement of White ethnics out of similar enclaves. It signals the upward mobility of Chinese Americans coupled with their growing acceptance by the rest of the population. This mobility and acceptance are especially evident in their presence in managerial and professional occupations noted earlier.

However, with their problems and constant influx of new arrivals, we should not lose sight that first and foremost Chinatowns are communities of people. Originally, in the nineteenth century, they emerged because the Chinese arriving in the United States had no other area in which they were allowed to settle. Today, Chinatowns represent cultural decompression chambers for new arrivals and an important symbolic focus for long-term residents. Even among many younger Chinese Americans, these ethnic enclaves serve as a source of their own identity. In "Listen to Their Voices" (on pp. 364–365), Henry Han Xi Lau, a student at Yale University, reflects on his roots in New York City's Chinatown, acknowledging that many of his generation will eventually live far from the ethnic community but still regard it always as their home.

FAMILY LIFE

Family life and religious worship are major forces shaping all immigrant groups' experience in the United States. Generally, with assimilation, cultural behavior becomes less distinctive. Family life and religious practices are no exceptions. For Chinese Americans, the latest immigration wave has helped preserve some of the old ways; but traditional cultural patterns have undergone change even in the People's Republic of China, and so the situation is very fluid.

The contemporary Chinese American family is often indistinguishable from its White counterpart, except that it is victimized by prejudice and discrimination. Older Chinese Americans and new arrivals often are dismayed by the more American behavior patterns of Chinese American youths. The lifestyle of Henry Han Xi Lau is typical of many urban youth, regardless of their race or ethnicity. Change in family life is one of the most difficult cultural changes to accept. Children questioning parental authority, which Americans grudgingly accept, is a painful experience for tradition-oriented Chinese.

Where acculturation has taken hold less strongly among Chinese Americans, the legacy of China remains. Parental authority, especially the father's, is more absolute, and the extended family is more important than is typical in middle-class families. Divorce is rare, and attitudes about sexual behavior tend to be strict because the Chinese generally frown on public expressions of emotion. We noted earlier that Chinese immigrant women in Chinatown survive a harsh existence. A related problem beginning to surface is domestic violence. While the available data do not indicate that Asian American men are any more abusive than men in other groups, their wives, as a rule, are less willing to talk about their plight and to seek help. The nation's first shelter for Asian women was established in Los Angeles in 1981, but increasingly, the problem is being recognized in more cities (Commission on Civil Rights 1992; D. Rubien 1989).

Another problem for Chinese Americans is the rise in gang activity since the mid–1970s. Battles between opposing gangs have taken their toll, including the lives of some innocent bystanders. Some trace the gangs to the tongs and thus consider them an aspect, admittedly destructive, of the cultural traditions some groups are trying to maintain. However, a more realistic interpretation is that Chinese American youth from the lower classes are not part of the model minority. Upward mobility is not in their future. Alienated, angry, and with prospects of low-wage work in restaurants and laundries, they turn to gangs such as the Ghost Shadows and Flying Dragons and force Chinese American shopkeepers to give them extortion money. Asked why he became involved in crime, one gang member replied, "To keep from being a waiter all my life" (R. Takaki 1989:451; see also K. Chin 1996).

The extended family is an important part of the Chinese American community.

LISTEN TO THEIR VOICES

I Was a Member of the Kung Fu Crew

Henry Han Xi Lau

Chinatown is ghetto, my friends are ghetto, I am ghetto. I went away to college last year, but I still have a long strand of hair that reaches past my chin. I need it when I go back home to hang with the K.F.C.—for Kung Fu Crew, not Kentucky Fried Chicken. We all met in a Northern Shaolin kung fu class years ago....

By the time my friends and I were in the eighth grade, we were able to do 20-plus push-ups on our knuckles and fingers. When we practiced our crescent, roundhouse and tornado kicks, we had 10-pound weights strapped to our legs. Someone once remarked, "Goddamn—that's a freaking mountain!" when he saw my thigh muscles in gym class.

Most Chinatown kids fall into a few general categories. There are pale-faced nerds who study all the time to get into the Ivies. There are the recent immigrants with uncombed hair and crooked teeth who sing karaoke in bars. There are the punks with highlighted hair who cut school, and the gangsters, whom everyone else avoids.

Then there is the K.F.C. We work hard like the nerds, but we identify with the punks. Now we are reunited, and just as in the old days we amble onto Canal Street, where we stick out above the older folks, elderly women bearing leaden bags of bok choy and oranges. As an opposing crew nears us, I assess them to determine whether to grill them or not. Grilling is the fine art of staring others down and trying to emerge victorious....

In the afternoon, we decide to eat at the Chinatown McDonald's for a change instead of the Chinese bakery Maria's, our

Japanese Americans

The nineteenth century was a period of vast social change for Japan: it brought the end of feudalism and the beginning of rapid urbanization and industrialization. Only a few pioneering Japanese came to the United States before 1885, because Japan prohibited emigration. After 1885, the numbers remained small relative to the great immigration from Europe at the time.

With little consideration of the specific situation, the American government began to apply against Japan the same prohibitions it applied to China. The early feelings of yellow peril were directed at the Japanese as well. The Japanese who immigrated into the United States in the 1890s took jobs as laborers at low wages under poor working conditions. Their industriousness in such circumstances made them popular with employers but unpopular with unions and other employees.

dear old hangout spot. "Mickey D's is good sit," Nel says. I answer: "But the Whopper gots more fat and meat. It's even got more bun." Nel agrees. "True that," he says. I want the Big Mac, but I buy the two-cheeseburger meal because it has the same amount of meat but costs less.

We sit and talk about ghettoness again. We can never exactly articulate what being ghetto entails, but we know the spirit of it. In Chinatown toilet facilities we sometimes find footprints on the seats because F.O.B.'s (fresh off the boats) squat on them as they do over the holes in China. We see alternative brand names in stores like Dolo instead of Polo, and Mike instead of Nike.

We live by ghettoness. My friends and I walk from 80-something Street in Manhattan to the tip of the island to save a token. We gorge ourselves at Gray's Papaya because the hot dogs are 50 cents each. But one cannot be stingy all the time. We leave good tips at Chinese restaurants because our parents are waiters and waitresses, too.

We sit for a long time in McDonald's, making sure that there is at least a half-inch of soda in our cups so that when the staff wants to kick us out, we can claim that we are not finished yet. Jack positions a mouse bite of cheeseburger in the center of a wrapper to support our claim.

After a few hours, the K.F.C. prepares to disband. I get in one of the no-license commuter vans on Canal Street that will take me to Sunset Park in Brooklyn, where my family lives now. All of my friends will leave Chinatown, for the Upper East Side and the Lower East Side, Forest Hills in Queens and Bensonhurst in Brooklyn. We live far apart, but we always come back together in Chinatown. For most of us, our homes used to be here and our world was here.

Source: Henry Han Xi Lau. "I Was a Member of the Kung Fu Crew," Reprinted by permission of the author.

Japanese Americans distinguish sharply among themselves according to the number of generations an individual's family has been in the United States. Generally, each succeeding generation is more acculturated, and each is successively less likely to know any Japanese. The **Issei** (pronounced "EE-say") are the first generation, the immigrants born in Japan. Their children, the **Nisei** ("NEE-say") are American-born. The third generation, the **Sansei** ("SAHN-say"), must go back to their grandparents to reach their roots in Japan. The **Yonsei** ("YAWN-say") are the fourth generation. Because Japanese immigration is relatively recent, these four terms describe virtually the entire contemporary Japanese American population. Some Nisei are sent by their parents to Japan for schooling and to have marriages arranged, after which they return to the United States. Japanese Americans expect such people, referred to as **Kibei** ("KEE-boy"), to be less acculturated than other Nisei. These terms are sometimes used rather loosely, and occasionally Nisei is used to describe all Japanese Americans. However, we will use them as they were intended—to differentiate the four generational groups.

The Japanese had unfortunate timing in arriving just as bigotry toward the Chinese had been legislated in the harsh Chinese Exclusion Act of 1882. For a time after the act, the Issei were welcomed by powerful business interests on the west coast. They replaced the dwindling number of Chinese laborers in some industries, especially agriculture. In time, however, anti-Japanese feeling grew out of the anti-Chinese movement. The same Whites who disliked the Chinese made the same charges about the new yellow peril. Eventually, a stereotype developed of Japanese Americans as lazy, dishonest, and untrustworthy.

The attack on Japanese Americans concentrated on limiting their ability even to earn a living. In 1913, California enacted the Alien Land Act, which 1920 amendments made still stricter. The act prohibited anyone who was ineligible for citizenship from owning land and limited leases to three years. The anti-Japanese laws permanently influenced the form that Japanese American business enterprise was to take. In California, the land laws drove the Issei into cities. In the cities, however, government and union restrictions prevented large numbers from obtaining the available jobs, leaving self-employment as the only option. Japanese, more than other groups, ran hotels, grocery stores, and other medium-sized businesses. Although this specialty limited their opportunities to advance, it did give urban Japanese Americans a marginal position in the expanding economy of the cities (E. Bonacich 1972; I. Light 1973; S. Lyman 1986).

THE WARTIME EVACUATION

Japan's attack on Pearl Harbor on December 7, 1941, brought the United States into World War II and marked a painful tragedy for the Issei and Nisei. Almost immediately, public pressure mounted to "do something" about the Japanese Americans living on the west coast. Many feared that if Japan attacked the mainland, Japanese Americans would fight on behalf of Japan, making a successful invasion a real possibility. Pearl Harbor was followed by successful Japanese invasions of one Pacific island after another. A Japanese submarine actually attacked a California oil-tank complex early in 1943.

Rumors mixed with racism rather than facts explain the events that followed. Japanese Americans on Hawaii were alleged to have cooperated in the attack on Pearl Harbor by using signaling devices to assist the pilots from Japan. Front-page attention was given to pronouncements by the Secretary of the Navy that Japanese Americans had the greatest responsibility for Pearl Harbor. Newspapers covered in detail FBI arrests of Japanese Americans allegedly engaging in sabotage to assist the attackers. They were accused of poisoning drinking water, cutting patterns in sugarcane fields to form arrows directing enemy pilots to targets, and blocking traffic along highways to the harbor. None of these charges was substantiated, despite thorough investigations. It made no difference. In the 1940s, the treachery of the Japanese Americans was a foregone conclusion regardless of evidence to the contrary (Y. Kimura 1988; A. Lind 1946; ten Brock et al. 1954).

Executive Order 9066 On February 13, 1942, President Franklin Roosevelt signed Executive Order 9066. It defined strategic military areas in the United States and authorized the removal from those areas of any people considered threats to national security. The events that followed were tragically simple. All people on the west coast of at least one-eighth Japanese ancestry were taken to assembly centers for transfer to evacuation camps. These camps are identified in Figure 12.1. This order covered 90 percent of the 126,000 Japanese Americans on the mainland. Of those evacuated, two-thirds were citizens, and three-fourths were under age twenty-five. Ultimately, 120,000 Japanese Americans were in the camps. Of mainland Japanese Americans, 113,000 were evacuated, but to those were added 1,118 evacuated from Hawaii, 219 voluntary residents (Caucasian spouses, typically), and, most poignantly of all, the 5,981 who were born in the camps (M. Weglyn 1976).

The evacuation order did not arise from any court action. No trials took place. No indictments were issued. Merely having a Japanese great-grandparent was enough to mark an individual for involuntary confinement. The evacuation was carried out with little difficulty. For Japanese Americans to have fled or militantly defied the order would only have confirmed the suspicions of their fellow Americans. There was little visible objection initially from the Japanese Americans. The Japanese American

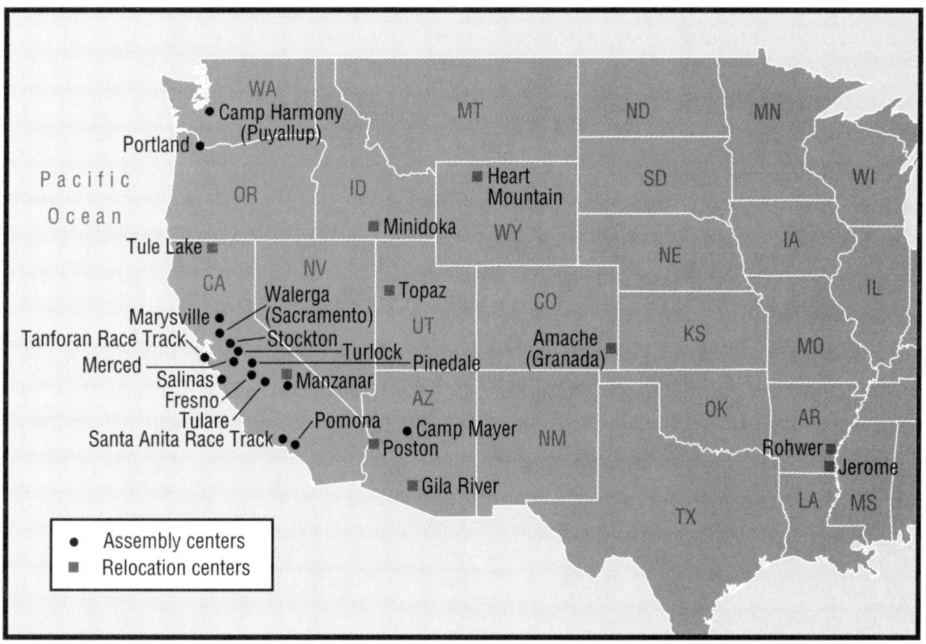

Figure 12.1 Evacuation Camps

Japanese Americans were first ordered to report to "assembly centers," from which, after a few weeks or months, they were resettled in "relocation centers."

Source: Adapted from Michi Weglyn, *Years of Infamy: The Untold Story of America's Concentration Camps.*

Citizens League (JACL), which had been founded by the Nisei as a self-help organization in 1924, even decided not to arrange a court test of the evacuation order. The JACL felt that cooperating with the military might lead to sympathetic consideration later when tensions subsided.

Even before reaching the camps, the **evacuees,** as Japanese Americans being forced to resettle came to be called officially, paid a price for their ancestry. They were instructed to carry only personal items. No provision was made for shipping their household goods. The federal government took a few steps to safeguard the belongings they left behind, but the evacuees assumed all risks and agreed to turn over their property for an indeterminate length of time. These Japanese Americans were destroyed economically. Merchants, farmers, and business owners had to sell all their property at any price they could get. Precise figures of the loss in dollars are difficult to obtain, but after the war, the Federal Reserve Bank estimated it to be $400 million. To place this amount in perspective, one estimate stated that, in 1995 dollars, the economic damages sustained, excluding personal income, would be in excess of $3.7 billion (Bureau of the Census 1996:483; Commission on Wartime Relocation and Internment of Civilians 1982a, 1982b; B. Hosokawa 1969; Thomas and Nishimoto 1946).

The Camps Ten camps were established in seven states. Were they actually concentration camps? Obviously, they were not concentration camps constructed for the murderous purposes of those in Nazi Germany, but such a positive comparison is no compliment to the United States. To refer to them by their official designation, relocation centers, ignores these facts: the Japanese Americans did not go there voluntarily, they had been charged with no crime, and they could not leave without official approval.

Japanese Americans were able to work at wage labor in the camps. The maximum wage was set at $19 a month, which meant that camp work could not possibly recoup the losses incurred by evacuation. The evacuees had to depend on the government for food and shelter, a situation they had not experienced in prewar civilian life. More devastating than the economic damage of camp life was the psychological damage. Guilty of no crime, the Japanese Americans moved through a monotonous daily routine with no chance of changing the situation. Forced community life, with such shared activities as eating in mess halls, weakened the strong family ties that Japanese Americans, especially the Issei, took so seriously (Kitsuse and Broom 1956).

Amid the economic and psychological devastation, the camps began to take on some resemblance to U.S. cities of a similar size. High schools were established, complete with cheerleaders and yearbooks. Ironically, Fourth of July parades were held, with camp-organized Boy Scout and Girl Scout troops marching past proud parents. But the barbed wire remained, and the Japanese Americans were asked to prove their loyalty.

A loyalty test was administered in 1943 on a form all had to fill out, the "Application for Leave Clearance." Many of the Japanese Americans were undecided how to respond to two questions:

> *No. 27. Are you willing to serve in the armed forces of the United States on combat duty, wherever ordered?*

> *No. 28. Will you swear to abide by the laws of the United States and to take no action which would in any way interfere with the war effort of the United States? (R. Daniels 1972:113)*

The ambiguity of the questions left many confused about how to respond. For example, if Issei said yes to the second question, would they then lose their Japanese citizenship and be left stateless? The Issei would be ending allegiance to Japan but were unable, at the time, to gain U.S. citizenship. Similarly, would Nisei who responded yes be suggesting that they had been supporters of Japan? For whatever reasons, 6,700 Issei and Nisei, many because of their unacceptable responses to these questions, were transferred to the high-security camp at Tule Lake for the duration of the war (R. Bigelow 1992).

Overwhelmingly, Japanese Americans showed loyalty to the government that had created the camps. In general, security in the camps was not a problem. The U.S. Army, which had overseen the removal of the Japanese Americans, recognized the value of the Japanese Americans as translators in the war ahead. About 6,000 Nisei were recruited to work as interpreters and translators, and by 1943, a special combat unit of 23,000 Nisei volunteers had been created to fight in Europe. The predominantly Nisei unit was unmatched, and it concluded the war as the most decorated of all American units.

Japanese American behavior in the concentration camps can be seen only as reaffirming their loyalty. True, some refused to sign an oath, but that was hardly a treasonous act. More typical were the tens of thousands of evacuees who contributed to the U.S. war effort.

A few Japanese Americans resisted the evacuation and internment. Several cases arising out of the evacuation and detention reached the U.S. Supreme Court during the war. Amazingly, the Court upheld lower court decisions on Japanese Americans without even raising the issue of the whole plan's constitutionality. Essentially, the Court upheld the idea of the collective guilt of an entire race. Finally, after hearing *Mitsuye Endo* v. *United States,* the Supreme Court ruled, on December 18, 1944, that the detainment was unconstitutional and consequently the defendant (and presumably all evacuees) must be granted their freedom. Two weeks later, Japanese Americans were allowed to return to their homes for the first time in three years and the camps were finally closed in 1946 (ten Brock et al. 1954).

The immediate postwar climate was not pro-Japanese American. Whites terrorized returning evacuees in attacks similar to those against Blacks a generation earlier. Labor unions called for work stoppages when Japanese Americans reported for work. Fortunately, the most blatant expression of anti-Japanese feeling disappeared rather quickly. Japan stopped being a threat as the atomic bomb blasts destroyed Nagasaki and Hiroshima. For the many evacuees who lost relatives and friends in the bombings, however, it must have been a high price to pay for marginal acceptance (M. Maykovich 1972a, 1972b; W. Petersen 1971).

The Evacuation: What Does It Mean? The wartime evacuation cost the U.S. taxpayers a quarter of a billion dollars in construction, transportation, and military expenses. Japanese Americans, as already noted, effectively lost at least several billion dollars. These are only the tangible costs to the nation. The relocation was not justifiable

The postwar welcome to evacuees returning home from the camps was generally not pleasant. A *Nisei* family is shown in 1945 in front of their home in Seattle, Washington, which they found had been vandalized while they were in an Idaho relocation center.

on any security grounds. No verified act of espionage or sabotage by a Japanese American was recorded. How could it happen?

Racism cannot be ignored as an explanation. Japanese Americans were placed in camps, though German Americans and Italian Americans were ignored by comparison. Many of those whose decisions brought about the evacuation were of German and Italian ancestry. The fact was that the Japanese were expendable. Placing them in camps posed no hardship for the rest of society, and, in fact, some profited by their misfortune. That Japanese Americans were evacuated because they were seen as expendable is evident from the decision not to evacuate Hawaii's Japanese. In Hawaii, the Japanese were an integral part of the society; removing them would have destroyed the islands economically (B. Hosokawa 1969; Y. Kimura 1988; S. Miyamoto 1973).

Some argue that Japanese lack of resistance made internment possible. This seems a weak effort to transfer guilt—to "blame the victim." In the 1960s, some Sansei and Yonsei were concerned about the alleged timidity of their parents and grandparents when faced with evacuation orders. Rather, many, if not most, evacuees probably did not really believe what was happening. "It just cannot be that bad," they may have thought. At worst, the evacuees can be accused of being naive. But even if they did see clearly how devastating the order would be, what alternatives were open? None (G. Haak 1970; H. Kitano 1976; Y. Takezawa 1991).

The Commission on Wartime Relocation and Internment of Civilians in 1981 held hearings on whether additional reparations should be paid to evacuees or their heirs. The final commission recommendation in 1983 was that the government formally apologize and give $20,000 tax-free to each of the approximately 66,000 surviving internees. Congress began hearings in 1986 on the bill authorizing these steps, and President Ronald Reagan signed the Civil Liberties Act of 1988, which authorized the payments. The payments, however, were slow in coming, because other federal expenditures had higher priorities. Meanwhile, the aging internees were dying at a rate of 200 a month. In 1990, the first checks were finally issued, accompanied by President Bush's letter of apology. Many Japanese Americans were disappointed by and critical of the begrudging nature of the compensation and the length of time it had taken to receive it (Commission on Wartime Relocation and Internment of Civilians 1982a, 1982b; T. Squitieri 1989; Y. Takezawa 1991).

Perhaps actor George Takei, of *Star Trek* fame, sums up best the wartime legacy of the evacuation of Japanese Americans. As a child, he had lived with his parents in the Tule Lake, California, camp. In 1996, on the fiftieth anniversary of the camp's closing, he reflected on his arrival at the camp. "America betrayed American ideals at this camp. We must not have national amnesia; we must remember this" (S. Lin 1996:10).

THE ECONOMIC PICTURE

The socioeconomic status of Japanese Americans as a group is very different from that of Chinese Americans. Many of the latter are recent immigrants and refugees, who have fewer of the skills that lead to employment in higher-paying positions. In contrast, the Japanese American community is more settled and less affected by new arrivals from the home country but continues to operate in a society in which tensions remain with Japan. We will first consider the Japanese American economic situation, which, on balance, has been very positive.

The camps left a legacy with economic implications; the Japanese American community of the 1950s was very different from that of the 1930s. Japanese Americans were more widely scattered. In 1940, 89 percent lived on the west coast. By 1950, only 58 percent of the population had returned to the west coast. Another difference was that a smaller proportion than before were Issei. The Nisei and even later generations accounted for 63 percent of the Japanese population. By moving beyond the west coast, the Japanese Americans seemed less of a threat than if they had remained concentrated. Furthermore, by dispersing, Japanese American businesspeople had to develop ties to the larger economy rather than do business mostly with other Japanese Americans. While ethnic businesses can be valuable initially, those who limit their dealings to those from the same country may limit their economic potential as well (Oliver and Shapiro 1995:46).

After the war, some Japanese Americans continued to experience hardship. Some remained on the west coast and farmed as sharecroppers in a role similar to the freed slaves after the Civil War. Sharecropping involved working the land of others, who provided shelter, seeds, and equipment and who also shared any profits at the time of harvest. The Japanese Americans used the practice to gradually get back into farming after being stripped of their land during World War II (M. Parrish 1995).

However, perhaps the most dramatic development has been the upward mobility that Japanese Americans collectively and individually have accomplished. By occupational and academical standards, two indicators of success, Japanese Americans are doing very well. The educational attainment of Japanese Americans as a group, as well as their family earnings, is higher than those of Whites, but caution should be used in interpreting such group data. Obviously, large numbers of Asian Americans, as well as Whites, have little formal schooling and are employed in poor jobs. Furthermore, Japanese Americans are concentrated in areas of the United States, such as Hawaii, California, Washington, New York, and Illinois, where both wages and the cost of living are far above the national average. Also, the proportion of Japanese American families with multiple wage earners is higher than that of White families. Nevertheless, the overall picture for Japanese Americans is remarkable, especially for a racial minority that had been discriminated against so openly and so recently (M. Inoue 1989; H. Kitano 1980; S. Nishi 1995; E. Woodrum 1981).

The Japanese American story does not end with another account of oppression and hardship. Today, Japanese Americans have achieved success by almost any standard. We must qualify, however, the progress that *Newsweek* (1971) once billed as their "Success Story: Outwhiting the Whites." First, it is easy to forget that several generations of Japanese Americans achieved what they did by overcoming barriers that U.S. society had created, not because they had been welcomed. However, many, if not most, have become acculturated. Nevertheless, successful Japanese Americans are still not wholeheartedly accepted into the dominant group's inner circle of social clubs and fraternal organizations. Second, Japanese Americans today may represent a stronger indictment of society than economically oppressed African Americans, Native Americans, and Hispanics. There are few excuses apart from racism that Whites can use to explain why they continue to look on Japanese Americans as different, as "them."

FAMILY AND RELIGIOUS LIFE

The contradictory pulls of tradition and rapid change that we found charactersitic of Chinese Americans is very present among Japanese Americans today. Surviving Issei see their grandchildren as very nontraditional. Change in family life is one of the most difficult cultural changes for any immigrants to accept in the younger generations.

As cultural traditions fade, the contemporary Japanese American family seems to continue the success story. The divorce rate has been low, although it is probably rising. Similar conclusions apply to crime, delinquency, and reported mental illness. Data on all types of social disorganization show that Japanese Americans have a lower incidence of such behavior than all other minorities; it is also lower than that of Whites. Japanese Americans find it possible to be good Japanese and good Americans simultaneously. Japanese culture demands high in-group unity, politeness, respect for authority, and duty to community, all traits highly acceptable to middle-class Americans. Basically, psychological research has concluded that Japanese Americans share the high achievement orientation held by many middle-class White Americans. One might expect, however, that, as Japanese Americans continue to acculturate, the breakdown in traditional Japanese behavior will be accompanied by a rise in social deviance (S. Nishi 1995).

As is true of the family and other social organizations, religious life in these groups has its antecedents in Asia, but there is no single Japanese faith. In Japan, religious beliefs tend to be much more accommodating than Christian beliefs are: one can be Shinto, but also Buddhist at the same time. Consequently, when they came to the United States, immigrants found it easy to accept Christianity, even though doing so ultimately meant rejecting their old faiths. In the United States, a Christian cannot also be a Shintoist or a Buddhist. As a result, with each generation, Japanese Christians depart from traditional ways.

Although traditional temples are maintained in most places where there are large numbers of Japanese Americans, many exist only as museums, and few are places of worship with growing memberships. Religion is still a source of community attachment, but it is in the Protestant Chinese church, not in the temple. At the same time, some Eastern religions, such as Buddhism, are growing in the United States, but the new adherents are overwhelmingly Whites who are attracted to what they perceive as a more enriching value system. This has led to friction between more traditional Buddhist centers and those associated with the more Americanized Zen Buddhism (Kosmin and Lachman 1993; *Religion Watch* 1996).

Remnants of Prejudice and Discrimination

The Fu Manchu image may be gone, but its replacement is not much better. In popular television series, Asian Americans, if they are present, are usually either karate experts or technical specialists involved in their work. Chinese Americans are ignored or misrepresented in history books. Even past mistakes are repeated. When the transcontinental railroad was completed in Utah in 1869, Chinese workers were barred from attending the ceremony. Their contribution is now well known, one of the stories of true heroism in the West. However, in 1969, when Secretary of Transportation John Volpe made a speech marking the hundredth anniversary of the event, he neglected to mention the Chinese contribution. He exclaimed, "Who else but Americans could drill tunnels in mountains 30 feet deep in snow? Who else but Americans could chisel through miles of solid granite? Who else but Americans could have laid 10 miles of track in 12 hours?" (A. Yee 1973:100). The Chinese contribution was once again forgotten.

Today, young Japanese Americans and Chinese Americans are very ambivalent about their cultural heritage. The pull to be American is intense, but so are the reminders that, in the eyes of many others, Asian Americans are "they," not

News media treat Asian Americans, such as Olympic figure skater Michelle Kwan, a Chinese American, as if they are foreigners. The cable news network MSNBC, an affiliate of the NBC network, covered the 1996 Olympics when Tara Lipinski defeated Kwan and then proclaimed "American Beats out Kwan."

"we." Sansei youth indicate that they would like to learn Japanese. It is questionable whether many will. The very success of Japanese Americans seems to argue that they will not maintain a unique cultural tradition. In fact, their success has been in part the result of their assimilating and in the process forsaking the cultural heritage of Japan. Their emphasis on college education and advanced training makes it likely that Japanese Americans will scatter throughout the country. Dispersal will make it harder to maintain cultural ties. Little Tokyos do exist, but even in some major cities, such a basic symbol of ethnic solidarity is absent (N. Onishi 1995).

Chinese Americans and Japanese Americans believe that prejudice and discrimination have decreased in the United States, but subtle reminders remain. Third-generation Japanese Americans feel insulted when they are told, "You speak English so well." Adopting new tactics, Asian Americans are now trying to fight racist and exclusionary practices (K. Lem 1976).

Marriage statistics also illustrate the effects of assimilation. At one time twenty-nine states prohibited or severely regulated marriages between Asians and non-

Asians. Today, intermarriage, though not typical, is legal and certainly more common, and more than one-fourth of Chinese Americans under twenty-four marry someone who is not Chinese. The degree of intermarriage is even higher among Japanese Americans—1990 census data showed that two-thirds of all children born to a Japanese American had a parent of a different race.

The increased intermarriage indicates that Whites are increasingly accepting of Chinese Americans. It also suggests that Chinese and Japanese ties to their native cultures are weakening. As happened with the ways of life of European immigrants, the traditional norms are being cast aside for those of the host society. In one sense, these changes make Chinese Americans and Japanese Americans more acceptable and less alien to Whites. But this points to all the changes in Asian Americans rather than any recognition of diversity in the United States. As illustrated in Figure 12.2, intermarriage patterns reflect the fusion of different racial groups, but compared to examples of assimilation and pluralism they are a relatively limited social process at the present time (S. Fong 1965, 1973; N. Onishu 1995).

The Japanese American community struggles to maintain its cultural identity. Despite being viewed as racially different, young Japanese Americans are readily adopting mainstream culture. Nisei Week celebrations have been held in August since 1934 as a festive effort to showcase traditions such as the tea ceremony, bonsai ornamental plant techniques, and Kamans (family crests). But other customs, such as eating traditional foods like sushi (uncooked fish) and namasu (radish and carrots marinated in vinegar), are fading in popularity (M. Becker 1995).

It would be incorrect to interpret assimilation as an absence of protest. Because a sizable segment of the college youth of the 1960s and early 1970s held militant

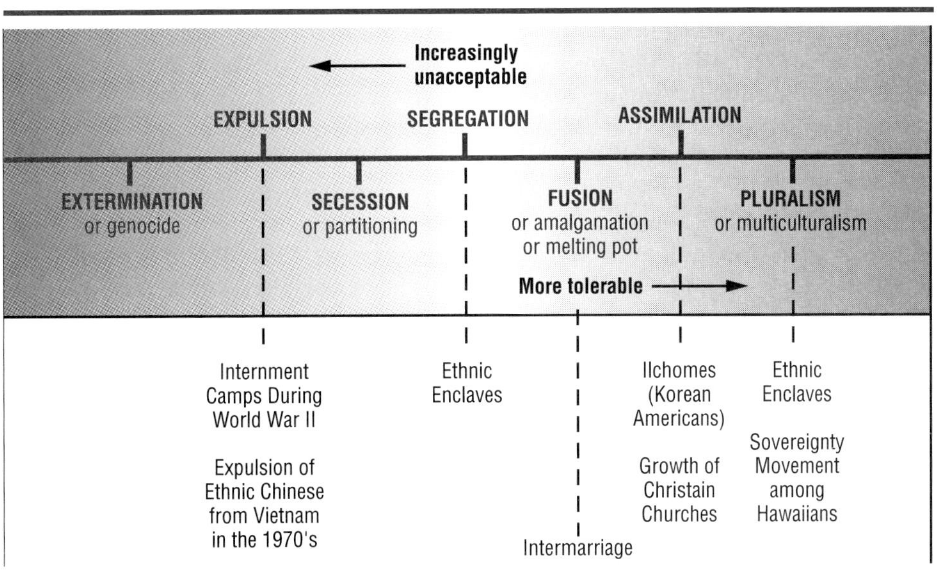

Figure 12.2 Intergroup Relations Continuum

Since 1934, Nisei Week activities in Los Angeles and some other cities have tried to reaffirm the ancestral heritage of Japanese Americans.

attitudes, and because the Sansei are more heterogeneous than their Nisei and Issei relatives, it was to be expected that some Japanese Americans, especially the Sansei, would be politically active. For example, Japanese and other Asian Americans have emerged as activists for environmental concerns ranging from contaminated fish to toxic working conditions, and the targets of Japanese Americans' anger have included the apparent rise in hate crimes in the United States against Asian Americans in the 1990s. They also lobbied for passage of the Civil Rights Restoration Act, extending reparations to the evacuees. They have expressed further activism through Hiroshima Day ceremonies, marking the anniversary of the detonation in World War II of the first atomic bomb over a major Japanese city. Also, each February, a group of Japanese American youths makes a pilgrimage to the site of the Tule Lake evacuation camp in a "lest we forget" observance. Such protests are modest, but they are a militant departure from the almost passive role played by the Nisei (G. Shaffer 1994; Y. Takezawa 1991; W. Wei 1993).

Is pluralism developing? Japanese Americans show little evidence of wanting to maintain a distinctive way of life. The Japanese values that have endured are attitudes, beliefs, and goals shared by and rewarded by the White middle class in America. All Asian Americans, not only Japanese Americans, are caught in the middle. Any Asian American is culturally a part of a society that is dominated by a group that excludes him or her because of racial distinctions.

CONCLUSION

Most White adults are confident that they can distinguish Asians from Europeans. Unfortunately, though, White Americans frequently cannot tell Asians apart from their physical appearance and are not disturbed about their confusion.

There are, however, definite differences in the experience of the Chinese and the Japanese, as we have seen, in the United States.

One obvious difference is in the degree of assimilation. The Chinese Americans have maintained their ethnic enclaves more than the Japanese Americans have. Chinatowns live on, both as welcomed halfway points for new arrivals and also as enclaves where many make very low wages. Little Tokyos, however, are few, because of the differences in the cultures of China and Japan. China was almost untouched by European influence, but even by the early 1900s, Japan had already been influenced by the West. Relatively speaking, then, the Japanese arrived somewhat more assimilated than their Chinese counterparts. The continued migration of Chinese in recent years has also meant that Chinese Americans as a group have been less assimilated than Japanese Americans (W. Beach 1934; S. Lyman 1974, 1986).

Both groups have achieved some success, but this success has not extended to all members. For Chinese Americans, a notable exception to success can be found in Chinatowns, which, behind the tourist front, are much like other poverty-stricken areas in American cities. Neither Chinese Americans nor Japanese Americans have figured prominently in the executive offices of the nation's large corporations and financial institutions. Compared to other racial and ethnic groups, Asian Americans have shown little interest in political activity on their own behalf.

The relative success of Asian Americans, however, especially that of the Japanese Americans, belongs to them, not to U.S. society. First, Asian Americans have been considered successful only because they conform to the dominant society's expectations. Their acceptance as a group does not indicate growing pluralism in the United States. Second, the ability of the Nisei, in particular, to recover from the camp experience cannot be taken as a precedent for other racial minorities. The Japanese Americans left the camps a skilled group, ambitious to overcome their adversity, and placing a cultural emphasis on formal education. They entered a booming economy in which Whites and others could not afford to discriminate even if they wished to. African Americans after slavery and Hispanic immigrants have entered the economy without skills at a time when the demand for manual labor has been limited. Many of them have been forced to remain in a marginal economy, whether that of the ghetto, the *barrio*, or subsistence agriculture. For Japanese Americans, the post-World War II period marked the fortunate coincidence of their having assets and ambition when they could be used to full advantage. Third, some Whites use the success of the Asian Americans to prop up their own prejudice. Asian American success is twisted by bigoted individuals to show that racism cannot possibly play a part in another group's subordination. If the Japanese or Chinese can do it, why cannot African Americans, the illogical reasoning goes. More directly, Japanese Americans' success may serve as a scapegoat for another's failure ("They advanced at my expense") or as a sign that they are clannish or too ambitious. Regardless of what a group does, a prejudiced eye will always view it as wrong.

As for other racial and ethnic minorities, assimilation seems to be the path most likely to lead to tolerance but not necessarily to acceptance. However, assimilation has a price that is well captured in the Chinese phrase, *Zhancao zhugen:* "To eliminate the weeds, one must pull out their roots." To work for acceptance means to uproot all traces of one's cultural heritage and former identity (L. Wang 1991).

KEY TERMS

evacuees 368
hui kuan 359
Issei 365
Kibei 365
Nisei 365
Sansei 365
tongs 359
tsu 359
Yonsei 365

REVIEW QUESTIONS

1. What has been the legacy of the "yellow peril"?
2. What made the placement of Japanese Americans in internment camps unique?
3. In what respects does diversity characterize Chinatowns?
4. How has Japanese American assimilation been blocked in the United States?
5. What are the most singificant similarities between the Chinese American and Japanese American experience? Differences?

CRITICAL THINKING

1. Considering the past as well as the present, are the moves made to restrict or exclude Chinese and Japanese Americans based on economic or racist motives?
2. What events can you imagine could cause the United States to again identify an ethnic group for confinement in some type of internment camps?
3. What stereotypical images of Chinese Americans and Japanese Americans can you identify in the contemporary media?

INTERNET EXERCISES

1. The text of the 1882 Chinese Exclusion Act can be found by following these steps. Log onto the site (http://www.yahoo.com), and type the words "Chinese Exclusion Act" into the search box. Press the search key, and you will be provided with a link to the act. Read over this act of the 47th Congress and review the discussion on it in Chapter 4. Why was this act passed? What were some of the prevailing feelings/perspectives toward Chinese immigrants at the time? When was the act rescinded? Imagine that you are a Chinese person living in 1882. What kind of work might you be doing? How would you feel about the act? What rights and freedoms did the act deny Chinese persons? Can you find points of similarity between the treatment of Chinese immigrants and immigrants from other countries?

2. Pictures, timelines, and a glossary about the Japanese American internment are available for viewing at (http://www.geocities.com/Athens/8420/main.html). What reasons were given for the removal of Japanese Americans from their homes? In which states were the internment camps located? Read the section on "Memories" and view the online photographs of camps and posters to answer the following questions: What was daily life like in the camps? How long were the camps open? What other forms of discrimination and prejudice did Japanese Americans experience before, during, and after World War II? Click on the "Glossary" section to explore these issues: What were loyalty questionnaires? What was Terminal Island? What was the WRA? What lasting impact and legacy have these internment camps had?

FOR FURTHER INFORMATION

Bill Hosokowa. *JACL in Quest of Justice*. New York: Morrow, 1982.

A well-illustrated, detailed account of the Japanese American Citizens League (JACL) from its founding through its efforts to gain reparations in the 1980s.

Jan Lin. *Reconstructing Chinatown: Ethnic Enclave, Global Change*. Minneapolis: University of Minnesota Press, 1998.

An ethnographic study of Manhattan's Chinatown that places it in the context of the global economy.

Eric Liu. *The Accidental Asian: Notes of a Native Speaker*. New York: Random House, 1998.

A young Chinese Americans, now enrolled in Harvard Law School following a role as a presidential speech writer, reflects on assimilation and the American experience.

13

Jewish Americans: Quest to Maintain Identity

CHAPTER OUTLINE

HIGHLIGHTS

The Jewish people are an ethnic group. Their identity rests not on the presence of physical traits or religious beliefs, but on a sense of belonging that is tied to Jewish ancestry. The history of anti-Semitism is as ancient as the Jewish people themselves. Today, evidence suggests that this intolerance persists today in both thought and action. Jews in the United States may have experienced less discrimination than did earlier generations in Europe, but some opportunities are still denied them. Contemporary Jews figure prominently in the professions and as a group exhibit a strong commitment to education. Many Jews share a concern about either the lack of religious devotion of some members or the division within American Judaism over the degree of orthodoxy. Jews in the United States practice their faith as Orthodox, Conservative, or Reform. Paradoxically, the acceptance of Jews by Gentiles has made the previously strong identity of Jews weaker with each succeeding generation.

Billings, Montana, does not have a large Jewish population although it does have an established community of Jews. Therefore, it would not be surprising that Billings had no history of visible anti-Jewish hostility. However, beginning in 1992, swastikas appeared outside a Jewish temple, tombstones in a Jewish cemetery were toppled, and bomb threats were made to a synagogue. Then, in the fall of 1993, rocks and bottles were thrown through the windows of homes of prominent members of the Jewish community in Billings. Police advised one of the victim households to remove the "Happy Hanukkah" pictures from their front windows. In light of this tension, local ministers encouraged their members to place menorahs in their windows. Stores instantly sold out of them, and local newspapers printed color pictures of them for people to hang in their window. As Christmas Day came in this overwhelmingly Christian community, home after home displayed symbols of Judaism, defying those who had attacked the Jews. The culprits were never identified but they had succeeded in bringing a city together (S. Cohon 1995).

The United States has the largest Jewish population in the world. This nation's 6 million Jews account for 44 percent of the world's Jewish population. Jewish Americans not only represent a significant group in the United States but also play a prominent role in the worldwide Jewish community. The nation with the second-largest Jewish population, Israel, is the only one in which Jews are in the majority, accounting for 81 percent of the population, compared to less than 3 percent in the United States. Figure 13.1 depicts the worldwide distribution of Jews.

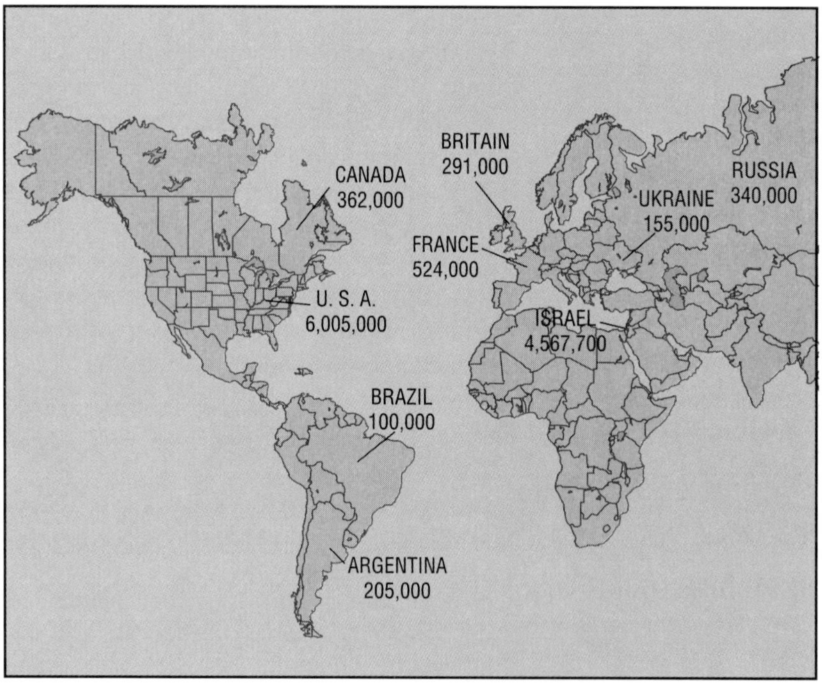

Figure 13.1 Worldwide Distribution of Jews

Note: Data are for 1996 and include all nations with at least 100,000 Jews.

Source: Copyright ©1998, *Los Angeles Times*. Reprinted by permission.

The Jewish people form a contrast to the other subordinate groups we have studied. At least 1,500 years had passed since Jews were the dominant group in any nation, until Israel was created in 1948. Even there, Jews are in competition for power. American Jews superficially resemble Asian Americans in that both are relatively freed from poverty, compared to Chicanos or Puerto Ricans. Unlike those groups, however, the Jewish cultural heritage is not nationalistic in origin. Perhaps the most striking difference is that the history of anti-Jewish prejudice and discrimination (usually referred to as **anti-Semitism**) is nearly as old as relations between Jews and Gentiles (non-Jews).

Statistical data on Jewish Americans are unreliable. Because the Bureau of the Census no longer asks people what their religion is, statistical information of this kind is not available on many other minority groups who are identified in the census. Estimates in 1998 placed the Jewish population at about 6 million. The Jewish birthrate remains well below the national average, so growth of the Jewish population during the 1990s did not keep pace with that of the nation as a whole. Indeed, the proportion of the U.S. population that is Jewish has been estimated to be the lowest since the first decade of the century. The most distinctive aspect of the Jewish population is its concentration in urban areas and in the Northeast. The most recent estimates place more than 40 percent of the Jewish population in the Northeast.

Jews are concentrated especially in the metropolitan areas of New York City, Los Angeles, and Miami where altogether they account for half of the nation's Jewish population.

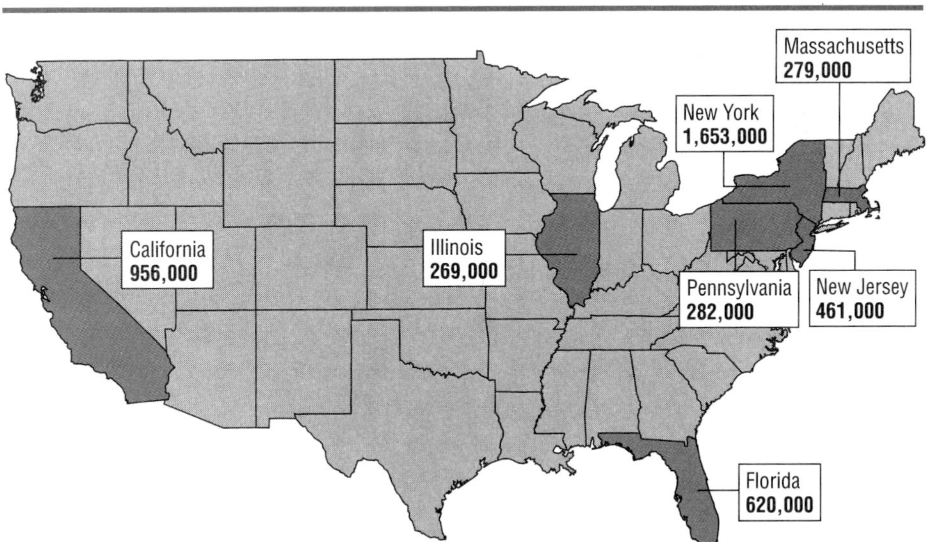

Figure 13.2 Jewish Population Distribution in the United States

Note: States highlighted have largest Jewish populations.

Source: American Jewish Congress 1998.

The Jewish People: Race or Religion or Ethnic Group?

Jews are a subordinate group. They fulfill the criteria set forth in Chapter 1.

1. Jewish Americans experience unequal treatment from non-Jews in the form of prejudice, discrimination, and segregation.
2. Jews share a cultural history that distinguishes them from the dominant group.
3. Jews do not choose to be Jewish, in the same way that Whites do not choose to be White or Mexican Americans to be Mexican American.
4. Jews have a strong sense of group solidarity.
5. Jewish men and women tend to marry one another rather than marrying outside the group.

The first criterion for classification as a subordinate group on this list requires special attention. What are the distinguishing traits? Are they physical features, thus making Jews a racial group? Are these characteristics matters of faith, suggesting that Jews are best regarded as a religious minority? Or are they cultural and social, making Jews an ethnic group? To answer these questions, we must address the ancient and perennial question: What is a Jew?

The issue of what makes a Jew is not only a scholarly question; in Israel it figures in policy matters. Following the 1988 general election, Israeli prime minister Yitshak Shamir was under great pressure from traditional Jews in both his own country and the United States to redefine Israel's Law of Return. This law defines who is a Jew and extends Israeli citizenship to all Jews. Currently, the law recognizes all converts to the faith, but pressure has grown recently to limit citizenship to those whose conversions were performed by Orthodox rabbis. While the change would have had little practical impact, symbolically this pressure shows the tension and lack of consensus even among Jews over who is a Jew (R. Watson 1988).

The definition of race used here is fairly explicit. The Jewish people are not physically differentiated from non-Jews. True, many people believe they can tell a Jew from a non-Jew, but actual distinguishing physical traits are absent. Jews today come from all areas of the world and carry a variety of physical features. Most Jewish Americans are descended from Northern and Eastern Europeans and have the appearance of Nordic and Alpine people. Many others carry Mediterranean traits that make them indistinguishable from Spanish or Italian Catholics. Many Jews reside in North Africa, and although they are not significantly represented in the United States, many people would view them only as a racial minority, Black. The wide range of variation among Jews makes it inaccurate to speak of a "Jewish race" in a physical sense (J. Gittler 1981; A. Montagu 1972).

To define Jews by religion would seem the obvious answer because there are Judaic religious beliefs, holidays, and rituals. But these beliefs and practices do not distinguish all Jews from non-Jews. To be a Jewish American does not mean that one is affiliated with one of the three religious groups: the Orthodox, the Reform, and the Conservative. A large segment of adult Jewish Americans, more than a third, do not participate in religious services or even belong, however tenuously, to a temple or synagogue. They have not converted to Christianity, nor have they ceased to think of themselves as Jews. Nevertheless, Jewish religious beliefs and the history of religious practices remain significant legacies for all Jews today, however secularized their everyday behavior. In a 1998 survey half of all Jews felt that a "shared history or culture" much more so than religion defined what it means to be Jewish (Los Angles Times Poll 1998).

The trend for some time, especially in the United States, has been toward a condition called **Judaization,** the lessening importance of Judaism as a religion and the substitution of cultural traditions as the ties that bind Jews. Depending on one's definition, Judaization has caused some Jews to become so assimilated in the United States that very traditional Jews no longer consider them acceptable spouses (H. Gans 1956).

Jewish identity is ethnic. Jews share cultural traits, not physical features or uniform religious beliefs. The level of this cultural identity differs for the individual Jew. Just as some Apaches may be more acculturated than others, the degree of assimilation varies among Jewish people. Judaization may base identity on such things as eating traditional Jewish foods, telling Jewish jokes, and wearing the Star of David. For others, this cultural identity may be the sense of a common

Jewish shoppers, many immigrants, crowd the streets of New York to buy food for the Passover feast in 1926.

history of centuries of persecution. For still others, it may be a relatively unimportant identification. They say, "I am a Jew," just as they say, "I am a resident of California."

The question of what constitutes Jewish identity is not easily resolved. The most appropriate explanation of Jewish identity may be the simplest. A Jew in contemporary America is an individual who thinks of himself or herself as a Jew. That also means that being a Jew is a choice and, as we will return to later in the chapter, many Jews may not be making that choice (Abrahamson and Pasternak 1998; H. Himmelfarb 1982).

Migration of Jews to the United States

As every schoolchild knows, 1492 was the year in which Christopher Columbus reached the Western Hemisphere, exploring on behalf of Spain. That year also marked the expulsion of all Jews from Spain. The resulting exodus was not the first migration of Jews nor was it the last. This is but one illustration of several of the social processes in the Intergroup Relations Continuum illustrated in Figure 13.3. Other examples will be presented throughout this chapter.

One of the most significant movements among Jews is the one that created history's largest concentration of Jews: the migration to the United States. The first Jews arrived in 1654 and were of Sephardic origin, meaning that they were originally from Spain and Portugal. These immigrants sought refuge after they had been expelled from other European countries.

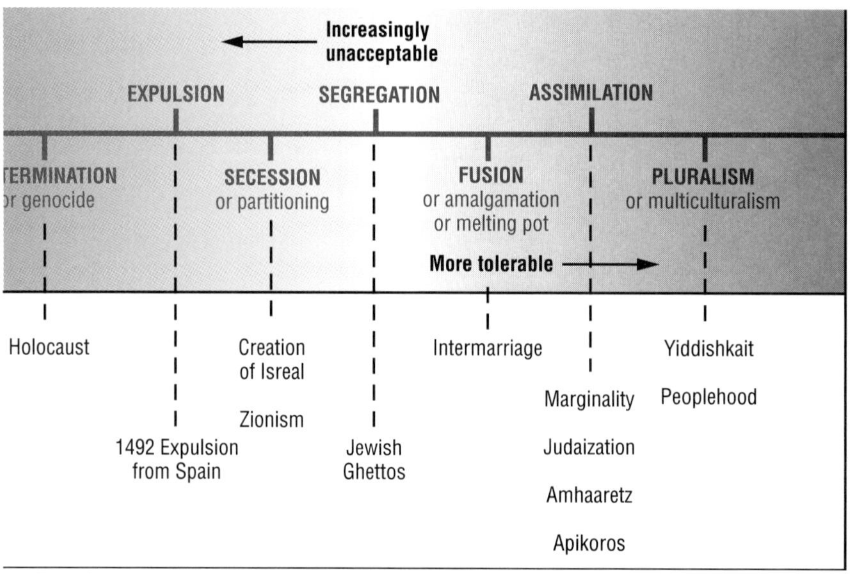

Figure 13.3 Intergroup Relations Continuum

When the United States gained its independence from Great Britain, only 2,500 Jews in the population lived here. By 1870 the Jewish population had climbed to about 200,000, supplemented mostly by Jews of German origin. They did not immediately merge into the older Jewish American settlements any more than the German Catholics fused immediately with native Catholics. Years passed before the two groups' common identity as Jews overcame nationality differences (L. Dinnerstein 1994; F. Jaher 1994).

The greatest migration of Jews to the United States occurred around the end of the nineteenth century and was simultaneous with the great European migration described in Chapter 4. Because they arrived at the same time does not mean that the movement of Gentiles and of Jews was identical in all respects. One significant difference was that Jews were much more likely to stay in the United States; few returned to Europe. Although between 1908 and 1937, one-third of all European immigrants returned, only 5 percent of Jewish immigrants did. The legal status of Jews in Europe at the turn of the century had improved since medieval times, but their rights were still revoked from time to time (C. Sherman 1974).

Despite the legacy of anti-Semitism in Europe, past and present, most of the Jews who migrated to the United States up to the early twentieth century came voluntarily. These immigrants tended to be less pious and less observant of Judaic religious customs than those who remained in Europe. As late as 1917, there were only five small day schools, as Jewish parochial schools were called, in the entire nation. Nevertheless, although the earliest Jewish immigration was not a direct response to fear, the United States had special meaning for the Jewish arrivals. This nation had no history of anti-Semitism like that of Europe. Many Jews must have felt a new sense of freedom, and many clearly demonstrated their commitment to their new nation by becoming citizens at a rate unparalleled in other ethnic groups (W. Herberg 1983; M. Sklare 1971).

The immigration acts of the 1920s sharply reduced the influx of Jews, as it did that of other European groups. Beginning in about 1933, the Jews arriving in the United States were not merely immigrants; they were also refugees. The tyranny of the Third Reich began to take its toll well before World War II. German and Austrian Jews fled Europe as the impending doom became more evident. Many of the refugees from Nazism in Poland, Hungary, and the Ukraine tended to be more religiously orthodox and adapted slowly to the ways of the earlier Jewish immigrants, if they adapted at all. As Hitler's decline and fall came to pass, the concentration camps, the speeches of Hitler, the atrocities, the war trials, and the capture of Nazi leaders undoubtedly made all American Jews—natives and refugees, the secular and the orthodox—acutely aware of their Jewishness and the price one may be required to pay for ethnicity alone.

Because the Immigration and Naturalization Service does not identify an immigrant's religion, precise data are lacking for the number of people of Jewish background migrating recently to the United States. Estimates of 500,000 have been given, however, for the number of Jews who made the United States their home during the 1960s and 1970s. The majority came from Israel, but 75,000 came from the Soviet Union and another 20,000 from Iran, escaping persecution in those two nations. As the treatment of Jews in the Soviet Union improved in the late 1980s, the U.S. immigration officials began to scrutinize requests for entry to see if refugee status was still merited. While some Soviet Jews had difficulty demonstrating that they had a "well-founded fear of persecution," the United States admitted over 13,600 in 1988 (through the processing center in Rome alone). The situation grew more complicated with the collapse of the Soviet Union in 1991. Throughout the period, the immigrants' arrival brought about a growth in the Jewish community in the United States (S. Gold 1988).

Anti-Semitism Past and Present

The history of the Jewish people is a history of struggle to overcome centuries of hatred. Several religious observances, like Passover, Hanukkah, and Purim commemorate the past sacrifices or conflicts Jews have experienced. Anti-Jewish hostility, or anti-Semitism, has followed the struggle of the Jewish people since before the beginning of the Christian faith to the present.

ORIGINS

Many anti-Semites justify their beliefs by pointing to the role of some Jews in the crucifixion of Jesus Christ, though he was also a Jew. For nearly 2,000 years various Christians have argued that all Jews share in the responsibility of the Jewish elders who condemned Jesus Christ to death. Much anti-Semitism over the ages bears little direct relationship to the crucifixion, however, and has more to do with the persisting stereotype that sees Jews as behaving treacherously to members of the larger society in which they live. Studies show that many Gentiles believe that Jews use underhanded methods in business and finance and that Jewish people tend to be clannish (T. Smith 1991; T. Wilson 1996).

What truth is there in such stereotypes? Even prominent political leaders have publicly expressed stereotyped opinions about Jews. In 1974, the chairman of the Joint Chiefs of Staff of the U.S. armed forces declared that Jews "own, you know, the banks in this country" (*Time* 1974b:16). Yet the facts show that Jewish Americans are dramatically underrepresented in management positions in the nation's leading banks. Even in New York City—where Jews account for half the college graduates—Jewish Americans represent only 4 percent of that city's senior banking officials (Slavin and Pradt 1979, 1982). Similarly, a 1998 national survey found that 8 percent of Jews were business owners compared to 9 percent of the total U.S., population (J. Getlin 1998:A26).

If the stereotype that Jews are obsessed with money is false, how did it originate? Social psychologist Gordon Allport (1979), among others, advanced the **fringe-of-values theory.** Throughout history, Jews have occupied positions economically different from those of Gentiles, often because laws forbade them to farm or practice trades. For centuries, the Christian church prohibited the taking of interest in the repayment of loans, calling it the sin of usury. Consequently, in the minds of Europeans, the sinful practice of money lending was equated with the Jew. In reality, most Jews were not moneylenders, and most of those who were did not charge interest. In fact, many usurers were Christians, but because they worked in secret, it was only the reputation of the Jews that was damaged. To make matters worse, the nobles of some European countries used Jews to collect taxes, which only increased the ill feeling. To the Gentile, such business practices by the Jews constituted behavior on the fringes of proper conduct. Hence, this theory about the perpetuation of anti-Semitism is called fringe of values (American Jewish Committee 1965, 1966a, 1966b; *Time* 1974a).

A similar explanation is given for other stereotypes, such as the assertion that Jews are clannish, staying among themselves and not associating with others. In the ancient world, Jews in the Near East area were frequently under attack by neighboring peoples. Throughout history, Jews have also at times been required to live in closed areas, or ghettos. This experience naturally led them to unify and rely on themselves rather than others. More recently, the stereotype of clannishness has gained support because Jews have been more likely to interact with Jews than with Gentiles. But this behavior is reciprocal because Gentiles have tended to stay among their own kind, too. It is another example of **in-group virtues** becoming **out-group vices.** Sociologist Robert Merton (1968) described how proper behavior by one's own group becomes unacceptable when practiced by outsiders. For Christians to take their faith seriously is commendable; for Jews to withstand secularization is a sign of backwardness. For Gentiles to prefer Gentiles as friends is understandable; for Jews to choose other Jews as friends suggests clannishness. The assertion that Jews are clannish is an exaggeration and also ignores the fact that the dominant group shares the same tendency. It also fails to consider to what extent anti-Semitism has logically encouraged—and indeed, forced—Jews to seek out other Jews as friends and fellow workers (G. Allport 1979).

This only begins to explore the alleged Jewish traits, their origin, and the limited value of such stereotypes in accurately describing several million Jewish people. Stereotypes are only one aspect of anti-Semitism: another has been discrimination against Jews. In A.D. 313, Christianity became the official religion of Rome. Within another two centuries, Jews were forbidden to marry Christians or to try to convert them. Because Christians shared with Jews both the Old Testament and the origin of Jesus, they felt ambivalent toward the Jewish people. Gentiles attempted to purge themselves of their doubts about the Jews by projecting exaggerated hostility onto the Jews. The expulsion of the Jews from Spain in 1492 is only one example. Spain was merely one of many countries, including England and France, from which the Jews were expelled. During the middle of the fourteenth century, the bubonic plague wiped out a third of Europe's population. Because of their social conditions and some of their religious prohibitions, Jews were less likely to die from the plague. Anti-Semites pointed to this as evidence that the Jews were in league with the devil and had poisoned the wells of non-Jews. Consequently, from 1348 to 1349, 350 Jewish communities were exterminated, not by the plague, but by Gentiles.

THE HOLOCAUST

The injustices to the Jewish people continued for centuries. It would, however, be a mistake to say that all Gentiles were anti-Semitic. History, drama, and other literature do record daily, presumably friendly, interaction between Jew and Gentile. At particular times and places, anti-Semitism was an official government policy. In other situations, it was the product of a few bigoted individuals and sporadically became very widespread. Regardless of the scope, anti-Semitism was a part of Jewish life, something that Jews were forced to contend with. By 1870, most legal restrictions aimed at Jews had been abolished in western Europe. Since then, however, Jews have again been used as scapegoats by opportunists who blame them for a nation's problems.

The most tragic example of such an opportunist was Adolf Hitler, whose "final solution" to Germany's problems led to the Holocaust. The **Holocaust** refers to the state-sponsored systematic persecution and annihilation of European Jewry by Nazi Germany and its collaborators. The move to eliminate Jews from the European continent started slowly with Germany gradually restricting the rights of Jews—preventing them from voting, living outside the Jewish ghetto, and owning businesses. Much of the anti-Semitic cruelty was evident before the beginning of the war. If there was any doubt, "Night of Broken Glass" or Kristallnacht in Berlin on November 9, 1938, ended any doubt. Some 90 Berlin Jews were murdered, hundreds of homes and synagogues were set on fire or ransacked, and thousands of Jewish store windows were broken.

Despite the obvious intolerance, Jews desiring to immigrate were turned back by government officials in the United States and elsewhere. Just a few months after Crystal Night, some 907 Jewish refugees aboard the liner *St. Louis* were denied entry to Cuba. Efforts to gain entry in the United States, including special appeals to Congress and President Roosevelt, were useless. Ultimately the ship returned with many of the Jews later dying in the death camps. Between 1933 and 1945, two-thirds of Europe's total Jewish population was killed; in Poland, Germany, and Austria, 90 percent were murdered. Even today, there are still 17 percent fewer Jews than in 1940.

Many eyewitnesses to the events of the Holocaust have served to remind us of the human tragedy involved. Among the most eloquent has been the writings and speeches of Nobel Peace Prize winner Elie Wiesel. In "Listen to Their Voices," he recalls as a teenager the moments before he and other Jews were freed from the Buchenwald concentration camp.

Despite the enormity of the tragedy, a small but vocal proportion of the world community, perhaps 3 percent, are **Holocaust revisionists** who claim that the Holocaust did not happen. Debates also continue between those who contend that this part of modern history must be remembered and others, in the United States and Europe, who feel that it is time to put the Holocaust behind us and go on. However, the poignant statements by Holocaust survivors such as Elie Wiesel as well as the release of such films as *Schindler's List* (1993) keep the tragedy of the destruction of European Jews in our minds (L. Collette 1994; L. Dawidowicz 1967, 1975).

With the 1991 collapse of eastern European Communist governments and the Soviet Union, a concern has emerged that the absence of authoritarian states will allow old hatreds to resurface. The fear is that, with freedom of speech, bigotry is beginning to be expressed openly. Yet more than a half-century after Nazi Germany mounted its war on the Jews of eastern Europe, the Jewish population in this region is relatively small. Many of the 1.5 million Jews in the countries formerly controlled by Moscow continue to leave facing new outbreaks of anti-Semitism as they become scapegoats for the economic collapse throughout much of the former Soviet empire. Even in western Europe where Jews have generally

LISTEN TO THEIR VOICES

Night

Elie Wiesel

On April tenth, there were still about twenty thousand of us in the camp, including several hundred children. They decided to evacuate us all at once, right on until the evening. Afterward, they were going to blow up the camp.

So we were massed in the huge assembly square, in rows of five, waiting to see the gate open. Suddenly, the sirens began to wail. An alert! We went back to the blocks. It was too late to evacuate us that evening. The evacuation was postponed again to the following day.

We were tormented with hunger. We had eaten nothing for six days, except a bit of grass or some potato peelings found near the kitchens.

At ten o'clock in the morning the SS scattered through the camp, moving the last victims toward the assembly place.

Then the resistance movement decided to act. Armed men suddenly rose up everywhere. Bursts of firing. Grenades exploding. We children stayed flat on the ground in the block.

The battle did not last long. Toward noon everything was quiet again. The SS had fled and the resistance had taken charge of the running of the camp.

At about six o'clock in the evening, the first American tank stood at the gates of Buchenwald.

Our first act as free men was to throw ourselves onto the provisions. We thought only of that. Not of revenge, not of our families. Nothing but bread.

And even when we were no longer hungry, there was still no one who thought of revenge. On the following day, some of the young men went to Weimar to get some potatoes and clothes—and to sleep with the girls. But of revenge, not a sign.

Three days after the liberation of Buchenwald I became very ill with food poisoning. I was transferred to the hospital and spent two weeks between life and death.

One day I was able to get up, after gathering all my strength. I wanted to see myself in the mirror hanging on the opposite wall. I had not seen myself since the ghetto.

From the depths of the mirror, a corpse gazed back at me.

The look in his eyes, as they stared into mine, has never left me.

Source: Elie Wiesel. Excerpt from *Night* by Elie Wiesel, translated by Stella Rodway.

felt well-treated during the last forty years, new revelations emerged beginning in the mid–1990s how European governments and leading financial institutions had for decades assisted in hiding the assets that had been stripped from Jews (J. McGeary 1997; M. Reynolds 1998).

UNITED STATES ANTI-SEMITISM: PAST

Compared to the brutalities of Europe from the time of the early Christian church to the rule of Hitler, the United States cannot be described as a nation with a history of severe anti-Semitism. Nevertheless, the United States has also had its outbreaks of anti-Semitism, though none have begun to approach the scope of western Europe's. An examination of the status of Jewish Americans today indicates the extent of remaining discrimination against Jews. Contemporary anti-Semitism, however, must be seen in relation to past injustices.

In 1654, the year Jews arrived in colonial America, Peter Stuyvesant, governor of New Amsterdam (the Dutch city later named New York), attempted to expel them from the city. Stuyvesant's efforts failed, but they were the beginning of an unending effort to separate Jews from the rest of the population. Because the pre–1880 immigration of Jews was relatively small, anti-Semitism was little noticed except, of course, by Jews. Most nineteenth-century movements against minorities were targeted at Catholics and Blacks and ignored Jews. In fact, Jews occasionally joined in such movements. By the 1870s, however, signs of a pattern of social discrimination against Jews had appeared. Colleges limited the number of Jewish students or excluded Jews altogether. The first Jewish fraternity was founded in 1898 to compensate for the barring of Jews from campus social organizations. As Jews began to compete for white-collar jobs early in the twentieth century, job discrimination became the rule, rather than the exception (J. Higham 1966; M. Selzer 1972).

The 1920s and the 1930s were the period of the most virulent and overt anti-Semitism. During these decades, the myth of an internationally organized Jewry took shape. According to a forged document entitled the *Protocols of the Elders of Zion,* Jews throughout the world planned to conquer all governments, and the major vehicle for this rise to power was communism, said by anti-Semites to be a Jewish movement. Absurd though this argument was, some respected Americans accepted the thesis of an international Jewish conspiracy and believed in the authenticity of the *Protocols.* Henry Ford, founder of the automobile company that bears his name, was responsible for the publication of the *Protocols. The Dearborn Independent,* a weekly newspaper owned by Ford, published anti-Semitic material for seven years. Finally in 1927, faced with several million dollars' worth of civil suits for slandering well-known Jewish Americans, he published a halfhearted apology. In his later years, Ford expressed regret for his espousal of anti-Semitic causes, but the damage had been done; he had lent an air of respectability to the most exaggerated charges against Jewish people.

It is not clear why Henry Ford—even for a short period of his life—so willingly accepted anti-Semitism. But Ford was not alone. Groups like the Ku Klux Klan and the German American Bund, as well as radio personalities like the Catholic priest Charles E. Coughlin, preached about the Jewish conspiracy as if it were fact. By the 1930s, those who held such sentiments usually expressed a fondness for Hitler and showed little concern about Germany's actions against Jews. Even the famed aviator Charles Lindbergh made speeches to gatherings claiming that Jews were forcing the United States into a war so that Jewish people could profit by wartime production. When the barbarous treatment of the Jews by Nazi Germany was exposed, most Americans were horrified by such events, and individuals like Lindbergh were as puzzled as anyone about how some Americans could have been so swept up by the pre-World War II wave of anti-Semitism (G. Meyers 1943; M. Selzer 1972).

The next section examines anti-Semitic feelings in contemporary America. Several crucial differences between anti-Semitism in Europe and in the United States need to be considered. First, and most important, the U.S. government has never promoted anti-Semitism. Unlike its European counterparts, the U.S. government has never embarked on an anti-Semitic program of expulsion or extermination. Second, because anti-Semitism was never institutionalized in the United States as it sometimes has been in Europe, American Jews have not needed to develop a defensive ideology to ensure the survival of their people. A Jewish American can make a largely personal decision about how much to assimilate or how secular to become. For Jewish Europeans, on the other hand, the major question of life has more often been how to survive, not whether to assimilate (B. Halpern 1974).

CONTEMPORARY ANTI-SEMITISM

Next to social research on anti-Black attitudes and behavior of Whites, anti-Semitism has been the major focus of studies of prejudice by sociologists and psychologists. Most of the conclusions described in Chapter 2 apply equally to the data collected on anti-Semitism. Relatively little concern was expressed by Jews in the United States about anti-Semitism immediately after World War II. From the latter 1960s into the 1990s, however, anti-Semitism has again appeared to be a threat in many parts of the world. For example, the infamous *Protocols,* used earlier to promote the notion of an international conspiracy of Jews, resurfaced in the Soviet Union in the 1970s and in Japan in the 1980s (D. A. Harris 1987; G. Johnson 1987; T. Smith 1994).

The Anti-Defamation League (ADL) of B'nai B'rith, founded in 1913, makes an annual survey of reported anti-Semitic incidents. Although the number has fluctuated, the 1994 tabulation reached the highest level in the seventeen years during which the ADL has been recording such incidents. It dropped slightly the next three years. Figure 13.4 shows the rise of harassment, threats, and assaults, which, adding episodes of vandalism, brings the total to 1,571 incidents for 1997. Some incidents were inspired and carried out by neo-Nazi skinheads—groups of young people who champion racist and anti-Semitic ideologies. Particularly disturbing has been the number of reported anti-Semitic incidents on college campuses. In 1997, 104 incidents were reported on eighty campuses. Anti-Jewish graffiti, anti-Semitic speakers, and swastikas affixed to predominantly Jewish fraternities were among the documented incidents. Particularly chilling is the Internet as a growing vehicle for anti-Semitism either by delivering such messages or serving as a means of reaching Web sites that spread intolerance (Anti-Defamation League of B'nai B'rith 1998).

Acts of anti-Semitic violence in the United States, along with the continuing Middle East conflict and the expression of anti-Semitic themes by some African Americans, have prompted renewed national attention to anti-Semitism.

American Jews and Israel When the Middle East became a major hot spot in international affairs in the 1960s, a revival of 1930s anti-Semitism occurred. Many

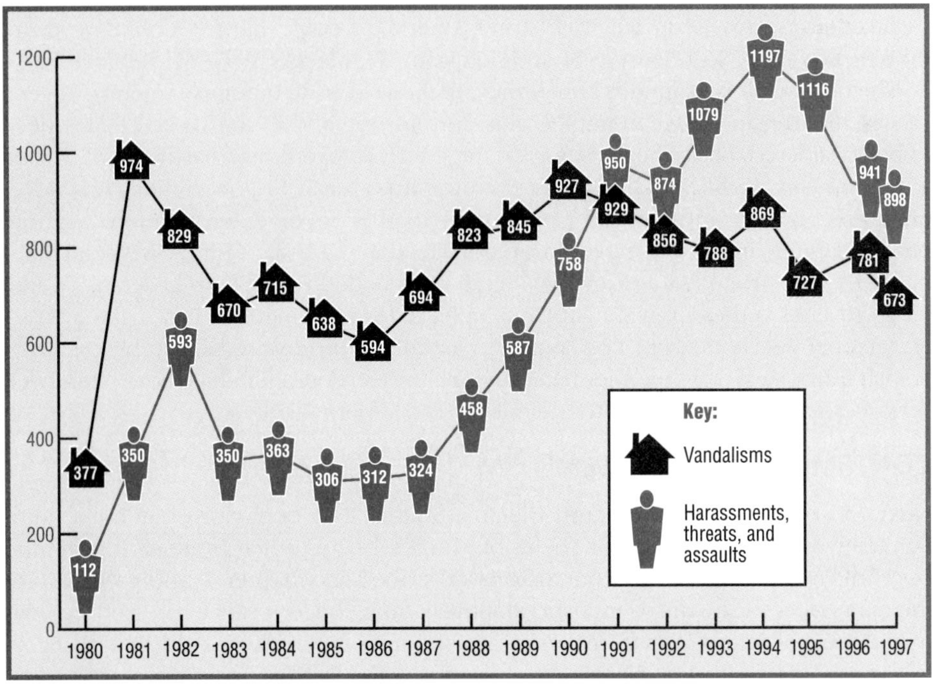

Figure 13.4 Anti-Semitic Incidents, 1980–1997

Source: Reprinted with permission of the Anti-Defamation League.

Jewish Americans expressed concern that, because Jews are freer in the United States than they have been in perhaps any other country in their history, they would ignore the struggle of other Jews. Israel's precarious status has proven to be a strong source of identity for Jewish Americans. Major wars in the Middle East in 1967, 1973, and 1991 reminded the world of Israel's vulnerability. Palestinian uprisings in the Occupied Territories and international recognition of the Palestine Liberation Organization (PLO) in 1988 eroded the strong pro-Israeli front among the Western powers. A few Jewish Americans have shown their commitment to the Israeli cause by actually emigrating to Israel. Although not all American Jews agree with Israel's actions, many Jews express support for Israel's struggles by contributing money and by trying to influence American opinion and policy to be more favorable to Israel.

The Anti-Defamation League has carefully watched for any trends signaling disfavor toward Israel. The 1973 oil embargo by the Arab states and the subsequent rise in American gasoline prices led to what some leaders of the ADL identified as an "oil backlash," when some people in the United States held Jews responsible for empty gas tanks. The ADL saw the oil embargo as signaling an end to "the golden age of Jewish life in America," when anti-Jewish feelings were minimal. Arab nations pressured American corporations not to invest in Israel and even not to place Jews in high management positions. The U.S. Army acknowledged in 1975 that it had not sent Jewish soldiers to Saudi Arabia because of that government's pressure. Such restrictions ended during the massive buildup for the 1991 Persian Gulf War (Lichtenstein and Denenberg 1975; T. Smith 1994).

In the year after the oil embargo (1974), the United Nations General Assembly ignored American and Israeli objections and passed a resolution declaring that "Zionism is a form of racism and racial discrimination." **Zionism,** which initially referred to the old Jewish religious yearning to return to the biblical homeland, has been expressed in the twentieth century in the movement to create a Jewish state in Palestine. Ever since the Diaspora, the exile of Jews from Palestine several centuries before Christianity, many Jews have seen the destiny of their people only as the establishment of a Jewish state in the Holy Land. The Zionism resolution, finally repealed by the UN in 1991, had no lasting influence and did not change any nation's foreign policy. It did, however, increase Jewish fears of reawakened anti-Semitism thinly disguised as attacks on Zionist beliefs. Even the development of agreements between Israel and its Arab neighbors and the international recognition of Palestinian autonomy in Israel did not end the concern of Jewish Americans that continuing anti-Israeli feeling reflected anti-Semitism (R. Carroll 1975; T. Smith 1994; I. Spiegel 1973a, 1973b).

American Jews and African Americans The contemporary anti-Semitism of African Americans is of special concern to Jewish Americans. There is no reason why anti-Semites should be exclusively White, but Jews have been especially troubled by Blacks expressing ethnic prejudices, given their own history of oppression. Jewish Americans have been active in civil rights causes and have contributed generously to legal defense funds. Jewish neighborhoods and employers have also been quicker than their Gentile counterparts to accept African Americans. There is, therefore, a positive Black-Jewish alliance with a long history. For these reasons, some Jews find it especially difficult to understand why another group experiencing prejudice and discrimination should express anti-Semitic sentiments.

Desecration of gravestones in Jewish cemeteries is one form that contemporary anti-Semitism takes in the United States.

Surveys do not necessarily show significant differences between Blacks and Whites in anti-Semitism, but studies do show a rise of anti-Semitism among African Americans. Added to this attitudinal component have been highly publicized events that have brought attention to Black anti-Semitism as well as anti-Black feelings among Jewish Americans (T. Smith 1990).

Beginning in the 1960s, some African American activists and the

Black Panther Party supported the Arabs in the Middle East conflict and called on Israel to surrender. Black-Jewish relations were again inflamed in 1984 by the Reverend Jesse Jackson during his campaign for the Democratic Party's nomination for the presidency. His off-the-record reference to Jews as "Hymies" and the publicly broadcast anti-Semitic remarks by one of his supporters, Nation of Islam minister Louis Farrakhan, gave rise to new tensions between Blacks and Jews. During the 1988 campaign, Jackson distanced himself from anti-Semitic rhetoric, stating, "The sons and the daughters of the Holocaust and the sons and the daughters of slavery must find common ground again" (W. Schmidt 1988:14).

In the 1990s, unrelated events again seemed to draw attention to the relationship between Jews and African Americans. On several college campuses, invited African American speakers made anti-Israeli statements, inflaming the Jewish students in attendance. In a 1991 New York City incident, a Hasidic Jew ran a red light, killing an African American child, and the ambulance that regularly serves the Hasidic community did not pick up the child. In the emotional climate that resulted, an Australian Jewish researcher was stabbed to death, and several days of rioting in the Brooklyn, New York, neighborhood of Crown Heights followed (Morris and Rubin 1993).

In response to these and other events, many Jewish and African American leaders perceived a crisis in intergroup relations, and calls for unity became very public. For example, in 1994, the Reverend Jesse Jackson sought to distance himself from the statements of Khalid Abdul Muhammad, an aide of Farrakhan, calling him "racist, anti-Semitic, divisive, untrue, and chilling" (A. Finder 1994:21).

African American resentment, in many situations attracting notoriety, has rarely been anti-Jewish as such but rather has been opposed to White institutions. As author James Baldwin (1967) said, Blacks "are anti-Semitic because they're anti-White" (p. 114). That racial prejudice is deep in the United States is shown by the fact that two groups suffering discrimination, groups that might unite in opposition to the dominant society, fight each other instead.

An old Yiddish saying, "Schwer zu sein a Yid" means "It is tough to be a Jew." Anti-Semitism past and present are related. The old hostilities seem to never die. The atrocities of Nazi Germany have not been forgotten nor should they be. Racial and ethnic hostility, against whatever group, unifies the group against its attackers, and Jewish Americans are no exception. The Jewish people of the United States have come together, regardless of nationality, to form a minority group with a high degree of group identity.

Position of Jewish Americans

Jewish Americans have an important role in contemporary America. They are active participants in the fight for civil rights and work on behalf of Israel. These efforts are important but only begin to describe their role in the United States. For a better perspective on Jewish people in the United States, the following summarizes their present situation with respect to (1) employment and income, (2) education, (3) organizational activity, and (4) political activity.

EMPLOYMENT AND INCOME

Discrimination conditions all facets of a subordinate group's life. Jews have experienced, and to a limited extent still experience, differential treatment in the American job market. A 1956 survey of employers in San Francisco showed that one out of four acknowledged that it either barred Jews altogether or limited their employment to a predetermined level. Civil rights acts and U.S. Supreme Court decisions have made it illegal to discriminate in employment. The results of a 1998 national survey showed that 71 percent of Jews viewed anti-Semitism as a problem in the United States, although not necessarily in hiring practices. As shown in Table 13.1, through perseverance and emphasis on education, Jewish Americans as a group have overcome barriers to full employment and now enjoy high incomes (Los Angeles Times Poll 1998).

Using a variety of techniques, social science studies have documented declining discrimination against Jews in the business world. Sociologist Samuel Klausner interviewed business school graduates, comparing Jews with Protestants and Roman Catholics who graduated from the same university in the same year. Klausner (1988) concludes that: "(1) Jewish MBAs are winning positions in the same industries as their Catholic and Protestant classmates; (2) they are rising more rapidly in corporate hierarchies than their Catholic and Protestant colleagues; (3) they are achieving higher salaries than their Catholic and Protestant colleagues" (p. 33). Klausner adds that researchers tested seven indicators of discrimination and, in each case, failed to find evidence of discrimination against Jewish executives. Interestingly, however, this same study detected substantial discrimination against African Americans and women.

The economic success of the Jewish people as a group obscures the poverty of many individual Jewish families. We reached a similar conclusion in Chapter 11 from income data on Asian Americans and their image as a model minority. Sociologists largely agree that Jews in 1930 were as likely to be poverty-stricken and to be living in slums as any minority group today. Most have escaped poverty, but what Ann Wolfe (1972) calls "the invisible Jewish poor" remains, invisible to the rest of society. Like Chinese Americans, the Jewish poor were not well served by the Economic Opportunity Act and other federal experiments to eradicate poverty in the 1960s and 1970s. Although the proportion of the poor among the Jews is not as substantial as among Blacks or Hispanics, it does remind us that not all Jewish families have affluent lifestyles (M. Gold 1965; A. Lavender 1977; Levine and Hochbaum 1974).

EDUCATION

Jews place great emphasis on education (see Table 13.1). This desire for formal schooling stems, it is argued, from the Judaic religion, which places the rabbi, or teacher, at the center of religious life. In the United States today, all Jewish congregations emphasize religious instruction more than Protestants typically do. The more religiously orthodox require instruction on Sundays as well as on weekday afternoons following attendance at public schools. Seventy-six percent of Jews have received some form of formal Jewish education before they reach thirty years of age. New Jewish schools have been built during the 1990s partly in recognition of the

Table 13.1 Profile of Jews in the United States

	Jewish Americans	All U.S.
Income		
Less than $40,000	28%	52%
$40,000–$59,999	18	21
$60,000 or more	38	20
Don't know/refused	16	7
Occupation		
Professional	40	15
Managers	24	20
White collar	19	19
Business owners	8	9
Unskilled blue collar	5	16
Skilled blue collar	3	19
Ideology		
Liberal	46	24
Moderate	28	31
Conservative	23	40
Political party		
Democrat	45	32
Independent	29	31
Republican	12	23
Education		
High school or less	13	59
Some college	27	21
College graduate	24	10
Graduate school	35	9

Source: Los Angeles Times Poll 1998.

desire to maintain the cultural ties but also because of dissatisfaction with the public schools. The Jewish-sponsored component of higher education is not limited to strict religious instruction such as found in rabbinical schools. Beginning in 1947, Jews founded graduate schools of medicine, education, social work, and mathematics, along with Brandeis University, which offers both undergraduate and graduate degrees. These institutions are nonsectarian (that is, admission is not limited to Jews) and are conceived of as a Jewish-sponsored contribution to higher education (A. Abrahamson 1997; *Los Angeles Times* Poll 1998).

The religiously based tradition of lifelong study has left as a legacy a value system that stresses education. The poverty of Jewish immigrants kept them from devoting years to secular schooling, but they were determined that their children do better. Despite their high levels of educational attainment, some members of the Jewish community express concern about Jewish education. They are disappointed with its highly secularized nature—not only because religious teaching has been limited, but because the Jewish sociocultural experience has been avoided altogether.

It may even contribute to Judaization, the lessening of Judaism. A group of sociologists (Glock et al. 1975; I. Spiegel 1975), after uncovering anti-Semitism among a sample of grade school and high school students, recommended that public schools not ignore the history of Judaism or sidestep anti-Semitism. There is no evidence that American public schools have changed curriculum materials to consider the Jewish experience as they have the role of Black Americans. Obviously the absence of dealing with the place of Jews in history only serves to contribute to Holocaust revisionism.

ORGANIZATIONAL ACTIVITY

The American Jewish community has encompassed a variety of organizations since its beginnings. These groups serve many purposes: some are religious, and others are charitable, political, or educational. No organization, secular or religious, represents all American Jews, but there are more than 300 nationwide organizations. Among the most significant are the United Jewish Appeal (UJA), the American Jewish Committee, the American Jewish Congress, and B'nai B'rith. The UJA was founded in 1939 and serves as a fund-raising organization for humanitarian causes. Recently, Israel has received the largest share of the funds collected. The American Jewish Committee (founded in 1906) and Congress (1918) work toward the similar purpose of improving Jewish–Gentile relations. B'nai B'rith (Sons of the Covenant) was founded in 1843 and claims 500,000 members in forty nations. It promotes cultural and social programs and, through its Anti-Defamation League, monitors and fights anti-Semitism and hate crimes directed at other groups.

Besides the national groups, many community-based organizations are active. Some local organizations, such as social and business clubs, were founded because the existing groups barred Jews from membership. The U.S. Supreme Court has consistently ruled that private social organizations like country clubs and business clubs may discriminate against Jews or any ethnic or racial group. Jewish

Young people gather at a Jewish school to study the Torah.

community centers are also prominent local organizations. To Gentiles, the synagogue is the most visible symbol of the Jewish presence at the community level. The Jewish community center, however, serves as an important focus of local activity. In many Jewish neighborhoods throughout the United States, it is the center of secular activity. Hospitals, nurseries, homes for the elderly, and child-care agencies are only a few of the community-level activities sponsored by Jewish Americans (S. Rabinove 1970; M. Sklare 1971).

POLITICAL ACTIVITY

American Jews play a prominent role in politics as both voters and elected officials. Jews as a group are not typical in that they are more likely than the general population to label themselves liberal (refer back to Table 13.1). Although upper-middle-class voters tend to vote Republican, Jewish voters in that category have been steadfastly Democratic. In fourteen presidential elections, beginning in 1940, Jews have voted at least 82 percent Democratic seven times and have always given the Democrats more of their votes than the Republicans. Jewish suburban voters, unlike those in the central cities, tend to be more supportive of Republican candidates but are still more Democratic than their Gentile neighbors. While the Democratic president, Bill Clinton, was successful in his reelection bid to defeat Bob Dole in 1996, with 49 percent of the vote, an estimated 78 percent of Jewish Americans supported Clinton.

Jews have long been successful in being elected to office, but it was not until 1988 that an Orthodox Jew from Connecticut was elected to the U.S. Senate. Joseph Lieberman refrained from campaigning on the Sabbath each week; his religious views were not an issue. However, the Jewish community does not automatically support Jewish candidates. For example, New York Senator Alfonse D'Amato in an earlier election was heavily backed financially by Jewish lobbyists over his contender, a Jewish candidate because of D'Amato's strong pro-Israeli position. Yet when Charles Schumer, a pro-Israeli Democrat challenger, successfully defeated D'Amato in 1998, the Republican only received 23 percent of the Jewish vote (J. Chanes 1994, J. Dao 1998; *New York Times* 1996).

As in all subordinate groups, the political activity of Jewish Americans has not been limited to conventional electoral politics. Radical Jewish politics has been dominated by college students. At the height of their involvement in the late 1960s, Jewish youths were active with Gentiles in the New Left movement as well as working alone for causes unique to Jews, like the support of Israel. Into the 1980s and 1990s, some Jews backed the more extreme responses to the friction between Israel and its Arab neighbors. A few even settled in Israel and, while small in number, were often vocal backers of resistance to any accommodation to the Arab nations or the Palestinian refugees (J. Porter 1970).

Religious Life

Jewish identity and participation in the Jewish religion are not the same. Many Americans consider themselves Jewish and are considered Jewish by others even though they have never participated in Jewish religious life. The available data indicate that

44 percent of American Jews are affiliated with a synagogue or temple, but only one-quarter attend services monthly. Even in Israel, only 30 percent of Jews are religiously observant. Nevertheless, the presence of a religious tradition is an important tie among Jews, even secular Jews (S. Cohen 1991).

The unitary Jewish tradition developed in the United States into three sects, beginning in the middle of the nineteenth century. The differences among Orthodox, Conservative, and Reform Judaism are based on their varying acceptance of traditional rituals. All three sects embrace a philosophy based on the Torah, the first five books of the Old Testament. The differences developed because some Jews wanted to be less distinguishable from other Americans. Another significant factor in explaining the development of different groups is the absence of a religious elite and bureaucratic hierarchy. This facilitated the breakdown in traditional practices.

Orthodox Jewish life is very demanding, especially in a basically Christian society like the United States. Almost all conduct is defined by rituals that require an Orthodox Jew to reaffirm his or her religious conviction constantly. Most Americans are familiar with **kashrut**, the laws pertaining to permissible and forbidden foods. When strictly adhered to, kashrut governs not only what foods may be eaten (kosher), but how the food is prepared, served, and eaten. Besides day-to-day practices, Orthodox Jews have weekly and annual observances. Marshall Sklare (1971) summarized the contrast between the Jewish faith and that of the dominant society: "The thrust of Jewish religious culture is sacramental [while] the thrust of American religious culture is moralistic" (p. 111, also see I. Shenker 1979).

Even Orthodox Jews differ in their level of adherence to traditional practices. Among the ultraorthodox are the Hasidic Jews, or Hasidim, who reside chiefly in several neighborhoods in Brooklyn. To the Hasidim, following the multitude of mitzvahs, or commandments of behavior, is as important today as it was in the time of Moses. They wear no garments that mix linen and wool. Men wear a yarmulka, or skullcap, constantly, even while sleeping. Attending a secular college is frowned on. Instead, the men undertake a lifetime of study of the Torah and the accompanying rabbinical literature of the Talmud. Women's education consists of instruction on how to run the home in keeping with Orthodox tradition (M. Abrahamson 1996).

Orthodox children attend special schools so as to meet minimal New York State educational requirements. The devotion to religious study is reflected in this comment by a Hasidic Jew: "Look at Freud, Marx, Einstein—all Jews who made their mark on the non-Jewish world. To me, however, they would have been much better off studying in a yeshivah [a Jewish school]. What a waste of three fine Talmudic minds" (H. Arden 1975:294). Although devoted to their religion, the Hasidim participate in local elections and politics and are employed in outside occupations. All such activities are influenced by their orthodoxy and a self-reliance rarely duplicated elsewhere in the United States (M. Danzger 1989; C. Liebman 1973; E. Schoenfeld 1976; R. Schultz 1974; *Time* 1972).

Reform Jews, though deeply committed to the religious faith, have altered many of the rituals. Women and men usually sit together in Reform congregations, and some congregations have introduced organ music and choirs. A few have even experimented with observing the Sabbath on Sunday. Circumcision for males is not mandatory. Civil divorce decrees are sufficient and recognized so that a divorce granted by a three-man rabbinical court is not required before remarriage. Reform Jews recognize the children of Jewish men and non-Jewish women as Jews with no need to convert. All these practices would be unacceptable to the Orthodox Jew.

Conservative Judaism is a compromise between the rigidity of the Orthodox and the extreme modification of the Reform. Because of the middle position, the national organization of Conservatives, the United Synagogue of America, strives to create its own identity and seeks to view its traditions as an appropriate, authentic approach to the faith.

A rabbi blesses a 13-year old at her Bat Mitzvah in the temple.

Table 13.2 displays some results of a national survey on Jewish identification. The three sects here include both members and nonmembers of local congregations. Reform Jews are the least likely of the three religious groups to participate in religious events, to be involved in the Jewish community, or to participate in predominantly Jewish organizations. Yet in Reform temples there has been an effort today to observe religious occasions such as Rosh Hashanah (*Religion Watch* 1995c; J. Wertheimer 1996).

The one exception in Reform Jews' relatively low levels of participation is on issues concerning world Jewry, such as Israel or the treatment of Jews in such nations as the former Soviet Union and Iran. For the Orthodox Jew these issues are less important than those strictly related to the observance of the faith. Although no nationwide organized movement advocates this, in recent years Reform Jews seem to have reclaimed traditions they once rejected.

Unlike most faiths in the United States, Jews historically have not embarked on recruitment or evangelistic programs to attract new members. Beginning in the late 1970s, Jews, especially Reform Jews, debated the possibility of outreach programs. Least objectionable to Jewish congregations were efforts begun in 1978 aimed at non-Jewish partners and children in mixed marriages. In 1981, the program was broadened to invite conversions by Americans who had no religious connection, but these modest recruitment drives are still far from resembling those that have been carried out by Protestant denominations for decades (K. Briggs 1978; *New York Times* 1982).

The Judaic faith embraces a number of factions or denominations that are similar in their roots but marked by sharp distinctions. No precise data reveal the relative numbers of the three major groups. Part of the problem is the difficulty of placing individuals in the proper group. It is common, for example, for a Jew to be a member of an Orthodox congregation but consider himself or herself Conservative. The following levels of affiliation are based on the 1998 national survey of Jewish

Americans (*Los Angeles Times* Poll 1998) and show ranges depending upon whether one considers only those born Jewish or also those who converted:

- Orthodox: 9 percent
- Conservative: 23 percent
- Reform: 29 percent
- Just Jewish: 18 percent
- Non-Jewish: 16 percent

As Protestant denominations, Jewish denominations are associated with class, nationality, and other social differences. The Reform Jews are the wealthiest and have the best formal education of the group; the Orthodox are the poorest and least educated in years of formal secular schooling; and the Conservatives occupy a position between the two, as shown in Table 13.2. A fourth branch of American Judaism, Reconstructionism, an offshoot of the Conservative movement, has only recently developed an autonomous institutional structure with ritual practices similar to the Reform. Religious identification is associated with generation: Immigrants and older Jews are more likely to be Orthodox, and their grandchildren are more likely to be Reform (*Los Angeles Times* Poll 1998).

Jewish Identity

Ethnic and racial identification can be positive or negative. Awareness of ethnic identity can contribute to an individual's self-esteem and give that person a sense of group solidarity with similar people. When a person experiences an identity only as a basis for discrimination or insults, the individual may want to shed his or her identity in favor of one more acceptable to society. Unfavorable differential treatment can also encourage closer ties among members of the community being discriminated against, as it has for Jews.

Most would judge the diminishing of out-group hostility and the ability of Jews to leave the ghetto as a positive development (G. Friedman 1967). However, the improvement in Jewish—Gentile relations also creates a new problem in Jewish social identity. It has become possible for Jews to shed their "Jewishness," or **Yiddishkait.** Many retain their Yiddishkait even in suburbia, but it is more difficult there than in

Table 13.2 Jewish Identification by Group (in percent)

Indices	Orthodox	Conservative	Reformed	"Just Jewish"
Ethnic pride	86	79	73	65
Closeness to Jews	90	83	71	54
Observance of Jewish holidays	73	42	28	18
Observance of Christian holidays	6	6	17	28
Pro-Israel	78	71	56	50

Source: S. Cohen 1991: 58, 63, 74.

the ghetto. In the end, however, Jews cannot lose their identity entirely. Jews are still denied total assimilation in the United States no matter how much the individual ceases to think of himself or herself as Jewish. Social clubs may still refuse membership and prospective non-Jewish in-laws may try to interfere with plans to marry.

Events in the world also remind the most assimilated Jew of the heritage left behind. A few such reminders in the past generation include Nazi Germany, the founding of Israel in 1948, the Six-Day War of 1967, Soviet interference with Jewish life and migration, the terrorist attack at the 1972 Munich Olympics, the Yom Kippur War of 1973, the 1973 oil embargo, the UNO's 1974 anti-Zionism vote, and the Scud missile attacks during the 1991 Gulf War.

A unique identity issue presents itself to Jewish women, whose religious tradition has placed them in a subordinate position. For example, it was not until 1972 the first female rabbi was ordained. Jewish feminism has its roots in the women's movement of the 1960s and 1970s, several of whose leaders were Jewish. There have been some changes in **halakha** (Jewish law covering obligations and duties), but it is still difficult for a woman to get a divorce recognized by the Orthodox Jewish tradition. Sima Rabinowicz of upstate New York has been hailed as the "Jewish Rosa Parks" for her recent bus battle. Rabinowicz refused to give up her seat in

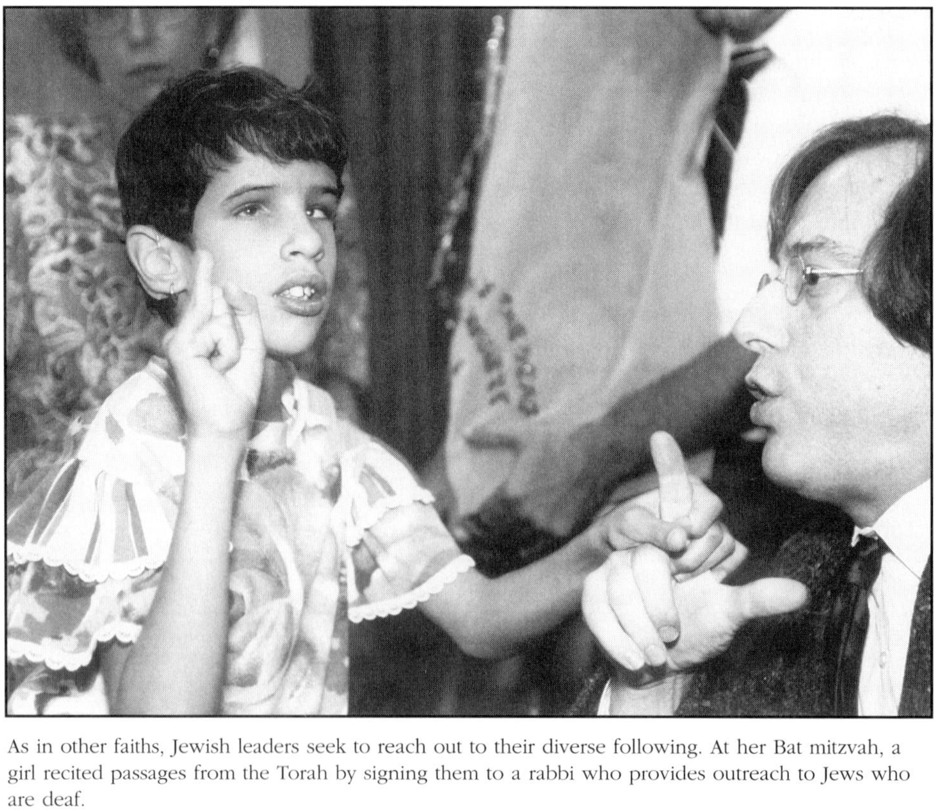

As in other faiths, Jewish leaders seek to reach out to their diverse following. At her Bat mitzvah, a girl recited passages from the Torah by signing them to a rabbi who provides outreach to Jews who are deaf.

the women's section of a Hasidic-owned, publicly subsidized bus to Orthodox men who wanted to pray in private, segregated from women as required by halakha. The courts defended her right to ride as she wished, just as an earlier court had ruled with Rosa Parks in the Birmingham bus boycott. Jewish women contend that they should not be forced to make a choice between their identities as a woman and as a Jew (G. Baum 1998; B. Frankel 1995a).

We will now examine three factors that influence the ethnic identity of Jews in the United States: family, religion, and cultural heritage.

ROLE OF THE FAMILY

In general, the family works to socialize children, but for religious Jews it also fulfills a religious commandment. In the past this compulsion was so strong that the shadchan (the marriage broker or matchmaker) fulfilled an important function in the Jewish community by ensuring marriage for all eligible people. The emergence of romantic love in modern society made the shadchan less acceptable to young Jews, but recent statistics show Jews more likely to marry than any other group.

Jews have traditionally remained in extended families, intensifying the transmission of Jewish identity. Numerous observers have argued that the Jewish family today no longer maintains its role in identity transmission and that the family is consequently contributing to assimilation. The American Jewish Committee released a report in 1976 identifying ten problems that are endangering "the family as the main transmission agent of Jewish values, identity, and continuity" (B. Conver 1976:A2). The following issues are still relevant to Jews nearly two decades later:

1. More Jews marry later than members of other groups.
2. Most organizations of single Jews no longer operate solely for the purpose of matching. These groups are now supportive of singles and the single way of life.
3. The divorce rate is rising; there is no presumption of the permanence of marriage and no stigma attached to its failure.
4. The birthrate is falling, and childlessness has become socially acceptable.
5. Financial success has taken precedence over child raising in importance and for many has become the major goal of the family.
6. The intensity of family interaction has decreased, although it continues to be higher than in most other religious and ethnic groups.
7. There is less socializing across generation lines, partly as a result of geographic mobility.
8. The sense of responsibility of family members to other family members has declined.
9. The role of Jewishness is no longer central to the lives of Jews.
10. Intermarriage has lessened the involvement of the Jewish partner in Jewish life and the emphasis on Jewish aspects of family life.

Data and sample surveys have verified these trends. Nevertheless, to use a term introduced in Chapter 10 in connection with the Hispanic family, Jewish Americans still have a higher than typical degree of familism. Jews are more likely than other ethnic or religious groups to be members of a household that interacts regularly with kinfolk. Nonetheless, the trend is away from familism, a trend that could further erode Jewish identity.

Without question, of the ten problems cited by the American Jewish Committee, intermarriage has received the greatest attention from Jewish leaders. Since Christianity's influence has grown, a persistent fear among Jews has been that their children or grandchildren would grow up to be *amhaaretz,* ignorant of the Torah. Even worse, a descendant might become *apikoros,* an unbeliever who engages in intellectual speculation about the relevance of Judaism. Intermarriage, of course, makes a decrease in the size of the Jewish community in the United States more likely. As the tolerance of mixed marriages rises in the United States, so, too, does Jewish leaders' concern over it, especially since the decrease in cultural differences between Jews and Gentiles makes such marriages a greater possibility. In marriages around 1970, over 70 percent of Jews married Jews or people who converted to Judaism. In marriages since 1985, that proportion has dropped to 48 percent. This change means that American Jews today are just as likely to marry a Gentile as a Jew. Three-quarters of the children of these Jewish-Gentile marriages are not raised as Jews (Kosmin et al. 1991; P. Steinfels 1992).

Several trends come together to lead to a stabilization or decline in the number of active Jews in the United States. As shown in Figure 13.5, the continuation of a Jewish tradition varies dramatically by denomination. Conservative and Orthodox Jews have larger families, encourage formal Jewish instruction, and are much less likely to witness intermarriage compared to Reform or unaffiliated ("just Jewish") Jewish Americans. Analysts of these data are concerned that Jews, especially if they are not Orthodox, cannot take it for granted that they will have grandchildren with whom to share Seders, Sabbath, and other Jewish moments (Gordona and Horowitz 1997).

Intermarriage, however, need not mean a decline in the number of the faithful. Non-Jewish spouses can convert to Judaism and raise their children in the faith. For example, 60 percent of intermarried Jews still participate in Passover rituals. However, some more traditional Jews question the integrity of these occasional ventures into the faith and see them as further evidence of Judaization. Yet many Jewish leaders respond that intermarriage is inevitable, and the Jewish community must build on whatever links the intermarried couple may still have with Jewish ethnic culture. The increase in intermarriage leads to further anxiety about the survival of religious and cultural traditions. Indeed, there are nearly 600 programs in the United States to help Gentile spouses of Jews feel welcome so that the faith will not lose them both. Yet other Jews feel that such efforts may be sending a dangerous signal that intermarriage is inevitable (D. Drin 1997; P. Steinfels 1992; J. Wertheimer 1994; K. Woodward 1991).

ROLE OF RELIGION

Devotion to Judaism appears to be the clear way to preserve ethnic identity. Yet Jews are divided about how to practice their faith. Many of the Orthodox see Reform Jews as little better than nonbelievers. Even among the Orthodox, some sects like the

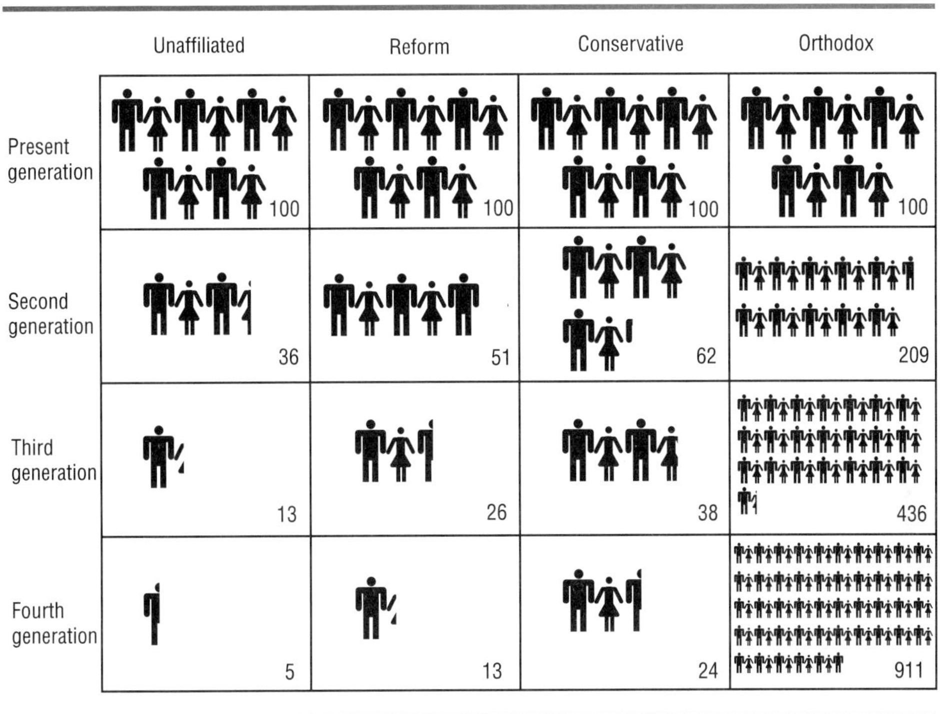

Figure 13.5 Generational Patterns by Denomination

Source: Gordon and Rabinowitz 1997. Based on the 1990 National Population Survey and the 1991 NY Jewish Population Study.

Lubavitchers try to awaken less observant Orthodox Jews to their spiritual obligation. Added to these developments is the continuing rise in Jewish out-marriages previously noted. Many Jewish religious rituals are centered in the home rather than in the synagogue, from lighting Sabbath candles to observing dietary laws. Jews are far more likely, therefore, to feel that children cannot be brought up in the faith without that family support.

The religious question facing Jews is not so much one of ideology as of observing the commandments of traditional Jewish law. The religious variations among the nearly six million Jewish Americans are a product of attempts to accommodate traditional rituals and precepts to life in the dominant society. It is in adhering to such rituals that Jews are most likely to be at odds with the Christian theme advanced in public schools, even if it appears only in holiday parties. In Chapter 1, we introduced the term **marginality** to describe the status of living in two distinct cultures simultaneously. Jews who give some credence to the secular aspects of Christmastime celebrations exemplify individuals' accommodating themselves to two cultures. For all but the most Orthodox, this acceptance means disobeying commandments or even accepting non-Jewish traditions by singing Christmas carols or exchanging greeting cards.

Is there a widespread pattern among Jewish Americans of reviving the "old ways"? Some Jews, especially those secure in their position, have taken up renewed orthodoxy. It is difficult to say whether the rise of traditionalism among Jews is a significant force or a fringe movement, as it was viewed in the 1960s. In the 1990s, Jewish leaders in North America and Europe are much more likely to express concern about the increase in the number of secularized Jews than to find reasons to applaud an increase in Yiddishkait (R. Gledhill 1992).

ROLE OF CULTURAL HERITAGE

For many Jews, religious observance is a very small aspect of their Jewishness. They express their identity instead in a variety of political, cultural, and social activities. For them, acts of worship, fasting, eating permitted foods, and the study of the Torah and the Talmud are irrelevant to being Jewish. Religious Jews, of course, find such a position impossible to accept (C. Liebman 1973).

Many Gentiles mistakenly suppose that a measure of Jewishness is the ability to speak Yiddish. Few people have spoken as many languages as the Jews through their long history. Yiddish is only one, and it developed in Jewish communities in eastern Europe between the tenth and twelfth centuries. Fluency in Yiddish in the United States has been associated with the immigrant generation and the Orthodox. Sidney Goldstein and Calvin Goldscheider (1968) reported that evidence overwhelmingly supports the conclusion that linguistic assimilation among Jews is almost complete by the third generation (see also I. Shenker 1974). The 1960s and 1970s, however, brought a slight increase in the use of Hebrew. This change was probably due to increased pride in Israel and a greater interaction between that nation and the United States.

Overall, the differences between Jews and Gentiles have declined in the United States. To a large extent, this reduction is a product of generational changes typical of all ethnic groups. The first-generation Mexican American in Los Angeles contrasts sharply with the middle-class White living in suburban Boston. The convergence in culture and identity is much greater between the fourth-generation Chicano and his or her White counterpart. A similar convergence is occurring among Jews. This change does not signal the eventual demise of the Jewish identity. Moreover, Jewish identity is not a single identity, as we can see from the heterogeneity in religious observance, dedication to Jewish and Israeli causes, and participation in Jewish organizations.

Being Jewish comes from the family, the faith, and the culture, but it does not require any one criterion. Jewishness transcends nation, religion, or culture. A sense of peoplehood is present that neither anti-Semitic bigotry nor even an ideal state of fellowship among all religions would destroy. American life may have drastically modified Jewish life in the direction of dominant society values, but it has not eliminated it. Milton Gordon (1964) refers to **peoplehood** as a group with a shared feeling. For Jews this sense of identity originates from a variety of sources, past and present, both within and without (S. Heilman 1982; H. Himmelfarb 1982; C. Liebman 1973).

CONCLUSION

Jewish Americans are the product of three waves of immigration originating from three different Jewish communities: the Sephardic, the western European, and the eastern European. They brought different languages and, to some extent, different levels of religious orthodoxy. Today, they have assimilated to form an ethnic group that transcends the initial differences in nationality.

Jews are not a homogeneous group. Among them are the Reform, the Conservative, and Orthodox denominations, listed in ascending order of adherence to traditional rituals. Nonreligious Jews make up another group, probably as large as any one segment, and still look on themselves as Jewish.

Jewish identity is reaffirmed from within and outside the Jewish community; however, both sources of affirmation are weaker today. Identity is strengthened by the family, religion, and the vast network of national and community-based organizations. Anti-Semitism outside the Jewish community strengthens the in-group feeling and the perception that survival as a people is threatened.

Today, American Jews face a new challenge: They must maintain their identity in an overwhelmingly Christian society in which discrimination is fading and outbreaks of prejudice are sporadic. Yiddishkait may not so much have decreased as changed. Elements of the Jewish tradition have been shed in part because of modernization and social change. Some of this social change—a decline in anti-Semitic violence and restrictions—is certainly welcome. While kashrut observance has declined, the vast majority of Jews care deeply about Israel, and many engage in pro-Israel activities. Commitment has changed with the times, but it has not disappeared (S. Cohen 1988).

Some members of the Jewish community view the apparent assimilation with alarm and warn against the grave likelihood of the total disappearance of a sizable and identifiable Jewish community in the United States. Others see the changes not as erosion but as an accommodation to a pluralistic, multicultural environment. We are witness to a progressive change in the substance and style of Jewish life. According to this view, Jewish identity, the Orthodox and Conservative traditions notwithstanding, has shed some of its traditional characteristics and has acquired others. The strength of this view comes with the knowledge that doomsayers have been present in the American Jewish community for at least two generations. Only the passage of time will divulge the nature of Jewish life in the United States (I. Finestein 1988; N. Glazer 1990).

Despite their successes, Jews experience discrimination and prejudice, as does any subordinate group. Michael Lerner (1993), editor of the liberal Jewish journal *Tikkun*, declares that "Jews can only be deemed 'white' if there is massive amnesia on the part of non-Jews about the monumental history of anti-Semitism" (p. 33). As we noted earlier, reported episodes of anti-Semitism are on the increase in Europe and North America, even on the college campuses in the United States.

Although discrimination against the Jews has gone on for centuries, far more ancient than anti-Semitism and the experience of the Diaspora is the subordinate role of women. Women were perhaps the first to be relegated to an inferior role and may be the last to work collectively to struggle for equal rights. Studying women as a subordinate group will reaffirm the themes in our study of racial and ethnic groups.

KEY TERMS

anti-Semitism 383
fringe-of-values theory 388
halakha 404
Holocaust 390
Holocaust revisionists 390
in-group virtues 389
Judaization 385
kashrut 401
marginality 407
out-group vices 389
peoplehood 408
Yiddishkait 403
Zionism 395

REVIEW QUESTIONS

1. Why are the Jewish people most accurately characterized as an ethnic group?
2. How have the patterns of anti-Semitism changed or remained the same?
3. Why do African American–Jewish American relationships receive special scrutiny?
4. Why is maintaining Jewish identity so difficult in the United States?
5. Why does the family play such a critical role in Jewish identity?

CRITICAL THINKING

1. Most minority groups regard acceptance as a positive outcome. Why do some Jewish Americans seem threatened by being accepted in contemporary Gentile society?
2. Using the Jewish experience as a basis for comparison, how has fusion functioned or not functioned for any other subordinate group when compared to Jews in the United States?
3. In Chapter 5 we presented Marcus Hansen's principle of third-generation interest. How does that apply or not apply to the generational differences displayed by denomination in Figure 13.5?
4. How different and similar have the experiences of women in organized religion been, compared with those of women in Jewish faith?

INTERNET EXERCISE

Jewish Americans have contributed much to the culture and history of the United States. To learn about the important role Jews played in the American Civil War, visit (http://www.jewish-history.com/civilwar.htm). Here you can read firsthand accounts by Jewish soldiers of Confederate and Union armies, as well as view photographs of the period. What was the 82nd Illinois Volunteer Infantry? Why was this an important and unique military unit? What was "General Orders #11"? Who issued this order, and what was the justification for doing so? What parallels are there between these orders and the recent experience of gays in the American military? What was it like to be a Jewish solider fighting during the Civil War? How were these experiences different and similar to those of other soldiers?.

FOR FURTHER INFORMATION

American Jewish Yearbook. New York: American Jewish Committee.
Published annually since 1899, this is the best available reference book on Jewish Americans. Each edition contains different articles plus updated biographies and bibliographies.

Alan Dershowitz. *The Vanishing Jew.* Boston: Little, Brown, 1997.
Outspoken attorney and law school professor looks at the challenge acceptance in a Gentile society affords to Jews who may be assimilating too rapidly.

Sidney Goldstein and Alice Goldstein. *Jews on the Move: Implications for Jewish Identity.* Albany, NY: State University of New York Press, 1996.
A detailed examination of the geographical mobility based on the 1990 National Jewish Population Survey, which points to a more dispersed population.

Michael Lerner and Cornel West. *Jews and Blacks: A Dialogue on Race, Religion, and Culture in America.* New York: Plume/Penguin, 1996.
A dialogue on the relations between African Americans and Jewish Americans led by two respected contemporary writers. This paperback edition contains a new epilogue that focuses on the state of Jewish-Black relations after the divisive O.J. Simpson verdict and the Million Man March led by Nation of Islam leader Louis Farrakhan.

PERIODICALS

The Jewish community is served by many newspapers and periodicals, including *Commentary* (established in 1946), *CommonQuest: The Magazine of Black Jewish Relations* (1996), *Moment: The Magazine of Jewish Culture and Opinion* (1975), and *Tikkun* (1986). Journals include *Judaism* (1952), *The Jewish Journal of Sociology* (1958), the *Jewish Review* (1946), *Contemporary Jewry* (1975), and *Jewish Social Studies* (1938).

14

Women: The Oppressed Majority

CHAPTER OUTLINE

HIGHLIGHTS

Subordinate status means confinement to subordinate roles not justified by an individual's abilities. Society is increasingly aware that women are a subordinate group. There are biological differences between males and females; however, one must separate differences of gender from those produced by sexism, distinctions that result from socialization. The feminist movement did not begin with the women's movement of the 1960s but has a long history and, like protest efforts by other subordinate groups, has not been warmly received by society. A comparison of the socioeconomic position of men and women leaves little doubt that they have unequal opportunities in employment and political power. Minority women occupy an especially difficult position in that they experience subordinate status by virtue of their race or ethnicity as well as their gender.

Women are an oppressed group even though they form the numerical majority. They are a social minority in the United States and throughout Western society. Men dominate in influence, prestige, and wealth. Women do occupy positions of power, but those who do are the exception, as evidenced by newspaper accounts that declare "she is the first woman" or "the only female" to be in a particular position.

Many people, men and women, find it difficult to conceptualize women as a subordinate group. After all, women do not live in ghettos. They no longer have to attend inferior schools. They freely interact and live with their alleged oppressors, men. How, then, are they a subordinate group? Let us reexamine the five properties of a subordinate or minority group introduced in Chapter 1:

1. Women do experience unequal treatment. Although they are not segregated by residence, they are victims of prejudice and discrimination.
2. Women have physical and cultural characteristics that distinguish them from the dominant group (men).
3. Membership in the subordinate group is involuntary.
4. Through the rise of contemporary feminism, women have become increasingly aware of their subordinate status and have developed a greater sense of group solidarity.
5. Women are not forced to marry; yet many women feel that their subordinate status is most irrevocably defined within marriage.

In this chapter, the similarities between women and racial and ethnic groups will become apparent.

The most common analogy about minorities used in the social sciences is the similarity between the status of African Americans and that of women. Blacks are considered a minority group, but, one asks, how can women of all groups be so similar in condition? We recognize some similarities in recent history; for example, an entire generation has observed and participated in both the civil rights movement and the women's movement. A background of suffrage campaigns, demonstrations, sit-ins, lengthy court battles, and self-help groups are common to the movement for equal rights for both women and African Americans. But similarities were recognized long before the recent protests against inequality. In *An American Dilemma* (1944), the famous study of race described in Chapter 1, Gunnar Myrdal observed that a parallel to the Blacks' role in society was found among women. Others, like Helen Mayer Hacker (1951, 1974), later elaborated on the similarities.

What do these groups have in common besides recent protest movements? The negative stereotypes directed at the two groups are quite similar: both groups have been considered emotional, irresponsible, weak, or inferior. Both are thought to fight subtly against the system: women allegedly try to outwit men by feminine wiles, as historically Blacks allegedly outwit Whites by pretending to be deferential or respectful. To these stereotypes must be added another similarity: neither women nor African Americans are accepting a subordinate role in society any longer.

Nearly all Whites give lip service to, even if they do not wholeheartedly believe, the contention that African Americans are innately equal to Whites. They are inherently the same. But men and women are not the same, and they vary most dramatically in their roles in reproduction. Biological differences have contributed to sexism. **Sexism** refers to the ideology that one sex is superior to the other. Quite different is the view that there are few differences between the sexes. Such an idea is expressed in the concept of **androgyny.** An androgynous model of behavior permits people to see that humans can be both aggressive and expressive, depending on the requirements of the situation. People do not have to be locked into the behavior that accompanies the labels masculine and feminine. In the United States, people disagree widely as to what implications, if any, the biological differences between the sexes have for social roles. We will begin our discussion of women as a subordinate group with this topic.

Gender Roles

Males and females are not biologically the same and neither are the sociocultural expectations and opportunities for men and women. How much do the biological differences of men and women contribute to their cultural differences? While research continues to unravel male-female differences, we already know the major distinctions: women can bear children, and men typically excel in physical strength. Even if these distinctions are clarified, their real meaning is dictated by the manner in which a society interprets and uses them (S. Bem 1994).

Gender roles are society's expectations of the proper behavior, attitudes, and activities of males and females. "Toughness" has traditionally been seen in the United States as masculine—and desirable only in men—while "tenderness" has been viewed as feminine. A society may require that one sex or the other take the primary responsibility for the socialization of the children, economic support of the family, or religious leadership.

Sociologist David Miller (1995, 1998) has studied the socialization of children by comparing the toys marketed to girls and boys in the United States. Toys created for girls tend to reinforce traditional female gender roles by focusing on familial relationships, nurturing and cooperative activity, fashion, style, and beauty. By contrast, toys created for boys are often action figures; these toys focus on command, control, aggression, and violence. There is even an entire category of assault toys for boys, ranging from plastic knives and grenades to multipurpose assault weapons.

Without question, socialization has a powerful impact on the development of females and males in the United States. Indeed, the gender roles first encountered in early childhood are often a factor in defining a child's popularity. Sociologists Patricia Adler and her colleagues (1992, 1998) observed elementary-school children and found that boys typically achieved high status on the basis of their athletic ability, "coolness," toughness, social skills, and success in relationships with girls. By contrast, girls gained popularity based on their parents' economic background and their own physical appearance, social skills, and academic success.

It may be obvious how males and females are conditioned to assume certain roles, but the origin of gender roles as we know them is less clear. Many studies have been done on laboratory animals, for example injecting monkeys and rats with doses of male and female hormones. Primates in their natural surroundings have been closely observed for the presence and nature of gender roles. Animal studies do not point to instinctual gender differences similar to what humans are familiar with as masculinity and femininity. Historically, women's work came to be defined as a consequence of the birth process. Men, free of child-care responsibilities, generally became the hunters and foragers for food. Even though women must bear children, men could have cared for the young. Exactly why women were assigned that

Women's roles have changed significantly since the early 1960s, when women were generally depicted in the media solely as wives and mothers, as shown in the popular television series of that time, *Leave it to Beaver.*

role in societies is not known. Women's role has not been the same cross-culturally. Furthermore, we know that acceptable behavior for men and women changes over time in a society. For example, the men in the royal courts of Europe in the late 1700s fulfilled present-day stereotypes of feminine appearance in their display of ornamental dress and personal vanity rather than resembling the men of a century later although they still engaged in duels and other forms of aggression. The social roles of the sexes have no constants in time or space (J. Bernard 1975; E. Kessler 1976; Martin and Voorhies 1975).

Sociological Perspectives

Sociologist Estelle Disch (1997) points out that gender differences are maintained in our culture through the systematic socialization of babies and infants, children, adolescents, and adults. Even though different subcultures and even each family vary in childrearing, we teach our children to be boys and girls, even though men and women are more alike than they are different. But she noted that gender socialization is not something that stops with youth. "From the time we are born until we die, gender socialization is a constant part of our lives" (p. 74). Gender training persists, and the larger institutional structures reinforce it. We are bombarded with expectations for behavior as men and women from many sources simultaneously. Many individual women hold positions involving high levels of responsibility and competence but may not be accorded the same respect as men. Similarly, individual men find the time to get involved with their children's lives only to meet with disbelief and occasional surprise from health care and educational systems accustomed to dealing only with mothers. Even when individuals are motivated to stretch the social boundaries of gender, social structure and institutions often impede them. Gender differentiation in our culture is embedded in social institutions—the family, of course, but also education, religion, politics, the economy, medicine, and the mass media.

Through this lifelong socialization, people are labeled by virtue of their sex. Certain activities and behaviors are associated with men and others with women. Besides the labeling perspective, we can also employ functionalist and conflict perspectives to grasp more firmly how gender roles develop.

Functionalists maintain that sex differentiation has contributed to overall social stability. Sociologists Talcott Parsons and Robert Bales (1955) argued that, to function most efficiently, the family requires adults who will specialize in particular roles. They believed that the arrangement of gender roles with which they were familiar had arisen because marital partners needed a division of labor.

The functionalist view is initially persuasive in explaining the way in which women and men are typically brought up in U.S. society. It would lead us, however, to expect even girls and women with no interest in children to still become baby-sitters and mothers. Similarly, males with a caring feeling for children may be "programmed" into careers in the business world. Clearly, such a differentiation between the sexes can have harmful consequences for the individual who does not fit into specific roles, while depriving society of the optimal use of many talented individuals who are confined by sexual labeling. Consequently, the conflict perspective is increasingly convincing in its analysis of the development of gender roles.

Conflict theorists do not deny the presence of a differentiation by sex. In fact, they contend that the relationship between females and males has been one of unequal

Suffragists struggled for many years to convince Congress and the states to pass the Nineteenth Amendment to the Constitution, extending to women the right to vote beginning in 1920.

power, with men being dominant over women. Men may have become powerful in preindustrial times because their size, physical strength, and freedom from child-bearing duties allowed them to dominate women physically. In contemporary societies, such considerations are not as important; yet cultural beliefs about the sexes are now long-established.

Both functionalists and conflict theorists acknowledge that it is not possible to change gender roles drastically without dramatic revisions in a culture's social structure. Functionalists see potential social disorder, or at least unknown social consequences, if all aspects of traditional sex differentiation are disturbed. Yet, for conflict theorists, no social structure is ultimately desirable if it has to be maintained through the oppression of a majority of its citizens (Miller and Garrison 1982; Schaefer and Lamm 2000).

The labeling approach emphasizes how the media, even in the present, display traditional gender-role patterns. For example, the portrayal of women and men on television has tended to reinforce conventional gender roles. In the United States, women have traditionally been presented on prime-time television as homemakers, nurses, and household workers—positions that reflect stereotyped notions of women's work. Even by 1995, only 19 percent of the characters on prime-time shows were women. Even when women are shown, the portrayal of women and men has tended to reinforce conventional gender roles. Similarly, a 1997 study documented that only 16 percent of stories on network evening newscasts are reported by female correspondents (Farhi 1995b; M. Moore 1997).

The Feminist Movement

Women's struggle for equality, like the struggles of other subordinate groups, has been long and multifaceted. From the very beginning, women activists and sympathetic men who spoke of equal rights were ridiculed and scorned.

In a formal sense, the American feminist movement was born in upstate New York in a town called Seneca Falls in the summer of 1848. On July 19, the first women's rights convention began, attended by Elizabeth Cady Stanton, Lucretia Mott, and other pioneers in the struggle for women's rights. This first wave of feminists, as they are currently known, battled ridicule and scorn as they fought for legal and political equality for women, but they were not afraid to risk controversy on behalf of their cause. In 1872, for example, Susan B. Anthony was arrested for attempting to vote in that year's presidential election.

All social movements—and feminism is no exception—have been marked by factionalism and personality conflicts. The civil rights movement and pan-Indianism have been hurt repeatedly by conflicts over what tactics to use and which reforms to push for first, as well as personality conflicts. Despite similar divisiveness, the women's movement struggled on toward its major goal: to gain the right to vote.

THE SUFFRAGE MOVEMENT

The **suffragists** worked for years to get women the right to vote. From the beginning, this reform was judged to be crucial. If women voted, it was felt, other reforms would quickly follow. The struggle took so long that many of the initial advocates of women's suffrage died before victory was reached. In 1879, an amendment to the Constitution was introduced that would have given women the right to vote. Not until 1919 was it finally passed, and not until the next year was it ratified as the Nineteenth Amendment to the Constitution.

The opposition to giving women the vote came from all directions. Liquor interests and brewers correctly feared that women would assist in passing laws restricting or prohibiting the sale of their products. The South feared the influence more Black voters (that is, Black women) might have. Southerners had also not forgotten the pivotal role women had played in the abolitionist movement. Despite the opposition, the suffrage movement succeeded in gaining women the right to vote, a truly remarkable achievement because it had to rely on male legislators to do so.

The Nineteenth Amendment did not automatically lead to other feminist reforms. Women did not vote as a bloc and have not themselves been elected to office in proportion to their numbers. The single-minded goal of suffrage was, in several respects, harmful to the cause of feminism. Many suffragists thought that any changes more drastic than granting the vote would destroy the home. They rarely questioned the subordinate role assigned to women. For the most part, agitation for equal rights ended when suffrage was gained. In the 1920s and 1930s, large numbers of college-educated women entered professions, but these individual achievements did little to enhance the rights of women as a group. The feminist movement as an organized effort that gained national attention faded, to regain prominence only in the 1960s (J. Freeman 1975; W. O'Neill 1969; A. Rossi 1964).

Nevertheless, the women's movement did not die out completely in the first half of the century. Many women carried on the struggle in new areas. Margaret Sanger fought for legalized birth control. She opened birth-control clinics because the medical profession refused to distribute birth-control information. Sanger and Katherine Houghton Hepburn (mother of actress Katharine Hepburn) lobbied Congress for reform throughout the 1920s and 1930s. Sanger's early clinics were closed by the police. Not until 1937 were nationwide restrictions on birth-control devices lifted, and some state bans remained in force until 1965.

THE WOMEN'S LIBERATION MOVEMENT

Ideologically, the women's movement of the 1960s had its roots in the continuing informal feminist movement that began with the first subordination of women in Western society. Psychologically, it grew in America's kitchens, as women felt unfulfilled and did not know why, and in the labor force, as women were made to feel guilty because they were not at home with families. Demographically, by the 1960s, women had attained greater control about when and if to become pregnant if they used contraception and hence had greater control over the size of the population (Heer and Grossbard-Shectman 1981).

Sociologically, several events delayed progress in the mid–1960s. The civil rights movement and the antiwar movement were slow to embrace women's rights. The New Left seemed as sexist as the rest of society in practice, despite its talk of equality. Groups protesting the draft and demonstrating on college campuses generally rejected women as leaders and assigned them traditional duties of preparing refreshments and publishing organization newsletters. The core of early feminists often knew each other from participating in other protest or reform groups that had initially been unwilling to accept women's rights as a legitimate goal. Beginning in about 1967, as Chapter 7 showed, the movement for Black equality was no longer as willing to accept help from sympathetic Whites. White men moved on to protest the draft, a cause not as crucial to women's lives. While somewhat involved in the antiwar movement, many White women began to struggle for their own rights, although at first they had to fight alone. Existing groups of women in nontraditional roles, like the 180,000-member Federation of Business and Professional Women, explicitly avoided embracing the feminist cause. Eventually, civil rights groups, the New Left, and most established women's groups endorsed the feminist movement with the zeal of new converts, but initially they resisted the concerns of the growing number of feminists (J. Freeman 1973, 1983).

A focal point of the feminist movement during the 1970s and early 1980s was the Equal Rights Amendment (ERA). First proposed to Congress in 1923, it was finally passed in 1972. The amendment declared that "Equality of rights under the law shall not be denied or abridged by the United States or by any State on account of sex." However, the ERA, like other constitutional amendments, required approval of three-fourths, or thirty-eight of the state legislatures. Ten years later, it had failed to meet this number by only three states. Clearly, the failure of the ERA effort was discouraging to the movement and its leaders. In many states, they had been outspent by their opponents, and in some states, they were outorganized by effective anti-ERA groups and insurance companies, which feared that their sex-differentiated insurance and pension plan payments would be threatened by the passage of an ERA. Ironically, these same insurance practices were overturned in the courts in 1983 (E. Langer 1976; J. O'Reilly 1982).

The movement has also brought about a reexamination of men's roles. Supporters of "male liberation" wished to free men from the constraints of the masculine value system. The masculine mystique is as real as the feminine one. Boys are socialized to think that they should be invulnerable, fearless, decisive, and even emotionless in some situations. Men are expected to achieve physically and occupationally at some risk of their own values, not to mention those of others. Failure to take up these roles and attitudes can mean that a man will be considered less than a man. Male liberation is the logical counterpart of female liberation. If women are to redefine their gender role successfully, men must redefine theirs as workers, husbands, and fathers (Cicone and Ruble 1978; W. Farrell 1974; L. Richardson 1981; J. Sawyer 1972; Schaefer and Lamm 2000).

Amid the many changing concerns since the mid–1960s, the feminist movement too has undergone significant change. Betty Friedan, a founder of the National Organization for Women (NOW), argued in the early 1960s that women had to understand the **feminine mystique,** recognizing that society saw them only as their children's mother and their husband's wife. Later, in the 1980s, though not denying that women deserved to have the same options in life as men, she called for restructuring the "institution of home and wife." Friedan and others now recognize that many young women are now frustrated when time does not permit them to do it all: career, marriage, and motherhood. Difficult issues remain, and feminists continue to discuss and debate over concerns such as the limits businesses put on careers of women with children, domestic violence, and male bias in medical research (Ferree and Hess 1994; B. Friedan 1963, 1981, 1991; C. Somners 1994).

Where are women's rights at the close of the twentieth century? In "Listen to their Voices," sociologist Arlie Russell Hochschild sees the women's movement as a stalled revolution where women may have more opportunities in the workplace but now are forced to do everything.

The Economic Picture

Women's lower status is visible in virtually all aspects of life in the United States. The passage in the Declaration of Independence proclaiming that all men are created equal has been taken too literally for too long. Women experience all the problems in employment associated with other subordinate groups and several that are especially acute for women. Women's subordinate role in the occupational structure is largely the result of institutional, rather than individual, discrimination. Women, more than any other group, are confined to certain occupations. Some sex-typed jobs for women pay well above the minimum wage and carry moderate prestige, like nursing and teaching. Nevertheless, they are far lower in pay and prestige than such stereotyped male positions as physician, college president, or university professor. When they do enter nontraditional positions, women as a group receive lower wages or salary.

The data in Table 14.1 present an overall view of the male dominance of high-paying occupations. Among the representative occupations chosen, men unquestionably dominate in those that pay well and managerial occupations. Women dominate as secretaries, seamstresses, health-care workers, and domestic workers. Trends show the proportions of women increasing slightly in the professions, indicating that some women have advanced into better-paying positions, but these gains have not significantly changed the overall picture.

Table 14.1 Employment of Women in Selected Occupations, 1950 and 1997

Women as a Percentage of All Workers in the Occupation

Occupation	1950	1997	Occupation	1950	1997
Professional workers	40	53	Managers	14	44
Engineers	1	10	Sales workers	35	44
Lawyers and judges	4	26	Clerical workers	62	81
Physicians	7	26	Machine operators	34	38
Registered nurses	98	94	Transport operatives	1	1
College teachers	23	43	Service workers	57	59
Other teachers	75	76			

Sources: Bureau of the Census 1998c: 417–419; Department of Labor 1980: 10–11.

LISTEN TO THEIR VOICES

"Time for Change"

Arlie Russell Hochschild

Nationwide, work absorbs more of a parent's time than it did 25 years ago. Women go back to work earlier after childbirth—in the 1960s, one in eight women returned to work less than a year after childbirth; in 1996, it was approximately one in two. Once back, more mothers now work full-time, year-round. Studies on hours vary, but one national study conducted by Families and Work Institute found that, of workers with children age 12 and under, only 4 percent of men and 13 percent of women worked less than 40 hours a week.

This is part of a larger pattern I refer to as "stalled revolution." In the last 25 years, women have changed, but everything else has not changed as fast or as much. Thus, tens of millions of women go out to work in offices and plants that demand long hours and inflexible schedules, live in a world without widespread quality child care, and come home to mates who don't share the domestic load. The family has become the shock absorber for the strains between faster-changing women and slower-changing men and workplaces. This was already true for some families in the 1950s and 1960s, but now it's true for most. And we've come to think of the family under these strained conditions as the "normal" family. Then we wonder why young people are scared to death to become working parents and why our divorce rate is one of the world's highest.

Thoughtful public discussion about this state of affairs has been oddly silenced by

How pervasive is segregation by gender in the workforce? To what degree are women and men concentrated in different occupations? Bureau of Labor Statistics researchers have compiled a "segregation index" to estimate the percentage of women who would have to change their jobs to make the distribution of men and women in each occupation mirror the relative percentage of each sex in the adult working population. This study showed that 54 percent of women and men workers would need to switch jobs in order to create a labor force without sex segregation. There has been a steady decline in such segregation, but the decrease had not been as great in the 1990s as in earlier decades (B. Wootton).

While occupational segregation by gender continues, women have increased their participation in the labor force. A greater proportion of women seek and obtain paid employment than ever before in United States history. In 1870, less than 15 percent of all workers were women, compared to 46 percent in 1997. The most dramatic rise in the female workforce has been among married women. In 1995, 61 percent of married women worked, compared to fewer than 5 percent in 1890.

two opposing parties, both of which divert our attention from the project of transforming the workplace. First, there are what I call the "accusatory traditionals," who have an eagle eye out for the problems of working mothers. If working mothers are tired, have troubled kids or tense marriages, the traditionals admonish women to junk their careers and stay home. Men, they don't touch.

Responding to these scolding traditionals are the "sunshine moderns," who get cornered into saying, "Two-, three-, and four-year-olds in nine- and ten-hour child care? Fine." "Middle-school children home alone after school? Let's call it 'self-care.'" The sunshiners' motto is "Don't bring me any bad news." Or at least no news that isn't strictly about the external world. Anything internal—like the idea that we can become complicit in the very cultural pressures that end up hurting us—is too dangerous, because if you admit such a thing, you're playing into the hands of the scolding traditionals and you're back to square one....

Other societies—Sweden, Norway, Canada—have led the way. And a number of organizations, inspired by the women's movement, are fighting the good fight here. The Women's Legal Defense Fund, for example, is trying to expand the 1993 Family and Medical Leave Act to cover more working people and more family needs, such as minor illnesses. It is also trying to make these leaves paid for low-wage workers. We can begin to think about a broader movement pressing for a shorter work-week and work-sharing as an alternative to layoffs. And we need men to join us in taking pressure off kids and putting it on the workplace. These are all ways we can unstall the feminist revolution in the next 25 years.

Source: Arlie Russell Hochshild. "Time for Change." Reprinted by permission of *Ms. Magazine,* copyright © 1997.

Nearly 65 percent of mothers with children under age six are working (Bureau of the Census 1975:129, 133; 1998c:403,409).

It is logical to assume that these percentages would be even higher if day care in the United States received more support. A number of European nations, including France, the Netherlands, Sweden, and the former Soviet Union, provide preschool care at minimal or no cost, although such benefits are underwritten through higher taxes. However, in the United States, these costs are borne entirely by the working parent. Recently, some employers have recognized the benefits of offering care and have begun to provide or subsidize this care, but they are the exception, not the rule (Schaefer and Lamm 2000).

A primary goal of many feminists is to eliminate sex discrimination in the labor force and to equalize job opportunities for women. Without question, women earn less than men. As we noted earlier, in Table 3.1 and Figure 3.2, women earn less than men even when race and education are held constant; that is, college-educated women working full time make less than comparably educated men. Even when

More women are gradually entering occupations previously held almost exclusively by men. In 1997, 18 percent of all engineers were women.

additional controls are introduced, like previous work experience, a substantial earnings gap remains. A detailed analysis of the wage gap, considering schooling, employment history, time with the current employer, and medical leaves of absence, found that all these factors can explain less than 42 percent of the wage differences between men and women (A. Wellington 1994; also see D. Tomaskovic-Devey 1993).

SOURCES OF DISCRIMINATION

If we return to the definition of discrimination cited earlier, are not men better able to perform some tasks than women, and vice versa? If ability means performance, there certainly are differences. The typical woman can sew better than the typical man, but the latter can toss a ball farther than the former. These are group differences. Certainly many women outthrow many men, and many men outsew many women, but society expects women to excel at sewing and men to excel at throwing. The differences in those abilities are due to cultural conditioning. Women are usually taught to sew, and men are less likely to learn such a skill. Men are encouraged to participate in sports requiring the ability to throw a ball much more than are women. True, as a group, males have greater potential for the muscular development required to throw a ball, but U.S. society encourages men to realize their potential in this area more than it encourages women to pursue athletic skills.

Today's labor market involves much more than throwing a ball and using a needle and thread, but the analogy to these two skills is repeated time and again. Such examples are used to support sexist practices in all aspects of the workplace. Just as African Americans can suffer from both individual acts of racism and institutional discrimination, women are vulnerable to both sexism and institutional discrimination.

Women are subject to direct sexism such as sexist remarks and also to differential treatment because of institutional policies.

Removing barriers to equal opportunity would eventually eliminate institutional discrimination. Theoretically, men and women would sew and throw a ball equally well. We say "theoretically" because cultural conditioning would take generations to change. In some formerly male jobs, like being a gas station clerk and attendant, society seems quite willing to accept women. In other occupations, like being president, it will take longer, and many years may pass before full acceptance can be expected in other fields, like professional contact sports.

Many efforts have been made to eliminate institutional discrimination as it applies to women. The 1964 Civil Rights Act and its enforcement arm, the Equal Employment Opportunity Commission, address cases of sex discrimination. As we saw in Chapter 3, the inclusion of sex bias along with prejudice based on race, color, creed, and national origin was an unexpected last-minute change in the provisions of the landmark 1964 act. Federal legislation has not removed all discrimination against women in employment. The same explanations presented in Chapter 3 for the lag between the laws and reality in race discrimination apply to sex discrimination: (1) lack of money, (2) weak enforcement powers, (3) occasionally weak commitment to using the laws available, and most important, (4) institutional and structural forces that perpetuate inequality.

What should be done to close the gap between the earnings of women and men? As shown in Figure 3.2 (see p. 84), the median income of year-round White female workers was only $26,470 in 1997, compared with $36,118 for White male workers—that is, a woman makes 73 cents for every man's dollar. Efforts to address the problem of wage discrimination have resulted in legislation and increased public awareness; yet women's salaries remain far lower than those of men. The federal Equal Pay Act of 1963, which mandates equal pay for equal work, applies to a relatively small proportion of female workers: those who perform the same job under the same roof as a male worker. Although these women's wages have increased as a result of the Equal Pay Act, most female workers, as we have seen, remain segregated in a few occupations in which no male workers do the same jobs. Therefore, these underpaid women cannot compare themselves with males.

During the 1980s, pay equity, or comparable worth, was a controversial solution presented to alleviate the second-class status of working women. It directly attempted to secure equal pay when occupational segregation by gender was particularly pervasive. **Pay equity** calls for equal pay for different types of work that are judged to be comparable by measuring such factors as employee knowledge, skills, effort, responsibility, and working conditions.

This doctrine sounds straightforward, but it is not so simple to put into operation. How exactly does one determine the comparability of jobs in order to identify comparable worth? Should a zookeeper be paid more than a child-care worker? Does our society pay zookeepers more because we value caretaking for children less than caretaking for animals? Or do zookeepers earn more than child-care workers because the former tend to be male and the latter are generally female?

Despite some local initiatives, pay equity has not received much support in the United States except from the feminist movement. From a policy perspective, pay equity would have to be initiated at the federal level, and in the 1990s, the government is backing away from affirmative action and is less likely to launch an initiative on pay equity (E. Sorensen 1994).

What about women aspiring to crack the "glass ceiling"? The phrase **glass ceiling,** as noted in Chapter 3 and illustrated in Figure 3.3, refers to the invisible barrier blocking the promotion of a qualified worker because of gender or minority membership. Despite debate in the 1990s over affirmative action, the consensus is that there is little room at the top for women and minorities. The glass ceiling operates so that all applicants may be welcomed by a firm, but when it comes to the powerful or more visible positions, there are limits—generally unstated—on the number of women and nonwhites welcomed or even tolerated. Women are doing better in top management positions than minorities, but they still lag well behind men according to a 1998 study that showed only 10.6 percent of the direct seats of the Fortune 500 companies are held by women. Still about one out of six companies have no women board members (Catalyst 1998; also see F. Blau 1998).

Women are still viewed differently in the world of management. In making hiring decisions, executives may assume that women are not serious about their commitment to the job and will be "distracted" by family and home. They assume that women are on a **mommy track**—an unofficial career track that firms use for women who want to divide their attention between work and family. Not only is this assumption false if applied to all women but it also implies that corporate men are not interested in maintaining a balance between work and family. Even competitive, upwardly mobile women are not always taken seriously in the workplace. A clear indicator of this was revealed in a 1996 study of top female executives and male CEOs. The vast majority of men, 82 percent, pointed to women's lack of general manage-

Table 14.2 Major Barriers to Women's Executive Advancement

- Initial placement and clustering in relatively dead-end staff jobs or highly technical professional jobs
- Lack of mentoring
- Lack of management training
- Lack of opportunities for career development
- Lack of opportunities for training tailored to the individual
- Lack of rotation to line positions or job assignments that are revenue producing
- Little or no access to critical developmental assignments, including service on highly visible task forces and committees
- Different stands for performance evaluation
- Biased rating and testing systems
- Little or no access to informal networks of communication
- Counterproductive behavior and harassment by colleagues

Source: Glass Ceiling Commission, cited in Department of Labor 1995a: 7–8.

ment experience as the primary factor preventing women from advancing into top corporate positions. However, 52 percent of the women who had succeeded listed male stereotyping and preconceptions about women as the problem (Catalyst 1996; Lipman-Blumen et al. 1996; F. Schwartz 1989, 1992).

SEXUAL HARASSMENT

Under evolving legal standards, **sexual harassment** is recognized as any unwanted and unwelcome sexual advances that interfere with a person's ability to perform a job and enjoy the benefits of a job. Increased national attention was given to harassment in the 1990s through allegations made against high-ranking military officers. These newsworthy events were overshadowed first by the allegations of Paula Jones of sexual harassment while Bill Clinton was governor and then, second, most dramatically, with the sexual relations between President Bill Clinton and White House intern Monica Lewinsky.

The most obvious example of sexual harassment is the boss who tells an employee: "Put out or get out!" However, the unwelcome advances that constitute sexual harassment may take the form of subtle pressures regarding sexual activity, inappropriate touching, attempted kissing, or sexual assault. Indeed, in the computer age, there is growing concern that sexually harassing messages are being sent anonymously over computer networks through e-mail (Price 1993).

Although estimates and definitions vary, a national survey conducted in 1992 found 23 percent of women indicated that they had been sexually harassed in their work outside the home, compared with 32 percent in a similar survey in October 1991. Part of the decrease can be attributed to the greater recognition of sexual harassment that emerged from the confirmation hearings of Supreme Court nominee Clarence Thomas, who was charged with repeatedly harassing a former aide, law professor Anita Hill. While Thomas was eventually confirmed, the nation became more sensitized to the widespread existence of harassment at all levels of employment (R. Morin 1993).

In light of many allegations that the military did not take charges of sexual harassment seriously, the armed forces made a hotline available to accept calls from victims.

In 1986, in a unanimous decision (*Meritor Savings Bank* v. *Vinson*), the Supreme Court declared that sexual harassment by a supervisor violates the federal law against sex discrimination in the workplace as outlined in the 1964 Civil Rights Act. Harassment, if sufficiently severe, is a violation even if the unwelcome sexual demands are not linked to concrete employment benefits such as a raise or promotion. Women's groups hailed the court's decisiveness in identifying harassment as a form of discrimination. A federal judge subsequently ruled that the public display of photographs of nude and partly nude women at a workplace constitutes sexual harassment. Despite these rulings, it is very difficult legally and emotionally for a person to bring forward a case of sexual harassment (Domino 1995).

Sexual harassment must be understood in the context of continuing prejudice and discrimination against women. Whether it occurs in the federal bureaucracy, the military, the corporate world, or universities, sexual harassment generally takes place where the hierarchy of authority finds White males at the top and in which women's work is valued less than men's. One survey of the private sector found that African American women were three times more likely than White women to experience sexual harassment. From a conflict perspective, it is not surprising that women—and especially women of color—are most likely to become victims of sexual harassment. These groups are typically an organization's most vulnerable employees in terms of job security (J. Jones 1988).

FEMINIZATION OF POVERTY

Since World War II, an increasing proportion of the poor in the United States have been female—many of them divorced or never-married mothers. This alarming trend has come to be known as the **feminization of poverty.** In 1996, female householders and their families accounted for 38 percent of the nation's poor (Bureau of the Census 1998c:480).

Poor women share many social characteristics with poor men: low educational attainment, lack of market-relevant job skills, and residence in economically deteriorating areas. Conflict theorists, however, believe that the higher rates of poverty among women can be traced to two distinct causes: sex discrimination on the job and sexual harassment place women at a clear disadvantage when seeking vertical social mobility.

The burden of supporting a family is especially difficult for single mothers, not only because of low salaries but because of inadequate child support as well. The average payment for child support in 1991 was a mere $2,961 per year, or about $57 per week. This level of support is clearly insufficient for rearing a child in the 1990s. Moreover, of the 4.9 million American women scheduled to receive child support payments from their former husbands in 1991, only 76 percent actually received any money. In light of these data, federal and state officials have intensified efforts to track down delinquent spouses and ensure the payment of child support. Policy makers acknowledge that such enforcement efforts have led to substantial reductions in welfare expenditures (Bureau of the Census 1996:385).

According to a study based on census data released in early 1994 by the advocacy group Women Work, single mothers and "displaced homemakers" are four times as likely to live in poverty as other households in the United States. **Displaced homemakers** were defined as women whose primary occupation had been homemaking but who did not find full-time employment after being divorced, separated, or widowed. Among the findings of the report were the following:

- The number of single mothers in the nation rose from 5.8 million in 1980 to 7.7 million in 1990. The number of displaced homemakers rose from 13.8 million in 1980 to 17.8 million in 1990.
- In 1990, 11 percent of all households in the United States lived in poverty. But the figure was 44 percent of households headed by single mothers and 42 percent of households headed by displaced homemakers.

Gilda Nardone, president of Women Work, noted that single mothers and displaced homemakers tend to work in service jobs, which offer low wages, few benefits, part-time work, and little job security. Moreover, single mothers and displaced homemakers are also more likely to have an unstable housing situation, including frequent changes of residence (Women Work 1998).

Many feminists feel that the continuing dominance of the political system by men contributes to government indifference to the problem of poor women. Patricia B. Reuss, a lobbyist for the Women's Equity Action League, has challenged male politicians who merely pay lip service to this issue: "I'm critical of the leaders of both parties who failed to take hold of the equity act and push the whole thing through. The things that have gotten through are nice beginnings, rather than real remedies" (S. Roberts 1984:A18). As more and more women fall below the official poverty line, policy makers will face growing pressure to combat the feminization of poverty.

Education

The experience of women in education has been similar to their experience in the labor force: a long history of contribution, but in traditionally defined terms. In 1833, Oberlin College became the first institution of higher learning to admit women, two centuries after the first men's college began in this country. In 1837, Wellesley became the first women's college. But it would be a mistake to believe that these early experiments brought about equality for women in education: at Oberlin, the women were forbidden to speak in public. Furthermore,

> *Washing the men's clothes, caring for their rooms, serving them at table, listening to their orations, but themselves remaining respectfully silent in public assemblages, the Oberlin "coeds" were being prepared for intelligent motherhood and a properly subservient wifehood. (Flexner 1959:30)*

The early graduates of these schools, despite the emphasis in the curriculum on traditional roles, became the founders of the feminist movement.

Today, research confirms that boys and girls are treated differently in school: teachers give boys more attention. In teaching students the values and customs of the larger society, schools in the United States have treated children as if men's education were more important than that of women. Professors of education Myra and David Sadker (1994b) documented this persistence of classroom sexism: the researchers noted that boys receive more teacher attention than girls, mainly because they call out in class eight times more often. Teachers praise boys more than girls and offer boys more academic assistance. Interestingly, they found this differential treatment was present with both male and female teachers.

Besides receiving less attention, girls are more likely to be encouraged to take courses that will lead them to enter lower-paying fields of employment. This has been the experience of girls who are exposed to courses that prepare them to be housewives and who, even when showing the aptitude for "men's work," are advised to pursue "women's work." Researchers have documented sexism in education in the books used, the vocational counseling provided, and even the content of educational television programs. Perhaps the most apparent result of sexist practices and gender-role conditioning in education is staffing patterns. Administrators and university professors are primarily male, and public school teachers are female.

At all levels of schooling, significant changes occurred with congressional amendments to the Education Act of 1972 and the Department of Health, Education, and Welfare guidelines developed in 1974 and 1975. Collectively referred to as Title IX provisions, the regulations are designed to eliminate sexist practices from almost all school systems. Schools must make these changes or risk the loss of all federal assistance:

1. Schools must eliminate all sex-segregated classes and extracurricular activities. This means an end to all-girl home economics and all-boy shop classes, although single-sex hygiene and physical education classes are permitted.
2. Schools cannot discriminate by sex in admissions or financial aid and cannot inquire into whether an applicant is married, pregnant, or a parent. Single-sex schools are exempted.
3. Schools must end sexist hiring and promotion practices among faculty members.
4. Although women do not have to be permitted to play on all-men's athletic teams, schools must provide more opportunities for women's sports, intramural and extramural. (*Federal Register,* June 4, 1975)

Title IX became one of the more controversial steps ever taken by the federal government to promote and ensure equality.

Efforts to bring gender equity to sports have been attacked as excessive, and they have fueled, as noted earlier, the "angry white men" perspective of men as victims. Conflict theorists maintain that such criticism reflects an underlying desire to protect the privileged positions of males rather than any genuine feeling about federal control and education. Feminists opposed government moves to soften some Title IX regulations, especially because Title IX fails to affect sex stereotyping in textbooks and curricula and exempts elementary schools and the military academies.

Family Life

"Does your mother work?" "No, she's a housewife."

This familiar exchange suggests that a woman is married to both a husband and a house and that homemaking does not constitute work. Our society generally equates work with wages and holds unpaid work in low esteem. Women who do such work through household chores and volunteer work are given little status in our society. Furthermore, the demands traditionally placed on a mother and homemaker are so extensive that simultaneously pursuing a career is extremely difficult. For women, the family is, according to sociologists Lewis Coser and Rose Laub Coser (1974) a "greedy institution." More recently, other social scientists have also observed the overwhelming burden of the multiple social roles associated with being a mother and working outside the home.

CHILD CARE AND HOUSEWORK

A man, boy, or girl can act as a homemaker and caretaker for children, but in the United States, these roles are customarily performed by women. Studies indicate that there continues to be a clear gender gap in the performance of housework, although the differences are narrowing. As shown in Figure 14.1, the most recent study finds women doing more housework and spending more time on child care than men, whether it be on a workday or when off work. Taken together, then, a woman's day on and off the job is much longer than a man's. Yet another challenge women disproportionately face is caring for aging parents. According to a Department of Labor (1998) study, 72 percent of caregivers are women typically spending around 18 hours per week caring for a parent.

Most studies on gender and child care focus on the time actually spent by women and men performing these duties. However, sociologist Susan Walzer (1996) was interested in whether there are gender differences in the amount of time that parents spend thinking about the care of their children. Drawing on interviews, Walzer found that mothers are much more involved than fathers in the invisible mental labor associated with taking care of a baby. For example, while involved in work outside the home, mothers are more likely to think about their babies and to feel guilty later if they become so consumed with the demands of their jobs that they fail to think about their babies.

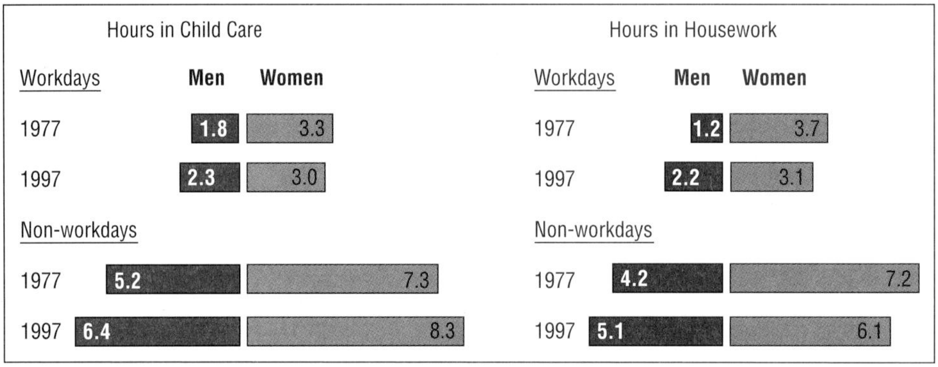

Figure 14.1 Child Care and Housework by Gender

Source: Bond, Galinsky and Swanberg. 1997 National Study of the Changing Workforce. Reprinted by permission of the Families and Work Institute.

Given the stresses of performing about two-thirds of all housework, why do married women accept this arrangement? Psychologist Mary Clare Lennon and sociologist Sarah Rosenfield (1994) studied this issue using interviews of adults from the same national sample discussed previously. When questioned in that survey, almost 61 percent of the women and more than 67 percent of the men suggested that this uneven distribution of housework is fair to both spouses. According to the researchers, those married women with the fewest alternatives and financial prospects outside marriage are most likely to accept unequal household arrangements as fair. Apparently, the more economically dependent a particular wife is, the more she will do (and justify) to preserve the marital relationship. In a striking finding, Lennon and Rosenfield reported that women who do view unequal housework as unjust experience more symptoms of depression.

Sociologist Arlie Hochschild (1989, 1990) has used the term **second shift** to describe the double burden—work outside the home followed by child care and housework—that many women face and that few men share equitably. On the basis of interviews with and observations of fifty-two couples over an eight-year period, Hochschild reports that the wives (and not their husbands) plan domestic schedules and play dates for children while driving home from the office—and then begin their second shift. Drawing on national studies, she concludes that women spend 15 fewer hours in leisure activities each week than do their husbands. In a year, these women work an extra month of twenty-four-hour days because of the second-shift phenomenon. Over a dozen years, they work an extra year of twenty-four-hour days.

Hochschild found that the married couples she studied were fraying at the edges, psychologically, and so were their careers and their marriages. The women she spoke with hardly resembled the beautiful young businesswomen pictured in magazine advertisements, dressed in power suits but with frilled blouses, holding briefcases in one hand and happy young children in the other. Instead, many of Hochschild's female subjects talked about being overtired and emotionally drained by the demands of their multiple roles. They were much more intensely torn by the conflicting demands of work outside the home and family life than were their husbands.

Fathers are taking on more responsibility for child care, but overwhelmingly, it remains the responsibility of mothers.

Hochschild (1990) concludes that "if we as a culture come to see the urgent need of meeting the new problems posed by the second shift, and if society and government begin to shape new policies that allow working parents more flexibility, then we will be making some progress toward happier times at home and at work" (p. 73). This view is shared by many feminists.

ABORTION

A particularly controversial subject affecting family life in the United States has been the call for women to have greater control over their bodies, especially their reproductive lives, through contraceptive devices and the increased availability of abortions. Abortion law reform was one of the demands NOW made in 1967, and the controversy continues despite many court rulings and the passage of laws at every level of government.

On January 22, 1973, the feminist movement received unexpected assistance from the U.S. Supreme Court decision in *Roe* v. *Wade*. The justices held, by a 7–2 margin, that the "right to privacy . . . founded in the Fourteenth Amendment's concept of personal liberty . . . is broad enough to encompass a woman's decision whether or not to terminate a pregnancy." However, the Court did set certain limits on a woman's right to abortion. During the last three months of pregnancy, the fetus was ruled capable of life outside the womb. Therefore, states were granted the right to prohibit all abortions in the third trimester except those needed to preserve the life, physical health, or mental health of the mother.

The Court's decision in *Roe* v. *Wade,* while generally applauded by "prochoice" groups, which support the right to legal abortions, was bitterly condemned by those opposed to abortion. For people who call themselves "prolife," abortion is a moral and often a religious issue. In their view, human life actually begins at the moment of conception rather than when the fetus could stay alive outside the womb. On the basis of this belief, the fetus is a human, not merely a potential life. Termination of this human's life, even before it has left the womb, is viewed essentially as an act of murder. Consequently, antiabortion activists are alarmed by the over one million legal abortions carried out each year in the United States (K. Luker 1984).

In recent years, influenced by the vote of conservative justices appointed by Ronald Reagan and George Bush, the Supreme Court has increasingly restricted the right to an abortion. The court has upheld a state's right to prohibit abortions in public facilities and block public employees from performing them. The justices have also allowed states to require minors to get the consent of a parent or judge before getting an abortion. It also has upheld state and federal funding bans and refused to require that public money be used for abortions for poor women (J. Greenburg 1998).

The early 1990s brought an escalation of violent antiabortion protests. Finally, a 1994 federal law made it a crime to use force or threats or to obstruct, injure, or interfere with anyone providing or receiving abortions and other reproductive health services. In signing the bill into law, President Clinton stated, "No person seeking medical care, no physician providing that care should have to endure harassments or threats or obstruction or intimidation or even murder from vigilantes who take the law into their own hands because they think they know what the law ought to be." A month later, the Supreme Court upheld most of a Florida state court injunction intended to prevent disruptive protesters from blocking access to abortion clinics. In a 6–3 ruling written by Chief Justice William Rehnquist, the Court's majority upheld the constitutionality of a thirty-six-foot "buffer zone" that keeps antiabortion protesters away from a clinic's entrance and parking lot. Abortion remains a disputed issue both in society and in the courts. The law has apparently had some impact, but acts of violence including deaths of clinic workers and physicians continue.

While courts restrict abortions and sporadic violence near clinics continues, public opinion has remained remarkably stable over the last thirty years. As shown in Figure 14.2, public opinion largely supports legalized abortion. However, underlying this general approval has been a shift from general acceptance to a "permit but discourage" model. For example, people are less likely to feel that a woman should get a legal abortion if her pregnancy would force her to interrupt her work, 37 percent said yes in 1989 to 25 percent in 1998 (Goldberg and Elder 1998).

Political Activity

Women in the United States constitute 53 percent of the voting population and 49 percent of the labor force but only 8 percent of those holding high government positions. In 1999, Congress included only fifty-nine women (out of 435 members) in the House of Representatives and only nine women (out of 100 members) in the Senate. As shown in Table 14.3, while the number of women in state legislatures in 1999 was more than five times larger than it was thirty years ago, only three states—Arizona, New Hampshire, and New Jersey—had a woman governor (S. Verhovek 1999).

Sexism has been the most serious barrier to women interested in holding office. Female candidates have had to overcome the prejudices of both men and women regarding women's fitness for leadership. Not until 1955 did a majority of people

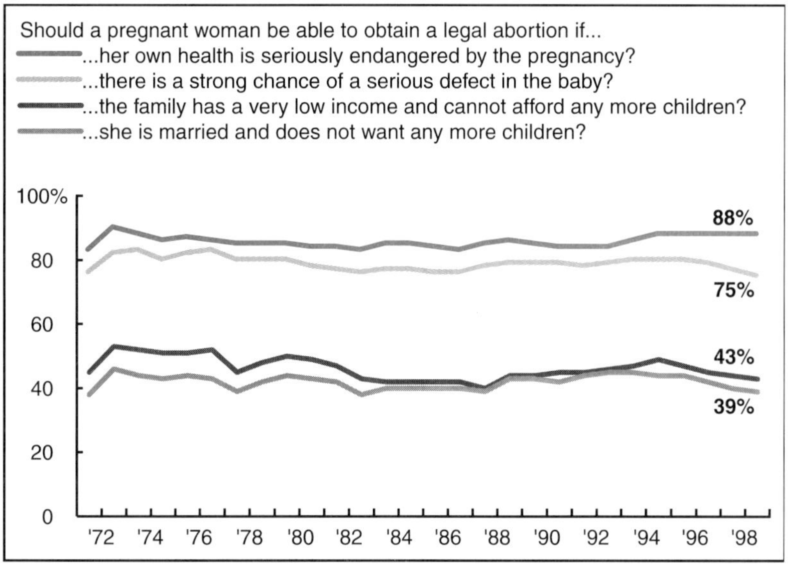

Figure 14.2 Public Opinion on Abortion, 1972–1998
Source: Reprinted by permission of New York Times Graphics.

in the United States indicate that they would vote for a qualified woman for president. Moreover, women often encounter prejudice, discrimination, and abuse after they are elected. In 1979, a questionnaire was circulated by male Oregon legislators asking them to "categorize the lady legislators" as to their "mouth, face, chest, dress, and so forth" (Shreve and Clemans 1980:105).

The low number of women office holders until recently has not been due to women's inactivity in politics. About the same proportion of eligible women and men vote in presidential elections. The League of Women Voters, founded in 1920, performs a valuable function in educating the electorate of both sexes, publishing newsletters describing candidates' positions, and holding debates among candidates.

Table 14.3 Women in Elected Office

	1969	1975	1981	1987	1999
House	10	19	21	23	58
Senate	1	0	2	2	9
Governors	0	1	1	2	3
State legislatures	301	604	908	1,170	1,605

Source: Reprinted by permission of the Center for the American Woman and Politics, Eagleton Institute of Politics, Rutgers University.

Data for state legislatures are for 1997.

In 1997, Madeleine Albright, shown here with Palestinian leader Yasser Arafat, became the first woman to be appointed as secretary of state.

Perhaps women's most visible role in politics until recently has been as unpaid campaign workers for male candidates: doorbell ringers, telephone callers, newsletter printers, and petition carriers. In addition, wives of elected male politicians play significant supportive roles and have increasingly spoken out in their own right, the most recent and visible example being Hillary Rodham Clinton. Campaigns in the 1990s showed women overcoming one of their last barriers to electoral office: attracting campaign funds. Running for office is very expensive, and women candidates have begun to convince backers to invest in their political future. Their success as fund-raisers will also contribute to women's acceptance as serious candidates in the future (Bledsoe and Herring 1990; McCormick and Baruch 1994).

Women have worked actively in both political parties, but women office holders are more likely to be Democrats—although by a slight margin. A recent, effective force is the National Women's Political Caucus (NWPC), which works to get more women elected. The NWPC was founded in 1971 by Betty Friedan, Gloria Steinem (founder of *Ms.* magazine), Bella Abzug, and Shirley Chisholm (the last two have been congresswomen from New York City). The NWPC oversees state caucuses that rally support for women's issues. The caucus finds it difficult to represent all politically active women because women's views encompass a whole range of ideologies and the NWPC includes women who are unmistakable antifeminists (CAWP 1994; J. Freeman 1975).

Double Jeopardy: Minority Women

We have seen the historical oppression of women that limits them by tradition and law to specific roles. Many women experience differential treatment not only because of their gender but because of race and ethnicity as well. These citizens face a **double jeopardy**—that of subordinate status twice defined. A disproportionate share of this low-status group also is impoverished so that the double jeopardy becomes a triple jeopardy. The litany of social ills continues for many as we add old age, ill health, disabilities, and the like.

Feminists have addressed themselves to the needs of minority women, but the oppression of these women because of their sex is overshadowed by the subordinate status that both White men and White women impose on them because of their race or ethnicity. The question for the Latinas (Hispanic woman), African American woman, Asian American woman, Native American woman, and so on appears to be whether she should unify with her brothers against racism or challenge them for their sexism. The answer is that society cannot afford to let up on the effort to eradicate both sexism and racism (E. Sutherland 1970; E. Vasquez 1970).

The discussion of gender roles among African Americans has always provoked controversy. Advocates of Black nationalism contend that feminism only distracts women from full participation in the African American struggle. The existence of feminist groups among Blacks, in their view, simply divides the Black community and thereby serves the dominant White society. By contrast, Black feminists such as bell hooks (1994) argue that little is to be gained by accepting the gender-role divisions of the dominant society that place women in a separate, subservient position. African American journalist Patricia Raybon (1989) has noted that the media commonly portray Black women in a negative light: as illiterate, as welfare mothers, as prostitutes, and so forth. Black feminists emphasize that it is not solely Whites and White-dominated media that focus on these negative images; Black men (most recently, Black male rap artists) have also been criticized for the way they portray African American women (S. Fulwood 1994).

Native Americans stand out as a historical exception to the North American patriarchal tradition. At the time of the arrival of the European settlers, gender roles varied greatly from tribe to tribe. Southern tribes, for reasons unclear to today's scholars, were usually matriarchal and traced descent through the mother. European missionaries sought to make the native peoples more like the Europeans, and this aim included transforming women's role. Some Native American women, like members of other groups, have resisted gender stereotypes (E. Pleck 1993).

The plight of Latinas is usually considered part of either the Hispanic or feminist movements, and the distinctive experience of Latinas is ignored. In the past, they have been excluded from decision-making in the two social institutions that most affect their daily lives: the family and the church. The Hispanic family, especially in the lower class, feels the pervasive tradition of male domination. The Roman Catholic Church relegates women to supportive roles, while reserving for men the leadership positions (De Andra 1996).

CONCLUSION

Women and men are expected to perform, or at least to prefer to perform, specific tasks in society. The appropriateness to one gender of all but a very few of these tasks cannot be justified by the biological differences between females and males any more than differential treatment based on race can be justified. Psychologists Sandra Bem and Daryl Bem (1970) make this analogy:

> *Suppose that a white, male college student decided to room with a black, male friend. The typical white student would not blithely assume that his roommate was better suited to handle all domestic chores. Nor should his conscience allow him to do so even in the unlikely event that his roommate would say, "No, that's okay. I like doing housework. I'd be happy to do it." We would suspect that the white student would still feel uncomfortable about taking advantage of the fact that his roommate has simply been socialized to be "happy with such an arrangement." But change this hypothetical black roommate to a female marriage partner, and the student's conscience goes to sleep. (p. 99)*

The feminist movement has awakened women and men to assumptions based on sex and gender. New opportunities for the sexes require the same commitment from individuals and the government as they make to achieving equality among racial and ethnic groups.

Women are systematically disadvantaged in both employment and the family. Gender inequality is a serious problem, just as racial inequality continues to be a significant social challenge. Separate, socially defined roles for men and women are not limited to the United States. Chapter 15 concentrates on the inequality of racial and ethnic groups in societies other than the United States. Just as sexism is not unique to this nation, neither is racism nor religious intolerance.

KEY TERMS

androgyny 414
displaced homemakers 428
double jeopardy 436
feminine mystique 420
feminization of poverty 428
gender roles 415
glass ceiling 426
mommy track 426
pay equity 425
second shift 432
sexism 414
sexual harassment 427
suffragists 418

REVIEW QUESTIONS

1. How is women's subordinate position different from that of oppressed racial and ethnic groups? How is it similar?
2. How has the focus of the feminist movement changed during the twentieth century?
3. How do the patterns of women in the workplace differ from those of men?
4. How has the changing role of women in the United States affected the family?
5. What are the special challenges facing women of subordinate racial and ethnic groups?

CRITICAL THINKING

1. Women have many characteristics similar to those of minority groups, but what are some differences? For example, they are not segregated from men residentially.
2. Earlier in the 1990s, the phrase *angry white men* was used by some men who viewed themselves as victims. In what respect may men see themselves as victims of reverse discrimination? Do you think these views are justified?
3. How are men's and women's roles defined differently when it comes to such concepts as *mommy track, second shift,* and *displaced homemaker*?

INTERNET EXERCISE

This chapter reveals the struggle that lead to the passage of the Nineteenth Amendment some 78 years ago. The History of the Suffrage Movement (http://www.rochester.edu/SBA/hisindx.html) provides further details about this era. What was the Seneca Falls Convention of 1848, and what consequences resulted from it? What are some of the changes proposed in the Declaration of Sentiments? Who were Susan B. Anthony and Elizabeth Cady Stanton? What were some of the most important events of the movement? What sacrifices did women make in order to gain the right to vote? Considering all the suffragettes went through, why do you believe that so many Americans today do not vote? Answer to yourself: Did you vote in the last election? Why or why not?

FOR FURTHER INFORMATION

Arlie Russell Hochschild. *Time Bind: When Work Becomes Home & Home Becomes Work.* New York: Metropolitan Books, Henry Holt, 1997.
The author of *Second Shift* describes the crunch that is taking place in time commitments to work and home and the social consequences it can have on both.

Laurel Richardson and Verta Taylor, eds. *Feminist Frontiers IV.* New York: McGraw-Hill, 1997.
A collection of fifty-three articles covering such topics as socialization, work, the family, health, violence, and social movement.

Barbara J. Risman. *Gender Vertigo: American Families in Transition.* New Haven: Yale University Press, 1998.
A sociologist considers changes taking place in gender roles and how some women are succeeding in creating more personal and feminist visions of family life.

Maxine Baca Zinn and Bonnie Thornton Dill, eds. *Women of Color in U.S. Society.* Philadelphia: Temple University Press, 1994.
Considers race, class, and gender, or interlocking systems of oppression.

PERIODICALS

Ms. (established in 1972) is a monthly mass-market publication that presents the feminist point of view. Similar publications are *Lilith* (1976), *Off Our Backs* (1970), and *Working Woman* (1976). The more traditional women's magazines have increasingly confronted the issues raised by the women's liberation movement. Journals devoted to women and men as social groups are *Feminist Studies* (1972), *Gender and Society* (1987), *Journal of Men's Studies* (1992), *Journeymen* (1991), *Masculinities* (1995), *Sex Roles: A Journal of Research* (1975), *Signs: Journal of Women in Culture and Society* (1972), *Women: A Cultural Review* (1990), *Women's Review of Books* (1983), and *Women's Studies* (1972).

15

Beyond the United States: The Comparative Perspective

CHAPTER OUTLINE

HIGHLIGHTS

Subordinating people because of race, nationality, or religion is not a phenomenon unique to the United States; it occurs throughout the world. In Mexico, the descendants of the Mayans as well as women are given second-class status. Despite its being viewed as a homogeneous nation by some, Canada faces racial, linguistic, and tribal peoples issues. Northern Ireland is a modern nation torn by religious strife. In Israel, Jews and Palestinians struggle over territory and the definition of each other's autonomy. In the Republic of South Africa, the legacy of apartheid dominates the future.

Ironically, modernization, by bringing more and more diverse groups of people into contact, has increased the opportunities for confrontation, both peaceful and violent, among culturally and physically different people. The decline in colonialism by European powers in the 1960s and the end of communist domination in eastern Europe during the 1990s have also allowed interethnic rivalries to resume. Throughout the world, groups defined by race, ethnicity, or religion confront other groups so defined. These confrontations, as Chapter 1 showed, can lead to extermination, expulsion, secession, segregation, fusion, assimilation, or pluralism. At the conclusion of this chapter, we will review how these processes have been illustrated in this chapter as we look beyond the United States.

Confrontations among racial and ethnic groups have escalated in frequency and intensity in the twentieth century. In surveying these conflicts, we can see two themes emerge—the previously considered world systems theory and ethnonational conflict. **World systems theory** considers the global economic system as divided between nations that control wealth and those that provide natural resources and labor. Historically, the nations we will be considering reflect this competition between "haves" and "have nots." Whether the laborers be poor Roman Catholics in Ireland or Black Africans, their contribution to the prosperity of the dominant group created the social inequality people are trying to address today. **Ethnonational conflict** refers to conflicts between ethnic, racial, religious, and linguistic groups within nations which are increasingly replacing conflicts between nations as the source of refugees and even death. These conflicts remind us that the processes operating in the United States to deny racial and ethnic groups rights and opportunities are at work throughout the world (W. Connor 1994; S. Olzak 1998; I. Wallerstein 1976).

The sociological perspective on relations between dominant and subordinate groups treats race and ethnicity as social categories. As social concepts, they can be understood only in the context of the shared meanings attached to them by societies and their members. Although relationships among dominant and subordinate groups vary greatly, there are similarities across societies. Racial and ethnic hostilities arise out of economic needs and demands. These needs and demands may not always be realistic; that is, a group may seek out enemies where none exist or where victory will yield no rewards. Racial and ethnic conflicts are both the results and the precipitators of change in the economic and political sectors (Barclay et al. 1976; L. Coser 1956).

Relations between dominant and subordinate groups differ from society to society, as this chapter will show. Intergroup relations in Mexico, Canada, Northern Ireland, Israel, and South Africa are striking in their similarities and contrasts. As shown in Figure 15.1, each society, in its own way, illustrates the processes of intergroup relations first introduced in Chapter 1. The examples range from the Holocaust which precipitated the emergence of Israel to the efforts to create a multiracial government in South Africa.

Another appropriate comparison is to consider the characteristics of the nations themselves under study. In Table 15.1, we offer an overview of these five nations as an introduction to understanding intergroup relations present within these countries. A study of these five societies, coupled with knowledge of subordinate groups in the United States, will provide the background from which to draw some conclusions about patterns of race and ethnic relations in the world today.

Mexico

Usually in the discussions of "race relations," Mexico is only considered as a source of immigrants to the United States. In questions of economic development, Mexico again typically enters the discussion only as it affects our own economy. However, Mexico, a nation of 95 million people (in the Western Hemisphere only Brazil and the United States are larger) is an exceedingly complex nation. It is therefore appropriate that

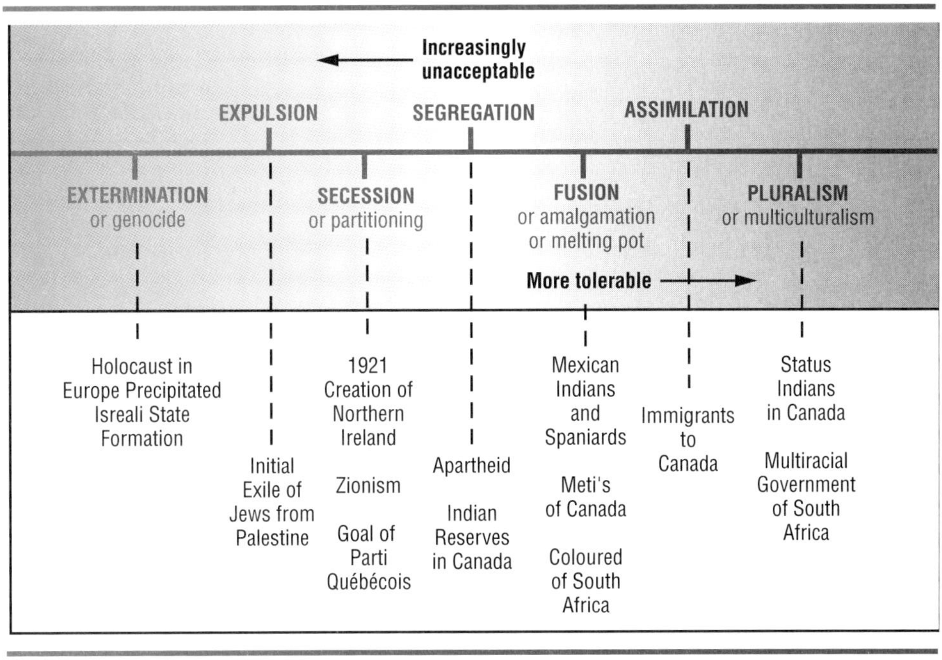

Figure 15.1 Intergroup Relations Continuum

we understand Mexico and its issues of inequality better. This understanding will also shed light on the relationship of its people to the United States.

In the 1520s, the Aztec Indian tribe that ruled Mexico was overthrown by Spain, and Mexico remained a Spanish colony until the 1820s. In 1836, Texas declared its independence from Mexico, and by 1846 Mexico was at war with the United States. As we described in Chapter 9, the Mexican-American War forced Mexico to surrender over half of its territory. In the 1860s, France sought to turn Mexico into an empire under the Austrian prince Maximilian but ultimately withdrew after bitter resistance led by a Mexican Indian, Benito Juárez, who later served as the nation's president.

THE MEXICAN INDIAN PEOPLE AND THE COLOR GRADIENT

In contemporary Mexico a major need has been to reassess the relations between the indigenous peoples—the Mexican Indians, many descended from the Mayas—and the government of Mexico. In 1900 the majority of the Mexican population still spoke Indian languages and lived in closed, semi-isolated villages or tribal communities according to ancestral customs. Many of these people were not a part of the growing industrialization in Mexico and were not truly represented in the national legislature. Perhaps the major change for them in this century was that many intermarried with the descendants of the Europeans, forming a *mestizo* class of

Table 15.1 Five-Nation Comparison, 1998

	Population (in millions)	GNP/per capita (USA = $28,020)	Groups represented	Current nation's formation
Mexico	98	$3,670	Mexican Indians, 15%	1823 Republic of Mexico declared independent from Spain
Canada	31	$19,020	French speaking, 25% Aboriginal people, 3–6% "Visible" minorities, 11%	1857 Dominion of Canada formed independent of England
Northern Ireland	1.6	Not available	Protestants, 54% Roman Catholic, 43%	1921 created from Ireland and becomes part of the United Kingdom
Israel	6	$15,870	Jews, 55% Others (citizens), 13% Moslems, Christians, Palestinians (non-citizens), 32%	1948 independence from British mandate of United Nations
South Africa	39	$28,020	Black Africans, 76% Whites, 13% Coloureds, 9% Asians, 3%	1948 independent from Great Britain

Sources: Author estimates based on Cornelius and Haub 1998; J. Dalburg 1998; C. MacMahon 1995; J. Redpath 1998; Rowley and Peres 1998; Statistics Canada 1998a, 1998b.

people of mixed ancestry. These mestizos have become increasingly identified with Mexico's growing middle class. Initially the subject of derision, the mestizos have developed their own distinct culture and, as the descendants of the European settlers are reduced in number and influence, have become the true bearers of the national Mexico sentiment.

Meanwhile, however, these social changes have left the Mexican Indian people even further behind the rest of the population economically. Indian cultures have been stereotyped as backward and resistant to progress and modern ways of living. Indeed, the existence of the many (at least fifty-six) Indian cultures has been seen in this century as an impediment to the development of a national culture in Mexico. In an effort to bring the indigenous people into the mainstream economy, in the late 1930s the Mexican government embarked on a government policy known as *indigenismo* or national integration. The Mexican Indians were given land rights to make them economically self-sufficient. This program was not unlike the U.S. policy in the 1880s with respect to the Native Americans (American Indians). However, *indigenismo* did not take place—the native people did not fade away culturally.

A legacy, both physical and cultural, of the Mayan people and other native peoples are today's Mexican Indians. Like their counterparts in the United States and, as we shall see later, in Canada, Mexican Indians occupy a subordinate position in their nation. As of 1996, while accounting for an estimated 15 percent of Mexico's population, Mexican Indians held no important offices in the central government and only a few of the more than 600 seats in the national assembly. About 60 percent of Mexican Indians are unemployed; most of those who are employed earn less than the minimum wage of about $2.50 per day. Only 12 percent of Mexican Indians complete even a sixth-grade education. The plight of Mexico's Indians is illustrated in Figure 15–2 (A. DePalma 1995a, 1995b; C. McMahon 1995).

The subordinate status of Mexico's Indians is only one reflection of the nation's color gradient. As noted in Chapter 9, a **color gradient** is the placement of people on a continuum from light to dark skin color rather than in distinct racial groupings by skin color. This is another example of the social construction of race in which social class is linked to the social reality (or at least the appearance) of racial purity. At the top of this gradient or hierarchy are the *criollos,* the 10 percent of the population who are typically White, well-educated members of the business and intellectual elites with familial roots in Spain. In the middle is the large, impoverished mestizo majority, most of whom have brown skin and a mixed racial lineage as a result of intermarriage. At the bottom of the color gradient are the destitute, full-blooded Mexican Indians and a small number of Blacks, some the descendants of 200,000 African slaves brought to Mexico. Ironically, while this color gradient is an important part of day-to-day life—enough so that some Mexicans use hair dyes, skin lighteners, and blue or green contact lenses to appear more European—nearly all Mexicans are considered part Mexican Indian because of centuries of intermarriage (J. Castañeda 1995; A. DePalma 1995a).

In 1992, an amendment to the Mexican Constitution recognized for the first time the diverse nature of the nation. The amendment stated that the languages, cultures,

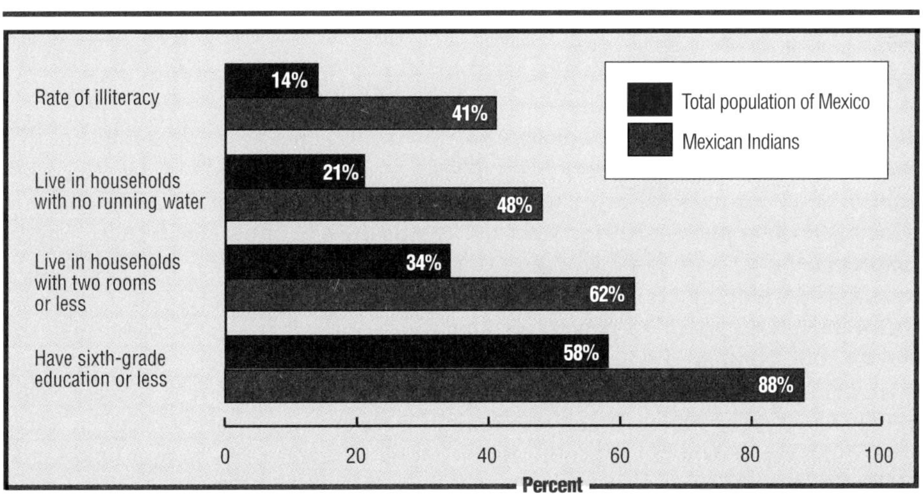

Figure 15.2 Position of Mexican Indians, 1990
Although Mexico has disturbing rates of poverty and illiteracy throughout its population, the situation is substantially worse for Mexican Indians.

Source: Data from 1990 Mexican census as reported in McMahon 1995, and World Bank 1995.

customs, and resources of indigenous Mexican Indian peoples would be protected. However, this reform did not satisfy members of Mexican Indian communities and had little practical effect on people's lives (R. Stavenhagen 1994).

The sense of frustration exploded two years later. On January 1, 1994, rebels from an armed insurgent group called the Zapatista National Liberation Army seized four towns in the state of Chiapas in southern Mexico. The rebels—who named their organization after Emiliano Zapata, a farmer and leader of the 1910 revolution against a corrupt dictatorship—were backed by 2,000 lightly armed Mayan Indians and peasants. Zapatista leaders declared that they had turned to armed insurrection to protest economic injustices and discrimination against the region's Indian population. The Mexican government mobilized the army to crush the revolt but was forced to retreat as news organizations broadcast pictures of the confrontation around the world. A cease-fire was declared after only twelve days of fighting, but 196 people had already died. Negotiations continue between the Mexican government and the Zapatista National Liberation Army (J. Darling 1995; A. DePalma 1996a).

The Zapatista rebels may represent only a small fraction of the Mexican Indian people, but there is widespread prejudice and discrimination against people of color that typically goes unrecognized. Schoolchildren are taught that the election of Benito Juárez, a Zapotec Indian, as president of Mexico in the nineteenth century proves that all Mexicans are equal. At the same time, Mexico's National Commission of Human Rights has never received a complaint alleging racial discrimination and has no process in place for handling such a complaint. Given this government indifference, there has been a marked growth in the last decade of formal organizations and voluntary associations representing Mexican Indians. The Zapatista revolt in Chiapas was an even more dramatic indication that those at the bottom of Mexico's color gradient are weary of inequality and injustice (A. DePalma 1995a, 1996a; Schaefer and Lamm 1998; R. Stavenhagen 1994).

THE STATUS OF WOMEN

Often in the United States we consider our own problems to be so significant that we fail to recognize that many of these social issues exist elsewhere. Gender stratification is an example of an issue we share with virtually the entire world, and Mexico is no exception. In 1975, Mexico City was the site of the first United Nations conference on the status of women. Much of the focus was on the situation of women in developing countries; in that regard, Mexico remains typical.

Currently, only about 74 percent of Mexican women stay in school through the fourth grade, compared with 95 percent of men. Only 17 percent of the administrative managers in Mexico's labor force are female, compared with 40 percent in the United States. As of 1995, women accounted for 8 percent of members of the lower house of Mexico's national assembly, 5 percent of members of the upper house, and 5 percent of the ministers of Mexico's national government (United Nations 1995: 172–175; World Bank 1995, 1996).

Even when Mexican women work outside the home, they are often denied recognition as active and productive household members, while men are typically viewed as heads of the household in every respect. As one consequence, women find it

The poverty of Mexican Indians is well documented and in some instances has led to violent protests for social change.

difficult to obtain credit and technical assistance in many parts of Mexico and to inherit land in rural areas.

In the larger economy in Mexico, women are often viewed as the "ideal workers." This appears to be particularly true of the foreign-owned factories or maquiladoras of the borderlands (discussed in Chapter 9) which rely heavily on women. For example, in a Tijuana electronics plant, women receive elementary training and work in the least-skilled and least-automated jobs because there is little expectation of advancement, organizing for better working conditions, or developing unions. Men are preferred over women in the more skilled jobs, and women lose out entirely as factories, even in developing nations such as Mexico, require more complex skills. In 1995, only 40 percent of women were in the paid labor force, compared to about 68 percent in Canada and 71 percent in the United States (Bureau of the Census 1998c:843; K. Kopinak 1995; E. Martelo 1996; G. Young 1993).

As is true in many developing countries, women in Mexico are more vulnerable than men to contracting the HIV virus and developing AIDS. In dealing with male sexual partners, women's subordinate social and economic position makes it difficult for them to assess their risk of infection and, even more important, to negotiate taking precautions. Interestingly, abortion is widely available in Mexico. Despite laws prohibiting abortion except in cases of rape or when necessary to save the woman's life, an estimated 400,000 abortions are carried out each year. Some women obtain abortions from practitioners of folk medicine, but many attempt to self-abort and then seek medical attention to prevent serious injury (A. Delriozolezzi 1995; M. Honey 1994).

In recent decades, Mexican women have begun to address an array of economic, political, and health issues. Often this organizing occurs at the grassroots level, outside traditional governmental forums. Because women continue to serve as household managers for their families, even when they work outside the home, they have been aware of the consequences of the inadequate public services in low-income urban neighborhoods. As far back as 1973, women in Monterrey—the nation's third-largest city—began protesting the continuing disruptions of the city's water supply. At first, individual women made complaints to city officials and the water authority, but subsequently, groups of female activists emerged. They sent delegations to confront politicians, organized protest rallies, and blocked traffic as a means of getting media attention. As a result of their efforts, there have been improvements in Monterrey's water service, although the issue of reliable and safe water remains a concern in Mexico and many developing countries (V. Bennett 1995; Schaefer and Lamm 1998).

Canada

Multiculturalism is a relatively recent term in the United States; it is used to refer to diversity. In Canada, it has been adopted as a state policy for over two decades. Still, many people in the United States, when they think of Canada, see it as a homogeneous nation with a smattering of Arctic-type people—merely a cross between the northern mainland United States and Alaska. This is not the social reality.

One of the continuing discussions among Canadians is the need for a cohesive national identity or a sense of common peoplehood. This need has been complicated by the immense size of the country, much of which is sparsely populated, and the diversity of its people.

In 1971, Canadian Prime Minister Pierre Trudeau presented to the House of Commons a policy of multiculturalism that sought to permit cultural groups to retain and foster their identity. Specifically, he declared that there should continue to be two official languages, French and English, but "no official culture" and no "ethnic group [taking] precedence over any other" (H. Labelle 1989:2). Yet it is not always possible to legislate a pluralistic society, as the case of Canada demonstrates.

THE ABORIGINAL PEOPLES

Canada, like the United States, has had an adversarial relationship with its native peoples. The Canadian experience, however, has not been as violent. During all three stages of Canadian history—French colonialism, British colonialism, and Canadian nationhood—there has been, compared to the United States, little warfare between Canadian Whites and Canadian Native Americans. Yet the legacy today is similar. Prodded by settlers, colonial governments and later Canadian governments drove the Native Americans from their lands. Already by the 1830s, Indian reserves were being established that were similar to the reservations in the United States. Tribal members were encouraged to renounce their status and become Canadian citizens. Assimilation was the explicit policy until relatively recently (D. Champagne 1994; C. Waldman 1985).

The 1.2 million native peoples of Canada are collectively referred to by the government as the Aboriginal Peoples and represent about 3–6 percent of the population, depending on the definition used. This population is classified into the following groups:

1. Status Indians: The 604 tribes or bands officially recognized by the government, numbering about 554,000, of whom the majority live on Indian reserves (or reservations).
2. Inuit: The 41,000 people living in the northern part of the country who typically have been referred to as the Eskimos.
3. Métis: Canadians of mixed ancestry, officially numbering 210,000; depending on definitions, they range in number from 100,000 to 850,000.
4. Non-Status Indians: Canadians of native ancestry who, because of voluntary decisions or government rulings, have been denied registration status. The group numbers about 423,000.

In a 1995 protest demonstration, Canadian Indians protest their living conditions on reserves by erecting teepees on Parliament Hill in Ottawa.

The Métis and non-Status Indians have historically enjoyed no separate legal recognition, but efforts continue to secure them special rights under the law, such as designated health, education, and welfare programs. The general public does not understand these legal distinctions, so if a Métis or non-Status Indian "looks like an Indian," she or he is subjected to the same treatment, discriminatory or otherwise (Statistics Canada 1998a).

The new Canadian Federal Constitution of 1982 included a Charter of Rights that "recognized and affirmed . . . the existing aboriginal and treaty rights" of the Canadian Native American, Inuit, and Métis peoples. This recognition received the most visibility through the efforts of the Mohawk, one of the tribes of Status Indians. At issue were land rights involving some property areas in Quebec that had spiritual significance for the Mohawk. Their protests and militant confrontations reawakened the Canadian people to the concerns of their diverse native peoples (Amnesty International 1993).

Some of the contemporary issues facing the Aboriginal Peoples are very similar to those faced by Native Americans in the United States. The Canadian Human Rights Commission has ruled that some native Inuit had their rights violated when they were forcibly relocated from northern Quebec to isolated areas in the Arctic in 1953. In response, the Department of Indian Affairs and Northern Development indicated in 1992 that it would facilitate transportation but rejected the possibility of compensation.

Another setback, also in 1992, occurred when a national referendum, the Charlottetown Agreement, was defeated. This constitutional reform package embraced a number of issues, including greater recognition of the Aboriginal Peoples. Canadian Native American and Inuit leaders expressed anger over the defeat, and Ron George, the leader of the Native Council of Canada, accused those who rejected the agreement of "perpetuating apartheid in this country" (Keesing's 1992:39126). However, the federal government has declared its willingness to accept the right of the Inuit and the other aboriginal people of Northern Canada to self-government (D. Champagne 1994).

The fate of urban Aboriginal Peoples is an equally difficult issue. Who is responsible for the hundreds of thousands of native peoples scattered across the country? In metropolitan Toronto alone there are an estimated 65,000 Aboriginal People from sixty tribal groups. The frustration that they face has led to the demand, not warmly greeted, for a House of Commons seat designated for Toronto's Aboriginal Peoples (E. Fulton 1992).

In 1996, the Royal Commission on Aboriginal People released a report after five years of study and hearings. Despite the opposition in Toronto to even one seat, the commission (among 440 recommendations) advanced the proposal of a separate advisory parliament for the native peoples. The general tone of the report was that 150 years of government policies had been a shameful failure. While the notion of a separate assembly has been largely dismissed, the government did release in 1998 a formal apology for 150 years of paternalistic assistance programs and racist residential schools that devastated Indian communities as thoroughly as any war or disease (A. DePalma 1998).

In a positive step, Canada created in 1999 a new territory in response to a native land claim in which the resident Inuit (formerly called Eskimos) dominated. Nunavut (NOO-nah-voot), as the territory was called, recognizes the territorial rights of the Inuit. Admirable as this event is, observers noted it was relatively easy to grant such economic rights and autonomy in the isolated expanse of northern Canada compared to the Aboriginal People of the more populated southern provinces of Canada (A. DePalma 1999).

THE QUÉBÉCOIS

Assimilation and domination have been the plight of most minority groups. The French-speaking people of the province of Quebec—the Québécois, as they are known—represent a contrasting case. Since the mid-1960s, they have reasserted their identity and captured the attention of the entire nation.

Quebec counts for about one-fourth of the nation's population and wealth. Reflecting its early settlement by the French, fully 80 percent of the province's population claims French as its first language, compared to only 25 percent in the nation as a whole (J. Fox 1994).

The Québécois have sought to put French Canadian culture on an equal footing with English Canadian culture in the country as a whole and to dominate the province. At the very least, this effort has been seen as an irritant outside Quebec and has been viewed with great concern by the English-speaking minority in Quebec (D. Salée 1994).

In the 1960s, the Québécois expressed the feeling that bilingual status was not enough. Even to have French recognized as one of two official languages in a nation dominated by the English-speaking population gave the Québécois second-class status in their view. With some leaders threatening to break completely with Canada and make Quebec an independent nation, Canada made French the official language of the province and the only acceptable language for commercial signs and public transactions. New residents are now required to send their children to French schools. The English-speaking residents felt as if they had been made aliens, even though many of them had roots extending back to the 1700s. These changes spurred residents to migrate from Quebec and some corporate headquarters to relocate to the neighboring English-speaking province of Ontario (J. Fox 1994; D. Salée 1994).

The long debate over how much independence Quebec should be permitted reached a stalemate with the Meech Lake Accords. In 1987, at Meech Lake, a group of constitutional amendments was developed that would recognize Quebec as a distinct society. Quickly, Quebec ratified the amendments, but two other provinces (Newfoundland and Manitoba) did not approve them within the three-year deadline. The accords died, but the effort did not.

In 1992, following a series of meetings and a new agreement, the Charlottetown Agreement, mentioned earlier as including provisions for the Aboriginal Peoples, was developed, but this time it was put to a national referendum following endorsement by all the provinces and territories. The proposal's rejection by a 55–45 percent margin in Canada as a whole has essentially closed constitutional debate on the topic. It has not, however, ended Quebec's quest for a unique role. There were many reasons for the referendum's defeat. For example, it was defeated even in Quebec, where many felt that the Charlottetown Agreement did not transfer sufficient powers to the province. Some Aboriginal Peoples were skeptical that their treatment would improve at the hands of the Québécois, and some leaders even vowed that they would secede as tribes if Quebec ever gained sovereignty (D. Farr 1993; C. Trueheart 1995a).

Through the past three decades of debate, the force both unifying and dividing the French-speaking people of Quebec has been the Parti Québécois. Since its establishment in 1968, the Parti Québécois has been a force in the politics of the provinces. It gained majority control of the province's assembly in 1994. The national version, Bloc Québécois, emerged second to the ruling party and therefore plays the role of the official opposition party within Canada's parliamentary government. The Bloc Québécois has advocated separatism—the creation of an independent nation of Quebec. Separatists contend that Quebec has the confidence, the natural resources, and the economic structure to stand on its own. However, not all Québécois who vote for the party favor this extreme position, although they are certainly sympathetic to preserving their language and culture.

In 1995, the people of Quebec were given a different referendum question that they would vote on alone—whether they wished to separate from Canada and form a new nation. In a very close vote, 50.5 percent of the voters indicated a preference to remain united with Canada. The vote was particularly striking given the confusion over how separation would be accomplished and its significance economically. Discussion over the referendum was further complicated by threats

Supporters of a Quebec separatist movement participate in a rally. In 1995, a referendum calling for separation from the rest of Canada was narrowly defeated.

from tribal people in Quebec that if secession were approved, the tribes themselves would secede from Quebec. About 60 percent of French-speaking people of Quebec favored secession, with 95 percent of English-speaking Québécois voting to preserve a united Canada. Separatists vowed to keep working for secession and called for another referendum in the future. This is particularly important since the Canada Supreme Court ruled in 1998 that Quebec cannot secede without seeking the consent of the central government. Canadians opposed to separation spoke of reconciliation following the bitter election debate, but it was unclear what further concessions they were prepared to make to the separatists (G. Lawson 1996; C. Trueheart 1995b).

Canada is characterized by the presence of two linguistic communities: the Anglophone and the Francophone, the latter occurring largely in one province, Quebec. Outside Quebec, Canadians are opposed to separatism, and within this province, they are divided. Language and cultural issues, therefore, both unify and divide a nation of 30 million people.

IMMIGRATION AND RACE

Immigration has also been a significant social force contributing to Canadian multiculturalism. In addition to Britain, France, and other European nations, the largest sources of ancestry in Canada, in descending order, are the Aboriginal Peoples, China, and Southeast Asia. Each of these groups accounts for 1–2 percent of the population. Collectively, the 3.2 million "visible minorities," as they are referred to in government reports of Blacks, Latin Americans, Arabs, and Asians, account for 11 percent of the population, but 87 percent are in three provinces: Ontario (Toronto), British Columbia (Vancouver), and Quebec (Montreal) (Statistics Canada 1998b).

People in the United States tend to view Canada's race relations in complimentary terms. In part, this view reflects Canada's role as the "promised land" to slaves escaping the U.S. South and crossing the free North to Canada, where they were unlikely to be recaptured. The social reality, past and present, is quite different. Africans came in 1689 as involuntary immigrants to be enslaved by French colonists. Slavery officially continued until 1833. It never really flourished because the Canadian economy did not require a large labor force, and therefore, most slaves worked as domestic servants. Blacks from the United States did flee to Canada before slavery ended, but some fugitive slaves returned following Lincoln's issuance of the Emancipation Proclamation in 1863. The early Black arrivals in Canada were greeted in a variety of ways. Often they were warmly received as fugitives from slavery, but as their numbers grew in some areas, Canadians grew concerned that they would overwhelm the White population (R. Winks 1971).

The view of Canada as a land of positive intergroup relations is also fostered by Canadians' comparing themselves to the United States. They have long been willing to compare their best social institutions to the worst examples of racism in the United States and to pride themselves on being more virtuous and high-minded (P. McClain 1979).

The contemporary Black Canadian population consists of indigenous Afro-Canadians with several generations of roots in Canada, West Indian immigrants and their descendants, and a number of post-World War II immigrants from the United States. Each of these groups has been significant. For example, in 1987, 60,000 Jamaicans lived in Toronto alone. Generally, Black Canadians, as well as Asians, do not experience the same degree of segregation as their counterparts in the United States (H. Denton 1987; E. Fong 1997).

Before 1966 Canada's immigration policy alternated between restrictive and more open, as necessary to assist the economy. As in the United States, there were some very exclusionary phases based on race. From 1884 to 1923, Canada levied a Chinese "head tax" that virtually brought Chinese immigration to a halt, though it had earlier been encouraged. Subsequent policies through 1947 were not much better. More recent immigration policy, while not explicitly racist, heavily favored White nationalities such as British, Australian, and New Zealander.

In 1967 favoritism by nationality was replaced by regulations that created a point system based on the prospective immigrant's education and occupational skill, in light of the occupational needs of Canada. These changes transformed the source of immigration to include greater numbers of Black immigrants from Jamaica and other Caribbean nations as well as from Asia (P. McClain 1979; Statistics Canada 1993; R. Winks 1971).

In 1977, in response to concerns about growing immigration and even outright racist calls to exclude non-Whites, Canada enacted Bill C–24, which allows immigration to be restricted to maintain the "safety and good order of Canadian society." While proponents argued that it was not race-specific, its passage was followed by a definite increase in the number of non-Whites denied entry or deported. Overall immigration dropped to the lowest levels since the end of World War II (Simmons and Keohane 1992).

Concerns over second-class status have led to organized protests, sometimes militant in nature. For example, after the initial verdict in the Rodney King case in Los Angeles, Black Canadians took to the streets of Toronto to protest police brutality in that city. The government and the courts have been far from silent on issues relevant to "the visible minorities" and the Aboriginal Peoples. Canadian courts have liberally interpreted their Charter of Rights and Freedoms to prevent systematic discrimination, and equal rights legislation has been passed. Yet institutional racism and continuing debates about immigration policy will remain a part of the Canadian scene for the next century (C. Farnsworth 1996; I. McKenna 1994).

It is difficult to escape the parallels with the United States. For example, the Ku Klux Klan spread into Canada in the 1920s and experienced a degree of resurgence in the 1980s. Its targets were Blacks, Asian immigrants, and Jewish Canadians. Similarly, in the 1990s, in Canada as well as in the United States, pressure increased to restrict the immigration of new arrivals from Central America seeking asylum. Public agitation to restrict immigration has been particularly intense when Latin Americans who have been denied permanent residence in the United States seek sanctuary in Canada (*Refugee Reports* 1992; J. Sher 1983).

In 1541, the Frenchman Jacques Cartier established the first European settlement along the St. Lawrence River, but within a year he withdrew because of confrontation with the Iroquois. Almost 500 years later, the descendants of the Europeans and Aboriginal Peoples are still trying to resolve Canada's identity as it is shaped by issues of ethnicity, race, and language.

Northern Ireland

Armed conflict between Protestants and Roman Catholics is difficult for many in the United States to understand. Our recent history in racial and ethnic relations makes it relatively easy for us to recognize that societies may be torn apart by differences based on skin color or even language. But atrocities among fellow citizens who share the bond of the Christian faith, even if in name only, can strike us as incredible. Yet newspapers and television news regularly recount the horrors from Northern Ireland—a very troubled land of only 1.6 million people.

PARTITION

The roots of today's violence lie in the invasion of Ireland by the English (then the Anglo-Normans) in the twelfth century. England, however, preoccupied with European enemies and hampered by resistance from the Irish, never gained complete control of the island. The northernmost area, called Ulster, received a heavy influx of Protestant settlers from Scotland and England in the seventeenth century following Oliver Cromwell's defeat of the Irish supporters of Britain's Roman Catholic monarch (see Figure 15.3).

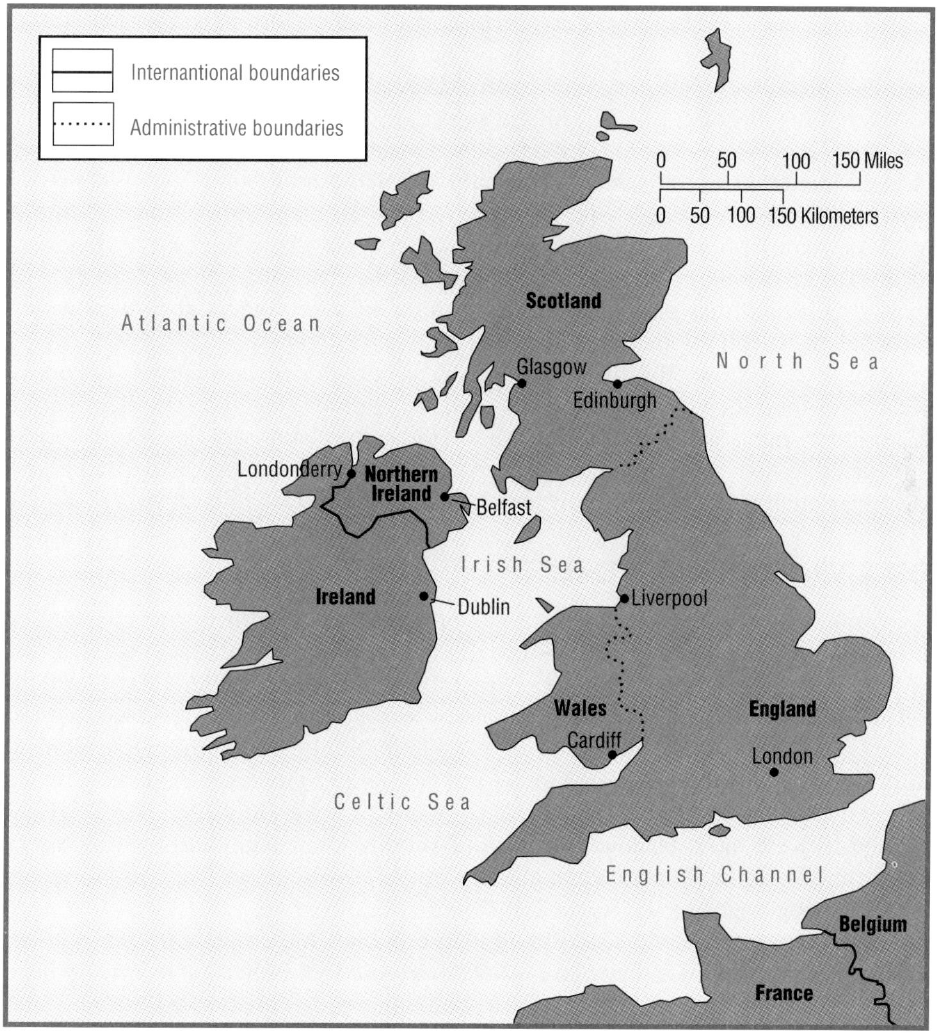

Figure 15.3 United Kingdom

Ireland was united with Great Britain (England, Scotland, and Wales) in 1801 to form the United Kingdom. Despite this union, Ireland was still governed as a colony. Most of the people of Ireland found it difficult to accept union and did not consider the government in London theirs. In secret, the native Irish continued to speak Irish (or Gaelic) and worship as Roman Catholics in defiance of the Protestant British government. Protestant settlers continued to speak English and to pay homage to the British monarch after the Restoration. Unhappy with their colonial status, the Irish, as they had done for the previous seven centuries, again pushed for independence or at least **home rule** with a local Irish parliament. Protestants in Ireland and most people in Britain objected to such demands, derisively referring to them as "Rome rule." During the latter 1800s, as home-rule bills were introduced, Irish Roman Catholics marched in support, only to be confronted by angry Protestants.

A very limited home-rule bill was passed in 1914, only to have its implementation delayed by World War I. Tired of waiting, a small group of militant Irish nationalists declared they would accept no compromises and no more delays. What could have been an isolated incident, unsupported by the majority of Roman Catholic and Protestant Irish alike, aroused an extreme reaction from England and escalated the Easter Rebellion of 1916 into the Anglo-Irish War of 1919–1921. In 1921, a treaty was signed that provided for establishing an independent sovereign nation in the south, which evolved into today's Republic of Ireland.

From 1921 through the present, the United Kingdom has retained its control over six of the nine counties of Ulster—today's Northern Ireland. The Republic of Ireland is 95 percent Roman Catholic, but Northern Ireland, with its population 54 percent Protestant and 43 percent Roman Catholic, is still a land divided. The partition was completed, but peace was not established (J. Dahlburg 1998).

THE CIVIL RIGHTS MOVEMENT

The immediate postpartition period was fairly peaceful, with fewer than twenty deaths through the late 1960s related to the Protestant-Roman Catholic conflict that had divided the island for centuries. Britain was relatively indifferent to Northern Ireland governance and looked the other way as the Protestants capitalized on their majority. Political districts were created that minimized the voting strength of Roman Catholics in sending representatives to Stormont, Northern Ireland's Parliament, while Protestant areas were divided to maximize electoral power. In some local elections, the abuses were more blatant, tying voting to home ownership and thereby disenfranchising large numbers of Roman Catholics, who were more likely to be renters or to be living with kin (R. Terchek 1977).

These political problems faced by Roman Catholics were compounded by other social problems. Because they had historically worked for Protestant factory owners, the Roman Catholics were more likely to be poor, live in substandard housing, and suffer from more and longer periods of unemployment. Residential segregation and separate schools further isolated the two groups from one another (Boal and Douglas 1982; J. Conroy 1981; J. Whyte 1986).

The civil rights movement of Northern Ireland began with a march in Londonderry (see Figure 15.3) in 1969, with Roman Catholics joined by some sympathetic Protestants, protesting the social ills described here. Marching in defiance of a police order, the demonstrators soon were confronted by the police, and violence broke out, leaving civilians injured. A year later, Belfast protests led to an escalation of violence, and ten demonstrators were killed. British troops were ordered into Northern Ireland the next day. Within two years, a well-organized guerrilla movement, the Irish Republican Army (IRA), rose on behalf of militant Roman Catholics. Simultaneously, terrorist Unionists, paramilitary Protestant groups, surfaced. The violence continued to escalate amid futile efforts by civil rights workers to have the issues discussed. In 1971, Britain initiated the policy of internment, allowing Britain to hold suspected terrorists, mostly Roman Catholics, without making charges against them.

In late 1994, peace was made in Northern Ireland as both the militant Unionists and the IRA forces declared cease-fires. This development followed months of intense effort between Great Britain and the Republic of Ireland, which pledged to involve the militant groups in negotiations that would bring a permanent end to the violence. The Irish Republic government also agreed to end its claim on Northern Ireland. The uneasy peace had held but a year when the IRA, critical of the exclusion of some Roman Catholic groups from peace talks, struck out at targets in England and British military installations in Northern Ireland.

THE NORTHERN IRELAND ACCORD

The continued violence, despite cease-fires on paper, led two nations to become involved in the negotiations which before had distanced themselves from the dispute—the United States and the Republic of Ireland. Momentum for a consensus came in 1994 when President Bill Clinton invited Gerry Adams, the leader of the Sein Fein, the political wing of the Irish Republic Army, to the United States. The British were outraged but it set in motion talks which involved not just official political leaders but also spokespersons for fringe groups as well.

In 1998, the Northern Ireland Accord was signed, calling for a new Northern Ireland Assembly which would have Protestants and Catholics share power—unlike the Protestant-dominated parliament abolished in 1972. A new North/South Ministerial (or Cabinet ministers) Council was called for as a forum

"NOW COMES THE TRICKY PART..."

where the Irish Republic government would meet to make policy with the new Northern Ireland Assembly. Other provisions called for the amending of the Irish Republic constitution where it had claimed the territory of Northern Ireland as its own (D. Balz 1998).

Within months of the Accord, one of the most violent attacks in recent history took place. A renegade group calling itself the Real IRA bombed a shopping area of Omagh, Northern Ireland leaving twenty eight dead—all civilians—including Protestants, Catholics, and even residents of the Republic of Ireland. In its aftermath some of the dissenters from the Accord said enough was enough and that it was time to push for peace (W. Underhill 1998).

Even with a guarded expectation for peace, problems continue to face Northern Ireland. Both Great Britain and the European Union have pledged to economically assist the strife-torn region. Assuming political equality is in the offering there is the issue of the persistence of social inequality. More Roman Catholic children leave school early and are much less likely to receive a university education. Consequently there is a significant difference in unemployment rates—23 percent of Catholic men are unemployed versus 9 percent of the Protestant men. As a result, more than twice as many Roman Catholic households are dependent on public assistance than are the Protestants. As is so often the case with ethnic tension, the basic characteristic of the minority experience is unequal treatment and its economic consequences (Cairns and Darby 1998).

Israel and the Palestinians

In 1991, when the Gulf War ended, hopes were high in many parts of the world that a comprehensive Middle East peace plan could be hammered out. The key element in any such plan was to resolve the conflict between Israel and its Arab neighbors and resolve the challenge of the Palestinian refugees. While the issues are debated in the political arena, the origins of the conflict can be found in race, ethnicity, and religion.

Nearly 2,000 years ago, the Jews were exiled from Palestine in the **Diaspora**. The exiled Jews settled throughout Europe and elsewhere in the Middle East. There, they often encountered hostility and the anti-Semitism described in Chapter 13. With the conversion of the Roman Empire to Christianity, Palestine became the site of many Christian pilgrimages. Beginning in the seventh century, Palestine gradually fell under the Muslim influence of the Arabs. By the beginning of the twentieth century, tourism had become established. In addition, some Jews had migrated from Russia and established settlements that were tolerated by the Ottoman Empire, which then controlled Palestine.

Great Britain expanded its colonial control from Egypt into Palestine during World War I, driving out the Turks. Britain ruled the land but endorsed the eventual establishment of a Jewish national homeland in Palestine. The spirit of **Zionism**, the yearning to establish a Jewish state in the biblical homeland, was well under way. From the Arab perspective, Zionism meant the subjugation, if not the elimination, of the Palestinians.

Thousands of Jews came to settle from throughout the world; even so, in the 1920s, Palestine was only about 15 percent Jewish. Ethnic tension grew as the Arabs of Palestine were threatened by the Zionist fervor. Rioting grew to such a point that, in 1939, Britain yielded to Palestinian demands that Jewish immigration be stopped. This occurred at the same time as large numbers of Jews were fleeing Nazism in Europe. Following World War II, Jews resumed their demand for a homeland, despite Arab objections. Britain turned to the newly formed United Nations to settle the dispute. In May 1948, the British mandate over Palestine ended, and the State of Israel was founded (A. Lesch 1983; Said et al. 1988).

The Palestinian people define themselves as the people who live in this former British mandate, along with their descendants on their fathers' side. They are viewed as an ethnic group, within the larger group of Arabs. They generally speak Arabic, and most of them are Muslim. With a rapid rate of natural increase, the Palestinians have grown in number from 1.4 million at the end of World War II to nearly 8 million worldwide (E. Bronner 1998).

ARAB-ISRAELI CONFLICTS

No sooner had Israel been recognized than the Arab nations, particularly Egypt, Jordan, Iraq, Syria, and Lebanon, announced their intention to restore control to the Palestinian Arabs, by force if necessary. As hostilities broke out, the Israeli military stepped in to preserve the borders, which no Arab nation agreed to recognize. Some 60 percent of the 1.3 million Arabs fled or were expelled from Israeli territory, becoming refugees in neighboring countries. An uneasy peace followed as Israel attempted to encourage massive new Jewish immigration. Israel also extended the same services that were available to the Jews, such as education and health care, to the non-Jewish Israelis. The new Jewish population continued to grow under the country's Law of Return, which gave every Jew in the world the right to settle permanently as a citizen. The question of Jerusalem remained unsettled, and the city was divided into two separate sections—Israeli Jewish and Jordanian Arab—a division both sides refused to regard as permanent (A. Lesch 1983).

In 1967, Egypt, followed by Syria, responded to Israel's military actions to take surrounding territory in what has come to be called the Six-Day War. In the course of defeating the Arab states' military, Israel occupied the Gaza Strip and the West Bank (see Figure 15.4). The defeat was all the more bitter for the Arabs as Israeli-held territory expanded.

The October 1973 war (called the Yom Kippur War by Jews and the Ramadan War by Arabs), launched against Israel by Egypt and Syria, did not change any boundaries, but it did lead to huge oil-price rises as Arab and other oil-rich nations retaliated for the European and U.S. backing of Israel. In 1979, Egypt, through the mediation of U.S. President Carter, recognized Israel's right to exist, for which Israel returned the Sinai, but there was no suggestion that the other occupied territories would be returned to neighboring Arab states. This recognition by Egypt, following several unsuccessful Arab military attacks, signaled to the Palestinians that they were alone in their struggle against Israel (P. Seale 1980).

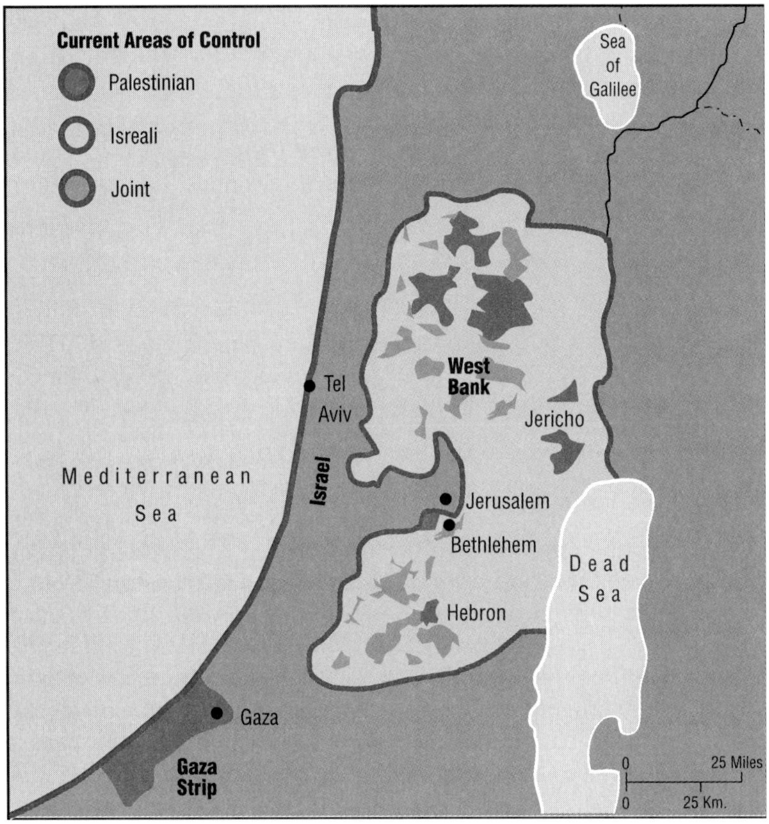

Figure 15.4 Israeli Settlements and Palestinian Lands

Source: From "The Shape of a State to Come" *Newsweek,* December 21, 1998.

While our primary attention here is on the Palestinians and the Jews, another significant ethnic issue is present in Israel. The Law of Return has brought to Israel Jews of varying cultural backgrounds. European Jews have been the dominant force, but a significant migration of the more religious observant Jews from North Africa and other parts of the Middle East has created what sociologist Ernest Krausz (1973) termed "the two nations." Not only are the various Jewish groups culturally diverse, but there are also significant socioeconomic differences, the Europeans generally being more prosperous, better represented in the Knesset (Israel's parliament), and better educated. The secular Jews feel pressure from the more traditional and ultra-Orthodox Jews who push for a nation more reflective of Jewish customs and law. Indeed in a 1998 survey, more Israeli Jews see the lack of unity within the state as a major shortcoming than a failure to end the Israeli-Arab conflict (*Los Angeles Times* Poll 1998; M. Miller 1998).

THE INTIFADA

The occupied territories were regarded initially by Israel as a security zone between it and its belligerent neighbors. By the 1980s, however, it was clear that they were also serving as the location of new settlements for Jews migrating to Israel, especially from Russia. Palestinians, while enjoying some political and monetary support of Arab nations, saw little likelihood of a successful military effort to eliminate Israel. Therefore, in December 1987, they began the **Intifada**, the uprising against Israel by the Palestinians in the occupied territories through attacks against soldiers, the boycott of Israeli goods, general strikes, resistance, and noncooperation with Israeli authorities. The target of the Intifada has been the Israelis. It should be realized that for several years the Intifada has been a grassroots, popular movement whose growth in support was as much a surprise to the Palestine Liberation Organization (PLO) and the Arab nations as it was to Israel and its supporters. The broad range of participants in the Intifada—students, workers, union members, professionals, and business leaders—showed the unambiguous Palestinian opposition to occupation.

Despite condemnation by both the United Nations and the United States, Israel continued to expel suspected activists from the occupied territories into neighboring Arab states. The Intifada began out of the frustration of the Palestinians within Israel, but the confrontations were later encouraged by the PLO, an umbrella organization for several Palestinian factions of varying militancy.

With television news footage of Israeli soldiers appearing to attack defenseless youths, the Intifada transformed world opinion, especially in the United States. Palestinians came to be viewed as people struggling for self-determination rather than as terrorists out to destroy Israel. Instead of Israel being viewed as the "David" and its Arab neighbors "Goliath," Israel came to take on the bully role and the Palestinians the sympathetic underdog role (A. Hubbard 1993).

Nearly half of the world's Palestinian people live under Israeli control. Of the Israeli Palestinians, about one-third are regarded as residents, and the rest live in the occupied territories. The Diaspora of Jews that the creation of Israel was to remedy has led to the displacement of the Palestinian Arabs. From the Israeli perspective, the continued possession of these lands is vital to serve as a buffer from bordering enemies, as evidenced by Iraq's firing of thirty-nine Scud missiles into Israel during the 1991 Gulf War. Yet despite this violence, there is a sense of stability today for Israeli Jews. An entire generation of Israelis and Palestinians has been born since the 1967 Six-Day War. A declining number of Israelis personally recall the time when the Jews did not have a homeland. The Intifada and international reaction propelled Israel and the PLO to reach an agreement in 1993 known as the Oslo Accords.

THE SEARCH FOR SOLUTIONS

The Oslo Accords between Israeli Prime Minister Yitzhak Rabin and PLO Chairman Yasser Arafat and subsequent agreements ended the state of war and set in motion the creation of the first-ever self-governing Palestinian territory in the Gaza Strip and the West Bank. Most of the Gaza Strip and about 27 percent of the West Bank has come under Palestinian civil control with security handled jointly by Israel and the Palestinians (Blow and Perry 1998).

Politically, the creation of a Palestinian Authority has been an unexpected achievement, but economically, the people are worse off. In the West Bank, the authority now operates education, health, welfare, and other services without the large Israeli subsidies of the past. In addition, many Palestinians who commuted to work in Israel have lost their jobs. Occasional closures of the Israel-Palestinian territory border also create economic problems for the former occupied territories.

The Israeli government must be constantly on guard against political attacks from within by those who feel that it sold out to the PLO. These right-wing Israelis also include residents in Jewish settlements who suddenly find themselves under Palestinian control. Indeed, in 1995, Prime Minister Rabin was assassinated at a peace rally by an Israeli who felt the government had given up too much. Israel is now offering financial incentives for Jewish settlements in the West Bank over the opposition of both the Palestinians and the United States. Also, sporadic attacks and protests by militant Palestinians and extremist Israelis make the unsettled situation even more tense. Arafat, once despised by Israel (and the United States), is viewed desperately as the key to keeping the peace.

The Israeli and PLO leaders continue to be concerned about their ability to control violence by those dissatisfied by the accord. Additional issues pending include:

- The status of Jerusalem. It is Israel's capital but is also viewed by Muslims as the third most holy city in the world.
- The future of the Jewish settlements in the Palestinian territories.

Within Jerusalem are places held sacred by the world's Christians, Jews, and Moslems.

- The future of Palestinians and other Arabs with Israeli citizenship.
- The creation of a truly independent Palestinian national state.
- The future of Palestinian refugees elsewhere.

Added worries are the uneasy peace between Israel and its Arab neighbors and the sometimes interrelated events in Iraq and Iran (Rouhanna and Bar-Tal 1998).

The last fifty years have witnessed significant changes: Israel has gone from a land under siege to a nation whose borders are recognized by virtually everyone. Now, as noted earlier, Israel relatively secure as a nation has come to terms with the various factions of religious and secular Jews trying to coexist. The Palestinian people have gone from disenfranchisement to becoming a people with territory who can now welcome back others from exile. The current solution is fragile and temporary, as is any form of secession, but the foundation for accommodation is stronger than at any time in recent memory.

Republic of South Africa

In every nation in the world, some racial, ethnic, or religious groups enjoy advantages denied to other groups. Nations differ in the extent of this denial and in whether it is supported by law or by custom. In no other industrial society has the denial been so entrenched in law as in the Republic of South Africa.

The Republic of South Africa is different from the rest of Africa because the original African peoples of the area are no longer present. Today, the country is multiracial, as shown in Table 15.2. The largest group is the Black Africans, or Bantus, who migrated from the north in the eighteenth century. Cape Coloureds, the product of mixed race, and Asians make up the remaining non-Whites. The small White community consists of the English and the Afrikaners, the latter descended from Dutch and other European settlers. As in all the other multicultural nations we have considered, colonialism and immigration have left their mark.

Table 15.2 Racial Groups in the Republic of South Africa (in percent)

	Whites	All Non-Whites	Black Africans	Coloureds	Asians
1904	22	78	67	9	2
1936	21	79	69	8	2
1951	21	79	68	9	3
1997	12	87	77	8	3
2010 (est.)	10	90	81	7	2

Sources: J. Redpath 1998; South African Institute of Race Relations 1992: 2, 3; P. van den Berghe 1978: 102.

Not all numbers sum due to rounding error.

THE LEGACY OF COLONIALISM

The permanent settlement of South Africa by Europeans began in 1652, when the Dutch East India Company established a colony in Cape Town as a port of call for shipping vessels bound for India. The area was sparsely populated, and the original inhabitants of the Cape of Good Hope, the Hottentots and Bushmen, were pushed inland like the indigenous peoples of the New World. To fill the need for laborers, the Dutch imported slaves from areas of Africa farther north. Slavery was confined mostly to areas near towns and involved more limited numbers than in the United States. The Boers, seminomads descended from the Dutch, did not remain on the coast but trekked inland to establish vast sheep and cattle ranches. The trekkers, as they were known, regularly fought off the Black inhabitants of the interior regions. Sexual relations between Dutch men and slave and Hottentot women were quite common, giving rise to a mulatto group referred to today as Cape Coloureds.

The British entered the scene by acquiring part of South Africa in 1814, at the end of the Napoleonic Wars. The British introduced workers from India as indentured servants on sugar plantations. They had also freed the slaves by 1834, with little compensation to the Dutch slave owners, and had given Blacks virtually all political and civil rights. The Boers were not happy with these developments and spent most of the nineteenth century in a violent struggle with the growing number of English colonists. In 1902, the British finally overwhelmed the Boers, leaving bitter memories on both sides. Once in control, however, they recognized that the superior numbers of the non-Whites were a potential threat to their power, as they had been to the power of the Afrikaners.

The growing non-White population consisted of the Coloureds, or mixed population, and the Black tribal groups, collectively referred to as Bantus. The British gave both groups the vote but restricted the franchise to people who met certain property qualifications. **Pass laws** were introduced, placing curfews on the Bantus and limiting their geographic movement. These laws, enforced through "reference books" until 1986, were intended to prevent urban areas from becoming overcrowded with job-seeking Black Africans, a familiar occurrence in colonial Africa (Barclay et al. 1976; G. Fredrickson 1981; J. Treen 1983; P. van den Berghe 1965; W. Wilson 1973).

APARTHEID

In 1948, South Africa was granted its independence from the United Kingdom, and the National Party, dominated by the Afrikaners, assumed control of the government. Under the leadership of this party, the rule of White supremacy, already well under way in the colonial period as custom, became more and more formalized into law. To deal with the multiracial population, the Whites devised a policy called apartheid to ensure their dominance. **Apartheid** (in Afrikaans, the language of the Afrikaners, it means "separation" or "apartness") came to mean a policy of separate development, euphemistically called multinational development by the government. At the time, these changes were regarded as cosmetic outside South Africa and by most Black South Africans.

A group of South Africans display their passbooks, which under apartheid were used to regulate the movements of Black people.

The White ruling class was not homogeneous. The English and Afrikaners belonged to different political parties, lived apart, spoke different languages, and worshipped separately, but they shared the belief that some form of apartheid was necessary. Apartheid can perhaps be best understood as a twentieth-century effort to reestablish the master-slave relationship. Blacks could not vote. They could not move throughout the country freely. They were unable to hold jobs unless the government approved. In order to work at approved jobs, they were forced to live in temporary quarters at great distances from their real homes. Their access to education, health care, and social services was severely limited (J. Burns 1978; J. Butler 1974; W. Wilson 1973).

During the 1980s, the United States and other nations increasingly isolated South Africa economically and politically. Of special embarrassment to South Africa was its virtual elimination from international sports competition, such as the Olympics, because of its apartheid athletic practices. Black and White athletes could not compete together.

Events took a significant turn in 1990, when South African Prime Minister F. W. De Klerk legalized sixty banned Black organizations and freed Nelson Mandela, leader of the African National Congress (ANC), after twenty-seven years of imprisonment. Mandela's triumphant remarks following his release appear in "Listen to Their Voices." The following year, De Klerk and Black leaders signed a National Peace Accord, pledging themselves to the establishment of a multiparty democracy and an end to violence. Following a series of political defeats, De Klerk called for a referendum

LISTEN TO THEIR VOICES

"Africa, It Is Ours!"

Nelson Mandela

The following excerpts are from 71-year-old Black nationalist leader Nelson Mandela's speech, delivered in front of the Cape Town City Hall following his being released from a 27-year imprisonment on February 12, 1990.

Amandla! Amandla! i-Afrika, mayibuye! [Power! Power! Africa, it is ours!]

My friends, comrades and fellow South Africans, I greet you all in the name of peace, democracy and freedom for all. I stand here before you not as a prophet but as a humble servant of you, the people.

Your tireless and heroic sacrifices have made it possible for me to be here today. I therefore place the remaining years of my life in your hands.

On this day of my release, I extend my sincere and warmest gratitude to the millions of my compatriots and those in every corner of the globe who have campaigned tirelessly for my release.

Negotiations on the dismantling of apartheid will have to address the overwhelming demand of our people for a democratic nonracial and unitary South Africa. There must be an end to white monopoly on political power.

And a fundamental restructuring of our political and economic systems to insure that the inequalities of apartheid are addressed and our society thoroughly democratized. . . .

in 1992 to allow Whites to vote on ending apartheid. If he failed to receive popular support, he vowed to resign. A record high turnout gave a solid 68.6 percent vote favoring the continued dismantling of legal apartheid and the creation of a new constitution through negotiation. The process toward power-sharing ended symbolically when De Klerk and Mandela were jointly awarded the 1993 Nobel Peace Prize (Ottaway and Taylor 1992).

THE MANDELA ERA

In April 1994, South Africa held its first universal election. Nelson Mandela's ANC received 62 percent of the vote, giving him a five-year term as president. The National Party's F. W. De Klerk is serving as one of two executive deputy presidents. The ANC is faced with making the transition from a liberation movement that for eighty years used boycotts, protests, and occasional sabotage as political statements to a governing party that needs to practice political compromise (F. Clines 1994; B. Nelan 1994).

The political and economic agenda is very full. Local and area elections are still to come in a country where local politicians are often not respected. The Black

Our struggle has reached a decisive moment. We call on our people to seize this moment so that the process toward democracy is rapid and uninterrupted. We have waited too long for our freedom. We can no longer wait. Now is the time to intensify the struggle on all fronts.

To relax our efforts now would be a mistake which generations to come will not be able to forgive. The sight of freedom looming on the horizon should encourage us to redouble our efforts. It is only through disciplined mass action that our victory can be assured.

We call on our white compatriots to join us in the shaping of a new South Africa. The freedom movement is the political home for you, too. We call on the international community to continue the campaign to isolate the apartheid regime. To lift sanctions now would be to run the risk of aborting the process toward the complete eradication of apartheid. Our march to freedom is irreversible. We must not allow fear to stand in our way.

Universal suffrage on a common voters' roll in a united democratic and nonracial South Africa is the only way to peace and racial harmony.

In conclusion, I wish to go to my own words during my trial in 1964. They are as true today as they were then. I wrote: I have fought against white domination, and I have fought against black domination. I have cherished the idea of a democratic and free society in which all persons live together in harmony and with equal opportunities.

It is an ideal which I hope to live for and to achieve. But if needs be, it is an ideal for which I am prepared to die.

Source: Mandela 1990:A10.

population itself is hardly homogeneous, speaking nine languages, holding ethnic rivalries that stretch back for centuries, and having political disputes across generations. At best, one-fifth of the nation's Blacks can compete in the nation's economy, while the balance, reflecting apartheid, form a huge underclass. Two-thirds live in homes without electricity or running water, and nearly a fifth are actually squatters or backyard slum dwellers (P. Taylor 1993, Treiman et al. 1996).

With the emergence of the new multiracial government in South Africa, we see a country with enormous promise but many challenges that are similar to those of our own multiracial society. Some of the controversial issues facing the Mandela government are very familiar to citizens in the United States:

- Affirmative action. Race-based employment goals and other preference programs have been proposed; yet critics insist that such efforts constitute reverse apartheid.
- Illegal immigration. Estimates ranging from 2 to 20 percent of the population are illegal immigrants, many of whom wish to escape the poverty and political turmoil of neighboring African states.

- Rights of Whites. Amid the enthusiasm for recognition of the rights of Blacks, Coloureds, and Asians, some South Africans have expressed a concern that the culture of Whites is being set aside. For example, debate has centered on the decline in Afrikaans-language television programming.
- Crime. While government-initiated violence has ended, the generations of conflict and years of intertribal attacks have created a climate for crime, ownership of illegal guns, and disrespect for law enforcement.
- Medical care. The nation is trying to confront the duality of private care for the affluent (usually Whites) and government-subsidized care (usually for people of color). AIDS is a major problem with, by 1998, 12 percent of the adult population having AIDS.
- School integration. Multiracial schools are replacing the apartheid system, but for some, the change is occurring too fast or not fast enough. As of 1998, 82 percent had no media equipment (television or computers) and 57 percent had no electricity.

The issues are to be addressed with minimal increases in government spending, as Mandela seeks to reverse deficit spending without an increase in taxes that would frighten away needed foreign investment. As difficult as all these challenges are, perhaps the most difficult is land reform (S. Daley 1997, 1998; L. Duke 1998; South African Institute of Race Relations 1998).

The Mandela government has pledged itself to addressing the issue of land ownership. Between 1960 and 1990, the government forced 3.5 million Black South Africans from their land and frequently allowed Whites to settle on it. Under the 1994 Restitution of Land Rights Act, these displaced citizens can now file for a return of their land. By early 1998, there had already been 23,000 claims filed. Where feasible, the government plans to restore the original inhabitants to their land; where this is not feasible, the government is to make "just and equitable compensation." The magnitude of this land reform issue cannot be minimized. Many claims will face objections by settled White families, and a special court has been created to resolve the inevitable land disputes that will occur (D. McNeil 1999; South African Institute of Race Relations 1998:325).

Despite the major achievements by the ANC, immense problems face the new government. Nelson Mandela enjoyed the advantage of wide personal support throughout the nation. He retired in 1999 when his second term ended and was succeeded by fellow ANC leader Thabo Mbeki who has much work to do in the 21st century because of the legacy of apartheid.

CONCLUSION

By looking beyond our borders, we gather new insights into the social processes that frame and define intergroup relationships. The colonial experience has played a role in all cases under consideration in this chapter, but particularly in South Africa. In Mexico and South Africa, which have long histories of multiethnic societies, intergroup sexual relations have been widespread but with different results. Mestizos in Mexico occupy a middle racial group and experience reduced tension, whereas in South Africa, the Cape Coloureds had freedoms under apartheid almost as limited as those of the Bantus. South Africa enforced de jure segregation, while Israeli communities seem to have de facto segregation. Israel's and South Africa's intergroup conflicts have involved the world community. Indigenous people figure prominently in Canada and Mexico. Complete assimilation is absent in all five societies and is unlikely to occur in the near future; the legal and informal barriers to assimilation and pluralism vary for those subordinate people choosing either option. Looking at the status of women in Mexico reminds us of the worldwide nature of gender stratification but also offers insight into the patterns present in developing nations.

If we add the United States to these societies, the similarities become even more striking. The problems of racial and ethnic adjustment in the United States have dominated our attention, but they parallel past and present experiences in other societies with racial, ethnic, or religious heterogeneity. The U.S. government has been involved in providing educational, financial, and legal support for programs intended to help particular racial or ethnic groups, and it continues to avoid interfering with religious freedom. Bilingual, bicultural programs in schools, autonomy for Native Americans on reservations, and increased participation in decision making by residents of ghettoes and barrios are all viewed as acceptable goals, although they are not pursued to the extent that many subordinate-group people would like.

The analysis of this chapter has reminded us of the global nature of dominant-subordinate relations along dimensions of race, ethnicity, religion, and gender. In the next chapter we will take an overview of racial and ethnic relations but also explore social inequality along the dimensions of age, disability status, and sexual orientation.

KEY TERMS

apartheid 464
color gradient 445
Diaspora 458
ethnonational conflict 442
home rule 456
Intifada 461
pass laws 464
world systems theory 442
Zionism 458

REVIEW QUESTIONS

1. Identify who are the native peoples and what has been their role in each of the societies discussed in this chapter.
2. On what levels can one speak of an identity issue facing Canada as a nation?
3. What role has secession played in Canada, Northern Ireland, and Israel?

4. How have civil uprisings affected intergroup tensions in Northern Ireland and Israel?
5. To what extent are the problems facing Nelson Mandela a part of apartheid's legacy?

CRITICAL THINKING

1. Social construction of race emphasizes how we create arbitrary definitions of skin color that then have social consequences. Drawing upon the societies discussed, select one nation and identify how social definitions are at work in other ways at defining group boundaries.
2. Apply the functionalist and conflict approaches of sociology first introduced in Chapter 1 to each of the societies under study in this chapter.
3. The conflicts summarized are examples of ethnonational conflicts, but how have the actions or inactions of the United States contributed to these problems?

INTERNET EXERCISES

1. To find out the latest on the political and religious conflicts in Northern Ireland that are covered in this chapter, visit (http://headlines.yahoo.com/Full_Coverage/World/Northern_Ireland_Conflict/). What is the current status of the conflict? Have any recent steps been made to secure and maintain peace? What challenges to peace still need to be overcome? Utilize the links provided to learn more about the IRA, Sinn Fein, and the Northern Ireland Accord. Why are marches, parades, and protests important in this conflict? What role do they play? Do you believe peace will come/stay in the region? Why or why not?
2. The Mandela Page (http://www.anc.org.za/people/mandela/) offers pictures, speeches, statements, and biographical information relating to Noble Peace Prize winner Nelson Mandela. Read his biography on this site to answer the following questions: Where and when was Mandela born? What is the ANC? What was the 1949 Programme of Action? What were some of the issues Mandela was concerned about? Why was Mandela nicknamed "The Black Pimpernel"? What was Mandela arrested and jailed for in the early 1960s? What role does Mandela now play in South African politics?

FOR FURTHER INFORMATION

Alfred McClung Lee. *Terrorism in Northern Ireland.* Bayside, NY: General Hall, 1983.
A sociohistorical analysis of the problems besetting the people of Northern Ireland.

Alan Paton. *Cry, the Beloved Country.* New York: Scribner, 1948.
Paton's widely acclaimed novel about an old Zulu parson who discovers that his sister is a prostitute and his son the murderer of a White industrialist.

Lynda Shorten. *Without Reserve: Stories from Urban Natives.* Edmonton, Alberta: NeWest Press, 1991.
A collection of autobiographical profiles of individual native people who live in a Western Canadian city.

Ronald Weitzer. *Transforming Settler States: Communal Conflict and Internal Security in Northern Ireland and Zimbabwe.* Berkeley: University of California Press, 1990.
A study of two settler groups, Protestants in Northern Ireland and Europeans in Zimbabwe, and the social change and political violence that followed.

PERIODICALS

Journals that cover race and ethnic relations from a cross-national perspective include *Ethnic and Racial Studies* (established in 1978), *Race and Class* (1959), and *Race Today* (1968). Other journals relevant to this chapter include *Israel Social Science Research* (1983), *Israeli Studies* (1981), *Journal of South African Studies* (1974), and *Palestine Refugees Today* (1960).

16

Overcoming Exclusion

CHAPTER OUTLINE

HIGHLIGHTS

The experience of social disadvantage is not limited to groups defined by race, ethnicity, gender, or religion. Despite an improving medical and financial situation, the elderly are still as a group at a disadvantage, given the ageism in our society. People with disabilities also have sought to achieve both respect and opportunities. While the Americans with Disabilities Act (ADA) is a significant step forward, serious advocacy efforts continue. Long-term homophobia has made it a challenge for gays and lesbians to go about their lives. Progress has been mixed; some civil rights legislation has been passed at the local level, but the federal government took positions against avowed homosexuals in the military and sought to prevent legal recognition of gay and lesbian marriage. For each of these groups, as well as the racial and ethnic minorities discussed earlier, it is easy to applaud the progress already made. However, given the level of inequality that still persists, the full agenda for further positive progress remains.

What metaphor do we use to describe a nation whose racial, ethnic, and religious minorities are on the way to becoming numerical majorities in cities and soon in states? For several generations the image of the *melting pot* has been used as a convenient description of our culturally diverse nation. The analogy of an alchemist's cauldron was clever, even if a bit ethnocentric. It originated in the Middle Ages, when the alchemist used a "melting pot" to attempt to change less costly metals into gold and silver.

The Melting Pot was the title of a 1908 play by Israel Zangwill. In this play, a young Russian immigrant to the United States composes a symphony that portrays a nation that serves as a crucible (or pot) where all ethnic and racial groups melt together into a new, superior stock.

The vision in the United States as a melting pot became popular in the first part of the twentieth century, particularly because it suggested that the United States had an almost divinely inspired mission to destroy artificial divisions and create a single humankind. However, the image did not mesh with reality, as the dominant group indicated its unwillingness to welcome Native Americans, African Americans, Hispanics or Latinos, Jews, and Asians, among many others, into the melting pot.

The image of the melting pot is not invoked so much today. Instead, people speak of a *salad bowl* to describe a country that is ethnically diverse. As we can distinguish the lettuce from the tomatoes from the peppers in a tossed salad, we can see ethnic restaurants and the persistence of "foreign" languages in conversations on street corners. The dressing over the ingredients is akin to the shared value system and culture, covering, but not hiding, the different ingredients of the salad.

Yet even the notion of a salad is wilting. Like the melting pot that came before, the image of a salad is static—certainly not indicative of the dynamic changes we see in the United States. It also fails to conjure up the myriad cultural pieces that make up the fabric or mosaic of our diverse nation.

The *kaleidoscope* offers another familiar and more useful analogy. Patented in 1817 by Scottish scientist Sir David Brewster, the kaleidoscope was a toy and then became a table ornament in the parlors of the rich. Users of this optical device turn a set of mirrors and observe the seemingly endless colors and patterns that are reflected off pieces of glass, tinsel, or beads. The growing popularity of the phrase "people of color" fits well with the idea of the United States as a kaleidoscope. The changing images correspond to the often bewildering array of groups found in our country (R. Schaefer 1992).

The images created by a kaleidoscope are hard to describe since they change dramatically with little effort. Similarly, in the kaleidoscope of the United States, we find it a challenge to describe the dynamic multiracial nature of this republic. Yet even as we begin to understand the past, present, and future of all the many racial and ethnic groups, we recognize that there are still other people who are stigmatized in society by virtue of group membership. In this chapter, we will continue our effort to understand those people excluded in varying degrees from society by considering the cases of the aged, people with disabilities, and the gay and lesbian community.

The Aged: A Social Minority

Older people in the United States form a paradox. They are a significant segment of the population who, as we shall see, are often viewed with negative stereotypes and are subject to discrimination. Yet they also have successfully organized into a potent collective force that wields significant political clout on certain social issues.

Unlike other social groups subjected to differential treatment, we all expect to become members of this social category someday. So in this one case, the notion of the elderly as "them" will eventually give way to "us."

The elderly share the priorities of subordinate or minority groups that we introduced in Chapter 1. Specifically,

1. The elderly experience unequal treatment in employment and may face prejudice and discrimination.
2. The elderly share physical characteristics that distinguish them from younger people. In addition, their cultural preferences and leisure-time activities are often at variance with those of the rest of society.
3. Membership in this disadvantaged group is involuntary.
4. Older people have a strong sense of group solidarity, as reflected in senior citizens' centers, retirement homes, and advocacy organizations.
5. When married, older people generally are married to others of comparable age, that is, within the group.

There is one crucial difference between older people and other subordinate groups, such as racial and ethnic minorities or women: all of us who live long will eventually assume the ascribed status of being an older person (M. Barron 1953; Levin and Levin 1980; Wagley and Harris 1958).

WHO ARE THE ELDERLY?

As is evident in Figure 16.1, an increasing proportion of the population is composed of older people. During the twentieth century, the number of people in the United States under the age sixty-five has tripled. At the same time, the number aged sixty-five or over has jumped by a factor of eleven. Consequently, men and women aged sixty-five and over, who constituted only 4 percent of the population in 1900, by 1997 made up 12.7 percent of the population.

These trends are expected to continue well into the next century as mortality declines and the postwar baby boomers age. It is currently projected that by the year 2025 more than 17 percent of the people in the United States will be sixty-five and older. Moreover, while the elderly population continues to increase, the "oldest old" segment of the population (that is, people eighty-five years old and over) is growing at an even faster rate. By 2050, the proportion of the population eighty-five and over will reach 4.8 percent, compared with only 0.2 percent in 1930 (N. Angier 1995; Bureau of the Census 1995b, 1996, 1998c:21; G. Kolata 1996).

Compared to the rest of the population, the elderly are more likely to be 1) female, 2) White, and 3) living in certain states. Men generally have higher death rates than women at every age. As a result, elderly women outnumber men by a ratio of 3 to 2. The difference grows with advancing age so that among the oldest old group, women outnumber men by a factor of 5 to 2. About 90 percent of the elderly are White. While the aged population is growing more racially and ethnically diverse, the higher death rates of members of racial and ethnic minorities, coupled with immigration to the United States of nonelderly Hispanics and Asians, are likely to keep

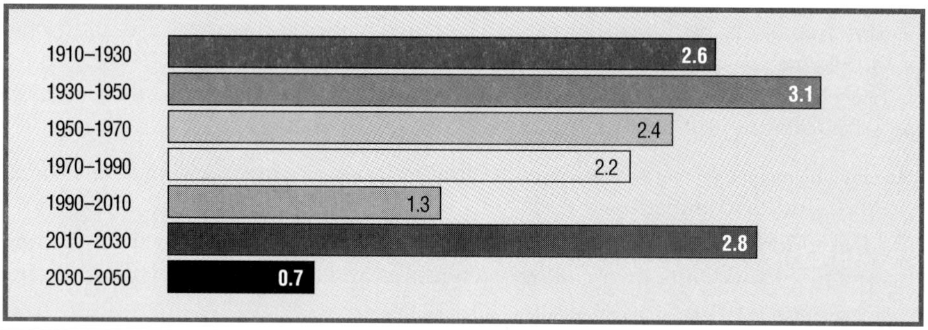

Figure 16.1 Growth Rate in Elderly Population, 1910–2050
The annual growth of the elderly population is projected to increase dramatically beginning about 2010, continue for about twenty years, and then level off for another twenty years.
Source: Bureau of the Census 1995b:2.

the older population more White than the nation as a whole. The aged tend to be found in larger numbers in certain states. While California may have the largest absolute number of elderly, the highest proportions are found in Florida and Pennsylvania, followed by several farm states such as Nebraska, Iowa, Missouri, and the Dakotas (Bureau of the Census 1995b).

AGEISM

Respected gerontologist Bernice Neugarten (1996) observed that negative stereotypes of old age are strongly entrenched in a society that prides itself on being oriented toward both youth and the future. In 1968, physician Robert Butler, the founding director of the National Institute on Aging, coined the term **ageism** to refer to prejudice and discrimination against the elderly. Ageism reflects a deep uneasiness among young and middle-aged people about growing old. For many, old age symbolizes disease and death; seeing the elderly serves as a reminder that they too may someday become old and infirm. By contrast, society glorifies youth seeing it as interchangeable with beauty and the future. Ageism is so common that Butler (1990:178) notes that it "knows no one century, nor culture, and is not likely to go away any time soon."

If there is any doubt how pervasive ageism is, we need only consider an experiment conducted by sociologist William Levin (1988). He asked such questions as, "Does this person appear to you to be competent or incompetent? Generous or selfish?" of college students in California, Massachusetts, and Tennessee after showing them photographs of men who appeared to be about twenty-five, fifty-two, and seventy-three years old. Levin's findings confirmed that a widespread age bias is evident across the United States.

The students questioned in Levin's experiment were not told that the three photographs were of the same man at different stages of his life. Special care was taken to select old photographs that had a contemporary look. Levin asked the college students to evaluate the "three men" for a job using nineteen measures. The twenty-five-year-old man was found to be active, powerful, healthy, fast, attractive, energetic, involved, and in possession of a good memory. Students thought that the fifty-two-year-old man had a high IQ and was reliable. By contrast, the seventy-three-year-old man was evaluated as inactive, weak, sickly, slow, ugly, unreliable, lazy, socially isolated, and possessing a low IQ and a poor memory. Clearly the negative stereotypes of older people evident in this study could contribute to discrimination in the paid labor force and other areas of our society.

How do these images develop? Partly, we tend to see the elderly only in situations that reinforce the image. For example, physicians see more sick old people, so "all old people are sick." Social workers see only the indigent; therefore, "all aged are poor." We see the aged sitting on park benches but do not notice them rushing to and from jobs or volunteer work, so "all old people are inactive with no interests to keep them involved with society." The needy aged have come to represent all the elderly in the public mind (Birren and Gribbin 1973; B. Neugarten 1996).

Yet in contradiction to these negative stereotypes present in an ageist society, researchers have found that older workers can be an asset for employers. According to a 1991 study, older workers can be retrained in new technologies, have lower rates of absenteeism than younger employees, and are often more effective salespeople. The study focused on two corporations based in the United States (the hotel chain Days Inns of America and the holding company Travelers Corporation of Hartford) and a British retail chain—all of which have long-term experience in hiring workers age fifty and over. Clearly the findings pointed to older workers as good investments (E. Fein 1996; K. Telsch 1991:A16).

However, this positive experience is not reflected in television programming. As with other subordinate groups, the elderly are not portrayed in a manner to counter stereotypes; in fact, they are hardly visible at all. An analysis of 1,446 fictional television characters revealed that only 2 percent were age sixty-five and over even though this age group accounts for more than 12 percent of the nation's population. In a second study, older women were found to be particularly underrepresented on television (Robinson and Skill 1993; J. Vernon et al. 1990).

The term "ageism" encompasses not only negative attitudes but also discrimination. In the last decade age discrimination has been increasingly evident in the disproportionate firing of older employees (often in their fifties and sometimes in their forties) during layoffs. In the five years from 1987 to 1992, the number of people aged fifty-five and older actively looking for work increased by 51 percent, while the proportion actually working declined (Besi and Kale 1996; E. Fein 1996).

The federal Age Discrimination in Employment Act, which went into effect in 1968, was passed to protect workers forty years of age or older from being fired because of their age and replaced with younger workers who presumably would receive lower salaries. According to the Equal Employment Opportunity Commission (EEOC), more than 17,000 complaints of age discrimination were filed in 1995. In early 1996, the Supreme Court strengthened federal protection against age discrimination, ruling unanimously that such lawsuits can be successful even if an older worker is replaced

Being older does not mean that employment is not available, although sometimes jobs that are open are unrelated to one's career work. LaFem Kuntz, 74, a retired medical lab employee, works at a fast food restaurant in suburban Chicago.

by someone older than forty. Consequently, if a firm unfairly fires a sixty-five-year-old employee to make way for a forty-five-year-old, this still can constitute age discrimination (L. Greenhouse 1996a).

The American Association of Retired Persons (AARP) conducted an experiment in 1993 that confirmed that older people often face discrimination when applying for jobs. Comparable resumes for two applicants—one fifty-seven years old and the other thirty-two years old—were sent to 775 large firms and employment agencies around the United States. In situations for which positions were actually available, the younger applicant received a favorable response 43 percent of the time. In contrast, the older applicant received favorable responses less than half as often (only 17 percent of the time). One Fortune 500 corporation asked the younger applicant for more information, while it informed the older applicant that no appropriate positions were open (Bendick et al. 1993).

While firing someone simply because they are old violates federal laws, courts have upheld the right to lay off older workers for economic reasons. Critics contend that later the same firms hire younger, cheaper workers to replace the experienced, older workers. Norman Matloff (1998), a computer science professor at the University of California, finds rampant age discrimination in the computer software industry, supposedly an understaffed field. Employers shunt aside midcareer programmers because they command higher salaries than recent college graduates. Companies defend their actions on grounds that the older workers lack skills in the latest software programs.

A degree of conflict is emerging along generational lines that resembles other types of intergroup tension. While the conflict involves neither violence nor the degree of subjugation found with other dominant-subordinate relations in the United

States, a feeling still prevails that what the elderly "get" is at the expense of younger generations. This is not unlike the "angry white men" view described in Chapter 14, in which it is assumed that benefits gained by racial minorities and women are at the cost of White males. Younger people are increasingly unhappy about paying Social Security taxes and underwriting the Medicare program, especially since they speculate that they themselves will never receive benefits from these fiscally insecure programs. Reflecting such concerns, Americans for Generational Equity (AGE) was established in 1984 to represent the interests of "younger and future generations of Americans."

Backed by contributions from banks, insurance companies, and corporations offering health-care services—all of which are private-sector competitors of Social Security and Medicare—AGE argues that the poor and the young suffer because society misappropriates too much funding for older people. AGE activists emphasize that while health-care costs for the elderly continue to rise, schools lack inadequate funding, and younger generations are being saddled with an increasing national debt. However, critics of this organization counter that AGE incorrectly and unfairly targets social services for the aged as the cause of their problems. Moreover, critics point out that in the early 1990s AGE openly lobbied to reduce Social Security benefits, yet was silent when social programs to benefit younger people were being debated (Hewitt and Howe 1988; J. Quadagno 1989, 1991).

THE ECONOMIC PICTURE

The elderly, like the other groups we have considered, do not form a single economic profile. The perception of the "elderly" and "poor" as practically synonymous has changed in recent years to a view that the noninstitutionalized elderly are economically better off than the population as a whole. Both views are too simplistic; income varies widely among the aged. For example, in 1996,

- The poverty rate—13.7 percent for all people—rose with age among the elderly, from 9 percent for those 65–74 to 13 percent for those seventy-five or older.
- Among those persons below the poverty level, the median length of poverty is 7.2 months for those over the age 64 compared to 4.7 months for other adults.
- The rate was higher for elderly African Americans (25 percent) and Hispanics (24 percent) than for Whites (9 percent). As Figure 16.2 shows, poverty became less prevalent during the 1980s for every racial and ethnic group.

The decline in poverty rates are welcome. However, advocates of the position that the elderly are receiving too much at the expense of the younger generations point to the rising affluence of the aged as evidence of an unfair economic burden placed on the young and future generations of workers (Bureau of the Census 1998c).

While part of this overall improved standard of living for older people stems from a greater accumulation of wealth—in the form of home ownership, private pensions, and other financial assets—much of the improvement is due to more generous Social Security benefits. While modest compared to some other countries' pension programs, Social Security in the United States nevertheless provides 38 percent of all income. Currently, about one-eighth of the nation's elderly

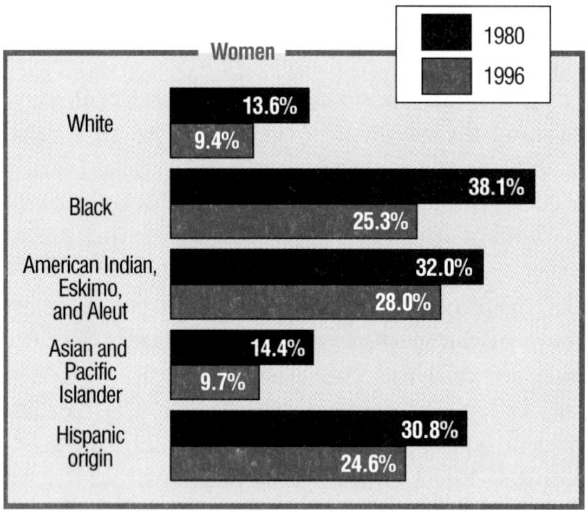

Figure 16.2 Poverty Rate among the Elderly
Note: American Indian data are for 1979 and 1989.

Source: Bureau of the Census 1995b:7, 1998c:478.

population is below the poverty line; without Social Security, that figure would rise to half.

As we can see in the previously mentioned data, the aged who are most likely to experience poverty are the same people more likely to be poor earlier in their lives: female-headed households and racial and ethnic minorities. While overall the aged are doing well economically, poverty remains a particularly difficult problem for the thousands of elderly who are impoverished annually through paying for long-term medical care (Quadagno 1999).

ADVOCACY EFFORTS BY THE ELDERLY

As we have seen with racial, ethnic, and gender groups, efforts to bring about desired change often require the formation of political organizations and advocacy groups. This is true with the elderly and, as we will see later, is also true for people with disabilities and gay men and lesbian women. One such group working on behalf of the elderly is the Gray Panthers. As of 1995, this organization had 40,000 members in thirty-two states and five foreign countries working to combat prejudice and discrimination against older people. In early 1995, Maggie Kuhn, the best known of the Gray Panthers' founders, died at the age of eighty-nine. Kuhn had spent the last twenty-five years of her life as a leader in the battle against ageism and other forms of injustice. Her desire to create an advocacy group for the elderly began when she was forced to retire at age sixty-five from her position on a church staff. Only two weeks before her death, she joined striking transit workers on a picket line (B. Folkart 1995; R. Thomas 1995).

The growing collective consciousness among older people also contributed to the establishment of the Older Women's League (OWL) in 1980. OWL focuses on access to health insurance, Social Security benefits, and pension reform. OWL leaders and the group's 20,000 members hope that the organization will serve as a critical link between the feminist movement described in Chapter 14 and activists for "gray power" (Hillebrand 1992).

The largest organization representing the nation's elderly is the American Association of Retired Persons (AARP), founded in 1958 by a retired school principal who was having difficulty obtaining insurance because of age prejudice. Many of AARP's services involve discounts and insurance for its 31.5 million members, but the organization also functions as a powerful lobbying group, working for legislation that will benefit the aged. For example, AARP has backed passage of a uniform mandatory-reporting law for cases of abuse of the elderly with enough federal funds to guarantee enforcement and support services.

The potential power of AARP is enormous; it represents one out of every four registered voters in the United States. AARP has endorsed voter registration campaigns, nursing home reforms, and pension reforms. Acknowledging its difficulties in recruiting members of racial and ethnic minority groups, AARP began a Minority Affairs Initiative. The spokeswoman for this initiative, Margaret Dixon, became the AARP's first African American president in 1996 (M. Fountain 1996; Mehren and Rosenblatt 1995).

People grow old in many different ways. Not all the elderly face the same challenges or enjoy the same resources. While the AARP lobbies to protect the elderly in general, other groups work in more specific ways. For example, the National Committee to Preserve Social Security and Medicare, founded in 1982, unsuccessfully lobbied Congress to keep Medicare benefits for the ailing poor elderly. Other large special interest groups represent retired federal employees, retired teachers, and retired union workers (J. Quadagno 1999).

The elderly in the Untied States are better off today financially and physically than ever before. Many of them have strong financial assets and medical care packages that will take care of most any need. But, as we have seen, a significant segment is impoverished, faced with the prospect of declining health and mounting medical bills. Older people of color may have to add being aged to a lifetime of discrimination. As in all other stages of the life course, the aged constitute a diverse group in the United States and around the world.

While organizations such as the Gray Panthers, OWL, and AARP are undoubtedly valuable, the diversity of the nation's older population requires many different responses to the problems of the elderly. For example, older African Americans and Hispanics tend to rely more on family members, friends, and informal social networks than on organizational support systems. Owing to their comparatively lower incomes and greater incapacity resulting from poor health, older Blacks and Hispanics are more likely to need substantial assistance from family members than are older Whites. In recent years, older people of color have emerged as a distinct political force—independent of the larger elderly population—in some urban centers and in the southwest. Advocacy groups for the aged are still in their early stages, and low-income elderly are often the least represented (W. Achenbaumm 1993; B. Neugarten 1996; also see Schaefer 2000).

People with Disabilities

Throughout history, people have been socially disadvantaged not because of the limits of their own skills and abilities, but because assumptions are made about them based on some group characteristics. People with disabilities are such a group. The very term "disabilities" suggests lack of ability in some area, but as we shall see, society often assumes that a person with a disability is far less capable than she or he is. Furthermore, society limits the life chances of people with disabilities in ways that are unnecessary and unrelated to any physical infirmity.

DISABILITY IN CONTEMPORARY SOCIETY

Societies have always had members with disabilities. Historically, they have dealt differently with people who had physical or mental limitations, but rarely have they been treated as equals. Today, an estimated 48 million people have disabilities, or about one in six in the population. **Disability** is considered a reduced ability to perform tasks one would normally do at a given stage in life. This includes everyone from the 16 million people who have difficulty carrying ten pounds to the 8 million people who require assistance leaving their homes. As shown in Table 16.1, about 12 percent of the population is estimated to have a severe disability (G. Albrecht 1997).

A significant stigma is attached to having a visible disability. Not wishing to present an image of a "disabled" president, Franklin Roosevelt enlisted the cooperation of the press corps to avoid being shown in a wheelchair or using crutches. This picture taken by a friend is only one of two such images known, according to Franklin Delano Roosevelt Library.

The proportion of people with disabilities continues to increase. Because of advances in medicine, many people who once would have died from an accident or illness now survive. Second, as more people live longer, they are more likely to experience diseases that have disabling consequences (G. Albrecht 1992).

Disabilities are found in all segments of the population, but racial and ethnic minorities are disproportionately more likely to experience them and also to have less access to assistance. Fewer African Americans and Hispanic people with disabilities are graduating from college compared to White people with disabilities. They also have incomes consistently lower than their White counterparts (J. McNeil 1997; Walker et al. 1996; R. Weitz 1995).

While disability knows no social class, about two-thirds of working-age persons with a disability in the United States are unemployed.

Table 16.1 Persons with Disabilities

Characteristic	Percent of Population 15 Years Old or Older
With any disability	24.0
Severe	12.5
Not severe	11.5
Has difficulty or is unable to:	
See words and letters	4.1
Hear normal conversation	4.8
Have speech understood	1.0
Lift or carry 10 pounds	7.9
Climb stairs without resting	8.9
Walk three city blocks	9.1
Has difficulty or needs personal assistance with:	
Getting around inside the home	1.7
Getting in/out of bed or a chair	2.7
Bathing	2.2
Dressing	1.6
Eating	0.5
Getting to or using the toilet	1.0
Needs personal assistance with:	
Going outside the home	4.0
Keeping track of money and bills	1.9
Preparing meals	2.1
Doing light housework	3.4
Using the telephone	1.3

Source: Census analysis released in 1998 based on 1994–1995 Survey of Income and Program Participation. See Bureau of the Census 1998f.

African Americans and Hispanics with disabilities are even more likely to be jobless. Most of them believe that they would be able to work if they were offered the opportunity or if some reasonable accommodation could be made to address the disability. These accommodations can be modest. Between 1978 and 1992, Sears Roebuck found that on average, it cost only $126 to accommodate a worker's disability with some measures involving little or no cost, such as flexible work schedules, back-support belts, and rest periods (P. Kirkpatrick 1994; B. Noble 1995; J. Shapiro 1993).

LABELING THE DISABLED

Labeling theorists, drawing on the work of sociologist Erving Goffman (1963), have suggested that society attaches a stigma to many forms of disability and that this stigma leads to prejudicial treatment. Indeed, people with disabilities frequently observe that people without disabilities see them only as blind, deaf, wheelchair users, and so forth, rather than as complex human beings with individual strengths and weaknesses whose blindness or deafness is merely one aspect of their lives.

In this regard, a review of studies of women with disabilities disclosed that most academic research on the disabled does not even differentiate by gender—thereby perpetuating the view that when a disability is present, no other personal characteristic can matter. When gender differences are recognized, it may only serve to deny a person's dignity. One study found that women with disabilities were more likely to be discouraged from having children and much more likely to be advised to have hysterectomies than women without disabilities but with similar medical conditions (Fine and Asch 1981, 1988a, 1988b; W. Gove 1980; B. Karkabi 1993).

As with other subordinate statuses, the mass media have contributed to the stereotyping of people with disabilities. Too often, they are treated with a mixture of pity and fear. Nationwide charity telethons promote a negative image of the disabled as being childlike and nonproductive, suggesting that until they are "cured" they cannot contribute to society like other people. At the very least, the poster child image proclaims that it is not okay to be disabled. By contrast, in literature and film, "evil" characters with disabilities—from Captain Hook to Dr. Strangelove to Freddy Krueger—reinforce the view that disability is a punishment for evil. Efforts to encourage sober driving or safety in the workplace use images of people with disabilities to frighten people into the appropriate behavior.

Even the more favorable treatments of disabled characters tend to focus on courageous and inspirational characters who achieve striking personal successes against great odds, such as Tiny Tim in *A Christmas Carol* or the idiot savant in the film *Rain Man,* rather than on the impact of prejudice and discrimination on "ordinary" disabled people. The press coverage received by people with disabilities who excel also serves to minimize the day-to-day reality of most persons with a disability (L. Bennetts 1993; Gartner and Joe 1987; M. Norden 1994).

Negative attitudes are not the only challenge facing people with disabilities. According to a 1998 national survey, only 29 percent of disabled people have a job compared to 79 percent of the nondisabled (National Organization on Disability 1998). Through institutional discrimination, society is sometimes organized in a way that serves to limit people with disabilities. Architectural barriers and transportation difficulties often add to the problems of disabled people when they seek and obtain employment. Simply getting around city streets can be quite difficult for people with mobility challenges. Many streets are not properly equipped with curb cuts for wheelchair users. A genuinely barrier-free building needs more than a ramp; it should also include automatic doors, raised letters and Braille on signs, and toilets that are accessible to the disabled. Even if a disabled person finds a job, and even if the job is in a barrier-free building, he or she still faces the problem of getting to work in a society where many rail stations and most buses remain inaccessible to wheelchair users and others with disabilities.

People with disabilities face challenges to being taken seriously as job applicants, and research shows that the problems intensify further for members of racial and ethnic minorities with disabilities. The Glass Ceiling Commission took a special look at employment opportunities for people with disabilities who are also members of racial and ethnic minorities. The analysis revealed that White individuals with disabilities are twice as likely to be employed on a full-time basis as African American or Hispanic people with disabilities. The primary reason for this is that minorities with disabilities experience dual sources of discrimination: subordinate group status as a member of a minority race and disability. The negative stereotype of being disabled is added on top of the stereotypes associated with racial and ethnic minorities (Braddock and Bachelder 1994; Stone et al. 1996).

ADVOCACY FOR DISABILITY RIGHTS

Until recently, the people with disabilities as a group have scarcely been thought of in any terms except perhaps pity. Often history has forgotten how deep the mistreatment has been. The United States Holocaust Museum is conducting research to better uncover the generally unknown aspect of the Holocaust of Nazi Germany. Before Europe's Jews were targeted for systematic extermination, German people with disabilities or mental illnesses—an estimated 70,000—were taken to be gassed at six "euthanasia" centers. Preliminary investigations suggest that 250,000 mentally and physically handicapped people were murdered from 1939 to 1945 (U.S. Holocaust Museum 1994).

Since World War II, there has been a steadily growing effort not only to ensure the survival of people with disabilities but also the same rights as enjoyed by others. In the early 1960s, Ed Roberts and some other young adults with disabilities wanted to attend the University of California at Berkeley. Reluctant at first, the university was eventually persuaded to admit them and agreed to reserve space in the

©J. D. Crowe

university infirmary as living quarters for disabled persons. These students and others eventually established their own student center and became known as the Rolling Quads. They eventually turned their attention to the surrounding community and established the Berkeley Center for Independent Living, which became a model for hundreds of independent living centers (R. Brannon 1995).

By the early 1970s, following the example of the Rolling Quads, a strong social movement for disability rights had emerged across the United States, which drew on the experiences of the Black civil rights movement and the feminist movement. This movement now includes a variety of organizations; some work on behalf of people with a single disability (such as the National Federation of the Blind) and others represent people with any of many disabilities (such as New York City's Disabled in Action). The large number of disabled Vietnam veterans who joined the effort gave a boost to advocacy efforts and a growing legitimacy in larger society.

Like other advocacy and resistance efforts, women and men involved in the disability rights movement are working to challenge negative views of disabled people; to gain a greater voice for the disabled in all agency and public-policy decisions that affect them; and to reshape laws, institutions, and environments so that people with disabilities can be fully integrated into mainstream society. Disability rights activists argue that there is an important distinction between organizations *for* disabled people and organizations *of* disabled people. The former include service providers, charitable associations, and parents' groups. Some activists maintain that because these organizations are not controlled by people with disabilities, they do not give priority to the goals of independence and self-help emphasized by the disability rights movement (R. Scotch 1984, 1989).

In 1990 many of these organizations worked for the passage of the Americans with Disabilities Act (ADA). This law in many respects represents the most sweeping antidiscrimination legislation since the 1964 Civil Rights Act. The ADA went into effect in 1992 covering people with a disability, defined as a condition that "substantially limits" a "major life activity" such as walking or seeing. It prohibits bias in employment, transportation, public accommodations, and telecommunications against people with disabilities. Businesses with more than twenty-five employees are forbidden to refuse to hire a qualified disabled applicant; these companies are expected to make a "reasonable accommodation" to permit such a worker to do the job. Commercial establishments such as office buildings, hotels, theaters, supermarkets, and dry cleaners are barred from denying service to people with disabilities (P. Kilborn 1992).

The ADA represents a significant framing of the issues of people with disabilities. Basically, we can see it taking a civil rights view of disabilities that seeks to humanize the way society sees and treats people with disabilities. The ADA does not take the perspective adopted in other nations, such as Great Britain, of seeing disability as totally an entitlement issue; that is, because you have a disability you automatically receive certain benefits. Rather, its perspective is that the disabled are being denied certain rights. As disability rights activist Mark Johnson said, "Black people fought for the right to ride in the front of the bus. We're fighting for the right to get on the bus" (J. Shapiro 1993:128; also see G. Albrecht 1995, 1997; C. Gooding 1994).

The ADA has generated public discussion on how to address the artificial limitations confronting people with disabilities. These limitations are not necessarily physical; they may also include the way we interact with and portray people with disabilities. For example, attendant services, where trained professionals assist people as needed, would provide limited services to particular needs to allow people to live independently and function in the workplace. The notion of independent living is based on the belief that persons with a disability should have the chance to live like other people and work independently. However, in the 1990s, as medical costs receive new scrutiny and businesses seek to limit their costs, such services are threatened even though the long-term financial benefits and savings could be substantial (G. Shapiro 1993).

The ADA has attracted much discussion as well as claims of discrimination—more than 18,000 annually filed with the Equal Employment Opportunity Commission (S. Armour 1998). In "Listen to Their Voices" (on pp. 488–489), writer Kathi Wolfe discusses her strong support for the ADA but also her concern that a backlash has begun to develop against people with disabilities.

Still, activists remain encouraged since the passage of the ADA. Although the act has been in effect for only a few years, studies reveal that people with disabilities feel empowered and perceive increased access to employment opportunities. However, one must remember that civil rights activists felt a measure of optimism after passage of the major civil rights legislation over thirty years ago (P. Bradley 1990; D. Pfeiffer 1996; R. Scotch 1988; also see Schaefer 2000).

Gays and Lesbians: Coming out for Equality

Homosexuality has been forbidden in most periods of western history, but it has always been a social issue. For example, at certain times in many societies, it was possible to acknowledge same-sex love and act upon it without necessarily encountering open hostility. Yet in general, societies have barely tolerated people who have sexual intimacy in any manner other than heterosexual.

BEING GAY AND LESBIAN IN AMERICA

There are anecdotal accounts of public recognition of homosexuality throughout United States history, but it was not until the 1920s and 1930s that it became visible. By that time, clubs for gays and lesbians were growing in number, typically in urban areas. Dramas, books, and organizations were written or created to meet the social needs of gays and lesbians. As homosexuality has become more visible, efforts to suppress it have been institutionalized. At about the same time, the United States Army hired psychiatrists to screen recruits for evidence of homosexuality and dismissed volunteers who were gay (P. Schwartz 1992).

The studies published by Alfred Kinsey (1948, 1953) and his research group shocked the general public when they documented that almost half of all men had had same-sex fantasies and that about one-third had experienced a homosexual encounter after childhood. While women reported less homosexual activity, the

LISTEN TO THEIR VOICES

Is the Disability Law Creating a Handicap?

Kathi Wolfe

In 1974, a Boston librarian wouldn't let me check out a record. "We don't want visually handicapped people here," she told me. "You cause too much trouble."

Years later, I tried, white cane in hand, to hail a cab near the Dirksen Senate Office Building on Capitol Hill. "I don't pick up no handicapped!" a cabby barked at me.

All my life, I've often felt like an uninvited dinner party guest in a society that largely prefers to keep disabled people away from the table. So on July 26, 1990, when the Americans With Disabilities Act (ADA) became law, I felt like I had died and gone to heaven. At last, I thought, I have civil rights! Libraries and restaurants can't refuse to serve me because I'm disabled. I'm protected from disability-based workplace discrimination. There's room for me at the table.

On the eighth anniversary, I'm taking stock. I now have decidedly mixed feelings about the ADA. In 1990, I believed the law would help disabled people become integrated into American life. Today, I'm concerned that abuse of the law is hurting people like me. A huge number of frivolous complaints brought under the ADA in recent years has contributed to the widespread impression that hiring disabled people is an invitation to trouble.

Don't get me wrong. I'm pleased that the ADA was passed. Not being a litigious person, I'm not likely to file a complaint under the law. But I do have this as an option if I'm kicked out of a library or cab again. The ADA has helped remake our public spaces as supermarkets, restaurants and sports arenas are made accessible to wheelchair users. There are more Braille signs; more and more restaurants offer large-type menus, which I greatly appreciate.

And the blind and wheelchair users are a small fraction of the beneficiaries. The language of the ADA is intentionally broad to ensure that all variety of disabilities are covered. As a result, the ADA has also

very fact that lesbian behavior was even raised in national discussion was unprecedented. The Kinsey reports also launched a public debate about the number of homosexuals in the United States. Given that the status of being either gay or lesbian is severely stigmatized, accurate data are hard to obtain. However, a 1992 national survey of human sexual behavior found that some 2.8 percent of men and 1.5 percent of women stated that they were homosexual or bisexual. In the nation's twelve largest cities, more than 9 percent of men identified themselves as gay, compared to 3 to 4 percent in the suburbs of those cities and only 1 percent in rural areas (Laumann et al. 1994a, 1994b).

Discussion and recognition did not bring any effort to promote understanding. The general focus was to explore ways to prevent and control homosexuality as contributed to improving life for people with conditions from learning disabilities to diabetes. . . .

One effect of the abuse of the ADA claims I have observed is that able-bodied people are becoming more, not less, anxious about dealing with the disabled. I recently asked a drugstore clerk for help in finding vitamins. He assisted me, then said, "Please don't sue us because we don't have Braille signs."

When I attended a conference on the care of the terminally ill, I listened to a group of hospital administrators talk about their fears of caring for and hiring the disabled. "We try to do the right thing, but we're terrified patients will sue us under the ADA," one woman said. "And who wants to hire them? You'd be afraid they'd sue every time somebody looked at them the wrong way."

Such attitudes are turning the ADA into another handicap for the disabled, particularly where it hurts us the most—in the hearts and minds of employers.

"I enjoy my work," says Fred Wild, a professor of communication at Lycoming College in Williamsport, Pa., who has had diabetes since he was a teenager. "But suppose I did have a job-related problem because of my diabetes. Perhaps I couldn't eat meals when I needed to. I wouldn't want to sue under the ADA. Even if I won my case, I'd be labeled a 'complainer.'

"I've observed what often happens in hiring committees," Wild says. "People are usually reluctant to hire disabled applicants. They're afraid that handicapped employees will develop health problems. Or demand too much—such as schedules that accommodate medical conditions. They don't understand the ADA, and they don't want to get sued."

I used to dream of a law that would dispel prejudice toward folks like me. Now, despite the good it does, the ADA is becoming a nightmare. If people don't stop using it to clog up the courts and excuse incompetence, the Americans With Disabilities Act will wind up reinforcing the discrimination it was designed to eradicate.

Source: Kathi Wolfe. "Is Disability Creating a Handicap?" Reprinted by permission of the author.

a disease, which is what psychiatrists thought it was. Well into the 1960s, discrimination against gays and lesbians was common and legal. Bars frequented by people seeking same-sex partners were raided and people jailed, with their names often published in local newspapers. While unusual in terms of the numbers involved, the events in Boise, Idaho, in 1955 illustrate how preoccupied the United States was with homosexuality. An initial arrest of three men who were accused of having sex with teenagers turned into a full-scale citywide search that resulted in thousands of men being hauled into police stations for questioning. Equally noteworthy is that neither citizens nor government officials were much concerned over the rights of the people or the targeting of the city's gay population (J. Gerassi 1966).

PREJUDICE AND DISCRIMINATION

Homophobia, the fear of and prejudice toward homosexuality, is present in every facet of life—the family, organized religion, the workplace, official policies, and the mass media. Like the myths and stereotypes of race and gender, those about homosexuality keep gay men and lesbian women subordinated as a group and may also serve to keep sympathetic members of the dominant group, the heterosexual community, from joining in support. It is considered a much more respectable form of bigotry than the voicing of ill-feelings against White ethnics described in Chapter 5. People still openly avoid homosexuals and group members are stereotyped in television and motion pictures. While strides are made, one is alarmed by the ease that people feel in expressing their homophobic feelings (Nava and Dawidoff 1994).

As we will see later, gays and lesbians have made extensive efforts to make their feelings known, to ask for respect and a variety of rights, and to have their sexual orientation accepted. However, their efforts seem to have had only a modest impact on public opinion. In 1982, 51 percent of the public felt that homosexuality should not be considered an acceptable alternative lifestyle, with 34 percent disagreeing and 15 percent expressing no opinion. In 1996, the proportion still stood at 50 percent, with 44 percent considering homosexual lifestyle acceptable and only 6 percent having no opinion (D. Moore 1996).

The stigmatization of gays and lesbians was seen as a major factor in the slow initial response to the presence of AIDS (acquired immune deficiency syndrome), which, when it first appeared in the United States, overwhelmingly claimed gay men as its victims. The inattention and the reluctance to develop a national policy forced gay communities in major cities to establish self-help groups to care for the sick, educate the healthy, and lobby for more responsive public policies. The most out-

Concerns about the rights of gays and lesbians often find support within other minority communities. Pictured is a contingent of Asian Americans participating in a 1994 anniversary march in New York City of the Stonewall Inn uprising.

spoken AIDS activist group has been ACT-UP, which has conducted controversial protests and sit-ins in the halls of government and at scientific conferences. While initially such efforts may have siphoned away participants from the broader gay rights effort, ultimately new constituencies of gay men and lesbians were created along with alliances with sympathetic supporters in the straight (heterosexual) community (B. Adam 1995; R. Shilts 1982).

In some instances, antigay prejudice has led to violence. Most notable were the 1978 killings of San Francisco Supervisor Harvey Milk (at one time the nation's most prominent openly gay public official) and Mayor George Moscone (a heterosexual supporter of gay rights) by a former police officer and supervisor. The National Coalition of Anti-Violence Programs and the New York City Gay (1997) released a report documenting more than 2,500 bias-motivated incidents against lesbians and gay men in the United States in 1996. Nationwide, 34 percent of the victims hurt in these attacks suffered injury or death. About 60 percent of the attacks were not reported to police because, in a rather sobering finding in another study, 14 percent of the victims feared more harm from the police. In 1998, the nation was shocked by the unprovoked brutal murder of Matthew Shepard, a University of Wyoming student, by two men. Subsequent investigation showed that Shepard's being gay was the reason for his attackers murdering him rather than leaving him alone after robbing the young man. Sociologist Valerie Jenness (1995b) notes that there has been unprecedented organizing against such violence in the lesbian and gay communities (Jenness and Broad 1994; Nava and Dawidoff 1994; Shilts 1982).

ADVOCACY FOR GAY AND LESBIAN RIGHTS

The first homosexual organization in the United States was founded in Chicago in 1924. Such groups grew steadily over the next fifty years, but they were primarily local and were more likely to be self-help and social rather than confrontational. The social movements of the 1950s and 1960s on behalf of African Americans and women caused lesbians and gay men also to reflect more directly on the oppression their sexual orientation caused (D'Emilio 1983; J. Katz 1992).

The contemporary gay and lesbian movement marks its beginning in New York City on June 28, 1969. Police raided the Stonewall Inn, an after-hours gay bar, and forced patrons into the street. Instead of meekly dispersing and accepting the disruption, the patrons locked police inside the bar and rioted until police reinforcements arrived. For the next three nights, lesbians and gay men marched through the streets of New York, protesting police raids and other forms of discrimination. Within months, gay liberation groups appeared in cities and campuses throughout the United States (M. Duberman 1993; R. Garner 1996; L. Humphreys 1972).

Despite the efforts of the lesbian and gay rights movement, in 1986 the Supreme Court in *Bowers* v. *Hardwick* ruled by a narrow 5–4 vote that the Constitution does not protect homosexual relations between consenting adults, even in the privacy of their own homes. The *Bowers* opinion dramatically illustrated the vast disparity between gay people's theoretical rights as citizens and their actual position in society. This decision underscored the fact that heterosexuality remains the socially approved form of sexual relations in the United States (Nava and Dawidoff 1994).

Despite this decision, gays and lesbians worked to establish the principle that sexual orientation should not be the basis for discrimination. As of the end of 1998, nine states had passed laws barring discrimination based on sexual orientation; however, a referendum had overturned such a law in Maine and it is feared other states may follow the effort (G. Goldberg 1998).

Issues involving gays and lesbians have always been present, but, because of advocacy efforts, the concerns are being advanced by political leaders and the courts. In 1993, President Bill Clinton, due to pressure from the gay community, reviewed the prohibition of homosexuals from the military. However, he encountered even greater pressure from opponents and eventually compromised in 1994 with the so-called "Don't Ask, Don't Tell" policy. The policy allows lesbians and gay men to continue to serve in the military as long as they keep their homosexuality secret, while commanders are prohibited from asking about a person's sexual orientation. Commanders can still investigate and dismiss military personnel if they find any evidence that they have committed homosexual acts. Indeed, according to a 1998 report, the military is discharging 67 percent more gay and lesbian troops today than before the new policy was enacted (T. Weiner 1998).

For many gay and lesbian couples, the inability to have their relationships recognized legally represents the most personal restriction that they have to face. Several dozen cities have begun to recognize domestic partnerships, defined as two unrelated adults who have chosen to share one another's lives in a relationship of mutual caring, who reside together and agree to be jointly responsible for their dependents, basic living expenses, and other common necessities. **Domestic partnership** benefits can apply to inheritance, parenting, pensions, taxation, housing, immigration, workplace fringe benefits, and health care. While the advocacy efforts for recognizing domestic partnerships legally have come from the lesbian and gay community, the majority of the relationships that would benefit would be cohabiting heterosexual couples. There is even a movement to allow homosexual couples to have legal marriages. Hawaii's highest court ruled that a ban on same-sex marriages violates the state's constitution. This decision was subsequently upheld by a federal court. More court battles will follow, but in anticipation that some states may allow gay and lesbian couples to legally marry, Congress enacted the Defense of Marriage Act in 1996, which would deny federal recognition of same-sex marriages. Despite criticism from the gay community and those supportive of legal recognition of same-sex marriage, the measure was immensely popular with the public. A 1998 survey showed that only 33 percent felt that same-sex marriages should be legal (B. Adam 1995; Kaplan and Klaidman 1996; M. Peyser 1998).

Reflecting the segmentation of our society, yet another manifestation of gay advocacy is the formation of organizations for elderly homosexuals. One such group, Senior Action in a Gay Environment (SAGE), was established in Manhattan in 1978 and now serves more than 4,000 lesbians and gay men in New York, New Jersey, and Connecticut. Like more traditional senior citizens' groups, SAGE sponsors workshops, classes, dances, and food deliveries to the homebound. At the same time, SAGE's activities provide a supportive gay environment where older lesbians and gay men can share their experiences. The vitality of such organizations helps to dispel the stereotype of aging homosexuals as inevitably isolated, lonely, and bitter (C. Leduff 1996).

Despite the stability of many same-sex couples, the same people who are concerned over family instability often are opposed to legal recognition of gay and lesbian couples.

Despite political criticism and even violent attacks, the advocacy for lesbian and gay rights has spread across the United States. Within this country, the prevailing image has long been that such efforts are confined to large and liberal cities, such as New York and San Francisco. Yet in 1995, about 5,000 people attended the annual gay pride march in conservative Salt Lake City. Moreover, according to the National Lesbian and Gay Task Force, there has been a noticeable increase in lesbian and gay visibility and advocacy efforts in small towns throughout the United States (Brooke 1996; D. Johnson 1996; also see Schaefer and Lamm 1998).

The Glass Half Empty

A common expression makes reference to a glass half full or half empty of water; those who see it as half full are optimists and those who see it as half empty are pessimists. For many people, the progress of subordinate groups or minorities—the half-full glass—makes it difficult to understand calls for more programs and new reforms (needed because it is also half empty). With the passage of the ADA, why is more assistance needed for people with disabilities? Is there not enough protection against sexism, racism, and ageism?

In absolute terms, the glass of water has been filling up, but people in the 1990s do not compare themselves to people in the 1960s. For example, Latinos and African Americans regard the appropriate reference group to be Whites today; compared to them, the glass is half empty at best.

In Figure 16.3, we have shown the present picture and recent changes by comparing African Americans and Hispanics to Whites. We see that the nation's largest minority groups—African Americans and Hispanics—have higher household income,

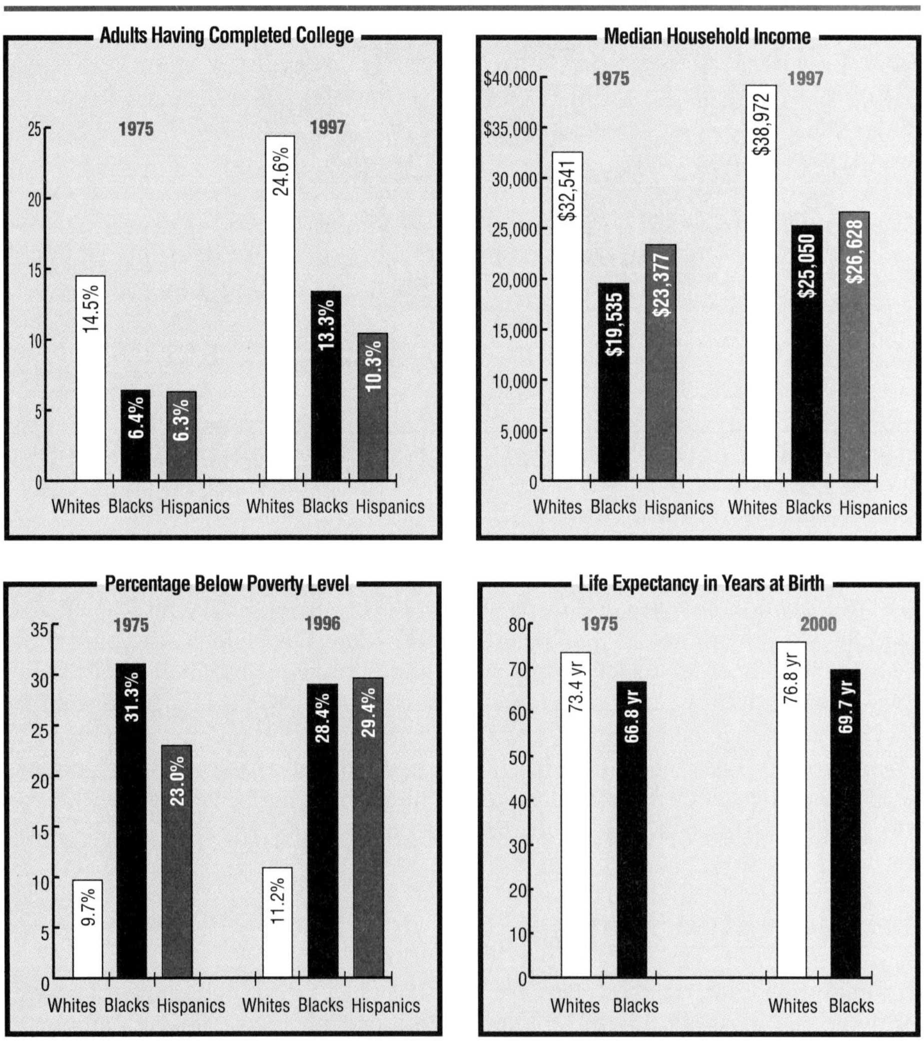

Figure 16.3 Recent Changes in Schooling, Income, and Life Expectancy

Notes: Education data include people twenty-five and over. Hispanic education 1975 data estimated by author from data for 1970 and 1980. The 2000 life expectancy data is a projection.

Source: Bureau of the Census 1998c:94, 167, 472, 756, 1988i:xvii.

complete more schooling, and enjoy longer life expectancy today than in 1975. White Americans have also made similar strides in all three areas. The gap remains and, if one analyzes it closely, has actually increased in some instances. Both Blacks and Hispanics in 1997 had yet to reach the income and educational levels that Whites had exceeded back in 1975. Also, Blacks today have barely matched the life expectancy that Whites had twenty-five years earlier. Similarly, many minority Americans remain entrenched in poverty—one out of three Hispanics and African Americans. Little has changed since 1975. True, Whites have experienced a rise in poverty during the recent troubled economic times, but the proportions of African Americans and Hispanics below the poverty threshold have also increased. We have chosen 1975 because that was a year for which we have comparable data for Hispanics (or Latinos) and Whites and African Americans. However, the patterns would be no different if we considered 1950, 1960, or 1970.

These data provide only the broadest overview. Detailed analyses do not yield a brighter picture. Since the early 1980s, the total number of doctoral degrees awarded has increased by 5.3 percent. Those held by African Americans have increased but still in 1996 made up 7 percent of the total. The increase in Black doctorates has been fueled entirely by women, as the number of Black men earning a doctorate has actually declined by 19 percent since the early 1980s. This dismal trend prompted Wade Henderson of the Washington NAACP to comment, "It certainly confirms our fears that black males are an endangered species in academia" (C. Manegold 1994). The prospect for Native Americans' doctorates is even more depressing. While these numbers have doubled, the actual number of Native Americans with doctorates in all fields was less than one percent of the total (Department of Education 1998).

CONCLUSION

As the United States promotes racial, ethnic, and religious diversity, it strives also to impose universal criteria on employers, educators, and realtors so that subordinate racial and ethnic groups can participate fully in the larger society. In some instances, to bring about equality of results—not just equality of opportunity—programs have been developed to give competitive advantages to women and minority men. Only more recently have similar strides been made on behalf of people with disabilities. These latest answers to social inequality have provoked much controversy over how to achieve the admirable goal of a multiracial, multiethnic society, undifferentiated in opportunity and rewards.

Relations among racial, ethnic, or religious groups take two broad forms, as situations characterized by either consensus or conflict. Consensus prevails where assimilation or fusion among groups has been completed. Consensus also prevails in a pluralistic society in the sense that members have agreed to respect differences among groups and not to demand conformity. Pluralism tolerates disagreement, but relations among groups are harmonious. By eliminating the contending group, extermination and expulsion also lead to a consensus society. In the study of intergroup relations, it is often easy to ignore conflict where there is a high degree of consensus because it is assumed that an orderly society has no problems. In some instances, however, this assumption is misleading. Through long periods of history, misery inflicted on a racial, ethnic, or religious group was judged to be appropriate, if not actually divinely inspired (D. Grove 1974; J. Horton 1966; R. Schermerhorn 1970).

In recent history, harmonious relations among all racial, ethnic, and religious groups have been widely accepted as a worthy goal. The struggle against oppression and inequality is not new. It dates back at least to the revolutions in England, France, and the American colonies in the seventeenth and eighteenth centuries. The twentieth century is unique in the extension of equality to the less privileged classes, many of whose members are racial and ethnic minorities. Conflict along racial and ethnic lines is especially bitter now because it evokes memories of slavery, colonial oppression, and overt discrimination. Today's African Americans are much more aware of slavery than contemporary poor people are of seventeenth-century debtors' prisons (P. Mason 1970a).

Racial and ethnic equality implies the right of the individual to choose his or her own way of life. As Hunt and Walker (1979) observed, however, individual rights may conflict with the group consensus. Gay and lesbian marriages and accommodating the needs of persons with disabilities in the workplace are the latest examples. This conflict makes the situation exceedingly complex; even if a society allows a group to select its own destiny, individual members of the group may then be unable to freely pursue their own course of action. If Native Americans as a group choose to emphasize their cultural distinctiveness, those individuals who wish to integrate into White society may be looked on by their peers as traitors to their tribe.

Unquestionably, the struggle for justice among racial and ethnic groups has not completely met its goals. Many people are still committed to repression, although they may see it only as the benign neglect of those less privileged. Such repression leads to the dehumanization of both the subordinated individual and the oppressor. Growth in equal rights movements and self-determination for Third World countries largely populated by non-White people has moved the world onto a course that seems irreversible. The old ethnic battle lines now renewed in Bosnia, Serbia, Rwanda, and the former Soviet Union have only added to the tensions. Philip Mason (1970b) acknowledged that people are more willing to reject stability if preserving it means inequality.

Self-determination, whether for groups or individuals, is often impossible in societies as they are currently structured. Bringing about social equality will therefore require significant changes in existing institutions. Because such changes are not likely to come about with everyone's willing cooperation, the social costs will be high. If there is a trend in racial and ethnic relations in the world today, however, it is the growing belief that the social costs, however high, must be paid to achieve self-determination.

It is naive to foresee a world of societies in which one person equals one vote, and all are accepted without regard to race, ethnicity, religion, gender, age, disability status, or sexual orientation. It is equally unlikely to expect to see a society, let alone a world, that is without a privileged class or prestigious job holders. Contact between different peoples, as we have seen numerous times, precedes conflict. Contact also may initiate mutual understanding and appreciation.

In a commencement address at American University in 1963, President John F. Kennedy declared, "If we cannot end now our differences, at least we can help make the world safe for diversity" (H. Cleveland 1995:23). In 1994, addressing the graduating class at the U.S. Naval Academy in Annapolis, President Bill Clinton (1994:1160) observed about current wars that "the hardest cases involved the many ethnic and religious conflicts that have erupted in our era." What may well emerge from contemporary and future unrest is the recognition by human beings that people are fundamentally alike and share the same abilities, weaknesses, and dreams.

KEY TERMS

ageism 476
disability 482
domestic partnership 492
homophobia 490

REVIEW QUESTIONS

1. What contributes to the changing image of diversity in the United States?
2. In what ways are the aged, people with disabilities, and gays and lesbians stereotyped?
3. What are common and differing aspects of the effort to mobilize the elderly, aged, and gay men and lesbians to achieve equality?
4. What has been the role of the federal government in the effort to achieve equality by the aged, people with disabilities, and the gay and lesbian community?
5. What does it mean to overcome exclusion?

CRITICAL THINKING

1. Sociologists use the term "master status" to describe a status that dominates others and thereby determines a person's general position within society. To what degree can that term be applied to the three groups considered in this chapter?
2. The media—in advertisements, humor, dramas, and situation comedies—portrays life in society. What are some examples, both positive and negative, of how the elderly, people with disabilities, and gays and lesbians are presented in the media? In what ways are these groups stereotyped?
3. How might advances in technology, including innovations for the home and computer chat rooms, have a unique effect on each of the groups trying to overcome exclusion discussed in this chapter?
4. How do policy makers trying to bring about change use the model of "half full" and "half empty" to either argue for change on behalf of minorities or use the same concepts to maintain that the status quo is adequate for addressing issues of social inequality?

INTERNET EXERCISES

1. The history and accomplishments of those with disabilities are the subject of the Disability Social History Project, found on-line at (http://www.disabilityhistory.org/dshp.html). Utilizing the timeline provided on the site, identify what you believe to be four key moments/events in the challenge for inclusion and equality. Why did you choose these four events over others? What is significant about them? Who were the main participants in the events? How did these events impact the rights of those with disabilities? Utilize other web sites to expand your knowledge of specific disabilities.
2. Based on the documentary Out of the Past, PBS offers a detailed timeline of over 400 years of gay and lesbian history (http://www.pbs.org/outofthepast/). Who are some of the earliest pioneers in the fight for gay and lesbian equality? What happened at the Stonewall Inn during 1969? What are some of the major contributions/achievements of homosexuals throughout history? What are some of the past and current forms of exclusion and discrimination? Considering the information in the timeline, can you see points of comparison between the experience of gays and lesbians in the 1600s and the 1990s? How have experiences stayed the same? How have they changed? What do you believe the future holds? Why?

FOR FURTHER INFORMATION

Barry D. Adam. *The Rise of a Gay and Lesbian Movement* (rev. ed.). New York: Twayne, 1995.
A sociological examination of the history of lesbian and gay social movements of the twentieth century.

David Deitcher (ed.). *The Question of Equality: Lesbian and Gay Politics in America Since Stonewall.* New York: Scribner. 1995.
This well-illustrated book documents the gay and lesbian movement and includes many first-person accounts of significant events.

Martin E. Norden. *The Cinema of Isolation: A History of Physical Disability in the Movies*. New Brunswick, NJ: Rutgers University Press, 1994.
An overview of how motion pictures have perpetuated stereotypes of people with disabilities.

Jill Quadagno. *Aging and the Life Course: An Introduction to Social Gerontology*. New York: McGraw-Hill, 1999. University of Chicago Press, 1995.
A sociological overview of the elderly and the manner in which they are treated by society.

JOURNALS

The topics considered in this chapter can be pursued in greater detail by consulting *Aging and Society* (established in 1981), *Disability Studies Quarterly* (1980), *Journal of Gay, Lesbian, and Bisexual Identity* (1996), and *Research on Aging* (1979).

INTERNET RESOURCE DIRECTORY

The following is a sample of the thousands of WEB sites that offer information on topics related to this book. Most of these sites have links to other resources.

GENERAL

Hate Crimes Laws
http://www.adl.org/frames/front_99hatecrime.html

Immigration and Naturalization Service
http://www.usdoj.gov/ins/index.html

Minority Studies Page
http://humanitas.ucsb.edu/shuttle/minority.html

PBS Background Reports
http://www.pbs.org/newshour/bb/race_relations/race_relations.html

Race Traitor (constructing whiteness)
http://www.postfun.com/racetraitor/

U.S. Census Bureau
http://www.census.gov

U.S. Commission on Civil Rights
http://www.usccr.gov

WebGEMS: Minorities
http://www.fpsol.com/gems/minorities.html

AFRICAN AMERICANS

Kwanzaa Information Center
http://www.melanet.com/kwanzaa/

MelaNET (The UnCut Black Experience)
http://www.melanet.com/

Quarterly Black Review of Books
http://www.bookwire.com/qbr/qbr.html

ASIAN AMERICANS

Asian Community Online Network
http://www.igc.apc.org/acon/

Asian American Network
http://www.aan.net/

Asian American Resources
http://www.mit.edu:8001/afs/athena.mit.edu/user/i/r/irie/www/aar.html

Hmong Home Page
http://www.stolaf.edu/people/cdr/hmong/

HISPANICS/LATINOS

CLNet (Chicano Studies Research Center, UCLA)
http://latino.sscnet.ucla.edu/

Institute for Puerto Rican Policy
http://www.iprnet.org/IPR/

Latino Web
http://www.latinoweb.com
United Farm Workers of America
http://www.ufm.org

JEWS AND JUDAISM

American Jewish Committee
http://www.ajc.org
Anti-Defamation League
http://www.adl.org
Judaism and Jewish Resources
http://shamash.org
Simon Wisenthal Center
http://www.wiesenthal.com/index.html

NATIVE AMERICANS

Bureau of Indian Affairs
http://www.doi.gov/bureau-indian-affairs.html
Nation of Hawai'i
http://hawaii-nation.org/
Native Americans and Environment
http://www.conbio.rice.edu/nae
Native WEB
http://www.nativeweb.org
Navajo Nation
http://www.navajos.com

WOMEN AND MEN

National Organization for Women
http://www.now.org
National Women's History Project
http:www.nwhp.org/
The Men's Issues Page
http://www.vix.com/men/
Womensnet
http://www.igc.apc.org/womensnet
Women World Leaders
http://web.jet.es/ziaorarr/00women.htm

OUTSIDE THE UNITED STATES

Abya Yala Net (South and Meso American Indian Rights Center)
http://abyayala.nativeweb.org
African National Congress (South Africa)
http://www.anc.org.za/
American-Israeli Cooperative Enterprise
http:www.us-israel.org/about/
First Perspective Canada's Source for Aborginees
http://www.mbnet.mb.ca/firstper/

Free Eire (Ireland)
http://www.free-eire.org/Free-Eire/
Information (general) on countries (CIA World Factbook)
http://www,odci.gov/cia/publications/factbook
Peace People (Northern Ireland)
http://www.peacepeople.com

ETHNIC GROUPS AND OTHER SUBORDINATE GROUPS

Administration on Aging
http://www.aoa.dhhs.gov
American Institute of Polish Culture
http://www.ampolinstitute.org
American Irish Historical Society
http://www.aihs.org
Catholics for a Free Choice
http://www.cath4choice.org
Disability Social History Project
http://www.disabilityhistory.org
German Americans (German Embassy site)
http://www.germany-info.org/
Human Rights WEB
http://www.hrweb.org
Interracial Voice (people of mixed racial background)
http://www.webcom.com/~intvoice
Polish American Association
http://www.polish.org
Queer Resource Directory (by and about gays and lesbians)
http://www.qrd.org/QRD/
SeniorLink
http://www.seniorlink.com/
Society and Culture: Disabilities (Yahoo)
http://www.yahoo.com/Society_and_Culture/Disabilities/
Sons of Norway
http://www.sofn.com

THE AUTHOR

Richard T. Schaefer (for e-mail correspondence)
schaeferrt@aol.com

GLOSSARY

Parenthetical numbers refer to the pages in which the term is introduced.

abolitionists Whites and free Blacks who favored the end of slavery. (212)

absolute deprivation The minimum level of subsistence below which families or individuals should not be expected to exist. (75)

affirmative action Positive efforts to recruit subordinate group members including women for jobs, promotions, and educational opportunities. (90)

Afrocentric perspective An emphasis on the customs of African cultures and how they have penetrated the history, culture, and behavior of Blacks in the United States and around the world. (34)

ageism Prejudice and discrimination against the elderly. (476)

AJAs Americans of Japanese ancestry in Hawaii. (348)

amalgamation The process by which a dominant group and a subordinate group combine through intermarriage to form a new group. (28)

androgyny The state of being both masculine and feminine, aggressive and gentle. (414)

anti-Semitism Anti-Jewish prejudice or discrimination. (383)

apartheid The policy of the South African government intended to maintain separation of Blacks, Coloureds, and Asians from the dominant Whites. (464)

assimilation The process by which an individual forsakes his or her own cultural tradition to become part of a different culture. (28)

authoritarian personality A psychological construct of a personality type likely to be prejudiced and to use others as scapegoats. (48)

bilingual education A program designed to allow students to learn academic concepts in their native language while they learn a second language. (276)

bilingualism The use of two or more languages in places of work or education and the treatment of each language as legitimate. (30, 276)

biological race The mistaken notion of a genetically isolated human group. (12)

Bogardus scale Technique to measure social distance toward different racial and ethnic groups. (55)

borderlands The area of a common culture along the border between Mexico and the United States. (281)

bracero Contracted Mexican laborers brought to the United States during World War II. (298)

brain drain Immigration to the United States of skilled workers, professionals, and technicians who are desperately needed by their home countries. (118, 290)

caste approach An approach that views race and social class as synonymous, with disadvantaged minorities occupying the lowest social class and having little, if any, opportunity to improve their social position. (49)

Chicanismo An ideology emphasizing pride and positive identity among Mexican Americans. (303)

civil disobedience A tactic promoted by Martin Luther King, Jr., based on the belief that individuals have the right to disobey unjust laws under certain circumstances. (221)

civil religion The religious dimension in American life that merges the state with sacred beliefs. (152)

class As defined by Max Weber, persons who share similar levels of wealth. (17, 255)

colonialism A foreign power's maintenance of political, social, economic, and cultural dominance over people for an extended period. (23)

color gradient The placement of people on a continuum from light to dark skin color rather than in distinct racial groupings by skin color. (288, 312, 445)

comparable worth *See* pay equity.

conflict perspective A sociological approach that assumes that the social structure is best understood in terms of conflict or tension among competing groups. (19)

contact hypothesis An interactionist perspective stating that intergroup contact between people of equal status in noncompetitive circumstances will reduce prejudice. (68)

creationists People who support a literal interpretation of the biblical book of Genesis on the origins of the universe and argue that evolution should not be presented as established scientific thought. (159)

crossover effect An effect that appears as previously high-scoring Native American children become below average in intelligence when tests are given in English rather than their native languages. (194)

culture of poverty A way of life that involves no future planning, no enduring commitment to marriage, and no work ethic; this culture follows the poor even when they move out of the slums or the barrio. (300)

curanderismo Hispanic folk medicine. (318)

de facto segregation Segregation that is the result of residential patterns. (241)

de jure segregation Children assigned to schools specifically to maintain racially separated schools. (220)

denomination A large, organized religion not officially linked with the state or government. (138)

Diaspora The exile of Jews from Palestine. (458)

differential justice Whites being dealt with more leniently than Blacks whether at time of arrest, indictment, conviction, sentencing, or parole. (260)

disability Reduced ability to perform tasks one would normally do at a given stage in life. (482)

discrimination The denial of opportunities and equal rights to individuals and groups because of prejudice or for other arbitrary reasons. (44, 75)

displaced homemakers Women whose primary occupation had been homemaking but who did not find full-time employment after being divorced, separated, or widowed. (428)

domestic partnerships Two unrelated adults who have chosen to share one another's lives in a relationship of mutual caring, who reside together, and who agree to be jointly responsible for their dependents, basic living expenses, and other community residents. (492)

double jeopardy The subordinate status twice defined, as experienced by women of color. (84, 436)

dual labor market Division of the economy into two areas of employment, the secondary one of which is populated primarily by minorities working at menial jobs. (79)

dysfunction An element of society that may disrupt a social system or lead to a decrease in its stability. (19)

Ebonics Distinctive dialect with a complex language structure found among many Black Americans. (211)

emigration Leaving a country to settle in another. (22)

English immersion Teaching in English by teachers who know the students' native language, but use it only when students do not understand the lessons. (277)

environmental justice Efforts to ensure that hazardous substances are controlled so that all communities receive protection regardless of race or socioeconomic circumstances. (90, 199)

ethclass The merged ethnicity and class in a person's status. (152)

ethnic cleansing Policy of ethnic Serbs to eliminate Muslims from parts of Bosnia. (24)

ethnic group A group set apart from others because of its national origin or distinctive cultural patterns. (9)

ethnicity paradox The maintenance of one's ethnic ties in a way that can assist with assimilation in larger society. (143)

ethnocentrism The tendency to assume that one's culture and way of life are superior to all others. (40)

ethnonational conflicts Conflicts between ethnic, racial, religious, and linguistic groups within nations replacing conflicts between nations. (442)

ethnophaulism Ethnic or racial slurs, including derisive nicknames. (44)

evacuees Japanese Americans interned in camps for the duration of World War II. (368)

exploitation theory A Marxist theory that views racial subordination in the United States as a manifestation of the class system inherent in capitalism. (49)

familism Pride and closeness in the family that result in placing family obligation and loyalty before individual needs. (316)

feminine mystique A woman's thinking of herself only as her children's mother and her husband's wife. (420)

feminization of poverty The trend since 1970 that has women accounting for a growing proportion of those below the poverty line. (428)

fish-ins Tribes' protests over government interference with their traditional rights to fish as they like. (184)

fringe-of-values theory Behavior which is on the border of conduct that a society regards as proper and which is often carried out by subordinate groups, subjecting those groups to negative sanctions. (388)

functionalist perspective A sociological approach emphasizing how parts of a society are structured in the interest of maintaining the system as a whole. (18)

fusion A minority and a majority group combining to form a new group. (28)

gender roles Expectations regarding the proper behavior, attitudes, and activities of males and females. (415)

genocide The deliberate, systematic killing of an entire people or nation. (24)

gerrymandering Redrawing districts bizarrely to create politically advantageous outcomes. (264)

glass ceiling The barrier that blocks the promotion of a qualified worker because of gender or minority membership. (97, 426)

glass wall A barrier to moving laterally in a business to positions that more likely lead to upward mobility. (100)

gook syndrome David Riesman's phrase describing Americans' tendency to stereotype Asians and to regard them as all alike and undesirable. (340)

halakha Jewish laws covering obligations and duties. (404)

Haoles Hawaiian term for Caucasians. (347)

Holocaust The state-sponsored systematic persecution and annihilation of European Jewry by Nazi Germany and its collaborators. (390)

Holocaust revisionists Individuals who deny the Nazi effort to exterminate the Jews or who minimize the numbers killed. (390)

home rule Britain's grant of a local parliament to Ireland. (456)

homophobia The fear of and prejudice toward homosexuality. (490)

hui kuan Chinese-American benevolent associations organized on the basis of the district of the immigrant's origin in China. (359)

ilchomose The 1.5 generation of Korean Americans—those who immigrated into the United States as children. (344)

immigration Coming into a new country as a permanent resident. (22)

income Salaries, wages, and other money received. (244)

informal economy Transfers of money, goods, or services that are not reported to the government. Common in inner-city neighborhoods and poverty-stricken rural areas. (78)

in-group virtues Proper behavior by one's own group ("in-group virtues") becomes unacceptable when practiced by outsiders ("out-group vices"). (389)

institutional discrimination A denial of opportunities and equal rights to individuals or groups resulting from the normal operations of a society. (77)

intelligence quotient (IQ) The ratio of an individual's mental age (as computed by an IQ test) divided by his or her chronological age and multiplied by 100. (13)

internal colonialism The treatment of subordinate peoples like colonial subjects by those in power. (24, 176)

Intifada The Palestinian uprising against Israeli authorities in the occupied territories. (461)

irregular economy *See* informal economy. (78)

Issei First-generation immigrants from Japan to the United States. (365)

Jim Crow Southern laws passed during the latter part of the nineteenth century that kept Blacks in their subordinate position. (213)

Judaization The lessening importance of Judaism as a religion and the substitution of cultural traditions as the tie that binds Jews. (385)

kashrut Laws pertaining to permissible (kosher) and forbidden foods and their preparation. (401)

Kibei Japanese Americans of the *Nisei* generation sent back to Japan for schooling and to have marriages arranged. (365)

kickouts or pushouts Native American school dropouts who leave behind an unproductive academic environment. (193)

kye Rotating credit system used by Korean Americans to subsidize the start of businesses. (345)

labeling theory A sociological approach introduced by Howard Becker that attempts to explain why certain people are viewed as deviants and others engaging in the same behavior are not. (20)

La Raza "The People," a term referring to the rich heritage of Mexican Americans and hence used to denote a sense of pride among Mexican Americans today. (299)

life chances People's opportunities to provide themselves with material goods, positive living conditions, and favorable life experiences. (150, 317)

maquiladoras Foreign-owned companies on the Mexican side of the border with the United States. (281)

marginality The status of being between two cultures at the same time, such as the status of Jewish immigrants in the United States. (33, 407)

Marielitos People who arrived from Cuba in the third wave of Cuban immigration, most specifically those forcibly deported by way of Mariel Harbor. The term is generally reserved for those refugees seen as especially undesirable. (284)

melting pot Diverse racial or ethnic groups or both forming a new creation, a new cultural entity. (28)

middlemen minorities Groups such as Japanese Americans that typically occupy middle positions in the social and occupational stratification system. (329)

migradollars (or remittances) The money that immigrant workers send back to families in their native societies. (125, 282)

migration A general term that describes any transfer of population. (22)

millenarian movements Movements, such as the Ghost Dance, that prophesy a cataclysm in the immediate future, to be followed by collective salvation. (175)

minority group A subordinate group whose members have significantly less control or power over their own lives than that held by the members of a dominant or majority group. (6)

model or ideal minority A group that, despite past prejudice and discrimination, succeeds economically, socially, and educationally without resorting to political or violent confrontations with Whites. (327)

mojados "Wetbacks;" derisive slang for Mexicans who enter illegally, supposedly by swimming the Rio Grande. (299)

mommy track The problematic corporate career track for women who want to divide their attention between work and family. (426)

nativism Beliefs and policies favoring native-born citizens over immigrants. (108)

neocolonialism Continuing dependence of former colonies on foreign countries. (308)

Neoricans Puerto Ricans who return to the island to settle after living on the mainland of the United States (also Nuyoricans). (306)

Nisei Children born of immigrants from Japan. (365)

normative approach The view that prejudice is influenced by societal norms and situations that serve to encourage or discourage the tolerance of minorities. (50)

out-group vices Proper behavior by one's own group ("in-group virtues") becomes unacceptable when practiced by outsiders ("out-group vices"). (389)

panethnicity The development of solidarity among ethnic subgroups as reflected in the terms "Hispanic" or "Asian American." (32, 272, 351)

pan-Indianism Intertribal social movements in which several tribes, joined by culture but not by kinship, unite in a common identity. (183)

pass laws Laws that controlled internal movement by non-Whites in South Africa. (464)

pay equity The same wages for different types of work that are judged to be comparable by such measures as employee knowledge, skills, effort, responsibility, and working conditions; also called comparable worth. (425)

pentecostal faiths Religious groups similar in many respects to evangelical faiths, which, in addition, believe in the infusion of the Holy Spirit into services and in religious experiences such as faith healing. (320)

peoplehood Milton Gordon's term for a group with a shared feeling. (408)

pluralism Mutual respect among the various groups in a society for one another's cultures, allowing minorities to express their own culture without experiencing prejudice or hostility. (30)

powwows Native American gatherings of dancing, singing, music playing, and visiting, accompanied by competitions. (187)

prejudice A negative attitude toward an entire category of people, such as a racial or ethnic minority. (44)

principle of third-generation interest Marcus Hansen's contention that ethnic interest and awareness increase in the third generation, among the grandchildren of immigrants. (142)

racial formation A sociohistorical process by which racial categories are created, inhibited, transformed, and destroyed. (15)

racial group A group that is socially set apart from others because of obvious physical differences. (8)

racism A doctrine that one race is superior. (15)

redlining The pattern of discrimination against people trying to buy homes in minority and racially changing neighborhoods. (258)

refugees People living outside their country of citizenship for fear of political or religious persecution. (127)

relative deprivation The conscious experience of a negative discrepancy between legitimate expectations and present actualities. (75, 225)

remittances (or migradollars) The monies that migrants return to their country of origin. (125, 282)

repatriation The program during the 1930s of deporting Mexicans. (298)

respectable bigotry Michael Lerner's term for the social acceptance of prejudice against White ethnics, when intolerance against non-White minorities is regarded as unacceptable. (145)

restrictive covenants Private contracts or agreements that discourage or prevent minority-group members from purchasing housing in a neighborhood. (219)

reverse discrimination Actions that cause better qualified White males to be passed over for women and minority men. (94)

riff-raff theory Also called the rotten-apple theory; the belief that the riots of the 1960s were caused by discontented youths, rather than by social and economic problems facing all African Americans. (225)

rising expectations The increasing sense of frustration that legitimate needs are being blocked. (225)

Sansei The children of the *Nisei,* that is, the grandchildren of the original immigrants from Japan. (365)

scapegoat A person or group blamed irrationally for another person's or group's problems or difficulties. (46)

secessionist minority Groups, such as the Amish, that reject both assimilation and coexistence. (159)

second shift The double burden—work outside the home followed by child care and housework—that is faced by many women and that few men share equitably. (432)

segregation The act of physically separating two groups; often imposed on a subordinate group by the dominant group. (26)

self-fulfilling prophecy The tendency of individuals to respond to and act on the basis of stereotypes, a predisposition that can lead to the validation of false definitions. (21)

set-asides Programs stipulating a minimum proportion of government contracts must be awarded to minority-owned businesses. (249)

setoffs Deductions from money due in U.S. government settlements with Native Americans, equal to the cost of federal services provided to the tribe. (180)

sexism The ideology that one sex is superior to the other. (414)

sexual harassment Any unwanted and unwelcome sexual advances that interfere with a person's ability to perform a job and enjoy the benefits of a job. (427)

sinophobes People with a fear of anything associated with China. (110)

slave codes Laws that defined the low position held by slaves in the United States. (207)

sociology The systematic study of social behavior and human groups. (17)

states' rights The principle, reinvoked in the late 1940s, that holds that each state is sovereign and has the right to order its own affairs without interference by the federal government. (87)

stereotypes Unreliable generalizations about all members of a group that do not take into account individual differences within the group. (20)

stratification A structured ranking of entire groups of people that perpetuates unequal rewards and power in a society. (17)

suffragists Women and men who worked successfully to gain women the right to vote. (418)

symbolic ethnicity Herbert Gans's term that describes emphasis on ethnic food and ethnically associated political issues rather than deeper ties to one's heritage. (143)

tongs Chinese American secret associations. (359)

total discrimination The combination of current discrimination with past discrimination created by poor schools and menial jobs. (76)

tracking The practice of placing students in specific curriculum groups on the basis of test scores and other criteria. (242, 315)

tsu Clans established along family lines and forming a basis for social organization by Chinese Americans. (359)

underclass Lower-class members who are not a part of the regular economy and whose situation is not changed by conventional assistance programs. (80)

underground economy *See* informal economy. (78)

underemployment Work at a job for which the worker is overqualified, involuntary part-time instead of full-time employment, or intermittent employment. (247)

victim discounting Tendency to view crime as less socially significant if the victim is viewed as less worthy. (260)

victimization surveys Annual attempts to measure crime rates by interviewing ordinary citizens who may or may not have been crime victims. (260)

Viet Kieu Vietnamese living abroad such as in the United States. (342)

wealth An inclusive term encompassing all of a person's material assets, including land and other types of property. (244)

White primary Legal provisions forbidding Black voting in election primaries, which in one-party areas of the South effectively denied Blacks their right to select elected officials. (213)

world systems theory A view of the global economic system as divided between nations that control wealth and those that provide natural resources and labor. (24, 172, 313, 442)

xenophobia The fear or hatred of strangers or foreigners. (129)

yellow peril A term denoting a generalized prejudice toward Asian people and their customs. (320)

Yiddishkait Jewishness. (403)

Yonsei The fourth generation of Japanese Americans in the United States, the children of the *Sansei*. (365)

Zionism Traditional Jewish religious yearning to return to the biblical homeland, now used to refer to support for the state of Israel. (395, 458)

zoning laws Legal provisions stipulating land use and the architectural design of housing, often used to keep racial minorities and low-income people out of suburban areas. (259)

References

Abelmann, Nancy, and Lie, John 1995 *Blue Dreams: Korean Americans and the Los Angeles Riots*. Cambridge, MA: Harvard University Press.

Aberbach, Joel D., and Walker, Jack L. 1973 *Race in the City*. Boston: Little, Brown.

Abrahamson, Alan 1997 School Growth: A New Chapter for U.S. Jews. *Los Angeles Times* (October 22), B2.

———; and Pasternak, Judy 1998 For U.S. Jews, Era of Plenty Takes Many Far from Roots. *Los Angeles Times* (April 20), pp. A1, A10–11.

Abrahamson, Mark 1996 *Urban Enclaves Identity and Place in America*. New York: St. Martin's Press.

Abron, JoNina M. 1986 The Legacy of the Black Panther Party. *The Black Scholar* 17 (November-December), pp. 33–37.

ACLU 1996a *Briefing Paper: Church and State*. New York: American Civil Liberties Union. 1996b *Racial Justice*. New York: American Civil Liberties Union.

Adam, Barry D. 1995 *The Rise of a Gay and Lesbian Movement*, rev. ed. New York: Twayne.

Adler, Patricia A.; Kess, Steven J.; and Adler, Peter 1992 Socialization to Gender Role: Popularity among Elementary School Boys and Girls. *Sociology of Education* 65 (July), pp. 169–187.

———; and Adler, Peter 1998 Peer Power: Preadolescent Culture and Identity. New Brunswick, NJ: Rutgers University Press.

Adorno, T. W.; Frenkel-Brunswik, Else; Levinson, Daniel J.; and Sanford, R. Nevitt 1950 *The Authoritarian Personality*. New York: Wiley

Aguillar-San Juan, Karin 1998 Creating Ethnic Places in "Little Saigon": History, Memory and Citizenship. Paper presented at American Sociological Association Annual Meeting, San Francisco.

Akwesasne Notes 1972 Columbus a Trader in Indian Slaves. 4 (Early Autumn), p. 22.
1988 Competing Sovereignties in North America and the Right-Wing and Anti-Indian Movements. 20 (Early Spring), pp. 12–13.

Alárcon, Odette 1995 An Interview. *Research Report* (Center for Research on Women, Wellesley College) 15 (Fall), pp. 3–4.

Alba, Richard D. 1985 *Italian Americans: Into the Twilight of Ethnicity*. Englewood Cliffs, NJ: Prentice-Hall.
1990 *Ethnic Identity: The Transformation of White America*. New Haven: Yale University Press.

Alba, Richard D., and Moore, Gwen 1982 Ethnicity in the American Elite. *American Sociological Review* 47 (June), pp. 373–382.

Albrecht, Gary L. 1992 *The Disability Business: Political Economy of Rehabilitation in America*. Beverly Hills, CA: Sage Publications.
1995 Review of Disabling Laws, Enabling Acts: Disability Rights in Britain and America. *Contemporary Sociology* 24 (No. 5), pp. 6\27–629.
1997 Disability Is Area Rich with Sociological Opportunity. *Footnotes* 25 (December, p. 6.

Allen, James Paul, and Turner, Eugene James 1988 *We the People: An Atlas of America's Ethnic Diversity*. New York: Macmillan.

Allen, Patricia A., and Adler, Peter 1998 *Peer Power: Preadolescent Culture and Identity*. New Brunswick, NJ: Rutgers University Press.

Allport, Gordon W. 1979 *The Nature of Prejudice, 25th Anniversary Edition*. Reading, MA: Addison-Wesley.

American Council on Education 1994 Students of Color Earn More Ph.D.s. *Higher Education and National Affairs* 43 (January 10), p. 3.

American Jewish Committee 1998 "Total Jewish Population." Cited in *Los Angeles Times*. (April 23), p. A26.

Amnesty International 1993 *Amnesty International Report 1993*. New York: Amnesty International.

Anderson, Dennis 1998 Judge Rules Rest of Prop. 187 is Unconstitutional. *USA Today* (March 19), p. 9A.

Anti-Defamation League 1996 The Web of Hate: Extremists Exploit the Internet. New York: Anti-Defamation League.

Anti-Defamation League of B'nai B'rith 1993 *Young Nazi Killers: The Rising Skinhead Danger*. New York: Anti-Defamation League.
1998 *Audit of Anti-Semitic Incidents 1997*. New York: Anti-Defamation League.

Aponte, Robert 1991 Urban Hispanic Poverty: Disaggregations and Explanations. *Social Problems* 38 (November), pp. 516–528.

Appelbome, Peter 1996 70 Years After Scopes Trial, Creation Debate Lives. *New York Times* (March 10), pp. 1, 22.
1997 Dispute Over Ebonics Reflects a Volatile Mix That Roils Urban Education. *New York Times* (March 1), p. 8.

Aran, Kenneth; Arthur, Herman; Colon, Ramon; and Goldenberg, Harvey 1973 *Puerto Rican History and Culture: A Study Guide and Curriculum Outline*. New York: United Federation of Teachers.

Archuleta, Glenda 1998 Interview with Archuleta (Council for Energy Resource Tribes) by Richard T. Schaefer. September 18.

ARDEN, HARVEY 1975 The Pious Ones. *National Geographic* 168 (August), pp. 276–298.

ARMOUR, STEPHANIE 1998 Disabilities Act Abused? *USA Today* (September 25), pp. B1, B2.

ARONSON, ELLIOTT 1999 *The Social Animal,* 8th ed. New York: Worth.

ASANTE, MOLEFI KETE 1987 *The Afrocentric Idea.* Philadelphia: Temple University Press.
1992 Afrocentric Systematics. *Black Issues in Higher Education* 9 (August 13), pp. 16–17, 21–22.
1996 Afrocentricity, Eurocentricity, and Multiculturalism: Toward the 21st Century. Address at Western Illinois University, Macomb, IL, February 13.

ASIAN AMERICAN JOURNALISTS ASSOCIATION 1991 *Project Zinger: The Good, the Bad and the Ugly.* Seattle: Center for Integration and Improvement Association.
1993 *Project Zinger: A Critical Look at News Media Coverage of Asian Pacific Americans.* Los Angeles: Center for Integration and Improvement Association.
1994 *News Watch: A Critical Look at Coverage of People of Color.* San Francisco: Center for Integration and Improvement Association.

ASSOCIATED PRESS 1997 Catholicism Embraces Native Culture in Mass. *Los Angeles Times* (January 4), pp. 84–85.

AYRES, IAN 1991 Fair Driving: Gender and Race Discrimination in Retail Car Negotiations. *Harvard Law Review* 104 (February), pp. 817–872.

BACON, JOHN 1987 Court Ruling Hasn't Quieted School Prayer. *USA Today* (April 3), p. 3A.

BADGETT, M. V. LEE, AND HARTMANN, HEIDI I. 1995 The Effectiveness of Equal Employment Opportunity Policies. In Margaret C. Simms, ed., *Economic Perspectives in Affirmative Action,* pp. 55–83. Washington, DC: Joint Center for Political and Economic Studies.

BAHR, HOWARD M. 1972 An End to Invisibility. In Howard M. Bahr, Bruce A. Chadwick, and Robert C. Day, eds., *Native Americans Today: Sociological Perspectives,* pp. 404–412. New York: Harper & Row.

BAKER, BOB 1992 Stereotype That Won't Go Away. *Los Angeles Times* (May 31), pp. A1, A18.

BALDWIN, JAMES 1967 Negroes Are Anti-Semitic Because They're Anti-White. *New York Times* (May 21), p. 114.

BALTZELL, E. DIGBY 1964 *The Protestant Establishment: Aristocracy and Caste in America.* New York: Vintage Books.

BALZ, DAN 1998 A Helping Hand From Across the Sea. *Washington Post National Weekly Edition* 15 (April 20), pp. 16–17.

BARBARO, FRED 1974 Ethnic Resentment. *Society* 11 (March-April), pp. 67–75.

BARCLAY, WILLIAM; KUMAR, KRISHNA; AND SIMMS, RUTH P. 1976 *Racial Conflict, Discrimination, and Power: Historical and Contemporary Studies.* New York: AMS Press.

BARNES, EDWARD 1996 Can't Get There from Here. *Time* 147 (February 19), p. 33.

BARRERA, MARIO; MUNOS, CARLOS; AND ORNELAS, CHARLES 1972 The Barrio as an Internal Colony. In Harlan Mahlan, ed., *People and Politics in Urban Society,* pp. 465–549. Beverly Hills, CA: Sage Publications.

BARRETT, DAVID B., AND JOHNSON, TODD M. 1998 Religious Adherents in the United States of America, AD 1900–2000. In David R. Calhoun, ed. *Britannica Book of Year,* p. 314. Chicago: Encyclopedia Britannica.

BARRETT, WAYNE, AND COOPER, ANDREW 1981 Koch's 99 Attacks Against the Other New York. *Village Voice* 26 (April 15–21), pp. 22–31.

BARRON, MILTON L. 1953 Minority Group Characteristics of the Aged in American Society. *Journal of Gerontology* 8, (October), pp. 477–482.

BASH, HARRY M. 1979 *Sociology, Race and Ethnicity.* New York: Gordon & Breach.

BASKIN, JANE A.; HARTWEG, JOYCE K.; LEWIS, RALPH G.; AND MCCULLOUGH, LESTER W., JR. 1971 *Race Related Civil Disorders: 1967–1969.* Waltham, MA: Lemberg Center for the Study of Violence, Brandeis University.

BASKIN, JANE A.; LEWIS, RALPH G.; MANNIS, JOYCE HARTWEG; AND MCCULLOUGH, LESTER W., JR. 1972 The Long, Hot Summer. *Justice Magazine* 1 (February), p. 8.

BASTIAN, LISA D., AND TAYLOR, BRUCE M. 1994 *Young Black Male Victims.* Washington, DC: U.S. Government Printing Office.

BAUER, RAYMOND A., AND BAUER, ALICE H. 1942 Day to Day Resistance to Slavery. *Journal of Negro History* 27 (October), pp. 388–419.

BAUM, GERALDINE 1998 New Power of Women Recasts Judaism. *Los Angeles Times* (April 21), pp. A1, A14, A15.

BAUMANN, MARTY 1992 Agreement on King, *USA Today* (May 11), p. 4A.

BAXTER, KEVIN 1998 Anaheim Angels Making Play for Latinos. *Los Angeles Times* (May 3), pp. A3, A34.

BBDO 1996 *Report on Black TV Viewing.* New York: BBDO.

BEACH, WALTER G. 1934 Some Considerations in Regard to Race Segregation in California. *Sociology and Social Research* 18 (March), pp. 340–350.

BECERRA, JOSÉ E., ET AL. 1991 Infant Mortality Among Hispanics: A Portrait of Heterogeneity. *Journal of the American Medical Association* 265 (January 9), pp. 217–221.

BECK, ROY 1994 The Ordeal of Immigration in Wausau. *Atlantic Monthly* (April), pp. 84–90, 94–97.

BECKER, MAKI 1995 Keeping Alive Culinary Customs of Japan. *Los Angeles Times* (January 3), p. B3.

BEDELL, KENNETH B., ED. 1997 *Yearbook of American and Canadian Churches 1997.* Nashville: Abingdon Press.

BELAIR, FELIX, JR. 1970 1965 Law Changes Ethnic Patterns of Immigration. *New York Times* (August 31), pp. 1, 37.

BELL, DANIEL 1953 Crime as an American Way of Life. *Antioch Review* 13 (Summer), pp. 131–154.

BELL, DERRICK 1994 The Freedom of Employment Act. *The Nation* 258 (May 23), pp. 708, 710–714.

BELL, WENDELL 1991 Colonialism and Internal Colonialism. In Richard Lachmann, ed., *The Encyclopedic Dictionary of Sociology,* 4th ed., pp. 52–53. Guilford, CT: Dushkin Publishing Group.

BELLAH, ROBERT 1967 Civil Religion in America. *Daedalus* 96 (Winter), pp. 1–21.
1968 Response to Commentaries on "Civil Religion in America." In Donald R. Cutler, ed., *The Religious Situation: 1968*, pp. 388–393. Boston: Beacon Press.
1970 *Beyond Belief: Essays on Religion in a Post-Traditional World.* New York: Harper & Row.
1989 Comment to Mathisen. *Sociological Analysis* 50 (Summer), p. 147.

BELLUCK, PAM 1997 A New Window to Run Welfare is a Tight Squeeze for Many Tribes. *New York Times* (September 9), pp. A1, A15.

BEM, SANDRA LIPSITZ 1994 In a Male-Centered World, Female Differences Are Transformed into Female Disadvantages. *Chronicle of Higher Education* 39 (August 17), pp. B1–B3.

BENDAVID, NAFTALI 1998 Violent, Frequent Crime Tearing at the Reservation. *Chicago Tribune* (May 3), pp. 1, 16.

BENDICK, JR., MARC; JACKSON, CHARLES W.; AND ROMERO, J. HORACIO 1993 *Employment Discrimination Against Older Workers: An Experimental Study of Hiring Practices.* Washington, DC: Fair Employment Council of Greater Washington.

BENJAMIN, ROBERT 1993 Illegal Chinese Immigrants Flood U.S. *Chicago Sun-Times* (February 28), p. 27.

BENNETT, CLAUDETTE E. 1995 The Black Population in the United States: March 1994 and 1993. *Current Population Reports,* Ser. P–20, No. 480. Washington, DC: U.S. Government Printing Office.

BENNETT, LERONE, JR. 1965 *Confrontation: Black and White.* Chicago: Johnson.
1966 *Before the Mayflower,* rev. ed. Baltimore: Penguin.

BENNETT, PHILLIP 1993 Ethnic Labels Fail to Keep Up with Reality. *The Cincinnati Enquirer* (November 18), p. A10.

BENNETT, VANORA 1998 Staying True to Their Roots. *Los Angeles Times* (April 10), p. A5.

BENNETT, VIVIENNE 1995 Gender, Class, and Water: Women and the Politics of Water Service in Monterrey, Mexico. *Latin American Perspective* 22 (September), pp. 76–99.

BENNETTS, LESLIE 1993 Jerry vs. the Kids. *Vanity Fair* 56 (September), pp. 83–84, 86, 90, 92, 94, 96, 98.

BERLIN, IRA 1998 *Many Thousands Gone: The First Two Centuries of Slavery in North America.* Cambridge, MA: Harvard University Press.

———, FAVREAU, MARC, AND MILLER, STEVEN F. 1998 *Remembering Slavery: African Americans Talk About Their Personal Experiences of Slavery and Emancipation.* Cambridge, MA: Harvard University Press.

BERNARD, JESSIE 1975 *Women, Wives, Mothers: Values and Options.* Chicago: Aldine.

BERNDT, RONALD M., AND BERNDT, CATHERINE 1951 *From Black to White in South Australia.* Melbourne: F. W. Chesire.

BERREMAN, GERALD D. 1973 *Caste in the Modern World.* Morristown, NJ: General Learning Press.

BERRY, JOHN 1995 VFW Skips Parade over Flag. *Peoria Star* (June 30), pp. A1, A7.

BESI, JOHN R., AND KALE, BALKRISHNA D. 1996 Older Workers in the 21st Century: Active and Educated a Case Study. *Monthly Labor Review* (June), pp. 18–28.

BETTELHEIM, BRUNO, AND JANOWITZ, MORRIS 1964 *Social Change and Prejudice.* New York: Free Press.

BEYETTE, BEVERLY 1995 Honoring Forgotten Victims of WWII. *Los Angeles Times* (February 10), p. E1.

BIELSKI, VINCE 1994 American Indians Walk for Justice. *The Daily Citizen* (February 18), pp. 1, 13.

BIGELOW, REBECCA 1992 Certain Inalienable Rights. *Friends Journal* 38 (November), pp. 6–8.

BILLINGSLEY, C. ANDREW 1992 *Climbing Jacob's Ladder: The Enduring Legacy of African-American Families.* New York: Simon & Schuster.

BILLSON, JANET MANCINI 1988 No Owner of Soil: The Concept of Marginality Revisited on Its Sixtieth Birthday. *International Review of Modern Sociology* 18 (Autumn), pp. 183–204.

BIRREN, JAMES E., AND GRIBBIN, KATHY 1993 The Elderly. In Don Spiegel and Patricia Keith-Spiegel, eds., *Outsiders USA.* San Francisco: Rinehart Press.

BISSIO, ROBERTO 1995 *The World 95/96.* Toronto: Garmond Press.

BLACKSTOCK, NELSON 1976 *COINTELPRO: The FBI's Secret War on Political Freedom.* New York: Vintage Press.

BLAU, FRANCINE D. 1998 Trends in the Well-Being of American Women, 1970–1995. *Journal of Economic Literature* 36 (March), pp. 112–165.

BLAUNER, ROBERT 1969 Internal Colonialism and Ghetto Revolt. *Social Problems* 16 (Spring), pp. 393–408.
1972 *Racial Oppression in America.* New York: Harper & Row.

BLEDSOE, TIMOTHY, AND HERRING, MARY 1990 Victims of Circumstances: Women in Pursuit of Political Office. *American Political Science Review* 84 (March), pp. 213–224.

BLOCH, HANNAH 1996 Cutting Off the Brains. *Time* 147 (February 5), p. 46.

BLOOM, LEONARD 1971 *The Social Psychology of Race Relations.* Cambridge, MA: Schenkman.

BLOW, CHARLES M., AND PERRY, JIM 1998 Portrait of a Land and Its People. *New York Times* (April 6), p. A13.

BOAL, FREDERICK W.; DOUGLAS, J.; AND NEVILLE, H. 1982 *Integration and Division: Geographical Perspectives on the Northern Ireland Problems.* New York: Academic Press.

BOBO, LAWRENCE 1998 Race, Interests, and Beliefs about Affirmative Action: Unanswered Questions and New Directions. *American Behavioral Scientist* 41 (April), pp. 985–1003.

———; KLUEGEL, JAMES R.; AND SMITH, RYAN A. 1997 Laissez-Faire Racism: The Crystallization of a Kinder, Gentler, Antiblack Ideology. In Steven A. Tuch and Jack K. Martin, eds., *Racial Attitudes in the 1990s: Continuity and Change,* pp. 15–42. Westport, CT: Praeger.

BOGARDUS, EMORY 1968 Comparing Racial Distance in Ethiopia, South Africa, and the United States. *Sociology and Social Research* 52 (January), pp. 149–156.

BOHLAND, JAMES R. 1982 Indian Residential Segregation in the Urban Southwest: 1970 and 1980. *Social Science Quarterly* 63 (December), pp. 749–761.

BONACICH, EDNA 1972 A Theory of Ethnic Antagonism: The Split Labor Market. *American Sociological Review* 37 (October), pp. 547–559.
1976 Advanced Capitalism and Black/White Race Relations in the United States: A Split Labor Market Interpretation. *American Sociological Review* 41 (February), pp. 34–51.
1988 The Social Costs of Immigrant Entrepreneurship. *Amerasia* 14 (Spring), pp. 119–128.

BONACICH, EDNA, AND MODELL, JOHN 1981 *The Economic Basis of Ethnic Solidarity*. Berkeley: University of California Press.

BOND, JAMES T.; GALINSKY, ELLEN; AND SWANBERG, JENNIFER E. 1998 *The 1997 National Study of the Changing Workforce*. New York: Families and Work Institute.

BONFANTE, JORDAN 1995 The Catholic Paradox. *Time* 146 (October 9), pp. 64–68.

BOOTH, WILLIAM 1993 Puerto Rico Rejects Statehood. *Washington Post* (November 15), pp. A1, A12.

BONILLA-SILVA, EDUARDO 1996 Rethinking Racism: Toward a Structural Interpretation. *American Sociological Review* 62 (June), pp. 465–480.

BORJAS, GEORGE 1990 *Friends or Strangers: The Impact of Immigrants on the U.S. Economy*. New York: Basic Books.

———, AND FREEMAN, RICHARD B. 1997 Findings We Never Found. *New York Times* (December 10), p. A23.

BORK, ROBERT H. 1995 What To Do About the First Amendment. *Commentary* 99 (February), pp. 23–29.

BOSITIS, DAVID A. 1996 The Farrakhan Factor. *Washington Post National Weekly Edition* 14 (December 16), p. 24.

BOSWELL, THOMAS D., AND CURTIS, JAMES R. 1984 *The Cuban-American Experience*. Totowa, NJ: Rowman & Allanheld.

BOUVIER, LEON F., AND GARDNER, ROBERT W. 1986 Immigration to the U.S.: The Unfinished Story. *Population Bulletin* 41 (November).

———, AND GRANT, LINDSAY 1994 *How Many Americans? Population, Immigration, and the Environment*. San Francisco: Sierra Club.

BOWEN, WILLIAM G., AND BOK, DERK 1998 *The Shape of the River: Long-Term Consequences of Considering Race in College and University Admissions*. Princeton, NJ: Princeton University Press.

BOWMAN, TOM 1998 Evangelicals Allege Bias in U.S. Navy, Marine Chaplain Corps. *Baltimore Sun* (August 23), p. A12.

BOWSER, BENJAMIN, AND HURST, RAYMOND G., EDS. 1996 *Impacts of Racism on White Americans*. Beverly Hills, CA: Sage Publications.

BOYER, EDWARD J. 1996 Life in a New Land: Illegal Immigrant Who Fled Deputies Reaches Goal: A Job in U.S. *Chicago Tribune* (May 7), p. 131, B8.

BRACEY, JOHN H.; MEIER, AUGUST; AND RUDWICK, ELLIOT, EDS. 1970 *Black Nationalism in America*. Indianapolis: Bobbs-Merrill.

BRADDOCK, D., AND BACHELDER, L. 1994 *The Glass Ceiling and Persons With Disabilities*. Washington, DC: The Glass Ceiling Commission. Washington, DC: U.S. Government Printing Office.

BRADLEY, MARTIN B.; GREEN, NORMAN M., JR.; JONES, DALE E.; LYNN, MAC; AND MCNEIL, LOU 1992 *Churches and Church Membership in the United States 1990*. Atlanta: Glenmary Research Center.

BRADLEY, PHIL 1990 The Growing Clout of Voters with Disabilities. *Illinois Issues* 16 (April), p. 34.

BRADSHER, KEITH 1997 Flight Response by Korean-Americans. *New York Times* (January 6), p. A7.

BRANIGIN, WILLIAM 1995 Sweatshops Reborn. *Washington Post National Weekly Edition* 12 (September 18), pp. 8–9.

BRANNON, RUTH 1995 The Use of the Concept of Disability Culture: A Historian's View. *Disability Studies Quarterly* 15 (Fall), pp. 3–15.

BRAUS, PATRICIA 1993 What Does "Hispanic" Mean? *American Demographics* 15 (June), pp. 46–49, 58.

BRESLAU, KAREN 1997 America's "Own Holocaust." *Newsweek* 130 (December 8), p. 61.

BRIGGS, DAVID 1996 Greeley Poll Says Catholics Want Democratic Church. *Chicago Tribune* (May 31), sect. 2, p. 9.

BRIGGS, KENNETH A. 1976 Churches Found Still Largely Segregated. *New York Times* (November 14), p. 26.
1978 Jewish Leader Urges a Program to Convert "Seekers" to Judaism. *New York Times* (December 3), pp. 1, 37.

BRIMELOW, PETER 1995 *Alien Nation*. New York: Random House.

BRIMMER, ANDREW 1995 The Economic Cost of Discrimination Against Black Americans. In Margaret C. Simms, ed., *Economic Perspectives in Affirmative Action*, pp. 9–29. Washington, DC: Joint Center for Political and Economic Studies.

BRIN, DINA WISENBERG 1998 Synagogues Ease the Way for Gentile Spouses. *Chicago Tribune* (July 10), sect. 2, p. 8.

BROOKE, JAMES 1995 Attacks on U.S. Muslims Surge Even as Their Faith Holds. *New York Times* (August 28), pp. A1, B7.
1996 To Be Young, Gay, and Going to High School in Utah. *New York Times* (February 28), p. B7.
1997 After Silence, Italians Recall the Internment. *New York Times* (August 11), p. A8.
1998 A Hot Issue in Northern New Mexico: Fine Print of an 1848 Treaty. *New York Times* (February 19), p. A10.
1998b Indians Striving to Save Their Languages. *New York Times* (April 9), pp. A1, A20.

BROOKS-GUNN, JEANNE; KLEBANOV, PAMELA K.; AND DUNCAN, GREG J. 1996 Ethnic Differences in Children's Intelligence Test Scores: Role of Economic Deprivation, Home Environment, and Maternal Characteristics. *Child Development* 67 (April), pp. 396–408.

BROOM, LEONARD 1965 *The Transformation of the American Negro*. New York: Harper & Row.

BROWN, CHRISTOPHER 1990 Discrimination and Immigration Law. *Focus* 18 (August), pp. 3–4, 8.

BROWN, DEE 1971 *Bury My Heart at Wounded Knee*. New York: Holt, Rinehart & Winston.

BRUGGE, DOUG, AND BENELLY, TIMOTHY 1998 Navajo Indian

Voices and Faces Testify to the Legacy of Uranium Mining. *Cultural Survival Quarterly* 22 (Spring), pp. 16–19.

BULLARD, ROBERT 1993 *Dumping in Dixie: Race, Class, and Environmental Quality.* 2d ed. Boulder, CO: Western Press.

BUREAU OF INDIAN AFFAIRS 1986 *American Indians Today: Answers to Your Questions.* Washington, DC: U.S. Government Printing Office.
1988 *Report of BIA Education: Excellence in Indian Education Through the Effective School Process.* Washington, DC: U.S. Government Printing Office.

BUREAU OF THE CENSUS 1975 *Historical Statistics of the United States, Colonial Times to 1970.* Washington, DC: U.S. Government Printing Office.
1982 *Statistical Abstract, 1982.* Washington, DC: U.S. Government Printing Office.
1988 *Statistical Abstract, 1988.* Washington, DC: U.S. Government Printing Office.
Statistical Abstract of the United States, 1992. Washington, DC: U.S. Government Printing Office.
1993a *We the American . . . Asians.* Washington, DC: U.S. Government Printing Office.
1993b *Money Income of Households, Families, and Persons in the United States: 1992,* Ser. P–60, No. 184. Washington, DC: U.S. Government Printing Office.
1993c *We the American . . . Hispanics.* Washington, DC: U.S. Government Printing Office.
1993d *We the . . . First Americans.* Washington, DC: U.S. Government Printing Office.
1994 *Statistical Abstract of the United States, 1994.* Washington, DC: U.S. Government Printing Office.
1995 *Sixty-Five Plus in the United States.* Washington, DC: U.S. Government Printing Office.
1996 *Statistical Abstract of the United States, 1996.* Washington, DC: U.S. Government Printing Office.
1997a Annual Demographic Survey. March Supplemt. Last revised September 29. Table 2. Accessed July 29, 1998.(http://Ferret.bls.Census.gov/macro/031997/perinc/02_025.htm)
1997b *Type of Residences by Total Money Income.* Last revised September 29. Accessed July 29, 1998. (http://Ferret.bls.census.gov/macro/031997/perinc/02_026.htm)
1997c Facts for Native American Month. News release. CB97-FS.11. Washington, DC: U.S. Government Printing Office.
1998a *United States Census 2000. Dress Rehearsal.* Washington, DC: U.S. Government Printing Office.
1998b Money Income in the United States: 1997 (with separate data on valuation of noncash benefits). *Current Population Reports,* pp. 60–200. Washington, DC: U.S. Government Printing Office.
1998c *Statistical Abstract of the United States 1998.* Washington, D.C. U.S. Government Printing Office.
1998d The Black Population of the United States, March 1997. *Current Population Reports.* Accessed August 4, 1998. (http://www.census.gen/population/socdemo/race/black/) Tables 12A and 12B.
1998e Hectic Lifestyles Make for Record-Low Election Turnout. *Census Bureau Reports.* Press Release. August 17.
1998f Disability Status of Persons 15 Years Old and Over. Special analysis provided to author on December 31.
1998g Young Adults Boost Asian College-Completion Levels. *Census Bureau Reports.* Press Release. June 29.
1998h Asians and Pacific Islanders Have Nation's Highest Median Household Income in 1997. *Census Bureau Reports.* Press Release. August 24.
1998i Money Income in the United States: 1997. *Current Population Reports,* Ser. P–60, No. 200. Washington, DC: U.S. Government Printing Office.
1998j Percent Reported Voted and Registered by Race, Hispanic Origin and Gender: November 1964 to Present. Internet release date: October 17, 1987. Accessed July 17, 1998. (http://www.census.gov/population/socdemo/voting/history/vot01.txt)
1998k Voting and Registration: November 1996. Internet release date: October 17, 1997. Accessed July 17, 1998. (http://www.census.gov/population/socdemo/voting/history/vot23.txt)

BURGESS, MIKE 1992 American Indian Religious Freedom Act Hearings. *News from Indian Country* (Late December), pp. 8–9.

BURNS, JOHN F. 1978 How Rules of "Petty Apartheid" Are Whittled Away. *New York Times* (June 4), pp. 1, 14.

BURRARD, ROBERT D. 1990 Ecological Inequities and the New South: Black Communities Under Siege, *Journal of Ethnic Studies* 17 (Winter), pp. 101–115.

BUTLER, JEFFREY E. 1974 Social Status, Ethnic Divisions and Political Conflict in New Nations: Afrikaners and Englishmen in South Africa. In Wendell Bell and Walter E. Freeman, eds., *Ethnicity and Nation-Building: Comparative, International and Historical Perspectives,* pp. 147–169. Beverly Hills, CA: Sage Publications.

BUTLER, JOHN SIBLEY 1996 The Return of Open Debate. *Society* 39 (March/April), pp. 11–18.

BUTLER, ROBERT N. 1990 A Disease Called Ageism. *Journal of the American Geriatrics Society* 38 (February), pp. 178–180.

BUTTERFIELD, FOX 1986 Bostonians Debating Drive to Carve Out a Black City. *New York Times* (October 12), p. 26.

CAIRNS, ED, AND DARBY, JOHN 1998 The Conflict in Northern Ireland. *American Psychologist* 56 (No. 7), pp. 754–760.

CALICA, PERRY 1995 Filipino Soldier: "We Were Abandoned." *Los Angeles Times* (February 4), p. B7.

CAMBRIDGE ECONOMIC GROUP 1998 *American Indian Gaming Policy and Its Socio-Economic Effects: A Report to the National Gambling Impact Study Commission.* Washington, DC: National Indian Gaming Association.

CARD, DAVID; DINARDO, JOHN; AND ESTES, EUGENIA 1998 The More Things Change: Immigrants and the Children of Immigrants in the 1940s, the 1970s, and the 1990s. Paper presented at the Joint Center for Poverty Research, Northwestern University of Chicago, April 9.

CARDAR, CHIARA, AND HAFFAJEE, FERIAL 1998 South Africa: Immigrants are Creating Work—Not Taking Out Jobs. *Africa News* (September 11).

CARNEGIE FOUNDATION FOR THE ADVANCEMENT OF TEACHING 1990 Native Americans and Higher Education: New Mood of Optimism. *Change* (January-February), pp. 27–30.

CARNEY, DAN 1996 As White House Calls Shots, Illegal Alien Bill Clears. *Congressional Quarterly Weekly Report* 54 (October 5), pp. 2864–2866.

CARRESE,, JOSEPH A.; AND RHODES, LORNA A. 1995 Western Bioethics on the Navajo Reservation. *Journal of American Medical Association* 274 (September 13), pp. 826–829.

CARROLL, RAYMOND 1975 An "Infamous Act" at the U.N. *Newsweek* 86 (November 24), pp. 51–54.

CARTER, DEBORAH J., AND WILSON, REGINALD 1993 *Minorities in Higher Education*. Washington, DC: American Council on Education.

CARTER, STEPHEN 1991 *Reflections of an Affirmative Action Baby*. New York: Basic Books.

CARVAJAL, DOREEN 1996 Diversity Pays Off in a Babel of Yellow Pages. *New York Times* (December 3), pp. 1, 23.

CASTAÑEDA, JORGE G. 1995 Ferocious Differences. *Atlantic Monthly* 276 (July), pp. 68–69, 71–76.
1996 A Tale of Two Islands. *Los Angeles Times* (February 12), p. B5.

CATALYST 1996 *Women in Corporate Leadership: Progress and Prospects*. New York: Catalyst.

CAUCHON, DENNIS 1991 Study Shows Bias in Sentencing Laws. *USA Today* (August 23), p. 8A.

CENTER FOR THE AMERICAN WOMAN AND POLITICS (CAWP) 1992 *Women in Elective Office, 1992*. New Brunswick, NJ: CAWP.
1994 Women State Legislators in 1995: A Tale of Two Parties. Press release.
1997 Fact Sheet. New Brunswick, NJ: CAWP.

CERAR, K. MELISSA 1995 *Teenage Refugees from Nicaragua Speak Out*. New York: Rosen Publishing.

CERT (COUNCIL OF ENERGY RESOURCE TRIBES). 1991 *15 Years*. Denver: Council of Energy Resource Tribes.

CHALFANT, H. PAUL, BECKLEY; ROBERT E.; AND PALMAR, C. EDDIE 1994 *Religion in Contemporary Society,* 3rd ed. Itasca, IL: F. E. Peacock.

CHAMPAGNE, DUANE 1994 *Native America. Portrait of the Peoples*. Detroit: Visible Ink.

CHANDLER, SUSAN 1998 Companies' Views Widely Divergent on Need for Diversity in Directors. *Chicago Tribune* (May 3), sect. 5, p. 1.

CHANES, JEROME A. 1994 Intergroup Relations. In David Singer, ed., *American Jewish Year Book, 1994,* pp. 113–152. New York: American Jewish Committee.

CHAPPELL, KEVIN 1995 Black Indians Hit Jackpot in Casino Bonanza. *Ebony* 50 (June), pp. 46–48

CHASE-DUNN, CHRISTOPHER, AND HALL, THOMAS D. 1998 World-Systems in North America: Networks, Rise and Fall and Pulsations of Trade in Stateless Systems. *American Indian Culture and Research Journal* 22 (No. 1), pp. 23–72.

CHAVEZ, LINDA 1996 The Hispanic Political Tide. *New York Times* (November 18), p. A17.

CHICAGO TRIBUNE 1993 Victors in Recall Plan to End School Busing. (December 16), p. 4.

CHIDEYA, FARAI 1993 Endangered Family. *Newsweek* 122 (August 30), pp. 16–27.

CHILDREN NOW 1998 A *Different World: Children's Perceptions of Race, Class, and the Media*. Oakland, CA: Children Now.

CHIN, KO-LIN 1996 *Chinatown Gangs: Extortion, Enterprise, and Ethnicity*. New York: Oxford University Press.

CHISWICK, BARRY R. 1992 *Immigration, Language, and Ethnicity: Canada and the United States*. Washington, DC: American Enterprise Institute Press.

CHRISTOPULOS, DIANA 1974 Puerto Rico in the Twentieth Century: A Historical Survey. In Adalberto Lopez and James Petras, eds., *Puerto Rico and Puerto Ricans: Studies in History and Society,* pp. 123–163. New York: Wiley.

CHUDACOFF, HOWARD P. 1989 *How Old Are You?* Princeton, NJ: Princeton University Press.

CICONE, MICHAEL V., AND RUBLE, DIANE N. 1978 Beliefs about Males. *Journal of Social Issues* 34 (Winter), pp. 5–16.

CLARK, KENNETH B., AND CLARK, MAMIE P. 1947 Racial Identification and Preferences in Negro Children. In Theodore M. Newcomb and Eugene L. Hartley, eds., *Readings in Social Psychology,* pp. 169–178. New York: Holt, Rinehart & Winston.

CLARY, MIKE 1997 A City That Still Is Consumed by Castro. *Los Angeles Times* (January 1), pp. A1, A26.

CLEAVER, KATHLEEN 1982 How TV Wrecked the Black Panthers. *Channels* (November-December), pp. 98–99.

CLEVELAND, HARLAN 1995 The Limits to Cultural Diversity. *Futurist* 29 (March-April), pp. 19, 22–26, 43–44.

CLIFFORD, FRANK 1998 Exploiters or Stewards of Nature? *Los Angeles Times* (January 10), pp. A1, A14.

CLINES, FRANCIS X. 1994 Dance for Joy! Come Dance a Toyi-Toyi! *New York Times* (May 11), pp. A1, A8.

CLINTON, WILLIAM J. 1994 Remarks at the United States Naval Academy Commencement Ceremony in Annapolis, Maryland. *Weekly Compilation* (May 25), pp. 1157–1162.

CODDINGTON, RON 1991 Native American Health Crisis. *USA Today* (November 12), p. 1A.

COHEN, KEN "BEAR HAWK" 1998 Witches in White Coats. *News from Indian Country* 12 (Mid March), pp. 14A, 15A.

COHEN, STEVEN M. 1988 *American Assimilation or Jewish Revival?* Bloomington: Indiana University Press.
1991 *Content or Continuity? Alternative Bases for Commitment*. New York: American Jewish Committee.

COHON, SAMUEL M. 1995 Not In Our Town. The Courage to Resist Hatred. *The Chronicle* (Issue 1995), pp. 6–9, 36, 38, 44, 48–50.

COLEMAN, JAMES S.; CAMPBELL, ERNEST Q.; HOBSON, CAROL J.; MCPARTLAND, JAMES; MOOD, ALEXANDER M.; WEINFOLD, FREDERIC D.; AND LINK, ROBERT L. 1966 *Equality of Educational Opportunity*. Washington, DC: U.S. Office of Education.

COLLETTE, LIN 1994 Encountering Holocaust Denial. *The Public Eye* 8 (September), pp. 1–15.

COMAS-DÍAZ, LILLIAN; LYKES, M. BRINTON; AND ALARCÓN, RENATO D. 1998 Ethnic Conflict and the Psychology of Liberation in Guatemala, Peru, and Puerto Rico. *American Psychologist* 53 (July), pp. 778–792.

COMER, JAMES P., AND POUSSAINT, ALVIN F. 1992 *Raising Black Children*. New York: Plume.

COMMISSION ON CIVIL RIGHTS 1972 *The Excluded Student: Educational Practices Affecting Mexican Americans in the Southwest*. Washington, DC: U.S. Government Printing Office.

1975 *Twenty Years After Brown: Equality of Economic Opportunity*. Washington, DC: U.S. Government Printing Office.

1976a *Fulfilling the Letter and Spirit of the Law: Desegregation of the Nation's Public Schools*. Washington, DC: U.S. Government Printing Office.

1976b *A Guide to Federal Laws and Regulations Prohibiting Sex Discrimination*. Washington, DC: U.S. Government Printing Office.

1977 *Window Dressing on the Set: Women and Minorities in Television*. Washington, DC: U.S. Government Printing Office.

1980a *Asian Americans: An Agenda for Action*. Washington, DC: U.S. Government Printing Office.

1980b *Characters in Textbooks: A Review of the Literature*. Washington, DC: U.S. Government Printing Office.

1980c *Success of Asian Americans: Fact or Fiction?* Washington, DC: U.S. Government Printing Office.

1981 *Affirmative Action in the 1980s: Dismantling the Process of Discrimination*. Washington, DC: U.S. Government Printing Office.

1992 *Civil Rights Issues Facing Asian Americans in the 1990s*. Washington, DC: U.S. Government Printing Office.

1995 *Briefing Paper from the U.S. Commission on Civil Rights Legislative, Executive and Judicial Development of Affirmative Action. Prepared by the Office of General Counsel, U.S. Commision oN Civil Rights*. Washington, DC: U.S. Government Printing Office.

COMMISSION ON WARTIME RELOCATION AND INTERNMENT OF CIVILIANS 1982a *Report*. Washington, DC: U.S. Government Printing Office.

1982b *Recommendations*. Washington, DC: U.S. Government Printing Office.

CONE, MARLA 1998 Sierra Club to Remain Neutral on Immigration. *Los Angeles Times* (April 26), pp. A1, A26.

CONFORTI, JOSEPH M. 1974 WASP in the Woodpile: Inequalities and Injustices of Ethnic Ecology. Paper presented at American Sociological Association Annual Meeting, Montreal.

CONGRESSIONAL QUARTERLY 1984 Democratic Party Rules, Mondale Delegates Lead. 42 (June 23), pp. 1504–1505.

CONNELLY, MARJORIE 1998 A Look at Voting Patterns of 115 Demographic Groups in House Races. *New York Times* (November 9), p. A20.

CONNOR, WALTER 1994 *Ethnonationalism: The Quest for Understanding*. Princeton, NJ: Princeton University Press.

CONOT, ROBERT 1967 *Rivers of Blood, Years of Darkness*. New York: Bantam.

CONRAT, MAISIE, AND CONRAT, RICHARD 1992 *Executive Order 9066*. Los Angeles: Los Angeles Asian American Studies Center.

CONROY, JOHN 1981 Ulster's Lost Generation. *New York Times Magazine* (August 2), pp. 16–21, 70–72, 74–75.

CONVER, BILL 1976 Group Chairman Lists Problems Endangering Jewish Family. *Peoria Journal Star* (December 4), p. A2.

CONYERS, JAMES L., JR. 1996 A Case Study of Social Stratification: An Afrocentric Edification. *Western Journal of Black Studies* 20 (Spring), pp. 9–15.

COOPER, KENNETH J. 1994 Wrong Turns on the Map? *Washington Post National Weekly Edition* 11 (February 6), pp. 14–15.

CORNACCHIA, EUGENE J., AND NELSON, DALE C. 1992 Historical Differences in the Political Experiences of American Blacks and White Ethnics: Revisiting an Unresolved Controversy. *Ethnic and Racial Studies* 15 (January), pp. 102–124.

CORNELL, STEPHEN 1984 Crisis and Response in Indian-White Relations: 1960–1984. *Social Problems* 32 (October), pp. 44–59.

1996 The Variable Ties that Bind: Content and Circumstance in Ethnic Processes. *Ethnic and Racial Studies* 19 (April), pp. 265–289.

COSE, ELLIS 1993 *The Rage of a Privileged Class*. New York: HarperCollins.

1996 Watch What They Do. *Newsweek* 128 (October 7), pp. 62–65.

COSER, LEWIS, AND COSER, ROSE LAUB 1974 *Greedy Institutions*. New York: Free Press.

COUNCIL ON SCIENTIFIC AFFAIRS 1991 Hispanic Health in the United States. *Journal of the American Medical Association* 265 (January 9), pp. 248–252.

COX, OLIVER C. 1942 The Modern Caste School of Race Relations. *Social Forces* 21 (December), pp. 218–226.

COZZETTO, DON A., AND LOROCQUE, BRENT W. 1996 Compulsive Gambling in the Indian Community: A North Dakota Case Study. *American Indian and Culture Research* 20 (No. 1), pp. 73–86.

CROSS, WILLIAM E., JR. 1991 *Shades of Black: Diversity in African-American Identity*. Philadelphia: Temple University Press.

CRULL, SUE R., AND BRUTON, BRENT T. 1985 Possible Decline in Tolerance Toward Minorities: Social Distance on a Midwest Campus. *Sociology and Social Research* 70 (October), pp. 57–62.

CULLEN, FRANCES T.; GENDREAU, PAUL; JARJOURA, G. ROGER; AND WRIGHT, JOHN PAUL 1997 Crime and the Bell Curve: Lessons from Intelligent Criminology. *Crime and Delinquency* 43 (October) pp. 387–411.

CUSHMAN, JOHN H., JR. 1998 Pollution Policy is Unfair Burden, States Tell E.P.A. *New York Times* (May 10), pp. 1, 20.

DAHLBURG, JOHN-THOR 1998 Deal Okd to End 30 Years of "Trouble" in Northern Ireland. *Los Angeles Times* (April 11), pp. A1, A8-A9.

DALEY, SUZANNE 1997 Reversing Roles in a South African Dilemma. *New York Times* (October 26), sect. WE, p. 5.
1998 A Post-Apartheid Agony: AIDS on the March. *New York Times* (July 23), pp. A1, A10.

DANIELS, ROGER 1972 *Concentration Camps, USA*. New York: Holt, Rinehart & Winston.
1990 *Coming to America*. New York: HarperCollins.

DAO, JAMES 1998 Looking Jubilant, if Bleary-Eyed, Schumer Sets His Priorities for the Senate. *New York Times* (November 5), p. B15.

DANZGER, M. HERBERT 1989 *Returning to Tradition*. New Haven: Yale University Press.

DARLING, JUANITA 1995 Cultural Rift Slows Pace of Chiapas Peace Talks. *Los Angeles Times* (April 28), p. A5.

DART, BOB 1998 Preserving America: Lancaster County, PA. *Atlanta Journal and Constitution* (June 28).

DART, JOHN 1994 A Closer Look at Islam in the West. *Los Angeles Times* (December 10), p. B4.

DAVIDSON, ROBERT C., AND LEWIS, ERNEST L. 1997 Affirmative Action and Other Special Consideration Admissions at the University of California, Davis, School of Medicine. *Journal of American Medical Association* 278 (October 8), pp. 1153–1158.

DAVIS, JAMES ALLAN, AND SMITH, TOM W. 1996 *General Social Surveys, 1972–1996: Cumulative Codebook*. Chicago: National Opinion Research Center.

DAWIDOWICZ, LUCY S. 1967 *The Golden Tradition: Jewish Life and Thought in Eastern Europe*. New York: Holt, Rinehart & Winston.
1975 *The War Against the Jews, 1933–1945*. New York: Holt, Rinehart & Winston.

DAY, JENNIFER CHESSEMAN 1996 Population Projections of the United States by Age, Sex, Race, and Hispanic Origin: 1995 to 2050. *Current Population Reports*, Ser. P–25, No. 1130. Washington, DC: U.S. Government Printing Office.

DE ANDRA, ROBERTO M. 1996 *Chicanas and Chicanos in Contemporary Society*. Boston: Allyn and Bacon.

DE BARROS, KYMBERLY, AND BENNET, CLAUDETTE 1998 The Black Population in the United States: March 1997 (Update). *Current Population Reports*, Ser. P–20–508. Washington, DC: U.S. Government Printing Office.

DE LA TORRE, ADELA 1998 Language Is a Bridge to Culture. *Los Angeles Times* (March 22), p. M5.

DEGLER, CARL N. 1969 The Negro in America—Where Myrdal Went Wrong. *New York Times Magazine* (December 7), p. 64.
1971 *Neither Black nor White: Slavery and Race Relations in Brazil and the United States*. New York: Macmillan.

DELORIA, VINE, JR. 1969 *Custer Died for Your Sins: An Indian Manifesto*. New York: Avon.
1971 *Of Utmost Good Faith*. New York: Bantam.
1992 Secularism, Civil Religion, and the Religious Freedom of American Indians. *American Indian Culture and Research Journal* 16 (No. 2), pp. 9–20.
1995 *Red Earth, White Lies*. New York: Scribner's.

———, AND LYTLE, CLIFFORD M. 1983 *American Indians, American Justice*. Austin: University of Texas Press.

DELRIOZOLEZZI, A., ET AL. 1995 The HIV AIDS Epidemic and Women in Mexico. *Salud Publica De Mexico* 37 (November-December), pp. 581–591.

D'EMILIO, JOHN 1983 *Sexual Politics, Sexual Communities*. Chicago: University of Chicago Press.

DEPALMA, ANTHONY 1995a Racism? Mexico's in Denial. *New York Times* (June 11), p. E4.
1995b For Mexico, Nafta's Promise of Jobs is Still Just a Promise. *New York Times* (October 10), pp. A1, A10.
1996 For Mexico Indians, New Voice but Few Gains. *New York Times* (January 13), pp. 1, 6.
1998 Indigenous Tribes in Canada Receive a Formal Apology. *New York Times* (January 8), pp. A1, A3.
1999 Canada's Eskimos Get a Land of their Own. *New York Times* (April 2), p.A3.

DEPARLE, JASON 1991 New Rows to Hoe in the "Harvest of Shame." *New York Times* (July 28), p. E3.

DEPARTMENT OF EDUCATION 1998 *Graduate and First-Professional Students. National Postsecondary Aid Study 1996*. Washington, DC: U.S. Government Printing Office.

DEPARTMENT OF JUSTICE 1996a *Crime in the United States, 1995*. Washington, DC: U.S. Government Printing Office.
1996b *Criminal Victimization 1994*. Washington, DC: U.S. Government Printing Office.
1997 *Crime in the United States, 1996*. Washington, DC: U.S. Government Printing Office.
1998 *Crime in the United States 1997*. Washington, DC: U.S. Government Printing Office.

DEPARTMENT OF LABOR 1965 *The Negro Family: The Case for National Action*. Washington, DC: U.S. Government Printing Office.
1980 *Perspectives on Working Women: A Databook*. Washington, DC: U.S. Government Printing Office.
1993 *Breaking the Glass Ceiling*. Washington, DC: U.S. Government Printing Office.
1995a *Good for Business: Making Full Use of the Nation's Capital*. Washington, DC: U.S. Government Printing Office.
1995b *A Solid Investment: Making Full Use of the Nation's Human Capital*. Washington, DC: U.S. Government Printing Office.

DERSHOWITZ, ALAN 1997 *The Vanishing American Jew*. Boston: Little, Brown.

DEUTSCHER, IRWIN; PESTELLO, FRED P.; AND PESTELLO, H. FRANCES 1993 *Sentiments and Acts*. New York: Aldine de Gruyter.

DE WITT, KAREN 1994 Wave of Suburban Growth Is Being Fed by Minorities. *New York Times* (August 15), pp. A1, A13.

DIAZ-VEIZADES, JEANETTE, AND CHENG, EDWARD T. 1996 Building Cross-Cultural Coalitions: A Case-Study of the Black-Korean Alliance and the Latino-Black Roundtable. *Ethnic and Racial Studies* 19 (July), pp. 680–700.

DILLON, SAM 1996 Mexico Drug Wars Advance Within Sight of U.S. Border. *New York Times* (October 10), pp. A1, A6.

DINNERSTEIN, LEONARD 1994 *Anti-Semitism in America*. New York: Oxford University Press.

DIONNE, E. J., JR. 1988 Jackson Share of Votes by Whites Triples in '88. *New York Times* (June 13), p. B7.

DISCH, ESTELLE 1997 *Reconstructing Gender: A Multicultural Anthology*. Mountain View, CA: Mayfield Publishing Company.

DOMESTIC COUNCIL COMMITTEE ON ILLEGAL ALIENS 1976 *Preliminary Report of the Domestic Council*. Washington, DC: Immigration and Naturalization Service, Department of Justice.

DOMINO, JOHN C. 1995 *Sexual Harassment and the Courts*. New York: HarperCollins.

DONOVAN, ROBERT J., AND LEVERS, SUSAN 1993 Using Paid Advertising to Modify Racial Stereotype Beliefs. *Public Opinion Quarterly* 57 (Summer), pp. 205–218.

DORNING, MIKE 1996 House Clears English-Only Measure after Emotional Debate. *Chicago Tribune* (August 2), sec. 1, p. 3.

DORSETT, ANDY 1994 America By the Numbers. *Ft. Lauderdale Sun-Sentinel* (October 30), p. 5S.

DRABELLE, DENNIS 1997 The Trade of the Tribes. *Washington Post National Weekly Edition* 14 (September 8), p. 34.

DROGIN, BOB 1995 Mandela After One Year: Public Acclaim, Private Pain. *Los Angeles Times*, (May 9), pp. 1, 4.

DUBERMAN, MARTIN 1993 *Stonewall*. New York: Dutton.

DUBLIN, THOMAS, ED. 1996 *Becoming American. Becoming Ethnic. College Students Explore Their Roots*. Philadelphia: Temple University Press.

DU BOIS, W. E. B. 1903 *The Souls of Black Folks: Essays and Sketches*. Reprinted in 1961 by New York: Facade Publications.
1939 *Black Folk: Then and Now*. New York: Holt, Rinehart & Winston.
1952 *Battle for Peace; The Story of My 83rd Birthday*. New York: Masses and Mainstream.
1961 *The Souls of Black Folk*. New York: Fawcett.
1968 *Dusk of Dawn*. New York: Schocken.
1969a *An ABC of Color*. New York: International Publications.
1969b *The Suppression of the African Slave-Trade to the United States of America, 1638–1870*. New York: Schocken.
1970 *The Negro American Family*. Cambridge: MIT Press.
1996 *The Philadelphia Negro: A Social Study*. Philadelphia: University of Pennsylvania Press (originally published in 1899).

DU BROW, RICK 1994 Portrayals of Latinos on TV Regressing. *Los Angeles Times* (September 7), p. A5.

DUFF, JOHN B. 1971 *The Irish in the United States*. Belmont, CA: Wadsworth.

DUGGER, CELIA W. 1996 A Tattered Crackdown on Illegal Workers. *New York Times* (June 3), pp. A1, B1.

DUKE, LYNNE 1996 Where a Promise Is Not a Home or even a House. *Washington Post National Weekly Edition* 13 (March 18), p. 18
1998 Where Education Is Failing the Students. *Washington Post National Weekly Edition* 15 (January 26), p. 16.

DUNCAN, GREG J., AND SMITH, KEN R. 1989 The Rising Affluence of the Elderly: How Far, How Fair, and How Frail. In W. Richard Scott and Judith Blake, eds., *Annual Review of Sociology, 1989*, pp. 261–289. Palo Alto, CA: Annual Reviews.

DUNN, ASHLEY 1994 Southeast Asians Highly Dependent on Welfare in U.S. *New York Times* (May 19), pp. A1, A20.

DURAND, JORGE; PARRADO, EMILIO A.; AND MASSEY, DOUGLAS S. 1996 Migradollars and Developments: A Reconsideration of the Mexican Case. *International Migration Review* 30 (Summer), pp. 423–444.

DURANT, THOMAS J., JR., AND LOUDEN, JOYCE S. 1986 The Black Middle Class in America: Historical and Contemporary Perspectives. *Phylon* 47 (December), pp. 253–263.

DWORKIN, ANTHONY GARY 1965 Stereotypes and Self-Images Held by Native-Born and Foreign-Born Mexican Americans. *Sociology and Social Research* 49 (January), pp. 214–224.

DYSON, MICHAEL ERIC 1995 *Making Malcolm: The Myth and Meaning of Malcolm X*. New York: Oxford University Press.

EARLY, GERALD 1994 Defining Afrocentrism. *Journal of Blacks in Higher Education* 1 (Winter), p. 46.

EDWARDS, HARRY 1970 *Black Students*. New York: Free Press.

EGAN, TIMOTHY 1998 New Prosperity Brings New Conflict to Indian Country. *New York Times* (March 8), pp. 1, 22.

EGERTON, JOHN 1971 Racism Differs in Puerto Rico. *Race Relations Reporter* 2 (July 6), pp. 6–7.

EL-BADRY, SAMIA 1994 The Arab-American Market. *American Demographics* 16 (January), pp. 22–31.

ELKINS, STANLEY 1959 *Slavery: A Problem in American Institutional and Intellectual Life*. Chicago: University of Chicago Press.

ELLIS, RICHARD N. 1972 *The Western American Indian: Case Studies in Tribal History*. Lincoln: University of Nebraska Press.

EL NASSER, HAYA 1996 Census Predicts California Will Grow 56% by 2025. *USA Today* (October 23), p. 7A.

ENG, MONICA 1998a Koreatown Crawl. *Chicago Tribune* (August 25), sect. 5, pp. 1, 5.
1998b Chinese-Americans Have Their Own Ways of Paying Respect. *Chicago Tribune* (May 28), sect. 5, pp. 1, 2.

EPSTEIN, JOSEPH 1972 Blue Collars in Cicero. *Dissent* 19 (Winter), pp. 118–127.

ERVIN, ALEXANDER M. 1987 Styles and Strategies of Leadership During the Alaskan Native Land Claims Movement: 1959–71. *Anthropologica* 39 (No. 1), pp. 21–38.

ESPIRITU, YEN LE 1992 *Asian American Panethnicity: Bridging Institutions and Identities*. Philadelphia: Temple University Press.
1996 Colonial Oppression, Labour Importation, and

Group Formation: Filipinos in the United States. *Ethnic and Racial Studies* 19 (January), pp. 29–48.
1997 *Asian American Women and Men: Labor, Laws, and Love.* Thousand Oaks, CA: Sage Publications.

FAIMAN-SILVA, SANDRA 1997 The Political Economy of "Gambling on Gambling" by States and Tribes: A Critical Comparative Perspective. Presentation at the annual meeting of the American Anthropological Association, November 19.

FARBER, M. A. 1975 Immigration Service Inquiry Ending; Results in Dispute. *New York Times* (April 27), p. 47.

FARHI, PAUL 1995 In Prime Time, It's She-TV. *Washington Post National Weekly Edition* 13 (November 20), p. 11.

FARLEY, REYNOLDS 1993 The Common Destiny of Blacks and Whites: Observations About the Social and Economic Status of the Races. In Herbert Hill and James E. Jones, Jr., eds., *Race in America: The Struggle for Equality,* pp. 197–233. Madison: University of Wisconsin Press.

FARLEY, REYNOLDS, AND ALLEN, WALTER R. 1987 *The Color Line and the Quality of Life in America.* New York: Russell Sage Foundation.

FARNSWORTH, CLYDE H. 1996 Canada's Justice System Faces Charges of Racism. *New York Times* (January 28), p. 3.

FARR, D. M. L. 1993 Canada. In *1993 Britannica Book of the Year,* pp. 463–465. Chicago: Encyclopaedia Britannica.

FARRELL, WARREN T. 1974 *The Liberated Man.* New York: Random House.

FEAGIN, JOE R. AND VERA, HERNAN 1995 *White Racism: The Basics.* New York: Routledge.

FEARS, DARRYL 1998 Koreatown Tolerance Is Model of Promise. *Los Angeles Times* (September 21), pp. A1, A16.

FEIN, ESTHER B. 1996 Companies are Biased Against Older Workers. In Charles P. Cozic, ed., *An Aging Population: Opposing Viewpoints,* pp. 188–199. San Diego, CA: Greenhaven Press.

FELDMANN, LINDA 1998 For Hmong Farmers, Help Wilts. *Christian Science Monitor* (May 21), p. 1.

FELDSTAR, STANLEY, AND COSTELLO, LAURENCE, EDS. 1974 *The Ordeal of Assimilation.* Garden City, NY: Anchor Books.

FERMI, LAURA 1971 *Illustrious Immigrants,* rev. ed. Chicago: University of Chicago Press.

FIELDS, GARY, AND PRICE, RICHARD 1990 Church Arsons: One Year Later. *USA Today* (December 23), pp. A1-A2

FINDER, ALAN 1994 Muslim Gave Racist Speech, Jackson Says. *New York Times* (January 23), p. 21.
1995 Despite Tough Laws, Sweatshops Flourish. *New York Times* (February 6), pp. A1, B4.

FINE, MICHELLE, AND ASCH, ADRIENNE 1981 Disabled Women: Sexism without the Pedestal. *Journal of Sociology and Social Welfare* 8 (July), pp. 233–248.
1988a *Women with Disabilities: Essays in Psychology, Culture, and Politics.* Philadelphia: Temple University Press.
1988b Disability Beyond Stigma: Social Interaction, Discrimination, and Activism. *Journal of Social Issues* 44 (No. 1), pp. 3–21.

FINESTEIN, ISRAEL 1988 The Future of American Jewry. *The Jewish Journal of Sociology* 30 (December), pp. 121–125.

FING, JING; MADHAVAN, SHANTHA; AND ALDERMAN, MICHAEL H. 1996 The Association between Birthplace and Mortality from Cardiovascular Causes among Black and White Residents of New York City. *New England Journal of Medicine* 335 (November 21), pp. 1545–1551.

FISHMAN, JOSHUA A.; HAYDEN, ROBERT G.; AND WARSHAVER, MARY E. 1966 The Non-English and the Ethnic Group Press, 1910–1960. In Joshua A. Fishman, ed., *Language Loyalty in the United States,* pp. 51–74. London and The Hague: Mouton.

FISKE, EDWARD B. 1988a Colleges Are Seeking to Remedy Lag in Their Hispanic Enrollment. *New York Times* (March 20), pp. 8, 16.
1988b The Undergraduate Hispanic Experience. *Change* (May-June), pp. 28–33.

FIXICO, DONALD L. 1988 The Federal Policy of Termination and Relocation, 1945–1960. In Phillip Weeks, ed., *The American Indian Experience,* pp. 260–277. Arlington Heights, IL: Forum Press.

FLEXNER, ELEANOR 1959 *Century of Struggle: The Women's Rights Movement in the United States.* Cambridge: Harvard University Press.

FLORES, WILLIAM V., AND BENMAYER, RINA, EDS. 1997 *Latino Cultural Citizenship: Claiming Identity, Space, and Rights.* Boston: Beacon Press.

FOLKHART, BART A. 1995 Maggie Kuhn, 89; Iconoclastic Founder of Gray Panthers. *Los Angeles Times* (April 23), p. A34.

FONG, ERIC 1997 A Systematic Approach to Racial Residential Patterns. *Social Science Research* 26, pp. 465–486.

FONG, STANLEY L. M. 1965 Assimilation of Chinese in America: Changes in Orientation and Perception. *American Journal of Sociology* 71 (November), pp. 265–273.

FONG, TIMOTHY P. 1994 *The First Suburban Chinatown.* Philadelphia: Temple University Press.

FORD, W. SCOTT 1986 Favorable Intergroup Contact May Not Reduce Prejudice: Inconclusive Journal Evidence, 1960–1984. *Sociology and Social Research* 70 (July), pp. 256–258.

FOUNTAIN, MONICA 1996 Not the Retiring Type. *Chicago Tribune* (April 14), sect. B, p. 6.

FOX, JIM 1994 Election Stirs Talk (in English and French) of Independence. *USA Today* (August 8), p. 4A.
1995 Tutsi, Hutu Alike Try to Rebuild Life. *USA Today* (January 6), p. 6A.

FOX, STEPHEN 1990 *The Unknown Internment.* Boston: Twayne.

FRANKEL, BRUCE 1995a N.Y.'s "Jewish Rosa Parks" Wins Bus Battle. *USA Today* (March 17), p. 4A.
1995b D'Amato Owns Up to "Sorry Episode." *USA Today* (April 7), p. 2A.

FRANKLIN, JOHN HOPE, AND MOSS, ALFRED A., JR. 1994 *From Slavery to Freedom,* 7th ed. New York: McGraw-Hill.

FRAZIER, E. FRANKLIN 1957 *Black Bourgeoisie: The Rise of a New Middle Class.* New York: Free Press.

1964 *The Negro Church in America.* New York: Schocken.

FREDRICKSON, GEORGE M. 1981 *White Supremacy: A Comparative Study in American and South African History.* New York: Oxford University Press.

FREEMAN, JAMES M. 1995 *Changing Identities: Vietnamese Americans, 1975–1995.* Boston: Allyn and Bacon.

FREEMAN, JO 1973 The Origins of the Women's Liberation Movement. *American Journal of Sociology* 78 (January), pp. 792–811.
1975 *The Politics of Women's Liberation.* New York: David McKay.
1983 On the Origins of Social Movements. In Jo Freeman, ed., *Social Movements of the Sixties and Seventies,* pp. 1–30. New York: Longman.

FREY, WILLIAM H. 1998 *Black Movement to the South, and Regional Concentration of the Races.* Report No. 98–412. Ann Arbor, MI: Population Studies Center, University of Michigan.

FRIEDAN, BETTY 1963 *The Feminine Mystique.* New York: Dell.
1981 *The Second Stage.* New York: Summit Books.
1991 Back to the Feminine Mystique? *The Humanist* 51 (January-February), pp. 26–27.

FRIENDS COMMITTEE ON NATIONAL LEGISLATION 1993 American Indian Religious Freedom. *News from Indian Country* (Mid-February), p. 8.

FUCHS, ESTELLE, AND HAVIGHURST, ROBERT J. 1972 *To Live on This Earth: American Indian Education.* Garden City, NY: Doubleday.

FULTON, E. KAYE 1992 Drumbeats of Rage. *Macleans* (March 16), pp. 14–17.

FULWOOD, SAM, III 1994 A Dilemma for Black Women. *Los Angeles Times* (August 27), pp. A1, A26.

GABACCIA, DONNA R. 1998 *We Are What We Eat: Ethnic Food and the Making of America.* Cambridge, MA: Harvard University Press.

GABLE, DONNA 1993 In Search of Prime-Time Faith. *USA Today* (July 12), p. 3D.

GALARZA, ERNESTO 1964 *Merchants of Labor: The Mexican Bracero Story.* Santa Barbara, CA: McNally & Loften.

GALLO, RICHARD J. 1998 Testimony before United States Senate, Committee on the Judiciary, Subcommittee on Immigration, July 29.

GALLUP, ALEC, AND MOORE, DAVID W. 1995 Americans Favor Constitutional Amendment to Permit Spoken Prayer in Schools. *Gallup Poll* 358 (July), pp. 14–16.

GALLUP ORGANIZATION 1997a *Black/White Relations in the U.S.* Princeton, NJ: Gallup Organization.
1997b *1997 Survey: The People's Republic of China Consumer Attitudes and Lifestyle Trends.* (http://www.gallup.com/Special_Reports/china.htm)
1998 Special Reports. *Black/White Relations in the U.S.* Full Report. June 10, 1997. Accessed on July 8, 1998 (http://www.gallup.com/Special_Reports/black-white.htm)

GALLUP POLL MONTHLY 1995 Gallup Short Subjects. 363 (December), pp. 38–48.
1998 Brief Questions. 388 (January), pp. 37–42.

GAMBINO, RICHARD 1974a *Blood of My Blood.* Garden City, NY: Doubleday.
1974b The Italian Americans. *Chicago Tribune Magazine* (May 5), pp. 56–58.

GANS, HERBERT J. 1956 American Jewry: Present and Future. *Commentary* 21 (May), pp. 424–425.
1979 Symbolic Ethnicity: The Future of Ethnic Groups and Cultures in America. *Ethnic and Racial Studies* 2 (January), pp. 1–20.
1995 *The War against the Poor: The Underclass and Antipoverty Policy.* New York: Basic Books.

GARFINKEL, HERBERT 1959 *When Negroes March.* New York: Atheneum.

GARNER, ROBERTA 1996 *Contemporary Movements and Ideologies.* New York: McGraw-Hill.

GARROD, ANDREW, AND LARIMORE, COLLEEN, EDS. 1997 *First Person First Peoples: Native American College Graduates Tell Their Life Stories.* Ithaca, NY: Cornell University Press.

GARTNER, ALAN, AND JOE, TOM, EDS. 1987 *Images of the Disabled, Disabled Images.* New York: Praeger.

GARY, LAWRENCE E.; BEATTY, LULA A.; BERRY, GRETA L.; AND PRICE, MARY D. 1983 *Stable Black Families: Final Report.* Washington, DC: Institute for Urban Affairs and Research, Howard University.

GARZA, MELITA MARIE 1995 Bilingual Bill Called Unconstitutional. *Chicago Tribune* (February 7), sect. 2, p. 4.

GATES, HENRY LOUIS, JR. 1989 TV's Black World Turns—But Stays Unreal. *New York Times* (November 12), sect. 2, pp. 1, 40.

GEDICKS, AL 1993 *The New Resource Wars.* Boston: South End Press.

GERASSI, JOHN 1966 *The Boys of Boise.* New York: Macmillan.

GERBER, DAVID A. 1993 *Nativism, Anti-Catholicism, and Anti-Semitism.* New York: Scribner's.

GIAGO, TIM 1998 Honor Another Race of People as Mascots. *News From Indian Country* (April 13).

GERTH, H. H., AND MILLS, C. WRIGHT 1958 *From Max Weber: Essays in Sociology.* New York: Galaxy Books.

GIBBONS, TOM 1985 Justice Not Equal for Poor Here. *Chicago Sun-Times* (February 24), pp. 1, 18.

GILENS, MARTIN 1996 "Race Coding" and White Opposition to Welfare. *American Political Science Review* 90 (September), pp. 593–604.

GILES, MICHAEL W.; GATLIN, DOUGLAS S.; AND CATALDO, EVERETTE F. 1976 Racial and Class Prejudice: Their Relative Effects on Protest Against School Desegregation. *American Sociological Review* 41 (April), pp. 280–288.

GITTLER, JOSEPH B., ED. 1981 *Jewish Life in the United States: Perspectives from the Social Sciences.* New York: New York University Press.

GLADWELL, MALCOLM 1996 Discrimination: It's Just a Bus Stop Away. *Washington Post National Weekly Edition* 13 (February 19), p. 33.

GLANCY, DIANE 1998 When the Boats Arrived. Hungry Mind Review. *The National Book Magazine* (Spring), p. 7.

GLASER, JAMES M., AND GILENS, MARTIN 1997 Interregional Migration and Political Resocialization: A Study of

Racial Attitudes under Pressure. *Public Opinion Quarterly* 61 (Spring), pp. 72–86.

GLAZER, NATHAN 1971 The Issue of Cultural Pluralism in America Today. In *Pluralism Beyond Frontier: Report of the San Francisco Consultation on Ethnicity,* pp. 2–8. San Francisco: American Jewish Committee.
1990 American Jewry or American Judaism? *Society* 28 (November-December), pp. 14–20.

GLAZER, NATHAN, AND MOYNIHAN, DANIEL PATRICK 1963 *Beyond the Melting Pot: The Negroes, Puerto Ricans, Jews, Italians, and Irish of New York City.* Cambridge: MIT Press.
1970 *Beyond the Melting Pot: The Negroes, Puerto Ricans, Jews, Italians, and Irish of New York City.* 2d ed. Cambridge: MIT Press.

GLEASON, PHILIP 1980 American Identity and Americanization. In Stephen Therstromm, ed., *Harvard Encyclopedia of American Ethnic Groups,* pp. 31–58. Cambridge: Belknap Press of Harvard University Press.

GLEDHILL, RUTH 1992 Losing the Chosen Race. *The Times (London) Saturday Review* (November 14), pp. 10–12.

GLOCK, CHARLES Y.; WUTHNOW, ROBERT; PILIAVIN, JANE ALLYN; AND SPENCER, METTA 1975 *Adolescent Prejudice.* New York: Harper & Row.

GOERING, JOHN M. 1971 The Emergence of Ethnic Interests: A Case of Serendipity. *Social Forces* 48 (March), pp. 379–384.

GOFFMAN, ERVING 1963 *Stigma: Notes on Management of Spoiled Identity.* Englewood Cliffs, NJ: Prentice-Hall.

GOLD, MICHAEL 1965 *Jews Without Money.* New York: Avon.

GOLD, STEVEN J. 1988 New Immigrant Organizations and Old Country Links: The Case of Soviet Jews in the U.S. Paper presented at the Annual Meeting of the American Sociological Association, Atlanta.

GOLDBERG, CAREY 1998 Maine Voters Repeal a Law on Gay Rights. *New York Times* (February 12), pp. A1, A16.

———, AND ELDER, JANET 1998 Public Still Backs Abortion, But Wants Limits, Poll Says. *New York Times* (January 16), p. A1.

GOLDSTEIN, SIDNEY 1981 Jews in the United States: Perspectives from Demography. In Joseph B. Gittler, ed., *Jewish Life in the United States,* pp. 31–102. New York: New York University Press.

———, AND GOLDSCHEIDER, CALVIN 1968 *Jewish Americans: Three Generations in a Jewish Community.* Englewood Cliffs, NJ: Prentice-Hall.

———, AND GOLDSTEIN, ALICE 1996 *Jews on the Move: Implications for Jewish Identity.* Albany, NY: State Unversity of New York Press. GOLEMAN, DANIEL
1990 As Bias Crime Seems to Rise, Scientists Study Roots of Racism. *New York Times* (May 29), p. C1.

GOMEZ, DAVID F. 1971 Chicanos: Strangers in Their Own Land. *America* 124 (June 26), pp. 649–652.

GOMPERS, SAMUEL, AND GUSTADT, HERMAN 1908 *Meat vs. Rice: American Manhood Against Asiatic Coolieism: Which Shall Survive?* San Francisco: Asiatic Exclusion League.

GONZALEZ, DAVID 1992 What's the Problem with "Hispanic"? Just Ask a "Latino." *New York Times* (November 15), p. E6.

GOODING, CAROLINE 1994 *Disabling Laws, Enabling Acts: Disability Rights in Britain and America.* Boulder, CO: Westview.

GOODSTEIN, LAURIE 1997 Has Television Found Religion? Not Exactly! *New York Times* (November 30), sect. AR, pp. 37, 43.

GOOZNER, MERRILL 1987 Age-old Tradition Bankrolls Koreans. *Chicago Tribune* (July 19), sect. 7, pp. 1–2.
1997 High Price of Success. *Chicago Tribune* (September 22), pp. 1, 10.

GORDAN, ANTHONY, AND HOROWITZ, RICHARD M. 1997 Will Your Grandchildren Be Jewish. Unpub. research based on a 1990 National Jewish Population Survey and the 1991 New York Jewish Population Study.

GORDAN, MICHAEL R. 1998 Black U.S. Marine Assaulted in Wave of Racism in Moscow. *New York Times* (May 5), p. A5.

GORDON, MILTON M. 1964 *Assimilation in American Life: The Role of Race, Religion, and National Origins.* New York: Oxford University Press.
1978 *Human Nature, Class, and Ethnicity.* New York: Oxford University Press.
1996 Liberal versus Corporate Pluralism. *Society* 33 (March/April), pp. 37–40.

GORDON, WENDELL 1975 A CASE FOR A LESS RESTRICTIVE BORDER POLICY. *SOCIAL SCIENCE QUARTERLY* 56 (DECEMBER), PP. 485–491.

GORNICK, MARIAN S., ET AL. 1996 Effects of Race and Income on Mortality and Use of Services among Medicare Beneficiaries. *New England Journal of Medicine* 335 (September 12), pp. 791–799.

GOULDNER, ALVIN 1970 *The Coming Crisis in Western Sociology.* New York: Basic Books.

GOVE, WALTER R. 1980 *The Labelling of Deviance,* 2d ed. Beverly Hills, CA: Sage Publications.

GRAHAM, LAWRENCE OTIS 1995 *Member of the Club: Reflections on Life in a Racially Polarized World.* New York: HarperCollins.

GRAHAM, WADE 1996 Masters of the Game: How the U.S. Protects the Traffic in Cheap Mexican Labor. *Harper's* 293 (July), pp. 35–50.

GRANT, NEIL, AND MIDDLETON, NICK 1987 *Atlas of the World Today.* New York: Harper & Row.

GREELEY, ANDREW M. 1974a *Ethnicity in the United States: A Preliminary Reconnaissance.* New York: Wiley.
1974b Political Participation among Ethnic Groups in the United States: A Preliminary Reconnaissance. *American Journal of Sociology* 80 (July), pp. 170–204.
1977 *The American Catholic.* New York: Basic Books.

GREENBERG, JAN CRAWFORD 1998 Roe vs. Wade at 25: America's Great Divide. *Chicago Tribune* (January 19), pp., 1, 16.

GREENBERG, JOEL 1996 Orthodoxy and Politics Mix in Israel. *New York Times* (June 14), p. A5.

GREENHOUSE, LINDA 1989 Court Bars a Plan Set up to Provide Jobs to Minorities. *New York Times* (January 24), pp. A1, A19.
1993a Court, Citing Religious Freedom, Voids a Ban on Animal Sacrifice. *New York Times* (June 12), pp. 1, 8.
1993b High Court Backs Policy of Halting Haitian

Refugees. *New York Times* (June 22), pp. 1, 8.
1996a Justices Say Age Bias Can Occur Even When One Over–40 Worker Replaces Another. *New York Times* (April 2), p. A14.
1996b Case on Government Interface in Religion Tied to Separation of Powers. *New York Times* (October 16), p. C23.

GREENHOUSE, STEVEN 1998a Equal Work, Less-Equal Perks. *New York Times* (March 30), p. 1.
1998b As Economy Booms, Migrant Workers' Housing Worsens. *New York Times* (May 31), pp. A1, A16.

GRIEGO, MANUEL GARCIA Y, AND JIMÉNEZ, ANDRÉS E. 1998 Making the Farm Worker's Life Even Harder. *Los Angeles Times* (October 10), p. A27.

GRIMSHAW, ALLEN D., ED. 1969 *Racial Violence in the United States*. Chicago: Aldine.

GROSS, JANE 1989 Diversity Hinders Asians' Power in U.S. *New York Times* (June 25), p. A22.

GROVE, DAVID JOHN 1974 *The Race vs. Ethnic Debate: A Cross-National Analysis of Two Theoretical Approaches*. Denver: University of Denver Press.

GWERTZMAN, BERNARD 1985 The Debt to the Indochinese Is Becoming a Fiscal Drain. *New York Times* (March 3), p. E3.

HAAK, GERALD O. 1970 Co-opting the Oppressors: The Case of the Japanese-Americans. *Society* 7 (October), pp. 23–31.

HACKER, ANDREW 1994 White on White. *The New Republic* 211 (October 31), pp. 12–13.
1995 *Two Nations: Black and White, Separate, Hostile, and Unequal*, exp. and updated ed. New York: Ballantine.

HACKER, HELEN MAYER 1951 Women as a Minority Group. *Social Forces* 30 (October), pp. 60–69.
1974 Women as a Minority Group: Twenty Years Later. In Florence Denmark, ed., *Who Discriminates Against Women*, pp. 124–134. Beverly Hills, CA: Sage Publications.

HAGAN, WILLIAM T. 1961 *American Indians*. Chicago: University of Chicago Press.

HALPERN, BEN 1974 America Is Different. In Marshall Sklare, ed., *The Jew in American Society*, pp. 67–89. New York: Behrman House.

HANDLIN, OSCAR 1951 *The Uprooted: The Epic Story of the Great Migrations That Made the American People*. New York: Grossett & Dunlap.
1957 *Race and Nationality in American Life*. Boston: Little, Brown.

HANSEN, KRISTEN A., AND BACHU, AMARV 1995 The Foreign-Born Population: 1994. *Current Population Reports*, Ser. P–20, No. 486. Washington, DC: U.S. Government Printing Office.

HANSEN, MARCUS LEE 1952 The Third Generation in America. *Commentary* 14 (November), pp. 493–500.

HARLAN, LOUIS R. 1972 *Booker T. Washington: The Making of a Black Leader*. New York: Oxford University Press.

HARRAH'S ENTERTAINMENT 1996 *Harrah Survey of Casino Entertainment*. Memphis, TN: Harrah's Entertainment.

HARRIS, DAVID A. 1987 Japan and the Jews. *Morning Freiheit* (November 8), pp. 1, 3.

HARVARD LAW REVIEW 1995 Unenforced Boundaries: Illegal Immigration and the Limits of Judicial Federalism. 108 (May), pp. 1643–1660.

HATCHETT, SHIRLEY J.; COCHRAN, DONNA L.; AND JACKSON, JAMES S. 1991 Family Life. In James S. Jackson, ed., *Life in Black America*, pp. 46–83. Newbury Park, CA: Sage Publications.

HAWAII 1994 *Vital Statistics Supplement 1991–1992*. Honolulu: Department of Health, State of Hawaii.

HAWKINS, HUGH 1962 *Booker T. Washington and His Critics: The Problem of Negro Leadership*. Boston: Heath.

HAYS, KRISTEN L. 1994 Topeka Comes Full Circle. *Modern Maturity* (April-May), p. 34.

HEALTH CARE FINANCING ADMINISTRATION 1995 *Monitoring the Impact of Medicare Physician Payment Reform on Utilization and Access: Summary Report*. Washington, DC: HCFA.

HECHINGER, FRED M. 1987 Bilingual Programs. *New York Times* (April 7), p. C10.

HEER, DAVID M., AND GROSSBARD-SHECTMAN, AMGRA 1981 The Impact of the Female Marriage Squeeze and the Contraceptive Revolution on Sex Roles and the Women's Liberation Movement in the United States, 1960 to 1975. *Journal of Marriage and the Family* 43 (February), pp. 49–76.

HEILMAN, SAMUEL C. 1982 The Sociology of American Jewry: The Last Ten Years. In Ralph H. Turner, ed., *Annual Review of Sociology, 1982*, pp. 135–160. Palo Alto, CA: Annual Reviews.

HEMLOCK, DOREEN A. 1996 Puerto Rico Loses Its Edge. *New York Times* (September 21), pp. 17, 30.

HENNEBERGER, MELINDA 1995 Muslims Continue to Feel Apprehensive. *New York Times* (April 14), p. B10.

HENRY, WILLIAM A., III 1994 Pride and Prejudice. *Time* 143 (February 28), pp. 21–27.

HENTOFF, NICHOLAS 1984 Dennis Banks and the Road Block to Indian Ground. *Village Voice* 29 (October), pp. 19–23.

HERBERG, WILL 1983 *Protestant-Catholic-Jew: An Essay in American Religious Sociology*, rev. ed. Chicago: University of Chicago Press.

HERO, RODNEY 1995 *Latinos and U.S. Politics*. New York: HarperCollins.

HERRING, CEDRIC, AND AMISSAH, CHARLES 1997 Advance and Retreat: Racially Based Attitudes and Public Policy. In Steven A. Tuch and Jack K. Martin, eds., *Racial Attitudes in the 1990s: Continuity and Change*, pp. 121–143. Westport, CT: Praeger.

HERRNSTEIN, RICHARD J., AND MURRAY, CHARLES 1994 *The Bell Curve: Intelligence and Class Structure in American Life*. New York: Free Press.

HERSKOVITS, MELVILLE J. 1930 *The Anthropometry of the American Negro*. New York: Columbia University Press.
1941 *The Myth of the Negro Past*. New York: Harper.

HEVRDEJS, JUDY, AND CONKLIN, MIKE 1995 Bradley May Wish Top of the Mornin' to Sinn Fein Leader. *Chicago Tribune* (May 16), p. 22.

HEWITT, PAUL S., AND HOWE, NEIL 1988 Future of Generational Politics. *Generations* (Spring), pp. 10–13.

HEYCK, DENIS LYNN DALY 1994 *Barrios and Borderlands: Cultures of Latinos and Latinas in the United States.* New York: Routledge.

HIGHAM, JOHN 1966 American Anti-Semitism Historically Reconsidered. In Charles Herbert Stember, ed., *Jews in the Mind of America,* pp. 237–258. New York: Basic Books.

HILL, HERBERT 1967 The Racial Practices of Organized Labor—The Age of Gompers and After. In Arthur M. Ross and Herbert Hill, eds., *Employment, Race, and Poverty,* pp. 365–402. New York: Harcourt, Brace & World.

HILL, KENT A., AND MORENO, DAVID 1996 Second-Generation Cubans. *Hispanic Journal of Behavior Sciences* 18 (May), pp. 175–193.

HILL, ROBERT B. 1972 *The Strengths of Black Families.* New York: Emerson Hall.
1987 The Future of Black Families. *Colloqui* (Spring), pp. 22–28.

HILLEBRAND, BARBARA 1992 Midlife Crisis. *Chicago Tribune* (May 10), sect. 6, pp. 1, 11.

HIMMELFARB, HAROLD S. 1982 Research on American Jewish Identity and Identification: Progress, Pitfalls, and Prospects. In Marshall Sklare, ed., *Understanding American Jewry,* pp. 56–95. New Brunswick, NJ: Transaction Books.

HIRSCHFELDER, ARLENE, AND MOLIN, PAULETTE 1992 *The Encyclopedia of Native American Religions.* New York: MJF Books.

HIRSCHMAN, CHARLES 1983 America's Melting Pot Reconsidered. In Ralph H. Turner, ed., *Annual Review of Sociology 1983,* pp. 397–423. Palo Alto, CA: Annual Reviews.

HIRSLEY, MICHAEL 1991 Religious Display Needs Firm Court. *Chicago Tribune* (December 20), sect. 2, p. 10.

HOCHSCHILD, ARLIE RUSSELL 1997a *Time Bind: When Work Becomes Home and Home Becomes Work.* New York: Metropolitan Books, Henry Holt.
1997b Time for Change. *Ms.* 8 (September/October), pp. 39–40.

HOCHSCHILD, ARLIE, WITH MACHUNG, ANNE 1989 *The Second Shift.* New York: Viking.
1990 The Second Shift: Employed Women Are Putting in Another Day of Work at Home. *Utne Reader* 38 (March-April), pp. 66–73.

HOLFORD, DAVID M. 1975 The Subversion of the Indian Land Allotment System, 1887–1934. *Indian Historian* 8 (Spring), pp. 11–21.

HOLMBERG, DAVID 1974 Pekin Isn't Ready to Give up "Chinks." *Chicago Tribune* (July 28), p. 24.

HOLMES, STEVEN A. 1996a Anti-Immigrant Mood Moves Asians to Organize. *New York Times* (January 3), pp. A1, A11.
1996b Education Gap Between Races Closes. *New York Times* (September 6), p. A8.

HONEY, MARTHA 1994 Mexico's Open Secret: Illegal Abortions. *The Nation* 259 (September 26), p. 312.

HOOKS, BELL 1994 Black Students Who Reject Feminism. *Chronicle of Higher Education* 60 (July 13), p. A44.

HORNBLUM, ALLEN M. 1998 *Acres of Slum: Human Experiments at Holmesby Prison.* New York: Routledge.

HORTON, JOHN 1966 Order and Conflict Theories of Social Problems as Competing Ideologies. *American Journal of Sociology* 71 (May), pp. 701–713.

———, WITH CALDERON, JOSE; PRADO, MARY; SAITO, LELAND; SHAW, LINDA; AND TSENG, YEN-FEN 1996 *The Politics of Diversity: Immigration, Resistance, and Change in Monterey Park, California.* Philadelphia: Temple University Press.

HOSOKAWA, BILL 1969 *Nisei: The Quiet Americans.* New York: Morrow.

HUBBARD, AMY S. 1993 U.S. Jewish Community Responses to the Changing Strategy of the Palestinian Nationalist Movement: A Pilot Study. Paper presented at the Annual Meeting of the Eastern Sociological Society, Boston.

HUDGINS, JOHN L. 1992 The Strengths of Black Families Revisited. *The Urban League Review* 15 (Winter), pp. 9–20.

HUFKER, BRIAN, AND CAVENDER, GRAY 1990 From Freedom Flotilla to America's Burden: The Social Construction of the Mariel Immigrants. *Sociological Quarterly* 31 (No. 2), pp. 321–335.

HUGHES, MICHAEL 1998 Symbolic Racism, Old-Fashioned Racism, and Whites' Opposition to Affirmative Action. In Steven A. Tuch and Jack K. Martin, eds., *Racial Attitudes in the 1990s: Continuity and Change,* pp. 45–75. Westport, CT: Praeger.

———, AND DEMO, DAVID H. 1989 Self-Perceptions of Black Americans: Self-Esteem and Personal Efficacy. *American Journal of Sociology* 95 (July), pp. 132–159.

HUMPHREYS, LAUD 1972 *Out of the Closets.* Englewood Cliffs, NJ: Prentice-Hall.

HURH, WON MOO 1990 The "1.5 Generation": A Paragon of Korean American Pluralism. *Korean Culture* 4 (Spring), pp. 21–31.
1994 Majority Americans' Perception of Koreans in the United States: Implications of Ethnic Images and Stereotypes. In H. Kwon, ed., *Korean Americans: Conflict and Harmony,* pp. 3–21. Chicago: Center for Korean Studies.
1998 The Korean Americans. Westport, CT: Greenwood Press.

HURH, WON MOO, AND KIM, KWANG CHUNG 1982 Race Relations Paradigms and Korean American Research: A Sociology of Knowledge Perspective. In E. Yu, E. Phillips, and E. Yang, eds., *Koreans in Los Angeles,* pp. 219–255. Los Angeles: Center for Korean American and Korean Studies, California State University.
1984 *Korean Immigrants in America: A Structural Analysis of Ethnic Confinement and Adhesive Adaptation.* Cranbury, NJ: Fairleigh Dickinson University Press.
1988 *Uprooting and Adjustment: A Sociological Study of Korean Immigrants' Mental Health.* Final Report submitted to National Institute of Mental Health. Macomb, IL: Western Illinois University.
1989 The "Success" Image of Asian Americans: Its Validity, and Its Practical and Theoretical Implications. *Ethnic and Racial Studies* 12 (October), pp. 512–538.

HUTCHINSON, EARL OFARI 1995 Racial Myths Reinforce White Fears. *Los Angeles Times* (October 22), p. M5.

IGNATIEV, NOEL 1994 Treason to Whiteness Is Loyalty to Humanity. Linterview with Noel Ignatiev. *Utne Reader* (November/December), pp. 83–86.
1995 *How the Irish Became White*. New York: Routledge.

IMMIGRATION AND NATURALIZATION SERVICE 1997 *1996 Statistical Yearbook of the Immigration and Naturalization Service*. Washington, DC: U.S. Government Printing Office.

INDIAN HEALTH SERVICE 1995 *Trends in Indian Health 1995*. Washington, DC: Indian Health Service.

INOUE, MIYAKO 1989 Japanese Americans in St. Louis: From Internees to Professionals. *City and Society* 3 (December), pp. 142–152.

INTER-PARLIAMENTARY UNION 1998 Women in National Parliaments. Situation as of 10 July 1998. Accessed July 13, 1998. (www.ipu.org/wmn-e/classif.htm)

ISHKANIAN, RAFFI 1996 Roots. Paper in Thomas Dublin, ed., *Becoming American Becoming Ethnic: College Students Explore Their Roots*, pp. 75–81. Philadelphia: Temple University Press.

IVERSON, PETER 1993 American Indian of the West. In Mary Kupiec Clayton, Elliot J. Gorn, and Peter W. Williams, eds., *Encyclopedia of American Social History*, pp. 667–680. New York: Scribner's.

JACOBS, JAMES B., AND POTTER, KIMBERLY 1998 Proposed Hate Crimes Bill Isn't Needed. *Los Angeles Times* (July 27), p. B5.

JACOBS, JERRY A. 1990 *Revolving Doors: Sex Segregation in Women's Careers*. Palo Alto, CA: Stanford University Press.

JAHER, FREDERIC CAPLE 1994 *A Scapegoat in the New Wilderness*. Cambridge: Harvard University Press.

JAIMES, M. ANNETTE 1992 *The State of Native America*. Boston: South End Press.

JAIN, ANJU, AND BELSKY, JAY 1997 Fathering and Acculturation: Immigrant Indian Families with young Children. *Journal of Marriage and the Family* 59 (November), pp. 873–883.

JAMES, KEITH, ET AL. 1995 School Achievement and Dropout among Anglo and Indian Females and Males: A Comparative Examination. *American Indian Culture and Research Journal* 19 (No. 3), pp. 181–206.

JENCKS, CHRISTOPHER, AND PHILLIPS, MEREDITH, EDS. 1998 *The Black-White Test Score Gap*. Washington, DC: Brookings Institution.

JENNESS, VALERIE 1995a Hate Crimes in the United States: The Transformation of Injured Persons into Victims and the Extension of Victim Status to Multiple Constituencies. In Joel Best, ed., *Images of Issues: Typifying Contemporary Social Problems*, 2d ed., pp. 213–237. New York: Aldine de Gruyter.
1995b Social Movement Growth, Domain Expansion, and Framing Process: The Gay/Lesbian Movement and Violence Against Gays and Lesbians as a Social Problem. *Social Problems* 42 (February), pp. 145–170.

———, AND BROAD, KENDAL 1994 Antiviolence Activities and the (In)visibility of Gender in the Gay/Lesbian and Women's Movements. *Gender and Society* 8 (September), pp. 402–423.

JENSEN, JOAN M. 1980 East Indians. In Stephen Thernstrom, ed., *Harvard Encyclopedia of American Ethnic Groups*, pp. 296–301. Cambridge: Belknap Press of Harvard University Press.

JETER, JON 1997 Death and Despair on the Reservation. *Washington Post National Weekly Edition* 15 (December 22), pp. 31–32.

JOHNSON, DIRK 1996 Gay-Rights Movement Ventures beyond Urban America. *New York Times* (January 21), p. 12.

JOHNSON, GEORGE 1987 The Infamous "Protocols of Zion" Endures. *New York Times* (July 26), p. E6.
1996 Indian Tribers' Creationists Thwart Archaeologists. *New York Times* (October 22), p. 1.

JOHNSON, KEVIN 1992 German Ancestry Is Strong Beneath Milwaukee Surface. *USA Today* (August 4), p. 9A.

JOHNSON, TROY R. 1996 Roots of Contemporary Native American Activism. *American Indian Culture and Research Journal* 20 (No. 2), pp. 127–154.

JOINT CENTER FOR POLITICAL STUDIES 1996 Affirmative Action Myths and Realities. *Focus* 24 (August), pp. 7–8.
1997 National Roster of Black Elected Officials, data; Washington, DC.

JOLIDON, LAURENCE 1991 Battle Builds over Indians' Fishing Rights. *USA Today* (March 21), pp. 1A–2A.

JONES, CHARISSE 1997 A World of Students. *USA Today* (September 24), pp. A1-A2.

JONES, JAMES M. 1972 *Prejudice and Racism*. Reading, MA: Addison-Wesley.

JONES-CARREA, MICHAEL 1998 *Between Two Nations: The Political Predicament of Latinos in New York City*. Ithaca, NY: Cornell University Press.

JOURNAL OF BLACKS IN HIGHER EDUCATION 1994 Are Nonresident Asian Students Displacing Black Ph.D.s in Science and Engineering? 1 (No. 2), p. 15.

KAGAN, JEROME 1971 The Magical Aura of the IQ. *Saturday Review of Literature* 4 (December 4), pp. 92–93.

KAHN, KATHERINE L., ET AL. 1994 Health Care for Black and Poor Hospitalized Medicare Patients. *Journal of the American Medical Association* 271 (April 20), pp. 1169–1174.

KAHNG, ANTHONY 1978 EEO in America. *Equal Opportunity Forum* 5 (July), pp. 22–23.

KALISH, SUSAN 1995 Multiracial Births Increase as U.S. Ponders Racial Definitions. *Population Today* 24 (April), pp. 1–2.

KANAMINE, LINDA 1992 Amid Crushing Poverty, Glimmers of Hope. *USA Today* (November 30), p. 7A.
1994 Tribal Leaders Now Feel They "Can Be Heard." *USA Today* (April 28), pp. 1A–2A.

KANG, K. CONNIE 1996 Filipinos Happy with Life in U.S., but Lack United Voice. *Los Angeles Times* (January 26), pp. A1, A20.

KAPLAN, DAVE 1993 Constitutional Doubt Is Thrown on Bizarre-Shaped Districts. *Congressional Quarterly Weekly Report* (July 3), pp. 1761–1762.

KAPLAN, DAVID A., AND KLAIDMAN, DAVID 1996 A Battle, Not the War. *Newsweek* 127 (June 3), pp. 24–30.

KARKABI, BARBARA 1993 Researcher in Houston Surveys Disabled Women about Sexuality. *Austin American-Statesman* (May 26), p. E8.

KASARDA, JOHN D. 1990 The Jobs-Skills Mismatch. *New Perspective Quarterly* 7 (Fall), pp. 34–37.

KASER, TOM 1977 Hawaii's Schools: An Ethnic Survey. *Integrated Education* 15 (May-June), pp. 31–36.

KATZ, DAVID, AND BRALY, KENNETH W. 1933 Racial Stereotypes of One Hundred College Students. *Journal of Abnormal Sociology and Psychology* 28 (October-December), pp. 280–290.

KEESING'S 1992 Canada: Rejection of Charlottetown Constitutional Reform Package. *Keesing's Record of World Events* (October), p. 39126.

KENNEDY, JOHN F. 1964 *A Nation of Immigrants.* New York: Harper & Row.

KENNY, KEVIN 1998 *Making Sense of the Molly Maguires.* New York: Oxford University Press.

KEPHART, WILLIAM M., AND ZELLNER, WILLIAM 1994 *Extraordinary Groups: The Sociology of Unconventional Life-Styles,* 5th ed. New York: St. Martin's Press.
1998 *Extraordinary Groups: An Examination of Unconventional Lifestyles,* 6th ed. New York: St. Martin's Press.

KESSLER, EVELYN S. 1976 *Women: An Anthropological View.* New York: Holt, Rinehart & Winston.

KIEH, GEORGE KLAY, JR. 1995 Malcolm X and Pan-Africanism. *Western Journal of Black Studies* 19 (No. 4), pp. 293–299.

KILBORN, PETER T. 1992 Big Change Likely as Law Bans Bias toward Disabled. *New York Times* (July 19), pp. 1, 24.

KILLIAN, LEWIS M. 1975 *The Impossible Revolution, Phase 2: Black Power and the American Dream.* New York: Random House.

KILSON, MARTIN 1995 Affirmative Action. *Dissent* 42 (Fall), pp. 469–470.

KIM, KWANG CHUNG, AND HURH, WON MOO 1984 The Wives of Korean Small Businessmen in the U.S: Business Involvement and Family Roles. Paper presented at the Annual Meeting of the American Sociological Association, San Antonio.
1985a Immigration Experiences of Korean Wives in the U.S: The Burden of Double Roles. Paper presented at the Annual Meeting of the National Council on Family Relations, Dallas.
1985b The Wives of Korean Small Businessmen in the U.S.: Business Involvement and Family Roles. In Inn Sook Lee, ed., *Korean-American Women: Toward Self-Realization,* pp. 1–41. Mansfield, OH: Association of Korean Christian Scholars in North America.

KIM, KWANG CHUNG, AND KIM, SHIN 1995 Korean Immigrant Churches in the United States. In Kenneth B. Bedell, ed., *Yearbook of American and Canadian Churches,* pp. 6–9. Nashville: Abingdon Press.
1998 Korean Middleman Merchants: A Conceptual Revision of Middleman Minority Theory. Paper presented at Midwest Sociological Society Annual Meeting, April 2.

KIMURA, YUKIKO 1988 *Issei: Japanese Immigrants in Hawaii.* Honolulu: University of Hawaii Press.

KING, MARTIN LUTHER, JR. 1963 *Why We Can't Wait.* New York: Mentor.
1967 *Where Do We Go from Here: Chaos or Community?* New York: Harper & Row.
1971 I Have a Dream. In August Meier, Elliott Rudwick, and Francis L. Broderick, eds., *Black Protest Thought in the Twentieth Century,* pp. 346–351. Indianapolis: Bobbs-Merrill.

KING, URSULA, ED. 1995 *Religion and Gender.* Oxford: Blackwell.

KINLOCH, GRAHAM C. 1974 *The Dynamics of Race Relations: A Sociological Analysis.* New York: McGraw-Hill.

KINSEY, ALFRED G.; POMEROY, WARDELL B.; AND MARTIN, CLYDE E. 1948 *Sexual Behavior in the Human Male.* Philadelphia: Saunders.

———; AND GEBHARD, PAUL H. 1953 *Sexual Behavior in the Human Female.* Philadelphia: Saunders.

KIRKPATRICK, P. 1994 Triple Jeopardy: Disability, Race and Poverty in America. *Poverty and Race* 3:1–8.

KITAGAWA, EVELYN 1972 Socioeconomic Differences in the United States and Some Implications for Population Policy. In Charles F. Westoff and Robert Parke, Jr., eds., *Demographic and Social Aspects of Population Growth,* pp. 87–110. Washington, DC: U.S. Government Printing Office.

KITANO, HARRY H. L. 1976 *Japanese Americans: The Evolution of a Subculture,* 2nd ed. Englewood Cliffs, NJ: Prentice-Hall.
1980 Japanese. In Stephen Thernstrom, ed., *Harvard Encyclopedia of American Ethnic Groups.* Cambridge: Belknap Press of Harvard University Press.
1997 *Race Relations.* Upper Saddle River, NJ: Prentice-Hall.

———, AND DANIELS, ROGER 1988 *Asian Americans: Emerging Minorities.* Englewood Cliffs, NJ: Prentice-Hall.

KITSUSE, JOHN I., AND BROOM, LEONARD 1956 *The Managed Casualty: The Japanese American Family in World War II.* Berkeley: University of California Press.

KLANWATCH 1997 Hate Groups in the United States in 1996. *Intelligence Report* (Winter): 20–21.

KLEINHUIZEN, JEFF 1991 Traditions Guard Hispanic Babies' Health. *USA Today* (February 4), p. 4D.

KLOEHN, STEVE 1997 Far from a Minority. *Chicago Tribune* (August 28), pp. 1, 18.

KNUDSON, THOMAS J. 1987 Zoning the Reservations for Enterprise. *New York Times* (January 25), p. E4.

KOMAROMY, MIRIAM 1996 The Role of Black and Hispanic Physicians in Providing Health Care for Underserved Populations. *New England Journal of Medicine* 334 (May 16), pp. 1305–1310.

KOPINAK, KATHRYN 1995 Gender as a Vehicle for the Subordination of Women Maquiladora Workers in Mexico. *Latin American Perspectives* 22 (Winter), pp. 30–48.

KORNBLUM, WILLIAM 1991 Who Is the Underclass? *Dissent* 38 (Spring), pp. 202–211.

KOSMIN, BARRY A. 1991 *The National Survey of Religious Identification*. New York: City University of New York.

———, AND LACHMAN, SEYMOUR P. 1993 *One Nation Under God*. New York: Harmony Books.

———, AND SCHECKNER, JEFFREY 1994 Jewish Population in the United States, 1993. In David Sanger, ed., *American Jewish Year Book, 1994*, pp. 206–226. New York: American Jewish Committee.

———, ET AL. 1991 *Highlights of the CJF 1990 National Jewish Population Survey*. New York: Council of Jewish Federations.

KOTLIKOFF, LAURENCE J., AND GOKHALE, JAGADEESH 1996 An Economic Burden Is Being Placed on Future Generations. In Charles P. Cozic, ed., *An Aging Population: Opposing Viewpoints*, pp. 32–37. San Diego, CA: Greenhaven Press.

KOZOL, JONATHON 1994 Romance of the Ghetto School. *The Nation* 258 (May 23), pp. 703–706.

KRAUSZ, ERNEST 1973 Israel's New Citizens. In *1973 Britannica Book of the Year*, pp. 385–387. Chicago: Encyclopaedia Britannica.

KRAYBILL, DONALD R. 1989 *The Riddle of Amish America*. Baltimore, MD: Johns Hopkins Press.

———, AND NOLT, STEVEN M. 1995 *Amish Enterprises: From Plows to Profits*. Baltimore, MD: Johns Hopkins Press.

KULETZ, VALERIE L. 1998 *The Tainted Desert: Environmental and Social Ruin in the American West*. New York: Routledge.

KUNEN, JAMES S. 1996 The End of Integration. *Time* 147 (April 29), pp. 39–45.

KWONG, PETER 1994 The Wages of Fear. *Village Voice* 39 (April 26), pp. 25–29.

LABELLE, HUGUETTE 1989 Multiculturalism and Government. In James S. Frideres, ed., *Multiculturalism and Intergroup Relations*, pp. 1–7. New York: Greenwood Press.

LACY, DAN 1972 *The White Use of Blacks in America*. New York: McGraw-Hill.

LADNER, JOYCE 1967 What "Black Power" Means to Negroes in Mississippi. *Transaction* 5 (November), pp. 6–15.

LAI, H. M. 1980 Chinese. In Stephen Thernstrom, ed., *Harvard Encyclopedia of American Ethnic Groups*, pp. 222–234. Cambridge: Belknap Press of Harvard University Press.

LAL, BARBARA BALLIS 1995 Symbolic Interaction Theories. *American Behavorial Scientist* 38 (January), pp. 421–441

LAMB, DAVID 1997 Viet Kieu: A Bridge between 2 Worlds. *Los Angeles Times* (November 4), pp. A1, A8.

LANDALE, NANCY S., AND OGENA, NIMFA B. 1995 Migration and Union Dissolution among Puerto Rican Women. *International Migration Review* 29 (Fall), 671–692.

LANDRY, BART 1987 *The New Black Middle Class*. Berkeley: University of California Press.

LANGDON, STEVE J. 1982 Alaskan Native Land Claims and Limited Entry: The Dawes Act Revisited. Paper presented at the Annual Meeting of the American Anthropology Association, Washington, DC.

LANGER, ELINOR 1976 Why Big Business Is Trying to Defeat the ERA. *Ms.* 4 (May), p. 64.

LAPIERE, RICHARD T. 1934 Attitudes vs. Actions. *Social Forces* 13 (October), pp. 230–237.
1969 Comment on Irwin Deutscher's "Looking Backward." *American Sociologist* 4 (February), pp. 41–42.

LAU, HENRY HAN XI 1997 I Was a Member of the Kung Fu Crew. *New York Times Magazine* (October 19), p. 54.

LAUERMAN, CONNIE 1993 Tribal Wave. *Chicago Tribune* (April 5), sect. 2, pp. 1–2.

LAUMANN, EDWARD O.; GAGNON, JOHN H.; AND MICHAEL, ROBERT T. 1994a A Political History of the National Sex Survey of Adults. *Family Planning Perspectives* 26 (February), pp. 34–38.

———; AND MICHAELS, STUART. 1994b *The Social Organization of Sexuality: Sexual Practices in the United States*. Chicago: University of Chicago Press.

LAUTER, DAVID 1995 Affirmative Action Poised to Become Political Divide. *Los Angeles Times* (February 21), pp. A1, A15.

LAVENDER, ABRAHAM D., ED. 1977 *A Coat of Many Colors: Jewish Subcommunities in the United States*. Westport, CT: Greenwood Press.

LAWSON, GUY 1996 No Canada? *Harper's* 292 (April), pp. 67–71, 74–78.

LAXSON, JOAN D. 1991 "We" See "Them" Tourism and Native Americans. *Annals of Tourism Research* 18 (No. 3), pp. 365–391.

LAZERWITZ, BERNARD 1993 Correspondence to Richard T. Schaefer. Data from Jewish Survey.

LEDERMAN, DOUGLAS, AND BURD, STEPHEN 1996 High Court Refuses to Hear Appeal of Ruling that Barred Considering Race in Admissions. *Chronicle of Higher Education* 43 (July 12), pp. A25, A29.

LEDUFF, CHARLIE 1996 When the Loneliness of Age Is Multiplied. *New York Times* (March 31), city sec., p. 9.

LEE, ALFRED MCCLUNG 1983 *Terrorism in Northern Ireland*. Bayside, New York: General Hall.

LEE, DON 1992 A Sense of Identity. *Kansas City Star* (April 4), pp. E1, E7.
1998 Asian Americans Finding Cracks in the Glass Ceiling. *Los Angeles Times* (July 15), pp. A1, A12–113.

LEE, ELISA 1993 Silicon Valley Study Finds Asian Americans Hitting the Glass Ceiling. *AsianWeek* (October 8), p. 21.

LEE, JOANN FAUNG JEAN 1992 *Asian Americans*. New York: The New Press.

LEE, ROSE HUM 1960 *The Chinese in the United States of America*. Hong Kong: Hong Kong University Press.

LEE, SHARON M. 1998 Asian Americans: Diverse and Growing. *Population Bulletin* 53 (June).

LEE, STACEY J. 1996 *Unraveling the Model Minority Stereotype: Listening to Asian American Youth*. New York: Teachers College Press.

LEEHOTZ, ROBERT 1995 Is Concept of Race a Relic? *Los Angeles Times* (April 15), pp. A1, A14.

LEHMAN, EDWARD C., JR. 1993 *Gender and Work: The Case of the Clergy.* Albany: State University of New York.

LEM, KIM 1976 Asian American Employment. *Civil Rights Digest* 9 (Fall), pp. 12–21.

LEMANN, NICHOLAS 1986a The Origins of the Underclass. *The Atlantic Monthly* 258 (June), pp. 31–43, 47–55.
1986b The Origins of the Underclass. *The Atlantic Monthly* 258 (July), pp. 54–68.

LEMOYNE, JAMES 1990 Most Who Left Mariel Sailed to New Life, a Few to Limbo. *New York Times* (April 15), pp. 1, 12.

LENNON, MARY CLARE, AND ROSENFIELD, SARAH 1994 Relative Fairness and the Division of Housework: The Importance of Options. *American Journal of Sociology* 100 (September), pp. 506–531.

LEON, SY 1996 *None of the Above: Why Non-Voters are America's Political Majority.* San Francisco: Fox and Wikes.

LERNER, MICHAEL 1969 Respectable Bigotry. *American Scholar* 38 (August), pp. 606–617.
1993 Jews Are Not White. *Village Voice* 38 (May 18), pp. 33–34.

———, AND WEST, CORNELL 1996 *Jews and Blacks: A Dialogue on Race, Religion, and Culture in America.* New York: Plume/Penguin.

LESCH, ANN M. 1983 Palestine: Land and People. In Naseer H. Aruri, ed., *Occupation: Israel Over Palestine,* pp. 29–54. Belmont, MA: Association of Arab-American University Graduates.

LESSINGER, JOHANNA 1995 *From the Ganges to the Hudson: Indian Immigrants in New York City.* Boston: Allyn and Bacon.

LEVIN, JACK, AND LEVIN, WILLIAM C. 1980 *Ageism.* Belmont, CA: Wadsworth.
1982 *The Functions of Prejudice,* 2d ed. New York: Harper & Row.

LEVIN, WILLIAM C. 1988 Age Stereotyping: College Student Evaluations. *Research on Aging* 10 (March), pp. 134–148.

LEVINE, NAOMI, AND HOCHBAUM, MARTIN, EDS. 1974 *Poor Jews: An American Awakening.* New Brunswick, NJ: Transaction Books.

LEVY, JACQUES E. 1975 *César Chávez: Autobiography of La Causa.* New York: Norton.

LEWINSON, PAUL 1965 *Race, Class, and Party: A History of Negro Suffrage and White Politics in the South.* New York: Universal Library.

LEWIS, NEIL 1996 Court Upholds Clinton Policy on Gay Troops. *New York Times* (April 6), pp. 1, 8.

LEWIS, OSCAR 1959 *Five Families: Mexican Case Studies in the Culture of Poverty.* New York: Basic Books.
1965 *La Vida: A Puerto Rican Family in the Culture of Poverty—San Juan and New York.* New York: Random House.
1966 The Culture of Poverty. *Scientific American* (October), pp. 19–25.

LI, WEN LANG 1976 Chinese Americans: Exclusion from the Melting Pot. In Anthony and Rosalind Dworkin, eds., *Minority Report,* pp. 297–324. New York: Praeger.

LICHTENSTEIN, EUGENE, AND DENENBERG, R. V. 1975 The Army's Ethnic Policy. *New York Times* (July 20), p. E2.

LICHTER, S. ROBERT, AND LICHTER, LINDA S. 1988 *Television's Impact in Ethnic and Racial Images.* New York: American Jewish Committee.

LIEBMAN, CHARLES S. 1973 *The Ambivalent American Jew.* Philadelphia: Jewish Publication Society of America.

LIGHT, IVAN H. 1973 *Ethnic Enterprise in America: Business and Welfare Among Chinese, Japanese, and Blacks.* Berkeley: University of California Press.
1974 From Vice District to Tourist Attraction: The Moral Career of American Chinatowns, 1880–1940. *Pacific Historical Review* 43 (August), pp. 367–394.
1996 A Self-Help Solution to Fight Urban Poverty. *American Enterprise Magazine* 7 (July/August), pp. 50–52.

———, AND BONACICH, EDNA 1988 *Immigrant Entrepreneurs: Koreans in Los Angeles 1965–1982.* Berkeley: University of California Press.

———; SABAGH, GEORGES; BOZORGMEHR, MENDI; AND DER-MARTIROSIAN, CLAUDIA 1994 Beyond the Ethnic Enclave Economy. *Social Problems* 41 (February), pp. 65–80.

LIN, JAN 1998 *Reconstructing Chinatown: Ethnic Enclave, Global Change.* University of Minnesota Press.

LIN, SAM CHU 1996 Painful Memories. *AsianWeek* 17 (July 12), p. 10.

LINCOLN, C. ERIC 1994 *The Black Muslims in America.* 3rd ed. Grand Rapids, MI: William B. Eerdmans.

———, AND MAMIYA, H. 1990 *The Black Church in the African American Experience.* Durham, NC: Duke University Press.

LIND, ANDREW W. 1946 *Hawaii's Japanese: An Experiment in Democracy.* Princeton: Princeton University Press.
1969 *Hawaii: The Last of the Magic Isles.* London: Oxford University Press.

LIND, MICHAEL 1998 The Beige and the Black. *New York Times Magazine* (August 18), pp. 38–39.

LINDNER, EILEEN W. 1998 *Yearbook of American and Canadian Churches 1998.* Nashville: Abingdon Press.

LINTHICUM, LESLIE 1993 Navajo School Working to Revive Language. *News From Indian Country* (Late June), p. 5.

LIPMAN-BLUMER, JEAN; FRYLING, TODD; HENDERSON, MICHAEL C.; MOORE, CHRISTINE WEBSTER; VECCHIOTTIE, RACHEL 1996 *Women in Corporate Leadership: Revising a Decade's Research.* Claremont, CA: The Claremont Graduate School Institute for Advanced Studies in Leadership.

LIU, ERIC 1998 *The Accidental Asian: Notes of a Native Speaker.* New York: Random House.

LLOYD, STERLING, AND MILLER, RUSSELL L. 1989 Black Student Enrollment in U.S. Medical Schools. *Journal of the American Medical Association* 261 (January 13), pp. 272–274.

LOAR, RUSS 1997 Native American Church Bridges Spiritual and Cultural Worlds. *Los Angeles Times* (January 7), p. B2.

LOGAN, RAYFORD W. 1954 *The Negro in American Life and Thought: The Nadir, 1877–1901*. New York: Dial Press.

LOMAX, LOUIS E. 1971 *The Negro Revolt*, rev. ed. New York: Harper & Row.

LONG, PATRICK DU PHUOC 1996 *The Dream Shattered: Vietnamese Gangs*. Boston: Northeastern University.

LOPEZ, DAVID, AND ESPIRITU, YEN 1990 Panethnicity in the United States: A Theoretical Framework. *Ethnic and Racial Studies* 13 (April), pp. 198–224.

LOPEZ, JULIE AMPARANO 1992 Study Says Women Face Glass Walls as Well as Ceilings. *Wall Street Journal* (March 3), pp. B1-B2.

LOS ANGELES TIMES POLL 1998 American and Israeli Jews. Los Angeles: *Los Angeles Times* and *Yedioth Ahronoth*.

LOURY, GLENN C. 1996 Joy and Doubt on the Mall. *Utne Reader* 73 (January–February), pp. 70–73.

LOVE, SPENCIE 1996 *One Blood: The Death and Resurrection of Charles R. Drew*. Chapel Hill, NC: University of North Carolina Press.

LUCE, CLARE BOOTHE 1975 Refugees and Guilt. *New York Times* (May 11), p. E19.

LUKER, KRISTIN 1984 *Abortion and the Politics of Motherhood*. Berkeley: University of California Press.

LUPSHA, PETER A. 1981 Individual Choice, Material Culture, and Organized Crime. *Criminology* 19 (May), pp. 3–24.

LYMAN, STANFORD M. 1974 *Chinese Americans*. New York: Random House.
1986 *Chinatown and Little Tokyo*. Milwood, NY: Associated Faculty Press.

MACK, RAYMOND W. 1996 Whose Affirmative Action? *Society* 33 (March/April), pp. 41–43.

MACKEY, WADE C. 1987 A Cross-Cultural Perspective on Perceptions of Paternalistic Deficiencies in the United States: The Myth of the Derelict Daddy. *Sex Roles* 12 (March), pp. 509–534.

MACRAE, C. NEIL; STANGOR, CHARLES; AND HEWSTONE, MILES 1996 *Stereotypes and Stereotyping*. New York: Guilford Press.

MAHLER, SARAH J. 1995 *American Dreaming: Immigrant Life on the Margin*. Princeton, NJ: Princeton University Press.

MAJKA, THEO J., AND MAJKA, LINDA C. 1996 Mexican Immigration, Transformation of California's Farm Labor and Decline of Unionization since 1980. Paper presented At The Annual Meeting of the American Sociological Association, Washington, DC.

MALCOLM X 1964 *The Autobiography of Malcolm X*. New York: Grove Press.

MANDEL, MICHAEL J., AND FARRELL, CHRISTOPHER 1992 The Immigrants. *Business Week* (July 13), pp. 114–120.

MANDELA, NELSON 1990 Africa, It Is Ours. *New York Times* (February 12), p. A10.

MANEGOLD, CATHERINE S. 1994 Fewer Men Earn Doctorates, Particularly among Blacks. *New York Times* (January 18), p. A14.

MANIGAN, KATHERINE S. 1991 Mexican Students, Including Commuters, Succeed at Texas Universities. *Chronicle of Higher Education* 37 (February 26), pp. A36–A37.

MANING, ANITA 1997 Troubled Waters: Environmental Racism Suit makes Waves. *USA Today* (July 31), p. A1.

MANNING, ROBERT D. 1995 Multiculturalism in the United States: Clashing Concepts, Changing Demographics, and Competing Cultures. *International Journal of Group Tensions* (Summer), pp. 117–168.

MANZO, KATHLEEN KENNEDY 1994 Flaws in Fellowships. *Black Issues in Higher Education* 41 (July 14), pp. 46–47, 52.

MARKLEIN, MARY BETH 1998 Tribal Colleges Bridge Culture Gap to Future. *USA Today* (April 13), p. 4D.

MARTELO, EMMA ZAPATA 1996 Modernization, Adjustment, and Peasant Production. *Latin American Perspective* 23 (Winter), pp. 118–130.

MARTIN, LYDIA 1996 A Question of Tolerance. *Miami Herald* (July 14), pp. 1L, 7L.

MARTIN, M. KAY, AND VOORHIES, BARBARA 1975 *Female of the Species*. New York: Columbia University Press.

MARTIN, PHILIP, AND WIDGREN, JONAS 1996 International Migration: A Global Challenge. *Population Bulletin* 5 (April).

MARTIN, SUSAN E. 1991 The Effectiveness of Affirmative Action: The Case of Women in Policing. *Justice Quarterly* 8, pp. 489–504.

MARTINEZ, RUBÉN 1998 An Evangelical Revival. *Los Angeles Times* (March 29), sect. 29, pp. M1, M3.

———, AND DUKES, RICHARD L. 1991 Ethnic and Gender Differences in Self-Esteem. *Youth and Society* 32 (March), pp. 318–338.

MARTY, MARTIN E. 1976 *A Nation of Behaviors*. Chicago: University of Chicago Press.
1985 Transpositions: American Religion in the 1980s. *Annals* 480 (July), pp. 11–23.

MARX, GARY 1995 Terrorism on Trial: Justice and the FALN. *Chicago Tribune Magazine* (October 22), pp. 22–23, 26, 28–30, 32–33.

MARX, KARL, AND ENGELS, FREDERICK 1955 *Selected Works in Two Volumes*. Moscow: Foreign Languages Publishing House.

MASAYESVA, VERNON 1994 The Problem of American Indian Religious Freedom: A Hopi Perspective. *American Indian Religions: An Interdisciplinary Journal* 1 (Winter), pp. 93–96.

MASON, PHILIP 1970 *Patterns of Dominance*. London: Oxford University Press.
1970b Race Relations. London: Oxford University Press.

MASSEY, DOUGLAS S., AND DENTON, NANCY A. 1993 *American Apartheid: Segregation and the Making of the Underclass*. Cambridge: Harvard University Press.

———, AND GROSS, ANDREW B. 1993 Black Migration, Segregation, and the Spatial Concentration of Poverty.

Paper, Harris Graduate School of Public Policy Studies, University of Chicago.

MASUD-PILOTO, FELIX 1996 From Welcomed Exiles to Illegal Immigrants: Cuban Migration to the U.S., 1959–1995 Lanham, MD: Rowan and Littlefield.

MATHEWS, TOM 1990 The Long Shadow. *Newsweek* 115 (May 7), pp. 34–44.

MATHISEN, JAMES A. 1989 Twenty Years After Bellah: Whatever Happened to American Civil Rights? *Sociological Analysis* 50 (Summer), pp. 129–146.

MATLOFF, NORMAN 1998 Now Hiring! If You're Young. *New York Times* (January 26), p. A21.

MATTHIESSEN, PETER 1991 *In the Spirit of Crazy Horse.* With a new epilogue. New York: Peking.

MATZA, DAVID 1964 *Delinquency and Drift.* New York: Wiley.
1971 Poverty and Disrepute. In Robert K. Merton and Robert Nisbet, eds., *Contemporary Social Problems,* 3rd ed., pp. 601–656. New York: Harcourt, Brace & World.

MAURO, TONY 1995 Ruling Helps Communities Set Guidelines. *USA Today* (December 21), pp. A1-A2.
1996 English-only Debate Lost in Legalese. *USA Today* (December 5), p. 4A.

MAYKOVICH, MINAKO KUROKAWA 1972a *Japanese American Identity Dilemma.* Tokyo: Waseda University Press.
1972b Reciprocity in Racial Stereotypes: White, Black and Yellow. *American Journal of Sociology* 77 (March), pp. 876–877.

MCCALL, NATHAN 1997 *What's Going On?* New York: Random House.

MCCLAIN, PAULA DENICE 1979 *Alienation and Resistance: The Political Behavior of Afro-Canadians.* Palo Alto, CA: R & E Research Associates.

MCCOLLOM, SUSANA 1996 Hispanic Immigrant Attitude Towards African Americans: A Study of Intergroup Contact. Paper presented at the Annual Meeting of the American Sociological Association, New York City.

MCCONAHAY, JOHN B., AND HOUGH, JR., J. C. 1976 Symbolic Racism. *Journal of Social Issues* 32 (No. 1), pp. 23–45.

MCCORMICK, JOHN, AND BEGLEY, SHARON 1996 How to Raise a Tiger. *Newsweek* 126 (December 9), pp. 52–59.

MCCORMICK, KATHERYNE, AND BARUCH, LUCY 1994 Women Show Strength as Campaign Fundraisers. *CAWP News and Notes* 10 (Winter), pp. 16–17.

MCCULLY, BRUCE T. 1940 *English Education and Origins of Indian Nationalism.* New York: Columbia University.

MCDONNELL, PATRICK J., AND RAMOS, GEORGE 1996 Latinos Make Strong Showing at the Polls. *Los Angeles Times* (November 8), pp. A1, A18.

MCFATE, KATHERINE 1994 The Grim Economics of Violence. *Focus* 22 (October), p. 4.

MCGREARY, JOHANNA 1997 Echoes of the Holocaust. *Time* 149 (February 24), pp. 36–40.

MCKENNA, IAN 1994 Legal Protection Against Racial Discrimination Law in Canada. *New Community* 20 (April), pp. 415–436.

MCMAHON, COLIN 1995 Mexican Rebels' Struggle in Chiapas is about the Future. *Chicago Tribune* (January 1), p. 6.

MCNEIL, DONALD G., JR. 1999 South Africa Limps Out of Bad Year for Police. *New York Times* (January 2), p. A6.

MCNEIL, JOHN M. 1998 Americans with Disabilities: 1994–95. *Current Population Reports,* Ser. P–70, No. 61. Washington, DC: U.S. Government Printing Office.

MCNICKLE, D'ARCY 1973 *Native American Tribalism: Indian Survivals and Renewals.* New York: Oxford University Press.

MCNULTY, TIMOTHY J. 1994 Conference on Violence Faces Reality. *Chicago Tribune* (January 9), p. 7.

MCVEIGH, ROY 1993 Creating Opportunities for Insurgency: The Case of the United Farm Workers Movement. Paper presented at the Annual Meeting of the American Sociological Association, Miami.

MEHREN, ELIZABETH, AND ROSENBLATT, ROBERT A. 1995 For AARP a Reversal of Fortune. *Los Angeles Times* (August 22), pp. A1, A10.

MEIER, AUGUST, AND RUDWICK, ELLIOTT 1966 *From Plantation to Ghetto: An Interpretive History of American Negroes.* New York: Hill & Wang.

MEIER, MATT S., AND RIVERA, FELICIANO 1972 *The Chicanos: A History of Mexican Americans.* New York: Hill & Wang.

MELÉNDEZ, EDWIN 1994 Puerto Rico Migration and Occupational Selectivity, 1982–1981. *International Migration Review* 28 (Spring), pp. 49–67.

MELENDY, HOWARD BRETT 1972 *The Oriental Americans.* New York: Hippocreme.
1980 Filipinos. In Stephen Thernstrom, ed., *Harvard Encyclopedia of American Ethnic Groups,* pp. 354–362. Cambridge: Harvard University Press.

MERL, JEAN 1997 City Still Viewed as Racially Split. *Los Angeles Times* (April 29), pp. A1, A18.

MERTON, ROBERT K. 1949 Discrimination and the American Creed. In Robert M. MacIver, ed., *Discrimination and National Welfare,* pp. 99–126. New York: Harper & Row.
1968 *Social Theory and Social Structure.* New York: Free Press.
1976 *Sociological Ambivalence and Other Essays.* New York: Free Press.

MEYERS, GUSTAVUS 1943 *History of Bigotry in the United States.* Rev. by Henry M. Christman, 1960. New York: Capricorn Books.

MIGRATION NEWS 1998a Mexico: Wages, Maquiladoros, NAFTA. *Migration News* 5 (February), pp. 12–14.
1998b Mexico, Dual Nationality. *Migration News* 5 (April), p. 8.

MILES, JACK 1992 Blacks vs. Browns. *The Atlantic Monthly* (October), pp. 41–68.

MILLER, DAVID L. 1995 Toys for Boys. In Richard T. Schaefer and Robert P. Lamm, *Sociology,* 5th ed., Annotated Instructor's Edition, pp. IM26–IM28. New York: McGraw-Hill.
1998 Toys Are Getting Better! Context Analysis of a Major Toy Catalog. In Richard T. Schaefer and Robert

P. Lamm, *Sociology,* 6th ed., Annotated Instructor's Edition, pp. IM30-IM33. New York: McGraw-Hill.

MILLER, DONALD E. 1997 *Reinventing American Protestantism.* Berkeley: University of California Press.

MILLER, JOANNE, AND GARRISON, HOWARD H. 1982 Sex Roles: The Division of Labor at Home and in the Workplace. In Ralph Turner, ed., *Annual Review of Sociology, 1982,* pp. 237–262. Palo Alto, CA: Annual Reviews.

MILLER, MARJORIE 1998 Cultural Battles Fall Along a Religious Divide. *Los Angeles Times,* (April 12), p. 59.

MILLER, NORMAN 1987 Hazards in the Translocation of Research into Remedial Interventions. *Journal of Social Issues* 43 (No. 1), pp. 119–126.

MIN, PYONG GAP 1987 Filipino and Korean Immigrants in Small Business: A Comparative Analysis. *Amerasia* 13 (Spring), pp. 53–71.

MINCY, RONALD B., ED. 1994 *Nurturing Young Black Males.* Washington, DC: Urban Institute Press.

MITCHEL, GARY 1996 Native Languages Go Silent. *News from the Indian Country* 10 (late April), pp. 1A, 7A.

MIYAMOTO, S. FRANK 1973 The Forced Evacuation of the Japanese Minority During World II. *Journal of Social Issues* 29 (No. 2), pp. 11–31.

MOGELONSKY, MARCIA 1995 Asian-Indian Americans. *American Demographics* 17 (August), pp. 32–39.

MOHL, RAYMOND A. 1986 The Politics of Ethnicity in Contemporary Miami. *Migration World* 14 (No. 3), pp. 7–11.

MONGE, JOSÉ TRIAS 1997 *Puerto Rico: The Trials of the Oldest Colony in the World.* New Haven: Yale University Press.

MONTAGU, ASHLEY 1972 *Statement on Race.* New York: Oxford University Press.
1975 *Race and IQ.* London: Oxford University Press.

MOORE, DAVID W. 1996 Public Opposes Gay Marriages. *Gallup Poll Monthly* 367 (April), pp. 19–21.

MOORE, HELEN A., AND IADICOLA, PETER 1981 Resegregation Processes in Desegregated Schools and Status Relationships for Hispanic Students. *Aztlan* 12 (September), pp. 39–58.

MOORE, JOAN W. 1970 Colonialism: The Case of the Mexican Americans. *Social Problems* 17 (Spring), pp. 463–472.

———, AND PACHON, HARRY 1985 Hispanics in the United States. Englewood Cliffs, NJ: Prentice-Hall.

———, AND PINDERHUGHES, RAQUEL, EDS. 1993 *In the Barrios: Latinos and the Underclass Debate.* New York: Sage.

MOORE, MARTHA T. 1997 Women, Minorities Fading out of News Picture. *USA Today* (March 17), p. 11A.

MOORE, STEPHEN 1998 *A Fiscal Report of the Newest Americans.* Washington, DC: National Immigration Forum and Cato Institute.

MOQUIN, WAYNE, AND VAN DOREN, CHARLES, EDS. 1971 *A Documentary History of the Mexican Americans.* New York: Praeger.

MORALES, FRANK, AND BONILLA, FRANK, EDS. 1993 *Latinos in a Changing U.S. Economy.* Newbury Park, NJ: Sage.

MORELLO, CAROL 1997 Opponents Chip Away at Prop. 209. *USA Today* (November 17), pp. A1-A2.

MORÍN, JOSÉ LUIS 1998 Hawai'i: Stirrings in the Colony. *CACL Report on the Americas* 31 (November/December), pp. 10–14.

MORIN, RICHARD 1993 Think Twice Before You Say Another Word. *Washington Post National Weekly Edition* 10 (January 3), p. 37.

MORRIS, ALDON D. 1993 Birmingham Confrontation Reconsidered: An Analysis of the Dynamics and Tactics of Mobilization. *American Sociological Review* 58 (October), pp. 621–636.

MORRIS, MILTON D., AND RUBIN, GARY E. 1993 The Turbulent Friendship: Black-Jewish Relations in the 1990s. *Annals* (November), pp. 42–60.

MORROW, DAVID J. 1996 Making Good On the Great Alaskan Windfall. *New York Times* (November 15), pp. C1, C6.

MORSE, SAMUEL F. B. 1835 *Foreign Conspiracy Against the Liberties of United States.* New York: Leavitt, Lord.

MOSKOS, CHARLES 1966 Racial Integration in the Armed Forces. *American Journal of Sociology* 72 (September), pp. 132–148.

MOULDER, FRANCES V. 1996 Teaching about Race and Ethnicity: A Message of Despair or a Message of Hope? Paper presented at the Annual Meeting of the American Sociological Association, New York City.

MURRAY, CHARLES, AND HERRNSTEIN, RICHARD J. 1994 Race, Genes, and I.Q.—An Apologia. *New Republic* 211 (October 31), pp. 27–37.

MUSCHKIN, CLARA G. 1993 Consequences of Return Migrant Status for Employment in Puerto Rico. *International Migration Review* 27 (Spring), pp. 79–102.

MUTISO, CLIVE 1998 Raising Hope. *Time* 151 (April 13), pp. 200–201.

MYDANS, SETH 1996 Returnees Ante Up Venture Capital: Their Ideas. *New York Times* (August 3), p. 4.

MYRDAL, GUNNAR 1944 *An American Dilemma: The Negro Problem and Modern Democracy.* With the assistance of Richard Steiner and Arnold Rose. New York: Harper.

NABOKOV, PETER 1970 *Tijerina and the Courthouse Raid,* 2d ed. Berkeley, CA: Ramparts Press.

NAGEL, JOANE 1988 The Roots of Red Power: Demographic and Organizational Bases of American Indian Activism 1950–1990. Paper presented at the Annual Meeting of the American Sociological Association, Atlanta.
1996 *American Indian Ethnic Renewal: Red Power and the Resurgence of Identity and Culture.* New York: Oxford University Press.

NAKANISHI, DON T. 1986 Asian American Politics: An Agenda for Research. *Amerasia* 12 (Fall), pp. 1–27.

NAKASHIMA, ELLEN 1996 Hawaii for the Hawaiians? *Washington Post National Weekly Edition* 13 (September 9), p. 30.

NASH, MANNING 1962 Race and the Ideology of Race. *Current Anthropology* 3 (June), pp. 285–288.

NATIONAL ADVISORY COMMISSION ON CIVIL DISORDERS 1968 *Report*. With introduction by Tom Wicker. New York: Bantam.

NATIONAL ASIAN PACIFIC AMERICAN LEGAL CONSORTIUM 1996 *1995 Audit of Violence Against Asian Pacific Americans*. Washington, DC: NAPALC.

NATIONAL CLEARINGHOUSE FOR BILINGUAL EDUCATION 1995 The Changing Face of America's Schools. *Forum* 18 (Fall), pp, 1, 5–7.

NATIONAL CONFERENCE OF CHRISTIANS AND JEWS (NCCJ) 1994 *Taking America's Pulse*. New York: NCCJ.

NATIONAL INDIAN GAMING ASSOCIATION 1995 *Speaking the Truth About Indian Gaming*—1995. Washington, DC: National Indian Gaming Association.
1996 Facts About Indian Gaming. *Indian Gaming Association* 1 (August), p. 43.

NATIONAL OPINION RESEARCH CENTER (NORC) 1996 *General Social Survey 1972–1996: Cumulative Codebook*. Chicago: National Opinion Research Center.

NATIONAL ORGANIZATION ON DISABILITY 1998 Study. Louis Harris and Associates.

NATIONAL PUBLIC RADIO 1992 Morning Edition (August 13).

NAVA, MICHAEL, AND DAWIDOFF, ROBERT 1994 *Created Equal: Why Gay Rights Matter to America*. New York: St. Martin's Press.

NAVARRO, MIREYA 1995 Puerto Rico Reeling Under Scourge of Drugs and Rising Gang Violence. *New York Times* (July 23), p. 11.
1997 As Older Cuban Exiles Die, Young Pragmatists Emerge. *New York Times* (December 6), p. A1.
1998 With a Vote for "None of the Above," Puerto Ricans Endorse Island's Status Quo. *New York Times* (December 14), p. A12.

NBC NEWS 1998 *Shopping Malls*. NBC Dateline, August 31.

NEE, VICTOR G., AND SANDERS, JIMMY 1985 The Road to Parity: Determinants of the Socioeconomic Achievements of Asian Americans. *Ethnic and Racial Studies* 8 (January), pp. 75–93.

NELAN, BRUCE W. 1994 Time to Take Charge. *Time* 143 (May 9), pp. 26–30, 34–35.

NEUGARTEN, BERNICE L. 1996 *The Meanings of Age. Selected Papers of Bernice L. Neugarten*. Ed. with a forward by Dail A. Neugarten. Chicago: University of Chicago Press.

NEWITZ, ANNALEE 1996 *White Trash: Race and Class in America*. New York: Routledge.

———, AND WRAY, MATT (EDS.) 1997 *White Trash. Race and Class in America*. New York: Routledge.

NEWMAN, WILLIAM M. 1973 *American Pluralism: A Study of Minority Groups and Social Theory*. New York: Harper & Row.

NEWS FROM INDIAN COUNTRY 1995 Devil's Tower a Devil of a Problem. (mid-March), p. 8.

NEWSWEEK 1971 Success Story: Outwhiting the White. 101 (June 21), pp. 24–25.

NEW YORK TIMES 1917a Illiteracy Is Not All Alike. (February 8), p. 12.
1917b The Immigration Bill Veto. (January 31), p. 210.
1982 Converts to Judaism. (August 29), p. 23.
1991 For 2, an Answer to Years of Doubt on Use of Peyote in Religious Rite. (July 9), p. A14.
1994 Arab-Americans Protest "True Lies." (July 16), p. 11.
1996 Portrait of the Electorate. (November 10), p. 16.

NICKERSON, STEVE 1971 Alaska Natives Criticize Bill. *Race Relations Reporter* 2 (November 15), pp. 7–10.

NIE, NORMAN H.; CURRIE, BARBARA; AND GREELEY, ANDREW M. 1974 Political Attitudes Among American Ethnics: A Study of Perceptual Distortion. *Ethnicity* 1 (December), pp. 317–343.

NEIBUHR, GUSTAV 1998 Southern Baptists Declare Wife Should "Submit" to Her Husband. *New York Times* (June 10), pp. A1, A20.

NISHI, SETSUKO MATSUNGA 1995 Japanese Americans. In Pyong Gap Min, ed., *Asian Americans: Contemporary Trends and Issues*, pp. 95–133. Thousand Oaks, CA: Sage Publications.

NOBLE, BARBARA PRESLEY 1995 A Level Playing Field, for Just $121. *New York Times* (March 5), p. F21.

NOBLE, HOLCOMB B. 1998 Struggling to Bolster Minorities in Medicine. *New York Times* (September 29), p. F7.

NORDEN, MARTIN E. 1994 *The Cinema of Isolation: A History of Physical Disability in the Movies*. New Brunswick, NJ: Rutgers University Press.

NOVAK, MICHAEL 1996 *Unmeltable Ethnics: Politics and Culture in American Life*, 2d. ed. New Brunswick, NJ: Transaction Books.

NOVELLO, ANTONIA C.; WISE, PAUL H.; AND KLEINMAN, DUSHANKA V. 1991 Hispanic Health: Time for Data, Time for Action. *Journal of the American Medical Association* 265 (January 9), pp. 253–257.

OAKES, JAMES 1993 Slavery. In Mary Kupiec Clayton, Elliot J. Gorn, and Peter W. Williams, eds., *Encyclopedia of American Social History*, pp. 1407–1419. New York: Scribner's.

OAKES, JEANNIE 1995 Two Cities' Tracking and Within-School Segregation. *Teachers College Record* 96 (Summer), pp. 681–706.

OBERSCHALL, ANTHONY 1968 The Los Angeles Riot of August 1965. *Social Problems* 15 (Winter), pp. 322–341.

O'CONNOR, ANNE-MARIE 1998 Church's New Wave of Change. *Los Angeles Times*(March 25), pp. A1, A16.

O'HARE, WILLIAM P., AND CURRY-WHITE, BRENDA 1992 Is There a Rural Underclass? *Population Today* 20 (March), pp. 6–8.

O'HARE, WILLIAM P., AND FELT, JUDY C. 1991 *Asian Americans: America's Fastest Growing Minority Group*. Washington, DC: Population Reference Bureau.

OHNUMA, KEIKO 1991 Study Finds Asians Unhappy at CSU. *AsianWeek* 12 (August 8), p. 5.

OJITO, MIRTA 1998 A Record Backlog to Get Citizenship Stymies 2 Million. *New York Times* (April 20), pp. A1, A16.

O'KANE, JAMES M. 1992 *The Crooked Ladder: Gangsters, Ethnicity, and the American Dream*. New Brunswick, NJ: Transaction Books.

OLIVER, MELVIN L., AND SHAPIRO, THOMAS M. 1995 *Black Wealth/White Wealth: New Perspectives on Racial Inequality*. New York: Routledge.

OLZAK, SUSAN 1998 Ethnic Protest in Core and Periphery States. *Ethnic and Racial Studies* 21 (March), pp. 187–217.

OMI, MICHAEL, AND WINANT, HOWARD 1994 *Racial Formation in the United States*. 2d ed. New York: Routledge.

O'NEILL, WILLIAM 1969 *Everyone Was Brave: The Rise and Fall of Feminism in America*. Chicago: Quadrangle.

ONG, PAUL, AND UMEMOTO, KAREN 1994 Diversity Within a Common Agenda. In Paul Ong, ed., *The State of Asian Pacific America*, pp. 271–276. Los Angeles: Leadership Education for Asian Pacific.

ONISHI, NORMITSU 1995 Japanese in America Looking Beyond Past to Shape a Future. *New York Times* (December 25), p. 1.
1996 New Sense of Race Arises Among Asian-Americans. *New York Times* (May 30), pp. A1, B6.

O'REILLY, JANE 1982 After the ERA: What Next? *Civil Rights Quarterly Perspectives* 14 (Fall), pp. 16–19.

ORFIELD, GARY; EATON, SUSAN E.; AND THE HARVARD PROJECT ON SCHOOL SEGREGATION. 1996 *Dismantling Desegregation: The Quiet Reversal of* Brown *v.* Board of Education. New York: The New Press.

ORLOV, ANN, AND UEDA, REED 1980 Central and South Americans. In Stephan Thernstrom, ed., *Harvard Encyclopedia of American Ethnic Groups*, pp. 210–217. Cambridge: Belknap Press of Harvard University Press.

OTTAWAY, DAVID S., AND TAYLOR, PAUL 1992 A Minority Decides to Stand Aside for Majority Rule. *Washington Post National Weekly Edition* 9 (April 5), p. 17.

OWEN, CAROLYN A.; EISNER, HOWARD C.; AND MCFAUL, THOMAS R. 1981 A Half-Century of Social Distance Research: National Replication of the Bogardus Studies. *Sociology and Social Research* 66 (October), pp. 80–97.

PARAL, ROB 1996 *Estimated Costs of Providing Welfare and Education Services to the Native Born and to Immigrants in Illinois*. Chicago: Latino Institute.

PARFIT, MICHAEL 1994 Powwows. *National Geographic* 185 (June), pp. 85–113.

PARK, ROBERT E. 1928 Human Migration and the Marginal Man. *American Journal of Sociology* 33 (May), pp. 881–893.
1950 *Race and Culture: Essays in the Sociology of Contemporary Man*. New York: Free Press.

PARK, ROBERT E., AND BURGESS, ERNEST W. 1921 *Introduction to the Science of Sociology*. Chicago: University of Chicago Press.

PARRISH, MICHAEL 1995 Betting on Hard Labour and a Plot of Land. *Los Angeles Times* (July 7), pp. A1, A20.

PARSONS, TALCOTT, AND BALES, ROBERT 1955 *Family, Socialization and Interaction Processes*. Glencoe, IL: Free Press.

PASSEL, JEFFREY S., AND CLARK, REBECCA L. 1996 *Taxes Paid by Immigrants in Illinois*. Washington, DC: The Urban Institute.

PASSELL, PETER 1996 Race, Mortgages, and Statistics. *New York Times* (May 10), pp. C1, C4.

PATON, ALAN 1948 *Cry, The Beloved Country*. New York: Scribner's.

PATTERSON, ORLANDO 1998 Affirmative Action. *Brookings Review* 16 (Spring), pp. 17–23.

PAYNE, CHARLES M. 1995 *I've Got the Light of Freedom*. Berkeley, CA: University of California Press.

PEASE, JOHN, AND MARTIN, LEE 1997 Want Ads and Jobs for the Poor: A Glaring Mismatch. *Sociological Forum* 12 (No. 4), pp. 545–564.

PEDDER, SOPHIE 1991 Social Isolation and the Labour Market: Black Americans in Chicago. Paper presented at the Chicago Urban Poverty and Family Life Conference, Chicago.

PERLSTEIN, LINDA 1998 A Half-Century of Change in Compton. *Washington National Post Weekly Report* 15 (May 18), p. 9.

PERUSSE, ROLAND I. 1990 *The United States and Puerto Rico: The Struggle for Equality*. Malabor, FL: Robert E. Krieger Publishing Company.

PETERSEN, WILLIAM 1971 *Japanese Americans: Oppression and Success*. New York: Random House.

PETERSON, ERIC D.; WRIGHT, STEVEN M.; DALEY, JENNIFER; AND THISAULT, GEORGE E. 1994 Racial Variation in Cardiac Procedure Use and Survival Following Acute Myocardial Infarction in the Department of Veterans Affairs. *Journal of the American Medical Association* 271 (April 20), pp. 1175–1207.

PETTIGREW, THOMAS F. 1958 Personality and Socio-Cultural Factors in Intergroup Attitudes: A Cross-National Comparison. *Journal of Conflict Resolution* 2 (March), pp. 29–42.
1959 Regional Differences in Anti-Negro Prejudice. *Journal of Abnormal and Social Psychology* 59 (July), pp. 28–36.

PETTIGREW, THOMAS F., AND MARTIN, JOANNE 1987 Shaping the Organizational Context for Black American Inclusion. *Journal of Social Issues* 43 (No. 1), pp. 41–78.

PEWEWARDY, CORNEL 1998 Our Children Can't Wait: Recapturing the Essence of Indigenous Schools in the United States. *Cultural Survival Quarterly* (Spring), pp. 29–34.

PEYSER, MARC 1998 Battling Backlash. *Newsweek* 132 (August 17), pp. 50–52.

PFEIFFER, DAVID 1996 A Critical Review of ADA Implementation Studies Which Use Empirical Data. *Disability Studies Quarterly* 16 (Winter), pp. 30–47.

PHELAN, THOMAS J., AND SCHNEIDER, MARK 1996 Race, Ethnicity, and Class in American Suburbs. *Urban Affairs Review* 31 (May), pp. 659–680.

PIDO, ANTONIO J. A. 1986 *The Filipinos in America*. New York: Center for Migration Studies.

PILEGGI, NICOLAS 1971 Risorgimento: The Red, White, and Greening of New York. *New York Times Magazine* (June 7), pp. 26–36.

PILLER, CHARLES 1998 The Gender Gap Goes High Tech. *Los Angeles Times* (August 25), p. A1.

PINDERHUGHES, RAQUEL 1996 The Impact of Race on Environmental Quality: An Empirical and Theoretical Discussion. *Sociological Perspectives* 39 (Summer), pp. 231–248.

PINKNEY, ALPHONSO 1975 *Black Americans,* 2d ed. Englewood Cliffs, NJ: Prentice-Hall.
1984 *The Myth of Black Progress.* New York: Cambridge University Press.
1994 *Black Americans,* 4th ed. Englewood Cliffs, NJ: Prentice-Hall.

PLECK, ELIZABETH H. 1993 Gender Roles and Relations. In Mary Kupiec Clayton, Elliot J. Gorn, and Peter W. Williams, eds., *Encyclopedia of American Social History,* pp. 1945–1960. New York: Scribners.

PORTER, JACK NUSAN 1981 *The Jew as Outsider.* Washington, DC: George Washington University Press.
1985 Self-Hatred and Self-Esteem. *The Jewish Spectator* (Fall), pp. 51–55.

PORTES, ALEJANDRO 1974 Return of the Wetback. *Society* 11 (March-April), pp. 40–46.
1996 (ed.). *The New Second Generation.* New York: Russell Sage Foundation.

———, AND MACLEOD, DAG 1996 What Shall I Call Myself? Hispanic Identity Formation in the Second Generation. *Ethnic and Racial Studies* 19 (July), pp. 523–547.

———, AND SCHAUFFLER, RICHARD 1996 Language and the Second Generation: Bilingualism Yesterday and Today. In Alejandro Portes, ed. *The New Second Generation,* pp. 8–29. New York: Russell Sage Foundation.

———, AND STEPICK, ALEX 1985 Unwelcome Immigrants: The Labor Market Experiences of 1980 (Mariel) Cuban and Haitian Refugees in South Florida. *American Sociological Review* 50 (August), pp. 493–514.

POWELL-HOPSON, DARLENE, AND HOPSON, DEREK 1988 Implications of Doll Color Preferences Among Black Preschool Children and White Preschool Children. *Journal of Black Psychology* 14 (February), pp. 57–63.

PRICE, DAVID ANDREW 1996 English-Only Rules: EEOC Has Gone Too Far. *USA Today* (March 28), p. 13A.

PRICE, WAYNE T. 1993 Low-Tech Problems Hits PC Networks. *USA Today* (August 6), pp. B1, B2,

PRINCETON SURVEY RESEARCH ASSOCIATES 1997 *State of the Union.* Washington: Pew Research Center for the People and the Press.

PUBLIC BROADCASTING SYSTEM 1998 Weekend Edition: National Public Radio with Eric Westervelt and Scott Simon. May 30.

PUENTE, MARIA 1994 A Real Melting Pot. *USA Today* (August 1), p. 3A.
1996a Immigration Numbers to Surge. *USA Today* (April 25), p. 3A.
1996b Naturalization at All-Time High. *USA Today* (July 5), p. 3A.

———, AND MORELLO, CAROL 1998 Bilingual Battle Still Rages in Class. *USA Today* (November 13), p. 4A.

QIAN, ZHENCHAO 1997 Breaking the Racial Barriers: Variation in Interracial Marriage Between 1980 and 1990. *Demography* 34 (May), pp. 263–276.

QUADAGNO, JILL 1989 Generational Conflict and the Politics of Class. *Politics and Society* 17 (September), pp. 353–376.
1991 Generational Equity and the Politics of the Welfare State,. In Beth B. Hess and Elizabeth W. Markson, eds., *Growing Old in America,* p. 341–351. New Brunswick, NJ: Transaction Books.
1999 *Aging and the Life Course: An Introduction to Social Gerontology.* New York: McGraw-Hill.

QUINTANILLA, MICHAEL 1996 The 1.5 solution. *Los Angeles Times* (January 12), pp. E1, E8.

RABINOVE, SAMUEL 1970 Private Club Discrimination and the Law. *Civil Rights Digest* 3 (Spring), pp. 28–33.

RACHLIN, CAROL 1970 Tight Shoe Night: Oklahoma Indians Today. In Stuart Levine and Nancy Oestreich Lurie, eds., *The American Indian Today,* pp. 160–183. Baltimore: Penguin.

RADA, JAMES A. 1995 Color Blind-Sided: Racial Bias in Network Television's Coverage of Professional Football Games. Paper presented at the annual meeting of the Association for Education in Journalism and Mass Communication Annual Convention in Washington, DC, August 1995.

RAKOW, LANA F., AND WACKWITZ, LAURA A. 1998 Communication of Sexism. In Michael L. Hecht, ed., *Communicating Prejudice,* pp. 99–111. Thousand Oaks, CA: Sage Publications.

RASPBERRY, WILLIAM 1991 Grim Reruns of the '60s. *Washington Post* (May 8), p. A3.

RAWICK, GEORGE P. 1972 *From Sundown to Sunup: The Making of the Black Community.* Westport, CT: Greenwood Press.

RAWLS, JAMES J. 1996 *Chief Red Fox is Dead: A History of Native Americans since 1945.* New York: Harcourt Brace.

RAYMOND, CHRIS 1991 Cornell Scholar Attacks Key Psychological Studies Thought to Demonstrate Blacks' Self-Hatred. *Chronicle of Higher Education* 37 (May 8), pp. A5, A8, A11.

REDPATH, JEAN 1998 A Witch's Brew for the Poor. *Frontiers of Freedom* (Third Quarter), pp. 15–16.

REESE, DEBBIE 1996 Teaching Young Children about Native Americans. *ERIC Digest* (May), p. EDO-PS-96-3.

REFUGEE REPORTS 1992 Canada Tightening Refugee Law, Takes Step Toward Turning Asylum Seekers Back to the United States. 13 (September 30), pp. 1–8.
1996 Administration Considers Final Chapter of Southeast Asian Refugee Crisis 17 (February 28), pp. 1–8.

REID, JOHN 1986 Immigration and the Future U.S. Black Population. *Population Today* 14 (February), pp. 6–8.

RELIGION WATCH 1995a Reform Synagogues Increasingly Adopting Orthodox Practices. 10 (March), p. 7.
1995b Japanese-American Buddhist Group Facing Decline and Dissension. 10 (March), p. 5.
1995c Women Religious Leadership Facing Mainline Decline, Conservative Growth. 11 (November), pp. 1–3.

REMNICK, DAVID 1998 Bad Seeds. *New Yorker* 74 (July 20), pp. 28–33.

RESKIN, BARBARA F. 1998 *The Realities of Affirmative Action in Employment.* Washington, DC: American Sociological Association.

REYNOLDS, MOURA 1998 Economic Ills Give Rise to Anti-Semitism in Russia. *Los Angeles Times* (November 22), pp. A20-A21.

RICHARDSON, LAUREL WALUM 1981 *The Dynamics of Sex and Gender*, 2d ed. Boston: Houghton Mifflin.

———; TAYLOR, VERTA; AND WHITTIER, NANCY, EDS. 1997 *Feminist Frontiers IV*. New York: McGraw-Hill.

RICHMAN, RUTH 1992 Glass Ceiling? Break It Yourselves, Federal Official Says. *Chicago Tribune* (August 16), sect. 6, pp. 1, 11.

RISMAN, BARBARA J. 1998 *Gender Vertigo: American Families in Transition*. New Haven, CT: Yale University Press.

RIVERA, GEORGE, JR. 1988 Hispanic Folk Medicine Utilization in Urban Colorado. *Sociology and Social Research* 72 (July), pp. 237–241.

RIVERA-BATIZ, FRANCISCO, AND SANTIAGO, CARLOS E. 1996 *Island Paradox: Puerto Rico in the 1990s*. New York: Russell Sage Foundation.

ROBERTS, BARI-ELLEN, AND WHITE, JACK 1998 *Roberts vs. Texaco: A True Story of Race and Corporate America*. New York: Avon.

ROBERTS, D. F. 1955 The Dynamics of Racial Intermixture in the American Negro—Some Anthropological Considerations. *American Journal of Human Genetics* 7 (December), pp. 361–367.

ROBERTS, STEVEN B. 1984 Congress Stages a Preemptive Strike on the Gender Gap. *New York Times* (May 23), p. A18.

ROBINSON, JAMES D., AND SKILL, THOMAS 1993 The Invisible Generation: Portrayals of the Elderly on Television. Paper, University of Dayton.

ROBLES, FRANCES, AND CASIMIR, LESLIE 1996 Legacies of a Shooting: Ethnic Tension, Boycott. *Miami Herald* (July 7), p. 1B.

RODRIGUEZ, CLARA E. 1989 *Puerto Ricans: Born in the USA*. Boston: Unwin Hyman.
1997 (ed.) *Latin Looks: Image of Latinos and Latinas in the U.S. Media*. Boulder, CO: Westview Press.

RODRIQUEZ, GREGORY 1996 *The Emerging Latino Middle Class*. Malibu, CA: Institute for Public Policy, Pepperdine University.
1998 Great Expectations. *Los Angeles Times* (January 11), pp. M1, M6.

RODRÍQUEZ, ROBERT 1994 Immigrant Bashing: Latinos Besieged by Public Policy Bias. *Black Issues in Higher Education* 10 (February 24), pp. 31–34.

RODRIQUEZ, ROBERTO 1993 Ingles: Si o No? Debate Rages on in Puerto Rico. *Black Issues in Higher Education* 9 (February 11), p. 13.

ROEDIGER, DAVID R., ED. 1998 *Black on White: Black Writers on What It Means to be White*. New York: Schocken Books.

ROHTER, LARRY 1993a Trade Pact Threatens Puerto Rico's Economic Rise. *New York Times* (January 3), pp. 1, 14.
1993b Rights Groups Fault Decision, As Do Haitians. *New York Times* (June 22), p. 18.

ROLLE, ANDREW F. 1972 *The American Indians: Their History and Culture*. Belmont, CA: Wadsworth.

ROSALES, F. ARTURO 1996 *Chicano! The History of the Mexican American Civil Rights Movement*. Houston, TX: Arte Pùblico Press.

ROSE, PETER I. 1981 *They and We*, 3d ed. New York: Random House.

ROSE, R. S. 1988 Slavery in Brazil: Does It Still Exist Today? Paper presented at the Annual Meeting of the American Sociological Association, Atlanta.

ROSENBAUM, JAMES E., AND MEADEN, PATRICIA 1992 Harassment and Acceptance of Low-Income Black Youth in White Suburban Schools. Paper presented at the Annual Meeting of the American Sociological Association, Pittsburgh.

ROSENBERG, MORRIS, AND SIMMONS, ROBERTA G. 1971 *Black and White Self-Esteem: The Urban School Child*. Washington, DC: American Sociological Association.

ROSS, ROBERT J. S. 1998 The New Sweatshops in the United States: How New, How Real, How Many, Why? Paper presented at the Annual Meeting of the American Sociological Association. San Francisco, CA, August.

ROSSI, ALICE S. 1988 Growing Up and Older in Sociology 1940–1990. In M. W. Riley, ed., *Sociological Lives*, pp. 43–64. Newbury Park, CA: Sage Publications.

ROTH, ELIZABETH 1993 The Civil Rights History of "Sex." *Ms.* 3 (March-April), pp. 84–85.

ROTHMAN, STANLEY 1996 Is God Really Dead in Beverly Hills? *American Scholar* 65 (Spring), pp. 272–278.

ROUHANA, NADIM N., AND BAR-TAL, DANIEL 1998 Psychological Dynamics of Intractable Ethnonational Conflicts: The Israeli-Palestinian Case. *American Psychologist* (July), pp. 761–770.

ROWLAY, STORER M., AND PERES, JUDY 1998 The War Within. *Chicago Tribune* (May 10), magazine section, pp. 32–35, 52.

RUBIEN, DAVID 1989 For Asians in U.S., Hidden Strife. *New York Times* (January 11), p. C1.

RUDWICK, ELLIOTT 1957 The Niagara Movement. *Journal of Negro History* 42 (July), pp. 177–200.

RUMBAUT, RUBÉN G. 1998 Coming of Age in Immigrant America. *Research Perspectives on Migration* 1 (January/February), pp. 1, 3–14.

RUSSELL, JAMES W. 1996 *After the Fifth Sun: Class and Race in North America*. Englewood Cliffs, NJ: Prentice-Hall.

RUSSELL, STEVE 1995 The Legacy of Ethnic Cleansing: Implementation of NAGPRA in Texas. *American Indian Culture and Research Journal* 19 (No. 4), pp. 193–211.

RYAN, WILLIAM 1976 *Blaming the Victim*, rev. ed. New York: Random House.

SAAD, LYDIA 1995 Immigrants See U.S. As Land of Opportunity. *Gallup Poll Monthly* 358 (July), pp. 19–33.
1998 America Divided Over Status of Puerto Rico. *Gallup Poll Monthly* 390 (March), p. 278.

———, AND MCANENY, LESLIE 1994 Most Americans Think Religion Losing Clout in the 1990s. *Gallup Poll Monthly* (April), pp. 2–4.

SADKER, MYRA, AND SADKER, DAVID 1994a Why Schools Must Tell Girls: "You're Smart, You Can Do It." *USA Weekend* (February 4), pp. 4–6.
1994b *Teachers, Schools, and Society,* 3rd ed. New York: McGraw-Hill.

SAID, EDWARD W., ET AL. 1988 A Profile of the Palestinian People. In Edward W. Said and Christopher Hitchens, eds., *Blaming the Victims,* pp. 235–296. London: Verso.

ST. PIERRE, STEPHANIE 1995 *Teenage Refugees From Cambodia Speak Out.* New York: Rosen Publishing Group.

SALÉE, DANIEL 1994 Identity Politics and Multiculturalism in Quebec. *Cultural Survival Quarterly* (Summer-Fall), pp. 89–94.

SALOPEK, PAUL 1996 Assimilation Puts Tribal Cultures at Loss for Words. *Chicago Tribune* (February 25), pp. 1, 13.

SANCHEZ, RENE 1998 The Winter of Their Discontent. *Washington Post National Weekly Edition* 16 (December), p. 20.

SANCHEZ, SANDRA 1991 Feelings of Frustration Boil Over. *USA Today* (May 8), p. 3A.

SANDEFUR, GARY D.; RINDFUSS, RONALD R; AND COHEN, BARNEY, EDS. 1996 *Changing Numbers, Changing Needs: American Indian Demography and Public Health.* Washington, DC: National Academy Press.

SANDERS, IRWIN T., AND MORAWSKA, EWA T. 1975 *Polish-American Community Life: A Survey of Research.* Boston: Community Sociology Training Program.

SAVAGE, DAVID G. 1995 Plan to Boost Firms Owned by Minorities Is Assailed. *Los Angeles Times* (April 2), p. A14.

SAWYER, JACK 1972 On Male Liberation. *Civil Rights Digest* 5 (Winter), pp. 37–38.

SCHAEFER, RICHARD T. 1971 The Ku Klux Klan: Continuity and Change. *Phylon* 32 (Summer), pp. 143–157.
1976 *The Extent and Content of Racial Prejudice in Great Britain.* San Francisco, CA: R & E Research Associates.
1980 The Management of Secrecy: The Ku Klux Klan's Successful Secret. In Stanton K. Tefft, ed., *Secrecy: A Cross-Cultural Perspective,* pp. 161–177. New York: Human Sciences Press.
1986 Racial Prejudice in a Capitalist State: What Has Happened to the American Creed? *Phylon* 47 (September), pp. 192–198.
1992 People of Color: The "Kaleidoscope" May Be a Better Way to Describe America Than "The Melting Pot." *Peoria Journal Star* (January 19), p. A7.
1996 Education and Prejudice: Unraveling the Relationship. *Sociological Quarterly* 37 (January), pp. 1–16.
2000 *Sociology: A Brief Introduction*, 3rd ed. New York: McGraw-Hill.

———, AND LAMM, ROBERT P. 1998 *Sociology,* 6th ed. New York: McGraw-Hill.

———, AND SCHAEFER, SANDRA L. 1975 Reluctant Welcome: U.S. Responses to the South Vietnamese Refugees. *New Community* 4 (Autumn), pp. 366–370.

SCHERMERHORN, R. A. 1970 *Comparative Ethnic Relations: A Framework for Theory and Research.* New York: Random House.

SCHMIDT, WILLIAM E. 1988 Religious Leaders Try to Heal Rift in Chicago. *New York Times* (November 27), p. 14.

SCHNEIDER, BART 1997 *An Anthology in the First Person.* New York: Crown Trade.

SCHOENFELD, EUGEN 1976 Jewish Americans: A Religo-Ethnic Community. In Anthony Dworkin and Rosalind J. Dworkin, eds., *The Minority Report: An Introduction to Racial and Ethnic Minorities,* pp. 325–352. New York: Praeger.

SCHULTZ, RAY 1974 The Call of the Ghetto. *New York Times Magazine* (November 10), p. 34.

SCHUMAN, HOWARD; STEEH, CHARLOTTE; BOBO, LAWRENCE; AND KRYSAN, MARIA 1997 *Racial Attitudes in America: Trends and Interpretation*, rev. ed. Cambridge, MA: Harvard University Press.

SCHWARTZ, FELICE 1989 Management Women and the New Facts of Life. *Harvard Business Review* 67 (January-February), pp. 65–76.

———, WITH ZIMMERMAN, JEAN 1992 *Breaking With Tradition: Women and Work, The New Facts of Life.* New York: Warner Books.

SCHWARTZ, JOHN 1994 Preserving Endangered Speeches. *Washington Post National Weekly Edition* 11 (March 21), p. 38.

SCHWARTZ, PEPPER 1992 Sex as a Social Problem. In Craig Calhoun and George Ritzer, eds., *Social Problems,* pp. 794–819. New York: McGraw-Hill.

SCOTCH, RICHARD K. 1988 Disability as the Basis For a Social Movement: Advocacy and the Politics of Definition. *Journal of Social Issues* 44 (No. 1), pp. 159–172.
1984 *From Good Will to Civil Rights: Transforming Federal Disability Policy.* Philadelphia: Temple University Press.
1989 Politics and Policy in the History of the Disability Rights Movement. *The Milbank Quarterly* 6 (Supplement 2), pp. 380–400.

SCOTT, ROBIN FITZGERALD 1974 Wartime Labor Problems and Mexican Americans in the War. In Manuel Servin, ed., *An Awakened Minority: The Mexican Americans,* 2d ed., pp. 134–142. Beverly Hills, CA: Glencoe Press.

SEALE, PATRICK 1980 Two Peoples—One Land. In *1980 Britannica Book of the Year,* pp. 64–69. Chicago: Encyclopaedia Britannica.

SEARS, DAVID O., AND KINDER, DONALD R. 1971 Racial Tensions and Voting Behavior in Los Angeles. In Werner Z. Hirsch, ed., *Los Angeles: Viability and Prospects for Metropolitan Leadership*, pp. 51–88. New York: Praeger.

———, AND MCCONAHAY, J. B. 1969 Participation in the Los Angeles Riot. *Social Problems* 17 (Summer), pp. 3–20.
1970 Racial Socialization, Comparison Levels, and the Watts Riot. *Journal of Social Issues* 26 (Winter), pp. 121–140.
1973 *The Politics of Violence: The New Urban Blacks and the Watts Riots.* Boston: Houghton-Mifflin.

SEGALL, REBECCA 1998 Sikh and Ye Shall Find. *Village Voice* 43 (December 15), pp. 45–48, 53.

SELZER, MICHAEL 1972 *"Kike"—Anti-Semitism in America.* New York: Meridian.

SENGUPTA, SOMINI 1997 Asians' Advances Academically Are Found to Obscure a Need. *New York Times* (November 9), p. 17.

SERVIN, MANUEL P. 1974 The Beginnings of California's Anti-Mexican Prejudice. In Manuel P. Servin, ed., *An Awakened Minority: The Mexican Americans,* 2d ed., pp. 2–26. Beverly Hills, CA: Glencoe Press.

SERWATKA, THOMAS S.; DEERING, SHARIA; AND GRANT, PATRICK 1995 Disproportionate Representation of African Americans in Emotionally Handicapped Classes. *Journal of Black Studies* 25 (March), pp. 492–506.

SEVERO, RICHARD 1970 New York's Italians: A Question of Identity. *New York Times* (November 9), pp. 43, 50.

SHAFFER, GWEN 1994 Asian Americans Organize for Justice. *Environmental Action* 25 (Winter 1994), pp. 30–33.

SHANKLIN, EUGENIA 1994 *Anthropology and Race.* Belmont, CA: Wadsworth.

SHARN, LORI 1996 Muslims Want a Place at Political Table. *USA Today* (August 23), p. 4A.

SHARP, DEBORAH 1994 A Culture Clash Divides Florida County. *USA Today* (May 18), p. 11A.

SHENKER, ISRAEL 1974 How Yiddish Survives at 2 New York City Schools. *New York Times* (January 16), p. 68.
1979 With Them, It's Always Strictly Kosher. *New York Times Magazine* (April 15), pp. 32, 33, 36–38, 40, 42.

SHENON, PHILIP 1996 Armed Forces Still Question Homosexuals. *New York Times* (February 27), pp. A1, A20.

SHER, JULIAN 1983 *White Hoods: Canada's Ku Klux Klan.* Vancouver, British Columbia: New Star Books.

SHERIF, MUSAFER, AND SHERIF, CAROLYN 1969 *Social Psychology.* New York: Harper & Row.

SHERMAN, C. BEZALEL 1974 Immigration and Emigration: The Jewish Case. In Marshall Sklare, ed., *The Jew in American Society,* pp. 51–55. New York: Behrman House.

SHERRY, LINDA 1992 New President at Chinese Six Co. *AsianWeek* (January 10), p. 3.

SHILTS, RANDY 1982 *The Mayor of Castro Street: The Life and Times of Harvey Milk.* New York: St. Martin's.

SHORTEN, LINDA 1991 *Without Reserve: Stories from Urban Natives.* Edmonton: NeWest Press.

SHUSTER, BETH 1996 Consulate Takes Activist Role for Mexicans in U.S. *Los Angeles Times* (April 9), pp. A1, A18–A19.

SIDDIQI, MOHAMMAD 1993 The Portrayal of Muslims and Islam in the U.S. Media. Paper presented at the Conference on the Expression of American Religion in the Popular Media, Indianapolis.

SIGELMAN, LEE, AND TUCH, STEVEN A. 1997 Metastereotypes: Blacks' Perception of Whites' Stereotypes of Blacks. *Public Opinion Quarterly* 61 (Spring), pp. 87–101.

———; BLEDSOE, TIMOTHY; WELCH, SUSAN; AND COMBS, MICHAEL W. 1996 Making Contact? Black-White Social Interaction in an Urban Setting. *American Journal of Sociology* 5 (March), pp. 1306–1332.

SINGER, DAVID; AND SELDEN, RUTH R. (EDS.) American Jewish Year Book 1998. New York: American Jewish Committee.

SILBERMAN, CHARLES E. 1971 *Crisis in the Classroom: The Remaking of American Education.* New York: Random House.
1985 *A Certain People.* New York: Summit.

SILVA, HELGA 1985 *The Children of Mariel.* Miami: Cuban American National Foundation.

SILVERSTEIN, STUART 1996 Glass Ceiling Over Women Still Intact In Workplace. *Los Angeles Times* (October 18), pp. A1, A21.

SIMMONS, ALAN B., AND KEOHANE, KIERAN 1992 Canadian Immigration Policy: State Strategies and the Quest for Legitimacy. *Canadian Review of Sociology and Anthropology* 29 (No. 4), pp. 427–451.

SIMPSON, JACQUELINE C. 1995 Pluralism: The Evolution of a Nebulous Concept. *American Behavioral Scientist* 38 (January), pp. 459–477.

SKLARE, MARSHALL 1971 *America's Jews.* New York: Random House.
1993 *Observing America's Jews.* Bedford, NH: Brandeis University Press.

SLAVIN, ROBERT E. 1985 Cooperative Learning: Applying Contact Theory in Desegregated Schools. *Journal of Social Issues* 41 (No. 3), pp. 45–62.

SLOAN, GEORGE 1980 30 Pekin High School Students Walk Out of Classes. *Peoria Journal Star* (September 4), p. 4.

SMITH, JAMES P., AND EDMONSTON, BARRY, EDS. 1997 *The New Americans: Economic, Demographic, and Fiscal Effects of Immigration.* Washington, DC: National Academy Press.

SMITH, M. ESTELLI 1982 Tourism and Native Americans. *Cultural Survival Quarterly* 6 (Summer), pp. 10–12.

SMITH, PAUL CHAAT, AND WARRIOR, ROBERT ALLEN 1996 *Like a Hurricane—The Indian Movement from Alcatraz to Wounded Knee.* New York: The New Press.

SMITH, TOM W. 1990 *Jewish Attitudes Toward Blacks and Race Relations.* New York: American Jewish Committee.
1994 *Anti-Semitism in Contemporary America.* New York: American Jewish Committee.

SMITH, WES 1997 Few to Feel Aid Cut More than the Struggling Hmong. *Chicago Tribune* (October 6), pp. 1, 14.

SNIPP, C. MATTHEW 1980 Determinants of Employment in Wisconsin Native American Communities. *Growth and Change* 11 (No. 2), pp. 39–47.
1989 *American Indians: The First of This Land.* New York: Sage.
1997 Some Observations About Racial Boundaries and the Experiences of American Indians. *Ethnic and Racial Studies* 20 (October), pp. 667–689.

SOCHEN, JUNE 1982 *Herstory: A Woman's View of American History,* 2d ed. Palo Alto, CA: Mayfield.

SOLOMON, JOLIE 1996 Texaco's Troubles. *Newsweek* 128 (November 25), pp. 48–50.

SOMNERS, CHRISTINA HOFF 1994 *Who Stole Feminism?* New York: McGraw-Hill.

SONG, TAE-HYON 1991 Social Contact and Ethnic Distance Between Koreans and the U.S. Whites in the

United States. Paper, Western Illinois University, Macomb.

SONTAG, DEBORAH 1993 Émigrés in New York: Work off the Books. *New York Times* (June 13), pp. 1, 42.

SOO, JULIE D. 1998 APAs Prefer Boxer in L.A., Poll Finds. *AsianWeek* 20 (October 29), p. 11.

SOUTH AFRICAN INSTITUTE OF RACE RELATIONS 1996 *South Africa Survey 1995/96*. Johannesburg: SAIRR.
1998 *South Africa Survey 1997/98*. Johannesburg: SAIRR.

SOUTHERN, DAVID W. 1987 *Gunnar Myrdal and Black-White Relations*. Baton Rouge: Louisiana State University.

SPIEGEL, IRVING 1973a Jewish Official Fears a Backlash. *New York Times* (October 27), p. 9.
1973b Jews Are Warned of Oil Backlash. *New York Times* (November 16), p. 35.
1975 Educators Called Remiss About Bias. *New York Times* (November 9), p. 63.

SQUITIERI, TOM 1989 Many Await Restitution. *USA Today* (September 13), p. 3A.

STAINS, LAURENCE R. 1994 The Latinization of Allentown, PA. *New York Times Magazine* (May 15), pp. 56–62.

STAMPP, KENNETH M. 1956 *The Peculiar Institution: Slavery in the Ante-Bellum South*. New York: Random House.

STAPLES, ROBERT, AND JOHNSON, LEANOR BOULIN 1993 *Black Families at the Crossroads: Challenges and Prospects*. San Francisco: Jossey-Bass.

STARK, RODNEY 1987 Correcting Church Membership Rates: 1971 and 1980. *Review of Religious Research* 29 (September), pp. 69–77.

STARK, RODNEY, AND GLOCK, CHARLES 1968 *American Piety: The Nature of Religious Commitment*. Berkeley: University of California Press.

STARR, PAUL, AND ROBERTS, ALDEN 1981 Attitudes Toward Indochinese Refugees: An Empirical Study. *Journal of Refugee Resettlement* 1 (August), pp. 51–61.

STATISTICS CANADA 1998a 1996 Census: Aboriginal Data. *The Daily* (January 13).
1998b 1996 Census: Ethnic Origin, Visible Minorities. *The Daily* (February 17).

STEDMAN, RAYMOND WILLIAM 1982 *Shadows of the Indian: Stereotyping in American Culture*. Norman: University of Oklahoma Press.

STAVENHAGEN, RUDOLFO 1994 The Indian Resurgence in Mexico. *Cultural Survival Quarterly* (Summer/Fall), pp. 77–80.

STEINBERG, STEPHEN 1977 *The Academic Melting Pot*. New Brunswick, NJ: Transaction Books.

STEINER, STAN 1968 *The New Indians*. New York: Harper & Row.
1976 *The Vanishing White Man*. New York: Harper & Row.

STEINFELS, PETER 1992 Debating Intermarriage, and Jewish Survival. *New York Times* (October 18), pp. 1, 16.

STODDARD, ELLYN R. 1973 *Mexican Americans*. New York: Random House.
1976a A Conceptual Analysis of the "Alien Invasion": Institutionalized Support of Illegal Mexican Aliens in the U.S. *International Migration Review* 10 (Summer), pp. 157–189.
1976b Illegal Mexican Labor in the Borderlands: Institutionalized Support of an Unlawful Practice. *Pacific Sociological Review* 19 (April), pp. 175–210.

STONE, DIANNA L.; EDDY, ERIK R; HOSUDA, MEGUINE; AND BEHSON, SCOTT 1996 The Interactive Effects of Disability, Race, and Gender on Job Placement Decision. *Disability Studies Quarterly* 16 (Spring), pp. 4–6.

STONEQUIST, EVERETT V. 1937 *The Marginal Man: A Study in Personality and Culture Conflict*. New York: Scribner's.

SUÁREZ, ZULIEMA 1998 Cuban-American Families. In Charles H. Mindel, Robert W. Hobenstein, and Roosevelt Wright, Jr., eds., *Ethnic Families in America: Patterns and Variations*, 4th ed. Upper Saddle River, NJ: Prentice Hall, pp. 172–198.

SULLIVAN, CHERYL 1986 Seeking Self-Sufficiency. *Christian Science Monitor* (June 25), pp. 16–17.

SUN, LENA H. 1995 A Cultural Park and Trust. *Washington Post National Weekly Edition* 12 (February 27), p. 9.

SUNG, BETTY LEE 1967 *Mountains of Gold: The Story of the Chinese in America*. New York: Macmillan.

SURATOS, WILLIAM H., JR., ED. 1994 *Gender and Religion*. New Brunswick, NJ: Transaction Books.

SUTHERLAND, ELIZABETH 1970 Colonized Women: The Chicano. In Robin Morgan, ed., *Sisterhood Is Powerful*, pp. 376–379. New York: Random House.

SVENSSON, CRAIG K. 1989 Representation of American Blacks in Clinical Trials of New Drugs. *Journal of the American Medical Association* 261 (January 13), pp. 263–265.

SWAGERTY, WILLIAM R. 1983 Native Peoples and Early European Contacts. In Mary Kupiec Clayton, Elliot J. Gorn, and Peter W. Williams, eds., *Encyclopedia of American Social History*, pp. 15–16. New York: Scribner's.

SWEET, JILL D. 1990 The Portals of Tradition: Tourism in the American Southwest. *Cultural Survival Quarterly* 14 (No. 2), pp. 6–8.

SWERDLOW, JOEL L. 1998 New York's Chinatown. *National Geographic*, 194 (August), pp. 58–77.

TACHIBANA, JUDY 1990 Model Minority Myth Presents Unrepresentative Portrait of Asian Americans, Many Educators Say. *Black Issues in Higher Education* 6 (March 1), pp. 1, 11.

TAKAGI, DANA Y. 1992 *The Retreat from Race: Asian-American Admissions and Racial Politics*. New Brunswick, NJ: Rutgers University Press.

TAKAKI, RONALD 1989 *Strangers from a Different Shore: A History of Asian Americans*. Boston: Little, Brown.

TAKEZAWA, YASUKO I. 1991 Children of Inmates: The Effects of the Redress Movement Among Third Generation Japanese Americans. *Qualitative Sociology* 14 (Spring), pp. 39–56.

TANNENBAUM, FRANK 1994 *Theories of Intergroup Relations: International Social Psychological Perspectives*, 2d ed. Westport, CT: Praeger.

TAYLOR, PAUL 1993 The Fault Line Between South Africa's Blacks. *Washington Post National Weekly Edition* 10 (November 22), p. 18.

TAYLOR, ROBERT JOSEPH; CHATTERS, LINDA M.; TUCKER, M. BELINDA; AND LEWIS, EDITH 1990 Developments in Research on Black Families: A Decade Review. *Journal of Marriage and the Family* 52 (November), pp. 993–1014.

TAYLOR, STUART, JR. 1987a High Court Backs Basing Promotion on a Racial Quota. *New York Times* (February 26), pp. 1, 14.
1987b High Court Voids Curb on Teaching Evolution Theory. *New York Times* (June 20), pp. 1, 7.
1988 Justices Back New York Law Ending Sex Bias by Big Clubs. *New York Times* (June 21), pp. A1, A18.

TEIJESEN, NANCY 1998 *Hmong American's Racial and Ethnic Relations in America*. Salem, MA: Salem Press.

TELSCH, KATHLEEN 1991 New Study of Older Worker Finds They Can Become Good Investments. *New York Times* (May 21), p. A16.

TEN BROCK, JACOBUS; BARNHART, EDWARD N.; AND MATSON, FLOYD W. 1954 *Prejudice, War and the Constitution*. Berkeley: University of California Press.

TENENBAUM, SHELLY 1993 The Jews. In Mary Kupiec Coyton, Elliot J. Gorn, and Peter W. William, eds., *Encyclopedia of American Social History*, pp. 769–781. New York: Scribner's.

TERCHEK, RONALD J. 1977 Conflict and Cleavage in Northern Ireland. *The Annals* (September), pp. 47–59.

TERRY, CLIFFORD 1975 Chicagoans—Pro Soccer. *Chicago Tribune Magazine* (May 5), p. 26.

TGAMAKI, JULIE 1998 Cultural Balancing Act Adds to Teen Angst. *Los Angeles Times* (July 13), pp. A1, A8-A9.

THIRD WORLD JOURNALISTS 1994 *Third World Guide 93/94*. Toronto: Garamond Press.

THOMAS, CURLEW O., AND THOMAS, BARBARA BOSTON 1984 Blacks' Socioeconomic Status and the Civil Rights Movement's Decline, 1970–1979: An Examination of Some Hypotheses. *Phylon* 45 (March), pp. 40–51.

THOMAS, DOROTHY S. 1952 *The Salvage*. Berkeley: University of California Press.

THOMAS, DOROTHY S., AND NISHIMOTO, RICHARD S. 1946 *The Spoilage: Japanese-American Evacuation and Resettlement*. Berkeley: University of California Press.

THOMAS, ROBERT MCG., JR. 1995 Maggie Kuhn, 89, the Founder of the Gray Panthers, Is Dead. *New York Times* (April 23), p. 47.

THOMAS, WAYNE P., AND COLLIER, VIRGINIA P. 1996 Language Minority Achievement and Program Effectiveness. Paper, George Mason University.

THOMAS, WILLIAM ISAAC 1923 *The Unadjusted Girl*. Boston: Little, Brown.

THORNTON, RUSSELL Demographic Antecedents of the 1890 Ghost Dance. *American Sociological Review* 46 (February), pp. 88–96.
1987 American Indian Holocaust and Survival: A Population History Since 1942. Norman: University of Oklahoma Press.
1991 North American Indians and the Demography of Contact. Paper presented at the Annual Meeting of the American Sociological Association, Cincinnati.

TILOVE, JONATHAN 1998 Face of the Nation. *Fort Lauderdale Sun-Sentinel* (July 12), sect. G, pp. 1, 2.

TIME 1972 What It Means to Be Jewish. 98 (April 10), pp. 54–64.
1974a Are You a Jew? 104 (September 2), pp. 56, 59.
1974b Brown's Bomb. 104 (November 25), pp. 16, 19.

TOMASKOVIC-DEVEY, DONALD 1993 The Gender and Race Composition of Jobs and the Male/Female, White/Black Pay Gaps. *Social Forces* 72 (September), pp. 45–76.

TOMLINSON, T. M. 1969 The Development of a Riot Ideology Among Urban Negroes. In Allen D. Grimshaw, ed., *Racial Violence in the United States*, pp. 226–235. Chicago: Aldine.

TORRES, VICKI 1996 The Great Wall of Chinatown. *Los Angeles Times* (March 31), pp. A1, A22.

TREEN, JOSEPH 1983 Apartheid's Harsh Grip. *Newsweek* 101 (March 28), pp. 31–32, 37.

TREIMAR, DONALD J.; MCKEEVER, MATTHEW; AND FODOR, EVA 1996 Racial Differences in Occupational Status and Income in South Africa, 1980 and 1991. *Demography* 33 (February), pp. 111–132.

TRIAY, VICTOR ANDRES 1998 *Fleeing Castro: Operation Pedro Pan and the Cuban Children's Program*. Gainesville, FL: University of Florida.

TRUEHEART, CHARLES 1995a In Quebec, Separation from Separatists Is the Goal. *Washington Post National Weekly Edition* 12 (February 13), p. 19.
1995b An Issue Left Unresolved. *Washington Post National Weekly Edition* 13 (November 16), p. 16.

TUCKER, M. BELINDA, AND MITCHELL-KERNAN, CLAUDIA, EDS. 1995 The Decline in Marriage among African Americans. New York: Russell Sage.

TURE, KWAME, AND HAMILTON, CHARLES 1992 *Black Power: The Politics of Liberation*. New York: Vintage Books.

TURNER, MARGERY; STRUYCK, RAYMOND J.; AND YINGER, JOHN 1991 *Housing Discrimination Study: Synthesis*. Washington, DC: Urban Institute.

TURNER, RALPH H. 1994 Race Riots Past and Present: A Cultural-Collective Approach. *Symbolic Interaction* 17 (No. 3), pp. 309–324.

TURNER, WALLACE 1972 New Hawaii Economy Stirs Minority Upset. *New York Times* (August 13), pp. 1, 46.

TWO SHOES, MINNIE 1996 AIM's Activism Agenda Still Full. *News from Indian Country* 10 (late March), p. 3A.

TYLER, GUS 1972 White Worker/Blue Mood. *Dissent* 190 (Winter), pp. 190–196.

TYLER, S. LYMAN 1973 *A History of Indian Policy*. Washington, DC: U.S. Government Printing Office.

TYSON, RAE 1996 Alabama Ferry to Bridge Racial Divide. *USA Today* (February 13), sect. 4, p. 4.

UNDERHILL, WILLIAM 1998 Bombing Backlash. *Newsweek* (August 31), p. 48.

UNITED NATIONS 1995 *The World's Women 1995: Trends and Statistics*. New York: United Nations U.S. Committee for Refugees.

1996a *World Refugee Survey 1996*. Washington, DC: Immigration and Refugee Services of America.
1996b 1996 Statistical Issue. *Refugee Reports* 17 (December 31), pp. 1–13.
1997 *The Rights of Indigenous Peoples*. Geneva: United Nations.

UNITED STATES HOLOCAUST MEMORIAL MUSEUM 1994 *Handicapped Victims of the Nazi Era 1933–1945*. Washington, DC: U.S. Government Printing Office.

UPI 1997 Carrier to Change Offensive Manual. *Chicago Defender* (August 21), p. 10.

USA TODAY 1994 Urban League Urges a "Marshall Plan." (January 21), p. 3A.

USDANSKY, MARGARET L. 1992a Old Ethnic Influences Still Play in Cities. *USA Today* (August 4), p. 9A.
1992b Asian Immigrants Changing Face of Rural USA. *USA Today* (September 10), p. 10A.
1993 Census: Languages Not Foreign at Home. *USA Today* (April 28), pp. A1, A2.

UTTER, JACK 1993 *American Indians: Answers to Today's Questions*. Lake Ann, MI: National Woodlands Publishing. American Indians: Answers to Today's Questions. Lake Ann, MI: National Woodlands Publishing.

VALENTINE, CHARLES A. 1968 *Culture and Poverty: Critique and Counter-Proposals*. Chicago: University of Chicago Press.

VASQUEZ, ENRIQUETA LONGAUEX Y 1970 The Mexican-American Women. In Robin Morgan, ed., *Sisterhood Is Powerful*, pp. 379–384. New York: Random House.

VEGA, WILLIAM A., ET AL. 1986 Cohesion and Adaptability in Mexican-American and Anglo Families. *Journal of Marriage and Family* 48 (November), pp. 857–867.

VERHOVEK, SAM HOVE 1995 Mother Scolded by Judge for Speaking in Spanish. *New York Times* (August 30), p. A12.
1997 Racial Tensions in Suit Slowing Drive for "Environmental Justice." *New York Times* (September 7), pp. 1, 16.
1999 Record for Women in Washington Legislature. *New York Times* (February 4), p. A14.

VERNON, JO ETTA A., ET AL. 1990 Media Stereotyping: A Comparison of the Way Elderly Women and Men Are Portrayed on Prime-Time Television. *Journal of Women and Aging* 2 (No. 4), pp. 55–68.

VIGIL, MAURILIO 1990 The Ethnic Organization as an Instrument of Political and Social Change: MALDEF, a Case Study. *The Journal of Ethnic Studies* 18 (Spring), pp. 15–31.

WAGLEY, CHARLES, AND HARRIS, MARVIN 1958 *Minorities in the New World: Six Case Studies*. New York: Columbia University Press.

WAITZKIN, HOWARD 1986 *The Second Sickness: Contradictions of Capitalist Health Care*. Chicago: University of Chicago Press.

WALKER, SAMUEL; SPOHN, CASSIA; AND DELONC, MIRIAM 1996 *The Color of Justice: Race, Ethnicity, and Crime in America*. Belmont, CA: Wadsworth.

WALKER, SYLVIA; SARAVANABHARAN, R. C.; AND ASBURY, CHARLES 1996 Prevalence of Disabling Conditions Among Minority Racial/Ethnic Groups: Implications for Current and Future Policies. *Disability Studies Quarterly* 16 (Spring), pp. 3–4.

WALLACE, STEVEN P. 1989 The New Urban Latinos: Central Americans in a Mexican Immigrant Environment. *Urban Affairs Quarterly* 25 (December), pp. 239–264.

WALLER, DAVID 1996 Friendly Fire: When Environmentalists Dehumanize American Indians. *American Indian Culture and Research Journal* 20 (No. 2), pp. 107–126.

WALLERSTEIN, IMMANUEL 1974 *The Modern World System*. New York: Academic Press.
1979 *The Capitalist World-Economy*. Cambridge, Eng.: Cambridge University Press.
1996a Social Change? Change is Eternal. Nothing Ever Changes. Paper presented at the III Congresso Português de Sociologia, Lisbon, Portugal.
1996b The ANC and South Africa: The Past and Future of Liberation Movements in the World-System. Paper presented at the annual meeting of the South African Sociological Association, Durban, South Africa.

WALSH, CATHERINE 1995 Perspectives. *America* 173 (October 14), p. 8.

WALZER, SUSAN 1996 Thinking About the Baby: Gender and Divisions of Infant Care. *Social Problems* 43 (May), pp. 219–234.

WANG, L. LING-CHI 1991 Roots and Changing Identity of the Chinese in the United States. *Daedalus* 120 (Spring), pp. 181–206.

WARD, DEBORAH L. 1996 Native Hawaiian Vote: the 'Aes have it. *Ka Wai Ola O Oha* (October 1996).

WARNER, R. STEPHEN 1993 Work in Progress Toward a New Paradigm for the Sociological Study of Religion in the United States. *American Journal of Sociology* 98 (March), pp. 1044–1093.

WARNER, SAM BASS, JR. 1968 *The Private City: Philadelphia in Three Periods of Its Growth*. Philadelphia: University of Pennsylvania Press.

WARNER, W. LLOYD, AND SROLE, LEO 1945 *The Social Systems of American Ethnic Groups*. New Haven: Yale University Press.

WARREN, PETER M; CLEELAND, NANCY; AND REYA, ILU 1996 Noncitizens Say They Voted in Orange County. *Los Angeles Times* (Decmber 27), pp. A1, A16–A17.

WARREN, ROBERT 1994 Immigration's Share of U.S. Population Growth: How We Measure It Matters. *Population Today* (September), p. 3.

WASHBURN, WILCOMB E. 1984 A Fifty-Year Perspective on the Indian Reorganization Act. *American Anthropologist* 86 (June), pp. 279–289.

WASHINGTON, BOOKER T. 1900 *Up from Slavery: An Autobiography*. New York: A. L. Burt.

WATERS, HARRY F. 1994 Listening to Their Latin Beat. *Newsweek* 123 (March 28), pp. 42–43.

WATERS, MARY 1990 *Ethnic Options. Choosing Identities in America*. Berkeley: University of California Press.

WATROUS, PETER 1996 Hispanic Stars Shining in the Pop Music Universe. *New York Times* (October 10), pp. B1, B5.

WATSON, RUSSELL 1988 Your Jewishness Is Not Good Enough. *Newsweek* 112 (November 28), p. 51.

WAX, MURRAY L. 1971 *Indian Americans: Unity and Diversity*. Englewood Cliffs, NJ: Prentice-Hall.

WAX, MURRAY L., AND BUCHANAN, ROBERT W. 1975 *Solving "the Indian Problem": The White Man's Burdensome Business*. New York: New York Times Book Company.

WEGLYN, MICHI 1976 *Years of Infamy*. New York: Quill Paperbacks.

WEI, WILLIAM 1993 *The Asian American Movement*. Philadelphia: Temple University Press.

WEINER, TIM 1998 Military Discharges of Homosexuals Soar. *New York Times* (February 12), p. A21.

WEITZ, ROSE 1992 College Students' Images of African American, Mexican American, and Jewish American Women. Paper presented at the Annual Meeting of the American Sociological Association, Pittsburgh.
1995 *A Sociology of Health, Illness, and Health Care*. Belmont, CA: Wadsworth.

WEITZER, RONALD 1990 *Transforming Settler States: Command Conflict and Internal Security in Northern Ireland and Zimbabwe*. Berkeley: University of California Press.
1997 Racial Prejudice Among Korean Merchants in African American Neighborhoods. *Sociologist Quarterly* 38 (No. 4), pp. 587–606.

WELLINGTON, ALISON J. 1994 Accounting for the Male/Female Wage Gap Among Whites: 1976 and 1985. *American Sociological Review* 59 (December), pp. 839–848.

WELLS, ROBERT N., JR. 1989 Native Americans' Needs Overlooked by Colleges. Paper, Canton, New York: St. Lawrence University.
1991 Indian Education from the Tribal Perspective: A Survey of American Indian Tribal Leaders. Paper, Canton, New York: St. Lawrence University.

WERNICK, ROBERT 1996 The Rise, and Fall, of a Fervid Third Party. *Smithsonian* 27 (November), pp. 150–152, 154–158.

WERTHEIMER, JACK 1994 Family Values and the Jews. *Commentary* 97 (January), pp. 30–34.
1996 *Conservative Synagogues and Their Members*. New York: Jewish Theological Seminary of America.

WHITE, JACK E. 1997 I'm Just Who I Am. *Time* 149 (May 5), pp. 32–34, 36.

WHITMAN, DAVID 1987 For Latinos, a Growing Divide. *U.S. News and World Report* 103 (August 10), pp. 47–49.

WHYTE, JOHN H. 1986 How Is the Boundary Maintained Between the Two Communities in Northern Ireland? *Ethnic and Racial Studies* 9 (April), pp. 219–234.

WICKHAM, DEWAYNE 1993 Subtle Racism Thrives. *USA Today* (October 25), p. 2A.
1996 Mayor's Task: Bridge Cuban-Black Gap. *USA Today* (October 7), p. 17A.
1998 Affirmative Action Not in Real Jeopardy. *USA Today* (April 7), p. 13A.

WIESEL, ELIE 1960 *Night*. New York: Bantam.

WILKINSON, GLEN A. 1966 Indian Tribal Claims Before the Court of Claims. *Georgetown Law Journal* 55 (December), pp. 511–528.

WILLIAM, PATRICIA J. 1998 *Seeing a Color-Blind Future: The Paradox of Race*. The Noonday Press/Farrar.

WILLIE, CHARLES V. 1978 The Inclining Significance of Race. *Society* 15 (July-August), pp. 10, 12–13.
1979 *The Caste and Class Controversy*. Bayside, NY: General Hall.

WILSON, JAMES Q., AND BANFIELD, EDWARD C. 1964 Public Regardingness as a Value Premise in Voting Behavior. *American Political Science Review* 58 (December), pp. 876–887.

WILSON, JOHN 1973 *Introduction to Social Movements*. New York: Basic Books.

WILSON, THOMAS C. 1996 Compliments Will Get You Nowhere: Benign Steroetypes, Prejudice and Anti-Semitism. *Sociological Quarterly* 37 (No. 3), pp. 465–479.

WILSON, TRACY 1996 Authorities Return Peyote to Indians in Ventura Country. *Los Angeles Times* (December 19), pp. A3, A50.

WILSON, WILLIAM J. 1973 *Power, Racism and Privilege: Race Relations in Theoretical and Sociohistorical Perspectives*. New York: Macmillan.
1980 *The Declining Significance of Race: Blacks and Changing American*. Institutions, 2d ed. Chicago: University of Chicago Press.
1988 The Ghetto Underclass and the Social Transformation of the Inner City. *The Black Scholar* 19 (May-June), pp. 10–17.
1996 *When Work Disappears: The World of the New Urban Poor*. New York: Knopf.

WINANT, HOWARD 1994 *Racial Conditions: Politics, Theory, Comparisons*. Minneapolis: University of Minnesota Press.

WINKLER, KAREN 1990 Researcher's Examination of California's Poor Latino Population Prompts Debate over the Traditional Definitions of the Underclass. *Chronicle of Higher Education* 37 (October 10), pp. A5, A8.

WINKS, ROBIN W. 1971 *The Blacks in Canada: A History*. Montreal, Quebec: McGill-Queen's University Press.

WINSBERG, MORTON 1994 Specific Hispanics. *American Demographics* 16 (February), pp. 44–53.

WIRTH, LOUIS 1928 *The Ghetto*. Chicago: University of Chicago Press.

WITT, SHIRLEY HILL 1970 Nationalistic Trends Among American Indians. In Stuart Levine and Nancy Oestreich Lurie, eds., *The American Indian Today*, pp. 93–127. Baltimore: Penguin.

WOLFE, ANN G. 1972 The Invisible Jewish Poor. *Journal of Jewish Communal Sciences* 48 (No. 3), pp. 259–265.

WOLFE, KATHI 1998 Is the Disability Law Creating a Handicap? *Washington Post National Weekly Edition* 15 (August 3), p. 23.

WOMEN WORK 1998 *Women Work: Poverty Persists*. Washington, DC: Women Work.

WONG, MORRISON G. 1995 Chinese Americans. In Pyong Gap Min, ed., *Asian Americans: Contemporary Trends and Issues*, pp. 58–94. Thousand Oaks, CA: Sage Publications.

WOO, ELAINE 1996 Immigrants, U.S. Peers Differ Starkly on Schools. *Los Angeles Times* (February 22), pp. A1, A19.

WOODRUM, ERIC 1981 An Assessment of Japanese American Assimilation, Pluralism, and Subordination. *American Journal of Sociology* 87 (July), pp. 157–169.

WOODWARD, C. VANN 1974 *The Strange Career of Jim Crow*, 3d ed. New York: Oxford University Press.

WOODWARD, KENNETH L. 1991 The Intermarrying Kind. *Newsweek* 118 (July 22), pp. 48–49.

WOODYARD, CHRIS 1995 Roadside Revival by the the Patels. *Los Angeles Times* (July 14), pp. A1, A40–A41.

WOOTON, BARBARA H. 1997 Gender Differences in Occupational Employment. *Monthly Labor Review* 120 (April), pp. 15–24.

WORLD BANK 1995 *World Development Report 1995: Workers in an Integrating World.* New York: Oxford University Press.
1996 *World Development Report 1996: From Plan to Market.* New York: Oxford University Press.

WORTHINGTON, ROGERS 1993 School Desegregation Efforts Divide Town. *Chicago Tribune* (December 13), p. 3.

WRIGHT, MARY BOWEN 1980 Indochinese. In Stephen Thernstrom, ed., *Harvard Encyclopedia of American Ethnic Groups*, pp. 508–513. Cambridge, MA: Belknap Press of Harvard University Press.

WRIGHT, PAUL, AND GARDNER, ROBERT W. 1983 *Ethnicity, Birthplace, and Achievement: The Changing Hawaii Mosaic.* Honolulu: East-West Population Institute.

WRIGHT, ROBERT 1995 Who's Really to Blame? *Time* 146 (November 6), pp. 33–37.

WRIGHT, SUSAN 1993 Blaming the Victim, Blaming Society, or Blaming the Discipline: Fixing Responsibility for Poverty and Homelessness. *Sociological Quarterly* 34 (No. 1), pp. 1–16.

WRONG, DENNIS H. 1972 How Important Is Social Class? *Dissent* 19 (Winter), pp. 278–285.

WU, CHENG-TSU 1972 *Chink!* New York: Meridian.

WYMAN, MARK 1993 *Round-Trip to America. The Immigrants Return to Europe, 1830–1930.* Ithaca, NY: Cornell University Press.

YANG, JOHN E. 1996 Drawing Outside the Lines. *Washington Post National Weekly Edition* 13 (April 22), pp. 15–16.

YBARRA, MICHAEL J. 1996 Limitations of Statuses: In the Light of Today. *New York Times* (June 9), p. E4.

YEE, ALBERT H. 1973 Myopic Perceptions and Textbooks: Chinese Americans' Search for Identity. *Journal of Social Issues* 29 (No. 2), pp. 99–113.

YINGER, JOHN 1995 *Closed Doors, Opportunities Lost: The Continuing Costs of Housing Discrimination.* New York: Russell Sage Foundation.

YIP, ALETHEA 1996 The Legacy of Chinatown. *AsianWeek* 17 (May 31), pp. 13–15.
1997 JUMP IN VIOLENCE AGAINST APAS. *ASIANWEEK* 17 (SEPTEMBER 19), PP. 11–12.

YOUNG, GAY 1993 Gender Inequality and Industrial Development: the Household Connection. *Journal of Comparative Family Studies* 124 (Spring), pp. 3–20.

YU, ELENA S. H. 1980 Filipino Migration and Community Organizations in the United States. *California Sociologist* 3 (Summer), pp. 76–102.

YU, HENRY 1996 How Tiger Woods Lost His Stripes. *Los Angeles Times* (December 2), p. B5.

ZACK, NAOMI, ED. 1995 *American Mixed Race: The Culture of Microdiversity.* London: Rowan and Littlefield.

ZHOU, MIN, AND KAMO, YOSHINORI 1994 An Analysis of Earnings Patterns for Chinese, Japanese, and Non-Hispanic White Males in the United States. *Sociological Quarterly* 35 (No. 4), pp. 581–602.

ZHOU, MIN, AND BANKSTON, III, CARL L. 1998 *Growing Up American: How Vietnamese Children Adapt to Life in the United States.* New York: Russell Sage Foundation.

ZIEGLER, DOLORES 1992 Family Associations: Role in a Racist American Society. *AsianWeek* (August 28), pp. 17, 19.

ZINN, MAXINE BACA, AND DILL, BONNIE THORNTON, EDS. 1994 *Women of Color in U.S. Society.* Philadelphia: Temple University Press.

ZINSMEISTER, KARL 1988 Black Demographics. *Public Opinion* 10 (January-February), pp. 41–44.

ZORN, ERIC 1995 American Justice Sees Black and White over Death Penalty. *Chicago Tribune* (May 4), sect. 2, p. 1.

PHOTO CREDITS

CHAPTER 1 Page 2: © Jill Hamilton/Monkmeyer; **5:** © Mannie Garcia; **10:** © Corbis-Bettmann; **18:** © AP/Wide World Photos; **26:** © Mark Burnett/Stock Boston; **29:** © Shelly Katz/Liaison International; **32:** © Lawrence Migdale/Photo Researchers

CHAPTER 2 Page 38: © David J. Phillip/AP/Wide World ; **41:** The Phillips Collection, Washington, D.C.; **47:** © Bernard J. "Barney" Gallagher; **52:** © Steve Allen/Gamma Liaison; **55:** © Bob Mahoney/The Image Works; **67:** © Dreamworks/Fotos International/Archive Photos

CHAPTER 3 Page 72: © Corbis-Bettmann; **74:** © Ted Hardin; **79:** © Michael Dwyer/Stock Boston; **82:** Courtesy University of Chicago; **89:** © Charles Kennard/Stock Boston; **95:** © Louis Balukoff/AP/Wide World Photos

CHAPTER 4 Page 104: © Chromosohm/Sohm/Photo Researchers; **110:** © UPI/Corbis-Bettmann; **113:** © George Eastman House Collection/Lewis W. Hine; **116:** Courtesy Raffi Ishkanian; **125:** © Denis Poroy/AP/Wide World Photos; **126:** © Richard R. Renaldi/Impact Visuals

CHAPTER 5 Page 132: © J. Nordell/The Image Works; **140:** © Larry Gus; **144:** © Robert Frerck/Tony Stone Images; **148:** © Philip Jon Bailey/Stock Boston/PNI; **151:** © Jose R. Lopez/New York Times Pictures; **153**: © Karin Shamsi-Sasha/Sygma

CHAPTER 6 Page 168: © Bernard Wolf/Monkmeyer; **170:** Chicago Tribune Photo by Jose Osorio; **175:** Montana Historical Society, Helena; **181:** © John Running/Stock Boston; **182:** © Ken Behrend/AP/Wide World Photos; **188:** Courtesy Indian Country Today; **191:** © Gary FandelAP Photo/Des Moines Register; **196:** © Bernard Wolf/Monkmeyer

CHAPTER 7 Page 204: © Matusow/Monkmeyer; **211:** © Lawrence Migdale; **214:** The New York Public Library, Astor, Lenox and Tilden Foundations; **216:** © Margaret Bourke-White/Life Magazine; **220:** © Carl Iwasaki/Life Magazine © Time, Inc.; **223:** © AP/Wide World Photos; **231:** © UPI/Corbis-Bettmann; **232:** © Dennis Brack/Black Star

CHAPTER 8 Page 236: © Rogers/Monkmeyer; **240:** © Bob Kramer/The Picture Cube; **247:** © Steve Kagan /NYT Pictures; **250:** © N.R. Rowan/The Image Works; **261:** © Bob Riha, Jr.; **265:** © Alan S. Weiner/New York Times Pictures; **267:** © Alan S. Weiner/New York Times Pictures

CHAPTER 9 Page 270: © Tony Arruza/Tony Stone Images; **275:** © Jill Connelly/Los Angeles Times; **277:** Courtesy Adela de la Torre; **282:** © L. M. Otero/AP/Wide World Photos; **284:** © AP/Wide World Photos; **286:** © Dezso Szuri/Miami Herald; **289:** © Bob Nickelsberg/Woodfin Camp & Associates

CHAPTER 10 Page 294: © Hazel Hankin/Stock Boston; **298:** © UPI/Corbis-Bettmann; **301:** © AP/Wide World Photos; **309:** © AP/Wide World Photos; **310:** © Marion Ettlinger; **313:** © Robert Fried/Stock Boston; **320:** © Phyllis Picardi/Stock Boston

CHAPTER 11 Page 338: Copyright Chicago Tribune 1998; **341:** © Doug Mills/AP/Wide World; **343:** © Mickey Pfleger/Photo 20-20/PNI; **346:** © Bart Bartholomew/New York Times Pictures; **349:** © Ken Sakamoto/Honolulu Star Bulletin

CHAPTER 12 Page 354: © Roy Gumpel/Gamma Liaison; **358:** © John Sotomayor/NYT Pictures; **361:** © Tom Wurl/Stock Boston; **363:** © Jean-Claude Lejeune; **364:** Courtesy Han Ix Lau; **370:** © AP/Wide World Photos; **374:** © Karin Cooper/Gamma Liaison; **376:** © Alon Reininger/Contact Press Images

CHAPTER 13 Page **380:** © Leland Bobbe/Tony Stone Images; **385:** © UPI/Corbis-Bettmann; **391:** © Ulf Andersen/Gamma Liaison; **395:** © Jim Bourg/Liaison International; **399:** © Lawrence Migdale/Tony Stone Images; **402:** © H. Gans/The Image Works; **404:** © Charles Cherney/Chicago Tribune

CHAPTER 14 Page **412:** © Claudia Kunin/Tony Stone Images; **416:** © Photo fest; **417:** © AP/Wide World Photos; **422:** © Sigrid Estrada/Courtesy Henry Holt and Company, Inc.; **424:** © Robert Reichert/Gamma Liaison; **427:** © The New York Times/New York Times Picture Service; **433:** © Dorothy Littel/Stock Boston; **436**: © Eyal Warshavsky/AP/Wide World Photos

CHAPTER 15 Page **440:** © Lionel Delevingne; **447:** © A. Duclos/M. Salaber/Liaison International; **449:** © Andrew Wallace/Gamma Liaison; **452:** © B. Kraft/Sygma; **462:** © Arlene Collilns/Monkmeyer; **465:** © Reuters/Corbis Bettmann; **466:** © UPI/Corbis-Bettmann

CHAPTER 16 Page 472: © Bob Daemmrich/Stock Boston/PNI; **478:**Chicago Tribune Photo by Jerry Tomaselli; **482:** © Margaret Suckley/FDR Library; **488:** Courtesy Kathi Wolfe; **490:** © Lee Snider/The Image Works

INDEX

Italicized letters "f" and "t" following page numbers indicate figures and tables respectively.